DEMOCRACY, POWER AND JUSTICE

DEMOCRACY, POWER AND JUSTICE

Essays in Political Theory

BRIAN BARRY

CLARENDON PRESS . OXFORD
1989

Oxford University Press, Walton Street, Oxford OX2 6DP
Oxford New York Toronto
Delhi Bombay Calcutta Madras Karachi
Petaling Jaya Singapore Hong Kong Tokyo
Nairobi Dar es Salaam Cape Town
Melbourne Auckland
and associated companies in
Berlin Ibadan

Oxford is a trade mark of Oxford University Press

Published in the United States
by Oxford University Press, New York

British Library Cataloguing in Publication Data
Barry, Brian
Democracy, power, and justice: essays in
political theory
1. Politics. Theories
I. Title
320'.01
ISBN 0–19–827298–7

Library of Congress Cataloging in Publication Data
Barry, Brian M.
Democracy, power, and justice: essays in political theory/Brian Barry.
Essays published between 1974 and 1988.
Includes index.
1. Democracy. 2. Power (Social sciences). 3. Justice. I. Title.
JC423.B26246 1989 321.8–dc19 89–2937
ISBN 0–19–827298–7

Set by Wyvern Typesetting Ltd, Bristol
Printed and bound in
Great Britain by Courier International Ltd
Tiptree, Essex

For Anni
and for Dammy and Julian
who brought us together

PREFACE

Of the twenty essays that make up this collection, nine have appeared in journals published in several different countries and spanning a number of disciplines. The remaining eleven have appeared in multi-authored books—a notoriously hit-and-miss form of disseminating one's work. It is therefore hardly surprising that most people who know of two or three things I have written are unaware of other pieces, even when these are equally relevant to their interests. For this reason I am pleased that the Clarendon Press is bringing out this selection.

As this volume contains only about two-fifths of my articles and review essays, the reader may wish to know something of the criteria used in making the selection. First, I have excluded anything that overlaps substantially with books that I have published. Second, I have excluded a couple of methodological pieces and one on the interpretation of Hobbes that did not seem to me to fit into the overall scheme for the volume. Third, I have endeavoured to include only those articles that continue to have significance and only those review essays that raise issues going beyond the criticism of the book in question. Inevitably, this third criterion raises the most difficulties, and the author is not necessarily the person best placed to make the judgements called for in applying it. I have been fortunate in having had guidance on these questions from Russell Hardin and David Miller, and it is my pleasure to thank them here for the time and thought that they have put into weighing the merits of a larger set of publications from which the present selection is drawn.

Readers of this volume are entitled to know how far what appears here has been altered from the form in which it originally appeared. A number of cross-references have been added. Spelling and punctuation have been brought into line with British usage wherever the original source was American. Such matters as italicization of words in foreign languages have been made uniform. So have symbolic conventions: actors are always *A*, *B*, and *C*, actions *x*, *y*, and *z*. Minor changes have been made throughout in the interests of euphony and clarity. In some cases new introductory or concluding material has been added in order to head off, as far as possible, misreadings that the pieces attracted in their originally published form. Various bits of academic shorthand acceptable in a learned journal have been expanded so as to make the pieces printed here accessible to non-professionals. I have also deleted a few paragraphs that, on rereading, seemed to me to hold up the argument rather than advance it. I have not, however, made any attempt to update anything, either to take account of later political events or later publications on the subject.[1] Doing this thoroughly would involve creating a quite different kind of book, and doing it sporadically would, I feel, reduce the value of the collection by leaving the reader unsure whether some successful prediction was a lucky shot or the result of an addition made with the benefit of hindsight. In place of such updating in the text, I have offered some remarks about subsequent developments in the Introduction to this volume.

Rather than preserving the original acknowledgements within individual chapters, I should like to thank here those whose comments improved the original versions of the pieces contained in this book: Bruce Ackerman, James Andrews, Chris Archibald, Benjamin Barber, Peter Brown, Hans Daalder, David Donaldson, Patrick Dunleavy, Jon Elster, John Ferejohn, James Fishkin, Bruno Frey, Robert Fullinwider, Allan Gibbard, Robert Goodin, Kenneth Goodpaster, John Gray, Russell Hardin, Albert Hirschman, Keith Hope, Samuel Huntington, Aanund Hylland, Robin Lovin, Douglas MacLean, John Maguire, Jane Mansbridge, Derek Parfit, Carole Pateman, Douglas Rae, Ronald Rogowski, Jim Sharpe, Charles Silver, Robert Simon, Miller Spangler, Arthur Stinchcombe, and Aristide Zolberg.

Finally, I am grateful to Claire Wilkinson for obtaining the permissions to reprint and helping with revisions for this volume, and to Anni Parker for making proof-reading as near to being a pleasure as is humanly possible.

[1] I have, however, on occasion substituted later and more accessible versions or reprints for articles originally published in obscure places or books that are now out of print.

ACKNOWLEDGEMENTS

I am grateful for permission to include the following in this collection:

'The Strange Death of Political Philosophy', originally published in *Government and Opposition*, 15 (1980), 276–88.

'Is Democracy Special?', originally published in Peter Laslett and James Fishkin (eds.), *Philosophy, Politics and Society*, Fifth Series (Oxford: Basil Blackwell; New Haven, Conn.: Yale University Press, 1979), 155–96, copyright © by Basil Blackwell.

'Does Democracy Cause Inflation? The Political Ideas of Some Economists', originally published in Leon N. Lindberg and Charles S. Maier (eds.), *The Politics of Inflation and Economic Stagnation* (Washington, DC: The Brookings Institution, 1985), 280–317, copyright © 1985 by The Brookings Institution.

'Political Accommodation and Consociational Democracy', originally published as a review article in *British Journal of Political Science*, 5 (1975), 477–505 (published by Cambridge University Press).

'The Consociational Model and its Dangers', originally published in *European Journal of Political Research*, 3 (1975), 393–412, copyright © 1975 by Martinus Nijhoff Publishers; reprinted by permission of Kluwer Academic Publishers.

'Self-Government Revisited', originally published in David Miller and Larry Siedentop (eds.), *The Nature of Political Theory* (Oxford: Clarendon Press, 1983), 121–54.

'Exit, Voice, and Loyalty', originally published as a review article in *British Journal of Political Science*, 4 (1974), 79–107 (published by Cambridge University Press).

'Power: An Economic Analysis', originally published in Brian Barry (ed.), *Power and Political Theory* (London: Wiley, 1975), 67–101, copyright © 1975 by John Wiley; reprinted by permission of John Wiley and Sons, Ltd.

'Is it Better to be Powerful or Lucky?', originally published in two parts in *Political Studies*, 28 (1980), 183–94 and 338–52.

'The Obscurities of Power', originally published in *Government and Opposition*, 10 (1975), 250–4.

'The Uses of "Power"', originally published as a review article in *Government and Opposition*, 23 (1988), 340–53.

'And Who is my Neighbour?', originally published as a review article in the *Yale Law Journal*, 88 (1979), 629–58, reprinted by permission of The Yale Law Journal Company and Fred B. Rothman & Company.

'Lady Chatterley's Lover and Doctor Fischer's Bomb Party: Liberalism, Pareto Optimality, and the Problem of Objectionable Preferences', originally published in Jon Elster and Aanund Hylland (eds.), *Foundations of Social Choice Theory* (Cambridge: Cambridge University Press, 1986), 11–43.

'Tragic Choices', originally published as a review article in *Ethics*, 94 (1984), 303–18, © 1984 by The University of Chicago; all rights reserved.

'Can States be Moral? International Morality and the Compliance Problem' has been published in two forms: in Anthony Ellis (ed.), *Ethics and International Relations* (Manchester: Manchester University Press, 1986, for the Centre for Philosophy and Public Affairs, University of St Andrews), and under the title 'Justice in International Society', in Robert J. Myers (ed.), *International Ethics in the Nuclear Age* (Ethics and Foreign Policy Series 4; Lanham, Md.: University Press of America, 1987, for the Carnegie Council on Ethics and International Affairs).

'Humanity and Justice in Global Perspective', originally published in J. Roland Pennock and John W. Chapman (eds.), *Ethics, Economics, and the Law* (Nomos, 24; New York and London: New York University Press, 1982), 219–52, copyright © 1982 by New York University.

'Justice as Reciprocity', originally published in Eugene Kamenka and Alice Erh-Soon Tay (eds.), *Justice* (London: Edward Arnold, 1979), 50–78, © Edward Arnold (Publishers) Ltd. 1979.

'Justice Between Generations', originally published in P. M. S. Hacker and J. Raz (eds.), *Law, Morality, and Society: Essays in Honour of H. L. A. Hart* (Oxford: Clarendon Press, 1977), 268–84.

'The Ethics of Resource Depletion', originally published as 'Intergenerational Justice in Energy Policy', in Douglas MacLean and Peter G. Brown (eds.) *Energy and the Future* (Totowa, NJ: Rowman and Littlefield, 1983), 15–30.

'The Continuing Relevance of Socialism', published in Robert Skidelsky (ed.), *Thatcherism* (London: Chatto & Windus, 1988), 143–58.

CONTENTS

INTRODUCTION

The three nouns in the title of this book—democracy, power, and justice—give a pretty accurate picture of its contents. The only chapter that forms an exception is the first, which is devoted to some reflections on the discipline of political philosophy. These reflections were occasioned by an invitation to contribute to a special issue of the journal *Government and Opposition* celebrating its twenty-fifth anniversary. We were asked to write about developments in our own subjects during the past quarter century, and the coincidence that I had taken up the study of political philosophy just a quarter of a century earlier explains and I hope excuses the way in which I allowed my response to take on an autobiographical form.

The four chapters following this one are all concerned in one way or another with the working of democratic political institutions. Chapter 2, 'Is Democracy Special?', tackles a broad question about the justification of such institutions—though not, as I shall point out below, the broadest question possible. The question it asks is as follows. Suppose we take as given the contents of a certain law or public policy. Is the strength of its claims on our obedience to it affected by the procedure which brought it into being? Specifically, what if it has been enacted by some procedure that in some way aggregates citizen preferences, either directly as in a referendum or indirectly as when representatives are elected under universal suffrage? Does the fact that a certain law or policy is the outcome of such a process provide a reason for obeying it that would not exist if the identical outcome had occurred under some different set of decisionmaking arrangements?

The argument of the chapter is that there is no virtue that can be claimed universally for an outcome simply on the basis of its democratic origins. I do, however, suggest that there is all the same a reason for obeying democratically arrived at laws that does not apply to others. This is that obedience to the laws helps to sustain the political system, and that system is itself valuable. Its value lies in the fact that, at any rate under modern conditions, the only determinate and generally acceptable basis for a right to rule is winning an open election. As a contingent matter, then, but one that is very solidly grounded, democracy is the only system of government compatible with at once political freedom and political stability. The basis for this claim is offered in the text of chapter 2.

It is important to get clear exactly what is the question being asked in this chapter. If this is misunderstood, the whole chapter is liable to be misinterpreted, and I have found that this has in fact happened on occasion. The question is not the very broad one: 'What in general can be said in favour of democracy?' That is a perfectly valid question but it is not the question asked here. Rather, the question I ask is: 'Do democratic procedures endow outcomes with a special claim to respect, holding constant the actual content of those outcomes?'

If we were asking the broader question, it would be very much to the point to argue that, at any rate under favourable conditions, democracy has a tendency to produce better outcomes than any other system of government. I think this is indeed true, and in chapter 2 I offer some account of what those favourable conditions are. But what has to be observed about this line of justification is that it flows not from procedure to outcome but from outcome to procedure. Since, on this view, the value of democracy is purely instrumental—that it tends to produce better laws and policies than alternative decision-making institutions—it follows that, if some other form of political institution offered better prospects, it should be preferred to democracy.

In contrast to this kind of justification by results, what I am concerned with in chapter 2 is justification in abstraction from outcomes, which I am here using quasi-technically to cover laws and policies. The negative part of my case is that there is no a priori argument in favour of outcomes simply in virtue of their democratic provenance. The positive part is that, if we look at the consequences of democratic government over and above outcomes in the sense defined, we can see that it is worth supporting. And since disobeying laws has a tendency to undermine a regime, this provides indirectly a special reason for obedience to democratically arrived at laws and policies.

Chapters 3 to 5 take up the question that was laid on one side in chapter 2. They ask under what conditions democracy has a tendency to produce good outcomes. They also ask whether institutional tinkering holds out hopes of improving the performance of democracies. It must be admitted immediately that there may be disagreement about what constitutes a good outcome. It is, indeed, such disagreement that gives substance to democratic politics. However, in these three chapters I attempt to finesse the difficulty by taking criteria that should be fairly uncontroversial.

In the first of them, 'Does Democracy Cause Inflation?', I assume that, whatever a good macroeconomic policy may be, a bad one is one that runs counter to the long-run interests of the vast majority of the population. The claim to be discussed in this chapter is that democratic government has built into it the feature that it tends to produce bad outcomes in precisely this sense. According to an influential school of 'public choice' theorists (mostly though not exclusively economists), there is a fatal flaw in democracy that results in governments persistently following policies that lead to levels of inflation that are too high, whether our standard be the interests or the policy preferences of their citizens.

The heyday of this school was the mid-1970s, when the chapter was originally written. As far as I am aware, however, none of the members of this school has publicly recanted. And in any case it is I think instructive to trace the shoddy reasoning by which people basically ill-disposed to democratic government for other reasons used the inflation bogey as a way of advancing their proposals for the hobbling of democratic governments. It is worth noting, incidentally, that in the USA the budget deficit has provided an excuse for dusting off what are essentially the same arguments. The hidden agenda remains the same: the entrenching of existing economic privilege against political majorities.

In chapters 4 and 5, the implicit criterion of a good outcome is different but I hope equally uncontroversial. Most people would agree that, whatever a good outcome may be, it does not include the oppression by one community within a country of another community within that country distinguished from the first by race, religion, language, or descent. In these two chapters, then, we are concerned with communally divided societies, where giving the majority what it wants is not the solution but the problem.

Because communal hostility can so easily lead to bloodshed and to the breakdown of constitutional government, the taming of communal conflicts is manifestly a matter of the greatest practical importance. These two chapters are devoted to the critical examination of a school of writers who claimed to have discovered a formula for the peaceful resolution of communal conflicts. The members of this school observed certain ways in which communal conflicts were successfully defused in some of the smaller Western European democracies, generated from these observations a model of 'consociational democracy', and proposed it as a scheme to be applied in other communally divided societies.

The theory of consociational democracy thus has two aspects, explanatory and prescriptive. Each of the chapters devoted to the theory focuses on one of these aspects. 'Political Accommodation and Consociational Democracy' is a critical review of the literature on the conceptualization of consociational democracy and on the operation of consociationalism in divided societies. 'The Consociational Model and Its Dangers' is addressed to the policy proposals deduced from studying consociational practices.

It is perhaps worth setting the second of these chapters in its historical perspective. At the time when it was written, in the mid-1970s, it was scarcely possible to open a newspaper such as the London *Times* without coming across an article recommending 'power sharing' as a solution to communal conflict in Northern Ireland and Cyprus, and pointing to its successes elsewhere. (These were held at that time to include the Lebanon.) The burden of my argument was that such claims for the enforcement of consociational devices were naïve. Provided the leaders of the communities wish for accommodation and can carry their communities with them, there is no question that devices such as a 'grand coalition' and proportional filling of sensitive offices can contribute to the stabilizing of whatever deal they strike. What I should have made more of, perhaps, was that the experience of collaboration can itself contribute to the process of stabilization by encouraging mutual trust among the partners. But what still has to be emphasized is that consociational devices cannot create the conditions for political accommodation where these do not exist. The leaders must want to make a deal to settle the issues in contention, and the followers must be prepared to follow them. That is fundamental, as the subsequent histories of Cyprus, Northern Ireland, and the Lebanon illustrate all too well.

In recent years, the claims of consociationalism have been advanced in another unpromising context, that of South Africa. Within the country, interest in consociational devices comes from Whites who recognize that the present system cannot endure indefinitely but wish to maintain as much as possible of their privileged position as a White minority in a multiracial political regime.[1] Outside the country, there are many figures in politics and business in Britain and the USA who fear that, after the many decades in which their governments have protected the White regime, a government based on a Black majority might not be very well disposed.

[1] See e.g. Denis Worrall, 'The Real Struggle in South Africa: An Insider's View', *Ethics and International Affairs*, 2 (1988), 115–37.

We are therefore beginning to hear suggestions for future constitutional development in South Africa that are reminiscent of the 'Bishop Muzorewa' constitution with which the British government sought to saddle an independent Zimbabwe. The essence of any such scheme is that, by some means or other (and there are many possibilities), the representatives of the Whites should have in effect a veto on any large-scale changes that might threaten their social and economic position. The fallacy here is patent. Consociational democracy is a device for freezing the status quo. It must therefore follow the achievement of a settlement that is satisfactory to all parties. But in South Africa the current situation is one of grotesque inequality, with the Whites owning all the best agricultural land, all the land with mineral deposits, and all the firms of any significant size. Whites also monopolize positions of power in the private as well as the public sector. Any kind of scheme that rules out in advance drastic measures to give Blacks their fair share of the society's resources and a dominant position in running its major institutions will inevitably be rejected by the African National Congress—and rightly so. (It is readily apparent that the mere abolition of official apartheid would do virtually nothing to redress these injustices.)

In some cases, a single state experiences conflict between different ethnic communities that occupy distinct territories, or would occupy distinct territories with some manageable transfers of population. A possible solution in such cases is for each community to have a state of its own. Although the principle of national self-determination has profoundly shaped politics in this century, it has received a generally bad press from political theorists. In the chapter 'Self-Government Revisited', I point out that this hostility to nationalism is quite understandable when one considers the biographies of most of those who have written on the subject. I argue, nevertheless, that nationalism is a defensible criterion for the drawing of state boundaries. I should add that the chapter originally appeared in a memorial volume for John Plamenatz, whose Montenegrin origins may well have accounted for his relatively favourable view of the principle of national self-determination.

Chapter 7, which follows this, forms a bridge between the analysis of democracy and the analysis of power, since it discusses Albert Hirschman's idea that people can respond to the unsatisfactory performance of organizations by two means: exercising 'voice' and engaging in 'exit'. Hirschman's *Exit, Voice, and Loyalty* is deservedly a classic of modern social theory. In my review article on it I took issue with some details of the theory but in the main tried to illustrate the fertility of the basic ideas.

The next four chapters are concerned with the concept and measurement of power. This is something I have wrestled with off and on over my entire career, and the four pieces reprinted here include the oldest and the newest in the collection. The first of these, chapter 8, offers an 'economic' analysis of power, by which I mean an analysis of getting people to do what they would not otherwise choose to do by the appropriate deployment of threats of sanctions and offers of rewards. There are other ways of getting people to do what they would not otherwise choose to do, and I begin with a general discussion of these. But the main focus is on threats and offers. Within the limitation that I consider only two parties to the transaction, the analysis is intended to be comprehensive.

Chapter 9, the next of the chapters devoted to the analysis of power, shifts away from the kind of power that flows from threats and offers to the kind of power that flows from participation in some formally specified system of collective decisionmaking, typically one in which decisions are taken by voting. A considerable literature has been devoted to the construction of 'power indexes', which are supposed to represent the relative power of actors in any given system. The subject has given rise to a good deal of nonsense, and I offer a way of thinking about power in a decisionmaking body that seems to me to avoid the pitfalls that the standard power indexes run into.

Chapter 10 is a fairly brief review of a very short book, Steven Lukes's *Power: A Radical View*. Lukes espouses the fashionable view that power is an 'essentially contested' concept. In my view the notion of essential contestability is not only mistaken but has pernicious effects on the quality of intellectual life. The review, however, does not take such high ground but argues that Lukes's own position is in any case self-contradictory. As far as the larger issue is concerned, rather than add to the heap of stuff already written on essential contestability I would rather try to show that the concept of power can be made clear and that what gives credence to the thesis of essential contestability is the prevailing confusion.

I have tried to make further progress towards this aim in the last of the pieces on power, which is entitled 'The Uses of "Power"'. This takes the form of a review of a recently published book on the analysis of power by Peter Morriss. A great strength of this book is that it brings together within a single framework the analysis of interpersonal power and power within committees or legislatures. I have therefore had the opportunity to show, picking up on themes from Morriss's book, how the topics of chapters 8 and 9 can be brought into relation with one another.

All but the last of the remaining essays are concerned with justice, or more generally with the allocation of rights and goods. Chapters 12 and 13 both deal in very different ways with the conflict between on one side individual rights and on the other side the principle that aggregate utility should be maximized (or its ordinal utility cousin the Pareto principle—see below). The first of these, 'And Who is my Neighbour?' provides a critical examination of the anti-utilitarian wave that has been the dominant force in moral philosophy in recent years. Although I do not argue for the reinstatement of utilitarianism, I do suggest that many of the alternatives on offer leave us with an impoverished conception of what human beings owe one another—hence its title. The chapter takes the form of a discursive discussion of one contribution to the genre, Charles Fried's *Right and Wrong*.

I should like, while on the subject of this chapter, to make a passing comment on the reception of it when it was originally published in an American law journal. The usual experience of publishing an article is that one has dropped it into the void. There used to be a trickle of reprint requests from medical schools in Eastern Europe but even that seems to have dried up in recent years. My experience with this review essay was quite different, however: I was deluged with appreciative notes from American Law professors. Clearly something in it touched a chord.

The other discussion of the conflict between rights and utility is 'Lady Chatterley's Lover and Doctor Fischer's Bomb Party'. The first part of this deals with Amartya Sen's claim that there is a conflict between the Pareto principle and any principle giving people a 'private sphere' over which they have exclusive control. The Pareto principle is a principle for judging between states of affairs. Suppose we want to compare situation x and situation y. If at least one person prefers x to y and nobody prefers y to x, then the Pareto principle tells us that x is better than y. This part of the chapter takes its title from the example which Sen originally used to illustrate his alleged 'liberal paradox'. This involved the reading or not reading of D. H. Lawrence's novel, at that time just legalized for sale in England. I argue that there is no contradiction between rights and Pareto optimality because they have different subject-matters: rights are concerned with what people should be allowed to do, Pareto optimality with what constitutes a good state of affairs.

The second part, 'Doctor Fischer's Bomb Party', deals with what I regard as the serious substantive issue arising from Sen's example. This is the moral status of offers that are freely, perhaps gratefully, accepted by the recipients, but are somehow suspect as degrading or corrupting. Its title is taken from Graham Greene's novel *Doctor Fischer of Geneva or The Bomb Party*, in which the eponymous doctor gives parties at which the guests, who are already quite wealthy, undertake degrading performances in order to receive large prizes.

Following these two fairly abstract analyses of individual rights and general welfare, chapter 14 is concerned with hard choices that societies have to make: whose life to save by the use of some expensive machine, whom to conscript to fight in a war, and so on. This chapter is in the form of a review of an original and influential book, *Tragic Choices*, by Guido Calabresi and Philip Bobbitt. Although I am critical of the authors' conception of a 'tragic choice' and of some of the details of their analysis, I believe that their discussion of alternative mechanisms for distributing benefits and burdens has much to offer, and I endeavour in this chapter to refine it and extend it in various directions.

The next five chapters are all concerned with the implications of distributive justice outside its usual sphere of relations among contemporary members of a single society. The first two of them focus on international justice, the last two on justice between different generations, while the one between discusses problems common to both. 'Can States Be Moral?' is devoted to the most basic issue that arises in international ethics, namely, the very possibility of holding states to account for their actions in the international arena. While conceding the strength of the case mounted by those who argue that international conditions preclude binding moral obligations on states, I maintain that there is nevertheless a good deal of room for such obligations. 'Humanity and Justice in Global Perspective' analyses two basic grounds for holding that rich countries have a moral obligation to transfer resources to poor ones: humanity and justice. The argument is made that both humanity and justice provide a grounding for obligations, but different ones in each case.

Much of everyday morality is concerned with reciprocity; in one way or another, one's obligations often arise from the requirement of repaying a benefit received or anticipating one expected. One of the features that makes moral relations between states (and even more between generations) problematic is the relative or absolute lack of reciprocity. 'Justice as Reciprocity' analyses the place of reciprocity in morality and asks what happens when it is weak or absent.

Chapters 18 and 19 are devoted to the peculiar problems that arise in the relations between different generations. Principles that we are familiar with and that work well enough among contemporaries are liable to have bizarre implications when applied to the obligations that one generation has to its successors. 'Justice between Generations' is a general survey of the problems that arise. Although much has been written on the topic (some of it by me) since this piece was originally published, I think that it still stands up as a useful introduction to a mind-bending topic.

'The Ethics of Resource Depletion' provides a sharp contrast with the preceding chapter in that it takes up just one issue concerning obligations to future generations. This is the question raised by the existence of non-renewable resources such as minerals and fossil fuels. To say that future generations should have the same stock of them as we have is a recipe for their never being used at all. But is there any alternative that is just between different generations? In this chapter I offer a general answer to the question, which has found favour with some other writers on the subject. I am well aware, however, of the difficulty of determining what its concrete implications are for a just policy on non-renewable resources.

The piece that I have chosen to be the final one in the collection stands a little apart from the others. It is based upon the text of a public lecture, and in preparing it for publication I have fought off the temptation to retrofit it with the usual scholarly armoury. I have not therefore added the qualifications that one would expect to find in a paper designed to anticipate all possible objections, nor indulged in the citation of authorities to back up my assertions.

'The Continuing Relevance of Socialism' was given as part of a series of public lectures on the theme of 'Thatcherism'. But I should say that, with the exception of the opening section, that lecture largely followed the text of the inaugural lecture that I gave (under the title 'Socialism Today') at the London School of Economics in December 1987 upon taking up the Chair of Political Science first held there by Graham Wallas. The Department of Government at the LSE has the reputation (completely justified) of being the most conservative in the United Kingdom. In trying to decide what to speak about, I reached the conclusion that it would be worth making it apparent that, at any rate as far as this chair was concerned, the pendulum that swung to the right when Michael Oakeshott succeeded Harold Laski had swung back again. A professor may be allowed once in a lifetime, I hope, to take the opportunity of professing. 'The Continuing Relevance of Socialism' is the result.

I

THE STRANGE DEATH OF POLITICAL PHILOSOPHY

All invitations to write something that come with far distant deadlines are a subtle exercise in entrapment (and I speak here from experience as both hunter and quarry), resting on the usual tendency to discount the future. How could anyone resist the temptation to talk about everybody's favourite subject—themselves—when it is enhanced by the flattery implicit in the suggestion that other people might be interested? So easy too: just a few thousand words about changes in the discipline in the last twenty-five years and the way in which one sees it.

It turns out not to be so easy after all. Exactly twenty-five years ago, in July 1955, I left school and in the following October became an Oxford undergraduate. How can I hope to distinguish changes between then and now in me from changes in the intellectual milieu over the same period? And can I hope to avoid reconstructing the past in the light of my current ideas and preoccupations?

In his study of R. G. Collingwood, Alan Donagan demonstrated that the famous *Autobiography* is more usefully viewed as an illustration of his later philosophical theories than as a veridical account of the process by which he came to hold them.[1] Collingwood, of course, made the mistake of having published the evidence on the basis of which his story could be judged. But perhaps that is the only feature that sets his case apart from that of the rest of us.

Thus, to take my own case, it is certainly my firm belief that there has been no substantial change in my basic outlook in the last twenty-five years—or even longer. I cannot remember any time when I was anything other than an atheist with a soft spot for the Church of England, a socialist exasperated with all sections of the Labour Party, and a sympathizer with the tribal vision of England à la Orwell ('a family with the wrong members in control') slightly suffocated by the reality of it. But who knows? It may be that these suspiciously neat ambivalences are just the latest attempt to impose order on chaos.

[1] Alan Donagan, *The Later Philosophy of R. G. Collingwood* (Oxford: Clarendon Press, 1962).

Well, this is all very fine, but it is hardly calculated to keep the printer in employment. What can be done? For an answer, I have resorted to the broom cupboard which passes for a filing system with me, and dug out a paper that I wrote in November 1961. It was called 'Has Political Philosophy a Future?' (How the title itself recalls those dim distant days!) I shall take it as the text for this chapter. First, I will say something about the background. Then I will summarize the argument, with enough extracts to recapture the flavour. Then in conclusion I will offer some comments from my present vantage-point, eighteen years later, in November 1979. As an exercise in multiple realities I must confess that the result is less gripping than *Rashomon*. But I hope at least that it has some of the awkward charm of those old snapshots that enliven books about Bloomsbury. (Was the inability to manage mechanical things like cameras part of the cult?)

To give the background of the paper, I need to say a little about the period between 1955 and 1961 (thus, rather neatly it seems to me, encompassing the required twenty-five-year span). Right from the start, as an undergraduate reading Philosophy, Politics, and Economics, I was drawn by both philosophy and economics and in the end chose between them because I thought I would get better teaching in philosophy. The study of politics, as conceived in Oxford, seemed to me a sad affair. The two required papers were British history from the mid-nineteenth century to 1945 and the politics of several countries since 1945. (Later, when I came back to Oxford, I was on one occasion privileged to be present at an apparently serious discussion among members of the politics subfaculty on the question of the date at which history ended and politics began. The majority view was that by then it had moved on to 1956, though there was also sentiment for 1951 and 1958.) Warmed-over facts with a topping of *Times* editorializing seemed to be the formula. If anybody had any notion that politics could be distinguished analytically rather than chronologically, it was a well-kept secret.

Philosophy, meanwhile, was an enormously exciting business. 'Bliss was it in that dawn to be alive . . .' It is hard to recapture in cold print the atmosphere of a place where people feel they have an approach that is paying off with solid results and is going to continue to do so. Normally it happens only in the natural sciences: Copenhagen in the twenties for physics, or Cambridge in the sixties for molecular biology, are perhaps the right kinds of analogue. Philosophy was visibly advancing—by minute steps perhaps but inexorably. You could see it happening as, say, Miss Anscombe wrestled with the concept of a want week after week.

This collective self-absorption may seem a little ridiculous, or even sinister, in retrospect. When you put together a number of bright people who write little and read less but talk a lot, you may unleash some powerful social dynamics. (I would reverse the usual Oxford view of Ernest Gellner's *Words and Things*:[2] the sociology is in my view better than the philosophy.) Still, there were three things that I got out of philosophy at Oxford in the late 1950s (I stayed on for two postgraduate years) that I still value.

The first was the idea that arguments should be pressed to the point at which the question is settled one way or the other. The second was that arguments must stand on their own feet and that one should avoid cluttering up the discussion with appeals to the authority of the illustrious dead. No faithful attender at Gilbert Ryle's 'informal instructions' could fail to learn that one. (They also taught one the pedagogical uses of silence—another very useful lesson.) The third was that philosophy is defined by its method rather than its subject-matter.

This last was of crucial importance to me because I have an extremely unspeculative turn of mind. I am a sucker for elegant structures of thought like those of physics and economics. (I have always regretted having to choose between 'arts' and 'sciences' at school and I'm glad my son doesn't have to make the same absurd choice.) But speculations that promise neither to explain a phenomenon nor to tell us how we should act leave me cold. Like Rickie in E. M. Forster's novel *The Longest Journey* I could never, even as an undergraduate, maintain more than a polite interest in questions such as where the cow is when nobody's looking at it. Naturally, this left me high and dry when the subject, even at Oxford, turned back to its traditional metaphysical concerns in the 1960s.

Only one more piece of background is needed. To provide it, I must move on to September 1961, when I settled in Cambridge, Mass. (or more precisely in an adjoining slum, since yuppified) for the year. The fellowship that I had allowed me to locate anywhere I liked, and I chose Cambridge because John Rawls was at that time at MIT. We did in fact have a couple of nice chats during the year, but the rest of the time I hung around at Harvard—something I was able to do thanks to

[2] Ernest Gellner, *Words and Things: A Critical Account of Linguistic Philosophy and a Study of Ideology* (London: Gollancz, 1959).

the good offices of C. J. Friedrich in fixing me up with an honorary fellowship for the year.

Since there seemed to be nothing much of interest going on in the philosophy department, I finished up by sitting in on Thomas Schelling's course on game theory and Edward Banfield's course on 'Political Economizing', which was a pioneering introduction to the 'public choice' perspective in political analysis. (I also started attending a course given by Henry Kissinger, but I'm pleased to say that I was thrown out for questioning the premisses: that American national interest was the only criterion of foreign policymaking and that the deployment of military force was the only means worth discussing.) These courses—and, equally, the conversation among graduate students in the lunch room at the top of the Littauer Building—had for me the force of a revelation. Politics didn't have to be the dull stuff we were taught at Oxford—it could actually have intellectual content!

These were, as far as I can now reconstruct them, the main experiences, positive and negative, that entered into the making of 'Has Political Philosophy a Future?' The paper was prepared for presentation to the philosophy department at Princeton, which had expressed some interest in hiring me. It opened as follows:

If a major war is somehow avoided, the next decade or two in English-speaking academic political philosophy could be interesting. This may at first glance appear eccentric to the point of perversity. Political philosophy is dead, we are told; indeed so moribund is it that even this has to be said by people who are not philosophers, because most philosophers are not even sufficiently interested in the subject to talk about it. Thus, in 1958, Robert Dahl wrote (in a review of Bertrand de Jouvenel's *Sovereignty* entitled 'Political Theory, Truth and Consequences', *World Politics* 1958, p. 89): 'In the English-speaking world, where so many of the interesting political problems have been solved (at least superficially), political theory is dead. . . . In the West, this is the age of textual criticism and historical analysis, when the student of political theory makes his way by rediscovering some deservedly obscure text or reinterpreting a familiar one.' And two years earlier, in 1956, Peter Laslett had written (in his introduction to the series of essays entitled *Philosophy, Politics and Society*): 'For the moment, anyway, political philosophy is dead. . . . A survey of our philosophical periodicals for the purposes of this collection gives the impression that their editors have often included articles on political subjects merely out of a sense of their conventional duty. Their contributors, too sometimes give the feeling that they have turned their attention to politics only because the curriculum of their university requires it.' Moreover, the essays reprinted in that series seemed intent on proving the editor's point. Even where they were of some individual quality they were entirely independent of each other and of any other contemporary work, representing the fruit of their authors' own ruminations and reading, rather than arising out of any current dialogue or debate.

If we turn from periodicals and essays to books of so-called 'political philosophy' or 'political theory' we find firstly the historical work mentioned by Dahl—e.g., the general works of Sabine, McIlwain, Strauss, Cobban, Cassirer, Coker and Vereker; and secondly, books of rather loosely-organized reflections of the kind which book reviews in the heavy press are likely to describe as 'mature', 'timely', 'thoughtful', etc. I refer to such authors as Barker, Field, Greaves and de Jouvenel. There is, of course, also Weldon's *Vocabulary of Politics*, but a book about the impossibility of political philosophy can hardly be counted as a portent of future life for it.

Why then do I nevertheless espouse a moderate optimism? For my answer I shall point as briefly as I can to four areas in which work has been produced which already has some achievements to its credit and promises more for the future. Academic philosophers have, however, had little hand in this work so far, and it has not been published or received much attention in their own journals.

What were these four areas? The first was 'work on the formal theory of voting'. I mentioned here first the work of Dahl, Downs, and Tullock as attempts to formalize Madison, James Mill, and Schumpeter; and then 'at a more abstract level' the work of Duncan Black and Kenneth Arrow, and the 'continuing discussion' of the latter's *Social Choice and Individual Values*.[3] I commented here that I hoped that eventually this field would become more transparent rather than more technically complicated, so that 'in ten or twenty years time we shall have a vocabulary in which it will be possible clearly to express our present gropings and see immediately which were right, which were wrong and which were so confused that they must be adjudged to have been meaningless'.

The second area I picked out was game theory.

Does it hold out any immediate prospect of enlightenment to a theoretically-minded student of society or is it merely a fashionable gimmick? Certainly the part which is most fruitful mathematically, the zero-sum part where one man's gain is another man's (equal) loss, has little application. Moreover, of the rest, the part seized on by R. B. Braithwaite, in his *Theory of Games as a Tool for the Moral Philosopher*, i.e. the problem of so-called 'games of fair division', seems to me more a branch of mathematical aesthetics than a more precise explication of ordinary notions of morality. As John Rawls has

[3] Kenneth J. Arrow, *Social Choice and Individual Values* (New Haven: Yale University Press, 1951; 2nd edn., 1963).

said '"To each according to his threat advantage" is hardly the principle of morality'. This work on so-called fair division is in fact closely related to the efforts of economists in the last two centuries to give precise mathematical content to the general idea of a 'fair' or 'equitable' tax burden in the theory of fiscal policy, of which Myrdal wrote (*The Political Element in the Development of Economic Theory*, p. 186): 'Bemused by the search for fictitious principles, it has succeeded in little more than in learned expositions and complex proofs of empty catch-phrases.'

The best chance lies in the direction of attempts to present formally ideas about threatening, bargaining, promising, deterring, etc. This study is still in its infancy. But already I think it is realistic to hope that this theory will find a framework within which a number of strands of thought, already worked out in other terms can be integrated. Duncan Black's treatment of conferences in *The Theory of Committees and Elections* and J. R. Hicks's treatment of collective bargaining in the *Theory of Wages* could be restated in game-theory terms. W. J. Baumol's *Welfare Economics and the Theory of the State* could, I think, go into the terminology of game-theory fairly easily. More precisely, it would come out as an extended application of the so-called 'Prisoners' Dilemma', that is, the kind of case where an enforceable agreement between two parties not to choose the most individually advantageous course makes both better off. It might also be instructive to try expressing the thought of, say, Hobbes, Hume and Rousseau in this form.

The third area, to which I devoted more time, was welfare economics which was, I remarked, like political philosophy 'periodically pronounced dead, having reached theoretical perfection and practical futility in the formulations of Bergson and Samuelson'. I argued that, although there was a lot in this, the abstract structure of welfare economics (and particularly the notion of trade-offs) was useful for thinking about policy questions, and that some of the ideas of economists about 'utility' were of philosophical significance.

The fourth and last source of input into political philosophy that I located was 'the attempts which some academic political scientists have made to appraise institutions in terms of stated principles or, if you like, "values"'. To illustrate the value of 'philosophical sophistication or philosophical criticism' I took up the fashionable notion that the concept of the public interest had no content and the curious notion that democrats must be procedure-fetishists. (Both of these points eventually turned up in *Political Argument*.[4]) I argued, of course, that the political scientists who had perpetrated these ideas could be shot down by appropriate theoretical reasoning.

[4] Brian M. Barry, *Political Argument* (London: Routledge and Kegan Paul, 1965).

I concluded, rather nervously, as follows:

> Even if it is granted that the research in these four areas is significant in itself, two questions still remain to be asked: is this a continuation of political philosophy as traditionally understood? and even if it is, should not philosophers renounce any claims to competence in it?
>
> The answer to the first question clearly turns on one's answer to the question: what was the subject of political philosophy as traditionally understood? I shall offer the answer that it was concerned with the nature and conditions of the good society, and, particularly, with the nature and conditions of good forms of government. If this characterization is accepted, then I think the relevance of my fourth category is immediately established since that is precisely what it is about. And the other three can I think be looked on as technical aids to clear-thinking about this traditional subject matter. We should no more spurn them because they are more technical than the conceptual apparatus used by Plato and Aristotle than we should spurn modern symbolic logic because *it* is technical.

In answer to the second question, I suggested that philosophy had a professional commitment to asking questions about the fundamentals of subjects that practitioners of them were liable to brush aside.

> The time is long past when philosophers were the people who supplied society with its quota of lofty speculation. Our contemporary Hegel is Professor Parsons, the two-by-two matrices of the latter replacing the triads of the former. Our contemporary scholastics are the welfare economists, the game theorists, and the voting analysts, drawing out with wonderful ingenuity the implications of axioms which themselves go largely uncriticized. Philosophers can best help, I suggest, by maintaining their characteristic critical posture.

After that, the Princeton philosophy department and I both independently decided against taking the matter any further, and I am sure we were both right. No self-respecting department of philosophy could have been too comfortable with the role of under-labourer's mate (relegated to carrying the tools) to which I had assigned philosophy in that paper. And for me it seemed to make more sense to be a theorist in a department of politics than a political philosopher in a department of philosophy—something which I arranged a year later.

Looking back now on that paper, one thing that seems undeniable is that I at any rate predicted the trend correctly. The description of the actual conditions in 1961 is, as far as I can see, absolutely accurate. Things were just as desperate as I then said they were. You really could turn over whole volumes of the philosophical journals and find nothing about political philosophy—indeed very little substantive moral philosophy except for an occasional piece of utilitarian casuistry.

I would also say that it was quite acute of me to have picked on not merely the paucity of material but the lack of any dialogue between the different contributions, such as they were. Comparing then and now, the biggest difference lies exactly here.

When I was writing my thesis (published in revised form as *Political Argument*) there simply wasn't a 'literature' to which one could relate one's work. There was nothing for it but to make the stuff up as one went along. Now, on just about every topic discussed in *Political Argument* there is an elaborate article literature of assertion, rebuttal, modified assertion, synthesis, and so on. This is, of course, what the professionalization of a field means.

If anything, the problem today is the opposite of the one I diagnosed back in 1961. I occasionally have a nightmarish feeling that 'the literature' has taken off on an independent life and now carries on like the broomsticks bewitched by the sorcerer's apprentice. Let me juxtapose the old snapshot with a recent one. I wrote in the October 1979 issue of *Ethics*, upon assuming the editorship of that venerable journal (founded as *The International Journal of Ethics* in 1890), that I was concerned at the tendency for submissions 'to recapitulate existing controversies or repeat with only slight variations points already made elsewhere'. I continued as follows:

> I can think of a number of perfectly understandable reasons why philosophers (who make up the great majority of our contributors) should be reluctant to break new ground. First, there are philosophically OK subjects, whose pedigree is established by their having been written about by OK philosophers, and one incurs a risk of professional oblivion by going outside them. Second, writing on a new topic may require a serious investment in learning the analytic techniques of some discipline and assimilating a mass of empirical material. And, third, it is damned hard work—much harder than reading six articles and pounding out a seventh on the same subject—with no guarantee of success.

These reactionary grumblings were, I hope, salutary in their context; but who would have imagined in 1961 that one would so soon have the luxury of being able to complain about a glut of political philosophy? The only thing wrong with the expression of 'moderate optimism' back then was that, while it was about right for the first decade, it was quite inadequate to the period since then.

In fact, 1971 is the key date. This is the year in which John Rawls's

A Theory of Justice was published.[5] And it is also the year in which the first issue of the journal *Philosophy & Public Affairs* appeared.

It is difficult to overemphasize the significance of the Rawls phenomenon. In the end it is of secondary importance whether one thinks his theories are right or wrong. What matters is that the book caught the imagination of scholars not only in philosophy but also in disciplines such as political science, sociology, economics, and law. *Political Theory* published a bibliography in its November 1977 issue which gives an indication in rough quantitative terms of the scale of the phenomenon. For 1972 there are 12 references. This rises sharply to 40 in 1973. 1974 is the peak year, with 52 entries. Then there is a decline to 35 in 1975 and 28 in 1976. This falling-off after 1974 (which would be continued if the list were extended to later years) is in a way misleading, however. For although 'Rawls articles' have become a drug on the market, this really reflects the way in which Rawls has now been thoroughly assimilated. His presence is therefore more ubiquitous than ever, but it is now more diffuse.

Why was this extremely long, poorly organized, and stylistically undistinguished book such a smash hit? It was immensely ambitious in its claims to deduce principles of justice from the construction of an 'original position' and at the same time could be regarded as constituting a massive synthesis of contemporary liberal political thinking. Those two points no doubt take one a long way. But in addition, I think that for many social scientists, reared on simple-minded logical positivism in graduate courses on 'methodology', the most exciting thing about Rawls was that he showed that one could sustain rational argument about questions of 'values' over 600 or so pages. Among philosophers, logical positivism, with its doctrine that all 'value judgements' are merely 'emotive utterances'—boos and hurrahs—had already been discredited. But Rawls was the first person to carry the message to non-philosophers. He thus got personal credit for a more general shift in philosophical ideas. But this was quite well deserved in that he was the first to do it on the grand scale rather than simply argue that in principle one could argue rationally about questions of political philosophy.

If Rawls's *A Theory of Justice* was the internal stimulus to the outpouring of political philosophy that we have witnessed since 1971, the Vietnam War was unquestionably the crucial external stimulus. Individual choices had to be made about draft resistance and other

[5] John Rawls, *A Theory of Justice* (Cambridge, Mass.: Harvard University Press, 1971).

forms of civil disobedience; and those who condemned the war had to develop the categories in which to show what was wrong with the means by which the war was being waged by the USA. Small wonder, therefore, that articles on the morality of civil disobedience, on the 'just war', and on the responsibilities of combatants proliferated.

This was the intellectual background out of which *Philosophy & Public Affairs* (like *The New York Review of Books*, with which it shares a certain common ambience) came into being. Thus, in the first issue, there was an article by Richard Wasserstrom on 'The Relevance of Nuremburg' and an early exposition by Michael Walzer of some of the ideas that were to appear six years later in *Just and Unjust Wars*.[6]

Philosophy & Public Affairs immediately settled down as a first-class journal devoted, as its 'statement of purpose' puts it, to 'philosophical discussions of substantive legal, social and political problems, as well as discussions of the more abstract problems to which they give rise'. To be hypercritical, one might say that in practice 'public affairs' have tended to be defined as issues before the US Supreme Court, especially abortion and reverse discrimination. But the range of subjects covered in the last eight years is quite impressive, and so is the consistently high quality of the contributions. *Philosophy & Public Affairs* has been central in creating the dense 'literature' of political philosophy to which I referred earlier.

Going back to my thoughts about the future of the subject in 1961, it is obvious that my big failure lay in missing out on the growth of self-sustaining normative political philosophy done by philosophers. I had, of course, identified Rawls as the most significant figure in contemporary political philosophy, which is why, as I have said, I was in Cambridge, Mass. in 1961 in the first place. But there had been no visible response to his article 'Justice as Fairness', which had been published in 1958. The bibliography of 'Rawls on Justice' already mentioned has no entries before 1963 (except one for 1957—i.e. *before* the article was published). And it records only fourteen items for the period between 1963 and 1970.

At our first meeting, Rawls had been kind enough to give me a copy of the book manuscript in its then existing form. (In those pre-Xerox days, getting hold of one was no easy matter.) But it seemed to me that the whole argument stood or fell by the validity of the derivation of the principles of justice from the original position, and that was, as far

[6] Michael Walzer, *Just and Unjust Wars* (New York: Basic Books, 1977).

as I could see, unsalvageable. I still think so, but it turned out that that did not preclude the fantastic reception that *A Theory of Justice* actually received.

The other stimulus to the growth of political philosophy was also on the Harvard campus, and I have already mentioned him, but I missed his true significance completely. I thought that Henry Kissinger was, as an academic, intellectually second-rate and dishonest. This was quite correct. But I did not foresee that, as the architect of the last and least defensible five years of the Vietnam War, he would drive a generation of Americans into a personal concern with the basic problems of political morality.

If one takes these developments as having engulfed my fourth category of incipient political philosophy, 'the attempts which some academic political scientists have made to appraise institutions in terms of principles', where does this leave my first three categories? I would say that here I score pretty well, though my time frame of 'a decade or two' was only just enough. Formal economic-style analysis of democratic institutions has, of course, taken off since 1961; and what I called the 'continuing discussion' of Arrow amounted in 1961 to only a dozen or so papers but is now numbered in the hundreds or even thousands. Yet I would say that it is only quite recently that there has begun to be any displacement of interest from making the applications more complicated to reflecting on the validity of the fundamental premisses and on the real implications of the formal theories for the evaluation of institutions. Similarly, it has taken longer than I expected for the crippling limitations of zero-sum game theory to be seen through and for it to be generally recognized that the central contribution of game theory is to the clarification of the analysis of problems of power and collective action.

Welfare economics, my third category, has developed in two directions since 1961, though both lines of development were already under way by then (and found their way into *Political Argument*). The first is cost-benefit analysis. In 1960 the kind of systems analysis that was to be brought to the Pentagon as PPBS was advocated by Hitch and McKean in *The Economics of Defense in the Nuclear Age*.[7] Since then cost-benefit analysis has, of course, proliferated. Its assumptions have been criticized by economists such as E. J. Mishan and academic lawyers such as Lawrence Tribe. Philosophers, whether because they allowed themselves to be blinded by science or thought it too crass to

[7] C. J. Hitch and R. N. McKean, *The Economics of Defense in the Nuclear Age* (Cambridge, Mass: Harvard University Press, 1960).

be worth attacking, have done little work on it. I think this was a missed opportunity.

The second direction in which welfare economics has moved was also foreshadowed in 1960, this time by the 'Coase theorem' set out in Coase's article 'The Problem of Social Cost'.[8] Since then an entire theology under the name 'economic analysis of law' has been developed, especially at the University of Chicago, based on the rather simple idea that all bargains are Pareto optimal. The Virginia school of constitutional engineering of James Buchanan represents an even more crude and ideological application of the same simple idea. Here lawyers and political scientists have contributed critiques, but philosophers have also been active to some extent.

However, as I emphasized (perhaps a little tactlessly) in my 1961 paper, political philosophy is political philosophy no matter who does it. The crucial difference between 1961 and now is that then it was a slogan—*in principle* it does not matter what department someone is in, so long as he does the right kind of thing. But in practice it almost always made a difference: the mind-sets, the authorities appealed to, and the standards of argument tended very strongly to vary according to departmental affiliation. Since then there has been an enormous change in just this respect, with a rapid growth in the number of interdisciplinary journals and associations and an increasing tendency of people to read and cite articles in journals outside their 'own' field. In the *Ethics* editorial from which I have already quoted my apprehensions about the risk of scholasticism, there followed the more cheerful thought that:

> Scholars in a variety of disciplines have started to become frustrated by the sterility of most 'mainstream' work and have begun to look for kindred spirits in other disciplines. I am thinking here, for example, of people interested in the theory of social choice who are not content to see its development either as a pure exercise in technical virtuosity or as the vehicle for a half-baked ideology of Pareto-optimality but who wish to bring its techniques into relation with the rich traditions of democratic theory and the theory of distributive justice. I am also thinking of people in public policy programs, law schools, and elsewhere, who are interested in the evaluation of public policy but are repelled by the arrogant naïveté of the standard works on cost-benefit analysis, public policy analysis, and so on. At the same time, philosophers have increasingly tired of their 'one-sided diet' of desert-island examples and have begun to bring the traditional concerns of social and

[8] R. H. Coase, 'The Problem of Social Cost', *Journal of Law and Economics*, 3 (1960), 1–44.

political philosophy into relation with the methods and findings of social science.

Coming from many directions, scholars in different disciplines are finding common ground. Already it is possible in certain contexts (for example at certain sessions of the Public Choice Society) to listen to a discussion without being able to tell from what is said that one speaker is from economics, another from law, another from philosophy, and another from political science. What we are seeing, in other words, is a new kind of interdisciplinary development: not a wary rapprochement across disciplinary boundaries but the creation of autonomous spheres of discourse that draw on existing disciplines but represent a genuine synthesis.

When I read my old paper again for the first time in eighteen years, I couldn't help being struck by how little my hopes for the future of political philosophy seem to have changed between then and now. There are, I suppose, two alternative explanations of that fact. One is that my hopes have continued on their own course oblivious of reality. The other is that reality has already been kind enough to them to make it quite rational to keep the faith. Time will tell. I look forward to having an opportunity to superimpose another snapshot on these in 2005 when we are asked to look back over fifty years.

2

IS DEMOCRACY SPECIAL?

Martin If government, in the sense of coercion, has hitherto been essential to society, that is because no society has yet been founded on equity. The laws have been made by one class for another; and there was no reason, other than fear, why that other class should obey them. But when we come to imagine an ideal society, would government, in this sense, be essential to it?

Stuart I suppose there would always be recalcitrant people.

Martin Why should there be? What makes people recalcitrant, save the fact that they are expected to obey rules of which they do not approve?

Stuart But make your institutions as just as you like, and your people as public-spirited as you like, there must always be differences of opinion as to this or that law or regulation; and if those differences become acute there must be a point at which coercion comes in. . . .

G. Lowes Dickinson, *Justice and Liberty: A Political Dialogue*

I

The question to which this essay is addressed is the following: does the fact that a law was passed by a democratic procedure provide a special reason for obeying it? Let me begin by explaining what I mean by 'a special reason'.

If we look at any law we can say that there are usually reasons for obeying it, such as fear of punishment, anxiety about the general effects of disobedience on social stability, and unwillingness to take advantage of the compliance of others (the essence of the John Rawls's 'duty of fair play'). There are also often reasons for disobeying it, of which personal advantage is the most obvious. In addition it seems plausible that approval of the content of the law makes the case for obeying it stronger than it would otherwise be, while disapproval makes it weaker. 'Approval' and 'disapproval', however, are anodyne generic terms, which conceal a range of relevantly different responses. It seems on the face of it reasonable to say, for example, that equally strong disapproval of two laws, one on the basis of its imprudence or inefficiency, the other on the basis of its injustice or immorality, should have different implications.

Exactly how and why all these factors provide reasons in favour of obedience or reasons telling against it is by no means straightforward. Nor, I am sure, would everyone agree that all of them should be reckoned as reasons at all. For the purpose of this chapter, however, I shall simply assume that at least some of these factors, and perhaps others like them, provide reasons for obeying or disobeying laws. My question then is whether an entirely different sort of consideration, namely, the procedure by which the law was enacted, or, in the case of long-standing laws, the procedure by which it might have been repealed and has not been, should be a reason for obeying a law.

More specifically, the question I wish to raise is whether or not a law's having been enacted (or not repealed) by a democratic procedure adds a reason for obeying it to whatever reasons exist independently of that. By a democratic procedure I mean a method of determining the content of laws (and other legally binding decisions) such that the preferences of the citizens have some formal connection with the outcome in which each counts equally. Let me make four comments on this definition.

First, I follow here those who insist that 'democracy' is to be understood in procedural terms. That is to say, I reject the notion that one should build into 'democracy' any constraints on the content of the outcomes produced, such as substantive equality, respect for human rights, concern for the general welfare, personal liberty, or the rule of law. The only exceptions (and these are significant) are those required by democracy itself as a procedure. Thus, some degree of freedom of communication and organization is a necessary condition of the formation, expression, and aggregation of political preferences. And in a state (as against a small commune, say) the only preferences people can have are preferences for general lines of policy. There are not going to be widely held preferences about whether or not Mr Jones should be fined £10 for speeding or Mrs Smith should get supplementary benefit payments of £3·65 per week. At most there can be preferences for a speeding tariff or for general rules about eligibility for supplementary benefit. If magistrates or civil servants are arbitrary or capricious, therefore, they make democracy impossible.

Second, I require that there should be a formal connection between the preferences of the citizens and the outcomes produced. My intention in specifying a formal connection is to rule out cases where the decisionmaking process is *de facto* affected by the preferences of the citizens but not in virtue of any constitutional rule. Thus, eighteenth-century England has been described as 'oligarchy tempered by riot'.[1] But, however efficacious the rioters might be, I would not say that their ability to coerce the government constituted a democratic procedure. In the concluding words of the judge appointed to enquire into riots in West Pakistan in 1953: 'But if democracy means the subordination of law and order to political ends—then Allah knoweth best and we end the report.'[2]

Third, by 'some formal connection' I intend deliberately to leave open a variety of possible ways in which democratic procedures might be implemented. In particular, I wish to include both voting on laws by the citizens at large and voting for representatives who exercise the law-making function. I shall take either of these to constitute 'some formal connection with the outcome' in the sense required by the definition: in the first case the citizens choose the laws and in the second they choose the law-makers (in both cases, of course, within the limits of the choice presented to them).

Finally, the phrase 'each counts equally' has to be read in conjunction with the preceding phrase 'some formal connection with the outcome'. That is to say, nothing is suggested by the definition of democratic procedure about equality of actual influence on outcomes. The equality is in the formal aspect: each adult citizen is to have a vote (only minor exceptions covering a tiny proportion of those otherwise eligible being allowed) and there are to be no 'fancy franchises' giving extra votes to some.

What about the notion that each vote should have an 'equal value'? This is valid if we construe it as a formal requirement. If there are two constituencies each of which returns one representative, the value of a vote is obviously unequal if one constituency contains more voters than another.[3] To talk about 'equal value' except in this a priori sense is sheer muddle. In recent years, for example, supporters of systems of proportional representation in Britain have succeeded in scoring something of a propaganda victory by pressing the idea that the vote for a candidate who comes third (or lower) in a plurality system is 'wasted' and the people who vote for the candidate are 'effectively

[1] W. J. M. Mackenzie, *Power, Violence, Decision* (Harmondsworth: Penguin, 1975), 151.

[2] Quoted in Hugh Tinker, *Ballot Box and Bayonet: People and Government in Emergent Asian Countries* (Chatham House Essays, 5; London: Oxford University Press, 1964), 83.

[3] This is, it may be noted, the line taken by the US Supreme Court in its decision requiring redistricting to secure approximately equal constituencies. (The leading case is *Reynolds* v. *Sims*, 377 US 533 (1964).)

disfranchised'. But then why stop there? The only way of making sense of this argument is by postulating that anyone who voted for a candidate other than the actual winner—even the runner-up—was 'effectively disfranchised'; and it was not long before some academics stumbled on this amazing theoretical breakthrough.[4] I do not think that anyone of ordinary intelligence would be found saying of an election for, say, the post of president of a club: 'I didn't vote for the winning candidate. In other words my vote didn't help elect anybody. And that means I was effectively disfranchised.' It is a little alarming that such palpably fallacious reasoning should have the power to impose on people when the context is a parliamentary election.

II

There is one simple, and on the face of it attractive, reason for giving special weight to laws arrived at by democratic procedures. This is that, on any given question about which opinion is divided, the decision must, as a matter of logic, accord with either the preferences of the majority or the preferences of the minority. And, by something akin to the rule of insufficient reason, it seems difficult to say why the decision should go in the way wanted by the minority rather than in the way wanted by the majority. Let us call this the majority principle.

Obviously, even if the majority principle were accepted, there would still be a gap between the majority principle and democratic procedures as I have defined them. The implication of the majority principle is, fairly clearly, that the best form of democratic procedure is that which permits a vote on issues by referendum. There is no guarantee that elected representatives will on every issue vote in such a way that the outcome preferred by a majority of citizens will be the one chosen. However much we cry up the effects of electoral competition in keeping representatives in line, there is no theoretical reason for expecting that a party or coalition of parties with a majority will always do what a majority of voters want. (Persistent non-voters will in any case have their preferences disregarded by competitive parties —though it may be noted that this is equally so in a referendum.) Even a purely opportunistic party would not necessarily be well advised to back the side on every issue that the majority supports, as Anthony

[4] An analysis with whose general line I concur is Paul E. Meehl's 'The Selfish Voter Paradox and the Thrown-Away Vote Argument', *The American Political Science Review*, 71 (1977), 11–30.

Downs pointed out.[5] And in practice no party is purely opportunistic —indeed a purely opportunistic party would in most circumstances be an electoral failure because it would be too unpredictable. The party or parties with a legislative majority are therefore always liable to have a package of policies approved of by a majority and policies opposed by a majority. (On many other issues there may be no single policy with majority support, but that is a complication in the specification of the majority principle that I shall discuss below.)

All this, however, is not as damaging for democratic procedures as might be supposed. For it may surely be said that no method of selecting law-makers and governments that was *not* democratic (in the sense defined) could provide a better long-run prospect of producing outcomes in accord with the majority principle. However disappointed an adherent of the majority principle might be in the actual working of democratic procedures, it is hard to see what he or she would stand to gain by helping to secure their overthrow. In principle, of course, this majoritarian might assist the rise to power of a group of dedicated majoritarians who would be committed to acting in accord with majority preferences as ascertained, say, by sophisticated opinion polling. But, once they were in power, what reason would there be for confidence in the good faith of these people, or, even more perhaps, of their successors?

I think, therefore, that an adherent of the majority principle would be prepared to disobey laws that were enacted (or not repealed) in the face of clear majority sentiment. But he or she would not take part in any activity either designed for or having the predictable consequence of bringing about the collapse of democratic procedures, because in the long run democratic procedures are more likely to produce majoritarian outcomes than are alternative procedures. Of course, it does not follow that a majoritarian who is satisfied that there is a clear majority against a piece of legislation is thereby committed to disobeying it. All the reasons for not breaking the law that I mentioned at the beginning of this chapter may still apply. The only thing that the absence of majority support does for a majoritarian is to remove one (conclusive) reason for obedience.

Can an adherent of the majority principle break the law in an attempt to get the majority to change its mind? I think that this may be done consistently with the principle if it is formulated so that not just any majority counts but only one based on a serious and informed

[5] A. Downs, *An Economic Theory of Democracy* (New York: Harper and Bros., 1957), 55–60.

consideration of the issue. Thus, on the facts as stated by him, Bertrand Russell's campaign against nuclear weapons could be consistent with a majoritarian standpoint.[6] But it is essential to the honesty of such a position that one must be prepared to specify what would constitute a fair test of 'real' majority opinion in a way that does not fall back on the proposition that 'No majority can *really* be in favour of *x*'.

I have suggested, then, that the majority principle provides fairly strong backing for democratic procedures. What now has to be asked, of course, is whether there is any reason for accepting the majority principle. The view that there is something natural and inevitable about it was expressed forcefully by John Locke in paragraphs 95–9 of the *Second Treatise*. The argument is tied up with Locke's consent theory of political authority but can, I think, be detached from it. The nub is that if there is going to be a body capable of making binding decisions then it 'must move one way' and 'it is necessary the Body should move that way whither the greater force carries it, which is the *consent of the majority*'. Locke adds that 'therefore we see that in Assemblies impowered to act by positive Laws where no number is set by that positive Law which impowers them, the *act of the Majority* passes for the act of the whole, and of course determines, as having by the Law of Nature and Reason, the power of the whole'.[7]

In my first book, *Political Argument*, I put forward the example of 'five people in a railway compartment which the railway operator has omitted to label either "smoking" or "no-smoking"', each of whom 'either wants to smoke or objects to others smoking in the vicinity'.[8] (I should have added that the carriage should be understood as one of the sort that does not have a corridor, so the option of changing compartments is not open.) I still think that the example was a good one. Unless all five can reach agreement on some general substantive principle—that in the absence of positive regulation there is a 'natural right' to smoke or a 'natural right' for any one person to veto

[6] 'Long and frustrated experience has proved, to those among us who have endeavoured to make unpleasant facts [about nuclear weapons] known, that orthodox methods, alone, are insufficient. By means of civil disobedience a certain kind of publicity becomes possible. . . . Many people are roused into inquiry into questions which they had been willing to ignore. . . . It seems not unlikely that, in the end, an irresistible popular movement of protest will compel governments to allow their subjects to continue to exist.' Bertrand Russell, 'Civil Disobedience and the Threat of Nuclear Warfare', in Hugo Adam Bedau (ed.), *Civil Disobedience: Theory and Practice* (New York: Pegasus, 1969), 153–9, at 157.

[7] John Locke, *Two Treatises of Government*, ed. Peter Laslett (New York: The New American Library, Mentor Books, 1965), 375–6.

[8] B. M. Barry, *Political Argument* (London: Routledge and Kegan Paul, 1965), 312.

smoking—it is difficult to see any plausible alternative to saying that the outcome should correspond to majority preference.

The position of someone who is outvoted but refuses to accept the decision is difficult to maintain. As I have suggested, quite persuasive arguments can be made for saying that the decision should not simply reflect the number of people who want to smoke as against the number who dislike being in the presence of smokers. But, since opposing principles can be advanced, the existence of relevant principles does not seem to offer a sound basis for resistance to a majority decision. Or suppose that one of the travellers happens to be the Archbishop of Canterbury. He might claim the right to decide the smoking question on the basis either of his social position or on the basis of his presumptive expertise in casuistry. If his claim is accepted by all the other passengers, no decisionmaking problem arises because there is agreement. If not all the fellow-passengers accept his claim, however, it again seems difficult to see how the question can be settled except by a vote. And if he finds himself in the minority it must be because he has failed to convince enough of the others of his claim to authority. He may continue to maintain that it should have been accepted, just as a believer in the natural right to smoke may continue to maintain that the others should have accepted that principle. But, in the face of actual non-acceptance, the case for bowing to the majority decision looks strong.

On further analysis, however, we have to recognize that the 'naturalness' of the majority principle as a way of settling the dispute rests on several features of the particular example which are not commonly found together. I am therefore now inclined to say that it was a good example in the sense that it illustrated well the case for the majority principle but that it was in another sense a bad example because of its special features. I shall single out four, the first three of which make the majority principle determinate while the fourth makes it acceptable. First, we implicitly assume that the people in the compartment have to make only this one decision. Second, only two alternatives are envisaged: smoking or non-smoking. Third, the decisionmaking constituency is not open to doubt. And fourth, nothing has been said to suggest that the outcome on the issue is of vital importance for the long-term well-being of any of those involved.

To begin with, then, let us retain the feature from the original case that the decisions to be made are dichotomous (that is to say, there are only two alternatives to choose between) but now say that several different decisions have to be taken. In addition to the question whether to permit smoking, the passengers also have to decide whether to allow the playing of transistor radios. Suppose that a vote is taken on each question and there is a majority against each. It may be that a majority of the passengers would nevertheless prefer permitting both to prohibiting both, if they were given a choice in those terms.

Let us assign the following symbols: *w* is no smoking, *x* is smoking allowed; *y* is no playing of radios, *z* is playing allowed. The preferences of the five passengers (*A*, *B*, *C*, *D*, and *E*) are in descending order as in Table 2.1.[9]

TABLE 2.1

Rank order	*A*	*B*	*C*	*D*	*E*
1	*wz*	*wz*	*xy*	*wy*	*wy*
2	*xz*	*xz*	*xz*	*wz*	*xy*
3	*wy*	*wy*	*wy*	*xy*	*wz*
4	*xy*	*xy*	*wz*	*xz*	*xz*

In a straight vote *A*, *B*, *D* and *E* all prefer *w* to *x*; and *C*, *D*, and *E* prefer *y* to *z*. The outcome would therefore be *w* and *y*. But the pair *wy* is less well liked than the opposite pair *xz* by *A*, *B*, and *C*.

We now ask: what does the majority principle prescribe in a situation like this? Are we committed to the view that neither smoking nor playing radios should be allowed, because there is a majority against each? Or can we take account of the fact that there is a majority in favour of overturning the result of the two separate votes and substituting their opposites?

A sufficient (though not necessary) condition of there being an outcome that is preferred by a majority to any other is that preferences should be what is called 'single-peaked'.[10] All this means is that it should be possible to arrange the alternative outcomes along a single line in such a way that, when we draw for each of the people involved a curve whose height represents their relative preference for each outcome, we get a curve with a single peak for each.

To illustrate this, let us allow for a choice with respect to smoking

[9] Adapted from Example 1 in Nicholas R. Miller, 'Logrolling, Vote Trading, and the Paradox of Voting: A Game-Theoretical Overview', *Public Choice*, 30 (1977), 49–75, at 69.

[10] The *locus classicus* is Duncan Black, *The Theory of Committees and Elections* (Cambridge: Cambridge University Press, 1963).

among three possibilities instead of two: no smoking at all, smoking of cigarettes but not pipes and cigars, and unrestricted smoking. Call the first policy x, the second y, and the third z. We may imagine the preference orderings of our five people to be as in Table 2.2, which corresponds to Figure 2.1. It will be seen that in this case the preferences are capable of being arranged along a single dimension (which can be labelled pro-smoking/anti-smoking) so that each person's preferences are single-peaked.

TABLE 2.2

Preference ranking	*A* and *B*	*C*	*D* and *E*
1	x	y	z
2	y	z	y
3	z	x	x

When preferences are single-peaked we know not only that a majority winner exists but we also know how to find it easily. The simple rule is that the outcome that is most preferred by the median person is the outcome that is preferred by a majority to any other. The median person is the one (for an odd number of participants) who has exactly as many others on one side as on the other. If there are n people (n being an odd number) whose preferences are to be taken into account, we should start counting at one end (it doesn't matter which since the answer will be the same) and stop when we get to $\frac{1}{2}(n+1)$. This will be the median person. In our example of five people $\frac{1}{2}(n+1)$

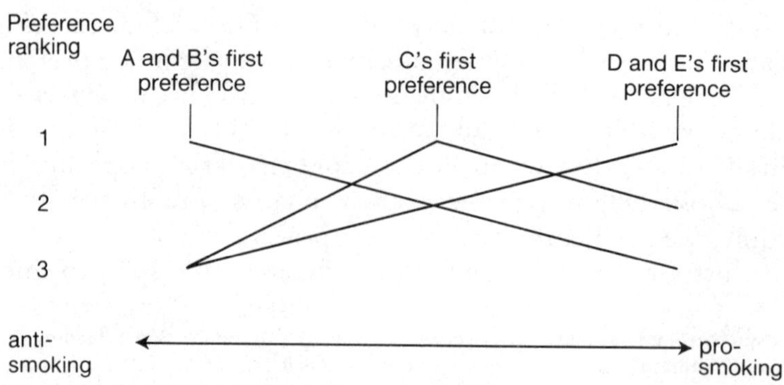

FIG. 2.1

= 3 and it will be seen that we get to *C*'s most preferred position by counting to three from either end. Where there is an even number of people there is no unique median but the people at $\frac{1}{2}n$ and $(\frac{1}{2}n) + 1$ (again counting from either end) occupy positions each of which is capable of gaining a majority against any other position. These two positions have an equal number of supporters when matched against each other so, on the majority principle, they may be regarded as equally good.

The trouble is that there may not be any outcome that is capable of getting majority support against any other (or, in the case of even numbers, two that are equally good in the sense just specified). Thus, suppose now that *D* and *E* do not like to smoke cigarettes and, if they cannot smoke their pipes, would prefer a smoke-free environment to one contaminated by *C*'s cigarette smoke. Then the preference matrix becomes as in Table 2.3. We now pit each possible outcome against each other in a series of three pairwise comparisons and get the result that *x* beats *y* (*A*, *B*, *D*, and *E* prefer it), *y* beats *z* (*A*, *B*, and *C* prefer it), and *z* beats *x* (*C*, *D*, and *E* prefer it). Thus, a quite plausible distribution of preferences generates a 'paradox of voting' in which the majorities arising from pairwise comparisons form a cycle.

TABLE 2.3

Rank order	*A* and *B*	*C*	*D* and *E*
1	*x*	*y*	*z*
2	*y*	*z*	*x*
3	*z*	*x*	*y*

The two sources of indeterminacy in the majority principle that I have so far been pointing out may be considered rather dull and technical, incapable of arousing political passions. This is by no means true. Consider, for example, the importance that both sympathizers of President Allende and apologists for the coup that overthrew him have attached in their polemics to the question whether or not he had majority support for his policies. Given a political set-up with three blocs, Allende was able to come into power as President on a bare plurality; and the Popular Unity Coalition that supported him never achieved a majority of votes cast. It was on the basis of these facts that the junta claimed legitimacy in terms of the majority principle for overthrowing the constitutional government. On the other side, however, it may be argued that 'one cannot infer that those who opposed Allende necessarily supported a military coup, especially the bloody one that ensued following his overthrow. Thus there is little evidence that a majority of Chileans wanted Allende overthrown by the military.'[11]

It is not my intention to join in this debate, merely to point out that, where the majority principle is indeterminate, generals find it worth appealing to it and scholars find it worth rebutting that appeal. However, if we measure the importance of a question by the blood spilt over it (and I find it hard to think of a better criterion) the importance of the third reason for the indeterminacy of the majority principle can hardly be denied. The question is the deceptively innocent one: majority of *what*?

In the railway carriage example this is not a problem. If the decision about permitting or prohibiting smoking is to be made according to majority preference there can be no doubt that the people whose preferences should be taken into account are the five people in the railway carriage who will be affected by the decision. But when the question is the boundaries of political entities—empires, supranational organizations, federations, nation-states, provinces, or other subdivisions—and their respective decisionmaking powers, the question 'who is included?' is an explosive one.

There is no need to labour the point. The briefest survey is enough. In Western Europe, after centuries of wars between states, civil wars, and heavy-handed centralizing government, Northern Ireland is paralysed by conflict, Scottish nationalism is a powerful force, the centralized Belgian state has been virtually partitioned, unfinished business from the nineteenth century still hangs over the Swiss Jura and the Alto Adige, while in Spain Basque and Catalan separatism are stirring again after the long freeze. In Eastern Europe almost every state has claims on the territory of at least one other. Order, of a kind, is maintained by the Soviet Union, which is itself a patchwork of nationalities held together by coercion. And nobody is taking bets on the existence of Yugoslavia in ten years' time. In North America, Quebec has a separatist government, and the unity of the country is in question. In the Middle East three wars have been fought over the boundaries of Israel and no end is in sight. In Africa, the boundaries bequeathed by the colonial powers, after a period of surprising stability (interrupted only by the Biafran and Katagan secessions), are

[11] James Petras and Morris Morley, 'Chilean Destabilisation and Its Aftermath', *Politics*, 11 (1976), 140–8, at 145.

coming under pressure in the Horn of Africa, and the trouble looks as if it may well spread further in coming years. The Indian subcontinent has seen first the convulsion of the creation of Pakistan and then the almost equally bloody process of its splitting into two; while in India the states have had to be reconstituted, amid a good deal of disorder, in an attempt to satisfy the aspirations of linguistic groups. There are few parts of the world where boundaries are not a potential source of serious conflict, and where we do not hear that they are (e.g. China) this is as likely to reflect our ignorance as the absence of potential conflict.

The only thing that has to be established, beyond the existence of conflicts over boundaries, is that the majority principle has no way of solving them, either in practice or in theory. In practice, the majority principle, so far from alleviating conflicts over boundaries, greatly exacerbates them. It may be tolerable to be ruled over by a cosmopolitan autocracy like the Austrian empire, or a more or less even-handed colonial power like the British in India. But to be subject to a majority of a different language, religion, or national identity is far more threatening. In an area where nationalities are intermingled, like the Balkans, every move to satisfy majority aspirations leaves the remaining minorities even more vulnerable.

On a theoretical level, any use of the majority principle in order to establish boundaries must involve begging the question. Locke, to do him credit, saw that the majority principle could come into play only after the constituency has been identified, but he finessed the problem by resorting to the fiction that those who are to form 'one body' all individually agree to do so. This approach obviously fails to provide any guidance in any situation where it is actually needed, that is to say where people are disagreeing about the 'body' they want to be members of.

The so-called 'principle of national self-determination' espoused by the Versailles Treaty of 1919 says, in effect, that if a minority within a state wishes to secede and the majority does not wish them to secede the minority should win—provided the minority is a 'nation'. As it stands, this is both question-begging (since the crucial judgement is packed into the question of whether the would-be secessionists constitute a 'nation') and contrary to the majority principle. But the attempt to reformulate it so as to derive it from the majority principle simply begs the question in a different way.

Suppose we say: the majority in any given territorial area should decide on the political status of that area. Then the question is thrown back one stage further. What is the relevant territorial area within which to count preferences? Consider, for example, the Irish question as it stood between 1918 and 1921. Simplifying somewhat, there was (probably) a majority in the UK as a whole (i.e. the British Isles) for the maintenance of the union; within Ireland (i.e. the whole island) there was a majority in favour of independence for the whole of Ireland; within the six provinces that became Northern Ireland there was a majority for partition as a second-best to union; but within two of those six counties there was a majority for unification with the south as a second best to independence for the whole of Ireland. But why stop at counties? Counties could have been further divided and some areas within them would have had one sort of majority and others other sorts.

A contemporary puzzle of the same sort is offered by Gibraltar: 'London insists that it will respect the wishes of the 25,000 Gibraltarians, a mixture of people who, for the most part, tend to favour retaining their colonial connection with Britain. Madrid insists on regaining sovereignty over what a broad spectrum of Spanish opinion considers a usurped segment of national territory'.[12] Is the majority of Gibraltarians the relevant one, or the majority of people in Spain plus Gibraltar?

It seems clear that the majority principle can offer no guidance. If we feel that (within limits of contiguity and feasibility) the right answer is to try to satisfy the wishes of as many people as possible to form a polity with those they wish to have in it and only those, we are moving beyond the majority principle to another, and in my view more defensible, notion. This is that what matters is not to satisfy the preferences of a majority but to respect the interests of all. I shall argue in the next section that democratic procedures can, under some conditions, be defended in terms of that conception.

Meanwhile, it should be noted that the upshot of the discussion is that any attempt to justify boundaries by appealing to the majority principle must be void. You can have as many referenda as you like, and show every time that over half of the people within the existing boundaries approve of them, but you cannot use that to prove to a minority that wants to secede that they ought to acquiesce in the status quo. If their loyalty is to be awakened, other and better arguments —backed by deeds rather than votes—are needed.

I shall take up the question of boundaries in chapter 6 below. For the

[12] James M. Markham, 'Talks on Gibraltar Due in October', *The New York Times* (25 Sept. 1977), 4.

purpose of the present chapter let us now assume that the composition of the group that is to be subject to a common policy is not at issue, and that the two more technical sources of indeterminacy are absent. Does that make the majority principle unassailable? Of course not. The fourth and last of the special features of the railway carriage case that I singled out was that, as the story had been told, we had no reason to suppose that the question of smoking or not smoking was of vital importance to any of the people involved. (It might be said that smoking is inherently a vital interest in that being smoked at lowers one's expectation of life; but, if we put it as a question of interests, is a few minutes more life a greater interest than the freedom of the addict from withdrawal symptoms?) Suppose, however, that one of the passengers suffers from severe asthma or emphysema, and that being subjected to tobacco smoke is liable to precipitate a dangerous attack. No doubt one would hope that this fact, when explained, would lead the others to agree not to smoke, however many of them would like to. But say that it does not. It seems clear to me that the person at risk would be behaving with an almost insane disregard for his or her interests in accepting a majority decision to allow smoking. The obvious recourse would be, I presume, to pull the communication cord and bring the train to a grinding halt.

It might be argued that nothing said here shows that the majority principle lacks universality. The majority principle, it may be said, always has a certain weight, but in some cases the reason it provides for obedience is overridden by a more pressing consideration, such as self-protection against a risk of substantial harm. This is not a correct representation of the position, however. Where the decision is sufficiently threatening to the vital interests of (some of) those affected by it, its pedigree is neither here nor there.

Take for example a group of youths like those in *A Clockwork Orange* who beat up strangers for fun. Would we be inclined to say 'Well, at least there's one redeeming feature: they choose their victims by majority vote'? I think not. This example of course raises the question of constituency, since the victim is outside the decisionmaking group. But if we modify it so that the members of a group decide by majority vote to beat up one of their own number the chosen victim has no less reason to resist or escape than he would if the decision were taken by a strong-arm leader. I do not see any significant respect in which my modified example of the railway passengers differs from that. Someone might adduce the difference between deliberately causing harm and doing something whose known but unintended consequences are harmful, but that is not in my view a morally relevant distinction. (See chapter 12 section III.)

The political parallels hardly need to be filled in. No minority can be, or should be, expected to acquiesce in the majority's trampling on its vital interests. Unfortunately the parallel to pulling the communication cord—bringing the state, or that part of its policy that is objectionable, to a grinding halt—is a much more messy business and carries the risk of incurring costs much higher than a £25 fine. But the principle is clear enough. Nobody but a moral imbecile would really be prepared to deliver himself over body and soul to the majority principle.

This is not to say that no reason can be found for giving weight to the fact that a law arose from a democratic procedure. But it is to say that the majority principle is a broken reed. The attraction of the majority principle lies in the claim that the majority 'naturally' is entitled to act for the whole. If it turns out that this 'naturalness' is contingent on the presence of a number of highly restrictive conditions, we must press our enquiries further and ask whether we can identify some more fundamental basis for saying that democratic procedures matter.

III

At several points in the preceding section, I gestured towards the lines on which an alternative defence of democratic procedures might be mounted. In arguing that the majority principle is helpless in the face of boundary disputes, I suggested that we might adopt the principle not of satisfying the preferences of the majority but of safeguarding the interests of everyone; and, in making the point that the majority principle cannot be regarded as sacrosanct even where it is perfectly determinate, I suggested that no minority should respect laws that disregard its vital interests. I now want to follow up those ideas and lay out systematically if sketchily the theory from which they can be derived.

It should be emphasized that the framework within which I am operating is not the familiar one of asking what is the 'best' decision-making system. Rather, I am concerned with the question that each person must ask: 'Given the procedure and the outcome, am I to obey this law?' The advantage of focusing on this practical question can be seen by reflecting on the discussion of the majority principle in the previous section. Social choice theorists often write as if all our problems would be over if (*per impossibile*) we could crack the Arrow General Possibility Theorem. Yet, for a single dichotomous choice, the majority principle satisfies all of Arrow's conditions for a satisfactory system of aggregating preferences into a 'social decision' and other stronger conditions as well. For all this, as we have seen, it is perfectly possible for a single dichotomous decision to be one that nobody with any elementary regard for self-preservation would voluntarily submit to. We thus get much deeper into the real problems of politics by asking not what is the best procedure but what one should do about actual decisions, taking account (among other things) of the procedures by which they were reached.

In order to offer any general statements we have to be able to imagine ourselves in all the possible positions that a person might get into, and ask what for someone in this position would be the right thing to do. A dramatic though not essential way of setting up the problem is to say that we are to imagine ourselves behind a Rawlsian veil of ignorance.[13] A person behind a veil of ignorance does not know his or her talents, aspirations, race, sex, etc., but must choose principles that will be binding on whoever he or she turns out to be. Unlike Rawls, I shall posit (and not suggest that I can derive it from the specification of the choice situation and the notion of rationality) that someone who is looking at all the possible positions he or she might turn up in will be particularly concerned with the protection of vital interests.

The first question to be asked is whether to have laws at all, and, if so, what is to be their status. One possibility is that there should be no rules of any kind. Another is that there should be rules but that they should have only the status of suggestions to aid interpersonal coordination. Alternatively, there might be a society in which laws carried sanctions but nobody ever considered anything except the sanction in deciding whether or not to obey the law (just as in our society we buy a bottle of Scotch if it is worth it to us after paying a large sum to the government); or there might be one in which the existence of a law was taken as a reason for obeying it but no sanction was attached to disobedience. Finally, the existence of a law might be taken as a reason for doing what it requires but there might be sanctions against disobedience too.

The question has been set up in classical 'social contract' terms, and the classical 'social contract' answer is that the last of these possibilities

[13] John Rawls, *A Theory of Justice* (Cambridge, Mass.: Harvard University Press, 1971), 136–42.

is preferable to any of the others: we need stable expectations that certain rules will be generally followed, we want there to be sanctions underwriting the rules, but we don't want people to keep the rules only when the sanctions are sufficiently probable to make obedience the course of action that pays on a prudential calculation. I think that in general this is a good answer.

But it is one thing to say that one would wish the standard situation to be one in which people accept the existence of a law as a reason for obeying it. That still leaves open the question whether or not something's being a law should always be taken as a decisive reason for obeying it. And, if the answer to that question is negative, it leaves open the question of particular concern here, namely, whether or not the law's origin in a democratic procedure should make a difference.

The first of these questions does not seem too difficult. Looking at the matter impartially, taking account of all the contingencies to which he or she could be exposed, it is surely apparent that our person choosing principles and institutions would not wish to be committed to unconditional obedience to law. In some cases open disobedience or rebellion may be right. I shall discuss these later. But I should like to say a word here for ordinary non-heroic disobedience, in other words crime, that is to say law-breaking undertaken for private rather than public ends and with the intention of avoiding detection if possible.

A typical reaction among political philosophers is that 'the ordinary criminal may be viewed as acting primarily out of motives of self-interest—motives which render him morally blameworthy and socially dangerous'.[14] Presumably it is not simply the self-interested motive that makes for a presumption against the moral acceptability of ordinary criminal law-breaking. Most market behaviour is motivated by self-interest but is not normally taken to be *ipso facto* reprehensible. I think that the basic reasons for condemning ordinary law-breaking are that breaking the law causes harm to the victim(s) and that it is unfair to take advantage of the forbearance of others to secure a private advantage. The criminal is, in Rawlsian terms, a 'free rider' on the scheme of social co-operation from which he or she benefits. This rationale, however, fails to apply in two kinds of cases:

[14] Jeffrie G. Murphy, in his Intro. to a book of readings on *Civil Disobedience and Violence* (Belmont, Calif.: Wadsworth, 1971), 2. Similarly, H. B. Acton, in 'Political Justification', repr. in Bedau (ed.), *Civil Disobedience*, pp. 220–39, having said that 'disobedience . . . may take a variety of forms', dismissed that of 'not obeying and of endeavouring to escape the legal consequences' as 'of no interest to us in this paper, since either it is nothing but a sort of unprincipled subterfuge or else it leads to [rebellion, i.e. the attempt to overthrow the government by force]' (p. 222).

where nobody is benefited by the actor's forbearance and where the whole scheme of social co-operation is not on balance beneficial to the actor.

We must, as Dr Johnson exhorted, clear the mind of cant. Will anyone seriously maintain that he or she has ever stopped drinking in a pub at exactly 10.40 p.m. (assuming that the landlord is prepared to go on serving) out of respect for the licensing laws rather than out of fear of possible unpleasantness with the police? There are a whole range of laws whose observance benefits nobody—laws against Sunday entertainment, laws prohibiting off-course betting, laws against contraception and abortion, laws regulating the sexual relations of consenting adults, and so on. There can be no unfairness to others in disobeying such laws, and it is surely significant that people break them on a massive scale without guilt feelings. The 'what if everybody did that?' argument against breaking the law has no force in such a case, as long as 'that' is understood as 'breaking the same law'.[15] For, *ex hypothesi*, the case is one where disobedience has no ill-effects whatever the scale. And in as far as mass disobedience has a tendency to bring about the demise of the law as a by-product, that is a plus factor in the reckoning. As Christian Bay has pointed out, the massive evasion of Prohibition in the USA had no high-minded motives 'for the Volstead act was usually evaded in secret, even if Clarence Darrow is said to have referred to bootleggers as fighters for American liberties and predicted the erection of statues to Al Capone in many a public park'.[16] But it still made repeal virtually unavoidable.

These are cases where nobody benefits from forbearance. The other cases are those where there are indeed beneficiaries from forbearance, but there is no mutual benefit. Thus, let us say that the system of apartheid in South Africa benefits (at least in the short run) the White minority. It clearly does not benefit the rest of the population and I can conceive of no reason other than concern for his or her own safety why anyone subject to this apparatus of legal oppression should pay it any respect. Published reports suggest that the hundreds of pass-law violators who are processed by the courts each day regard the inevitable fine as an incident of life in an unjust society rather than as the expiation of personal wrongdoing.[17] Turning T. H. Green on his

[15] Compare Richard A. Wasserstrom, 'The Obligation to Obey the Law', repr. in Bedau, *Civil Disobedience*, 256–62.

[16] Christian Bay, 'Civil Disobedience: Prerequisite for Democracy in Mass Society', repr. in Murphy, *Civil Disobedience and Violence*, 73–92, at 85.

[17] See Larry Garbus, 'South Africa: The Death of Justice', *The New York Review of Books* (4 Aug. 1977).

head (the time-honoured treatment for idealists), one may say that force, not will, is the basis of the state, and that this legitimates a purely pragmatic attitude to law on the part of the oppressed majority.

We now need to face the question whether a law's having been passed by a democratic procedure should provide a special reason for obeying it. A common argument for accepting an outcome reached by a democratic procedure even when you dislike it is that you should take the rough with the smooth: you can't win them all, but in the long run you can expect to win more than half the time because on each issue the majority principle ensures that more people win than lose. I want in the rest of this section to take this popular idea, see what it presupposes in order to be persuasive, and then ask what should be done where it breaks down.

As we have already seen, the majority principle cannot be equated with democratic procedures (as I equated it in presenting the view to be discussed), so it will make for clarity to split the analysis into two parts. First, I shall show that the application of the majority principle produces satisfactory results so long as the preferences to be taken into account are distributed in certain ways. Following that I shall try to establish a connection for such cases between the outcome required by the majority principle and the general tendency to be expected of democratic procedures.

Consider, then, a country in which all issues are dichotomous and in which the following characteristics hold: (1) each of those who are in the majority stands on the average to gain as much satisfaction from the passage of any given law as each of those in the minority stands to lose from it; and (2) on each issue there is an independent probability for each person of being in the majority that is equal to the proportion of the total number in the majority on that issue. The first condition says in effect that the stakes of each person are the same on any given issue (though they may not be the same on different issues). The second says in effect that, whatever we know of a person's previous voting record, we cannot do better than predict that he or she has a 0·6 probability of being in the majority if the majority is 60 per cent, a 0·7 probability of being in the majority if the majority is 70 per cent, and so on.

The second condition entails that, over a period sufficient for a number of issues to come up, decisions made in accordance with the majority principle can be expected to yield approximately equal satisfaction to each person. Adding the first condition, we can go further: if we count getting the outcome you want as +1 and getting the outcome you don't want as -1, then each person can expect $(x - 0{\cdot}5) \times 2$ units of satisfaction, where x is the average majority. (For example, if the average majority is 0·7, each person can expect 0·4 units of satisfaction.) But in addition the first condition alone tells us that the majority principle maximizes average satisfaction, for it can never increase average satisfaction to please fewer people rather than more, given that the average gain of each winner is the same as the average loss of each loser.

If the person choosing from behind the veil of ignorance were seeking to maximize the average of the levels of satisfaction of all the people he or she might turn out to be, the first condition alone indicates that the majority principle would be the one to pick. But suppose instead that the person behind the veil of ignorance were to follow Rawls's recommendation and choose a rule for aggregating preferences with the object of making the lot of the worst off of all those that one might turn out to be as desirable as possible. Then, because in the special case stated in the second condition everyone has the same expectation of satisfaction, it would still be best to pick the majority principle. For any other principle lowers the average and, since everyone's expectations are the same, that means that on any other principle each of the people he or she might turn out to be would be worse-off.

Let us take this idea and cash it out into the choice of sanctions for breaking the law and principles about obedience to the law. Obviously, when we say that people get satisfaction from getting a law they want or lose satisfaction from getting a law they do not want, we are speaking in shorthand. What people gain or lose satisfaction from is not the enactment itself but the operation of the law. If those who are in the minority on any law ignore it with impunity, they do not suffer the loss associated with it; but those in the majority do not experience the gain associated with it either, at any rate if the minority is large enough for its disobedience to undermine the law. But in the case as specified there is a net gain from each law (that is, from the operation of each law) and each person stands in the long run to share equally in these gains. Therefore, from behind the veil of ignorance it is advantageous both to support sanctions and to adopt the principle as binding on all that laws which have majority approval ought to be obeyed even in the absence of prudential motives.

Now, by contrast, suppose that the second condition does not hold, though the first still does. It still maximizes the average satisfaction of all the people one might turn out to be to endorse the majority principle. But if one is concerned to avoid the worst threats to one's interests, the majority principle is no longer so attractive. Take the opposite extreme from the atomistic society in which there is no association between one person's vote and any other's and consider a society permanently divided into two rigid groups. Each group always has monolithic preferences, so the same people are always in the majority and the minority. The average of all the people one might be is still $(x - 0{\cdot}5) \times 2$, though here x is simply the proportion of the whole constituted by the majority group. But the expectation of each member of the minority group is -1, since on every issue they lose.

If in addition we give up the first condition, we can no longer even be confident that the average satisfaction will be maximized by adopting the side on every issue that corresponds with the majority preference. Thus, suppose we assume that politics is a zero-sum game, so that on every issue the amount gained by those who are on the winning side is exactly equal to the amount lost by those on the losing side.[18] This entails, of course, under the majority principle, that winners always win less per head than losers lose. Then it would obviously be better to have no procedure for making laws. Anyone who wants gratuitous risks can always gamble privately—there is no point in forcing risks on everyone.

The upshot of this very crude analysis is that, from behind the veil of ignorance, a person of reasonable prudence would accept outcomes produced in accordance with the majority principle for an atomistic society or a pluralistic society, which we may take as the closest real-life approximation: that is to say, a society in which there are many groups and the relations between them are fluid. In such a society the majority principle gives each group a good chance of being in the majority over half the time. This description of the pluralistic society is, of course, recognizable as the picture of the USA drawn by the celebrants of the 1950s. It is probably a fair description of the way the system works for the best-placed 60 or 70 per cent of the adult population. Conversely, the more closely a society approximates to the model of a monolithic majority bloc facing a minority which is always on the losing side, the more would reasonably prudent people refuse to accept that, if they found themselves in such a society and in the minority group, they would be bound to respect the laws that had been passed by the majority over minority opposition.

The assumption that all issues are dichotomous is a very restrictive

[18] This assumption is implicit in William J. Riker, *A Theory of Political Coalitions* (New Haven, Conn.: Yale University Press, 1962).

and unrealistic one. Let me extend the analysis just one step, to the simplest case beyond: that where all preferences lie on one dimension. I have already, in section II, pointed out that in such a case the majority principle picks out one point as the unique one that is capable of gaining a majority in a pairwise comparison with any other. This is the point corresponding to the preference of the median person, in other words the person with exactly as many others on each side. In investigating the properties of the majority principle, then, all we need to do is examine the properties of the median.

Consider first a case in which these three things are true: (1) on any issue, each person experiences the same loss of satisfaction for any given distance between the most preferred outcome and the actual outcome; (2) for each person the loss of satisfaction is linear with distance, in other words it is always true that an outcome twice as far away represents twice as much loss of satisfaction; and (3) on each issue, each person has an independent probability of being in any position that is equal to the proportion of the total number of people in that position.

Here, conditions (1) and (2) correspond to the first stipulation for the dichotomous case. That said that winners always gain and losers always lose equal amounts per head. Conditions (1) and (2) entail that the aggregate loss from any given outcome can be obtained by summing over all the people concerned the distances between their ideal points and the outcome. In the dichotomous case, the first stipulation implied that we maximize gain by making the outcome the one preferred by a majority. In the present case, conditions (1) and (2) have the implication that loss of satisfaction is minimized when we make the outcome the one preferred by the person in the median position. This follows from the fact that the sum total of distances from the median position is the smallest possible, however people may be distributed along the line. The reason for this can be seen by imagining people standing at various points along a real line. Place yourself in front of the person at the median position and then move either to left or right. As you move, you get nearer to some people and further from others. But it must be true that you move away from more people than you move towards. Finally, condition (3) corresponds to the second stipulation for the dichotomous case. It guarantees that everyone in the long run loses the same amount, so that each person receives the average loss.

Analogously with what was said in the dichotomous case, conditions (1) and (2) alone would be sufficient to lead anyone who was concerned only with the average level of satisfaction to endorse the majority principle (here implemented by choosing the median position). Adding the third condition, which produces equal expectations for all, would also make the median position the choice either of a maximizer or of someone concerned to minimize the losses of the person losing the most.

At this point, however, the analogy with the dichotomous case breaks down. In dropping the second stipulation for the dichotomous case—the atomistic assumption—we went to the opposite extreme and imagined a society with no changing of places at all, and decided that a person of reasonable prudence would not endorse the majority principle for such a society. In the one-dimensional case, however, a similar total lack of fluidity in relative positions does not necessarily have such disturbing implications for the majority principle.

Consider the most neutral assumption about the way in which preferences are distributed: that they are evenly distributed along the dimension. If we plot the density of preferences on the vertical dimension, a distribution of this kind looks as in Figure 2.2. Now the interesting thing about this distribution is that the median position (marked m) not only minimizes average loss (as does the median with any distribution, given the first two assumptions) but also minimizes the maximum loss of any person. For, if we move away from it in either direction, the people at the far end are made worse off than they were when the outcome was at the median.

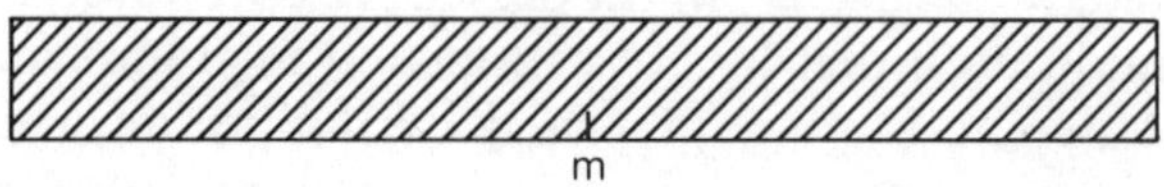

FIG. 2.2

As may be apparent, a rectangular distribution is not needed to generate this result. Any distribution such that the median point lies half-way between the extremes will do it. Therefore all symmetrical distributions—that is to say distributions such that one half of the line is a mirror-image of the other half—satisfy the requirement. Examples are Figures 2.3 and 2.4. Of course the average loss of satisfaction differs between the three distributions: it is greatest in Figure 2.4, least in Figure 2.3, and intermediate in Figure 2.2. The society depicted in Figure 2.3 has more ability to satisfy its average member

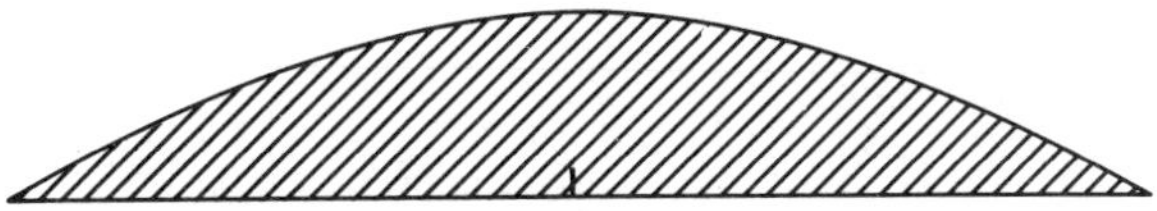

FIG. 2.3

FIG. 2.4

than the society in Figure 2.2, and that in Figure 2.2. more than that in Figure 2.4. Failing some realignment of preferences—the rise of a different issue, perhaps—it might be as well for the two groups in the last society to split off into separate polities, or form a federation allowing each the maximum autonomy; or if they are too geographically mingled for that they might at least try *verzuiling* (functional decentralization). But if there *is* going to be one set of policies binding on all of them, the median is the one that anybody choosing from behind a veil of ignorance will have to go for.

The natural reaction to Figure 2.4 is, I think, to dispute the analysis and suggest that the median position is unlikely to be the outcome. I agree, but mainly because the situation as depicted is so finely balanced. The tension between the two groups would be extreme because so much was at stake: changes in the birth-rates or the migration rates, or a little gerrymandering, could so easily swing the outcome a long way to one side or the other. The reasonably prudent person choosing from behind a veil of ignorance would not, I concede, give unqualified allegiance to the majority principle for a society so evenly balanced between two blocs, with so few people in the region of the median, as in Figure 2.4. The logic of the situation is illustrated by Figure 2.5. This shows how, once we move away from a symmetrical bimodal distribution like that in Figure 2.4, the median position leaves those in the minority group out in the cold. The average loss is still minimized but the maximum loss is great.

Notice in passing that moving the unimodal distribution of Figure

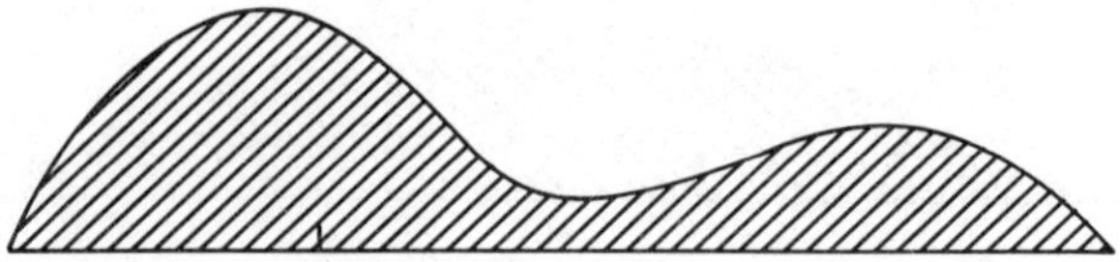

FIG. 2.5

2.3 away from symmetry does not have the same kind of drastic results. Figure 2.6 illustrates the way in which the median shifts a little away from the centre, but not dramatically. A distribution of this kind may be thought of as a rough sketch of a politics of economic interest in an otherwise homogeneous society, where income and status follow a pattern of continuous graduation (as against dichotomous classes) but where the distribution of income and status is in the traditional 'squashed diamond' shape.

How do these results relate to those we obtained for the dichotomous case? We can establish two fairly direct parallels. The atomistic society, in which people distribute themselves randomly on dichotomous issues, is, I suggested, a rose-tinted model of the USA in the 1950s. It might be realistic for other societies with a fluid social structure, perhaps the USA and other settler societies at a certain stage of development. The one-dimensional model with random placement may be thought of as a more complex version of the same thing, with the dichotomous assumption relaxed to allow a range of different positions on each issue. The alternative model of two rigid groups facing one another on successive dichotomous issues approximates the condition of a society with a deep structural cleavage running through it: a division based on ethnicity, language, race, or possibly (where there is a sharp gulf between landlords and peasants or owners and workers) on class. The one-dimensional model with a bimodal

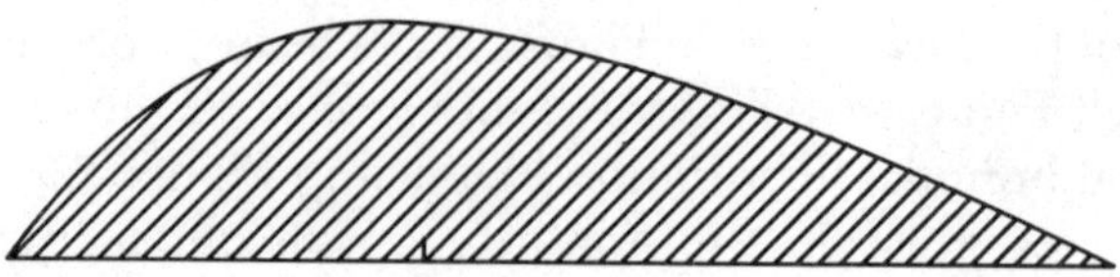

FIG. 2.6

distribution refines on this by allowing for a fixed range of positions within the groups and the possibility of some people holding intermediate positions. But the general implications are much the same as in the dichotomous case: outcomes in accordance with the majority principle may be highly injurious to the interests of the minority group.

Where we get something distinctively new from the one-dimensional analysis is in the case of a fixed unimodal distribution. For we can see here how fixed positions may be compatible with acceptable outcomes. Admittedly the people on the two tails of the distribution will be dissatisfied with the outcomes that the majority principle calls for, that is to say the outcomes preferred by the person in the median position. But what alternative can they seriously propose? Those in the minority group have a good cause for complaint when there is a bimodal distribution and the median person is in the majority group. But with a unimodal distribution any move towards one set of extremists leaves the extremists at the other end even more dissatisfied than they were in the first place. From behind the veil of ignorance it would be inconsistent to say that if one found oneself on one tail of a unimodal distribution one should resist outcomes corresponding to the median position without acknowledging that those at the other extreme should also resist them, for there is no way of distinguishing the two. 'The end I happen to be at' will not do.

Although we started from a defence of the majority principle that was expressed in terms of winning and losing, we have finished up with a case where the majority principle can be defended even though the line-up is the same on each question that comes up for decision. That is to say, on each question the same single dimension defines the positions of each of the actors and they find themselves in the same places. We got here by transforming the winning and losing in the dichotomous case into a value of getting the outcome you want and a (negative) value of getting the outcome other than the one you want. We then made a natural extension of that way of thinking so as to accommodate the analysis in one dimension by assuming that the distance between the preferred outcome and the actual outcome provides a measure of dissatisfaction with that outcome. We are thus able to evaluate the median position as an outcome in terms of the distribution of loss of satisfaction that it produces, without any need to refer to winning and losing.

To see that winning and losing is irrelevant, go back for a moment to the set-up depicted in Figure 2.1, where *A* and *B* take one position,

C a middle position, and *D* and *E* the position at the other end of the line. If the final vote on each issue is between *C*'s position and one of the others (which is what we would normally expect), *C* will always be on the winning side, but whether or not *A* and *B* 'win' or *D* and *E* 'win' depends on the way the choice is structured. If the choice is between the outcome preferred by *A* and *B* and the outcome preferred by *C*, then *C*, *D*, and *E* will vote together and *A* and *B* will go down to defeat. If the position preferred by *D* and *E* is set against that preferred by *C*, we will get the result that *A*, *B*, and *C* combine against *D* and *E*. Yet in both cases the outcome is the same: the outcome preferred by *C* is the one that gets a majority. This simple example illustrates the fallacy of counting up 'wins' and 'losses' where there are more than two possible positions. The only sound procedure is to compare the position preferred by each actor with the actual outcome.

The unimodal model of preference-distribution fits reasonably well the Scandinavian countries, New Zealand, Australia and Great Britain (but not Northern Ireland). Other countries are not adequately represented by this unimodal model, in which political differences reflect the socioeconomic stratification of an otherwise relatively homogeneous population. Yet at the same time they do not exhibit the radical pluralism of societies such as Guyana, the Lebanon, Indonesia, Nigeria, Cyprus, or Malaysia, in which different groups live side by side, sharing no common institutions except those of the state. These other societies, of which the Netherlands and Belgium are paradigmatic, have a division between 'spiritual families' (and, in the Belgian case, an ethnic cleavage) but are at the same time sufficiently integrated to have the potential for a politics of socioeconomic interest cutting across these ascriptive lines. An adequate model of preference-distribution in such societies requires two or even three dimensions. However, except for special cases, there is no longer a unique point picked out by the majority principle once we move away from one dimension. There is in general no Condorcet winner, no point capable of gaining a majority over all others. The problem of circularity rears its head once more. I cannot afford the space here to follow up the complexities that arise in analysing spaces of two or more dimensions, since I still have not made the connection, even for the one-dimensional cases, between the majority principle and democratic procedures. Having established that connection, however, I shall be in a position to take some short-cuts in the analysis of the politics of plural societies.

So far, then, I have been operating with the majority principle as the object of analysis. But if this analysis is to tie up with democratic procedures, I have to argue that democratic procedures have a tendency to produce the outcomes called for by the majority principle. This I believe to be true in general, and I think that theoretical arguments can be offered to show why it is not accidental that it happens, but I can do no more than sketch the argument here.

In the dichotomous case, I have already suggested in section II that democratic procedures are more likely to produce the outcomes desired by a majority than any alternative procedure. All that needs to be added here is that the case in which a purely opportunistic party would sometimes support minority policies is ruled out for any case where the per capita gains and losses of majority and minority are equal.

The one-dimensional case requires a little more analysis. With direct voting between all pairs of positions, we know that the median position can obtain a majority over all rivals. But even in a committee cruder devices are used. In a referendum, only two choices are commonly offered: to accept the proposal or reject it. This leaves a good deal of scope for manipulation to whoever is able to set the terms of the referendum. For, if preferences are one-dimensional, the option closer to the median will win; but, if both the options are some way off the median, the result will obviously not have the desirable properties attributed here to the median. This suggests that referenda are dubious unless either (*a*) the topic 'naturally' creates a dichotomy or (*b*) it is open to any group of fair size to place an alternative on the ballot and some form of preferential voting is employed.

Voting for representatives is not subject to the same difficulties because the parties in effect do the work of sifting issues and putting together a majority. Very crudely, let me divide the types of party system to be analysed into two-party and multi-party systems. In two-party systems, the parties will tend to converge towards the median voter's position if they are concerned with winning elections. This is because, if each voter votes for the party whose position is nearer his own, the party nearer the median voter must get the most votes.[19] The argument is, in my view, compelling, and can be extended by observing that even if parties are not trying to win elections (or have other aims as well) it is still true that the party nearer the median voter will win. So the tendency for the party that gets a majority to be somewhere in the neighbourhood of the median voter

[19] Downs, *An Economic Theory of Democracy*, ch. 8.

does not depend on strong assumptions about party motivation, only on the assumption that, for whatever reason, at least one party will usually be fairly near the median voter at an election. (See chapter 7, section VIII for an argument to the effect that even ideologically motivated parties will tend towards the median.)

The multi-party case is more controversial. Downs argues in effect that with multi-party systems no systematic relationship between voter preferences and the policies pursued by governments can be expected.[20] In my view this is false to experience and also contrary to the logic of parliamentary tactics. Downs assumed that if several parties formed a coalition government the policy of the government would be some sort of average of the positions of the parties making it up. But his assumption has no rational foundation. The same logic that leaves the median voter with the whip-hand in a direct vote leaves the party containing the median legislator (call it the median party) with the whip-hand. Give me the minimum assumption that, other things being equal, parties prefer to be in governments that pursue their own programmes to being in governments that pursue other parties' programmes. I can then show that for any majority coalition with a policy other than that of the median party there is another majority coalition (which must contain some overlapping members) with the policy of the median party, and that all the members of this coalition will prefer it to the first one. Qualifications are of course needed, and cannot be given here, to deal with anti-system parties, cartels, and so on. But I believe that the basic tendency of multi-party systems that fall along one dimension is towards implementing the policies desired by the median party.

It still has to be shown that the median party's position can be anticipated to be in the region of the median voter, but this can be done fairly easily. As in the two-party case, we can say immediately that, if each voter votes for the nearest party, the median party will have been voted for by the median voter. But, in a multi-party system, the median party is normally quite closely hemmed in by other parties, so the range within which it is closer to an elector than any other party is likely to be quite small. So there is good reason for expecting the median party and the median voter to be near one another.

The upshot of this analysis is that the earlier discussion of the strengths and weaknesses of the outcomes corresponding to the majority principle can be transferred to the outcomes that we can

[20] Ibid., ch. 9.

expect democratic procedures to produce. (To the extent that party competition and coalition formation do not operate in the way I have postulated, our confidence in the reliability of this coincidence must of course be weakened.) Thus, the tendency of democratic procedures in societies with a bimodal distribution of preferences will be to produce outcomes that are highly prejudicial to the interests of the minority group. And in the less extremely fragmented societies of Western Europe we can say that democratic procedures have the same tendency when the political parties draw their support on the basis of ethnic, religious, racial, or other ascriptive criteria rather than competing by offering alternative positions on the dimension of party preferences related to location in the system of socioeconomic stratification.

What would be a sensible attitude to adopt towards obedience to law? Although we do not observe people choosing from behind a veil of ignorance, we do see the way they choose in real life and from that we can infer the relative strength of different motives—information that would be needed before an intelligent choice could be made from behind the veil of ignorance. And if we look at the empirical evidence we find that people do in fact tend to deny the legitimacy of a regime—however much it may bolster itself up by appeals to the majority principle—if they find the group to which they belong systematically discriminated against, treated as second-class citizens, denied cultural expression or communal organization, and generally not dealt with in terms of equal partnership.

It does not follow from that, however, that disobedience should be prescribed from behind the veil of ignorance. We need to examine the evidence. It seems clear that resistance to the majority has in some instances produced a more acceptable outcome, especially where it was backed up by the threat that disunity within the country might result in its loss of independence. If we look at instances where majorities have drawn back from pressing their maximum claims and accepted minorities as equal partners in what has been called 'consociational democracy', we find that they come about when the minority has established (given the background of the international situation) a capacity to cause trouble to the majority. These conditions can be seen in the stock examples of the conciliation of a minority: the Swiss settlement in 1848 following the Sonderbund war, the Dutch 'pacification' of 1917, the complex Lebanese balancing act and the Austrian compromise between 'black' and 'red' in 1945. In two cases (Switzerland and Austria) the minority lost a civil war, and in the Lebanese case the possibility of a civil war was (as recent events have tragically proved) too clear to miss. At the same time, in all of them, the international situation was threatening. Switzerland's integrity was threatened by the growing idea that state boundaries should correspond to 'nationalities', with the prospect that Switzerland might be dismembered and the parts absorbed into national states. The risk to the survival of the Netherlands of harbouring a discontented minority predominantly located on its border with Germany are too clear to need spelling out. The position of the Lebanon has always meant that internal disturbances risked outside intervention—as in the recent civil war. And in Austria the country was under four-power occupation in the post-war period, the withdrawal of the Russians could not be taken for granted, and the country was bordered by states under Russian influence. (These points are extended in chapters 4 and 5 below.)

There are, it need hardly be said, other situations that are far less favourable to the minority, where the only effect of resistance is to increase the degree of injustice and repression. In such cases, the minority has prudential reasons (though no others) for refraining from resistance, and hoping that some new turn of the wheel of international politics will bring about a more propitious situation, in which the ability to create a disturbance will be a stronger bargaining counter.

IV

The premiss of the previous section was ruthlessly instrumental. The assumption made was that people were concerned to get the outcomes they wanted, and were interested in procedures only as a means to that end. The content of the laws, not the way in which they were brought into existence, was all that mattered. The case for democratic procedures was simply that, under favourable circumstances, they were likely to produce acceptable outcomes. But any other procedure that produced the same outcomes would be equally acceptable. I am convinced that there is more to be said for that view, both morally and as a way of predicting how people will actually behave, than there is for the 'majority principle'. And yet—wasn't there *something* in the idea mooted in section II that there is a certain naturalness about majorities as a basis for settling matters that are in dispute? I think there is and in this final section I shall try to say what I think it is.

Come back for a moment to the notion of consociational

democracy. The essence of it is that the élites may be able to prevent democratic procedures from exacerbating conflict if they co-operate (maybe but not necessarily in a formal 'grand coalition') to find an agreed solution to the divisive issues and then sell it to (or impose it on) the electorate. Arendt Lijphart, who was responsible for introducing the term into contemporary political science, remarked that 'consociational democracy violates the principle of majority rule, but it does not deviate much from normative democratic theory'.[21] But the whole idea of consociational democracy is clearly at odds with any notion that the point of democratic procedures is that the parties are forced by the exigencies of competition to articulate the preferences for public policies of their supporters. The defining characteristic of 'consociational democracy' is that the party leaders do *not* press for the interests of their supporters (as those supporters see them), but rather somehow manage to carry their followers along a path of compromise.

Obviously, if peace and stability can be achieved only by preventing the electoral pressure from deflecting the party leaders from compromise, it is natural to ask why they should have to put up with electoral sanctions at all. Why not just have 'consociation' and drop 'democracy'? In practice, it might be said, this is what does happen in some states: where representative institutions produce a clash between ethnic groups, a non-representative system permits controlled 'consociation' from the top in the shape of participation of members of different groups in the government. (Nigeria and Kenya could both be cited as examples.) But if there is in the literature of consociational democracy an implicit value judgement that, other things being (approximately) equal, it is better to have representative institutions, on what is that judgement based? Clearly, not on the majority principle, since the essence of 'consociational democracy' is to avoid finishing up with what the majority wants. The answer would, I think, have to be on the lines that, *if* the trick can be brought off, the combination in divided societies of elections and élite collusion is superior to either elections without collusion or collusion without elections, because it satisfies both the value of peace and stability and the value of freedom of speech and organization.

How would this claim be made out? I think the key is the following

[21] Arend Lijphart, 'Consociational Democracy', repr. in Kenneth McRae (ed.), *Consociational Democracy: Political Accommodation in Segmented Societies* (Toronto: McClelland and Stewart, 1974), 70–89, at 77. See also Arend Lijphart, *Democracy in Plural Societies: A Comparative Exploration* (New Haven, Conn.: Yale University Press, 1977).

assertion: once a society reaches a level of development in which there is widespread education and where the bulk of the population enjoys independence from grinding poverty and continuous toil, the choice can *only* be between repression (including arbitrary action against citizens, making political prisoners out of critics and tight restraints on freedom of publication, assembly, etc.) and a system of representative government. This may appear to be a quite banal generalization and yet if it is true (and it seems to stand up well empirically) it is surely a remarkable fact.

In principle, after all, any kind of regime might be able to establish itself with sufficient acceptance to allow freedom to its critics. One would gather, for example, from Michael Oakeshott's *On Human Conduct* that there is no particularly favoured basis for the legitimacy of regimes. Their authority simply rests on the fact of recognition. He offers as an 'analogue' the case of the Marylebone Cricket Club's having acquired over time recognition as the arbiter of the rules of cricket. Its authority 'has nothing to do with the recognition of the desirability of the rules or with the constitution of the committee'.[22] I am inclined to think that this analogue tells us more about Oakeshott's view of the world than about the world. Who cares, to put it bluntly, what the rules of cricket are? Certain modifications of, say, the lbw rule may provide special opportunities for bowlers with a particular technique to cramp the style of certain batsmen, but on the whole any rule leaves teams as well placed in relation to one another as they were before. It is in the nature of rules of a game (and therefore makes them highly tendentious paradigms of political decisions in general) that any rule, so long as it is simply applied impartially, defines a fair procedure for determining who wins. It is therefore less important what the rules are than that everyone plays by the same ones. I venture to suggest that if the MCC claimed jurisdiction over any matter that has anything in common with the normal stuff of politics—if, for example, it were able to levy a royalty on every game of first-class cricket played in the world and the question arose how the money raised were to be spent—it would not be long before the demand would arise for the body charged with disbursing the funds to be put upon some kind of representative basis.

Why is this? It would be easy to say that 'democratic ideology' is triumphant and therefore provides the only basis for general consent. But it would be so easy as to be worth very little. The use of 'ideology'

[22] Michael Oakeshott, *On Human Conduct* (Oxford: Clarendon Press, 1975), 154n.

in this context is an essentially irrationalist one and implies that some other basis of legitimacy with a different content altogether might just as well have become established in the world. Such a view would ignore the very real advantages of competitive election as a rationale for placing the government in one set of hands rather than another.

The point I am driving at was put more effectively than by anyone else I have come across by Sydney Smith in one of his 'Four Speeches on the Reform Bill'. The Reform Bill in question was that of 1832 and it was of course (considered in relation to universal suffrage) a very limited measure. But the logic of his argument shows how difficult it is to find any determinate stopping-place short of universal suffrage.

> It is not enough that a political institution works well practically: it must be defensible; it must be such as will bear discussion, and not excite ridicule and contempt. It might work well for aught I know, if, like the savages of Onelashka, we sent out to catch a king: but who could defend a coronation by chase? Who can defend the payment of £40,000, for the three-hundredth part of the power of Parliament, and the resale of this power to Government for places to the Lord Williams and Lord Charles's, and others of the Anglophagi? Teach a million of the common people to read—and such a government (work it ever so well) must perish in twenty years. It is impossible to persuade the mass of mankind that there are not other and better methods of governing a country.[23]

The most important point about a system of election for representatives is that it provides an intelligible and determinate answer to the question why these particular people, rather than others perhaps equally well or better qualified, should run the country. If people can be induced to believe in the divine right of kings or the natural superiority of a hereditary ruling caste, it may be possible to gain general acceptance for rule based on the appropriate ascribed characteristics. But once the idea of the natural equality of all men has got about, claims to rule cannot be based on natural superiority. Winning an election is a basis for rule that does not conflict with natural equality. Indeed, it might be said to flow from it. For if quality is equal (or, as Hobbes more exactly put it, quality must be taken to be equal as a condition of peace) the only differentiating factor left is quantity. Once we supply the premiss of natural equality, we can see why it seemed obvious to Locke that the majority 'necessarily' constitutes the 'greater force'. Justification for rule in terms of the specific achievements of the government lacks this essential feature of determinacy.

[23] Sydney Smith, *The Selected Writings of Sydney Smith*, ed. W. H. Auden (London: Faber and Faber, 1957), 346.

Others can always claim that their performance would be superior, and who is to say it would not be?

To express any confidence in the possibility of democratic institutions continuing to rest on a basis of mass acceptance is, of course, highly unfashionable. Theorists of the left and the right agree that the jig is up. There is a 'legitimation crisis' in the advanced capitalist societies: they have become 'ungovernable', governments are 'overloaded' by popular demands, and the 'economic contradictions of democracy' are revealing themselves ever more starkly.[24] Events may indeed prove these Cassandras right, but my own view is that they are grotesquely over-reacting to the disequilibriating effects of a sudden fourfold increase in the price of crude oil.

It seems to me that the only perspective from which things could be said to look sticky now for democratic institutions would be one from which the 1950s and the first half of the 1960s constituted the norm. But that period of prosperity and peace among all the advanced capitalist economies was historically unique. (I am not denying that favourable objective conditions help.) A simple exercise is to run back decade by decade to the beginnings of universal suffrage in each of the major countries and to ask in how many of these periods (except the 1950s) democratic institutions looked more firmly established in popular sentiment than they are today.

It is, of course, true that there is a tension between the formal political equality of one-man-one-vote and the inequalities of wealth, status, and actual power over the lives of others (especially their working lives) generated by the other institutions of these societies. But this is hardly a new thought: it was a commonplace to Victorian conservatives and was elaborated by ideologues of the privileged strata like Maine and Lecky. The tension is still there but I see no sign that the forces that have kept it within bounds until now are losing their efficacy.

I conclude, therefore, that there is a case for democratic procedures over and above the instrumental one developed in section III. It is related to the majority principle in one way: it makes use of the idea

[24] As a representative sample see: Jürgen Habermas, *Legitimation Crisis* (Boston, Mass.: Beacon Press, 1975); Alan Wolfe, *The Limits of Legitimacy: Political Contradictions of Contemporary Capitalism* (New York: The Free Press, 1977); Michel Crozier, Samuel P. Huntington, and Joji Watanuki, *The Governability of Democracies* (New York: New York University Press for the Trilateral Commission, 1975); Anthony King, 'Overload: Problems of Government in the 1970s', *Political Studies*, 23 (1975), 290–5; Samuel Brittan, 'The Economic Contradictions of Democracy', *British Journal of Political Science*, 5 (1975), 129–59; James O'Connor, *The Fiscal Crisis of the State* (New York: St Martin's Press, 1973); and Richard Rose and Guy Peters, *Can Government Go Bankrupt?* (New York: Basic Books, 1973).

that decision by majority has a natural attractiveness about it. But it really differs quite fundamentally. The majority principle, as I defined it following a whole body of 'social choice' literature, is that outcomes are legitimate if they correspond to majority preference and illegitimate if they run counter to majority preference. Democratic procedures are justified (to the extent that they can be) in terms of their tendency to bring about outcomes that correspond to majority preference. In contrast, the argument in this section has been that elections are a way of picking out, without reference to inherently arguable claims to superior competence, a unique set of rulers.

The implication is, I think, that a qualification has to be added to the results arrived at in section III. Laws that systematically violate the vital interests of a minority are still devoid of any claims to obedience except prudential ones. But we must expand the sphere of prudential reasons beyond sanctions to encompass long-term consequences. If the price of changing the laws is the collapse of a democratic system, that is a heavy price to pay because it will include the suppression of freedom of publication and political organization. In non-democratic systems, the choice between trying to prevent the government from implementing unjust policies and trying to overthrow the government is a purely tactical one: the only question is which route has the better chance of success and the lower expected cost. In democratic regimes, however, the choice is not purely tactical. There are strong reasons for aiming at a result that leaves the government resting on election but accommodating the interests of the minority as the recognized price of gaining their co-operation.

The course of the argument in this chapter is rather tortuous. I have found, when presenting these ideas in academic gatherings, that many people find difficulty in grasping the distinction between the argument in favour of democratic procedures that I reject and the one that I accept. Let me therefore juxtapose the two in the hope of making the contrast more apparent.

The first argument relates in the first instance to the relation of preferences to policies and only secondarily to institutions such as voting. The notion here criticized is that there is something natural, obvious, or almost inevitable in the principle that the policy put into effect ought to be that corresponding to the majority preference. I accepted the correctness of that claim for the special case of the five people in the railway carriage but went on to suggest that the obviousness of the principle was an artefact of a number of special features either specified or implied in the description of the case. If anything, I was perhaps too lenient with the principle. For we might imagine as alternatives to agreement on a substantive meta-principle (such as the right to breathe uncontaminated air) or some principle of authority (like the one that the Archbishop's decision should be binding) procedural solutions other than the majority principle. For example, the participants might agree in a more 'consociational' spirit to divide up the estimated length of the journey into five equal periods and give each passenger control of one segment.

What I wish to emphasize is, in any case, the difference between the majority principle and the rationale of voting for representatives put forward here in section IV. This argument does, like the first one, invoke the claim that a certain procedure appears natural or obvious. But the assertion in the second case is not that naturalness is in itself a justification for the procedure. Rather it is that, if voting for representatives settles the question of who should rule in a way that claims to superior competence or claims to inherent personal superiority do not, it permits freedom of speech and organization as no other regime does.

3

DOES DEMOCRACY CAUSE INFLATION?

The Political Ideas of Some Economists

> It is not the popular movement, but the travelling of the minds of men who sit in the seat of Adam Smith that is really telling and worthy of all attention.
>
> Lord Acton, letter to Mary Gladstone

Since inflation has ebbed but democratic institutions have not radically changed, some economists may prefer to forget one of their major themes of the 1970s, namely, the view that inflation is the inevitable outcome of the normal functioning of democratic political institutions. But even if the economists who maintained this view are bashful, it is worth recalling their analysis and, at least retrospectively, analysing the premisses that might once again be appealed to if high levels of inflation recur. Since none of this group has himself recanted, it seems reasonable to assume that their doctrines and prescriptions still stand. These economists proposed the simple view that political authorities create or permit inflation by their control of fiscal and monetary policy. Applying the standard methodology of economics to the analysis of political phenomena, this new school of 'political economists' (which is represented in this discussion principally by the work of James Buchanan and the Virginia School) went on to propose that central aspects of economic policymaking be removed from the control of elected representatives, such as governments in parliamentary systems.[1]

[1] See William D. Nordhaus, 'The Political Business Cycle', *Review of Economic Studies*, 42 (1975), 169–90; C. Duncan MacRae, 'A Political Model of the Business Cycle', *Journal of Political Economy*, 85 (1977), 239–63; Richard E. Wagner, 'Economic Manipulation for Political Profit', *Kyklos*, 30 (1977), 395–410; Assar Lindbeck, 'Stabilization Policy in Open Economies with Endogenous Politicians', *American Economic Review*, 66 (1976, *Papers and Proceedings*, 1975), 1–19; Michael Parkin, 'The Politics of Inflation', *Government and Opposition*, 10 (1975), 189–202; Larry A. Sjaastad, 'Why Stable Inflations Fail: An Essay in Political Economy', in Michael Parkin and George Zis (eds.), *Inflation in the World Economy* (Manchester: Manchester University Press, 1976), 73–95; James M. Buchanan and Richard E. Wagner, *Democracy in Deficit: The Political Legacy of Lord Keynes* (San Diego: Academic Press, 1977); Samuel Brittan, *The Economic*

Perhaps the remedy would have been worse than the disease; but, to establish that, it must first be determined whether the disease—what has been termed the 'democratic distemper'—was really so serious.

To decide that, three questions have to be asked. First, how important is it to ensure that inflation cannot occur? How bad are its economic, social, and political consequences? (The alternatives also have consequences.)[2] Second, is it true that representative institutions have built into them an inevitable tendency towards inflation? Third, in the light of the answers to these questions, how should the proposals for constitutional change that have been put forward be assessed? Because constitutional changes are relatively irrevocable, prudence demands that the arguments in their favour be subjected to the strictest scrutiny.

The methodological techniques that the expounders of the new political economy bring to the analysis of political phenomena constitute a serious encumbrance. Their adherence to a vulgarized Popperian methodology, particularly as represented in Milton Friedman's paper 'The Methodology of Positive Economics',[3] requires, as a matter of faith, that the assumptions used in theory-building not be subjected to direct test. A theory is taken to be true if its implications fit the facts sufficiently, and no effort is made to check the adequacy of the story it tells about the phenomena. In practice, no serious attempt is ever made to determine whether or not fundamental assumptions should be abandoned.[4] Since it is likely that, with enough ingenuity, *some* theory can be found that will incorporate them and give rise to implications that fit the facts sufficiently, the assumptions are in effect beyond challenge.

Consequences of Democracy (London: Temple Smith, 1977), 223–89, 'The Economic Contradictions of Democracy', *British Journal of Political Science*, 5 (1975), 129–59, and 'Can Democracy Manage an Economy?' in Robert Skidelsky (ed.), *The End of the Keynesian Era: Essays on the Disintegration of the Keynesian Political Economy* (New York: Holmes and Meier, 1977), 41–9.

[2] 'It may be true that if demand is sufficiently restricted, and unemployment correspondingly increased, collective bargaining will in time no longer operate to force up wages and prices, while other sources of inflation will prove unimportant. But restrictive policies can have other consequences that operate even more powerfully: governments may fall from power and entire societies be torn apart before inflation dies away. It is necessary, therefore, to weigh up the *total* consequences of policies recommended.' Alec Cairncross, *Inflation, Growth and International Finance* (State University of New York Press, 1975), 14.

[3] Milton Friedman, *Essays in Positive Economics* (Chicago: University of Chicago Press, 1953), 3–43 (Friedman does not refer to any philosopher later than John Maynard Keynes's father). See Brian Barry, 'On Analogy', *Political Studies*, 23 (1975), 208–24; Martin Hollis and Edward J. Nell, *Rational Economic Man: A Philosophical Critique of Neo-Classical Economics* (Cambridge: Cambridge University Press, 1975).

[4] Friedman, *Essays*, pp. 22–3, virtually admits this.

If the orthodox methodology of contemporary economics is a cut-down version of a fifty-year-old development in logical positivist doctrine,[5] the official theory of value subscribed to by most economists is an even more antique form of logical positivism. Many economists still treat 'value judgements' (statements, for example, that one form of society is better than another) as 'preferences', and follow Lionel Robbins in believing that the interpersonal comparison of utilities is impossible.[6] Since Kenneth Arrow has shown that the aggregation of ordinal preferences into a 'social welfare function' is impossible,[7] the only criterion left is unanimity of preferences, that is, roughly, Pareto optimality.[8] The consequences of professing an irrationalist theory of value are that economists do not engage in open discussion of questions of value. Rather, they smuggle their values into their analyses, where they are immune to rational criticism.

I ECONOMISTS' EVALUATION OF INFLATION

The orthodox approach of welfare economics has had great difficulty in identifying a welfare loss from inflation at all commensurate with that often loosely attributed to it. In terms of static allocational inefficiency, the only welfare cost that can be identified is that people keep smaller cash balances than they would choose to do in the absence of inflation, because they are, in effect, losing money by holding cash. Even this is not an unmitigated welfare loss, for taxes have to be raised somehow and a tax on cash holdings (which is one way of looking at inflation) is as good a tax as any other. An economist with impeccably orthodox credentials has therefore suggested that an inflation rate of, say, 5 per cent might be regarded as beneficial, in the 'second-best' world where taxation is a fact of life.[9]

[5] See Karl Popper, *Logik der Forschung* (Vienna: Julius Springer, 1935).

[6] Lionel Robbins, *An Essay on the Nature and Significance of Economic Science*, 2nd edn. (London: Macmillan, 1969).

[7] Kenneth Arrow, *Social Choice and Individual Values* (New Haven: Yale University Press, 1951; 2nd edn. 1963).

[8] This of course brings the economists' theory of value into contact with the venerable tradition of social contract theory. The connection has been made explicit by the Virginia School. See James M. Buchanan and Gordon Tullock, *The Calculus of Consent: Logical Foundations of Constitutional Democracy* (Ann Arbor: University of Michigan Press, 1962); James M. Buchanan, *The Limits of Liberty: Between Anarchy and Leviathan* (Chicago: University of Chicago Press, 1975). For a critique, see Brian Barry, 'Review', *Theory and Decision*, 12 (1980), 95–106.

[9] J. S. Flemming, *Inflation* (London: Oxford University Press, 1976), 112. David Laidler and Michael Parkin discuss inflation as a tax on money balances in 'Inflation: A Survey', *Economic Journal*, 85 (1975), 791–4.

Leaving aside the alleged social and political by-products of inflation, it is hard to maintain that the consequences of inflation are enormously serious, especially when that level of inflation is arrived at over a number of years so as to allow for some adjustments of expectations along the way. The difficulties with mortgage repayments, long-term leases, and so on, are not negligible, but there are expedients available for dealing with them. (There is no reason why people should not be assured a positive inflation-discounted return on their savings.) And although these expedients deal with the distributive effects of inflation only in a rough-and-ready way, the residual distributive effects seem relatively small when set beside problems like unemployment and the underemployment of resources generally, pollution, depletion of resources, and so on.[10]

Hyperinflation is another matter, in that a market economy breaks down if money has to be spent within a few hours before it loses its value. But experience suggests that there is no inexorable development of hyperinflation from ordinary inflation. In spite of quite severe inflation in most member countries of the Organization for Economic Co-operation and Development (OECD) in the 1970s, none let it get out of control and accelerate in the classic pattern of hyperinflation.

Even if the monetarists are right and there is no trade-off between unemployment and inflation in long-run equilibrium, there is no reason for expecting to get into long-run equilibrium. Meanwhile, the ill-effects of anti-inflationary policies are quite certain. There are clear losers—those who would be thrown out of employment (or who would lose overtime or piecework bonuses).[11] The anxieties of being unemployed may be partially allayed by institutional change (high unemployment benefits); nevertheless, unemployment has profoundly disrupting social and psychological effects that even full replacement of income would do nothing to obviate. It is not therefore necessary to depict governments as composed of cynical manipulators to explain why they have tended to choose economic policies that have inflation as one of their consequences. A sincere desire for the public good and a rational preference for the avoidance of certain evils in the near future rather than the avoidance of speculative evils in the distant

[10] Harold T. Shapiro, 'Inflation in the United States', in Lawrence B. Krause and Walter S. Salant (eds.), *Worldwide Inflation: Theory and Recent Experience* (Washington, DC: Brookings Institution, 1977), 290.

[11] The studiously non-controversial Congressional Budget Office suggested that in order to achieve a reduction of 1 per cent in the rate of inflation by 1980 it would be necessary to cut the Federal budget, beginning in 1978, by an amount that would decrease GNP by 3 to 4 per cent in each year (though the loss would decrease after peaking in 1979). US Congressional Budget Office, *Recovery with Inflation* (Washington, DC: CBO, 1977), 36, and Table 2, p. 37.

future would have led in the same direction. The assumption underlying much of the new political economy—that the economic outcomes of democratic politics diverge sharply from those that would be brought about by a wholly benevolent dictator—is not self-evident.

Inflation as 'moral rot'

Is there perhaps some evil of inflation so serious that economists might be justified in seeking institutional changes (such as the insulation of the central bank from political pressure) that would ensure a lower inflation rate than that produced by the workings of a competitive political system, responsive in broad terms to popular preferences? Are the citizens of the Western democracies so corrupt that their preferences can legitimately be disregarded in the higher pursuit of saving them from themselves?

To some academic economists, and to many social critics and journalists, inflation is both a reflection of and a major contributor to a general collapse of values. Buchanan and Wagner identified a '*zeitgeist*, a "spirit of the times" . . . at work in the 1960s and 1970s', that they described as 'a generalized erosion in public and private manners, increasingly liberalized attitudes toward sexual activities, a declining vitality of the Puritan work ethic, deterioration in product quality, explosion of the welfare rolls, widespread corruption in both the private and the governmental sector, and, finally, observed increases in the alienation of voters from the political process.' And they contended that inflation 'plays some role in reinforcing several of the observed behavior patterns. Inflation destroys expectations and creates uncertainty; it increases the sense of felt injustice and causes alienation. It prompts behavioral responses that reflect a generalized shortening of time horizons. "Enjoy, enjoy"—the imperative of our time—becomes a rational response in a setting where tomorrow remains insecure and where the plans made yesterday seem to have been made in folly.'[12] They cited in support Wilhelm Röpke's even more apocalyptic view that 'inflation, and the spirit which nourishes it and accepts it, is merely the monetary aspect of the general decay of law and respect for law. . . . Laxity about property and laxity about money are very closely bound up together; in both cases what is firm, durable, earned, secured and designed for continuity gives place to what is fragile, fugitive, fleeting, unsure and ephemeral.'[13]

[12] Buchanan and Wagner, *Democracy in Deficit*, pp. 64–5.

[13] Ibid. 65 n. 16, quoting Wilhelm Röpke, *Welfare, Freedom and Inflation* (Tuscaloosa, Al.: University of Alabama Press, 1964), 70.

Similarly, the editor of *The Times*, William Rees-Mogg, saw inflation as part of a general twentieth-century decay: 'The damage that Dr. Spock did was that he destroyed confidence in discipline for children; the damage that Freud did was that he destroyed belief in the necessity of discipline in sexual conduct; the damage of the explosion of science was that it destroyed discipline in man's dealings with nature.'[14] (The remedy, according to Rees-Mogg, was God and Gold in equal doses.) He was seconded by another conservative journalist, Robert Moss, who argued that 'the recent trends that are pulling us towards strato-inflation are related both to an inflation of expectations in the post-1945 consumer society, and to a loss of broader concepts of patriotism and citizenship. . . . The psychology of inflation is deeply implanted'.[15]

The fact that academic economists accepted this sort of diagnosis so readily just reflects the tendency of the Friedmanite 'methodology of positive economics' to divide the social realm sharply into one area where the deductive method can be put to work and another that is subject to no canons of science and is therefore open to unconstrained speculation.

Fortunately, data as well as assertions exist. A political scientist, Ronald Inglehart, has also studied the question of whether a fundamental shift in values is occurring in Western countries.[16] His findings support the notion of a generational shift in values away from hard work, self-discipline, production, public order, patriotism, and the like, towards such values as self-expression, self-realization, political participation, and concern with the 'quality of life'. His survey of post-materialist attitudes in the European Economic Community and the United States in 1973 produced a close correlation between the first set of values and a high priority on control of inflation. There was a strong relation between the proportion in each category of materialist interests and in ranking by age-group in the EEC countries.[17] In a simpler survey, respondents were asked to choose the two most desirable of four aims. Two pairs (of a possible six pairs) accounted for half the responses: 'maintaining order in the nation' combined with 'fighting rising prices', and 'giving the people

[14] William Rees-Mogg, *The Reigning Error: The Crisis in World Inflation* (London: Hamish Hamilton, 1974), 103. (In 1988, Rees-Mogg, now ennobled, was given the job by a grateful government of keeping smut off Britain's television screens.)

[15] Robert Moss, *The Collapse of Democracy* (London: Sphere Books, 1977), 69–70.

[16] Ronald Inglehart, *The Silent Revolution: Changing Values and Political Styles among Western Publics* (Princeton, NJ: Princeton University Press, 1977).

[17] Ibid. 54.

more say in important political decisions' combined with 'protecting freedom of speech'.[18] The first are termed materialist and the second post-materialist; the distribution of responses by age cohort is shown in Table 3.1 on page 68. In the post-materialist columns the growth of this outlook among the younger generation is striking: in West Germany and France it rises from a negligible 1 to 2 per cent among the oldest to 19 to 20 per cent among the youngest age-group.[19]

Suppose that the generational change is sufficiently established to be accepted. The under-thirties show a higher incidence of a complex of attitudes, including attributing a relatively low priority to fighting inflation. To that extent, the thesis of the emergence of a new *Zeitgeist* is confirmed (though even among the most susceptible age-group in only a fifth or less). But there are no good grounds for accepting the assertion that inflation is a significant factor in creating and reinforcing this *Zeitgeist*. It seems to be the experience of affluence rather than the experience of inflation that is responsible for post-materialist values. For example, France since 1948 has been persistently one of the most inflationary countries and West Germany one of the least, but both have undergone economic transformation and the two display remarkably similar profiles of age-related attitudes. It is surely reasonable to suppose that the quest for more control of one's life and for a satisfying rather than a merely lucrative job will be a result of experiencing the diminishing returns of affluence and not of a change in the numeraire. A check in the rate of inflation cannot be expected to reverse the process of change in values—except in so far as the measures taken to reduce the rate of inflation produced such a decline in production and employment as to raise the priority of material goods and economic security again.

What conservatives decry as a 'collapse of values' seems to be more accurately depicted as the result of two forces: a decline in respect for established hierarchies, which has been working itself out for several

[18] Ibid. 21.

[19] Inferring a change in values from one generation to another on the basis of cross-sectional data is, of course, always suspect. Inglehart suggests that the difference in distributions of materialist and post-materialist values between generations should be greater the more contrasting their experiences. Thus, intergenerational difference is least in Britain and the United States, neither of which has experienced defeat or change of regime in this century, and both of which were relatively wealthy countries in 1945 and have had a moderate rate of economic growth. Conversely, in Germany the older generation can remember the hyperinflation of the 1920s, the mass unemployment of the 1930s, and the ruin and chaos immediately after the war, while those in the youngest cohort have known only the prosperity of the post-1948 'economic miracle'. The differences between generations in Germany are extreme. For other countries also the degree of difference between generations correlates well with difference in the life experience of the generations.

TABLE 3.1. Materialist attitudes among respondents to surveys in ten countries, 1972–1973[a]

Country	Percentage point spread across age groups	Percent in age-group											
		19–28		29–38		39–48		49–58		59–68		Over 68	
		Materi-alist	Post-ma-terialist	Materi-alist	Post-ma-terialist	Materi-alist	Post-ma-terialist	Materi-alist	Post-ma-terialist	Materi-alist	Post-ma-terialist	Materi-alist	Post-ma-terialist
W Germany	56	24	19	39	8	46	5	50	5	52	7	62	1
France	51	22	20	28	17	39	9	39	8	50	3	55	2
Italy	42	26	16	41	8	42	7	48	6	49	4	57	5
Belgium	39	18	23	20	17	22	10	25	10	39	3	39	5
Ireland	36	24	13	31	9	41	6	37	6	45	2	51	4
Netherlands	35	27	14	22	17	28	9	40	10	41	12	51	5
Denmark	34	33	11	34	9	47	4	44	5	48	4	58	2
Switzerland	32	27	15	26	17	30	15	35	9	34	6	50	6
USA	26	24	17	27	13	34	13	32	10	37	6	40	7
UK	17	27	11	33	7	29	6	30	7	36	5	37	4

[a] Countries ranked by spread across age-groups.

Source: Inglehart, *The Silent Revolution*, Table 2.2, pp. 36–7.

centuries in the West, and an extension to wider sections of the population of aspirations for autonomy and personal fulfilment. There is no reason for supposing that these profound modifications in the expectations that people hold about the conditions of co-operation with others are affected much by the experience of inflation.

It might be argued that there is indeed a causal connection that runs in the opposite direction to that so far considered. Existing industrial and governmental structures that are not going to adapt to new demands may well respond to abnormal discontent by allowing pay increases, thus buying time even at the expense of increased inflation further down the road. The big (and inflationary) pay rises for French workers that the government oversaw following the events of May 1968 constitute a clear example of this. Or inflation may occur as a result of the weakening of group leaders' authority to bind their members to accept deals that have been struck in their names, thus unleashing competition between groups. In the Netherlands, for example, the elaborate system of parcelling out state functions among corporate groups has come under increasing attack and has in some matters begun to crumble. The Swiss almost carried an initiative to restrict drastically the number of foreign workers, in the face of opposition from almost every established organization, including all the political parties. In Norway, the referendum on joining the EEC produced a majority vote against, in spite of support for entry from most major organizations, including the political parties with all but a handful of seats in the parliament. In economic affairs high-level agreements on national wage and salary rates have been increasingly strained—even in Sweden, normally regarded as the country in which comprehensive national bargaining is most highly developed. To the extent that trade union leaders cannot bind their followers to a programme of mutual restraint, one might expect an increase in the rate of inflation, as different groups scramble for relative advantage.

If there is a causal connection running from sociocultural change to inflation, rather than the other way round, the possibility must be seriously entertained that inflation acts as a safety valve, blunting the impact of incompatible demands. Even if that is going too far, it may be that inflation is a by-product of other things that are happening and cannot be held responsible for them.

Inflation as a cause of regime collapse

However unreasonable the intense feelings against change may be, they can, under certain conditions, give rise to the overthrow of a democratic system and its replacement by a regime such as that of Franco, the Greek colonels, or the Chilean junta. In this sense, it is true that inflation poses risks to the continuance of democratic institutions. Those who adhere to the idea of a collapse of values tend to conclude that nothing can be hoped for from democracy, since democratic institutions result in public policies that reflect the majority outlook. Support for some kind of authoritarian regime is a natural (if not often acknowledged) implication of their views. The tension between economic freedom (as understood by the proponents of the market) and political freedom (the freedom to publish, to organize, and to vote governments out of office) goes back over a century. (See further on this chapter 20 below.) Milton Friedman was not the first enthusiast for the market to endorse a collection of thugs, with his support for Pinochet. Vilfredo Pareto, an admirer of Mussolini, was a distinguished predecessor.

Some observers who profess to favour the continuation of democratic institutions still express fear that inflation will result in the replacement of a democratic regime by one less benign. The lesson to be drawn, however, is not that inflation and other things that arouse the violent dislike of reactionary army officers are political evils; rather, that it is important not to have an officer caste drawn from a narrow sector perpetuating an ideology in which the military stand as saviours of 'the nation' from the politicians. Where such a state of affairs exists it is difficult to change it: for every Cárdenas there are many Allendes. And where it cannot be changed, or the risk of a counterstroke is too great, an honourable political leader may judge that it is better to run a hobbled democratic government than to provoke a coup. If so, then the things that are liable to result in a coup—whether they be long hair, rock music, strikes, or inflation—become things to be avoided for political reasons.

There is, however, another commonly expressed idea that inflation in a democratic system leads to massive popular discontent and thus to the collapse of the regime. The distinctive feature of the theory is that the overthrow would apparently be met with popular support, or at least acquiescence. Supporters of this hypothesis tend to rely heavily on the German hyperinflation of 1922–4 and the success of the Nazis in 1933 in securing almost half the popular vote. But the Weimar

Republic, despite the fact that it was never accepted by the leaders of most of the powerful institutions and early alienated many of its natural supporters in the working class, survived the trauma of the Great Inflation. And the Nazis failed miserably in their attempts to attract support in the early 1920s. The obvious candidate for an economic explanation for their success is surely the very high level of unemployment in the early 1930s. The lesson to be drawn would thus seem to be that massive unemployment rather than hyperinflation is the serious threat to democratic institutions.[20]

None of this is to deny that hyperinflation is normally followed by the collapse of the regime under which it occurred. In this respect, the Weimar case is an exception. But the explanation is that the hyperinflation is one of the most dramatic signs of the government's failure. Hyperinflation typically occurs when government, because of war, revolution, the antagonism of powerful groups in the society, or the incapacity of its own administrative apparatus, is unable to collect sufficient taxes to finance its expenditures and therefore resorts to the printing press. It thereby buys a year or two of time, but it would be quite misleading to say that the hyperinflation led to its eventual downfall.[21]

The difficulty is one that bedevils much analysis in social science, namely, that of impossible counterfactuals. Roughly speaking, to say that *a* caused *b* is to say that, if everything else had been the same except that *a* had not occurred, *b* would not have happened either.[22] In many instances it makes perfectly good sense to pose questions about politics in those terms—for example, 'Would Nixon have completed his term of office if the Watergate break-in had not been discovered?' The question can properly be posed because the possibility that the 'plumbers' might have been less sloppy or the guards less vigilant is not inconsistent with the way the world works. But questions about the effects of large-scale social phenomena are liable to run into trouble.

John Stuart Mill set this point out in the course of his argument that the methods of agreement and difference are inapplicable to social

[20] For recognition that the collapse of Weimar followed on unemployment, but an argument that inflation had already eroded its democratic centre, see Brian Griffiths, *Inflation: The Price of Prosperity* (New York: Holmes and Meier, 1976), 177.

[21] For an analysis on these lines of the Indonesian hyperinflation of 1965–6 (in which President Sukarno lost power), see Dudley Jackson, H. A. Turner, and Frank Wilkinson, *Do Trade Unions Cause Inflation?* (Cambridge: Cambridge University Press, 1972), 52–4.

[22] See J. L. Mackie, *The Cement of the Universe: A Study of Causation* (London: Oxford University Press, 1974), 29–58.

phenomena.[23] His example—the effect of a protective tariff on a country's prosperity—is precisely the kind of association between two macro-level variables that is involved in the question about the relation between inflation and regime collapse. 'Two nations which agreed in everything except their commercial policy would agree also in that. Differences of legislation are . . . effects of pre-existing causes.'[24] Similarly, it does not in general make sense to ask what would have happened if everything else had been the same in a country except the inflation rate.[25]

Especially in Latin America inflation has been widely understood as a way of accommodating conflict by displacing an explicit zero-sum conflict over the distribution of the social product into a more loosely structured scramble for competitive advantage. Of course, at some point (which has been suggested to lie at an inflation rate of about 50 per cent per annum), 'demands develop for drastic government action',[26] and one consequence may well be the fall of the regime and its replacement by a more repressive one, either as a prelude to stabilization or as a reaction to the unpopularity of the government's efforts at stabilization. None of this entails the view—which members of the monetarist school are fond of attributing to others—that inflation is 'caused' by conflict, as if the supply of money had nothing to do with it. To be sure, though, inflation may be a response to conflict—including in this a response by the monetary authorities.

From interests to preferences

It has so far been proposed that there is no objective basis for the scaremongering of those who would like to use inflation as the occasion for removing economic policymaking from the province of ordinary politics. It might be argued, however, that inflation is so unpopular with the public that the institutions of democracy must

[23] John Stuart Mill, *A System of Logic: Ratiocinative and Inductive* (University of Toronto Press, 1974), bk. 6, ch. 7. Most social scientists whom I have polled informally have the impression that Mill *advocated* the use of these methods in the social sciences! One eminent political scientist has cited 'the influence of J. S. Mill's *Logic*' as one of the main reasons why 'the comparative observation of unmanipulated cases could ever have come to be regarded as any sort of equivalent of experimental method in the physical sciences.' Harry Eckstein, 'Case Study and Theory in Political Science', in Fred I. Greenstein and Nelson W. Polsby (eds.), *Handbook of Political Science*, vol. vii: *Strategies of Inquiry* (Reading, Mass.: Addison-Wesley, 1975), 117.

[24] Mill, *Logic*, bk. 6, ch. 7, p. 882.

[25] For a sophisticated contemporary treatment of counterfactuals, see Jon Elster, *Logic and Society: Contradictions and Possible Worlds* (Chichester: Wiley, 1978), ch. 6. I have criticized some aspects of Elster's treatment in Brian Barry, 'Superfox', *Political Studies*, 28 (1980), 136–43.

[26] Jackson, Turner, and Wilkinson, *Do Trade Unions Cause Inflation?*, p. 35.

therefore have been failing in periods of high inflation. The notion that democratic institutions are justified because they are the most efficient way of ensuring that there is some match between the policy preferences of the citizens and the policy outputs of government naturally appeals to market-oriented economists because it parallels the standard defence of a market economy.[27] The concept of consumer sovereignty—originally imported from the political vocabulary to suggest that consumers, merely by choosing how to spend their money, 'control' producers—has been reimported into politics, to suggest that voters 'control' elected representatives merely by deciding how to dispose their votes. In the process the concept of sovereignty in politics loses its original meaning of the power to give authoritative commands.

On the basis of the theory that political systems are to be judged by the extent to which they produce policy outcomes corresponding to the preferences of voters (ignoring the question of how those preferences are to be aggregated), democratic institutions can be condemned if politicians adopt policies that bring about inflation despite its unpopularity. That opens the way for proposals to limit the fiscal and monetary discretion of elected governments so as to ensure that the citizens get the outcomes that they really want. Requirements of a balanced budget or of a fixed (and small) rate of increase in the money supply can prevent politicians from getting between the people and the outcomes they wish to have brought about. 'Just as an alcoholic might embrace Alcoholics Anonymous, so might a nation drunk on deficits and gorged with government embrace a balanced budget and monetary stability.'[28]

But is inflation so unpopular that its existence can be taken as evidence for the failure of democratic institutions to work as they should? Buchanan and Wagner wonder how the 'ordinary democratic process' can seemingly produce 'a regime of continuous and mounting deficits, with subsequent inflation, along with a bloated public sector [that] can scarcely be judged beneficial to anyone. . . . Where is the institutional breakdown?'[29] This blithely assumes that the size of

[27] Arrow, *Social Choice and Individual Values*, p. 5, says that 'voting and the market mechanism' can both be regarded as 'special cases of the more general category of collective social choice'.

[28] Buchanan and Wagner, *Democracy in Deficit*, p. 159. This sample of their rhetoric is by no means atypical.

[29] Ibid. 94. It is a consequence of the antique logical positivist faith that Buchanan is committed officially to the view that no 'value judgement' can be made about any change unless everyone stands to benefit from it, or at any rate some benefit and none lose.

the deficit, of the public sector, and of the rate of inflation are too large by 'social choice' standards. Is this true? It is noteworthy that the bulk of the big increase in government expenditures in the 1970s was accounted for by transfer payments rather than by the government's spending a larger share of the gross national product on collective goods such as defence, roads, and other public services.[30] Since transfer payments simply place spending money in the hands of different people from those who had it before tax (including social security contributions here as a tax), it may be presumed that those who receive such payments do not object, nor do those who would otherwise have to care for them, or those who regard such transfers as just or as socially and politically stabilizing.

Collective expenditures raise more difficult questions. I believe that most people would find it very difficult to estimate the value to them of collective expenditures, still less of alternatives departing widely from the status quo.[31] It is conceivable (as Buchanan and Wagner apparently believe) that, in a fully informed judgement, most people would conclude that they are getting more public provision than they would be willing to pay for. But that could hardly be the case for the United States, where the lack of collective expenditure on the amenities of civilized life is painfully apparent. It would certainly be rash to assert dogmatically that the size of the US budget constitutes evidence for the failure of the democratic process to give people what they want. Of course people dislike paying taxes, but they also (as the tax-cutting enthusiasts often complain) value the services the government provides.

Some people believe that if 'waste' were eliminated from public expenditure, the same services could be provided with less taxation. But by the standards according to which public authorities waste billions, private consumers waste hundreds of billions. If a public authority builds a facility costing 10 million dollars that turns out to be

[30] Old age and other insurance plus public welfare payments in the United States rose from $15.3 billion (10 per cent of total government expenditure) in 1960 to $70.5 billion (18 per cent) in 1972; Michel Crozier, Samuel P. Huntington, and Joji Watanuki, *The Crisis of Democracy* (New York: New York University Press for the Trilateral Commission, 1975), Table 2, p. 69. Huntington (ibid., pp. 71–2) notes that these transfer payments are popular with the public, which seems to cast direct doubt on the Buchanan and Wagner conspiracy theory of public expenditure. For the United Kingdom, see James Alt and Alec Chrystal, 'Endogenous Government Behaviour: Overture to a Study of Public Expenditure', Discussion Paper 108 (Colchester: University of Essex, Dept. of Economics, Dec. 1977).

[31] This makes implausible the contention of Albert Breton that political discontent occurs when people are failing to get (in their own estimation) value for money from their taxes: see *The Economic Theory of Representative Government* (London: Macmillan, 1974), 71–3.

unnecessary, or spends 10 million dollars more than the minimum to do the job, that is excoriated as waste; if a million people spend 10 dollars on dud appliances or spend 10 more dollars than they needed to spend to achieve the same end equally effectively, that is regarded as a normal incident of a market society. Of course, it may be possible for either governments or individual consumers to do better, but campaigning against 'waste in government' should be recognized for what it is—campaigning against government.

The assertion that inflation 'can hardly be judged beneficial to anyone' is extraordinarily implausible. To the extent that inflation is purely redistributive, there are (by definition) net gainers as well as net losers. To the extent that it has effects that are not cancelled out in this way, the news is still not all bad. Against the 'welfare loss' arising from people keeping smaller cash balances than they would like and the 'cost' attributable to uncertainty about the future price level must be set the losses of real income and employment created by attempts to reduce inflation by the use of monetary or fiscal policy.

It may nevertheless be said that, whether beneficial or harmful, inflation is provably unpopular and that this is enough to condemn democratic institutions for failing to deliver the outcomes that are desired by citizens. But how exactly are the preferences of ordinary citizens for economic outcomes established? When answers to public opinion poll questions are accepted as evidence that inflation is the country's number one problem, what does that actually mean? It ought to mean that people dislike increases in the price level. But do most people have such a clear grasp of economic concepts as this requires? Such studies of popular understanding of economic terms as have been made suggest that it would be rash to assume so. People often have a hazy idea that, in the absence of inflation, they would have been able to have their latest pay increase and keep its purchasing power through the whole of the subsequent year. Thus, a 10 per cent inflation is looked on as equivalent to a 10 per cent loss of real income. In endorsing the absence (or reduction) of inflation, they are opting for a state of affairs in which nominal incomes would have gone up but prices would not have risen at all, or at any rate as fast as they actually had done.

The deliberate confusion of inflation with a corresponding loss of real income is pervasive. For instance, Michael Blumenthal, less than a week before his dismissal as treasury secretary, was reported to have said that inflation had 'cut sharply into workers' real incomes', and to have warned that 'workers should not try to make up for their loss in income because that would only result in higher prices and worse inflation'.[32] Obviously, if inflation were a gratuitous deduction from an otherwise attainable level of real income, it would be perfectly reasonable to respond by restoring the level of real income. But why should it be assumed that increases in nominal incomes would be wiped out in real terms by price increases if it makes sense to imagine that workers could have had their present money incomes *without* inflation?

Blumenthal's successor, G. William Miller (while he was chairman of the Federal Reserve Board), had similarly beclouded the relation between inflation and real income. '"What is the social benefit for programs that are well meaning but wreck the wealth and incomes of all Americans", Miller asked. "An 8 percent inflation is a $160 billion tax."'[33]

Another, more indirect way of estimating public opinion about inflation is to correlate changes in voting intentions or in support for incumbents with changes in economic indicators. The rates of inflation, unemployment, and change in real income (the usual aggregate indicators used in regression equations) are not, however, brute facts of experience but are mediated by newspaper and television reporting. Even inflation is an abstraction from the movements of all prices. In the absence of standard indexes, people might be aware over time of a trend in prices, but they could no more say whether the inflation rate was 5 per cent or 10 per cent than most people could say whether the outside temperature is 85° or 90° without looking at a thermometer. Until Stanley Jevons constructed the first index,[34] apparently nobody had noticed that the rises in some prices and falls in others between 1845 and 1862 in England had not balanced out, but amounted to an inflationary trend. Aggregate unemployment rates and changes in real income in a society are, obviously, even less plausibly regarded as immediate data of experience.

Scholars who analyse public opinion are well aware that the popularity of incumbents depends on more than the state of the economy. They attempt to remove disturbing factors by introducing dummy variables such as 'Watergate'. But when all the major changes

[32] *New York Times* (14 July 1979).

[33] Patrick R. Oster, *Chicago Sun-Times* (21 Nov. 1978). The notion of the whole loss of purchasing power of a given nominal income as an inflationary 'tax' is, of course, to be distinguished from the more sophisticated idea of inflation as a tax on cash balances.

[34] W. Stanley Jevons, *A Serious Fall in the Value of Gold Ascertained, and Its Social Effects Set Forth* (London: Edward Stanford, 1863), cited in *The Collected Writings of John Maynard Keynes*, vol. x: *Essays in Biography* (London: Macmillan, 1972), 119–22.

in public opinion over a period are 'explained' by political events involving the actions of incumbents or their opponents, one may wonder how much faith to have in assurances that the residual changes should be laid to the account of the economy. And precise claims about the way in which, say, 1 per cent more inflation changes government support, other things being equal, should be viewed cautiously. They never are equal, and that is just what creates the measurement problem in the first place.

Furthermore, there is no reason for expecting that the state of the aggregate economic variables will have a fixed relation to the popularity of incumbents. Even if there is no change in the pleasantness or unpleasantness of a particular mix of those variables in people's minds, there may be a change in the degree to which they hold the government responsible for that mix. A government may improve its standing in the polls either by improving the state of the economy or by convincing people that it is doing as well as can be expected. Hence, for example, the (not wholly unreasonable) efforts of successive administrations to attribute much of the responsibility for the stagflations of 1973–4 and 1979–80 to the Organization of Petroleum Exporting Countries (OPEC). People may (as seems to have happened in Britain) continue to give a fair degree of support to governments that have presided over varying combinations of high inflation, high unemployment, and declining real income that would earlier have been a guarantee of political suicide, not because they like it but because most of the time they despair of any other government doing any better.[35]

This again, however, raises the question of why politicians persist in making inflation more of a bogey than it deserves to be. If the alternative to doing better is to make people feel that what you are doing already is not so bad, why pile on the agony in this gratuitous way? My answer is, admittedly, speculative.

There are three ways in which governments can seek to control inflation in an economy where the key economic decisions remain in private hands. The first is to deflate the economy enough for economic activity to decline to a point at which people will be glad to take jobs at any rate of pay, and prices will begin to fall. A second route is through neocorporatism or, more prosaically, tripartite agreement between business, labour, and government. In the United States particularly there is an obvious problem of ideological incompatibility between

[35] See Alt and Chrystal, 'Endogenous Government Behaviour'.

this kind of high-level fix and the ethos of antitrust, business unionism, and limited government. But there is also a simple problem of feasibility. The institutions do not exist: no organization can speak for all workers or all employers and deliver on any deal that is struck. The roots of societal collaboration in countries such as Austria and the Netherlands go back centuries; such understandings and practices cannot be wished into existence. Moreover, it may not be an accident that the examples of successful neocorporatism are all countries with only a few million inhabitants. Perhaps the sheer size and diversity of the United States (or even Britain) rule out corporatist solutions.

The only remaining path is exhortation, and it is not therefore surprising that this is the chosen instrument of governments whose concern for popularity (or even governability) leads them to eschew the first course and whose ideological commitments or practical necessities rule out the second. But exhortation requires that the evils of inflation be painted so dramatically that people will voluntarily take less than the market will bear, out of deference to the anti-inflation guidelines. Since inflation is not really evil enough to lead a rational person to pass up the chance of making a buck, creative confusion steps in to fill the gap.

To summarize, I do not believe it is realistic to hope for very exact guidance about public attitudes to inflation. But even if there were agreement that inflation *is* unpopular, does it really follow that the institutions of democracy have been failing to work as they should? I do not believe so. There has, of course, been inflation (at widely differing rates) in all the economically advanced democracies. And governments have taken harsh contractionist measures in the hope of reducing the rate of inflation in their societies—measures that inevitably have adverse effects on employment and real income. Assuming that people care about unemployment and loss of real income as well as inflation, have governments in general been too lax about fighting inflation, taking as a criterion the preferences of the public? I can see no reason for thinking that, given the choices, politicians opt for more inflation than their constituents, if they understood the choices, would opt for. My own suspicion is the reverse. I cannot prove it. But I maintain that the whole presumption that underlay the economists' criticism that democracy produces more inflation than the citizens want has rested on extremely shaky foundations.

II THE 'NEW POLITICAL ECONOMY'

Economists have attempted to shore up their conclusions with models of electoral behaviour. But the premisses of these also deserve careful scrutiny. In fact, there is not just a single theory of the effects of electoral competition on the rate of inflation, but a family of models that share certain basic features. At the core of their economic component is the idea, whose essentials can be traced back to David Hume's essay 'Of Money', that an increase in the quantity of money has an initial effect of raising the level of economic activity and only later dissipates itself in a general rise in prices. At first the extra money will be used to buy and sell more at the old prices, and only later will the shortfall of supply drive prices up. 'It is easy to trace the money in its progress through the whole commonwealth; where we shall find, that it must first quicken the diligence of every individual, before it increases the price of labour.'[36] In modern terms: people act on expectations about future prices that are doomed to be disappointed, and it is the mismatch that makes for the increase in activity.[37] It follows, then, that the more sluggish the response of inflationary expectations to the actual experience of inflation, the more a government can stimulate the economy in a certain period (for example, in the run-up to an election) without the bulk of the inflationary effects showing until a later period.

The same analysis can be expressed using the device of the Phillips curve—a curve relating the inflation rate (on the vertical axis) and the level of unemployment (on the horizontal axis). The original Phillips curve was plotted from the observed levels of change in money wage rates against unemployment in the United Kingdom from 1861 to 1957.[38] Since the points fell on a single curve, the implication was that to every level of unemployment there corresponded a unique level of increase in money wage rates, and it was hypothesized that this relationship might be accounted for by labour market conditions—the tighter the labour market, the more wages go up.[39] On the view underlying the theory of the politico-economic cycle, however, this

[36] David Hume, *Essays: Moral, Political and Literary* (London: Oxford University Press, 1963), 294.

[37] See the strikingly Humean formulation of the 'new macroeconomics' in D. E. W. Laidler, *Essays on Money and Inflation* (Chicago: University of Chicago Press, 1975), 9–10.

[38] A. W. Phillips, 'The Relation between Unemployment and the Rate of Change of Money Wage Rates in the United Kingdom, 1861–1957', *Economica*, 25 (1958), 283–99.

[39] Richard G. Lipsey, 'The Relation between Unemployment and the Rate of Change of Money Wage Rates in the United Kingdom, 1862–1957: A Further Analysis', *Economica*, 27 (1960), 1–31.

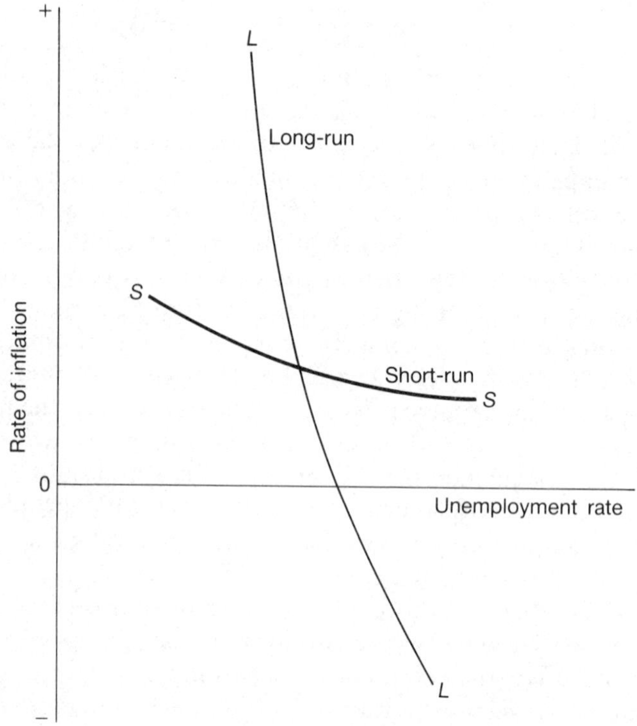

FIG. 3.1. Short-run and long-run Phillips curves relating inflation to unemployment

idea of a single curve must be abandoned for a pair of short-run and long-run Phillips curves. In the short run, a given increase in employment is associated with a smaller increase in wages (or prices) than in the long run, so the short-run Phillips curve has a flatter slope than the long-term one. Thus, in Figure 3.1, if the economy is at the point where the two curves intersect, the shape of the curves implies that the government could reduce unemployment in the short run (by moving the economy leftward along the curve *SS*) at a lower cost in inflation than could be sustained in the long run. Any point below and to the left of the long-run curve *LL* designates a combination of inflation and unemployment that is better than can be achieved in long-run equilibrium, when expectations have had a chance to adjust fully and behaviour is in accord with those expectations.

Conversely, of course, the shapes of the curves also imply that a government wishing to reduce inflation must accept a move to the right along the short-run curve *SS* until expectations have adjusted to the new conditions. Since this means moving to a point above and to the right of the long-run curve, the analysis implies that the economy will in the short term have a worse combination of inflation and unemployment than could be maintained indefinitely once the economy had settled down and expectations had once again adjusted.

Since the long-run curve is a theoretical entity, its shape is subject to theoretical arguments. Modern monetarists suggest that it must be vertical because, at any level of unemployment except one (the 'natural rate' for that economy), the rate of inflation will (in the long run) tend to go up or down. Any stable inflation rate is compatible with the same unemployment rate. The actual rate of inflation itself will be a function of the rate at which the money supply increases in relation to the real national income. While the deduction is logically impeccable, it says nothing about the world. Maybe this 'long run' is never reached; that would mean, for instance, that it is never true that all contracts could be negotiated in such a way as to cancel out the rate of inflation. Even if the long run does exist, it may be measured in decades or even centuries. I therefore follow the convention of making the long-run curve steep but not vertical.

Economists who venture into formal analysis of the political system tend to assume that politicians are conscienceless seekers of power, those in office being prepared to inflict any amount of damage on their countries in order to increase, however fractionally, their share of the vote. At the same time, politicians are assumed (for the purpose of model-building) to be consummately skilful at manipulating the levers of economic policy in pursuit of the end of re-election. Voters, by contrast, are assumed to have barely any cognitive or ratiocinative capacities. They are hardly able to remember the economic record of the current government when election time comes round, and have no ability to anticipate the future (or if they do then somehow this anticipation does not affect their actions). Within the limits set by their defective memories, these zombies react with approval or disapproval to past experience of inflation and unemployment rates and also perhaps to the direction in which those rates are changing; but they do not attempt to make any estimates of the future course of these variables.

If these are the premisses, it is hardly surprising that the conclusion turns out to be that democracy is a flawed form of government. What could anyone hope for from a system characterized by a collection of rogues competing for the favours of a larger collection of dupes? Characteristically, the premisses of politico-economic models developed by economists are baldly stated, with little discussion of their plausibility.[40] And only anecdotal evidence at best is normally adduced in support of the conclusions. Yet, for no democratic country do the economists' assumptions appear to approximate to the truth. Studies of national-level politicians in democratic countries suggest that they are motivated either by policy concerns or by service of a personal kind to their constituents.[41] These 'satisfactions of office' are derived from doing something with the office that is thought to be worthwhile. Moreover, political leaders are very often highly motivated by the thought of their reputations in history and may well be unwilling to pay a price of ignominy for doing something with predictably bad consequences in order to secure some short-run electoral gain. Even Richard Nixon, by risking further obloquy in his subsequent attempts to justify himself, illustrates the importance of reputation to politicians.

Voting studies suggest that voters try to decide which candidates would do better on the issues that they care most about and tend to vote according to the answers they come up with.[42] They also try to form estimates of the competence of alternative candidates, something way beyond the picture of voters merely responding to the 'goodness or badness of the times' by voting for the ins or the outs.[43] If voters sometimes find it hard to make clear judgements about policy differences between candidates, this may reflect the reluctance of politicians to go beyond generalities. When politicians differentiate themselves clearly on an issue, the evidence suggests that voters are usually aware of it.[44]

There is no lack of evidence that voters give extra weight to the

[40] 'Once it is recognized that macroeconomic policy is made by self-interested, not disinterested or other-interested politicians, a new perspective on macroeconomic policy appears, particularly if politicians believe that economic conditions can affect their survival prospects.' Wagner, 'Economic Manipulation', pp. 396–7. (Note: *recognized* rather than *postulated*.)

[41] See Robert D. Putnam, *The Beliefs of Politicians: Ideology, Conflict, and Democracy in Britain and Italy* (New Haven: Yale University Press, 1973).

[42] See V. O. Key, *The Responsible Electorate: Rationality in Presidential Voting, 1936–1960* (Cambridge, Mass.: Harvard University Press, 1966); Samuel Popkin *et al.*, 'Comment: What Have You Done for Me Lately?' *American Political Science Review*, 70 (1976), 779–805.

[43] Popkin *et al.*, 'Comment', show convincingly how much George McGovern was hurt in the 1972 presidential campaign by perceptions of lack of competence following the Eagleton affair.

[44] See Benjamin I. Page, *Choices and Echoes in Presidential Elections: Rational Man and Electoral Democracy* (Chicago: University of Chicago Press, 1978).

more recent performance of the economy, but if they are trying to decide whether to endow the government with another term of office, that does not seem an unreasonable thing to do. After all, for a year or even two, a government can with some legitimacy blame troubles on its predecessor; but the longer it has been in office, the better the case for judging its priorities and capabilities on the current state of the economy. Pessimistic analyses of democratic political economy imply that a government might find it advantageous to stage a massive deflation in its first two years if it could get the unemployment rate down again and combine it with a lower rate of inflation by election day. But I think that kind of gratuitous deflation would be remembered because it would be important information about the way the government worked. The Republicans, to give the most obvious example, were distrusted by many people for a whole generation because of what 1929–32 was taken to have told about their complacency in the face of mass unemployment.

The political business cycle

The basic idea of the political business cycle can be explained using the apparatus of short-run and long-run Phillips curves. Figure 3.2 illustrates the characteristic clockwise loop that the theory seeks to explain. Starting at *A*, the government brings about a pre-election boom, moving the economy along the short-run curve S_1S_1 to *B*. As expectations adapt, this favourable combination of unemployment and inflation cannot be maintained and both deteriorate (presumably after the election) to *C*. But suppose that *C* is too high in inflation to be popular electorally. The government therefore wishes to bring down the rate of inflation, which it can do only by moving the economy along the short-run curve S_2S_2 to *D*. This brings the economy back onto the long-run curve at *A*, but of course if there is time before the next election to stage a boom, it will be possible to get to *B* for it (assuming the intervening experience has not changed the shape of the short-run curve—an important proviso), and so the cycle is set off again.[45]

In principle the political business cycle thus generated could occur even if the voters based their decisions at election time on the experience of the whole period since the previous election, equally

[45] Compare Nordhaus, 'Political Business Cycle'; Lindbeck, 'Stabilization Policy'; MacRae, 'Political Model'; Bruno S. Frey, *Modern Political Economy* (Chichester: Wiley, 1978).

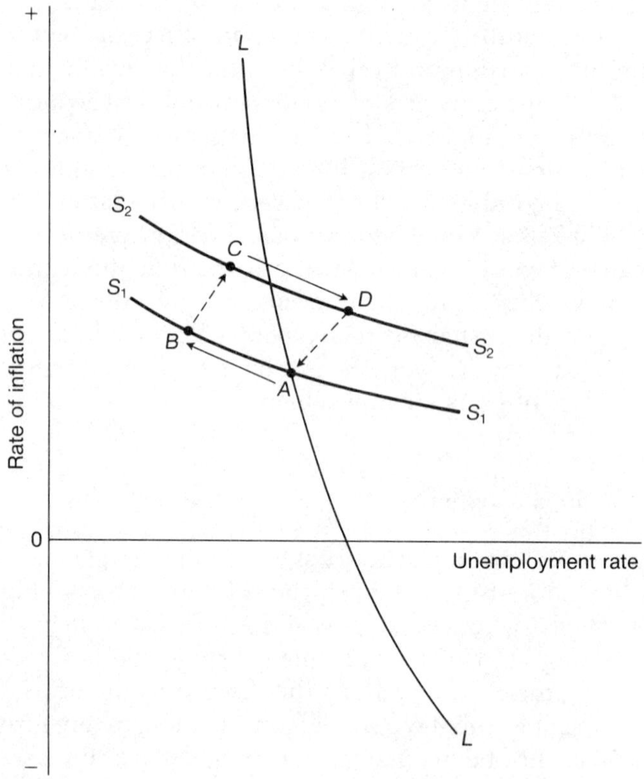

FIG. 3.2. Short-run and long-run Phillips curves and the clockwise loop of the political business cycle

Note: Solid arrows represent moves along the short-run Phillips curve brought about by government policy decisions; dashed arrows represent subsequent adjustments in the economy that shift it from one short-run Phillips curve to another.

weighted. The driving mechanism is the possibility of producing an advantageous combination of inflation and unemployment before the election and the assumption that the long-run rate of inflation arising after the election is unpopular. However, it is clear that the motivation for government to engage in the kind of behavour depicted is enhanced if the voters discount the early years in office when judging the government's economic performance. For then the high unemployment of stage *D*, an 'investment' in getting lower on the long-run curve, carries a reduced electoral penalty.

The simplest test of the notion that a political business cycle is endemic in democracies is to see whether the rates of inflation and unemployment correspond with the predictions of the model. The unemployment rate would be expected to increase as soon after an election as the government could get its policy instruments to work, and then to decline as the next election approached. The course of inflation is more difficult to predict on the basis of the theory. Because the new government inherits inflationary pressures, the rate of inflation should increase to begin with, but then it should decline as the increase in unemployment begins to take effect. However, it is compatible with the theory that inflation should turn upwards again as the government boosts the economy in the run-up to the next election.

Tests of the theory are relatively crude. They focus on the predictions about unemployment, since these are more definite, and make comparisons between a period before the election (one month, one year, two years, or half the inter-election period, for example) and the rest of the time since the preceding election. Bruno Frey has tested the hypothesis that unemployment rates are lower on the average in the two years preceding general elections in Britain and presidential elections in the United States than the rest of the time. Assuming, as Frey[46] and Nordhaus[47] do, that unemployment can be increased quickly after an election and will then decline steadily, the path of unemployment should be saw-toothed, and the average level in the first half of an inter-election period higher than in the second. Frey concludes that for Britain the reverse tended to be true if anything from the mid-1950s to the mid-1970s, while for the United States the evidence points in no particular direction.

Edward Tufte claims better success with trends rather than averages of US unemployment from 1948 to 1976, except in the period of the Eisenhower presidency. He claims that, excluding the 1956 and 1960 elections, unemployment was lower in November of each election year than for most of the preceding twenty-four months—results he describes as 'phenomenal'.[48] But, during the whole of the eight years of the Democratic administrations of Kennedy and Johnson, there is

[46] See Frey, *Modern Political Economy*, p. 131.

[47] See Nordhaus, 'Political Business Cycle', p. 185.

[48] Edward R. Tufte, *Political Control of the Economy* (Princeton, NJ: Princeton University Press, 1978), 21.

no sign of any cycle: unemployment fell almost continuously month by month. The Nixon–Ford record Tufte himself describes as 'mixed', which leaves only the Truman administration of 1948–52 and the Nixon 'game plan' of 1968–72, both of which do show the rise and then fall in unemployment. Looking at the unemployment chart armed only with the theory of the political business cycle, it would be very hard to guess where the elections came.

William Nordhaus has tested the proposition that unemployment has a rising trend for the first half of the inter-election period and a falling trend for the second half, against post-war data for nine countries in which 'a cursory examination of macro-economic policies pointed to the possibility that the three conditions for the political business cycle would be met'. His conditions were 'that the government be chosen in periodic competitive elections', that it 'have sufficient economic control and sophistication to move the economy in the desired direction', and that voters should evaluate governments purely on the basis of the performance of the economy since the previous election. But Nordhaus was able to claim only three countries in which 'the coincidence of business and political cycles is very marked', namely, the Federal Republic of Germany, New Zealand, and the United States.[49] (The other countries tested were Australia, Canada, France, Japan, Sweden, and the United Kingdom.)

Even then his conclusions have to be treated with caution, for he misleadingly excludes results that do not negate his theory even if they do not confirm it. Nordhaus gives for each country the number of times the trend was downward in the second half of the inter-election period (confirming the theory) and upward (disconfirming the theory), and the number of times in the first half that the overall trend was upward (confirming the theory) and downward (disconfirming the theory). But the numbers fall far short of the number of post-war elections for some countries. The missing cases are presumably those where the unemployment rate was the same throughout or where it went both up and down in the period. But if the theory of the political business cycle predicts a rising unemployment rate and the unemployment rate does not rise, that is a negative result for the theory.

To see that this makes a difference, take the two countries where Nordhaus claims to have found 'some modest indications of a political cycle', France and Sweden.[50] For France, Nordhaus claims six hits and three misses. But the nine periods add up at the most to eighteen of the

[49] Nordhaus, 'Political Business Cycle', pp. 185, 186. [50] Ibid. 186.

twenty-six years covered by his study. Thus the confirmatory experiences total at best only twelve of the twenty-six years—hardly a robust demonstration. In the case of Sweden, Nordhaus counts seven hits and five misses, and even this slender margin of success would disappear if the omitted periods were added and counted as failures for the theory.

A deeper problem is the role of caprice in deciding whether to count a set of twenty-four monthly unemployment figures as an upward trend, a downward trend, or neither. Thus, in the 1946–72 period in the United States, Nordhaus counts 1954–6 as a success for the theory, whereas Tufte does not, while Tufte counts 1960–2 and 1966–8 as successes but Nordhaus does not. Both count 1948–52 as a success, but the two-year period following the 1948 election shows a fairly symmetrical rise and fall back to the election-day level, so it hardly represents a rising trend. At any rate, it does not fit Nordhaus's hypothesis of a trend over the two years. Tufte gives unemployment as 'rising' in the two years after the 1960 election, on the basis of an infinitesimal increase in the few months after the election, followed by a substantial drop sustained through the whole of the second year, whereas in 1972 a fall in unemployment extending over almost a year after the election followed by a substantial rise is also described as 'rising'.

In another study Tufte purports to show that, in twenty-seven democracies (some with rather dubious credentials), there were nineteen in which 'short-run accelerations in real disposable income per capita were more likely to occur in election years than in years without elections',[51] between 1961 and 1972. However, a number of the differences appear trivial. For example, in Belgium and also in Ireland real disposable income is shown as having increased in 67 per cent of election years and 63 per cent of non-election years—in both countries, two out of three election years and five out of eight non-election years. Five-eighths represents the closest it is possible to come to two-thirds.

It does look as if there is a political-economic cycle for about half the countries. However, this is a cycle in real disposable income and not necessarily in the overall level of economic activity. It could be consistent with a uniform level of unemployment and economic growth if governments tended to raise taxes early in their term, start building roads, schools, and so forth, in time to have something to

[51] Tufte, *Political Control*, p. 11.

show by the next election, and tried to reduce taxes or give out increased cash benefits in their final year. The cycle would then be one of public as against private consumption.

That the two phenomena are different is suggested by the fact that Nordhaus concluded that 'for the entire period a political cycle seems to be implausible as a description for Australia, Canada, Japan and the U.K.', whereas these four countries are among the most striking examples of the disposable real income cycle, the ratio of percentage increases in election years to those in non-election years being, respectively, 75:29, 100:57, 100:29, and 67:38. Conversely, West Germany, one of Nordhaus's three cases of a 'marked' cycle, does not have a disposable real income cycle: disposable real income is shown as increasing in a slightly smaller proportion of election years than of non-election years.[52] Similarly, Tufte cites a study of the Philippines describing the economy as moving in a 'biennial lurch', with real income rising and falling within the electoral cycle;[53] yet the Philippines are shown in his table as not having increases of real disposable income more frequently in election years.

The Tufte data on changes in real disposable income are, therefore, suggestive in their own right but do not do anything to add to the limited support that the Nordhaus evidence provides for the theory of the political business cycle.

Politico-economic models of inflation

The theory of the political business cycle leads to the conclusion that inflation and unemployment should both rise immediately after an election, to be followed by a period of high unemployment accompanied by a falling inflation rate, and then a period of falling unemployment extending to the next election accompanied by a rate of inflation that, whether continuing to fall or starting to rise again at the end, is lower than could be combined with that rate of unemployment in the long run. No country shows this complex sequence more than occasionally, which is hardly surprising in view of the exogenous shocks to which an economy is subject. Apparently only a few show even disjointed bits of it.

Even if the theory were better supported than it is, however, it would do nothing to suggest that democracy has any built-in tendency to produce inflation. The rate of inflation, according to the

[52] Nordhaus, 'Political Business Cycle', p. 186; Tufte, *Political Control*, p. 12.
[53] Tufte, *Political Control*, pp. 13–14.

theory, will fluctuate within the electoral cycle, but that is not to say either that it will fluctuate around a rising trend or, if around some constant level, whether that level will be high rather than low. The most natural expectation, assuming that vote-maximizing governments manipulate the economy for their own purposes, might seem to be that the rate will fluctuate around the level corresponding to the point on the long-run Phillips curve that is most popular with the electorate. And the clockwise loop described by the economy would cycle around that point.

The combinations of inflation and unemployment that might gain, respectively, 50, 51, and 52 per cent of votes are depicted in Figure 3.3 on p. 90. On the assumption that inflation and unemployment are both disliked, these isopsephic curves slope down to the right;[54] the further they are from the origin, the smaller the share of the popular vote the government will garner if it comes up to an election with the economy in that state. The best point on the long-run Phillips curve for the government to pick is that tangent to the highest attainable isopsephic curve—in Figure 3.3 the point *T*—which gives the government 51 per cent of the vote. Thus, the rate of inflation will depend on the shapes of the Phillips curve and the isopsephic curve. Other things being equal, the steeper the Phillips curve, the lower the inflation rate that will be chosen by a vote-maximizing government. (If the long-run Phillips curve is vertical, as monetarists claim, the most popular position attainable will be one with stable prices, assuming that isopsephic curves bend back at zero inflation—that is, if voters dislike falling prices as well as rising prices.) And, other things being equal, the steeper the slope of the isopsephic curves the higher the rate of inflation that will maximize votes. For a steep slope would mean that the voters were relatively tolerant of inflation as compared with unemployment.

The conclusion to be drawn is that voters get the rate of inflation that has the most support and that it is not necessarily high or low. And though they might prefer to do without the occasional clockwise loops of the electoral cycle, there is no evidence that the welfare losses from the part of the cycle that lies above and to the right of the long-run Phillips curve outweigh the gains from the part that lies below and to the left of it.[55] In any case, adding the political business cycle would

[54] I call these *isopsephic* curves rather than using the customary but barbarous term, *isovote* curves.

[55] Lindbeck, 'Stabilization Policy', p. 13, says that 'the experiences of recent years have shown how high the economic and social costs are during this deflationary phase of the policy cycle', but he does not mention in the same breath the gains from the good part of the cycle.

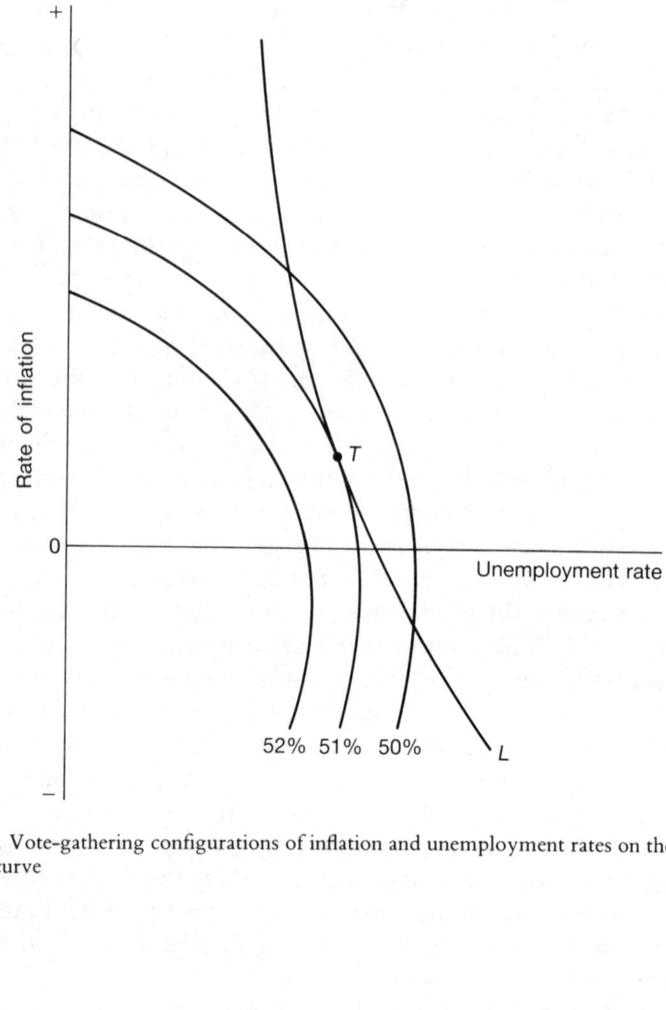

FIG. 3.3. Vote-gathering configurations of inflation and unemployment rates on the long-run Phillips curve

not raise the average level of inflation or cause it to increase over time without limit. Yet economists and journalists and other commentators on current events frequently suggest that the level of inflation produced by electoral competition tends to be higher than most people want, or indeed that there is some inexorable process tending to make the rate of inflation go up over time.

The Nordhaus model

Critics, it is apparent, are often expressing disapproval for what voters allegedly want (supposedly, higher inflation), rather than solicitude for their failing to get what they want. None the less, William Nordhaus has sought to make a narrower case—namely, that vote-maximizing among a myopic electorate brings about an inflation rate higher than the amount that would get the biggest majority out of all points on the long-run Phillips curve. He has tried, unsuccessfully I believe, to formalize the idea that vote-maximizing by governments produces a level of inflation that is higher than the most popular rate. His model supposes that, if the economy is on the short-run Phillips curve S_1S_1 after an election, the government picks the point E_1 on the curve that is at a tangent with the 53 per cent isopsephic curve (Figure 3.4). However, it cannot in fact keep the economy at any point that lies off the long-run Phillips curve, which is by definition the series of points at which any particular mix of unemployment and inflation can remain constant. By the time of the next election, therefore, the position will have deteriorated so that the short-run Phillips curve S_2S_2 applies. The new government will do the best it can electorally, again on the assumption that it cannot shift the short-run curve before the next election, so it will pick the point E_2. Since this too is off the long-run Phillips curve, it cannot be maintained for an extended period either, so the economy will slip to the short-run Phillips curve S_3S_3 by the next election. The point of tangency with the highest attainable isopsephic curve, E_3, now lies on the long-run Phillips curve. And the story stops there, for no government can do better than pick E_3—provided the relations between the macroeconomic variables remain the same. A government, however, can be too pessimistic as well as over-sanguine. If an election is held at a time when the short-run curve S_5S_5 applies, the government will pick E_5, and be pleasantly surprised by the move to S_4S_4. It will hence move to E_4 and thence to the improved curve S_3S_3 and point E_3.

Nordhaus also views the long-run equilibrium point E_3 as the solution to a problem in collective choice, the purely myopic point U_M (Figure 3.5). It is the point that would be chosen by the biggest majority if the future were wholly discounted. If the future were not discounted at all, the point that would gain the biggest majority *on average* over an indefinitely long period would be U_G, where the isopsephic curve V_2V_2 is at a tangent to the long-run Phillips curve. For, over a long enough period, the cost of getting to that point

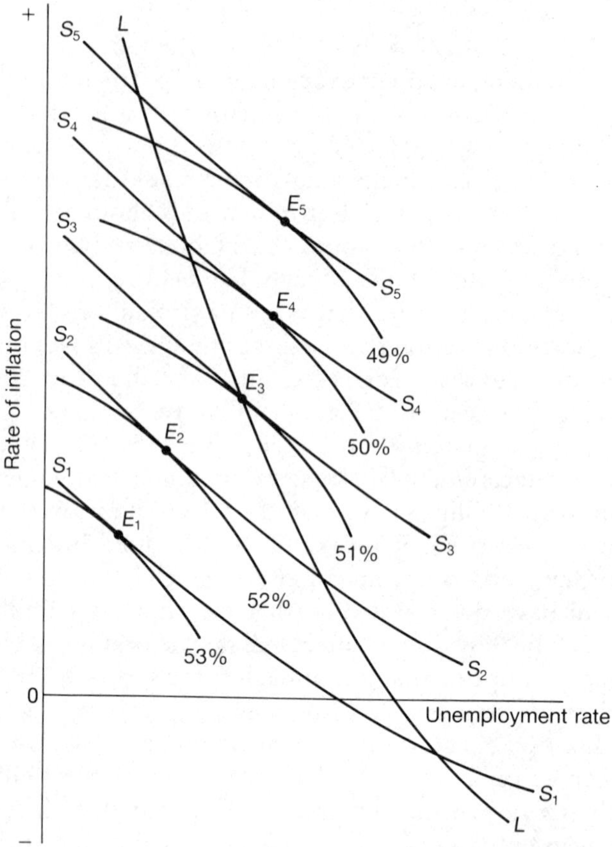

FIG. 3.4. Nordhaus model of vote-maximizing governments' effect on inflation
Source: Nordhaus, 'Political Business Cycle', Fig. 4, p. 179.

becomes relatively insignificant. Somewhere between U_M and U_G lies U_W, the point that would win by the biggest majority, given the 'appropriate' rate of time discount. This point is taken by Nordhaus to be the 'general welfare optimum'.[56] Its exact location obviously depends on what is taken to be the appropriate discount rate, and

[56] Ibid. 177.

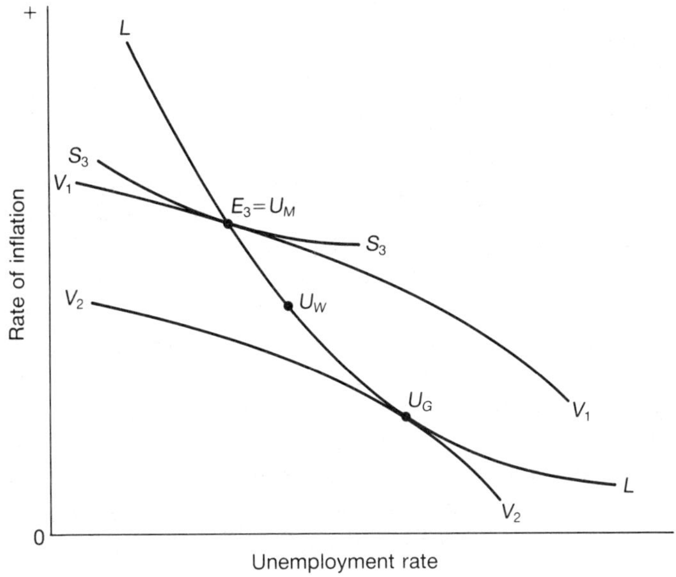

FIG. 3.5. Nordhaus model of the relation of an economy in equilibrium to various rates of time discount
Source: Nordhaus, 'Political Business Cycle', Fig. 5, p. 179.

Nordhaus does not discuss that question. I am doubtful of the propriety of discounting future welfare: as Sidgwick said, 'the time at which a man exists cannot affect the value of his happiness from a universal point of view'.[57] Economists often appear to move without adequate justification from the point that \$100 now is worth more than \$100 in ten years' time (which is true if only because the \$100 could be invested now so as to come to more in ten years' time) to the quite different notion that the same amount of welfare has more value now than in ten years' time.

Of course, for an individual it makes sense to discount his own future welfare because the further ahead it lies the more doubtful it must become that he will be around to enjoy it. But in spite of the menace of nuclear holocaust and the possibility that a chance asteroid may destroy the earth, it seems to me that the only morally acceptable

[57] Henry Sidgwick, *The Methods of Ethics* (London: Macmillan, 7th edn., 1907), 414.

course is to attach equal weight to the interests of all generations.[58]

Still, there is a more general difficulty. Nordhaus raises the following question: 'In the absence of political constraints what are the optimal levels of unemployment and inflation?' In alternative terms, what is the 'appropriate criterion, or social welfare function' to use in order to evaluate the alternative possible states of the economy that might confront 'a planning agency constructing a medium-term plan for a mixed economy?'[59] Nordhaus suggests using the aggregate voting function, represented graphically by the system of isopsephic curves. This means in effect that the ideal planner is to try to maximize the votes for economic outcomes expressed by the aggregate voting function, discounted over time by whatever is the appropriate factor. But in general it is surely clear that vote-maximizing outcomes have no necessary connection with welfare, in any sense of welfare satisfying the condition that more of it is better than less. In a divided society, the overall vote-maximizing policy may be one that oppresses the minority in the interests of the majority, for example. (See below, chapter 4.)

What can, however, be more plausibly claimed is that vote-maximization is an appropriate criterion for assessing the operation of a democratic political system. It can, of course, be questioned whether 'giving people what they want' is something that should be asked of political leaders; and it may also be questioned whether, when some want one thing and others something else, the best form of aggregating those conflicting wants is to see what policy would get the biggest majority. Whatever the answers to these questions, it is important to know whether the forces of electoral competition can be expected to operate in some systematic way to give people what they do not want, or more specifically to give them something that would be defeated by some alternative in a straight vote. For this would suggest that there is some kind of internal flaw in democracy, so that it turns out not even able to do the one thing that might be claimed for it as against other forms of regime, namely, to give people what they want (in the majoritarian sense specified).

If a vote-maximizing welfare criterion is used in this way, then it is apparent that the future should be discounted at whatever rate the

[58] Uncertainty may, however, enter into a social welfare calculation in a different and more acceptable way, namely, as uncertainty about the future course of events. If a government creates unemployment now in the hope of moderating inflation in the future, the unemployment is certain, whereas the moderation of inflation is hypothetical. There is therefore some reason for discounting the future benefits, not because they are future but because they are uncertain.

[59] Nordhaus, 'Political Business Cycle', p. 175.

voters actually discount it. The policy U_W will thus be the one that would get the biggest majority if the voters were (contrary to Nordhaus's assumption) knowledgeable about the macroeconomic structure of the economy and thus able to compare all possible alternative policies over an indefinitely long future. Provided the rate of time discount used by most voters is neither zero nor infinity, the result arrived at by Nordhaus can be reaffirmed: U_W will lie between U_M and U_G on the long-run Phillips curve.

If the rest of his analysis is correct, then, it will have been proved that the tendency of electoral competition is to produce more inflation and less unemployment than the voters want. But is it correct?

The model put forward by Nordhaus to show the inflationary tendencies of democracy is independent of his model of the political business cycle. It is, indeed, incompatible with his or any other model of the political business cycle. It is also internally inconsistent. The key result reached by Nordhaus requires the assumption that, over its term of office, a government is restricted to choosing a point on the short-run Phillips curve.[60] Yet the notion of the political business cycle makes no sense unless a government can, within its term of office, shift the position of the short-run Phillips curve. Moreover, the model purporting to show the inflationary tendency of democracy incorporates a shift in the short-run Phillips curve from one election to the next, so long as the economy is off the long-run Phillips curve. Thus, the model actually requires that the position of the short-run Phillips curve shift between elections but at the same time has the government acting as if it did not.

The conclusion by which Nordhaus sets great store is that in equilibrium the 'democratic outcome' is a rate of inflation that is 'purely myopic . . . where the implicit rate of time preference is infinite'.[61] This conclusion will obviously hold true if a government is seeking to maximize votes at the next election and can choose only points on the short-run Phillips curve. For the vote-maximizing point is the point at which the short-run Phillips curve is at a tangent with the isopsephic curve. But this conclusion is completely dependent on the assumption that the government operates over its whole term of office as if it had a time horizon of zero. This is obviously not consistent with vote-maximizing behaviour on the part

[60] 'In a two-party system the incumbent party chooses economic policies consistent with the current short-run trade-off, but it cannot move the short-run trade-off substantially in its incumbency.' Ibid. 178.

[61] Ibid. 179.

of the government, which requires (if it does not look beyond the next election) that its time horizon begin with the number of years to the next election and decline steadily to zero on the next election day.

The model of the political business cycle depends precisely on the idea that government has foresight. It

> predicts that the government will usually cut back aggregate demand after the election in order to bring down the rate of inflation, to squeeze out inflationary expectations and hence to shift down the short-term Phillips curve, as well as to reduce the deficits in the current account, well in time before the next election, so that new expansionary actions can be undertaken again before that election without immediately running into high inflation and a large current account deficit.[62]

Clearly, the government would not take unpopular actions after the election unless it was following a strategy for the whole inter-election period.

Nordhaus has, in effect, produced a theory of the rate of inflation where a vote-maximizing government always expects the next election to take place tomorrow. That the economic outcome will be 'completely myopic' in such conditions is a trivial consequence. Perhaps its only relevance is to cast doubt on the wisdom of Lindbeck's tentative suggestion ('a theoretical possibility') to 'let the exact time of elections be determined by a random process'.[63] The idea underlying this is obviously that if the government does not know when the next election is going to come, it has no incentive to run a political business cycle, because it cannot plan ahead for a non-inflationary boom timed for just before the next election. But if the government reacts to this inability to plan ahead by acting all the time so as to be in the best possible position to fight an election, the result would be like that produced by Nordhaus, at any rate for governments unconstrained by any considerations except vote-maximization. More generally, the greater the time between elections the bigger the cycles would be (especially if voters heavily discount the path of the economy to its election-day position), but the shorter the period between elections the higher the average rate of inflation. Thus, even on its own terms, Nordhaus's model fails because it is incoherent. It presupposes both that positions on the short-run Phillips curves (except where they intersect the long-run curve) cannot be maintained

62 Lindbeck, 'Stabilization Policy', p. 13.
63 Ibid. 18 n. 8.

over an inter-election period[64] and that governments nevertheless behave as if they could.

III INFLATION AND DEMOCRACY

There is no reason for attributing to inflation of the kind experienced in the advanced industrial societies in recent decades any ill-effects over and above the patent ones: the inconvenience of constant price adjustments, the uncertainty about future changes in the price level, and, to the extent that the inflation is not anticipated or compensated for by deliberate policy, a certain degree of redistribution along lines that have no particular ethical attraction. However, to the extent that the distribution of wealth and income in these societies is ethically unattractive in the absence of inflation anyway, it seems unreasonable to worry very much about a crosscutting and relatively minor form of unjust enrichment.

There is a common argument to the effect that inflation in the United States in the 1970s was particularly hard on the poor, because the highest price rises were in things whose purchase constituted a large proportion of their expenditure and that could not easily be done without. This rests on confusion between inflation and changes in relative prices. If the things the poor buy more of, like heating oil, become more expensive in relation to other things, then the poor will inevitably become worse off, whatever happens to the general price level. Suppose that the overall price level had remained unchanged over a year, with a few prices going up a lot and the rest going down a little to keep the consumer price index level. The poor would be poorer to exactly the same extent as in an inflationary period. The only way of compensating for changes in relative prices is to give the poor relatively more money. Inflation is (as so often) a red herring.

On objective grounds, there is no basis for saying that democratic institutions, by permitting inflation, can be shown to have failed and should be superseded. As for the argument that democratic institutions can be seen to have failed in terms of their own justification, because they produce outcomes that are in conflict with citizens' preferences, there is no factual evidence for the assumption, and the kind of model from which it is to be deduced rests on highly dubious premisses and even then does not entail any such conclu-

[64] In fact, the slopes of the short-run curves in Fig. 3.5 are if anything flatter than the slope Nordhaus gives for an empirically derived curve for the US economy that is claimed to be a 'first quarter or impact' short-run Phillips curve. Nordhaus, 'Political Business Cycle', pp. 170, 171.

sion. Once again, therefore, the case against democracy must be dismissed.

I shall close by suggesting that, for most of the economist constitution-mongers discussed in this chapter, inflation was never really the main issue anyway. The economists who make proposals to require balanced budgets, to fix the money supply automatically according to some formula, to go back to the gold standard, to make central banks more autonomous, and so on, are, for the most part, economic liberals in the nineteenth-century sense. That is, they believe that collective action carried out through the state should be kept to a minimum and that the market should determine what gets produced and who receives what income. There is, as both defenders and critics of the market have been forced to recognize over the last hundred years or so, a built-in tension between liberalism (in the nineteenth-century sense) and democracy.[65] Monetarism, and, more generally, market liberalism, is, as Ernest Gellner has written, inevitably betrayed by democratic governments.[66] For the workings of the market are not in fact conducive to the well-being of the majority of the population, and any government concerned with re-election finds itself intervening, whatever its official doctrine, to cushion people from the effects of unconstrained market forces. The demand management, guidelines, statutory controls over wages and prices, and other devices that governments use in order to try to moderate inflation are simply an aspect of this general phenomenon.

Anyone whose primary commitment is to the market must, therefore, look on the democratic state, with its inevitable tendency to regulate, make collective provision, and redistribute, with antipathy. The political problem facing that person is how to get democratic approval for tying the hands of elected governments in perpetuity. Such problems do not of course arise in non-democratic regimes, and it is not therefore surprising that it is territories with authoritarian

[65] Sir Henry Sumner Maine, *Popular Government* (London: John Murray, 1885; Liberty Classics, 1976) made the point a century ago. The quotation from Lord Acton at the opening of this chapter is from his letter of 11 Nov. 1885 to Mary Gladstone, commenting on *Popular Government*. He continued: 'Maine tells me that his book, A Manual of Unacknowledged Conservatism, is selling well. It is no doubt meant to help the enemy's cause, and more hostile to us [liberals] than the author cares to appear. For he requested me not to review it.' Quoted in George Feaver, *From Status to Contract: A Biography of Sir Henry Maine, 1822–1888* (London: Longmans, Green, 1969), 237. William Edward Hartpole Lecky, in *Democracy and Liberty* (London: Longmans, Green, 1896; Indianapolis: Liberty Classics, 1981), carried the argument further and injected a greater note of stridency. The same ideas inform the views of their descendants, the so-called Mont Pelerin group, including von Mises, Hayek, and de Jouvenel.

[66] 'A Social Contract in Search of an Idiom: The Demise of the Danegeld State?', *Political Quarterly*, 46 (1975), 127–52.

regimes such as Hong Kong, Taiwan, and South Korea that are often the apple of the market economist's eye.

The beauty of inflation is that it can be used as a rallying cry to sweep up people who might otherwise be chary of plans to cripple the ability of governments to make economic policy. A perfect example is James Buchanan's decade-long call for a 'constitutional counterrevolution' to undo the work of the New Deal and the Warren Court.[67] Anti-inflationary hysteria is an opportunity to mobilize behind proposals that would, in calmer times, be widely recognized as reactionary twaddle. That is in the end the only reason why inflation is important.

[67] Buchanan, *Limits of Liberty*; James M. Buchanan, *Freedom in Constitutional Contract: Perspectives of a Political Economist* (College Station, Tex.: Texas A & M University Press, 1977); Barry, 'Review'.

4

POLITICAL ACCOMMODATION AND CONSOCIATIONAL DEMOCRACY

SHALLOW. Better accommodated! it is good; yea, indeed, is it. Good phrases are surely, and ever were, very commendable. Accommodated! it comes of *accommodo*. Very good; a good phrase.

BARDOLPH. Pardon, sir; I have heard the word. Phrase call you it? By this day, I know not the phrase; but I will maintain the word with my sword to be a soldier-like word, and a word of exceeding good command, by heaven. Accommodated; that is, when a man is, as they say, accommodated; or when a man is, being, whereby he may be thought to be accommodated: which is an excellent thing.

Henry IV, Pt. 2.

I

As my Shakespearian quotation shows, the word 'accommodate' gradually entered into English usage in the sixteenth century and, if Bardolph's efforts are any guide, the problems of definition to which I shall draw attention are not new. 'Accommodation' as a noun came a little later, the first use found by the *Oxford English Dictionary* (actually in *Othello*) being recorded in 1604. There it meant lodgings, and this has remained its most common use. Indeed, I have come across a number of people who are firmly convinced that Arend Lijphart's book *The Politics of Accommodation* is a study of Dutch housing policy. But the meaning relevant here—referring to the process, the outcome, or the spirit of mutual conciliation—is well established and can be traced back to the seventeenth century. The *OED* cites this from a pamphlet on *Liberty of Conscience* published in 1645: 'By accommodation I understand an agreement of dissenters with the rest of the Church in practical conclusions' (*sub* 'accommodation' 4). This use is, however, rarely found in popular speech or writing, and, as far as I know, it has never become common currency in politics by being attached to a particular issue, like 'appeasement' (of Germany and Italy in the 1930s) or '*détente*' (with China and the Soviet Union in the 1970s). My own casual observations on contemporary usage suggest that it is employed in order to introduce deliberate vagueness about the form and content of any possible agreement. Thus, the most frequent application I have found is in the context of the Arab–Israeli conflict, when the writer wants to speculate about whether the two sides might reach an 'accommodation', without committing himself on whether this would be a signed treaty or a gradual acceptance of some status quo, or on what the terms (written or unwritten) would be.

'Consociation' is a much rarer word than 'accommodation', though with an equally long pedigree, and indeed I do not believe I have ever seen it used outside the writings of contemporary political scientists. According to the *OED* it can be used as an abstract noun for 'the action or fact of associating together; union in fellowship; combination' or to refer to actual associations, unions, and combinations. In the sense of 'an alliance or confederation' it is now said by the *OED* to be obsolete, but it seems that its main use at any time (and now its sole use) as a concrete noun has been in the context of formal co-operative arrangements among Churches and in particular to refer to confederal ties among Presbyterians and (in the USA) Congregationalists.

The point of this philological excursion is to show that 'accommodation' is a word of extremely general application, referring to any kind of agreement or settlement, while 'consociation' is simply a more or less obsolete word meaning much the same as 'association' and sharing with it the characteristic that it can be used both as an abstract noun (for the fact of association) and a concrete one (for actual associations). So what? It is no part of my intention to play the linguistic conservative and suggest that words should never be redefined for scholarly purposes so as to make them more specific. But it is very easy to run into formidable conceptual difficulties by doing so, and we need to be aware of these.

The problem is particularly great where, as here, an expression ('political accommodation' or 'consociational democracy') encapsulates a theory. The existence of 'theory-laden' terms occurs in all sciences as soon as they get beyond classifying objects according to observable similarities. Thus, to give a simple example, a phylum is defined as a group of organisms descended from a common ancestral form, so the word encapsulates the theory of the differentiation of species through evolution. In the 'hard' sciences, the difficulties are kept at bay during periods of 'normal science' by general acceptance of the underlying theory. If, however, the underlying theory comes to be questioned, the elements that have been yoked together in a single word dependent on that theory come apart. Thus, suppose that the idea of the evolution of species were to be rejected. We would then have two criteria for phyla: the definition in terms of common ancestry and the lists of species arranged under phyla. We could either say there are no phyla or we could drop the definition in terms of ancestry and keep the word 'phyla' for the classification.

In the social sciences, as has often been pointed out (with either relish or distress), we do not enjoy the conditions of 'normal science', and the introduction of 'theory-laden' terms is therefore much more hazardous. Let me try to illustrate the problem in connection with 'political accommodation' and 'consociational democracy'.

In *The Politics of Accommodation* we read:

> Dutch politics is a politics of accommodation. That is the secret of its success. The term accommodation is here used in the sense of settlement of divisive issues and conflicts where only a minimal consensus exists. . . . A key element of this conception is the lack of a comprehensive political consensus, but not the complete absence of consensus. . . . The second key requirement is that the *leaders* of the self-contained blocs must be particularly convinced of the desirability of preserving the system. And they must be willing and capable of bridging the gaps between the mutually isolated blocs and of resolving serious disputes in a largely nonconsensual context.[1]

It would be naïve to say that the third sentence in this quotation is a definition and the rest empirical statements. It would be more sensible to say that the use of the deceptively simple assertion 'Dutch politics is a politics of accommodation' commits one to all these ideas:

(*a*) divisive issues are settled in the Netherlands;
(*b*) the settlements are between blocs that have a low level of consensus between them;
(*c*) the settlements are between blocs that are 'self-contained' and 'mutually isolated';
(*d*) these blocs have leaders, who are responsible for negotiating settlements; and
(*e*) the bloc leaders are convinced of the need for settlements.

Finally, although it is not made explicit in the quotation, I think we may, in the light of the earlier theoretical discussion in the book, add the 'cross-cutting cleavage' hypothesis in its 'associational' form:

[1] Arend Lijphart, *The Politics of Accommodation: Pluralism and Democracy in the Netherlands* (Berkeley and Los Angeles: University of California Press, 1968), 103–4.

(*f*) there is a causal connection between the fact that the blocs are 'self-contained' and the fact that there is a low level of consensus between them.

The term 'political accommodation', as used by Lijphart, encapsulates all these ideas. What I mean by this is that we would no longer be able to speak of the Netherlands (or some other country) as the site of a 'politics of accommodation' if we came to disbelieve any of these propositions. For example, it would not be enough that divisive issues were settled if they were not between isolated blocs, if the blocs did not have low consensus, if the settlement were not by bloc leaders, or if the bloc leaders were not convinced of the need for a settlement.

The same line of analysis can be applied to 'consociational democracy', and Lijphart in his paper with that title is very clear about the fact that he is putting forward a complex theoretical construction encapsulated in the term. An often quoted sentence from this paper runs: 'Consociational democracy means government by élite cartel designed to turn a democracy with a fragmented political culture into a stable democracy.'[2] What is less often noticed is that Lijphart goes on to say that consociational democracy has four requirements (in brief, that the 'élites of rival subcultures' are willing and able to 'accommodate the divergent interests and demands' because they are committed to the maintenance of the system and they see the need for accommodation as a means to this) and that '*these four requirements are logically implied by the concept of consociational democracy as defined in this paper*'.[3]

In addition, Lijphart speaks in the paper of 'consociational devices', which correspond to the 'rules of the game' in *The Politics of Accommodation*. Examples are grand coalition and proportionality or circulation of certain posts over time according to some formula. This expression 'consociational devices' packs further theoretical baggage, since anyone using the phrase is in effect committing himself to the idea that these devices (or variants on them) are essential aspects of the élite accommodation that is a defining characteristic of 'consociational democracy'. An illustration of the problem is provided by Val Lorwin, who, in a postscript written to Kenneth McRae's collection of articles, refers to 'the structures of segmented pluralism or

[2] A. Lijphart, 'Consociational Democracy', *World Politics*, 21 (1969), 207–25. Repr. in Kenneth McRae (ed.), *Consociational Democracy: Political Accommodation in Segmented Societies* (Toronto: McClelland and Stewart, The Carleton Library, 1974), 70–106. I shall give page references for this and other articles in McRae's convenient collection, citing it as 'McRae'. The quotation in the text appears on p. 79.

[3] Lijphart, 'Consociational Democracy', in McRae, p. 79 (my italics).

consociational democracy in Belgium' in a context where the whole point is the *increasing inadequacy* of the structures to contain conflict.[4]

The crucial point that has to be grasped about Lijphart's definition of 'consociational democracy' is that a consociational democracy is necessarily stable and successful in mediating conflicts. This follows from the way in which the term was introduced by him as a modification of Gabriel Almond's typology of political systems, put forward in the well-known 'Comparative Political Systems' article in 1956. In Almond's typology, cultural homogeneity and overlapping memberships are associated with stable and effective government, while separate subcultures and segmentation (reinforcing memberships) are associated with unstable and ineffective (*immobiliste*) government. Lijphart advocates the recognition of a third category of countries, like Switzerland and the Netherlands, which combine the political characteristics (stability and effectiveness) of Almond's first category with the socio-cultural characteristics (separate subcultures and segmentation) of his second. 'These deviant cases of fragmented but stable democracies will be called "consociational democracies."'[5] (The logic of this two-by-two matrix suggests that we should also look for countries which are culturally homogeneous, with overlapping memberships, but whose politics are unstable and ineffective. I suppose some people would put forward Britain and the USA as candidates.)

'Consociational democracy' as conceptualized by Lijphart puts together in a package stability, dissensus, segmentation, élite accommodation, and some mix of the 'consociational devices'. As the genesis of the typology makes clear, there is underlying this concept the implicit theory that under conditions of dissensus and segmentation *only* élite accommodation institutionalized in consociational devices can produce stability. This yoking together can be seen from the way in which 'consociational democracies' are first defined as 'fragmented but stable democracies' and then as countries with 'government by élite cartel'. Obviously, there could in principle be countries which were 'fragmented but stable' and where nevertheless this stability had not been brought about by 'government by élite cartel'. This possibility is ruled out by the typology, just as the

[4] Val R. Lorwin, 'Belgium: Conflict and Compromise', printed for first time in McRae, pp. 179–206, at p. 206.

[5] Lijphart, 'Consociational Democracy', in McRae, p. 75. Almond's article 'Comparative Political Systems' appeared in the *Journal of Politics*, 18 (1956), 391–409.

possibility of *any* 'fragmented but stable' democracy was ruled out by the Almond typology.

In the introduction to his collection of articles *Consociational Democracy*, Kenneth McRae speaks of 'the four "classic" cases of consociationalism among developed Western democracies, namely the Netherlands, Austria, Belgium, and Switzerland'. Although this is perhaps the most explicit statement we could find of the paradigmatic status of these four countries, Lijphart writes of 'the Low Countries, Switzerland and Austria' as the 'deviant cases . . . to be called "consociational democracies"', and Lorwin's 'segmented pluralist' countries are these plus Luxembourg.[6] I propose to argue in this chapter for the following propositions: (1) that Switzerland provides no support for the theory of consociational democracy; (2) that the Austrian case is less clear-cut than is often assumed; (3) that Belgium and the Netherlands, although plausible supporting cases, still fall short of fully bearing out the theory; and (4) that the relevance of the 'consociational' model for other divided societies is much more doubtful than is commonly supposed.

It may be asked—and it is a fair question—who am I to cross swords with the experts on these countries? I do not claim any expertise, but it is not my intention to produce any facts of my own. My information will be drawn almost entirely from the writings of those identified with what Hans Daalder has called the 'incipient school' of adherents to the theory of consociational democracy, and it will be on this information that I base my arguments.[7] This seems to me fair enough. In Anglo-Saxon jurisprudence it is considered to be the job of the advocate to produce his own supporting facts, and although this may not be a good way of organizing a legal system it seems to have served well enough in scholarly debates.

II

My analysis of the Swiss case will be based mainly on Jürg Steiner's book *Amicable Agreement versus Majority Rule*.[8] This is an ambitious and fertile book, with many more interesting ideas in it than can be discussed here. The point on which I shall focus is this: that, although

[6] McRae, p. 13; Lijphart in McRae, pp. 74–5; Lorwin, p. 36 in McRae.

[7] H. Daalder, 'The Consociational Democracy Theme', *World Politics*, 26 (1974), 604–21, at 609.

[8] J. Steiner, *Amicable Agreement versus Majority Rule: Conflict Resolution in Switzerland* (Chapel Hill: University of North Carolina Press, rev. and enlarged edn. 1974, tr. from German edn. of 1970).

Steiner identifies himself closely with other members of the 'consociational democracy' school, he does not show—or indeed really try to show—that Switzerland fits the model of 'consociational democracy' as a theoretical construction. Switzerland does, of course, have consociational devices and in *that* sense is a consociational democracy (though even this statement has to be qualified), but these devices do not function in the way postulated by the theory.

The object of Steiner's study is to explain why 'strong subcultural segmentation' does not lead to 'intersubcultural hostility' in Switzerland. These terms are defined as follows. Subcultures are defined in Robert Dahl's words as 'distinctive sets of attitudes, opinions, and values that persist for relatively long periods of time in the life of a country and give individuals in a particular subculture a sense of identity that distinguishes them from individuals in other subcultures'.[9] The strength of subcultural segmentation, Steiner adds, depends on the intensity of self-identification of the different subcultures. 'Possible indicators are responses to attitudinal survey questions, frequency of interactions among the members of a subculture, and organizational ties within a subculture.'[10] 'Subcultural hostility' exists 'if two or more subcultures perceive one another in such negative terms that they have a desire or at least a readiness to damage one another.'[11]

What, then, is the explanation? 'Along with Lehmbruch and Lijphart I consider the predominant pattern of decision-making the key explanatory variable.'[12] In the light of my earlier discussion it is important to notice that Steiner refers to Lijphart's terms 'consociationalism' and 'accommodation' as referring to a 'peculiar type of decision-making' and goes on: 'Other concepts to describe roughly the same decision-making model are *contractarianism* [Bluhm], *amicable agreement* [Lehmbruch], and *Konkordanzdemokratie* [Lehmbruch and Reich].'[13] Thus, for Steiner, a 'consociational democracy' would be identifiable by the presence of 'consociational devices', whether or not these were carrying out the role of conflict-prevention ascribed by Lijphart. What we have to ask, however, is whether the 'consociational devices' function in the way postulated by the theory encapsulated in the term 'consociational democracy'.

First, though, it is worth making sure that Switzerland really is

[9] R. A. Dahl (ed.), *Political Oppositions in Western Democracies* (New Haven, Conn.: Yale University Press, 1966), 371.

[10] Steiner, *Amicable Agreement*, p. 3.

[11] Ibid. 4. [12] Ibid. 6. [13] Ibid. 4–5.

'consociational' in the descriptive sense as against the theory-laden sense. Is decisionmaking predominantly by the model of 'amicable agreements' rather than by the model of 'majority rule', to use the terms preferred by Steiner? There is the convention that the major parties are represented (since 1959 on a roughly proportional basis) in the seven-man executive, the Federal Council. But these men are thought of as individuals administering departments rather than as party oligarchs reaching concordats binding on their followers. The representatives of a party elected to the Federal Council may not always be those nominated by the party and the fact that a party is represented does not inhibit it (or some section of it) from voting against a proposal put forward in the name of the Federal Council. As Steiner says, 'It is even doubtful that it makes sense to talk about the Federal Council as a coalition government.'[14] What is much more to the point is the tendency, which Steiner emphasizes and illustrates with several case studies of policymaking, for new legislation or policy initiatives to be hammered out among the 'interests' involved (probably in secret) and a single unanimous proposal presented. This is the core of 'amicable agreement': there is indeed 'élite accommodation', in which representatives of the parties play a part, though it is only very partially mediated through the Federal Council.

This, however, does not entail that the method of political decision-making in Switzerland is one of 'amicable agreement', because of the existence of the referendum and the popular initiative. Thus, one of Steiner's case studies is of the decision to create a university in the Aargau canton, in which he was closely involved himself. In thirty-five pages he describes in detail the way in which the proposal was developed to the point at which all the party spokesmen were favourable (only two members of parliament voted against it) and every conceivable pressure group had been squared. As he rather naïvely says, 'since there was no organized opposition to the university project, the estimates of public opinion were diffuse and hard to make'.[15] But in spite of all this the proposal was carried in the referendum by only 31,460 votes to 28,945. Thus, although one way of describing the outcome would be to say that it was one of 'amicable agreement' among the élite, another would be to say that it was one in which 52 per cent of those voting imposed their will on 48 per cent. Or, more pointedly, one in which 52 per cent of the people plus the whole of the carefully solidified élite imposed their will on 48 per cent of the people.

[14] Ibid. 37. [15] Ibid. 199.

This is of course a cantonal example, but an important federal case with much the same characteristics was the constitutional amendment promoted by James Schwarzenbach ('Over-foreignization Initiative II'), designed to 'limit the number of foreigners in any given canton (except Geneva) to 10 per cent of the population'.[16] This came too late to be mentioned by Steiner, whose book appeared in German in 1970, but is discussed by Benjamin Barber in his admirable work on the canton of Graubünden (Grisons). The Aargau university case was one with the 'establishment' solidly in favour; the Schwarzenbach initiative showed it equally solidly against.

The Federal Council . . . was implacably opposed to the measure; the National Council, presumably representative of popular opinion, voted 136 to 1 against it (prior to the referendum); the Council of States (*Standerat*, representing the cantons) rejected it 39 to 0. Manufacturing, trade, and industrial interests were unanimously critical and funded a record-breaking publicity campaign urging defeat of the proposal and defaming its supporters [as Nazis and racists]. . . . Not a single major political party, not one significant pressure group or voluntary association could be found that was favourable to the amendment. . . . Yet on June 7 [1970], no less than 46 per cent of a postwar record turnout (over 74 per cent of the electorate) voted yes on the amendment, while in seven of the twenty-two cantons the proposal actually carried.[17]

The picture that emerges is one of 'amicable agreement' among the élite (either painfully cobbled together as in the Aargau university case or spontaneous as in the Schwarzenbach case) but at the same time a pattern in which binding collective decisions may be taken on very small popular majorities. Indeed, although this is speculative, is it not possible that some of the élite practices described in such detail by Steiner (and in some of which he was an active participant) are responses to the existence of the referendum and the initiative? I am thinking here particularly of the attempts to co-opt all the relevant experts and to 'homogenize' the statistics and estimates produced by different sources, so that only one set of figures ever becomes publicly available. Surely this kind of conspiratorial behaviour is typical of those who wish to maximize their influence over an outcome while knowing that they do not have the final say. Thus, Royal Commissions in Britain always attach great importance to making a unanimous report. Those who insist on rocking the boat and produ-

[16] Benjamin R. Barber, *The Death of Communal Liberty: A History of Freedom in a Swiss Mountain Canton* (Princeton, NJ: Princeton University Press, 1974), 252.

[17] Barber, *Death of Communal Liberty*, pp. 253–4.

cing a minority report seem almost invariably to run into the hostility of their fellows. Recent examples may be drawn from the Royal Commission on Local Government (Maud) and the Royal Commission on the Constitution (Kilbrandon).

In other countries with 'consociational' devices we also find co-optation and suppression of information, in order to minimize the chance that people outside the élite will have enough ammunition to be able to stir up trouble against negotiated agreements. But in these other countries there is not the same possibility of a challenge through constitutional channels, and the emphasis on these features is perhaps less. The leaders can afford to let it be known that there are differences of view so long as they can hold their own supporters in line behind them organizationally. They do not have to fear repudiation in the privacy of the polling booth.

To the extent, however, that consociational democracy (in the purely descriptive sense) entails restriction of information, this may help to explain why it has so far existed only in small countries. The reason usually assigned, that consociationalism requires a 'low foreign affairs load', has recently, and rightly, come under fire. There seems to be no reason why 'consociationalism' should make the conduct of foreign affairs especially difficult and it is significant that most non-consociational countries have all-party coalitions in wartime, presumably the better to deal with external threats. Nor is it obvious that a small country in general needs less agility than a large in adapting to its environment if it is to survive. But what must be true is that a small country will have a relatively small élite and only a small number of experts on any given subject, and this must make much more feasible the project of co-opting all those with expertise on a subject and thus pre-empting their right to oppose the agreed line.

Perhaps, also, the presence of representatives of all the major parties in the Federal Council might be looked on as partially a response to the initiative and referendum. According to Steiner, because of the cost of obtaining the necessary signatures and carrying out a propaganda campaign, 'although it is technically possible for a small party to make use of the right to initiative and referendum, it is improbable on a practical level'.[18] A 'large party' might therefore be defined as one that could upset the apple-cart by demanding a referendum. To put it another way, the existence of such a further decisionmaking stage invalidates the usual parliamentary formula for a 'minimum winning

[18] Steiner, *Amicable Agreement*, p. 19.

coalition'. If we define a 'minimum winning coalition' as one that can with high probability ensure that what its members support will stick, it will have to be one including all those parties capable of routinely financing referenda and, as we have seen, that would (on Steiner's evidence) correspond exactly to the four-party coalition that Switzerland has had. (Incidentally, I think it ought to be emphasized that highly inclusive governments of the Swiss sort are not necessary for consociational democracy in the descriptive sense. Belgium, which, with the Netherlands, is one of the two indisputable cases, has since 1944 almost always had minimum winning coalitions of two parties, and—when the Catholic party won an absolute majority—of one party.)

As I have said, Steiner does not explicitly try to relate the institutions of the popular initiative and the referendum to the model of 'amicable agreement' into which he claims the Swiss system fits. He seems to regard 'amicable agreement' as defined by élite behaviour and the initiative and referendum as something else: a safety-valve (page 236) or a counterbalance (page 283). No doubt it is quite correct to say that in practice these popular votes operate primarily negatively and as ways of registering more or less diffuse protest. But this is not inherent in the procedures themselves. It simply reflects the particular political situation: a highly-unified élite committed to modernization, rationalization, economic growth, and so on facing a people large sections of which are acutely uneasy at such developments.[19]

The crucial point is that the institution of collective decisionmaking by a simple majority of the popular vote is in itself the antithesis of 'amicable agreement'. 'Amicable agreements' must be negotiated among people who either trust one another or do not need to because they can apply sanctions against defaulters. This entails that only a small number of people can be involved in the decisionmaking process. Even more important, 'amicable agreement' requires that the same people should be involved in a number of different decisions and that they should be able to make deals with one another. This makes it possible for a decision favourable to one group to be taken today on the understanding that a decision favourable to another group will be taken tomorrow. This is the process called 'log-rolling' in the USA and in Austria *Junktim*. As Lehmbruch says: 'this procedure means that one of the actors offers a concession he detests in exchange for a concession by his opponent that the latter detests equally strongly'.[20]

[19] For this interpretation, see Barber, *Death of Communal Liberty*, pp. 258–74.

[20] Gerhard Lehmbruch, 'A Non-Competitive Pattern of Conflict Management in Liberal

Popular voting strikes at the roots of log-rolling. One issue is decided at a time and there is no way in which a mass electorate voting by secret ballot could set up an enforceable or even plausible agreement whereby one set of people would vote for something they didn't want on one occasion in return for a promise from another set to vote for something *they* didn't want on a future occasion (or even on another item at the same time). Of course, even in a legislature promises are not strictly enforceable, so that if the items of a package are voted on sequentially it would be possible for those due to make the last concession to renege. But the actors in a legislature know they may have to continue to deal with one another into the indefinite future, so the sanction of exclusion from future deals is a potent one.

If, then, the institutions of the referendum and popular initiative are not the instrument whereby those in the majority on some line of cleavage oppress those in the minority, this is not because the institutions themselves would not lend themselves to it but, presumably, because the Swiss do not choose to employ them for such a purpose. This means, though, that we must reject Steiner's central thesis: that the 'predominant pattern of decision-making' is the 'key explanatory variable' in explaining the low 'level of intersubcultural hostility'.[21] The alternative explanation of the low level of intersubcultural hostility is that (except for the Jura question) the members of these subcultures do not have any cause for hostility. They do not have incompatible aspirations such that the fulfilment of one section's aims would spell a threat to the material well-being, cultural survival, or social honour of another. As William Keech observed succinctly in his shrewd research note on 'Linguistic Diversity and Political Conflict', 'an absence of sharp conflict [between linguistic or religious groups] may not necessarily be the result of patterns of conflict resolution, but possibly stem from the absence of sources of conflict, or perhaps a mixture of both'.[22] Steiner cites this note but fails to draw the relevant conclusion: that before the pattern of decisionmaking can be made the explanation for a lack of hostility, it is necessary to rule out the alternative hypothesis that there are no sources of serious conflict anyway.

In fact, if we go back again to the model of 'consociational

Democracies: the Case of Switzerland, Austria and Lebanon', printed for the first time in McRae, pp. 90–106, at p. 92.

[21] Steiner, *Amicable Agreement*, p. 4.

[22] William R. Keech, 'Linguistic Diversity and Political Conflict: Some Observations Based on Four Swiss Cantons', *Comparative Politics*, 4 (1972), 387–404, at 388.

democracy' spelt out at the beginning of this chapter, it seems to me that Switzerland fails to fit it at every point. In a 'consociational democracy' there are groups with a low level of consensus between them and that are mutually isolated. The sharply incompatible aspirations of these groups are articulated by different political parties, which fight elections by appealing to the loyalty of their own client group through whipping up group sentiment and making play with the group ideology. The leaders of these parties, having disciplined their supporters into following them by emphasizing the need to unite to fight the others, then use the free hand this gives them to settle the issues dividing the groups in a pragmatic way.

Steiner's own analysis demolishes any notion that Switzerland corresponds to this model. He mentions with approval Girod's statement 'that there is a strong consensus among the Swiss parties on all important questions—even on the question of the relation between church and state and problems related to economic and social policy'.[23] The parties do not therefore articulate dissensual ideologies, as in the 'consociational democracy' model. Nor do the parties appeal exclusively to different subcultural groups in the society. Steiner goes on to 'suggest that the demands of the Swiss parties coincide to such an extent partly because the party cleavages crosscut other important cleavages—in particular, the cleavages of occupational groups, linguistic groups, religious groups, regional groups, cantons, economic interest groups, and voluntary associations'.[24] He then states the classic argument for the moderating effect on party extremism of cross-cutting between party support and membership of ascriptive groups.

> A party that draws its supporters from different social groups cannot afford to cater to the interests of one group only. . . . If, for example, party and language lines crosscut, a party cannot afford to represent one-sidedly the interests of a specific language group. On the contrary, every party attempts to articulate demands that pay heed to the needs of all linguistic groups.[25]

I think that the general 'cross-cutting cleavage hypothesis', that all cross-cutting cleavages moderate conflict, is unproven, as Eric Nordlinger argues.[26] But the thesis that cross-cutting between political parties and socio-cultural cleavage lines moderates conflict seems to me much more plausible and better supported. It may well be, even

[23] Steiner, *Amicable Agreement*, p. 49.
[24] Ibid. [25] Ibid.
[26] In *Conflict Regulation in Divided Societies* (Cambridge, Mass: Center for International Affairs, Harvard University, Occasional Papers in International Affairs, No. 29, 1972).

so, that the causal link is mainly in the reverse direction, so that the fact of parties drawing support across cleavage lines is evidence for the relatively low salience of issues related to ascriptive group membership rather than the cause of it. (Thus, the institution of the ethnically balanced ticket in US local politics is, in effect, a sign that politicians do not see any advantage in fighting on ethnically related issues. If the parties did want to fight on such issues they would, obviously, clear the decks by choosing ethnically homogeneous tickets.) But if the link runs mainly in this direction, the cross-cutting between party support and ascriptive groups simply provides evidence that there are no crucial issues dividing these groups.

The picture could not be more different from the 'consociational democracy' model. In that model, the parties articulate the divergent demands of different groups, and the possibilities of immobilism or conflict opened up are deliberately averted by overarching élite co-operation. In Switzerland, the process of stifling conflict between groups (if there is really any potential for it) is carried out by the parties right at the stage of electoral competition when they aggregate support across the lines of cleavage. There is therefore nothing left to be done after the election: there are no parties elected on a solidary group basis facing one another.

I queried in parentheses whether there is a basis at the mass level for conflict between the ascriptive groups in Switzerland. Steiner does not give any survey evidence about mass attitudes to possible inter-group issues, but it is certainly hard to imagine that Switzerland is a country where the groups are itching to oppress one another and kept from it only by the manipulations of the political élite. We must, I think, reject the applicability of the item in the 'consociational democracy' model that says there is a low level of consensus between members of the ascriptive groups. The almost perfect consensus among the parties on intercommunal issues probably reflects a high (though less perfect) consensus in the population at large.

Finally, on Steiner's evidence, the linguistic and religious groups are not 'isolated' or 'self-contained' as in Lijphart's model of 'consociational democracy'. As a matter of strict logic, it does not seem to me that this feature is necessary to the model. Surely the politically important aspect of relations between the groups is a low level of consensus. If this were to coincide with the absence of isolation between them it would still pose a problem of reconciliation for the élites. It is for this reason that I suggested adding to the model as set out earlier the sixth item (*f*), the cross-cutting cleavage hypothesis in its 'associational' form, to the effect that there is a causal connection between the fact that the blocs are 'self-contained' and the fact that there is a low level of consensus between them. Adding this makes the factor of isolation relevant to the rest of the model by making it a cause (or perhaps more plausibly a sustaining condition) of dissensus.

As I have already mentioned, I do not think the hypothesis is well substantiated. Inasfar as there is an empirical connection, it may reflect the tendency for conflict to lead to segregation rather than for segregation to lead to conflict. But if so it is further indirect evidence for the relatively low level of division between the subcultures in Switzerland. Thus, for example, in sharp contrast with Belgium or with Austria, sporting activities are carried on primarily in organizations that do not follow subcultural cleavage lines. (Nor do they follow lines of party support.) The organizations are, rather, inclusive.[27]

In short, then, we may say: (1) if we give full weight to the potentialities of the referendum and the popular initiative, it is highly doubtful whether the decisionmaking system in Switzerland can be said to be preponderantly one of 'amicable agreement' or 'élite accommodation'; and (2) there is no evidence that there is a low level of consensus between members of the subcultural groups, so even if we allowed that the system were one of 'amicable agreement' this would not be necessary to explain the low level of intersubcultural hostility. These two points show clearly that Swiss politics do not fit the model of 'consociational democracy'. They do not, however, entirely refute Steiner's Hypothesis I, which reads: 'In a system with strong subcultural segmentation, the more often political decisions are made by amicable agreement, the more probable is a low level of intersubcultural hostility.'[28] This kind of probabilistic statement is extremely difficult to test since it requires a large number of cases before we can begin to say whether one thing makes another more probable. By contrast, Lijphart's theory of consociational democracy would be disproved by one case of a society characterized by isolated and dissensual blocs plus stable and effective democracy minus the practices of élite accommodation constituting 'consociational democracy' as a description of a pattern of decisionmaking.

Steiner's hypothesis is so weak that it may be true without being important. That is to say, other things being equal, it may be that the more 'amicable agreement' there is, the less intersubcultural hostility.

[27] Steiner, *Amicable Agreement*, p. 257. [28] Ibid. 252.

But where, as in Switzerland, the parties cross-cut the subcultures, the effect of 'amicable agreement' among the party leaders (compared with parliamentary majoritarianism) is likely to be slight. To put it concretely, if Swiss parties were to drop the 'magic formula' and instead the Federal Council were to be made up of representatives of parties with a majority of seats only, it may be that intersubcultural hostility would go up a little (since the parties are not exact microcosms of the electorate), but surely not much. Of course, this speculation is flawed by the fact that it does not really make sense to say 'other things being equal', since we have to suppose some prior upheaval to lead to that change. (See above, chapter 3 section I.) But we may at least say that we are assuming that the change, whatever its cause, is not a reaction to some increase in hostility or polarization of opinion between the subcultures.

To conclude this section I should like to take up one argument that is not made by Steiner himself but is parallel to one that has been made in relation to the Netherlands and Belgium. It has been suggested (by Lijphart and Lorwin, for example) that in these countries the 'consociational' mode of decisionmaking is no longer required to mediate conflicts between the 'spiritual families' because these conflicts have died down anyway. Consociational devices are now a sort of institutional hangover. But they were needed in the past. Could the same argument be made for Switzerland?

The strongest counter-argument is that, during the period when the institutions of 'amicable agreement' were presumably needed, they did not exist. 'From the founding of the federal state in 1849 until 1891 the Federal Council consisted entirely of Free Democrats who had won a military victory over the Christian Democrats (then called Conservatives).'[29] For forty-two years after the Sonderbund war, then, the stability of the state was maintained while the victors monopolized the executive. Only in 1891 was a Christian Democrat elected to the Federal Council. The same story applies to the Socialists, who qualified on a proportional basis for a seat in the Federal Council in 1919 but did not receive one until 1943 or their proportional share of two until 1959.[30] Although Steiner does not draw attention to the coincidence in dates, he later quotes Girod as saying: 'the present program of the Social Democratic Party (adopted in 1959) is frankly reformist and pragmatic. It does not refer at all to the principle of class struggle, and there is no allusion to marxism.'[31]

[29] Ibid. 33. [30] Ibid. [31] Ibid. 54–5.

Thus, 'amicable agreement', at the level of the Federal Council, has never operated as an instrument for reconciling differences between parties. Rather, parties are included in the system of 'amicable agreement' only when, and to the extent that, they have shed their distinguishing features. Indeed, I would suggest that there are good a priori reasons for thinking that the relation in Switzerland between the executive and the legislature (especially the fact that the members of the Federal Council are elected individually and do not agree on a common programme in advance) makes multi-party governments much *less* possible if the parties disagree fundamentally than does the usual kind of cabinet/parliament relationship. Perhaps the very survival of the system in Switzerland is a further sign of the high level of consensus among parties participating in government, since it could not function without it.

III

Austria is the jewel in the 'consociational' crown because it 'presents virtually the only example of a European state in which an initially unsuccessful parliamentary system turned into a successful one, and in which constitutional and party-structural factors can be held constant over half a century (1919–1969)'.[32] What made the difference between the collapse of democratic government in the post-1918 First Republic and its stabilization in the post-1945 Second Republic? The special ingredient, according to the 'consociational democracy' school, was the practice of 'élite cartel', institutionalized in the grand coalition of the two major parties between 1945 and 1966. According to Lijphart, it is one of the two 'clearest examples', the other being the first years of the Belgian state.[33]

There can, I think, be no question that what happened in Austria during those years completely satisfied the conditions for 'government by élite cartel'. As William Bluhm summarizes the position:

> For the whole period from 1945 to 1966 the two great parties renewed their agreement to cooperate following each parliamentary election by signing a pact of coalition (*Koalitionspakt*), by which they divided between them the offices of state at the ministerial level and by which they established a rubric for the day-to-day conduct of policy making during the subsequent legis-

[32] P. G. J. Pulzer, 'The Legitimizing Role of Political Parties: The Second Austrian Republic', *Government and Opposition*, 4 (1969), 324–44, repr. in McRae under title 'Austria: the Legitimizing Role of Political Parties', 157–78, at 158.

[33] Lijphart, 'Consociational Democracy', in McRae, p. 75.

lative period. Included in this was a unanimity rule and an agreement on a system of proportionalism (*Proporz*) for staffing government corporations and nationalized industries whereby each party received positions for its members in proportion to its strength in the electorate.[34]

The significance of the Austrian 'grand coalition' was quite different from that of the Swiss one. In Switzerland, as we saw, a member of the Federal Council is elected as an individual, not as a party leader who thereby commits his party to a common programme. Indeed, some of the parties do not *have* a definite structure of leadership at the federal level. But in Austria the 'grand coalition' was a deal between the leaders of highly-disciplined political parties.

The pacts provided for a coalition commission (*Koalitionsausschuss*) with power to decide any matters of interpretation. Except for the two party leaders (who would be the Chancellor and Vice-Chancellor of the government) the delegates to the commission were whips and party functionaries, not cabinet members. It is evident that in terms of policy-making power the cabinet was subordinate to the commission, as parliament was subordinate to both, since it was the duty of the parliamentary whips to ensure compliance with the decisions of the commission.[35]

The contrast in the method of decisionmaking with that in force during the lifetime of the First Republic is also clear, since the Christian Social Party monopolized the government between the first election in 1920 and the promulgation of a new, authoritarian, constitution in 1934. Equally, there can be no doubt that the tensions between the *Lager* during the existence of the First Republic form a genuine contrast to the relatively harmonious development of the Second Republic. At the same time, 'constitutional and party-structural factors' were, as Pulzer stated, similar in the two Republics. Both were, in formal terms, parliamentary democracies; and the stability of support for the two major political groupings over the periods 1918–34 and 1945–66 was extraordinary when one considers the turnover of the electorate in almost fifty years and the political upheaval in the middle.[36]

We have, it may appear, all the requisites for a 'natural experiment': we hold constant the background conditions (constitutional and party-structural), we vary the élite behaviour (élite conflict in the First Republic, élite cartel in the Second), and we observe a difference in the

[34] William T. Bluhm, *Building an Austrian Nation: the Political Integration of a Western State* (New Haven and London: Yale University Press, 1973), 71.

[35] Pulzer, 'Austria', in McRae, pp. 173–4.

[36] See ibid. 168–9.

result (collapse of the First Republic, stability of the Second). Is there any room, then, for doubting Lijphart's categorical assertion that 'The fragmented and unstable Austrian First Republic of the interwar years was transformed into the still fragmented but stable Second Republic after the Second World War by means of a consociational solution'?[37]

It would be a bold man who would undertake to show that the 'consociational solution' was *not* the explanation of the difference between the experience of the First and Second Republics. I do not propose to be that man. But I do want to argue that there is room for doubt. There were other potentially relevant differences between the First and Second Republics than the behaviour of the political élite; and even if élite behaviour is accepted as a crucially important difference, it may be that a smaller shift than that from a '*Lager* mentality' to a 'consociational solution' would have been sufficient to bring about stability within the same constitutional and party-structural framework.

Expressed formally in terms of the logic of 'natural experiments', the main point is that the *ceteris paribus* condition for ascribing the change in outcome to the 'experimental' change in treatment is not met. Therefore we cannot assert with confidence that the change in treatment (consociational democracy) was either (*a*) a necessary or (*b*) a sufficient condition of the change in outcome (stable democracy). It may be helpful to set out in detail the implications of this for the Austrian case.

(*a*) *Necessary condition*. Given the other changes between the two periods, it may be that the Second Republic would have survived where the First Republic collapsed without the 'consociational solution'. This does not entail the extreme proposition that the Second Republic could have survived if élite behaviour had been exactly the same as it was under the First Republic. Indeed, since the formal end of the First Republic was constituted by a piece of élite behaviour—Dollfuss's coup in 1934—this alternative scarcely makes sense. But what we are saying is that it may be that some less formally institutionalized change from the extremely conflictual attitude of the inter-war period (perhaps no more than a degree of self-restraint) would have been enough, combined with other favourable conditions, to give the Second Republic the same lease of life as it has actually enjoyed.

(*b*) *Sufficient condition*. Given the other changes between the two

[37] Lijphart, 'Consociational Democracy', in McRae, p. 75.

periods, the survival of the Second Republic does not show that the First Republic would have survived if the 'consociational solution' had been adopted by the political élite. It is possible that conditions were too unfavourable between the wars for any pattern of élite behaviour to have ensured the survival of the First Republic.

Notice that it is logically possible to take a mixed position. Thus, one might say that the 'consociational solution' was necessary *plus* the other favourable factors to create a stable democracy in 1945, whereas the 'consociational solution' *without* these other favourable factors would not have been enough to create a stable democracy in 1918. Although he does not explicitly commit himself on the second half, this would appear to be Bluhm's position. But it should be made clear that it falls far short of the proposition that the 'consociational solution' was sufficient to transform the First Republic into the Second.

A subsidiary logical point to which I should like to draw attention is this. Even if we allowed that such changes as there were between the inter-war and post-war periods were of no relevance in determining the a priori prospects for the survival of a democratic regime, we could still assert no more than that the change in treatment (consociational democracy) was a sufficient condition of the change in outcome. We could not say that it was a necessary condition because it is possible that alternative treatments to the one actually applied would have produced the same outcome. The Duke of Clarence was drowned in a butt of Malmsey, but we should be unwise to deduce from that that water would not have been just as effective. For many purposes a sufficient condition is adequate. If we are interested in the cause of the Duke of Clarence's death, it is enough to know that he was drowned in a butt of Malmsey. But if we are interested in finding out how to drown people it is highly relevant to know whether the cheaper and generally more readily available substitute of water would have done as well. Similarly, if we wish to extract lessons from the 'consociational democracies' for application to other deeply divided societies, we need to know not only that a 'consociational solution' has caused stability in certain cases but also whether any alternative patterns of élite behaviour (maybe more attainable) would have done so.

Of course, even if we believe the answer to be that no alternative pattern of élite behaviour would have been effective, this is not enough to enable us to recommend a 'consociational solution' to another society. Here my main point comes in again: there may be differences between divided societies that enable a 'consociational solution'—or perhaps other 'solutions' too—to bring about stability in one and not another. I shall enlarge on these problems of extrapolation in the next section of this chapter and in chapter 5.

So far I have merely stated logically possible objections to the thesis that the 'consociational solution' explains the success of the Second Republic in contrast to the failure of the First. What I have to do now is to argue that these objections are not only possible but plausible. What, then, are the alternative explanations of the success of the Second Republic that involve factors other than élite behaviour? I make no claim for originality in adducing two relevant differences between the inter-war and post-war periods: the altered international setting and the contrast between the economic dislocation after the First World War and the growing prosperity of Western Europe (in which Austria fully shared) after the Second.

I have already mentioned William T. Bluhm's *Building an Austrian Nation*. Bluhm places great explanatory emphasis on élite behaviour, and mentions with approval the ideas of Lijphart, Lorwin, and Nordlinger.[38] And he commits himself to a strong claim for the 'consociational solution': that it was a necessary condition of stability. 'If the existence of opposing armies [the great political parties] was not to result in catastrophic conflict, if they *had* to be brought to agreement, this could only be by a procedure resembling a continuous treaty or contract negotiation, a constant conclave of their chiefs, resolving issues through compromise and unanimous decision—a "Grand Coalition".' The words 'could only' entail that if the People's party, after winning an absolute majority of seats in the elections of 1945, had not invited the Socialist party to join them in forming a government, or if the Socialists had refused, the result would have been 'catastrophic conflict'.

At the same time, however, Bluhm presents the evidence on the basis of which this claim can be doubted. The First Republic was born in defeat, as a by-product of the dismemberment of the Austro-Hungarian Empire. It was 'the state that nobody wanted'. 'On November 12, 1918, the Provisional National Assembly unanimously voted a constitutional law declaring that "German Austria is a part of the German Reich".'[39] Refused *Anschluss* by the Allies, the inhabitants of the newly-created Austria had to live together, but without any commitment to doing so.

Compare the situation in 1945. The experience of *Anschluss* had

[38] Bluhm, *Building an Austrian Nation*, p. 68 n. 37.

[39] Ibid. 25.

hardly been encouraging, and, by dissociating itself from Germany, Austria had the opportunity of being treated, if not as an honorary victor, at least as a liberated victim. Nor did it make much sense now to regret the loss of the eastern territories. In spite of partial Russian occupation, one might just dare to hope for a unified Austria, but a unified 'Danubian confederation' (the ideal of some after the First World War) was obviously out of the question. Although, as Bluhm shows, there would still be widespread doubts about the existence of an 'Austrian nation', there was little room for disagreement about the necessity for an Austria state.

The contrast in economic performance is just as clear. Indeed, one of the main forces behind the demand for *Anschluss* was the belief that the Austria created in 1918 was economically non-viable.

> Everything seemed to point to a need for integration into some kind of a larger political unit. Heavy industry . . . was virtually non-existent. The centers of the empire had been in Bohemia and Moravia, which now were foreign territory. . . . The empire had not formed or accumulated capital to anything like the degree typical of western European industrial states during the second part of the nineteenth century. . . . The Austrian republic, fifteen years after its inception, found itself with a structural unemployment problem; there was a labor force of two million but only 1·4 million jobs.[40]

In 1945 the Second Republic inherited the fruits of an industrial build-up, partly thanks to Hitler, and was further helped by the Marshall Plan. 'During 1948–52 one-third of the net investment was financed by ERP counterpart funds.'[41] The 'soaring productivity and consumer affluence' have 'disproven once and for all the myth of economic nonviability'.[42]

It should be recognized at once that those who wish to assert the unique causal efficacy of élite behaviour in explaining the collapse of the First Republic and the stability of the Second are not thereby committed to denying the relevance of these international or economic factors. But if they are to be consistent they can allow them only as a cause of the cause, not as an independent cause. In other words, they can say that the changed conditions of 1945 provided an incentive to the party leaders to make a go of the Second Republic that was lacking after 1918 when neither side saw the First Republic as more than an unsatisfactory and unviable stopgap.

Even this, however, is dangerous ground. For, if we were to say that the party leaders in 1918 and in 1945 could not have behaved

[40] Ibid. 24. [41] Ibid. 86. [42] Ibid. 85.

differently from the way they did, the whole 'consociational democracy' thesis collapses. As Lijphart makes very clear (and he is here followed by Nordlinger), the essence of the theory is to assert that political leaders have an autonomous influence on events and to deny that they are merely the passive instruments of 'social forces' or 'political cleavages'. In a broader setting, the 'consociational democracy' thesis can be seen as part of the movement among political scientists in recent years towards a reassertion of politics as the 'master science', in reaction to the socio-economic reductionism implicit in the explanatory claims of political sociology.

If, therefore, anything significant is to be left of the 'consociational democracy' theory, we have to believe that it makes sense to ask what would have happened if the party leaders had behaved co-operatively in the First Republic or competitively in the Second. Even if the behaviour of the actual leaders was determined by circumstances, we have to be prepared to believe that other leaders (similar in all other respects, perhaps) might have chosen to behave differently. The question to be asked is: what difference would this difference of behaviour have made to the stability and survival of the two Austrian Republics?

The answer can be no more than a matter for speculation, and this must be so where we have only one case from which to draw conclusions. But it can be informed speculation. The information may be about Austria or about other countries. Although it is a truism that every country is unique, this does not entail that there are no valid generalizations in politics, nor does it prevent us from making particular comparisons that are at least highly suggestive.

One of the best-established generalizations in political science is, surely, that a prosperous country is more likely to be stable than one with high unemployment and stagnant or falling production. This is true whatever the regime but, because of the peculiar dependence of representative democracy on widespread consent among the population, it is especially true of that form of regime. On the strength of this generalization and the facts already mentioned concerning Austria's economic performance in the inter-war and post-war periods, we would predict, without any further information, that the First Republic would be less healthy than the Second.

Of course, it could be argued that the contrasting economic performance was itself the result of the difference between one-party and two-party governments. Even if this were so, it would not, strictly speaking, support the thesis that consociational democracy is a way of overcoming otherwise unfavourable conditions. At most, it would suggest that consociational democracy helps create favourable conditions. But in any case the overriding fact is that every Western European country suffered economic dislocation in the inter-war period and every Western European country shared in a sustained boom after the Second World War. In the face of this it seems out of place to look for an explanation of the general features of Austria's economic performance in the two periods by looking for specifically Austrian causes.

If we turn from economic to political conditions, we are again led to wonder how much is left to be explained by the presence or absence of consociational devices. In having its own brand of authoritarian clerical corporatist state (established on 1 May 1934), Austria was in phase with the rest of Western Europe in the 1930s, just as it was after the Second World War in remaining a functioning parliamentary democracy.

More specifically, the Nazi momentum in Germany would have posed a threat to Austrian democracy however its institutions had been operated by the politicians of the Christian Social and Socialist parties. Bluhm speaks of 'the identification of German nationalism with Nazi ideology' and notes that in the local elections of 1932 the National Socialists polled over 200,000 votes in Vienna, winning fifteen seats (fourteen of them Christian Social), while 'Christian Social majorities in Lower Austria and Salzburg had been destroyed by the Nazis'.[43] The end of the First Republic was a Christian Social coup, not against the threat of the Socialists, but against the further erosion of the Christian Social Party's position by the Nazis.

Obviously, we can play the game of 'might have been' in greater elaboration, and suggest that the two major parliamentary parties might have co-operated to check the growth of Nazism. But the essence of consociational *democracy* is that the parties taking part in the collaborative enterprise should be able to hold the support of their followers in free elections. Manifestly, the Christian Social party was failing to hold its support in 1932, and (extrapolating from German experience, which seems reasonable here) one would expect the Nazi surge to have continued if further elections had been held. I can see no reason for supposing that a Christian Social/Socialist 'grand coalition' would have reduced the growth in Nazi support. And it might have increased it: as has often been pointed out, a 'grand coalition' of the

[43] Ibid. 34.

pro-system parties may be counterproductive in driving discontent into anti-system channels.

The threat to the Christian Social electoral position could have been avoided by a bilateral 'red-black' authoritarian regime instead of the unilateral 'black' one. But this would not be consociational *democracy*, nor would it really be *consociation* since it would be co-operation by two political forces to suppress the rise of a third one. For the same reasons, incidentally, I am unwilling to accept the alleged South American examples of consociational democracy that are sometimes put forward. To say, for example, of the agreement in 1958 between the *Blancos* and the *Colorados* in Colombia that it was a 'consociational arrangement', although 'the efficacy of the right to vote is severely restricted', might at best be regarded as heavy irony, since the agreement had the effect that, regardless of the distribution of political sentiment in the population, the two parties would share power in predetermined ways.[44]

As far as the inter-war period is concerned, then, the basic facts are as follows. The First Republic lasted from 1918 until 1934 (or 1933 if we count the dissolution of the National Assembly *sine die* by the President as the effective end of the regime), with a competitive rather than consociational system of parliamentary government. In 1938 Hitler invaded Austria and brought Austrian independence to an end. Since I take it that no previous history of co-operation between the Christian Social and Socialist parties would have enabled Austria to resist this invasion for long, we can say that the only question at issue is whether consociational democracy could have saved the First Republic for an extra four or five years. And this, as we have seen, is quite problematic given the strength of the Nazi challenge within the country. When we reflect on the disadvantages under which the First Republic laboured, we should perhaps be more impressed with the fact that it survived as long as it did than with the fact that it eventually fell.

The relevant question for the inter-war period is: given the economic and political conditions, could the First Republic have survived longer than it did if the two major parties had acted in a 'consociational' fashion? The relevant question for the post-war period is: given the economic and political conditions, could the Second Republic have lasted until now if the two major parties had not acted in a 'consociational' fashion from 1945 until 1966? As I have already

[44] See Lijphart, 'Consociational Democracy', in McRae, p. 77.

mentioned, the general economic conditions were more benign, and so were the general political conditions. Democratic institutions in Western Europe were faced in the 1930s with the challenge of Fascism, and it was predictable that the Nazi success in Germany would be reflected within Austria. After the Second World War the parallel threat to democratic institutions was the Communist surge, but indigenous support for Communism in Austria was vanishingly small as a result of the experience of Russian occupation.

The comparison with West Germany seems to me very suggestive, and it is rather surprising that more has not been made of West Germany as a 'control'. The contrast between the precarious existence and ignominious downfall of the Weimar Republic on the one hand and the stability and widespread acceptance of the Federal Republic on the other is surely at least as striking as the contrast between the First and Second Republics in Austria. Yet the West German regime has not been claimed by anyone for the ranks of the consociational democracies.

Perhaps this in itself ought to be a little surprising, since the expression 'cartel of élites', used by Lijphart as one characterization of consociational democracy, was itself borrowed from Ralf Dahrendorf's book *Society and Democracy in Germany*.[45] But Dahrendorf did not mean by this 'universal participation', as Lijphart glosses it. Rather, he intended the expression to refer to the unwillingness of the members of the German élite to take individual responsibility for sweeping policy initiatives.

> By the cartel of elites I do not mean any explicit, much less written agreement between generals, entrepreneurs, bishops and party chairmen; the idea would be absurd as the social contract certified by a notary public. [Yet this is exactly what the Austrian *Koalitionspakt* was—B.B.] What I mean is that the elites behave as if they had agreed to cease from all initiative, to distribute social power according to a certain rule and not to dispute this rule. The 'cartel' in this social-political sense is a conceptual implication, not a real institution. . . .[46]

We should not allow ourselves to get sidetracked here by Dahrendorf's belief in the virtues of conflict and his consequently negative evaluation of the respect shown for vested interests in the Federal Republic. We may wish to say that both in Germany and in Austria a certain caution and forbearance among the members of the

[45] See ibid. 76.
[46] Ralf Dahrendorf, *Society and Democracy in Germany* (London: Weidenfeld and Nicolson, 1968), 269.

political élite was a prudent reaction to the excesses of the inter-war period. But the significance for our purpose of the West German case is that it shows us a country establishing a stable and widely accepted regime of parliamentary democracy without the use of consociational devices. The Austrian People's party invited the Socialists to join the government in 1945 although they had won a majority of seats, and the 'grand coalition' continued until 1966. In West Germany, by contrast, the same formative years (until the 'grand coalition' of 1966) were years in which Christian Democrats ruled either alone or in coalition with the small Free Democrat party.

Obviously, the relevance of the West German case can be disputed. Since no two countries are exactly alike, it is always possible to deny that what happened in one is a valid guide to what would have happened in another. And it is certainly true that a sceptic can point to two changes between Weimar and Bonn that do not have parallels in Austria: first a reconstitution of the boundaries of the state and second a change from a fragmented party system to a two-and-a-half party system. But, at the same time, it must be observed that both of these changes make the analogy between post-war Germany and post-war Austria more convincing. The party systems of the two countries have been remarkably similar: a large Social Democratic party, a large Conservative/Christian party, and a small middle-class liberal party sometimes holding the balance of seats in parliament. And, although I would not want to make too much of the point, the loss of Prussia surely left the truncated West Germany more culturally similar to Austria than the whole of Germany had been.

The conclusion towards which I am driving is this. When we set the post-war experience of Austria in a comparative context, we must doubt whether the 'consociational solution'—the combination of a 'grand coalition' and a very strict *Proporz* principle for all sorts of appointments—was really a necessary condition of stable democracy. To put it concretely, suppose that in November 1945, after the Austrian People's party had won a narrow overall majority in elections to the National Assembly, their leader had *not* approached the Socialists with the offer of a coalition but had instead installed himself as Chancellor of a one-party government. Would the result, within a few years, have been either a civil war or a potential civil war averted at the cost of the suppression of free institutions?

Bluhm commits himself firmly to this proposition. 'Parliamentary elections . . . tallied . . . the strength of opposing armies. If the existence of opposing armies was not to result in catastrophic conflict, if they *had* to be brought to agreement, this could only be by a procedure resembling a continuous treaty or contract negotiation, a constant conclave of their chiefs, resolving issues through compromise and unanimous decision—a "Grand Coalition".'[47] But is this apocalyptic vision of the inevitable alternative plausible?

We might concede to those who emphasize the importance of leadership behaviour that, if the leaders of the two major parties had been determined to maximize conflict and had organized their followers to carry on an extra-parliamentary struggle, they could probably have made the Second Republic collapse. Even this much, however, may be doubted if we are prepared to draw any general conclusions from G. Bingham Powell's study of a small town near Salzburg (Hallein).[48] Town council politics are quite rancorous in Hallein (though Powell does seem to be rather easily shocked), and the leaders of the two main parties view one another with a great deal of hostility. In spite of this, and the extent to which party supporters are segregated in economic, cultural, and sporting organizations, the level of hostility among the population at large is not high. Of the whole sample in Powell's survey, about 7 per cent would be displeased at the prospect of a child marrying across party lines, and about 14 per cent thought that if the other party came to power nationally it would 'endanger the nation'.[49]

This suggests that the mass is a restraining influence on the élites and not (as in the classic 'consociational' vision) that the élites have to collaborate to keep their supporters away from one another's throats. Strong support for this impression is provided by Powell himself, who reports 'the attitude expressed by the overwhelming majority of survey respondents (more than 75% in both major parties) who thought the political parties should cooperate more at the local level'.[50]

However, let us concede that, with sufficiently determined efforts to produce chronic confrontation at the national level, the party leaders could probably have made the Second Republic unworkable. What follows from this? Not much that is to the point. For there is obviously a wide range of possible élite behaviour between all-out conflict and the peculiarly comprehensive suppression of conflict that was actually instituted in post-war Austria.

It is here, surely, that the West German example is relevant. For it

[47] Bluhm, *Building an Austrian Nation*, p. 70.

[48] G. Bingham Powell, jun., *Social Fragmentation and Political Hostility: An Austrian Case Study* (Stanford, Calif.: Stanford University Press, 1970).

[49] Calculated from Table 19, p. 61, of Powell, *Social Fragmentation*.

[50] Ibid. 71.

provides a model of an alternative line of development based on mutual forbearance among the leaders of the main parties rather than on the consociational devices employed in Austria. We should qualify this a little to allow for the use of a kind of *Proporz* in West Germany for manning certain especially sensitive posts, as Lehmbruch has pointed out in an interesting article.

Judges of the Federal Constitutional Court are elected by a parliamentary majority of two-thirds. This rule guarantees a quasi-proportional share of 'black' and 'red' on the bench. Public institutions of political education . . . are placed under all-party supervisory boards, and the supervisory boards of radio and television are formed by representatives of the political parties, large interest groups and churches in order to establish the political neutrality of these media.'[51]

This fairly modest degree of *Proporz* was little increased during the period of the 'grand coalition'; according to Lehmbruch (p. 561), only one ministry was staffed on a proportional basis and that was the Federal Press and Information Office.

As always, we cannot assert, simply on the strength of the fact that they existed, that these modest concessions to consociational management were necessary to the creation of a stable state. But it is easy to see why in these particular areas control by a single party might cause anxiety. If we wish, therefore, we can transfer the West German practice in these matters to our alternative scenario for post-war Austria. We are still left with a quite sharp contrast with what actually happened in Austria.

This discussion raises two points that bear on the consociational theorists' emphasis on the explanatory significance of élite behaviour. The first point arises from the contrast drawn by de Tocqueville between the 'men of letters who are always inclined to find general causes' and the 'politicians' who 'are prone to imagine that everything is attributable to particular incidents, and that the wires they pull are the same as move the world'.[52] Tocqueville added: 'It is to be presumed that both are equally deceived.' But we could more reasonably say that both may be equally correct.

The consociational theorists—Nordlinger is especially explicit about this—are concerned to reverse what they see as the excessive

[51] Gerhard Lehmbruch, 'The Ambiguous Coalition in West Germany', *Government and Opposition*, 3 (1968), 181–204, repr. in abridged form in Mattei Dogan and Richard Rose (eds.), *European Politics: A Reader* (London: Macmillan, 1971), 549–63, at 553.

[52] Quoted by Graham T. Allison in the front of *Essence of Decision* (Boston: Little, Brown, 1971), no ref. supplied.

weight given to 'general causes' by orthodox political science, as when the 'political culture' or the 'cleavage structure' are taken as the key explanatory variables. Orthodoxy—as represented for example by Gabriel Almond—is changing too, for in Almond's most recently published project the emphasis is placed on the creative role of politicians in shaping events.[53]

It seems to me, though, that there is a danger of underplaying the 'general causes' and that the consociational theorists fall into this danger. Of course, we can describe in detail how things happen by focusing on the behaviour of politicians, and there is no substitute for this. But we must step back from this level of detail to appreciate the constraints on these actors and the opportunities open to them. The constraints are particularly severe in a democratic system. Rival politicians may get together to suppress dissent and we may if we wish call the result 'consociation'; but if it is to be consociational *democracy*, they must carry their supporters with them voluntarily. Lijphart and Nordlinger both mention this point but treat it as subsidiary. Yet it seems to me crucial. We know that in post-war Austria the two major parties were able to keep their supporters in line while they co-operated. We do not know whether they could have done so in the inter-war period, but we do know that the Nazis were making big inroads into the Christian Social vote in the 1930s. More generally, the 1950s and 1960s have been uniquely favourable for parliamentary democracy in Western Europe. It is hardly a parsimonious explanation to attribute this to the simultaneous decisions of political élites in over a dozen countries.

The second point about the explanatory significance of élite behaviour is that, even if we allow that something about élite behaviour is critically significant, we have to be careful in specifying what it is. Thus, in the post-war Austrian case, perhaps the important thing was the willingness of the party leaders to co-operate rather than the institutionalization of that co-operation through consociational machinery. In other words, it may be that what mattered was the attitude manifested in the offer and acceptance of a 'grand coalition', and that the same attitude without any consociational institutions could also have produced a stable democratic system.

[53] G. A. Almond, S. C. Flanagan, and R. J. Mundt (eds.), *Crisis, Choice and Change: Historical Studies of Political Development* (Boston: Little, Brown, 1973). I have reviewed this work in *The British Journal of Political Science* as follows: Part I, 'Plus ça change?', 7 (1977), 99–113; Part II, 'Games theorists play', 7 (1977), 217–53.

IV

We may summarize the upshot of the previous two sections as follows. (1) We eliminated Switzerland as an exemplar of the consociational democracy thesis. Because of the referendum, we argued that it does not even provide a pure case of consociational institutions. But in any case it does not fit the model of deep divisions articulated by different political parties. The political parties cross-cut cleavages in the society and provide a picture of remarkable consensus rather than a highly structured conflict of goals. (2) We accepted without demur that Austria was from 1945 until 1966 a fully-fledged consociational democracy, in the purely descriptive or non-theoretical sense that it had a panoply of consociational devices. But we questioned whether it satisfied the consociational democracy thesis in that the consociational devices may not have been necessary to keep conflict down to a manageable level.

The result is to halve the number of 'classic cases' of consociational democracy from four to two, the remaining members of the class being the Netherlands and Belgium. Both of the Low Countries have been indubitably consociational in their method of conflict-management. This is not exhibited primarily in a tendency to 'grand coalition': the Netherlands often has 'oversized', though far from all-inclusive, coalitions, while Belgium conforms as much as most Western European countries to the 'minimum winning coalition' model. Rather, what makes them consociational is the way in which the composition of the government is not the determinant of major changes in public policy, as it is in Britain, for example.

The government manages the day-to-day affairs of the country, of course. But major developments—especially when they involve relations between the socio-religious blocs—are drawn up by the representatives of the interested parties (parliamentary and extra-parliamentary) in private negotiation and then presented to parliament for ratification. Examples of this process are the Dutch 'pacification' of 1917 and the Belgian school pact of 1958.

How far the Netherlands and Belgium support the theory of consociational democracy cannot be decided simply by a description of what happens in them. As we have seen, we are inevitably involved in a counterfactual conditional when we attempt to answer the question. Nordlinger expresses some qualms about the Dutch 'pacification' on this score: was the degree of conflict sufficient for it to provide a case of 'conflict regulation in divided societies'?

For the present purpose, however, let us accept that the pattern of consociational settlements in the Netherlands and Belgium has contributed to the stability and general acceptability of the system in a way that a more majoritarian pattern of conflict-management would not. There is still a problem. The diminution in the range of 'classic cases' has serious implications for the wider applicability of the model of consociational democracy to other divided societies. Our two surviving cases are contiguous countries and the divisions that have been subjected to consociational management are of the same kind: the Church–State question and the challenge posed by the rise of the working-class movement. The potentially explosive quality of these issues is not to be belittled: even within twentieth-century Western Europe they underlay the tragedy of the Spanish civil war, for example. But we should be cautious in extending the formula to other divisions and in particular to those involving ethnic identity.

In chapter 5 below, I argue for this claim in detail, taking as examples Canada and Northern Ireland. Here I want to offer four general reasons why divisions based on ethnic identity are more likely than others to be resistant to consociational management. First, it simply does seem to be the case that acts of gross inhumanity are more readily engaged in or supported when the victims are members of an ethnically defined out-group than when the basis of differentiation is class or religion, especially when sympathetic identification with the out-group is reduced by large physical or cultural differences.

Second, religious and class conflict is a conflict of organizations. Ethnic conflict is a conflict of solidary groups. Whether these groups have an organizational embodiment is a contingent matter, but in any case they do not need organization to work up a riot or a pogrom so long as they have some way of recognizing who belongs to which group. The importance of this factor for the viability of consociational democracy is clear when we recall the point that the leaders of the blocs must be able to hold the support of their followers for any deal that they agree to.

Ethnic groups may of course have leaders, but an ethnic group is not defined by the fact that it follows certain leaders. If the present leaders agree to something on behalf of their followers it is always open to some rival to denounce the terms as a sell-out and to seek to gather support for repudiating them. By contrast, a Roman Catholic is, by definition, someone who accepts the authority of the Church. Although the Bishops may therefore have trouble with lay organizations that want to be 'more Catholic than the Pope'—more intransigent than the official line—these can usually be brought to heel by an instruction being issued to the faithful. Protestant Churches and working-class organizations obviously differ among themselves in the degree of control that the leaders can exert over the followers. Leaders may be more or less easily replaced, followers may find it more or less difficult or costly to leave. But, to the extent that the leaders do have control, they can, again, take part in consociational arrangements with confidence that they can 'deliver' their supporters.

Third, and related to this, someone can feel confidently that he knows what the advancement of the collective interest of an ethnic group calls for in a certain situation, without the benefit of any complex scheme for interpreting the world. No elaborate theoretical argument is needed to establish that some policy would provide material and symbolic gratifications for the members of one group while inflicting deprivation and degradation on the members of the other. By contrast, the question of whether or not some policy is or is not in the interests of some religion clearly depends on the answer to the prior question of what the religion itself requires. In some religions there is an authoritative source for determining the answer to that question. Although laymen may wish to be 'more Catholic than the Pope', for example, they are in a difficult position to make an effective challenge because the distinguishing characteristic of Roman Catholics *is* precisely that they accept the authority of the Pope, and more generally of the hierarchy. Even where there is no final authority in the hands of the leaders, the fact that the 'right answer' depends on a process of more or less subtle reasoning clearly gives a built-in advantage to the leaders as experts.

Similarly, it is by no means self-evident what constitutes the collective interest of the 'working class' in any given situation, and the same analysis applies as to religion. Either (as in the Communist party) it is a question to be decided authoritatively by the hierarchy, and anyone who dissents is by definition a bad Communist (and if he persists may find himself not a Communist at all), or it is a matter of argument, in which experts presumably have an advantage. Because of this contrast between the apparent clarity of ethnic issues on the one hand and religious or class issues on the other, we should expect that it will be easier for deals to be made by leaders in connection with religious or class issues with some confidence that they will be able to carry their followers with them.

Fourth and last, the question in dispute in class or religious issues is how the country is to be run. The question is thus: how are *we* to get along together? Naturally, a question so posed lends itself to consociational methods of resolution. But where the basis of division is ethnic the question may not be how the country is to be run but whether it should be a country at all. Should one group secede and become an independent state? Should it merge with an ethnically cognate neighbour state? Or should the whole of the existing state absorb or be absorbed by another? These are questions which allow little room for negotiation because at least one party may not want a solution within the existing framework.

The relative potency of ethnic identification as a basis for conflict is brought out well by William Keech in his research note on 'Linguistic Diversity and Political Conflict'. Keech himself uses 'ethnic differences' as a synonym for 'linguistic and religious differences'[54] but I shall not follow him in this, reserving the concept of 'ethnic identification' for the sense of being a 'people' or a 'race' (in the old-fashioned sense in which people used to talk about the 'English race'). The central question raised in Keech's note is why relations between French and German speakers have been so much worse in the Bern canton of Switzerland than in the Fribourg canton, in spite of the objectively worse discrimination suffered by the German minority in Fribourg than by the French minority in Bern. And the answer that he gives is in terms of what I am calling ethnic identification.

> A strong case can be made that it is the Jura per se rather than language which is the main basis of separatism, and that language complicates the problem by being more or less congruent with the boundaries of the Jura, rather than vice versa. . . . The attitude seems to be 'It is not because we happen to speak French, but because we are not Bernese and can never become Bernese that we want to be separate from Berne'. . . . Although the German Freiburger has grievances, he does not see them as inconsistent with loyal citizenship in the multilinguistic canton. . . . They think of themselves as Freiburgers and they do not want separatism but, rather, complete equality in the canton. . . . Instead of having no real traditional alternative to membership in the canton, as in Fribourg, the Jura had an 800-year history as a separate political unit, the memory of which emphatically competed with Bern for the loyalty of the Jurassian citizens.[55]

It may well have occurred to the reader that I should already have mentioned the Walloons and the Flemings in Belgium. They are indeed relevant, but mainly in the context of my argument that consociational methods are better adapted to moderating religious or

[54] See Keech, 'Linguistic Diversity', p. 387.
[55] Ibid. 400, 401, 402.

class conflicts than ethnic ones. The claim of Belgium to rank as a 'classic consociational' case rests on its handling of the divisions between its 'spiritual families', not on its handling of relations between its two constituent ethnic groups.

The demands of the ethnic groups have not been articulated by the party system, as required by the consociational model. The major parties have continued to be based on 'spiritual' cleavages, and the rise of parties standing explicitly on ethnic platforms—representing Flemings, Walloons, and Francophone Bruxellois—has been seen by the other parties not as an encouraging sign that the problems are on their way to being solved but as a deadly threat to the system. The action that has been taken to defuse the ethnic conflict has not been based on negotiating between the ethnic parties but has been taken by the other parties in pursuit of a common interest in preventing the growth of these parties by stealing their clothes. And, finally, it has taken the form of unscrambling the unitary state set up in 1830 and giving much more autonomy to the ethnically defined regions of the country. To the extent therefore that there is inter-ethnic agreement it is an agreement to go separate ways: a friendly divorce rather than a more complete marriage.

The implications of the Flemish–Walloon conflict for the theory of consociational democracy are obscure because the method has not on the whole been used. It may be argued that that is the problem. Val Lorwin in effect took this line in a paper first presented in 1965. In asking why 'by the mid-1960s the linguistic-regional tensions appeared more intractable than those of ideological difference or social class' his first answer was as follows.

> The sentimental and practical interests of the linguistic communities were not effectively organized, and the geographical regions had no administrative or formal political existence as yet. There were no recognized representatives qualified to formulate demands, to negotiate, and to fulfil commitments. The 1962–1963 language laws were negotiated within and between the PSC and the PSB [Catholics and Socialists], the two governing parties. This aggregation of linguistic and regional claims by the governing parties was challenged, not only by the leading opposition party and by the regional and linguistic parties, but also by self-designated linguistic and regional spokesmen within the governing parties.[56]

As I have already pointed out, it is the nature of the case that rival leaders are more likely to spring up when the issue is an ethnic one than

[56] Lorwin, 'Belgium: Conflict and Compromise', in McRae, p. 197.

when it is a religious or class one. But would it be a contribution to social harmony if each ethnic group were represented by a single monolithic organization? If it were so in Belgium, then Belgium would be, as far as I know, unique in the annals of human history. Except where it is the prelude to peaceful fission of the state, a situation in which conflicting ethnic groups are mobilized behind monolithic organizations is a situation of potential civil war or of civil war averted by effective oppression by one group of the other. The clearest contemporary examples of political systems with elections dominated by ethnically based political parties are probably Guyana, Sri Lanka, and Northern Ireland. Nigeria, during its career as a parliamentary system, was another example. None of these is exactly an advertisement for such a system.

It is possible to explain why this should be so if we recall the earlier discussion of the way in which religious and class issues allow more scope for the leaders to impose their interpretation of the collective interests of their followers than do ethnic issues. Because of this we can predict that, if there is to be a leadership of an ethnic group that is not in constant danger of being undercut by challengers, it must inevitably be seen to be taking up an extreme position in defence of the group's interests. And, having done this to gain and then maintain its position, it is not likely to be able to afford to counsel moderation later. Once ethnic feeling has been whipped up, it has a terrifying life of its own, as communal massacres on the Indian subcontinent and in Indonesia since the Second World War illustrate. Cyprus and Northern Ireland provide examples on a far smaller but still depressing scale.

5

THE CONSOCIATIONAL MODEL AND ITS DANGERS

> 'What curious attitudes he goes into!' 'Not at all,' said the King. 'He's an Anglo-Saxon Messenger—and those are Anglo-Saxon attitudes.'
>
> Lewis Carroll, *Alice Through the Looking Glass*

I THE CONSOCIATIONAL VOGUE

In a review article on 'The Consociational Democracy Theme', Hans Daalder wrote that the model of 'consociational democracy' challenged 'prevailing normative views, based mainly on American or British perspectives' about 'the conditions of effective and stable democratic rule'.[1] I should like to make two remarks about this claim. First, I question whether the attitudes to which Daalder refers are really 'prevalent', at any rate in America or Britain themselves. And, second, I should like to suggest that the battle has not only been won but is in some danger of turning into a rout. Less metaphorically, the 'consociational democracies' are no longer likely to be written off as being 'isolated phenomena, mainly of folkloristic interest',[2] but their relevance to other societies may now be exaggerated.

In the past few years in Britain the aspects of the political system which have come under fire most frequently are precisely those where it deviates most clearly from the 'consociational' model: the artificial opposition of parties whose members (it is said) largely agree on what should be done (and even more on the limits of what anyone could do), and the tendency for alternating party governments to spend much of the time undoing the work of their predecessors and the rest preparing legislation, much of which does not even reach the statute book before the next election puts it back at square one. It is also worth noting that at any time in the last few years anything from a quarter to a half of the electorate with an opinion has been shown by public

[1] Hans Daalder, 'The Consociational Democracy Theme', *World Politics*, 26 (1974), 604–21, at 605.

[2] Ibid. 604.

opinion polls to agree with statements on the lines of 'Politicians should co-operate together to solve the nation's problems', or specifically to say that they would welcome coalition government. So far, then, from the prevailing mood in Britain being one in which the 'consociational democracies' are regarded as aberrations, it might be nearer the truth to say that there is a great deal of doubt about what had been thought of as the distinctive merits of the system: the electoral system that usually creates a majority party out of only a plurality of votes, and the winner-take-all allocation of political power to the party with a majority of seats in the House of Commons.

It is, in the nature of the case, difficult to prove that this chastened mood about our long-established political habits and political institutions is widespread. But the clearest sign was probably an active correspondence in *The Times* which took place between the February and October elections in 1974, when the unsettled parliamentary situation (the two major parties holding almost equal numbers of seats, the balance being held by minor parties) made reform appear a practical possibility. I pick one as an example, almost at random.

The first paragraph of the letter runs as follows:

> Electoral reform seems nowadays to meet with general approval by the public if not by professional MPs. It would, presumably, generally lead to minority or coalition governments and this might be no bad thing. It will, however, be quite ineffective in imposing upon the politicians the necessity for genuine consensus government unless it is accompanied by a major change in the constitutional arrangements of the United Kingdom. This is the removal from the Prime Minister of the day of the power to require a dissolution of parliament.[3]

The significant part of this letter for the present purpose is the idea that minority or coalition government is desirable as a means to genuine consensus government. The writer's own piece of constitutional *bricolage* is significant only as a symptom of the tendency to cast around for foreign devices to import that people usually engage in when they are dissatisfied with their own institutions. But it is a nice irony that the device imported into France—dissolution of parliament before its full term expires—with the object of making the system function more like the British one should now have its abolition proposed in Britain with the avowed object of making the system more 'continental'.

The situation in the USA is, of course, in all kinds of ways different.

[3] Letter from Mr Anthony Sumption, *The Times* (21 Sept. 1974), p. 15, col. 7.

This is clearly illustrated by the fact that the Anglophile supporters of 'a more responsible two-party system' such as Schattschneider and Beer have, correctly, seen themselves as going against the American grain. The norm in Congressional committees is one of businesslike co-operation, with unanimity highly valued and very little overt partisanship except on organizational matters. And the rule requiring a two-thirds majority for *clôture* in the Senate (combined with the reluctance of Senators to invoke it) is an embodiment of Calhoun's notion of the 'concurrent majority', an essentially 'consociational' idea. The only 'majoritarian' feature of the federal system is the Presidency itself, and those who have in the past decried the 'deadlock of democracy' in the USA have tended to pin their hopes on a reconstruction of the parties behind the leadership of the President and (more difficult to institutionalize) a Presidential candidate-designate for the other side. But, under the impact of the abuses of Johnson and Nixon, the emphasis has recently been on cutting the Presidency down to size rather than building it up further. Restraining the Presidency inevitably means building up Congress: that is to say, trying to find ways in which Congress, through its committees, can gain some greater control over what is done by or in the name of the President.

In the intellectual climate I have described, I do not think that any further Anglo-Saxon breast-beating over past hubris in relation to our political institutions is called for. What worries me at present is that attempts to apply the 'consociational model' outside its original areas (especially in ethnically divided societies such as Northern Ireland or Canada) may make things worse. There is always a risk that proposals for institutional transfer from one country to another will partake more of sympathetic magic than of sober science. Maurice O'Sullivan, in his delightful autobiographical book *Twenty Years a'Growing*, quotes an apposite Irish saying: 'Live horse and you'll get grass'.[4] 'Have proportional representation and a grand coalition and you'll become Swiss or Dutch' is not perhaps so different as a mode of reasoning. Let me hasten at once to acquit the exponents of 'consociational democracy' of peddling it as a panacea. But I do think that someone who does not read the small print may go away with the impression that, in order to turn a conflict-ridden democracy into a harmonious one, all that is required is an effort of will by political leaders. Insufficient attention may be paid to the fact that, if the

[4] Maurice O'Sullivan, *Twenty Years a'Growing* (London: Oxford University Press. The World's Classics, 1953), 17.

country is a democracy, the leaders can continue to be leaders only so long as they have followers.

I should like to explore briefly the cases of two divided Western societies: Canada and Northern Ireland. It is clearly of considerable practical importance to know whether an attempt to introduce consociational democracy into these societies would be likely to make for more harmonious inter-communal relationships or exacerbate a situation that is already uneasy in Canada and really grave in Northern Ireland. And, although one can have only limited confidence in these matters, I think the balance of probability is on the latter.

II THE CANADIAN CASE

For Canada, I refer to Kenneth D. McRae's collection entitled *Consociational Democracy*.[5] This book is a useful source of articles on the idea of consociational democracy in general and on the four 'classic cases' of Belgium, the Netherlands, Switzerland, and Austria. But the last quarter of the book is taken up with a section entitled 'Applications and Illustrations: Canada'. The editor, like many Anglophone academics in Canada, is deeply committed to the cause of maintaining the territorial integrity of Canada. In practical terms what this comes to is that he is committed to trying to prevent Quebec from seceding.

The political implications that follow have been set out very clearly by John Meisel in his *Working Papers on Canadian Politics*. He states an 'axiom' as follows: 'when two or more groups of people have it in their power to survive within independent political entities, the only workable basis on which they can arrange the political relations between them is compromise'.[6] And he then fills out the axiom in a way that makes it clearly tautological. (This is not a criticism: tautologies may be illuminating.) The choice, he says, is separation, force, or accommodation. If force is ruled out and separation is to be avoided then 'the sole basis on which accommodation between the two communities can rest is an agreement acceptable to both'.[7] But what form should this 'accommodation' take? 'Accommodation' is a word of very non-specific meaning in this kind of context. If the parties to a dispute 'reach an accommodation' this means that *some* terms of agreement have been reached, but it does not entail that they should take any particular form.

[5] Kenneth McRae, *Consociational Democracy: Political Accommodation in Segmented Societies* (Toronto: McClelland and Stewart. The Carleton Library, 1974).

[6] John Meisel, *Working Papers on Canadian Politics* (Montreal and London: McGill—Queen's University Press. Enlarged edn. 1973), 184–5.

[7] Ibid. 185.

There are two possible directions in which accommodation may be pursued that are compatible with the existing party system and are indeed on the political agenda. The first is the attempt to make the Federal government truly 'bilingual' and 'bicultural' by selective recruitment, use of scrupulously bilingual forms and notices, and so on. The second is to allow Quebec more autonomy so that French Canadians can feel that they are in charge of its economic and cultural destiny wthout concluding that they need complete independence to achieve their goals. I mention these because it seems clear that McRae's object is to advocate something different—though not necessarily incompatible with either of them. He takes 'accommodation' to entail the reconstruction of Canadian politics to make it fit the consociational model.

McRae puts his case in the Epilogue to the book with quite a rhetorical fervour. He describes a 'majoritarian attitude' as the 'Achilles heel of the Canadian political system' and 'the *damnosa hereditas* of Anglo–American democracy and Lockean political theory and liberal society'.[8] His argument is that the only alternative to 'a more explicitly consociational political system' is 'the separation or quasi-separation of Quebec', which 'would still leave substantial minorities in Quebec and the rest of Canada'.[9]

McRae never makes it clear quite what he means by 'modifying [Canada's] formal institutions along more consociational lines'. But in the article by himself that he prints on 'Consociationalism and the Canadian Political System'[10] he states the objections to the existing system from the 'consociational' point of view by saying that the two 'weaknesses of the Canadian political system may be summarized by borrowing the terminology of Lijphart: *adequate articulation of the interests of the subcultures* is not guaranteed at cabinet level because of uncertainty and distortion in the electoral system, and *internal political cohesion of the subcultures* is not strong enough to assure that agreements reached in cabinet will be accepted by the electorate'.[11] I want to argue that both general theoretical considerations and the experience of other countries, properly interpreted, combine to suggest that the kind of political realignments that McRae is looking for could only be the consequence of and at the same time an accelerating factor in producing exactly the kind of breakdown in Anglo-French relationships that he is seeking to prevent. And the intellectual origin of this

[8] McRae, *Consociational Democracy*, p. 301.
[9] Ibid. [10] Ibid. 238–61.
[11] Ibid. 252–3, italics in original.

error is the mechanical transfer of supposed lessons from the experience of consociational democracy in Europe.

'Adequate articulation of the interests of the subcultures' and their stronger 'internal political cohesion' (so that whatever the leaders agreed to could be counted on as acceptable to the followers) could, I suggest, occur only as a concomitant of increased polarization between the English-speaking and French-speaking communities, with each community lining up solidly behind extremist leaders. Unity and an absence of challenge to leaders can come about when the issues involve communal conflict, as I pointed out in chapter 4. To wish deliberately to create such conditions so as to create the possibility of resolving the conflict by 'consociational' means is, to say the least, reckless.

The existing Canadian party system is, as everyone agrees, one of 'catch-all' or 'brokerage' parties. Each party's support is, to an unusual degree even by the standards of other members of the 'Anglo-American' political systems—in Almond's famous (or infamous) typology—spread across regional, occupational, religious and linguistic lines. In particular, the Liberal party, which must be regarded as the dominant party for more than a generation past, depends for its position on its ability to attract heavy support in Quebec without forfeiting it in the rest of Canada. The primary site of inter-ethnic accommodation may thus be said to be the Liberal party.

I suggest that the politicians of the major national parties are right to regard this kind of set-up as the best hope for the continuation of the existing federation. As in Belgium, they see the rise of exclusively ethnic parties not as the prelude to smoother co-operation but as the beginning of the end of the existing state. I think they are right. It is *not* necessarily an advantage for the most salient (or potentially salient) line of cleavage to be reproduced by the structure of political division. Communal cleavages are so potentially explosive that they can probably only be accommodated in the interstices of politics, while the politicians ostensibly fight one another over quite different issues.

I have not referred to the way in which McRae ties up his preference for better 'articulation of the subcultures' with a reform of the electoral system designed to replace the first-past-the-post single-member constituency system by some other more proportional system. It seems to me that the desirability or undesirability of the kind of realignment McRae advocates is independent of any question about the way in which such a realignment might be brought about. I have no wish to get drawn deeply into that question unnecessarily, but for what it is worth I offer the comment that there does not seem to be any *general* reason for expecting a more proportional electoral system to bring about an alignment into monolithic blocs along the most salient line of cleavage in the society.

It is surely excessively simple-minded to say that, because the 'Anglo-American' countries tend to have single-member constituencies and broadly-aggregating parties, the first is the cause of the second. The structure of cleavages must also be taken into account. Where there are cross-cutting cleavages, but one is more salient than the other, the logic of a single-member system is to suppress the less salient line of cleavage and create monolithic communal blocs of the kind McRae apparently wants to see.

Northern Ireland provides a perfect test of this proposition, and it is worth noticing that practical politicians have been quite well aware of the way in which the political articulation of potential bases of division may be affected by the manipulation of the electoral system. Northern Ireland came into being with a system of elections in multi-member constituencies (by single transferable vote) to its own parliament. In the first general election, held in 1921 under conditions of great inter-communal tension, the established Unionist party was able to monopolize the Protestant representation. But at the next election, in 1925, 'in Belfast there were four four-member constituencies. Eight candidates appealed for a Protestant anti-Unionist vote. Only one failed to get elected. There were three Labour and four Independent Unionist MPs in the new Parliament. Unionist representation went down from 40 to 32.'[12]

The response of the Unionist government was to introduce legislation providing for elections to be held in single-member constituencies. It is important to recognize that this was not necessary to ensure a comfortable majority of Protestant representatives. With proportional representation, Protestants were assured of two-thirds of the seats in accordance with their two-to-one ratio in the population. And although the eventual outcome of the change was indeed to increase the proportion of Protestant representatives, the condition for this to occur was that the Protestant vote should not be split between rival candidates in any constituency where the Catholic minority exceeded a third of the electorate. The Unionist leaders thus accepted a change from a system that made a Protestant majority certain to one that made a Catholic majority a theoretical possibility,

[12] Eamonn McCann, *War and an Irish Town* (Harmondsworth: Penguin, 1974), 192.

in the hope (which was fully justified in the event) that the risk of letting in a Catholic on a split Protestant vote would force Protestant voters to unify behind the Unionist party.

Every general election would thus be simply a plebiscite on the issue of the border: there would be no way in which a voter could simultaneously vote for or against partition and for or against alternative socioeconomic policies that might cut across the Protestant–Catholic division. The Prime Minister, Sir James Craig, was quite explicit about the objective of suppressing any cleavages cross-cutting the Protestant–Catholic one. Introducing the bill to abolish proportional representation early in 1929, he said: 'What I have been afraid of under the proportional representation system was that certain members might be returned to the house who in a crisis on the one point of vital importance to Ulster might not stand on whichever side it was intended they should stand when they were elected to this house. Therefore, I personally will welcome this opportunity to get down to simple issues instead of the complicated ones that are inevitably brought before us under the old plan'.[13] McCann's comment seems apt in the light of the forty years of political ossification that followed: 'The "simple issues" were the border, whether Catholics should be allowed to sweep the floor in the City Hall, and so on. The "complicated ones" were unemployment, houses, rents, wages and such things, irritatingly being "brought before us under the old plan".'[14] In the election held in 1929 the Unionist representation went up to 37, the Independent Unionists lost one seat, and the Labour party two seats.[15]

The experiment was given a further work-out in 1973 when elections were held for the new Northern Ireland Assembly that came into being at the beginning of 1974. For this purpose the British government reverted to the pre-1929 system of election by the single transferable vote in multi-member constituencies. The objective was explicit: to reduce the pressures towards a monolithic Protestant vote and give a chance to parties (the Northern Ireland Labour party and the newly formed Alliance party) that attempted to play down the Protestant–Catholic line of division.

The strategy succeeded to the extent that the Protestant vote was split between extremists and supporters of the 'power-sharing' constitution, while the Alliance party, although it polled poorly, managed to obtain a few seats—something it could not have achieved

[13] Hansard (N.I.) (1929), vol. 10, p. 29.
[14] McCann, *War and an Irish Town*, pp. 192–3.
[15] Ibid. 193.

in a single-member constituency system. Then, as if to allay any remaining doubts about the mechanics of the process, the British government called a general election for February 1974. This was held in Northern Ireland under the usual UK rules, and the single-member constituency system produced its usual effect of solidifying the Protestant vote, though this time behind a loose alliance of Protestant parties opposed to the pro-power-sharing Unionists.

In Canada, it seems to be a safe bet that the main effect of introducing a more proportional electoral system would be simply to spread the elected representatives of the existing parties more evenly round the country. As Cairns has pointed out,[16] the single-member system greatly exaggerates regional differences of support between parties, so that in terms of parliamentary representation the parties are much more regionally concentrated than is their distribution of the popular vote. Thus, except in a good year, the New Democratic party is almost entirely a highly geographically concentrated party in parliamentary terms, though it has minority support spread widely through the country, in just the same way as in Britain the Liberal party is, except in a good year, almost entirely a party of the 'Celtic fringe', even though there are few constituencies in which it cannot now obtain over a fifth of the votes cast.

The change to a more even geographical spread of party representation might be regarded as desirable from various points of view, but McRae is not interested in minor changes in the representation at the Federal level of parties aligned on the existing 'catch-all' basis. I suggest that there is no reason to suppose that a change in the electoral system would have any tendency to further the kind of realignment that McRae is looking for. On the contrary, the example of Northern Ireland seems to imply that, once parties are aligned on the basis of communal cleavage, the single-member system is highly conducive to maintaining the kind of monolithic ethnic party that McRae apparently wishes to see in Canada.

III THE NORTHERN IRELAND CASE

The question posed for the theory of consociational democracy by Northern Ireland is quite different from that posed by Canada. In the case of Canada the question is whether it would be desirable for the party system to articulate the communal cleavage as a precondition to

[16] Alan C. Cairns, 'The Electoral System and the Party System in Canada, 1921–1965', *Canadian Journal of Political Science*, 1 (1968), 55–80.

applying 'consociational' techniques of conflict-management. In Northern Ireland the main line of party division has articulated the Protestant–Catholic cleavage ever since the Province was set up with its present boundaries and a quasi-autonomous status in 1921. Writing in 1971, Richard Rose observed that 'The two major parties are exclusive on religious grounds—95 percent of Unionist supporters are Protestants, and 99 percent of Nationalist supporters are Catholics'.[17] Although the Unionist party has splintered since then and the Catholics have unified behind a new party, the incidence of voting across religious lines is probably if anything even lower now. It is possible to imagine, if we could run the time machine back to the mid-1920s and cancel the change in the electoral system, that there might have been an alternative line of development. One could imagine a situation in which the pro-partition MPs (and perhaps also anti-partition MPs) were divided on internal socioeconomic issues, and in which there were tactical voting alliances across communal lines. One could even imagine that this could lead to inter-communal governments within a framework of pragmatic acceptance of the border.

This would not necessarily, of course, have eliminated 'nationalist' aspirations among the Catholics, even over many years. But it is interesting to note that, even after forty years—with the border as the main issue dividing the parties in Northern Ireland—Richard Rose's 'loyalty survey' in 1968 showed that only 14 per cent of the Catholic sample definitely disapproved of the existing constitutional arrangements because they wanted a united Ireland. It may be added that, although a total of a third (34 per cent) of the Catholics expressed disapproval of the constitutional arrangements, the majority of them either expressed a preference for some new political deal within the boundaries of Northern Ireland or were pretty vague about what they wanted. Perhaps even more striking is the fact that another third (34 per cent) expressed themselves satisfied with the existing constitutional arrangements and the remaining third (33 per cent) said they didn't know. If these figures mean anything, they do not suggest that the Catholics formed a unified nationalistic bloc in 1968.

However, there is no practical profit now in speculating about what might have happened in the past if the Unionist party had not succeeded in structuring the politics of Northern Ireland along a single dimension of cleavage. The current situation is obviously one of great inter-communal discord, and it is unrealistic to expect any electoral

[17] Richard Rose, *Governing Without Consensus: An Irish Perspective* (London: Faber and Faber, 1971), 235.

system to do anything except mirror it (proportional system), as against exaggerating it (single-member system).

We might offer this as a tentative generalization. It is sometimes possible to maintain a system of party alignments cutting across a line of communal cleavage. It is usually possible to shift from this to a system where parties articulate the communal cleavage. But it is extremely difficult if not impossible to move in the reverse direction, because of the primitive psychological strength of communal identification and the effects of social reinforcement on maintaining the political salience of communal identification. Sri Lanka in 1956 provides an instructive example of a case where politicians exploited the ethnic issue (Sinhalese hostility to the Tamil minority) in order to win an electoral advantage and then found that the powerful communal sentiments they had aroused could not be contained.[18]

There is, then, no realistic alternative in Northern Ireland to a system in which the interests and aspirations of the two communities are articulated directly by political parties. This being so, the choice is between repression and accommodation. The first of these was, on the whole, the chosen instrument from 1921 until 1963. The Prime Minister from 1921 until his death in 1940, Sir James Craig (Lord Craigavon), 'himself spoke of the regime as "a Protestant government" and called it "a Protestant Parliament for a Protestant People"'.[19] No attempt was made to cater for the sentiments or the interests of Catholics, and the government relied for its maintenance on the ability and willingness to coerce the minority, notably through the paramilitary Protestant force, the 'B Specials'.

In 1963 Captain Terence O'Neill acceded to the post of Prime Minister and attempted to win the allegiance rather than the coerced compliance of the Catholic minority. Unfortunately, his efforts were largely symbolic (allowing himself to be photographed with nuns, etc.), and the result was that he lost support among Protestants without gaining it among Catholics. Apart from this he pinned his hopes heavily on economic development as a solvent of traditional hostilities, but did nothing to meet the real political grievances of the Catholics: the unequal franchise and gerrymandered constituencies for elections to local authorities and the lack of any statutory protection against job and housing discrimination. At the same time the new atmosphere (reinforced perhaps by the *Zeitgeist* of the 1960s) led to a

[18] Alvin Rabushka and Kenneth A. Shepsle, *Politics in Plural Societies: A Theory of Democratic Instability* (Columbus, Ohio: Charles E. Merrill Publishing Co., 1972), 135–6.

[19] Rose, *Governing Without Consensus*, p. 92.

systematic and determined Catholic demand for improvement, in the shape of the Civil Rights movement. Illegal 'civil rights' marches, and the undisciplined reaction of the regular police (the RUC) and the B Specials, led to a deterioration in relations between the communities. After O'Neill resigned in 1969, the British government became more and more heavily involved in the affairs of the Province, and in March 1972 took direct control of it.

The lesson that has been drawn from this experience by the British political élite is that political accommodation in Northern Ireland is inseparable from the institutions of consociational democracy. Specifically, the official position of both Conservative and Labour parties, in government and in opposition, has been and remains one of exclusive attachment to the notion of a 'power-sharing executive' as the key to the salvation of Northern Ireland. The White Paper of March 1973[20] declared that the British government would devolve power on to a new Northern Ireland Assembly only on condition that there was an 'agreed understanding' to the effect that 'executive powers will not be concentrated in elected representatives from one community only'.[21] A 'power-sharing' executive was set up under the provisions of the White Paper and took office at the beginning of 1974, but it collapsed at the end of May under the impact of a general strike by Protestant workers that paralysed the Province. In spite of this, both parties remain committed to the power-sharing formula, and the constitutional convention elected in May 1975 was told in advance that its proposals must incorporate a power-sharing executive. Since the elections to the convention produced a majority firmly committed to the rejection of power-sharing the prospect is one of deadlock.

It is not my intention to suggest that I have any alternative panacea to offer. In fact my own view of the prospects is extremely bleak. The experiment in accommodation launched by O'Neill has ended in disaster. At the same time a return to the pre-1963 formula of coercion by armed and ill-disciplined Protestant forces would, after all that has happened since 1969, be the signal for a massacre of Catholics (especially in Belfast), rather than a mere return to the status quo ante.

These are the logically exhaustive possibilities for self-government in the existing Province. It is therefore hardly surprising that people should be casting around for alternatives to self-government in the existing Province. One alternative is to keep the existing boundaries

[20] Cmnd. 5259.

[21] *The Times* (21 Mar. 1973), p. 5, col. 1.

of Northern Ireland but to try to lower the stakes of inter-communal politics by integrating it completely into the United Kingdom. It would then retain local government authorities but these would have only the relatively weak powers of local authorities elsewhere in the UK—and even these might be further reduced by legally enforceable guarantees of non-discrimination in the allocation of jobs and houses by local councils. But would this save the British Army from being shot at by men of violence on both sides, and in any case is it really feasible in the long run to go in that direction in Northern Ireland, at the same time as Scotland and Wales achieve partial self-government under elected national assemblies?

Alternatively, self-government might be retained, but the area of the existing Province changed.[22] There are of course many precedents for partition and transfer of populations as ways of alleviating conflict between different communal groups in a single polity. In the case of Northern Ireland this would entail re-drawing the boundary between North and South so as to transfer to the South those tracts of the present Northern Ireland that are predominantly occupied by Catholics, and some arrangement for the evacuation of the Catholic enclave in Belfast to the South or to the mainland of Britain. The truncated Northern Ireland could then either be semi-autonomous within the UK or could form a small independent state. Although this may now be the best hope of restoring stability in Ireland, it is certainly not an easy solution. The human cost of uprooting people must never be underestimated, and in any case an attempt to implement any proposal to transfer territory from Northern Ireland to the Republic might itself occasion bloody resistance from the Protestants.

It is not necessary to pursue these possibilities further here. I mention them only to make the point that there is no easy alternative to accommodation between the two communities. It is therefore important to decide whether the British political élite is right to insist on a power-sharing Constitution as a guarantee that the Catholic minority will be accommodated. I believe that they are probably mistaken, and that this insistence makes some sort of accommodation less likely rather than more likely.

It is always tempting to seize on the visible institutional embodiments of accommodation and to attribute to them an exaggerated influence. The willingness of the leaders of the Austrian People's party

[22] See Arend Lijphart, 'Review Article: The Northern Ireland Problem; Cases, Theories, and Solutions', *British Journal of Political Science*, 5 (1975), 83–106, at 105–6.

in 1945 to offer a 'grand coalition' and the willingness of the leaders of the Socialist party to accept the offer was deeply significant because it showed that they were prepared to act in an accommodating way. But the same attitudes might well have served to create a stable polity if the People's party had formed a moderate government and the Socialist party a moderate opposition. Before 1966, when the People's Party did form a government by itself, some writers in Austria had predicted disaster if the 'grand coalition' came to an end: they had made the mistake of taking as essential the formal framework of accommodation. What really mattered was that both sides behaved with restraint: the government did not threaten the position of the opposition, nor the opposition the position of the government. (According to Bluhm,[23] the People's party sent a deputation to London to find out from the Conservative party how to conduct a one-party government!)

In an exactly similar way there can be no question that it would be enormously encouraging for the future of Northern Ireland if a party representing a substantial proportion of the Protestant vote in Northern Ireland were voluntarily to offer a coalition to a party representing a substantial proportion of the Catholic vote and if this party were to accept. For it would show in the clearest possible way that representatives of both sides recognized the necessity for reaching an accommodation.

But the same real desire to reach an accommodation might be shown by a Protestant government trying seriously to remove the grievances of the Catholics and a Catholic party acknowledging the genuineness of the government's attempt and accepting the role of 'loyal opposition'. The beginning of just such a process of normalization did in fact occur in the early years of the O'Neill period. 'The Nationalist Party . . . took half a step toward co-operation within Ulster in 1965 by accepting the title of official opposition'.[24] All this was swept away (and so was the Nationalist party) with the rise of violence, but it illustrates the way in which co-operation can develop without co-optation.

More specifically, there are two reasons why the experience of, say, the Netherlands does not support the constitutional requirement of power-sharing in Northern Ireland. The first is the difference in the basis of cleavage. This is a tricky point in the case of Northern Ireland

[23] William T. Bluhm, *Building an Austrian Nation: The Political Integration of a Western State* (New Haven and London: Yale University Press, 1973).

[24] Rose, *Governing Without Consensus*, p. 99.

because the contending groups are defined in religious terms as Protestants and Catholics. Does this not mean that we can assimilate it to the religious cleavage in the Netherlands? Richard Rose, in the interesting last chapter of *Governing without Consensus*, which briefly pursues a number of comparisons between Northern Ireland and other countries, appears to take just this line:

> Among fully legitimate European regimes, the Netherlands, superficially at least, appears to have much in common with Northern Ireland. Within Dutch society religious differences are of major political and social importance: in addition to a Catholic party there are two Protestant parties—one fundamentalist and one middle-of-the-road—and two secular parties—one liberal and one Socialist. Each of these three major *zuilen* (literally, pillars) —the Catholic, Protestant and secular—has its own schools, newspapers, television stations and other institutions. These are meant to segregate each group from their fellow subjects.[25]

In spite of this, Rose continues, 'modern Dutch politics is a record of peaceful, if sometimes incessant, bargaining about political differences among politicians who give full allegiance to the regime'.[26]

In seeking to show why, although both have 'distinctive and multiple differences', Dutch experience does not offer much comfort for Northern Ireland, Rose picks on what I suggest is a mere epiphenomenon: the number of blocs, and in particular the fact that none of them can hope to form a majority by itself:

> In consequence of the necessity of coalition government, even that most controversial of issues—the relationship of church and state in education—was capable of compromise in the Netherlands. The two Christian groups combined to assure state subsidies to separate denominational schools. Either group, in combination with the secular *zuil*, could prevent the monopoly of the other sectarian groups. In a complementary fashion, the secular *zuil* secured the creation of a secular school system, paralleling the sectarian ones. By contrast, the division of Northern Ireland people into two groups, with one permanently in the majority, removes the need or possibility of coalition government with an alternation of groups in power.[27]

This explanation, in terms of formal structural facts (fragmentation of groups, cross-cutting cleavages, etc.), is of a kind that had a general vogue in social science in the 1960s. A typical example was the reduction of a belief that one is a victim of injustice to a feeling of

[25] Ibid. 448. [26] Ibid.

[27] Ibid. 449. See also Richard Rose and Derek Urwin, *Regional Differentiation and Political Unity in Western Nations* (London and Beverly Hills, Calif.: Sage Publications, 1975), 49.

'relative deprivation' and the explanation of that in terms of the frequency of interaction with those better-off than oneself. This kind of mechanical approach has not been generally very successful and it would be surprising if it were. Contact with someone better-off than oneself is not a simple stimulus clocking up the relative deprivation count: its impact depends entirely on the framework of beliefs into which it is fitted. Similarly, the place to start in analysing the effects of social cleavage is not its formal characteristics but its content.

By this criterion, the most important thing to notice about the Dutch blocs referred to by Rose is that they are divided on religious, or more generally cultural, questions. The only reason why there is ever any occasion for dispute between blocs differentiated in this way is that at least one is seeking to use political means to expand its membership while the rest are at least committed to maintaining their existing position. In the Netherlands, the secular liberals were seeking a hegemonic position in the nineteenth century, while in Belgium, where evenly-matched Catholic and secular blocs faced one another, both were in an expansionist mood.[28] The Dutch 'pacification' of 1917 was made possible by the willingness of all parties to dig in behind their existing lines and forswear the possible gains of a *Kulturkampf*. Given this willingness to settle for a neutralization of the conflict, the obvious principle on which to do so was that of the caucus race in *Alice in Wonderland*: 'All have won and all must have prizes'. It has indeed been pointed out that the lush development of *verzuiling* in the Netherlands is the consequence rather than the cause of the settlement of 1917. There is nothing more conducive to the growth of organizations than the existence of patronage to be distributed.

The crucial point to notice is that the whole cause of the disagreement was the feeling of some Dutchmen or (until the linguistic/regional issue displaced the 'spiritual' issue) Belgians that it mattered what *all* the inhabitants of the country believed. Demands for policies aimed at producing religious or secular uniformity presuppose a concern (even if a misguided one) for the state of grace of one's fellow citizens. By contrast, the inhabitants of Northern Ireland have never shown much concern for the prospects of the adherents of the other religion going to hell. There has been no attempt at proselytizing, and the question of schools has not been a serious source of division between the communities. The Protestants use the state system, while the Catholics patronize privately run but heavily state-aided schools,

[28] See the respective contributions by Daalder and Lorwin in Robert A. Dahl, *Political Oppositions in Western Democracies* (New Haven and London: Yale University Press, 1966).

and the official representatives of both sides are apparently happy to keep it that way.[29] As far as I am aware, even in the current state of extreme hostility between the communities, the school question has not been reopened by either side. Perhaps it would even be an encouraging sign if it were.

Since Rose is surely correct in describing 'the relationship of church and state in education' as the 'most controversial issue' where religious values are at stake, we should have to be puzzled by the lack of conflict on this score in Northern Ireland if we saw the dispute there as religious in origin. But it is not. 'Protestant' and 'Catholic' are ways of designating two distinct peoples, whose divergent histories are constantly kept before each succeeding generation: the descendants of the settlers, mainly from Scotland, planted in the seventeenth century as an act of British policy, and the descendants of the indigenous inhabitants.

The two sides are communal groups identified by religious affiliation, rather than religious groups. There are two issues between them. One is the national issue: Catholics tend to be attached to the idea of a united Ireland politically separate from the rest of the British Isles; Protestants are attached to union with the UK or, failing that, an independent Ulster. It is, of course, a little too simple to say that this is a national issue rather than a religious one. One of the standing objections of the Ulster Protestants to the idea of incorporation in the Republic is the very reasonable one that the Constitution of the Republic of Ireland which was introduced by the de Valera government in 1937 (specifically claiming validity for all thirty-two counties) is avowedly a Catholic constitution. The *Derry Journal* hailed it as 'a magnificent confession of Faith',[30] which is accurate but displays a frightening lack of understanding of the kind of constitution that would really be needed to enable a thirty-two-county Ireland to live in peace.

However, I believe that it is still correct to place the emphasis on the factor of national identity for this reason. Suppose that the offending parts of the existing constitution were repealed and in addition that the right to divorce and birth control and to non-Catholic schooling were constitutionally entrenched in their place, would the Ulster Protestants drop their objections to joining the Republic? I find it very difficult to believe that they would. And if we ask why, we come back to the matter of a separate identity. This is manifested in a lack of

[29] Rose, *Governing Without Consensus*, p. 336.
[30] McCann, *War and an Irish Town*, p. 179.

sympathy for other aspects of public policy in the Republic, such as the attempt to build up the status of Gaelic, but it is not reducible to that.

The other issue dividing the two sides is that of relations between the communities in Northern Ireland, not in cultural terms but in terms of power and material advantage or disadvantage. It is incidental to the second issue that the differentiation between the communities is religious: it could just as well be in terms of language or skin colour. In principle, the basis of differentiation might be no more than descent alone, though I believe it would be very unusual for a politically salient characteristic not to be marked in some way in addition to bare descent. That Roman Catholics were discriminated against under the Stormont regime (for example in relation to jobs and houses controlled by public authorities) is not in question. But the point is that the *content* of the discrimination was in no way intrinsically connected with their religious status, as would be a ban or tax on the observance of Roman Catholic worship or some other kind of action peculiarly enjoined by the Roman Catholic religion. By contrast, a job (as distinct from being out of work) and a place to live (as distinct from no place to live) may be said to be extremely widespread objects of human desire, and in the particular context of Northern Ireland their desirability was certainly not a matter on which members of the two communities disagreed. The disagreement was about who should have them.

There is also a political implication of this kind of communal conflict as against one between religious denominations that should be noted: the greater chance of recognized leaders being in a position to 'deliver' the consent of their followers to any deal they may make where the content of the issue is bound up with organizations. If the Catholic hierarchy approves of a settlement of the school question it is hardly open to lay activists to denounce it. But the relation between the Catholic Church and Irish nationalism has been much more equivocal. Nationalist aspirations are not defined by the Church and extreme nationalists have not been deterred by denunciation or even excommunication. 'Loyalism' among Protestant clergy reflects rather than leads 'loyalism' among their congregations and in any case there is more room for Protestants to transfer from one sect to another if they find their current one distasteful politically. The Revd Ian Paisley, for example, is not a member of any established sect.

The second problem in applying the experience of 'consociational' countries to Northern Ireland is that the consociational democracies of

Western Europe are not countries in which the constitutional rules prescribe that governments should have more than a simple majority in parliament. It is one thing for the leaders of a number of parties to decide that stability requires them to join in an 'oversized' government. It is another thing altogether if the constitution requires them to join in an 'oversized' government or have no government at all. The second is a recipe for instability because it means that any group of people (whether represented in parliament or not) who want to bring down the regime know that all they have to do to achieve their end is to make an 'oversized' government unworkable.

This point seems to me to have escaped one political scientist, Cornelius O'Leary of the Queen's University, Belfast, who has explicitly defended the mandatory power-sharing provisions of the 1973 Constitution by invoking '"the politics of accommodation" or "consociational democracy" as practised in these [Switzerland, Canada, and Holland] and other segmented societies (about which there is a rapidly growing literature)'.[31] The confusion emerges plainly when he says that in these 'segmented' societies 'the political arrangements ensure that minorities do share in power'. To the extent that minorities share in power this is because the structure of electoral competition encourages it, given the existing alignments, or because the politicians choose to do things that way, either out of a sense of collective self-preservation (where the collectivity in question may be politicians versus other actors or the state versus other states) or because they believe that that is the way things *ought* to be done.[32]

Apart from the short-lived experiment in Ulster, there are two other examples of *compulsory* power-sharing that can be studied. One, which O'Leary draws attention to (while admitting that it was a failure), is the Cyprus constitution of 1959; the other is some experiments at provincial and national level during the closing years of British rule on the Indian subcontinent. These were likewise not encouraging. An analysis of these two cases concluded that:

> the most important lesson of all from experience . . . is this: power-sharing must stem from the will of the communities involved; it cannot be durably imposed upon them. . . . Should we not recognize now that *mandatory* power-sharing and democratic majority rule are incompatible aims, and that no exercise in squaring constitutional circles can replace a painfully-won desire

[31] Letter to *The Times* (4 Oct. 1974), p. 17, cols. 6 and 7.

[32] Daalder has emphasized the importance of historical traditions in this matter. See his article 'On Building Consociational Nations', repr. in McRae, *Consociational Democracy*, pp. 107–24.

by both Protestants and Catholics to work together? Consensus, not prescriptive power-sharing, is the right objective.[33]

If I am right, then, the lessons of consociational democracy have to be applied with great care in Northern Ireland. Since the parties do articulate the most salient cleavage in the society, that between Protestants and Catholics, there is, I suggest, no question that the future would be relatively bright if the leaders of the two communities saw the desirability of consociational devices (say a 'grand coalition' plus a *Proporz* for various appointive positions) and were able to carry their followers with them in instituting them. But if it were possible in the near future for leaders of both communities to carry their followers with them on such a programme, and not be displaced by more extreme rivals, the situation in Northern Ireland would not be half as bad as it is anyway. Assuming that these relatively benign conditions are not met in the current Northern Ireland, the attempt to create power-sharing by fiat is attractive but, I suggest, ultimately misguided. If, however, there is a recognition by both sides that some sort of accommodation has to be reached so as to avoid an indefinite continuation (probably of steadily increasing intensity) in the present communal violence and the disruption of ordinary life, this could be done without any special political arrangements, simply by the Protestant majority making conciliatory moves and the Catholic minority responding. Unfortunately, however, many Protestants probably believe that total victory can be achieved at an acceptable cost. So long as they continue to believe this (and it is not obviously an irrational belief) there can be no very bright prospect of accommodation in Northern Ireland.

33 H. V. Hodson, 'Cyprus: The lesson is that people cannot be forced into power-sharing', *The Times* (31 July 1974), 16.

6

SELF-GOVERNMENT REVISITED

The least-known of any of John Plamenatz's books is, it seems safe to say, *On Alien Rule and Self-Government.*[1] This may, indeed, be its first citation in a scholarly article. There are, I suspect, two reasons for this lack of influence or (probably) readers. The first is that it must have jarred the expectations of any of its three natural audiences. Those who came to it from Plamenatz's mature work hoping for more of the same must have found that it contained little, at any rate explicitly, on the history of political thought. Devotees of 'conceptual analysis', looking for something on the lines of *Consent, Freedom and Political Obligation,*[2] must have been disappointed by its relative lack of concern for definitions and distinctions. And political scientists, who would in other respects have found its substantive concerns with such topics as nationality congenial, must have been put off by its total indifference to any modern empirical literature and its substitution of 'conversations with Margery Perham' for more conventional source citations. The second reason is that it was overtaken by events. The argument was primarily focused on the case for self-government among peoples who were still under colonial rule, and within a few years of publication the argument had been settled, as far as Britain was concerned (and to a large extent altogether), by history.

In spite of these disadvantages, I would like to suggest that *On Alien Rule and Self-Government* is worth resuscitating. Indeed, I would go so far as to say that the present intellectual climate ought to be more propitious than the one existing when the book was originally published. Nobody can now read the political science of the period without squirming, so Plamenatz's disregard of it means that the book is free of what would otherwise have turned out to be an incubus. Nobody now thinks that conceptual analysis pursued in the absence of some definite theoretical problem is worth doing. And the rise of the contextualists, such as John Pocock and Quentin Skinner, has cast into a (perhaps temporary) eclipse the approach typified by John

[1] John Plamenatz, *On Alien Rule and Self-Government* (London: Longman, 1960).

[2] John Plamenatz, *Consent, Freedom and Political Obligation* (London: Oxford University Press, 2nd edn. 1968).

Plamenatz, which was essentially that of a very intelligent and serious man sitting down with a text and trying to make sense of it. But for an intelligent and serious man to sit down with a substantive problem can never be anything but a good thing, however fashions may change. As far as subject-matter is concerned, the question of topicality has by now entirely faded away and what is left is a contribution to an enduring question: that of the basis of the claims that are persistently made by the people in some area to be associated together in an independent state.

Plamenatz took the view, which one might think on the face of it rather commonplace, that there was quite a lot to be said for the principle of self-determination, and that national feeling was a force that should as far as possible be accommodated. In fact, however, such a line was rather heretical for a political theorist in Plamenatz's age-group. Native Englishmen tended not to regard the problem as salient. From the supposed end of the Irish Question in 1921 until its revival in the 1960s, problems of boundary-making and nationalism had little personal significance. This is not, of course, to say that the English are not chock-full of nationalism, but it takes the form of that unconscious assumption of superiority that so infuriates foreigners: Shakespeare is not easily mistaken for Fichte. So, Michael Oakeshott, the leading native English theorist of that generation, takes the existence of a 'society'—with all that that entails—for granted and focuses on the question of the appropriate 'arrangements' for managing such a society.

It becomes more and more striking, as the main outlines of our century begin to emerge, that an extraordinary amount of what makes it intellectually distinctive is the achievement of members of two groups: assimilated German-speaking Jews and Viennese—and, indeed, that an amazingly high proportion is owed to those in the intersection of the two sets. This is true in social and political theory as in other basic subjects. And it is hardly to be wondered at if, in the circumstances, the doctrines of nationalism and self-determination have been treated as inimical to civilized values. Self-determination reduced Vienna from the status of the cosmopolitan capital of an empire to something closer to that of a provincial town. And for assimilated Jews the rise of nationalism obviously threatened at best remarginalization after the emergence from the ghetto and at worst, under Hitler, physical destruction.

One way of meeting the situation was indeed to embrace Zionism. The rise of nationalism in others is then countered by Jewish nationalism. (This is another twentieth-century theme that can be chalked up to Vienna.) Michael Walzer, in the next generation, illustrates the way in which dedication to the cause of Israel can give rise to a general protectiveness towards the claims of the nation-state to autonomous development. This, however, was not the route followed by the distinguished Central European refugees who dominated English-speaking political theory during the quarter century following the Second World War. Karl Popper's attack on what he tendentiously called 'tribalism' (actually nationalism) in *The Open Society and Its Enemies*[3] is the most comprehensive example, but I think that one could find the same basic antipathy to the use of political means for any collective ends—the same repugnance to the idea of a society as anything except the result of individual actions in pursuit of individually defined ends—in Hayek, Talmon, Kohn, and (with more shading) Berlin.

Cold war liberalism was a response not only to the post-war situation but also to the pre-war one. The popularity of the dubious concept of 'totalitarianism' to cover not only Stalinism, Nazism, and Fascism but also (in terms such as 'totalitarian tendencies') any kind of collectivistic thinking is perhaps the best indicator. In the lexicon of, say, *Encounter* in its heyday, charges of 'totalitarian tendencies' could be deployed against a wide variety of targets with remarkable rhetorical effectiveness.

As far as I can tell, Plamenatz adhered to the tenets of what I have here called cold war liberalism except in one respect: he did not share the antipathy to nationalism or more generally to the idea that people might properly use political means to determine the conditions of their common life. As he wrote in *On Alien Rule and Self-Government*, he 'belong[ed] by birth and affection to a "backward" nation',[4] and his sympathy with the aspirations of colonial peoples in the rest of the world is evident. In this chapter I want to undertake an enquiry of a rather abstract kind that I think relates to the concerns that separated Plamenatz from his contemporaries. I want to ask how far, starting from individualist premisses, we can hope to say anything definite about the appropriate criteria for political boundaries. In particular, I want to ask if there is any way of fitting in the characteristic doctrines of nationalism that can be reconciled with individualist ideas.

For the purpose of this chapter, I understand the individualist principle to be that the only way of justifying any social practice is by

[3] K. R. Popper, *The Open Society and Its Enemies* (London: Routledge and Kegan Paul, 1962).
[4] Plamenatz, *On Alien Rule and Self-Government*, p. viii.

reference to the interests of those people who are affected by it. By a 'social practice' I mean to include social institutions such as marriage, organizations such as schools or businesses, or methods of reaching collectively binding decisions such as elections and rules of legislative assemblies. The concept of interests is notoriously controversial and the individualist principle takes on a rather different coloration depending on the interpretation adopted. Conceptions of interest fall into three categories: those that identify it with the satisfaction of preferences (perhaps only of certain kinds, e.g. for states of oneself, or only under certain conditions, e.g. perfect information about alternatives); those that identify interest with pleasure, happiness, etc., as in Bentham's statement that 'a thing is said to promote the interest, or to be *for* the interest, of an individual, when it tends to add to the total sum of his pleasures: or, what comes to the same thing, to diminish the sum total of his pains';[5] and, finally, those that identify interests with opportunities to act and with access to material advantages (Rawlsian primary goods are this kind of thing). I intend my definition of individualism to cover all three ways of understanding 'interest'. (Indeed, it is apparent that there are potentially close connections, conceptual and/or empirical, between them.) The individualist principle, understood in this way, may seem so hospitable as to exclude very little, but that appearance simply illustrates its contemporary predominance. It rules out appeals on behalf of God, Nature, History, Culture, the Glorious Dead, the Spirit of the Nation, or any other entity—unless that claim can somehow be reduced to terms in which only individual human interests appear.

From the present broad perspective, all three of the doctrines which are currently regarded in mainstream Anglo-American philosophy as the primary contenders—utilitarianism, rights theories, and contractarian theories—are to be seen as variants on the principle of individualism, as set out above. Utilitarianism in its classical Benthamite form is the most straightforward. It starts from the basic idea of individualism—that interests are what matter—and, indeed, Bentham's most general statement of the principle of utility is simply what I am callng the individualist principle: 'By the principle of utility is meant that principle which approves or disapproves of every action whatsoever, according to the tendency which it appears to have to augment or diminish the happiness of the party whose interest is in question. . . .'[6]

[5] Jeremy Bentham, *An Introduction to the Principles of Morals and Legislation* (New York: Hafner Publishing Co., 1948), 3.

[6] Ibid. 2.

Bentham then provides the simplest possible rule for bringing the interests of different people into relation with one another, namely that we sum the total interest-satisfaction over all the people concerned and adopt the criterion that one arrangement is better than another if it produces a larger total.

On the surface, rights theories stand in opposition to utilitarianism; for rights, whatever their foundation (or lack thereof), are supposed to trump claims that might be made on behalf of the general welfare. The point here, however, is that the whole notion of rights is simply a variation on utilitarianism in that it accepts the definition of the ethical problem as conterminous with the problem of conflicting interests, and replaces the felicific calculus (in which the interests are simply added) with one which does not permit certain interests to be traded off against others.

Contractarian thinking is a further twist on the basic individualist principle. We arrive at it by starting again from the general formulation and stipulating that a social arrangement may be justified only by showing that it operates in the interests of each and every participant in it. This contractarian version of individualism may take a variety of forms, depending on the way in which certain key questions are answered. Is the contract taken to be actual or hypothetical? Is weight attached to the contract itself or is the contract significant only as an indication of mutual gain? Must the mutual gain be realized or is it enough for it to be anticipated? If anticipated, what are the circumstances in which the *ex ante* estimation is to be made? And, either way, what is the standard against which 'mutual gain' is to be counted? My object in mentioning these puzzles within contractarian thinking is not to pose them as subjects for present discussion but once again to observe that common to all strands of contractarian thought is the individualist principle that interests are what matter, and that the content of political theorizing is exhausted by the question of how potential or actual conflicts of interest are to be resolved.

Each of the three varieties of individualism—utilitarian, rights, and contract—may be (and has been) advanced as an all-embracing theory. Alternatively, a contract framework may be used to derive one (or some mix) of the other two; or it may be claimed that one can derive (some version of) rights from (some version of) utilitarianism. It is beside my present purpose to follow up these possible lines of analysis. But I think it is worth pointing out that the enduring appeal of the three versions of the individualist principle can readily be explained if we appreciate that each of them speaks to a moral consideraton of undeniable power. However we want to put them together, it seems awfully hard to deny that (in some circumstances at least) the greater aggregate gain should be preferred to the less, that the pursuit of that aggregate gain should be qualified by certain limitations on the way in which people can permissibly be treated, and that one test for the legitimacy of an arrangement is reciprocity of benefit from it.

I myself find it implausible that, even taking all three together, we exhaust the sphere of morally relevant considerations. But it is important to notice that those who share my scepticism are certainly not committed to the rejection of the individualist principle. It is perfectly reasonable to take the position that moral issues should always be conceived of in terms of individual interests, while at the same time denying that the relevant criteria for adjudicating between interests are adequately reflected in any one of the three theories just discussed or in any combination of them.

Having said something about the meaning to be attached, for the purpose of this chapter, to the term 'individualist', let me now ask what illumination theorists within the individualist tradition have provided in their treatment of one question: the criteria appropriate for determining membership within a common state. I think that we can pick out three standard responses, all of which are, I must confess, so weak as to be a serious embarrassment to anyone sympathetic to the general individualist enterprise.

The first, which is simply a refusal to take the question seriously, is Locke's contract of association: people somehow got together to form a political society and this society then set up a particular form of government. There was, indeed, a certain truth obscurely embodied in this idea of a contract to set up a society, namely, that in some circumstances there may be general agreement on the boundaries of the polity, so that disagreement about the form it should take does not always have to entail reopening the question of boundaries. The notion of a contract of association thus functioned in Locke's theory to legitimate the assumption that any change of regime in England would leave the same boundaries. But, as a theory about the way to set about determining on the basis of some principle the boundaries of a state where there is in fact disagreement, some wanting one boundary and others some other, Locke's piece of fiction is obviously quite useless.

A second approach is to assert a right to self-determination. However, if this is put forward as a right of each individual, it hardly makes any sense, except as an alternative way of expressing the

Lockean consent theory; and it breaks down in just the same way wherever there is a lack of agreement because some people want one boundary and others want another—which is, of course, the only context in which there is any problem in the first place.

It is tempting, and the temptation has not always been resisted, to reformulate the individual right as a right to take part in a plebiscite to determine the boundaries of the state that is to include one's current place of residence. But what moral significance could such a right have? Suppose that a majority of the people in an area want the boundaries of that area to be the boundaries of a state, and a minority do not—whether they want to carve a separate state out of that area, attach the whole area or some part of it to another state, or whatever—the question is what claim the majority has in that case. The issue is in effect decided by the choice of the area of the plebiscite, and the minority would presumably begin by dissenting from that. Locke's contract of association, however absurd, did at least correspond to the logic of constructing states out of individual rights. What we have here is in effect an attempt to bypass the step from individuals to a collectivity.[7] We can avoid the impasse by saying that the right is to be attributed not to individuals but to nations. Thus, Article 1 and Article 55 of the United Nations Charter make reference to 'the principle of equal rights and self-determination of peoples'.[8] And the Draft Covenant on Civil and Political Rights shares with the Draft Covenant on Economic, Social, and Cultural Rights a common Article 1, whose first clause runs: 'All peoples have the right of self-determination. By virtue of this right they freely determine their political status and freely pursue their economic, social and cultural development.'[9] But attributing rights to collectivities is incompatible with the individualist principle. As Cobban wrote:

> it is one thing to recognize rights, and another to attribute them to a collective body such as a nation. Before allowing that there is a right of national self-determination, we should have to admit that the nation is a self, capable of determining itself. . . . Further, even if we accept the idea of a nation as a single self with a single will, can it have rights as such?[10]

The third position is that it is possible to specify in universal terms

[7] See Henry Sidgwick, *The Elements of Politics* (London: Macmillan and Co., 1891), 621–2.

[8] Robert E. Asher *et al.*, *The United Nations and the Promotion of the General Welfare* (Washington, DC: Brookings, 1957), 1084, 1092. The term 'nations' is already pre-empted as an equivalent to 'states'.

[9] Ibid. 1112, 1123.

[10] Alfred Cobban, *The Nation State and National Self-Determination* (London: Collins, Fontana Library, 1969, first pub. 1945), 106.

the interests that states exist to protect, and that we can deduce their appropriate boundaries from that. There are several variants. One is that, since all states ought to do the same things, it should not matter what the boundaries are. Thus, from a Lockean perspective we can say that states exist to maintain property rights (which are not created by the state—hence the prohibition on conquerors appropriating the property of their new subjects), so the laws should be the same everywhere and it ought not to matter to anyone what state his property happens to be in. Naturally, if you happen to live in a country whose government is violating the laws of nature and (say) taxing your property without your consent, you may wish that you lived in some other state; and I suppose that, if you despaired of any improvement from within, you might wish for your state to be absorbed by a better-run state. But the point is that you would be concerned with boundaries purely as a means to getting the same laws honestly administered, not because you cared who else was in the same state or because you expected differently composed states to have different policies.

Elie Kedourie's *Nationalism* argues this kind of case. He claims that, until the French Revolution declared that 'the principle of sovereignty resides essentially in the Nation', nobody believed in nationality as a basis for statehood.

> The philosophy of the Enlightenment prevalent in Europe in the eighteenth century held that the universe was governed by a uniform, unvarying law of Nature. With reason man could discover and comprehend this law, and if society were ordered according to its provisions, it would attain ease and happiness. The law was universal, but this did not mean that there were no differences between men; it meant rather that there was something common to them all which was more important than any differences. It might be said that all men are born equal, that they have a right to life, liberty, and the pursuit of happiness, or, alternatively, that men are under two sovereign masters, Pain and Pleasure, and that the best social arrangements are those which maximize pleasure and minimize pain: whichever way the doctrine is phrased, certain consequences can be drawn from it. The state, on this philosophical view, is a collection of individuals who live together the better to secure their own welfare, and it is the duty of rulers so to rule as to bring about—by means which can be ascertained by reason—the greatest welfare for the inhabitants of their territory. This is the social pact which unites men together, and defines the rights and duties of rulers and subjects. Such is not only the view of the *philosophes*, for which they claimed universal validity, but also the official doctrine of Enlightened Absolutism.[11]

[11] Elie Kedourie, *Nationalism* (London: Frederick A. Praeger, 1960), 10.

Kedourie affirms (without offering any supporting arguments) these ideas, and thus finds it incomprehensible that 'a young man of good family' like Mazzini should conspire against 'a government which, as governments go, was not really intolerable: it did not levy ruinous taxation, it did not conscript soldiers, it did not maintain concentration camps, and it left its subjects pretty much to their own devices'.[12] The only explanation he can offer is a psychological one: 'restlessness'. This kind of psychological reduction is indeed inevitable if there is no rational basis for favouring one set of boundaries over another. 'Frontiers are established by power, and maintained by the constant and known readiness to defend them by arms. It is absurd to think that professors of linguistics and collectors of folklore can do the work of statesmen and soldiers.'[13]

If we say that the task of the state is not only to enforce property rights but also to cope with externalities (or what are sometimes called spillovers), we can come up with a criterion for boundaries, namely that a state should cover an area such that (*a*) most of the externalities generated within that area impinge on the area, and (*b*) most of the externalities impinging on the area are generated within it. Thus, if a lake is potentially subject to pollution, there is, by this criterion, an a priori case in favour of the whole shore of the lake being contained within a single jurisdiction. The basic idea is still that states are in the business of protecting a standard set of interests. Boundaries, on this view, are to be determined on a technical basis, and not with any reference to the desires of the inhabitants to be associated politically with some people and not others. Such ideas are characteristic of market-oriented economists, whose only use for the state is as a remedy for 'market failure', but we can find their influence in political science too, as in this passage:

> If, because of its boundaries, a political system lacks authority to secure compliance from certain actors whose behavior results in significant costs (or loss of potential benefits) to members of the system, then the boundaries of the system are smaller than the boundaries of the problem.[14]

The central image in the book, by Robert Dahl and Edward Tufte, from which this quotation is drawn, is of an individual with a set of fixed desires for his personal security and prosperity looking around for political units that will deliver them and favouring boundaries on

[12] Ibid. 97.

[13] Ibid. 125.

[14] Robert A. Dahl and Edward R. Tufte, *Size and Democracy* (Stanford, Calif.: Stanford University Press, 1974), 129.

the basis of the 'capacities' of alternative units to do so. There is a glancing reference to the 'problem of loyalty in a complex polity that begins to transcend the nation-state',[15] but this is presented as a complication in the creation of political units based on technical criteria, although in other works Dahl has shown a good deal of understanding of the importance of communal identifications in politics.[16]

Starting from the same idea, that states should administer a common set of basic services and no more, Lord Acton, in his famous essay on 'Nationality',[17] drew the singular conclusion that it did not matter how states were composed—so long as they were heterogeneous.

> Private rights, which are sacrificed to the unity, are preserved by the union of nations. . . . Liberty provoked diversity, and diversity preserves liberty by supplying the means of organization. . . . This diversity in the same State is a firm barrier against the intrusion of the government beyond the political sphere which is common to all into the social department which escapes regulation and is ruled by spontaneous laws.[18]

Hence,

> If we take the establishment of liberty for the realisation of moral duties to be the end of civil society, we must conclude that those states are substantially the most perfect which, like the British and Austrian Empires, include various distinct nationalities without oppressing them.[19]

This 'if' is, it need hardly be said, crucial: what Acton is pointing out here is that the best way of confining a state to the pursuit of negative liberty is to ensure that its citizens cannot put together a majority for anything more positive. As Madison said in the tenth *Federalist*, the greater the area and diversity of a political authority, the more difficult it is for it to pursue 'an improper or wicked project' such as redistribution of wealth.[20] This principle has clearly worked pretty

[15] Ibid. 'Epilogue', 141.

[16] e.g. Robert A. Dahl (ed.), *Political Oppositions in Western Democracies* (New Haven and London: Yale University Press, 1966); and *Polyarchy: Participation and Opposition* (New Haven and London: Yale University Press, 1971).

[17] Lord Acton (John E. E. Dalberg-Acton), *The History of Freedom and Other Essays* (London: Macmillan, 1909), 270–300.

[18] Ibid. 289, 290.

[19] Ibid. 298.

[20] 'The smaller the society, the fewer probably will be the distinct parties and interests composing it; the fewer the distinct parties and interests, the more frequently will a majority be found of the same party. . . . Extend the sphere, and you take in a greater variety of parties and interests; you make it less probable that a majority of the whole will have a common motive to invade the rights of other citizens; or if such a common motive exists, it will be more difficult for who feel it to discover their own strength, and to act in unison with each other. . . . A rage for

effectively in the USA and, indeed, Acton's principle came to the support of Madison's in that the ethnic diversity of later immigrants frustrated class-based organization. Today it has potential applications in Western Europe. The attraction of the EEC to some of the more clear-sighted supporters of British entry was that it would hamper the attempts of British governments to manage the economy by using selective import controls or subsidies to industries while at the same time being too divided for there to be any risk of positive community-level intervention. If you are opposed to positive state action, accept that legitimacy must in contemporary societies rest ultimately on universal suffrage, and fear that majorities cannot be persuaded to share your anti-statism, the best bet is to go for a weak and heterogeneous confederation.

Unlike the contract and rights theories, this third attempt as an individualist theory of citizenship cannot simply be dismissed out of hand. Admittedly, there are objections to each formulation of it: the Lockean theory of property (recently warmed over by Nozick) is palpable nonsense; Kedourie's idea that until the French Revolution everybody believed in Enlightened Despotism is grotesque;[21] it is a fallacy to suppose, as Dahl does, that the only way of assuming that externalities can be taken care of is to have a single authoritative body covering all the producers and all the consumers of the externality;[22]

paper money, for an abolition of debts, for an equal division of property, or for any improper or wicked project, will be less likely to pervade the whole body of the Union than a particular member of it. . . .' Alexander Hamilton, James Madison, and John Jay, *The Federalist* (London: J. M. Dent [Everyman], 1911), 46–7. See also Robert A. Dahl, *A Preface to Democratic Theory* (Chicago: University of Chicago Press, 1956), esp. 29–30.

[21] 'Mayor Bilandic showed us a new and surprising side of his personality last week—he is a keen student of world history.

'In an emotional lecture to a gathering of precinct captains, he demonstrated his scholarship by comparing criticism of his administration [much criticized for its inactivity in the face of a record snowfall] with the crucifixion of Christ, the Jewish Holocaust, the enslavement of American blacks, the frequent occupation of Poland, the oppression of Latin Americans and the revolution in Iran. . . . The fact is, history bears out what Bilandic has said. The parallels between history's most famous persecutions and the attacks on his leadership are amazingly appropriate. . . .

'As for Poland, Bilandic was incredibly perceptive when he compared criticism of himself with the foreign oppression of Poland, which has been going on for more than 300 years.

'As most historians have pointed out, when Russia seized part of Poland in 1772, the Russian czar said: "Now we will plow your alleys."

'In 1914, when the Russians were driven out of Poland, Gen. Pilsudski proclaimed: "Now we will plow our own alleys."

'But in 1947, when the Russians took over again, they said: "We have come here because you have not plowed your alleys. We will plow them. We will also clear the cross walks. Rock salt for everyone!"' Mike Royko, 'Plowing into history', *Chicago Sun-Times* (18 Feb. 1979), p. 2. If Kedourie were correct, it would be impossible to explain why this is funny.

[22] If there are, say, two or three states around the lake, and pollution of the lake is bad for all of them, they have a common interest in agreeing to control pollution, and there is a built-in

and Acton's idea that the Austrian and British empires were not oppressive is pretty quaint. But, leaving all that on one side, there is nothing demonstrably wrong with the claim that the role of states should be confined to protecting the property and physical security of their citizens against invasions by one another or by others outside.

It may be objected, of course, that many important human desires that require the state for their fulfilment are going to be frustrated by such a narrow conception of the state's mission. But that does not make it incompatible with the individualist principle, which, it may be worth recalling, I defined as the principle 'that the only way of justifying any social practice is by reference to the interests of those people who are affected by it'. For the interpretation of interests that identifies them with all desires is only one conception. (Note, incidentally, that 'Nothing is to count except desires' does not entail 'All desires are to count'. A strong and widespread wish to (say) burn heretics at the stake does not have to be accepted as an interest by someone who endorses the individualist principle.)

Anyone who is content with the view of the state that flows from conceiving of interests as being confined to protection against loss and harm may stop here. It is no part of the present project to consider what kinds of moves might be made in arguing for or against alternative conceptions of interest. For those who are still with me, however, what I propose to do in the remainder of the chapter is to ask how more full-bodied conceptions of the state articulate with individualist premisses. I shall divide up the additional criteria for common citizenship that are to be considered into three kinds: first, those that are so totally at variance with the spirit of the individualist principle as to be clearly ruled out of court by it; second, those that are equally clearly compatible with the individualist principle (given an appropriate conception of interest); and, third, those that present an

sanction (assuming compliance can be monitored) in that any state violating the agreement can expect the others to abandon it too. (For a sophisticated treatment, see Michael Taylor, *Anarchy and Cooperation* (London: John Wiley & Sons, 1976), revised as *The Possibility of Cooperation* (Cambridge: Cambridge University Press, 1987).) The solution will not work where the states are not symmetrically situated, as when several states border a great international river such as the Rhine or the Danube. Here an upstream state that pollutes cannot be threatened in kind by a downstream state. However, if we are concerned only with efficiency, the well-known 'Coase theorem' reminds us that the downstream state can always pay the upstream state not to pollute the water. This is objectionable from the point of view of equity, but the downstream state may instead be able to threaten to withold some benefit from the upstream state in some other matter unless it refrains from polluting the river. In any case, the question is whether considerations such as these, even where they have a certain substance, should determine the boundaries of a state.

interesting problem and challenge us to think again about the principle of individualism itself.

First, then, what I shall call ethnicity seems to me clearly excluded by individualist premisses as a basis for political association in a state. In the several years in which I have been reading around in this area I have reached the conclusion that many apparent disagreements of substance actually reflect differences in the meaning given to words such as 'ethnicity' and 'nationality'. Let me therefore try to say as precisely as possible here what I intend to have understood by the term 'ethnicity'.

The narrowest (and etymologically primitive) definition of an ethnic group would make it equivalent to a tribe, in the sense of 'the largest social group defined primarily in terms of kinship'.[23] I shall extend it to include (as the Greeks came to do) a group defined by descent without requiring (even the myth of) common descent from a single ancestor. Ethnicity is thus to be understood as a sort of extended analogue of kinship (e.g. the references in the British Press to Rhodesian Whites as 'our kith and kin' at the time of UDI). The essence is the conception of oneself as belonging to a common 'stock' or 'race' (either in the contemporary sense or the older sense in which people spoke of French and English 'races' in Canada). Needless to say, conceptions of ethnicity have usually been tied up with phoney biology, sociology, and history, but (unless one wants to load the dice—which it appears many scholars do) there is no need to include any of these notions in the specification.

The significant point about ethnicity is negative: that it is not (generally speaking) possible to join an ethnic group by an act of will. 'Men may change their clothes, their politics, their wives, their religions, their philosophies, they cannot change their grandfathers. Jews or Poles or Anglo-Saxons, in order to cease being Jews or Poles or Anglo-Saxons, would have to cease to be.'[24] This definition of ethnicity in terms of descent is quite compatible with the emphasis of much recent scholarship on the mutability of ethnicity: that ethnic identities can be created, can merge into more inclusive ones, or can be differentiated. The plasticity of ethnic identities that we find in Eastern Europe in the nineteenth century and in post-Second World War Africa is not a chance for *individuals* to choose their ethnicity (or only very exceptionally).[25] Nor am I intending to deny that ethnic groups

[23] Anthony D. Smith, *Theories of Nationalism* (London: Duckworth, 1971), 180.

[24] Quoted by Carlton J. H. Hayes, *Essays on Nationalism* (New York: The Macmillan Company, 1933), 249–50.

[25] For nineteenth-century Europe, see Eugene Kamenka (ed.), *Nationalism* (New York: St

are often identified by traits such as language; but the point is that the language in question is not the one the person actually speaks, but (as it is revealingly called) the 'mother tongue'.[26]

The reason why ethnicity cannot in itself be a basis for the composition of a state on individualist premisses is quite simply that there is no necessary connection between descent, which is a matter of biology, and interest, which is a matter of the fulfilment of human needs and purposes. To this extent Acton was correct: 'our connection with the race is merely natural and physical, whilst our duties to the political nation are ethical'.[27] Saying 'You're a member of the X ethnic group' cannot in itself constitute a ground for saying you should be in a state with (all of and/or nothing but) other members of the X ethnic group if, as the individualist principle holds, an arrangement can be justified only in terms of the interests of those affected by it. We can invoke God, Nature, or History if we choose but that clearly takes us outside the realm of individualism. Thus, Herder (although there is more to his ideas than this, and I shall return to him later) wrote that 'a nationality is as much of a plant of nature as a family, only with more branches' and that 'a kingdom consisting of a single nationality is a family, a well-regulated household; it reposes on itself, for it is founded by nature, and stands and falls by time alone'.[28] This appeal to what is 'natural' and the tell-tale analogy to the family are clearly in contradiction to the idea that any form of association must be referred to the test of human interests. 'Individualism, political conventionalism, and rational justification were the counterpart to the family/state distinction', Gordon Schochet wrote in his study of patriarchalism.[29] All that has to be added is that, as individualism (which in my sense includes conventionalism and rational justification) has strengthened its grip, the family has been assimilated to a voluntary association.[30] James I, in *The Trew Law of Free Monarchies*, 'insisted that, as children

Martin's Press, 1976), 13–14. For the post-Second World War phenomenon of ethnic transformation, especially in sub-Saharan Africa, see Crawford Young, *The Politics of Cultural Pluralism* (Madison, Wisc.: University of Wisconsin Press, 1976).

[26] Cf. Kedourie, *Nationalism*, pp. 71–2: 'a nation's language was peculiar to that nation only because such a nation constituted a racial stock distinct from other nations'. (Kedourie rather characteristically equates the 'racial' theory with Nazism.)

[27] Acton, *History of Freedom*, p. 292.

[28] R. R. Ergang, *Herder and German Nationalism* (New York: Columbia University Press, 1931), 243, 244–5.

[29] Gordon J. Schochet, *Patriarchalism in Political Thought* (New York: Basic Books, 1975), 76.

[30] See David Gauthier, 'The Social Contract as Ideology', *Philosophy & Public Affairs*, 6 (1977), 130–64. Although contractarian thinking is only one form of individualism, much of Gauthier's analysis applies to individualism in general rather than the contractarian variant in particular.

could not rise up against their fathers even when their acts were wicked or foolish, so subjects could not resist their rulers'.[31] Clearly, the antecedent no longer holds, and the Swedes have, quite consistently, begun to think of giving children the right to shop around for alternative parents if they don't get on with their biological parents.

I went to some trouble to give a precise definition of ethnicity because I wanted to ensure that in my usage ethnicity would be distinguished from nationality. For the next stage in my argument is that nationality is a basis for the composition of states that is unambiguously compatible with the individualist principle. However, to anticipate the third stage of the argument for a moment, I shall go on to qualify this by drawing attention to some manifestations of nationalism that pose problems for the individualist principle.

The question is, then: 'What is a nation?', and the answer I wish to employ is the subjective one that Renan gave in his famous lecture with that title.

> A nation is a grand solidarity constituted by the sentiment of sacrifices which one has made and those one is disposed to make again. It supposes a past, it renews itself especially in the present by a tangible deed: the approval, the desire, clearly expressed, to continue the communal life. The existence of a nation (pardon this metaphor!) is an everyday plebiscite; it is, like the very existence of the individual, a perpetual affirmation of life.[32]

More austerely, we may take Max Weber's definition of nationalism as 'a common bond of sentiment whose adequate expression would be a state of its own, and which therefore normally tends to give birth to such a state'.[33] My only reservation about calling this subjective is that subjectivity is often confused with arbitrariness. But a sentiment of common nationality is not something people just happen to have. Loyalty to a nation—a wish for it to have a state if it does not have one, a wish for it to continue to have one if it does have one, and a willingness to make sacrifices to those ends—tends to grow out of a habit of co-operation between different groups within the nation. For this gives rise to stable expectations about future group behaviour, and especially to some degree of trust that a concession made today without a precise quid pro quo being specified will be reciprocated at some future time, when the occasion arises.

[31] Schochet, *Patriarchalism*, p. 87.

[32] Ernest Renan, 'Qu'est-ce qu'une nation?' in Louis L. Snyder, *The Dynamics of Nationalism* (New York: Van Nostrand, 1964), 9–10.

[33] Hans Kohn, *The Idea of Nationalism* (New York: Macmillan, 1946), 583 n. 16.

Scholars who have packed into the concept of the 'nation-state' such things as an integrated economy, common social institutions, and a single status of citizen have often been motivated by suspect ideas about 'political development', but I think we can say simply that the lack of such factors—feudal relations, an estates system, or a Furnivall-type 'plural society', for example[34]—must inhibit the development of habits of co-operation, mutual trust, or fellow-feeling. The same goes for such matters as common language or common culture: they are predisposing conditions but not necessary conditions. It is a commonplace that trust and co-operation are facilitated by communication—which is not only a question of language but of shared outlook. (Thus, it has been found that letting people talk together—about anything—before playing an *n*-person prisoners' dilemma game increases co-operation.[35]) We can also understand how it is that the sheer survival of a state over a long period tends to bring about a sense of common nationality among those within its territory. The experience of co-operation tends to create a preparedness to co-operate in the future. As Weber observed, nations without states often formed political units—or more precisely were formed by political units—at some time in the past.

There is a tendency in the literature, I find, to assimilate the nation to either the state or the ethnic group.[36] Reducing the number of elements to two in either way leads to strange consequences. Thus, Reinhard Bendix, in *Nation-Building and Citizenship*, appears (although I can find no explicit definitions) to regard a nation-state as a state that successfully claims sovereignty in the Bodin/Hobbes sense (see especially chapter 4). A nation-state is, it seems, one with 'a minimum of long-run stability, that is, minimal agreement concerning the rules that are to govern the resolution of conflicts'; but it should be noted that this 'agreement' is hardly equivalent to what I am calling a sense of nationality, for Bendix also writes just before that:

Only the total disloyalty or ostracism of a section of the population is a genuine hazard to the underlying agreement of such a community, though

[34] For Furnivall, see Leo Kuper and M. G. Smith (eds.), *Pluralism in Africa* (Berkeley: University of California Press, 1971); and M. G. Smith, *The Plural Society in the British West Indies* (Berkeley: University of California Press, 1974).

[35] Robyn Dawes, 'Experimental Analysis of Commitment to Group Benefit in a Commons Dilemma Situation' (Paper presented to The American Political Science Association meetings, Sept. 1976, at Chicago). See also Anatol Rapoport, 'Prisoner's Dilemma: Recollections and Observations' in Anatol Rapoport (ed.), *Game Theory as a Theory of Conflict Resolution* (Dordrecht: D. Reidel, 1974), 17–34, esp. 22–3.

[36] Smith, *Theories of Nationalism*, p. 176.

coercion can make a nation-state endure even in the presence of that hazard to its foundations, as South Africa demonstrates.[37]

If South Africa constitutes a 'nation-state' then indeed the idea of a 'nation' has no independent content. A nation-state is simply a state in which the government is able to make its writ run within its territory. (This identification of 'nation' with 'state' is quite common, as in the name of the United Nations Organization, which is neither united nor made up of nations.)

Going in the other direction, Karl Popper's hysterical attacks on nationalism in *The Open Society and Its Enemies* (especially chapters 9 and 12) presuppose that the only basis of nationality is some kind of bogus claim that nations are natural:

> The attempt to find some 'natural' boundaries for states, and accordingly, to look upon the state as a 'natural' unit, leads to the *principle of the national state* and to the romantic fictions of nationalism, racialism, and tribalism. But this principle is not 'natural', and the idea that there exist natural units like nations, or linguistic or racial groups, is entirely fictitious.[38]

The assimilation of nationality to ethnicity is also illustrated by Orlando Patterson's book, *Ethnic Chauvinism*, though he confuses the issue even further by treating ethnicity as a matter of descent-group but then identifying it with common cultural characteristics, thus finishing up with the assertion that 'the idea of the nation-state is the view that a state ought to consist of a group of people who consciously share a common culture'. Therefore, in terms of this definition, 'Britain, the United States, Canada, and Switzerland are not nation-states. Ireland, France, and most of the other European states are nation-states; so is Japan.'[39] Assuredly, 'Britain was never a unified tribal or cultural entity';[40] but this is not equivalent to denying that Britain has been a nation, except on the basis of Patterson's peculiar conception of nationality. Similarly, if America and Switzerland are not nations, what are they? They are, of course, states, and that would apparently be Patterson's answer; but surely that is not all we can say about them. To share a state with someone is after all merely to recognize a legal fact. Surely Swiss or Americans share more than that: what they share is precisely nationality.

[37] Reinhard Bendix, *Nation-Building and Citizenship: Studies of our Changing Social Order* (London: John Wiley & Sons, 1964), 22.

[38] Popper, *Open Society*, i. p. 288 n. 7.

[39] Orlando Patterson, *Ethnic Chauvinism: The Reactionary Impulse* (New York: Stein and Day, 1977), 80.

[40] Ibid. 75.

Patterson's list of 'nation-states' is also dubious. Presumably even he could not face the paradox of denying that France is a nation; but it is hardly a state inhabited by a single (even mythical) descent-group, and even on the criterion of common culture it was a nation before it could seriously be described as culturally unified:

In 1876, a student at a Teacher's College in Limoges couldn't say more than two words about Joan of Arc; as late as 1906, only one military conscript in four could explain why July 14 was a national holiday. When the Marseillaise was written, most Marseillais barely spoke French. At the time of the Third Republic's founding, French was a foreign language for over one-quarter of the population.[41]

For the reasons already set out, one would indeed expect an increase in cultural unity to bring about a higher level of identification with all one's fellow countrymen, and a tendency to weaken loyalties to smaller units. The only point to make is that cultural unity is not *identical* with nationhood. As far as Ireland is concerned it is important to recall that Irish nationalism in the eighteenth and nineteenth centuries was focused on all the people of Ireland: there were Protestant as well as Catholic Irish nationalists (including Parnell and Yeats) though the mass of votes came from Catholics.[42] The effort to create an Irish nationality failed, and politics in Ireland developed along ethnic lines, producing the Ulster problem. But it is too easy to say that it was bound to fail. Again, we need, in order to talk about the phenomena, to be able to distinguish between nationality and ethnicity.

We can see how both the statist and the ethnic definition of nationality bedevil analysis by thinking about the new states in sub-Saharan Africa that inherited the boundaries originally created by the European colonial powers. These boundaries were either drawn as straight lines on a map or followed the lines of rivers. Since in Africa rivers act as a means of bringing communities together rather than separating them, both methods of boundary-creation had the same effects. They split ethnic groups between different territories and brought together in a single territory members of different ethnic groups.

What, then, would be involved in making such territorial entities into nations? According to the statist conception, all that is needed is

[41] Peter Gourevitch, review of Eugene Weber, *Peasants into Frenchmen: The Modernization of Rural France, 1870–1914*, *The American Political Science Review*, 72 (1978), 1140.

[42] See Kohn, *Idea of Nationalism*, pp. 467–74, for the United Irishmen.

that the successor regime should succeed in filling the shoes of the colonial administrators by maintaining 'law and order' and suppressing separatist movements. According to the ethnic conception, on the other hand, creating a nation, so far from being relatively easy, is impossible: the whole idea is an absurdity. According to Patterson, 'the idea of the nation-state was . . . an astonishingly stupid one in these states'.[43] Obviously, if nationality is the same as ethnicity, this is undeniable. But, rather than lunge around in this way, I suggest that it would have been better to ask whether the stupidity does not lie in Patterson's interpretation.

Patterson's alternative to the nation-state is what he calls the juridical state. This is rather ironic in someone who regards 'reactionary' as a term of abuse, since he is in effect calling for a return to the *ancien régime*, under which 'the state was a juristic and territorial concept', defined in terms of a ruler and the land over which he ruled, rather than as the embodiment of a political community.[44] Patterson claims that such a state could have 'referential symbols': 'A state's flag is such a symbol. So are symbols such as a monarch, or titular head of state, or such ritual symbols as independence day celebrations.'[45] But a symbol presumably must be a symbol *of* something. Why should anybody form an attachment to an administrative apparatus with a monopoly of legitimate force within a certain territory? Symbols like this would be infused with life only if they became symbols of the nation rather than symbols of the state: what is important is not the machinery of government but that the people should have a sense of shared political destiny with others, a preference for being united with them politically in an independent state, and preparedness to be committed to common political action.[46]

I hope that, once nationality has been distinguished from ethnicity and statehood, it is not necessary to take a lot of time to belabour the advantages, from an individualist perspective, of nation-states over states that do not satisfy the principle of nationality. First, given the definition of nationality with which I am working, it is a necessary truth that a nation-state fulfils the aspirations of those who belong to the nation embodied in the state. Second, the presence of fellow-feeling obviously facilitates co-operation on common projects and

[43] Patterson, *Ethnic Chauvinism*, p. 82.
[44] Cobban, *Nation State*, p. 35.
[45] Patterson, *Ethnic Chauvinism*, pp. 83–4.
[46] See, for a sensitive discussion of what is really entailed in 'nation-building' (as distinct from state-building), W. T. Bluhm, *Building an Austrian Nation: The Political Integration of a Western State* (New Haven and London: Yale University Press, 1973).

makes redistribution within the polity more acceptable. (This is in effect the obverse of the Acton/Madison case in favour of heterogeneity.) Both of these points were taken account of by Bentham, who defined national patriotism as 'sympathy for the feelings of a country's inhabitants, present, future, or both, taken in the aggregate', and insisted that 'as devotion to the commonweal, and especially, to its improvement and reform, national patriotism can be of great service in promoting the greatest good of the greatest number'.[47]

Moreover, as I have already remarked, if trust and understanding have developed between the members of a state, this makes it more possible to carry out policies that apply universalistic criteria and have the result of helping certain regions or groups more than others, because there is some expectation that other policies another time will have the effect of benefiting other groups. Trust might be defined as the willingness to wait: hence the impossibility, according to Hobbes, of covenants in a state of nature. In all kinds of different cultures, paying back gifts or services too quickly is regarded as a refusal of social relations, and in traditional Irish peasant society, where loans among neighbours were common, the first thing one did upon falling out with somebody was to pay off any outstanding loan.

If we put together the lack of sympathetic attachment to the interests of all those within the polity and the lack of trust in the willingness of others to reciprocate benefits when the need arises, we can see why policies such as those designed to help big cities get diluted in the US Congress until they are so non-selective as to be virtually useless. We can also understand how rational decision-making in countries such as Belgium or (pre-civil war) Lebanon is bedevilled by the political necessity of matching each benefit for one group by an exactly equal one for the other(s)—whether it makes sense as an efficient use of resources or not.

What can be said on the other side, from a similarly broad utilitarian standpoint? Sidgwick, who laboured under the moral and intellectual handicap of being a Liberal Unionist, offered several considerations in *The Elements of Politics* in favour of the 'forcible suppression' of any attempt of a national group to secede 'merely on the ground that the interests of the seceders would be promoted or their sentiments of nationality gratified by the change'. There would have to be 'some serious oppression or misgovernment of the seceders by the rest of the community,—i.e. some unjust sacrifice or grossly incompetent

[47] Carlton J. H. Hayes, *The Historical Evolution of Modern Nationalism* (New York: Macmillan, 1950), 128.

management of their interests, or some persistent and harsh opposition to their legitimate desires' (where presumably suppressing their national aspirations does not count).[48]

Sidgwick's arguments boil down to four. First, the state may be concerned for its security 'either through increased danger of war from the addition of the seceding community to the number of possible foes, or from the mere loss of strength and prestige'.[49] Second, there may be a minority within the territory that is opposed to the secession. Third, the loss of the seceding district might be specially serious, from its containing mines or other natural resources, in which the rest of the state's territory was deficient.[50] Finally, 'over and above these calculations of expediency, justifying resistance to disruption, we must recognise as a powerful motive the dislike of the community from which the secession is opposed to lose territory that has once belonged to it, and to which it has a claim recognised by foreigners'.[51]

The last of these points raises in an acute form the question of whether we wish to employ a version of the individualist principle that counts all desires equally if they are of equal strength—the desire to speak and the desire to suppress another's speech, the desire to be free and the desire to oppress, and so on. In any version of the individualist principle that I should be prepared to take seriously, there would have to be some discrimination according to the worth of different desires, and I should therefore regard the desire to hold territory for no reason other than that one has a strong desire to do so as morally irrelevant.

The other three arguments have some force but would presumably be just as strong in defending the annexing of territories against the wishes of a majority of their inhabitants so long as it would increase military security, accord with the wishes of a minority, or make available raw materials. Just about every international atrocity of the past two centuries could be justified on one or other of those grounds —and usually was. Rather than accept Sidgwick's arguments, therefore, I think that we should advocate changes in the international regime that would reduce the importance of ownership of territory for military security and access to natural resources. The problem of minorities is, of course, an intractable one; but if one accepts Sidgwick's claim that a minority loyal to the larger state should have its wishes respected even if this entails overriding the wishes of the local majority, how is one to condemn Mussolini's claims on Dalmatia or

[48] Sidgwick, *Elements of Politics*, p. 217.
[49] Ibid. 218.
[50] Ibid. 218–19.
[51] Ibid. 219.

Hitler's on Czechoslovakia? Only, it would seem, by sanctifying the status quo; but I can see no reason why, if every other relevant factor is the same, force used to defend the status quo is more morally legitimate than force used to change it.

Manifestly, these questions cry out for more careful treatment, but I hope that I have established what I set out to, namely, that there is a strong prima facie case on individualist premisses for drawing state boundaries so that they correspond with nationality, as I have defined it. I now want, in conclusion, to take up the aspect of nationalism that seems to me to pose some problems for the individualist principle. This is cultural nationalism, the core of the romantic nationalism of the late eighteenth and early nineteenth centuries.

By no means all the claims that might be associated with cultural nationalism appear to me to create difficulties for individualism, and I shall begin by disposing of two that do not. First, there is nothing contrary to the individualist principle in saying that cultural similarity is a good basis for association. Anne Cohler, in her book *Rousseau and Nationalism*, treats similarity as a 'non-political' factor and draws all kinds of horrendous implications from such a factor's being the basis of political association.[52] Yet there are two quite straightforward advantages in cultural similarity. First, there is a strong causal link between cultural similarity and trust. Hans Kohn quotes Rudyard Kipling's poem 'The Stranger' as an illustration of a 'primitive feeling'.[53] But there is nothing primitive in the idea that the ability to interpret the behaviour of other people depends on a mass of shared understandings.

A second reason for having political units that are as culturally homogeneous as possible is that the provision of public goods is more feasible and their funding from tax revenues more equitable the more similar the tastes of the public. Again, this is simply the same analysis as Acton's, with the opposite conclusion: Acton favoured heterogeneity to avoid any collective action beyond the bare minimum of 'law and order'; but if one takes the view that it is appropriate for states to provide collective benefits, especially where they are 'non-excludable' so that it would otherwise be difficult to raise the money for them, then it clearly follows that the more homogeneous the taxing unit the more scope there is for collective provision. It should, however, be said that this point bears on tax and service-provision units rather than on states, and could be met by making subordinate

[52] Anne Cohler, *Rousseau and Nationalism* (New York: Basic Books, 1970).
[53] Kohn, *Idea of Nationalism*, p. 5.

units correspond to areas with different cultures. Even where cultural differences do not cut along convenient geographical boundaries, it is possible to go some way towards public provision for each cultural group by having each person pay a tax (thus avoiding the 'free rider' problem), but permitting each to designate whether the money is to go (say) to a Catholic or Protestant school system or television system, as in the Netherlands. Thus, the public goods argument for a culturally homogeneous state is not very strong in itself.

As far as linguistic homogeneity is concerned, we can again emphasize the relation between communication and trust, and press the view that, for democratic politics to work, the citizens must be able to communicate with one another, and must have access to the same forums of political debate. This was one of the bases of J. S. Mill's endorsement of linguistically defined frontiers, in *Considerations on Representative Government*; but Mill did not make it sufficiently clear that the rationale of linguistic homogeneity here has nothing to do with the usage of language (in the form of 'mother tongue') to establish ethnic group membership, that is to say, nationality in the 'objective' sense in which the sentiments of the people concerned do not count. The California Supreme Court has dealt a blow to this conception of the requirement of intercommunication by permitting the registration to vote of citizens lacking the ability to speak English, and it is quite likely that the requirement of competence in English for naturalization will come under attack in the courts in coming years. The basis for the California decision was that there were (in the Los Angeles area, where the case was brought) a sufficient number of Spanish newspapers, magazines, and television channels to enable monoglot Spanish speakers to collect enough information to be in a position to cast an informed vote. The model underlying this decision is clearly that of the voter having fixed interests which he looks around for a means of satisfying through the political system. The idea that there is an overriding collective interest in the maintenance of a single political community among those formally entitled to take part in political affairs is lacking in such reasoning. One can hardly avoid asking oneself what is the expected longevity of a political system in which the norm of politics as a means for the pursuit of individual interests (rather than as a process in which the conception of one's interests is constantly open to modification through societal communication) has penetrated so deeply that one of the most respected courts acts on it.

The aspect of cultural nationalism that seems to me to create some problems within the individualist paradigm is the claim that the state should be used to preserve the culture of the nation as it has come down and transmit it to the next generation. There are two variants on this which, whatever their merits, do not run into conflict with the individualist principle as I define it. The first is the one that Rousseau advanced in the *Considerations on the Government of Poland*. As Judith Shklar has emphasized, 'quite unlike the later nationalists Rousseau did not believe that the national self had any basis in nature'.[54] But he regarded it as essential for a country like Poland to have a national identity distinct from all others, and insisted that the educational system should stress national peculiarities, even if they were quite devoid of intrinsic value.

Rousseau's advice has begun to be taken in recent years by the governments of some Third World countries, which

> have discovered that independence must be taken a stage further [than that of formal political independence] into the cultural fold and pressure must be placed on the radio and television companies (which are normally state-owned) and on the newspapers (which are state-influenced and sometimes state-owned) to indigenize their output, to play down the imported entertainment material and emphasize local news, local and regional culture, indigenous entertainment.[55]

This may be regarded as the obverse of the notion that cultural uniformity within the country makes for the kind of solidarity necessary for politics to work smoothly: the idea here is that difference from other countries also helps. It may be said that this other side is a good deal more sinister in that it seems inescapably bound up with the view that states are to be defined as being in (actual or potential) conflict with others. The situation of Poland in the eighteenth century was perhaps desperate enough to warrant extraordinary measures to play up national peculiarities. The conflict with neighbours was only too apparently present. But it seems hard to justify the fomenting of national peculiarities for purely political reasons as anything but a response to a dire threat of national extinction. The point for our present purpose is, however, that there is no difficulty in seeing how, if the appropriate factual assumptions are supplied, cultural nationalism can be derived from individualistic rather than holistic premisses, since it can be argued to be conducive to individual interests.

The other notion of cultural nationalism that is consistent with the

[54] Judith N. Shklar, *Men and Citizens* (London: Cambridge University Press, 1969), 161.

[55] Anthony Smith, *The Geopolitics of Information: How Western Culture Dominates the World* (New York: Oxford University Press, 1980), 38.

individualist principle is that of cultural imperialism. If you believe that German culture is better than Slav or that European culture is better than that of the 'natives' of India or Africa, in the sense that it is better *for people*, then you could deduce a 'civilizing mission' for the bearers of the superior culture from individualist premisses. This should perhaps count as another variant on the theory that it does not matter what the boundaries are so long as those within them are culturally heterogeneous: that it is a positively good thing for the culturally 'more advanced' to dominate the more 'backward races'. Acton, indeed, believed this too, and much of the essay 'Nationality' is devoted to that theme.[56] It is a common idea among Victorian liberals: we can also find it in Mill and Sidgwick, for example. Clearly, in order to make this go, from an individualist standpoint, one must have a conception of interest that detaches it from preference, since 'natives' have usually had the poor taste to resist colonization. Most of us lack the certainties of the Victorians that we know what is best for alien peoples, though Americans seem to have continued to struggle with the White Man's Burden long after the European powers gave it up. Anyway, there is no need here to evaluate the theory of cultural imperialism. All we have to do is to note that, again with suitable adjuncts, it can be fitted into the individualist framework.

The version that does cause trouble is, ironically, one that is neither manipulative for ulterior political ends like Rousseau's nor arrogant like that of the cultural imperialists. This is the idea that each culturally distinct group has a legitimate interest in maintaining the integrity of that culture and passing it on intact to the next generation. Notice that this is different in a basic respect from either of the views just canvassed because it posits that people attach an intrinsic value to their own culture. On Rousseau's theory, it would be perfectly all right to assimilate to a different culture if this were politically necessary. Separate cultures are important only as the underpinnings of separate polities. And on the cultural imperialist theory it would be positively desirable if the culture to which one was assimilating had a language capable of handling more complex discriminations and a richer

[56] As well as the cultural imperialist strand, one also has to take account of the Roman Catholic strand in Acton's thought. This comes out more clearly in another essay, where he wrote: 'Thus the theory of nationality, unknown to Catholic ages, is inconsistent both with political reason and with Christianity, which requires the dominion of race over race, and whose path was made straight by two universal empires. The missionary may outstrip, in his devoted zeal, the progress of trade or of arms; but the seed that he plants will not take root, unprotected by these ideas of right and duty which first came into the world with the tribes who destroyed the civilisation of antiquity, and whose descendants are in our day carrying those ideas to every quarter of the world.' Acton, *History of Freedom*, p. 247.

literature. The view in question is, however, distinct from both of these. According to it, my culture is best for me and yours is best for you. Each of us should preserve and transmit our own culture and respect the culture of others.

Now, it is quite clear that much resistance to assimilation can be related to (whether 'accounted for by' is another question) economic advantage. Cultural nationalism produces 'jobs for the boys', because the criteria for becoming a schoolteacher or a civil servant change so that, instead of competing at a disadvantage in a second language, the members of the newly enfranchised language are at a comparative advantage. But it is impossible to explain the whole phenomenon in this way. Assimilation over a generation or so can be perfect, so that the disadvantage would be transitional: in Belgium, for example, part of the tension in linguistic politics arose from Dutch-speaking parents in the Brussels area choosing to send their children to schools in which French was the language of instruction so that they could obtain better jobs in a French-speaking environment. The Fleming concerns taken up collectively through political action were not for the well-being of individual Flemings, many of whom were happy to have their children assimilate to French, but for the maintenance of the Fleming identity and culture. Similarly, in Quebec, one may explain in terms of self-interest the explosion of pressure on firms to create promotion opportunities for French speakers in the 1960s and 1970s. However, the same self-interest would dictate discouragement of assimilation to French among the rest of the population, yet the current education policies are designed to produce assimilation. Thus, there is (I almost apologize for having to say it) a desire for a French-speaking province over and above the economic considerations.

The school of German nationalism stemming from Herder is the obvious place to look for the arguments. I have already cited Herder's notion of nations as natural growths, but his primary concern, as I understand it, was with the idea that 'the individual can attain his highest self-development only in the life of the group as a whole'.[57] Clearly, if it were true that Germans (say) were naturally (in the sense of biologically) suited to German language and German culture, it would be easy to see why it was important to stick to them. It may be that some people (perhaps including Herder) said things like this, though I suspect that we tend to read into them more differentiated ideas than they had, but anyway such an idea is too stupid to be worth

[57] Ergang, *Herder*, p. 248.

attention. Even if we drop any such notion of the biological basis of particular cultures, we can of course agree that as a matter of biological necessity an individual, to flourish, must grow up and live in *some* culture.[58] But that still leaves us with the question of why it is worth trying to protect one's own culture from being swamped by outside influences—as many people believe it is—and worth trying to ensure that subsequent generations grow up sharing its ideas, reading its literature, and so on.

One possible answer would be that in practice cultural mixing is almost always for the worse. Rousseau's attacks on 'cosmopolitan' culture would obviously align him with this claim. In a contemporary version, it might be argued that what will tend to be picked up are the quickly gratifying, non-demanding, effort-saving, bland, and tasteless aspects of other cultures, at the expense of the more physically, intellectually, and morally strenuous features of the indigenous culture. This is the root of the widespread antipathy around the world to 'Americanization'. And the key to the invasive success of American culture is, perhaps, that it is itself the product of generations of assimilation and has thus selected out for exactly the features mentioned above: American food is notoriously lacking in sharp flavour or distinctive texture; American entertainment tends to require little cultural context to appreciate it; and even American language is designed to minimize the need for a grasp on grammar, so that its sentences are typically assembled out of pre-formed phrases.[59]

I find this argument broadly persuasive, and thus sympathize strongly with the efforts of weaker countries to control the flow of communications across their borders—especially restricting the import of American television programmes.[60] The standard American criticisms of this seem to me to miss the point that, because tastes are changed by exposure, individual 'freedom to consume' cultural artefacts gives rise over time to a pervasive cultural drift within the society, which is a collective phenomenon and a legitimate subject of collective concern and regulation. Of course, to say that something is

[58] See Mary Midgley, *Beast and Man: The Roots of Human Nature* (Ithaca, NY: Cornell University Press, 1978), 285–305. 'A culture is a way of awakening our faculties. Any culture does this to some extent. People proficent in one culture can usually make sense of another. There is no prison. We can always walk on if we want to enough. What we cannot do is something which is no loss—namely be nobody and nowhere. I do not mean that some people may not be very unlucky in their culture, either because it is generally bad, or because it suits them badly. But this is still nothing to the misfortune of having no culture at all' (p. 291).

[59] See Tibor Scitovsky, *The Joyless Economy* (New York: Oxford University Press, 1967).

[60] 'The free flow of one section of the globe merely swamps the culture of others.' Smith, *Geopolitics of Information*, p. 37.

a legitimate matter for political intervention is not to underwrite any and every form of intervention, and most actual ones are open to criticism. But the point is simply that, on a broad conception of interest, individual interests are certainly at stake here.

The argument up to this point is that, whatever the existing culture is, it is probably better, not than alternative cultures, but than what would most likely result from the (inevitably partial) assimilation of this one to another. As Sir Arthur Evans said of the culture of the inhabitants of Knossos, the Palace of which he had excavated, 'A poor thing but Minoan'.

Surely, however, this cannot be the whole story. Many people care a lot about the preservation and transmission of their culture as an end in itself. They see themselves as standing in a position of trust between past and future generations. This notion of a culture as something continuous through time, with those currently alive as trustees, recalls to English-speaking readers Edmund Burke. But the idea is more fully developed by the German Romantic nationalists. We can find it in Herder, but it is much more fully expressed in Fichte's *Addresses to the German Nation*, especially the eighth where he asks if the 'man of noble mind' does not 'wish to snatch from the jaws of death the spirit, the mind, and the moral sense' that he displayed in his own life? He invokes the German resistance to assimilation to Rome: 'All those blessings which the Romans offered them meant slavery to them —they assumed as a matter of course that every man would rather die than become half a Roman, and that a true German could only live in order to be, and to remain, just a German and to bring up his children as Germans.'[61] If we steer clear of the references to laws of nature and laws of divine development with which Fichte's text is strewn, we may ask whether we can make any sense of what is left from within the individualist framework.

Here again, everything has to be referred back to the crucial concept of interest. If my interest is identified with my happiness or pleasure (or any other state of myself), it must be the case that I can have no interest in what happens on earth after my death—assuming that death is the termination of consciousness. By the same token, those who are no longer alive can have no interest in what happens now. However, it seems perfectly natural to say that our interests are for states of the world rather than only for states of ourselves. If I want something to happen, I do not merely want the satisfaction of believing that it

[61] Johann Gottlieb Fichte, *Addresses to the German Nation*, tr. R. F. Jones and G. H. Turnbull (Chicago: Open Court, 1922), 132, 144.

happens; and if it happens, I have got what I want even if I never have the satisfaction of hearing about it. If it is reasonable to include in interests having certain things happen (whether one knows about them or not) while one is alive, it seems strange to draw the line at one's death.[62] If interests can include states of the world after one is dead, we have a possible way of justifying, on individualistic premisses, a collective decision to try to pass on our own culture intact, even if we believe that it could be transformed without being damaged. (It may be questioned whether such a judgement could be made, since the criteria for damage have to come from somewhere and the obvious candidate is the existing culture, in which case all change will be bad automatically. However, I assume that it is possible to gain some degree of detachment from one's culture and to conclude that some changes impoverish it and others enrich it.)

Obviously, the move to bring cultural nationalism within the individualist fold depends on the actual desire on the part of past and present people to pass on their culture. If that desire exists (or existed), we can talk about an interest and thus get to the answer that cultural transmission satisfies individual interests. What we cannot do, however, is say that people ought to have an interest in passing on their culture even if they do not in fact have any such interest. We could try to persuade them that their lives would take on greater significance if they were to care about the texture of their descendants' lives. But if they still do not care, we have, I take it, reached the outer bounds of individualistic political philosophy. If we want to say that they are *wrong* not to care, then we have to be prepared to say that cultures have a value of their own and that human beings are, as it were, their biological instruments. At a pinch, I could perhaps bring myself to believe this, but on the whole I am gratified to find how far one can get without having to resort to this kind of move.

What I have been saying in these last pages presupposes that it does make sense to talk about people having interests that survive them, and this is, in some people's view, an odd and paradoxical notion. Let me break it down, however, into two parts. The first is the assertion that people have interests in what happens after their deaths. For example, they may want their children to be well provided for, rather than simply wanting the pleasure of believing now that their children

[62] See Joel Feinberg, 'Harm and Self-Interest' in P. M. S. Hacker and J. Raz (eds.), *Law, Morality, and Society: Essays in Honour of H. L. A. Hart* (Oxford: Clarendon Press, 1977), 285–308; repr. in Joel Feinberg, *Rights, Justice and the Bounds of Liberty: Essays in Social Philosophy* (Princeton, NJ: Princeton University Press, 1980), 45–68.

will be well provided for. This seems to me fairly incontrovertible. If it were not true, large parts of human behaviour would be simply unintelligible. The second assertion, which is what some people gag on,[63] is that when a person is dead he still has an interest in what happens. I think that Feinberg is right in supposing that, when one really thinks about it, it is actually quite hard to accept the first without accepting the second—or, to put it the other way round, the premisses required to reject the second will jeopardize the first as well.

Both are required if we wish to say that the interests of past as well as present generations are involved in cultural transmission. But only the first is required if we confine ourselves to saying that the members of the present generation have an interest in what happens to their culture in the future, including the time after they are dead. Moreover, it may be argued that we can still bring in the previous generations indirectly. For we can say that the present generation has more chance of having its own current interests with respect to what happens in the future served by future generations if it itself makes a point of carrying out the wishes that previous generations had for the future while they were alive.[64]

However, I am bound to say that for me this proposal brings out the difficulty of accepting the first assertion without the second. Suppose that those now alive (the *A*s) really care about what happens after they are dead and would like their descendants (the *D*s) to regard the *A*s' present concerns for the future as a basis for the *D*s' actions then. Why in that case should the *A*s not accept the past concerns for the present of earlier generations as a basis for the *A*s' actions now?[65] Thus, I do

[63] See e.g. Ernest Partridge, 'Posthumous Interests and Posthumous Respect', *Ethics*, 91 (1981), 243–64.

[64] This is Partridge's own answer.

[65] An illustration of this point is provided by the case of Roger Lapham, a keen golfer who wanted to be cremated and have his ashes buried on his favourite golf course—Cypress Point, on the Monterey Peninsula. 'He died in 1966, at the age of eighty-three, and Lewis, on receiving the news of his father's death, hurried out to the family home in San Francisco. Shortly after his arrival, he was informed by his brother that there had been a hitch in the plans: their mother had stated forcefully that she would not permit her husband's body to be cremated or to be buried at Cypress Point. "Under California law at that time, a person did not control the disposition of his remains," Lewis Lapham has recalled. "His executors could disregard his stipulations if they wished to. When I got together with my mother, I suggested that we have a shot of sherry—that seemed a good idea. Then we began discussing things, and I said to her, 'I don't think your position is reasonable. For example, I'm your heir and executor. What would you think if I were to disregard the instructions set down in your will?' 'You wouldn't dare,' she said. 'But consider this,' I went on. 'That is exactly what you are going to do with someone you lived with for fifty-nine years.' I suggested we have another sherry. The upshot was that my mother came round, and my father was cremated and buried on that little ridge overlooking Cypress Point, in sight of the tide rolling in on a small beach."' Herbert Warren Wind, 'The Sporting Scene: From Linksland to Augusta', *The New Yorker* (22 June 1981), 96–111, at 104.

This *could* be interpreted in 'intergenerational social contract' terms, so that the widow

not myself see that the halfway house is a satisfactory resting-point. But I offer it in case it can be shown by some further argument to be internally consistent to accept the first assertion and deny the second.

I have in this chapter traversed a large area, and I shall not attempt to summarize. Let me conclude, then, with the observation that the individualist moral theory, in its general form, is capable of generating a wide variety of alternative conclusions about the rights and wrongs of nationalism in various forms. Ultimately, the disagreements turn on the conception of interest that one plugs into the basic doctrine and on the ways of life that one believes conduce to human interests so understood. Although my main intent here has been to explore the ways in which the argument can go, my not-so-hidden agenda has been to suggest that nationalism has been given a bum rap in recent political theory, and to try to show that the efforts of the Viennese liberals to conflate ethical individualism and anti-nationalism will not withstand scrutiny.

complied with her late husband's wishes *in order to* get the son to comply with hers. But surely the way the story runs makes it clear that the crucial move is an argument from equity: that if you really care about what happens after your own death there is no valid reason for refusing to pay the same attention to the wishes that others had for what would happen after their deaths. And this is exactly the point advanced in the text.

7

EXIT, VOICE, AND LOYALTY

I

My primary purpose in this chapter is to provide a detailed critique of the internal logic of Albert Hirschman's *Exit, Voice, and Loyalty*.[1] Before doing this, however, I should like to consider briefly the phenomenon of which it is an exemplar: the 'in' book, for this raises some general questions of interest.

One important manifestation of the self-conscious professionalism of American academics is the way in which a corpus of ideas—often in severely stripped-down form—is at any given time common property. Indeed, the possession of the current stock of ideas, at least in rudimentary form, sufficient to enable references to be identified, might be said to be the badge that distinguishes the professionals and would-be professionals (advanced graduate students) from the dilettantes, the drop-outs, and the inside-dopesters.[2] The way in which the corpus is built up would repay investigation by a sociologist of knowledge, but I shall hazard a few guesses. First, the idea itself must have the dual characteristic that its essence can be expressed very simply while at the same time its ramifications are great. Second, the process of dissemination is almost certainly by word of mouth rather than by formal channels such as book reviews or footnote citations. So long as the channels of communication across and within departments exist in any case, all that is then required is a fairly widespread desire (whether normatively or prudentially motivated) to 'keep up with the field'.

The reception of *Exit, Voice, and Loyalty* points up with peculiar sharpness the difference in the workings of academic political science

[1] Albert O. Hirschman, *Exit, Voice, and Loyalty: Responses to Decline in Firms, Organizations, and States* (Cambridge, Mass.: Harvard University Press, 1970).

[2] One result of the lack of this common professional range of reference in Britain is that practising politicians, in their relations with professional political scientists, are able to regard themselves not as the raw materials but as the experts. The same phenomenon can, of course, be looked at the other way round and one can say that the unquestioned acceptance by many political scientists of the validity of the actor's point of view (which thus makes the politician's claim to expertise indefeasible) is one of the main inhibitions on the development of a distinctive discipline.

between the USA and Britain. In the USA the book became a talking-point upon publication and by now its basic ideas have entered the article literature, while at least one Ph.D. thesis is based upon their application. My impression, which is of course based on only a limited sample, is that relatively few political scientists in Britain have heard of the book and that this is not because there is some *other* book that everyone is talking about but rather reflects the fact that the phenomenon of the 'in' book does not exist.

But the absence of 'in' books is itself only one manifestation of the whole style of British political science, which is characterized by the absence in almost all areas of the subject of 'invisible colleges' composed of those actively engaged on research in this area keeping in touch by exchanging papers as well as through formal and informal meetings and visits;[3] by the lack of common reference points either in the form of a shared conception of a discipline or a shared body of ideas; and (a natural consequence of these) by a tendency to define research as 'about' some place or event or person and not in relation to problems arising from some area of the discipline.

One rather mechanical explanation which must, I think, be rejected as too simple is the 'critical mass' theory, according to which the answer lies in the small total number of academics in the subject and in particular the average size of the departments. This theory would entail that the position should have improved dramatically with the expansion of the past decade, and—to take a *reductio ad absurdum* —would predict that Oxford's sixty or more full-time politics teachers should be far and away the most active and discipline-orientated group in the country. More fundamentally, what has to be explained is why there is so little need felt for regular contact with colleagues who have similar interests. After all, a large proportion of political scientists in Britain can get to a meeting in London and back in a day, and most departments are within travelling distance of several others. Why are departments so isolated from one another, and why has the Political Studies Association failed to develop viable sections?[4] How could we explain why, if the smallness of departments or of the aggregate size of the profession were perceived as a problem, British universities should have been so behindhand in joining the

[3] D. de Sola Price, *Little Science, Big Science* (New York: Columbia University Press, 1963).

[4] One simple quantitative comparison is that the American Political Science Association, with twenty times the membership of the Political Studies Association of the UK, has about forty times the number of papers at its annual convention, and this leaves out of account the annual meetings of the regional associations, each of which regularly has more papers presented than are given at the PSA conference.

European Consortium for Political Research, which is designed precisely to get round these problems?

The general lines of the answer must, I think, be those laid down by Halsey and Trow:[5] the continuing strength of the ideal of the academic as one devoted primarily to teaching undergraduates by labour-intensive methods and spending much of the remainder of his time on academic administration of a kind that elsewhere would be in the hands of full-time administrators. This still has to be supplemented, however, by observing that the grip of such a conception of the academic role varies from one subject to another. Physical scientists are much more closely attuned to international norms of professional postgraduate training, research, and intensive communication. And even within the social sciences there appear to be variations, with political science showing a significantly more marked degree of parochialism and inertia than economics. Exactly why this should be I am not sure, but I would suggest that one relevant fact is the one referred to by Edward Shils in his essay on 'British Intellectuals in the Mid-Twentieth Century' when he wrote that 'Outside the China of the Mandarins, no great society has ever had a body of intellectuals so integrated with, and so congenial to, its ruling class, and so combining civility and refinement.'[6] This assimilation is, as Shils points out, a major contributing factor to the stability of British society. The effect on the study of politics is, however, debilitating in that a close identification with the outlook of decisionmakers is inimical to the detachment which is the necessary condition of abstraction and generalization.

To the extent that the differences in intellectual style between the countries have deep-seated cultural causes, they are not amenable to deliberate change. But it seems reasonable to suppose that something could be done to increase the level of intellectual interdependence in Britain if resources were devoted to it. The work of the American Social Science Research Council (especially perhaps its Committee on Comparative Politics) would well repay study in this context. It is, therefore, a real question whether this is a direction in which it would be desirable to move.

The pros and cons are easy enough to set out; the difficulty is to decide on their relative weight. Thus, it would seem that in principle a rapid and intensive circulation of ideas should speed up the development of the subject by allowing everyone to make use of a new idea in

[5] A. H. Halsey and M. A. Trow, *The British Academics* (London: Faber and Faber, 1971).

[6] Edward Shils, *The Intellectuals and the Powers and Other Essays* (Chicago: University of Chicago Press, 1972), 152.

his own work instead of leaving each person to struggle along on his own for many years working on some monograph until eventually the relevant work of others (also in monograph form) comes to his attention.[7] Conversely, the obvious potential disadvantage of an effective communication network is the danger of faddism: the risk that the energies of the profession may be dissipated in scrambling aboard successive intellectual bandwagons, thus crippling the organic growth processes inherent in sound scholarship.[8]

Which of these forces one regards as more significant depends, I think, on two things. The first is whether one believes that the process by which some ideas are selected and others fall by the wayside has an element of rationality in it or whether the rise and fall of ideas is to be explained either in terms of chance or in terms of power. The second is how one evaluates the actual record so far. My own inclination is to believe that, at least in the context of academic discourse, Milton was right in proclaiming the superior survival value of good ideas over bad ones, and also to believe that—if only by exciting a reaction in some cases—ideas such as cross-cutting cleavages, veto groups, the paradox of voting, the prisoner's dilemma, interest articulation and aggregation, Downsian competition, non-decisionmaking, the Olson problem, and Allison's 'three models' have served the discipline well.

My object in this chapter is to ask whether the concepts of exit, voice, and loyalty (and the framework in which they are embedded) form a worthy addition to the list. My answer will be that, in spite of shortcomings in the detail of the book, Hirschman has identified and given shape to an important phenomenon.

[7] A helpful way to think about the relative effectiveness of different modes of communication in fostering the transmission of ideas might be in terms of 'reaction time'. This we may define as the average amount of time that elapses from the time when *A* has a new idea until *B* has had an opportunity to react to *A*'s idea and allow it to modify or inspire work which becomes available to *A* or some further person *C*. Consider first a system in which the prevailing mode of communication is the book. If it takes *A* an average of five years from conception to completion and another year to publication, and then an average of a couple of years before *B* hears about the book, we have a reaction time of fourteen years. In these circumstances slow theoretical development will hardly be surprising. A move to article publishing, as is now gradually taking place in Britain, cuts down the reaction time greatly, to perhaps four years—two years from inception to publication for *A* and *B*, and no intervening time, provided that *B* reads the journal *A* publishes in. But clearly the existence of a dense network of personal communications, face to face and by circulation of manuscripts, makes reaction times of a matter of months quite easy, while the attainable minimum from *A* to *B* to *C* is a matter of a few seconds.

[8] I am not here intending to echo F. M. Cornford's remark that '"Sound scholar" is a term of praise applied to one another by learned men who have no reputation outside the University, and a rather queer one inside it.' *Microcosmographia Academica*, 6th edn (London: Bowes and Bowes, 1964), 19.

II

There is no doubt that *Exit, Voice, and Loyalty* has the features necessary for an 'in' book mentioned earlier: the theory can be stated in a few words, but at the same time has an unlimited range of application. The theory can indeed be stated almost out of the words in the title, as follows. There are two alternative responses to decline in firms, organizations, and states, namely exit and voice. ('Exit' simply means leaving; 'voice' means trying to get the managers to reverse the decline by complaining, protesting, or organizing internal opposition.) Loyalty affects the individual calculus by making voice, as against exit, more probable than it would otherwise have been, all else remaining the same.

'Big deal!' may well be the initial reaction to this piece of intelligence. But such a reaction would, I think, be out of place for two reasons. First, Hirschman succeeds by the use of this simple framework in drawing together a number of apparently disparate phenomena. The second reason is that the book represents a development of the 'economic' approach to political analysis. This point highlights the enormous long-run advantage to a discipline in having a core of common intellectual possessions: once a certain body of analytical material has been acquired it is possible to add to it at low cost. I shall take up these two points in turn, in the present section and the next one.

As I said earlier, the 'in' book exists, for most political scientists, not in its full complexity but in a stripped-down form. Hirschman's book, in this form, simply consists of the idea that exit and voice are alternatives. This is one of those ideas that are obvious once they are stated, but which need to be set out explicitly before they can be used to organize the unlimited body of relevant observations. Indeed, the idea that exit and voice are alternatives, and in particular that ease of exit makes voice less likely, is one that has often been put forward in particular contexts, and once one has been sensitized to the notion one finds examples of it all over the place.

Thus, to give a couple of examples that I came across: Eric Wolf, speaking of seventeenth- and eighteenth-century Russia, says that 'peasants in Cossack-dominated areas became Cossacks, thus escaping from the peasantry rather than solving the problem of peasant oppression', and Samuel Huntington has pointed out that it has been to the advantage of newly established Communist regimes in North Vietnam, East Germany, and Cuba to allow dissidents to leave, since they might otherwise cause trouble.[9] Similarly, it has often been pointed out that the internal peace of the new American republic was helped by the exodus of the supporters of the British connection to Canada, and Hirschman himself suggests that the ease with which defeated opposition leaders in Latin America can slip across the border to a culturally similar state has weakened the development of a coherent opposition.[10]

Again, Huntington has argued that 'outside opportunities for horizontal mobility (urbanization) contribute to the relative stability of the countryside in most modernizing countries',[11] and specific support for this idea is provided by a study which showed an inverse correlation between militancy and emigration from rural Italian provinces before the First World War.[12] It would be interesting to know whether there would be a similar inverse correlation between Black emigration from Southern counties in the USA and political participation by Blacks, but this would seem likely. Indeed, it is worth noticing that Matthews and Prothro, in their discussion of emigration, emphasize the point which is also Hirschman's main concern: that exit may operate as a dampener of voice and thus leave those who are left behind worse-off than they could otherwise have been. They observe that 'those who have paid some attention to this matter generally have concluded that the South is better off without these millions of Negroes', but then add that

> the allegedly benign effects of Negro emigration for the South are cast in an entirely new light when we consider its effects on the region's Negro leadership. The South will probably lose from a third to a half of its most highly trained potential leaders as a result of emigration. . . . Without leadership in adequate quantity and quality, the Negro masses will not participate in politics as frequently or as effectively as they otherwise would. The flight from the South by educated Negro youths may prove to be a major—perhaps *the* major—deterrent to the southern Negroes' full and expeditious realization of racial and political equality.[13]

The same inverse relation between geographical mobility (exit) and political participation (voice), this time in an urban setting, is sug-

[9] Eric R. Wolf, *Peasant Wars of the Twentieth Century* (New York: Harper and Row, 1969), 52; Samuel P. Huntington, *Political Order in Changing Societies* (New Haven, Conn: Yale University Press, 1968), 310–11.

[10] Hirschman, *Exit, Voice, and Loyalty*, pp. 60–1.

[11] Huntington, *Political Order*, p. 54.

[12] J. S. MacDonald, 'Agricultural Organization, Migration and Labour Militancy in Rural Italy', *Economic History Review*, 2nd ser., 16 (1963–4), 61–75.

[13] Donald R. Matthews and James W. Prothro, *Negroes and the New Southern Politics* (New York: Harcourt, Brace and World, 1966), 449, 450.

gested by one study which explicitly relates itself to Hirschman's terminology. The authors found that Blacks in Columbus, Ohio, were 'more likely to voice in response to problems than are whites of similar status who live in similar urban areas'.[14] And this can, of course, be plausibly related to the much lower chances for Blacks of moving away if they do not like the place where they live.

The sentence following that quoted from Huntington above brings in another important aspect of the exit/voice relationship. In contrast to the high rate of horizontal mobility (migration to the towns) in the rural areas, he suggests that 'there are few opportunities for vertical mobility (occupational and income) within the cities', and that this lack of mobility 'contributes to their greater instability'.[15] This, of course, immediately relates to the parallel idea, put forward for industrial societies, that the belief in the possibility of social mobility depresses support for radical political movements which offer to recast the system so as to improve the lot of the worse-off collectively.

In fact, the statement of the case in what is generally thought of as the *locus classicus* for this kind of idea is a bit more subtle than this. It still, however, falls within the exit/voice framework and thus illustrates the kind of intellectual joy-ride one can get led into by following up Hirschman's idea. For what Lipset and Bendix actually suggest is that the *supposed* possibility of exit from a poor position in the society has the effect of stultifying voice even if the individual does not himself think he will ever exit by upward social mobility; instead he exits either by vicarious social mobility (the belief that his children will do better) or by withdrawal into religion, with its promise of posthumous upward mobility, both literal and metaphorical.[16] Thus,

[14] John M. Orbell and Toro Uno, 'A Theory of Neighborhood Problem Solving: Political Actions *vs*. Residential Mobility', *American Political Science Review*, 66 (1972), 471–89, at 484.

[15] Huntington, *Political Order*, p. 54.

[16] Seymour Martin Lipset and Reinhard Bendix, *Social Mobility in Industrial Society* (London: Heinemann, 1959). The key passage runs as follows:

> Cultures which emphasize egalitarian values and the possibility of success for all, such as those of the United States and the Soviet Union, presumably expose 'failures' to greater problems of adjustment. . . . Both ['transvaluational religion' and 'high aspirations for children'] may be reviewed as a means of safeguarding society against instability. In America, for example, the depressed strata seem to have turned to evangelical religion rather than to radical politics; in Russia, where political protest is forbidden, there is also some evidence of a 'return to religion' among the poorer strata: and both societies—each in its own way—seem to place an extraordinarily high emphasis on a better life for children. It is in the societies of Europe and Asia where less emphasis is placed on equality of opportunity that left-wing political movements are strong among the lower strata—presumably because they teach that traditional inequalities can be done away with by changing the social system (pp. 262–3).

a sort of choice between voice and exit is presented by Lipset and Bendix as practically invariable: 'In general, it seems to be true that the depressed and the failures who have little hope of individual success have a strong faith either in radical politics or in an emotional religiosity, so that almost nowhere are the lower classes both moderate in their politics *and* indifferent to religion.'[17] This of course leads us on to the debate among historians as to whether Methodism operated as an alternative to political agitation in England and Wales in the first half of the nineteenth century. But I think I have already presented enough examples to illustrate the versatility and fecundity of the basic idea of exit and voice as alternative options.

Since this has been my aim in the present section, I have been content simply to show how the idea has cropped up in a number of widely differing contexts. No doubt readers will doubt some of the alleged correlations and, perhaps even more, wonder whether in some cases the same factors make for exit *and* for lack of voice among those remaining. However, such doubts (which I share) do not seriously detract from the effectiveness of the demonstration, since the fact remains that an inverse relation between exit and voice has been asserted often enough to make the phenomenon worth examination at a general level.

What is more serious is the question of the unity of the phenomenon itself. Although I have set out the cases as neutrally as possible, I hope that readers will have been becoming uneasy and asking themselves whether there is really a common process underlying all these cases, even if they are all accepted as instances of a non-spurious connection between exit and lack of voice. Unlike the other two kinds of scepticism, this one goes directly to the usefulness of the framework for analysis set out in *Exit, Voice, and Loyalty*. It is to that framework that I now turn.

III

I want to begin by asking what *kind* of analysis Hirschman offers of the relation between exit, voice, and loyalty and the effects of their interaction on the performance of firms, organizations, and states. The answer is, I think, that it falls broadly within the sphere of the 'economic approach' to the study of society.

In a book that was published in the same year as Hirschman's, I said that *The Logic of Collective Action* was 'the only book fit to rank with

[17] Lipset and Bendix, *Social Mobility*, p. 263.

Downs's *Economic Theory of Democracy*, as an exemplar of the virtues of the '"economic" approach' outside the conventional subject-matter of economics, and added: 'Both books, as may be expected in pioneering works, suffer from obscurities and ambiguities which become apparent on close examination. But it is greatly to their advantage that, unlike so many books on political and sociological theory, they stimulate and repay this degree of careful attention.'[18] If I venture to quote myself now it is because what I said there about both the strengths and weaknesses of Downs and Olson seems to me so exactly to fit Hirschman as well.

It is interesting, however, to notice that this interpretation of the significance of his work—as a contribution to the 'economic' analysis of politics—is not the one that Hirschman himself offers. On the contrary, he professes an ecumenical spirit which—fortunately for the coherence of the book—he at no point allows to get in the way of a straight 'economic' approach to the phenomena under consideration. In his Preface he says that 'this book does not use the tools of one discipline for the purpose of annexing another. As is shown particularly in the appendixes, the concepts I develop can be translated into the language of traditional economic analysis, and may possibly enrich it; but by no means do they uniquely belong there' (p. vii).[19] Leaving aside the emotive word 'annexing', the state of affairs described in the second sentence is precisely what one would expect where economic modes of analysis are being applied to political phenomena.

A little later Hirschman says that he hopes 'to demonstrate to political scientists the usefulness of economic concepts *and to economists the usefulness of political concepts*' (p. 19, italics in original). There seems to be an equivocation here on the words 'political concepts' and 'economic concepts', between on the one hand political and economic *mechanisms* and on the other hand political and economic *methods of analysis*. The sentence before that quoted clearly rests on the first interpretation: here Hirschman says that 'exit and voice, that is, market and non-market forces, that is, economic and political mechanisms, have been introduced as two principal actors of strictly equal rank and importance' (p. 19). All this says is that economists (not

[18] Brian Barry, *Sociologists, Economists and Democracy* (London: Collier-Macmillan, 1970; repr. Chicago: Chicago University Press, 1978), 24, referring to Anthony Downs, *An Economic Theory of Democracy* (New York: Harper and Bros., 1957) and Mancur Olson, Jr., *The Logic of Collective Action: Public Goods and the Theory of Groups* (Cambridge, Mass.: Harvard University Press, 1965).

[19] All quotations with page references in this form are from *Exit, Voice, and Loyalty*.

defined but presumably conventionally understood as people concerned with goods and services) need to look at non-market mechanisms such as protest; and political scientists (again not defined but presumably understood as people concerned with parties, pressure groups, states, and all that) need to look at the possibility of leaving organizations. Left open entirely by this is the question of whether both the market and non-market phenomena can be studied by using a characteristically 'economic' approach, in the second sense that I distinguished. The 'public choice' school (which started life, be it recalled, by publishing 'Papers in Non-market Decision-Making') is of course dedicated to the presupposition that 'economic' methods can cover the whole lot. And, as I have noted, Hirschman in practice proceeds on exactly the same assumption, never explicitly using any assumption about motivation that would take him outside an individualistic maximizing framework of analysis.

In its more or less formal aspects, then, the book offers two things. The first is an analysis from an 'economic' viewpoint of non-market mechanisms ('voice') affecting the quality of goods and services offered by a firm in a market situation. The second is an analysis, again from an 'economic' viewpoint, of both voice and exit in organizations other than those supplying goods and services in a market situation. I shall consider the book as an exemplification of both the virtues and the deficiencies of the 'economic' approach when it is applied outside the analysis of market forces. My general conclusion will be that, as in the case of Downs and Olson, Hirschman's 'economic' approach is as useful for what it fails to explain as for what it explains successfully, since such failures point to phenomena which require explanations of a different kind.

IV

To illustrate this let us begin (as Hirschman does) with firms producing in a market—not necessarily a competitive market but simply a situation in which its revenues come from sales to customers rather than (to take the obvious alternative) being raised by taxation. Hirschman's main point here is that the 'discipline of the market' may fail to work very effectively, so 'voice' is needed as an antidote to declining quality and may in some circumstances be a rational response by consumers. The idea of the 'discipline of the market' is supposed to be that, when a firm's products or services deteriorate in quality, enough dissatisfied customers switch to the competing firms or give up the product or service altogether to make a dent in the delinquent firm's sales and thus profits, and that this leads to an improvement in performance so as to restore the status quo ante.

As Hirschman points out, this scenario can go wrong at a number of points. Thus, there can be a stable situation in which a small number of firms simply take in one another's dissatisfied clients (Hirschman cites General Motors and Ford) so that, although individual customers switch, the net effect is nil since the switches simply cancel one another out. This is reminiscent of the reply attributed to Keynes on being asked why, if businessmen were as stupid as he maintained, they succeeded in making profits: 'Because they only have to compete with other businessmen.' An alternative point of slippage in the 'market discipline' model is what Hirschman calls 'organizational slack'. At the level of the state this corresponds to Adam Smith's remark that there is a lot of ruin in a nation. In relation to firms we can put it by saying that there is a great distance between maximizing profits and going bankrupt, and a firm whose managers prize a quiet life may be able to steer a course between the two for an indefinitely long period of time.

All this leads to the conclusion that voice—direct attempts to modify the policies of firms—may be necessary in order to reverse a deterioration in products or services supplied on a market. And from this conclusion Hirschman deduces other conclusions of a less obvious kind. Thus, in a chapter entitled 'How Monopoly Can be Comforted by Competition', he points out that the mediocre management of a firm with a monopoly in the supply of some good or service may actually welcome the arrival of a competing firm offering better quality at a higher price, thus drawing off exigent customers who would otherwise make life miserable for them by their constant complaints about poor quality. Competition—of the right sort—thus provides the 'lazy monopolist' with the 'freedom to deteriorate'.

From the point of view of public policy, Hirschman suggests that this may make it desirable, where competition has the effect only of leaving the predominant supplier free of his most demanding customers, to enforce a total monopoly. Although Hirschman does not put it in quite this way, what the proposal amounts to is that the more quality-conscious consumers should be required to provide the 'public good' of agitation against poor quality for all consumers of the product or service. This same line of recommendation can be extended beyond firms to other organizations, on the basis of a similar analysis, and this Hirschman in fact does.

> Suppose at some point, for whatever reason, the public schools deteriorate. Thereupon, increasing numbers of quality-education-conscious parents will send their children to private schools. This exit may occasion some impulse toward an improvement of the public schools; but here again this impulse is far less significant than the loss to the public schools of those member-customers who would be the most motivated and determined to put up a fight against the deterioration if they did not have the alternative of the private schools (pp. 45–6).

A similar argument might be made against allowing a private sector of medicine to coexist with a state-provided health service.

I shall take up later the value premisses which are required in order to generate the judgements expressed in the book that one outcome is desirable and another undesirable, and the recommendations (addressed to various actors) which are made. These value premisses are at no time stated, still less defended, but it is possible to infer them. The question that I want to raise now, however, concerns the logic of the argument just set forth. Let us accept the possibility that 'market discipline' may fail to keep firms at full stretch and that public services provided out of tax revenues may feel even less pressure from the withdrawal of quality-conscious consumers. It then follows (since 'voice' comprises everything except 'exit' that might be done by consumers) that if anything is done it will have to be done by means of voice. But how likely is voice to appear in sufficient volume to make it worth the while of managers to improve their performance? The fact that something is 'needed' if some postulated desirable end-state is to be achieved does not, on the face of it, provide any reason for expecting it to happen.

Of course, it would be possible to adopt some sort of functionalist assumption, according to which 'society' is conceived of as a homeostatic mechanism—as having, in some mysterious way, built-in recuperative properties. Hirschman dabbles in this kind of thing to the extent of quoting Arrow as follows: 'I propose the view that, when the market fails to achieve an optimal state, society will, to some extent at least, recognize the gap, and nonmarket social institutions will arise attempting to bridge it . . . this process is not necessarily conscious' (pp. 18–19). However, as the author of *Social Choice and Individual Values* is presumably as aware as anyone, 'society' is an abstraction and any recognizing and acting that is to be done has to be done by people.

The 'plain man', uncorrupted by acquaintance with micro-economics, would probably take this in his stride and say that all we have to do to make things logically watertight is to add a missing link connecting social needs to individual action in the form of an assertion that individuals will recognize the existence of social needs and will strive to see that something is done to satisfy these social needs. But, in spite of his brief unconsummated flirtation with teleological functionalism, Hirschman does not follow this logically respectable reformulation. For it introduces a kind of motivation—direct concern for the social good—that lies outside the scope of ordinary economic analysis.

Thus, although he never explicitly raises the matter, Hirschman's formal discussion of the circumstances in which the voice option will be chosen rests on the assumption that each individual is concerned only with the quality of goods or services that he himself buys or receives. The fact that any general improvement in quality which his exercise of 'voice' may bring about will presumably benefit many others besides himself is not treated as a possible motivating factor.

The calculation facing the individual consumer or citizen when deciding whether or not to exercise 'voice' takes a form familiar from Downs and Olson, complicated only by the assumed alternative of exit. (See for a formal statement Appendix B, pp. 132–7.) Suppose that a consumer is faced with a decline in the quality of the goods provided by his usual supplier, and that by exercising voice he has a 0·6 probability of reversing 30 per cent of the decline. Leaving out the alternative of exit, we can say that it will pay him to exercise voice if the certain cost of exercising voice is less than the value to him of a 0·6 chance of improving quality by 30 per cent of the amount it has declined. To take account of the possibility of exit all we have to do is to add to the cost of voice the opportunity cost of forgoing the best available alternative product. We thus say it will pay to exercise voice only if the value of a given probability of a given improvement is higher than the value of the best alternative *plus* the cost of exercising voice.

This analysis can be complicated in three ways. First, a point which Hirschman mentions only in passing, though it is obviously crucial: the choice is not normally merely between voice and no voice but between larger and smaller amounts of voice (including zero), each associated with a given cost. Thus, the question may be whether the extra cost of making a bigger effort to get a change is warranted by, say, an increase in the probability of a given improvement in quality from 0·6 to 0·7.

Second, a given level of voice may be thought of as having not just a 0·6 probability of producing a 30 per cent recovery but of having a 0·8 probability of at least a 10 per cent recovery, a 0·5 probability of at least a 35 per cent improvement, and so on. This is in fact the way Hirschman presents the analysis, and he allows it to make the results indeterminate by suggesting that whether or not voice is chosen may depend on whether the actor is more interested in low probabilities, medium probabilities, or high probabilities. All this complication can be disposed of, however, as Hirschman mentions in a footnote (p. 135n.), by boiling down the various combinations of probabilities and pay-offs into a single 'expected value' for that level of voice.

The third complicating point is one that applies to the whole book, namely that there is not in general anything logically distinctive about deterioration from a previously superior quality as against a consistently low (or at any rate improvable) quality. The only distinctive feature of deterioration is that, if the quality has been low all along, a member or customer would not have a motive for exit (all else remaining the same) unless he simply discovered that he had made the wrong choice from the available alternatives earlier on.

The *ceteris paribus* proviso is important. Thus, suppose that the product you usually buy stays the same in quality but a new higher-quality contender becomes available, either in the form of a new entrant or an improvement in an old-established rival. You may simply decide to exit, but you might reason that the superiority of another firm's product is prima facie evidence that your usual supplier could do better than he is doing. If there is any reason for thinking that he might be able to do even better than the new opposition, there would be a potential motive for exercising voice, so one would have the choice between exit and voice in a way exactly parallel to that which arises when the usual supplier declines and the rivals stay as good as they were before.

It is also worth spelling out a little more fully the way in which exit is an option even if all else remains the same if you believe not that the product has deteriorated but that you made a mistake about its quality in the first place. For this is, I think, the real logic of the Ford *vs.* General Motors example: the man who buys a lemon from Ford and switches to General Motors for his new car (and vice versa) does not believe that Fords were better than General Motors but have deteriorated; rather, he believes that he overestimated the quality of Ford cars when he bought one.

The most useful way of thinking about the book is to say that it is about situations in which quality can be improved. No doubt one good piece of evidence that quality might be better than it is now is that it was better in the past. But this is not the only form of evidence: there may be other indications of 'organizational slack', such as a situation (as sometimes arises) where the value of the physical assets of a firm is higher than the value placed by the stock market on the company as a going concern. Again, there may be deficiencies in the design or the manufacture of a product which are obviously in principle remediable even if they have never actually been remedied. Or it may simply be possible to *see* by direct examination that a firm or organization is badly run.

Thus, voice should be conceived of not only as a possible 'response to decline' but as a possible response to the belief that a firm or other organization could do better. It is this belief which is a necessary condition (though not, of course, a sufficient condition) for the exercise of voice to be rational—in *any* means–end conception of rationality—since there is no point (though there may be some expressive satisfaction) in exercising voice where it is not believed possible that any improvement could occur. The connection between the belief that improvement could conceivably be brought about and the experience of deterioration is purely contingent.

I have just argued that constant quality may be associated with the belief that improvement is possible; equally, deteriorating quality need not produce a belief that the decline can be reversed, or perhaps even arrested. Thus, Alessandro Pizzorno has suggested that the weakness in Edward Banfield's attribution of collective inaction in Montegrano to 'amoral familism' is that it presupposes that there is something to explain, namely that the inhabitants of this southern Italian village fail to co-operate to improve conditions. But, he points out, Banfield himself admits that 'even if the Montegranians did everything suggested, and the prefects, the government etc., did many others, the conditions in Montegrano would not improve. Consequently, the Montegranians are right in not doing anything, because no one is silly enough to do things that serve no purpose!'[20]

[20] Allesandro Pizzorno, 'Amoral Familism and Historical Marginality', *International Review of Community Development*, 15 (1966), 55–66, repr. in Mattei Dogan and Richard Rose (eds.), *European Politics: a Reader* (London: Macmillan, 1971), 87–98, at 92. This point is of course relevant to the study of rural Italy mentioned earlier, and illustrates my remark that the connection between exit and absence of voice may not be that they are alternatives. It is surely plausible that the apparent impossibility of achieving much of an improvement in conditions even if voice were wildly successful in getting action would itself be a strong incentive to exit.

> It is of fundamental importance to consider the fact that the whole world does not appear equally hopeless to the peasant. In fact, he applies this concept of inability solely to himself and to the environment in which he is living at the moment. . . . He feels that he could improve his situation if he could find work in a northern factory or could emigrate to America.

Quoted by Pizzorno, in Dogan and Rose, *European Politics*, from Cancian, 'Il contadino

Let us go back to the most basic formulation of Hirschman's idea. This can be expressed most comprehensively as follows: voice will occur when the expected value of the quality resulting from the exercise of the optimal amount of voice minus the cost of exercising it is higher than the value of the best that can be obtained without using voice. Where the best that can be obtained without using voice is the present product the question reduces to the simple one of whether the expected value of any improvement is greater or smaller than the cost of exercising the corresponding amount of voice. Where there is another currently available alternative it is necessary to make the more complex calculation comparing the value of the present product, the expected value of the present product after exercising voice minus the cost of exercising it, and the value of the alternative product.

This way of putting the criterion for rational action makes it clear that to speak of a choice between exit and voice is in fact to collapse two separate choices into one another. One choice is between exit (leaving) and non-exit (staying), the other is between voice (activity, participation) and silence (inactivity, non-participation). In any situation, one choice has to be made out of each pair of options, even if only by default. Thus, as well as silent exit and non-exiting voice, there is also silent non-exit, and this may well be the rational course to follow if exit is unattractive, even if it is believed that things could be done better by the firm, organization, or state concerned. The fourth combination is exit plus voice and would correspond to a case where someone campaigns for improvements after leaving. An example —though not a very good one—which Hirschman discusses is that of public officials freeing themselves to attack government policy by resigning. I deal with this below, in Section VII.

V

In this section I want to back up the idea just put forward that, in the absence of exit, silence will often be more rational (on 'economic'

meridionale: comportamento politico e visione del mondo', *Bollettino delle richerche sociali* (Oct. 1961), 269. An earlier exit available to peasants in some areas such as Lucania was to become brigands: this might be compared with the case mentioned earlier of Russian peasants becoming Cossacks. (See e.g. Carlo Levi, *Christ Stopped at Eboli* (London: Cassell, 1948).) Becoming a bandit, as Hobsbawm points out, is almost always initially an exit phenomenon, though the role may acquire secondary 'voice' aspects, of the 'Robin Hood' variety: 'The State shows an interest in a peasant because of some minor infraction of the law, and the man takes to the hills because how does he know what a system which does not know or understand peasants, and which peasants do not understand, will do to him?' E. J. Hobsbawm, *Primitive Rebels* (Manchester: Manchester University Press, 1959), 16.

premisses) than voice. I also want to suggest that the type of analysis offered by Hirschman fails to explain most actual occurrences of voice, both in the positive sense of failing to predict them and in the *verstehen* sense of failing to capture the nature of the actors' intentions. The first argument provides a foundation for the second so I shall begin with it.

The essence of the first argument is that only in very small groups—of less than a dozen, say—is the expected benefit *to oneself* from the exercise of voice in pursuit of the 'public good' of an improvement in general quality likely to outweigh the costs of exercising it. This is, of course, the theme of Olson's *The Logic of Collective Action*, but although Hirschman mentions it in a footnote he does not seem to me to have appreciated its force in relation to his own work. For, if it is true that voice is rarely an option that a rational person would choose, the idea that the potentialities of voice have been neglected by economists falls to the ground. Similarly, this undermines the notion that it might be advantageous from the point of view of public policy to 'lock in' the customers of a 'lazy monopolist' so that the most quality-conscious customers are forced to deal with him. Although voice may be 'needed' socially in such cases, the logic of collective action suggests that it will not be forthcoming on the basis of any calculations of rational self-interest and that the quality-conscious consumers, denied exit, will simply suffer in silence.

How does Hirschman manage to overlook this apparently serious gap in his theory? The answer is, I think, that he is helped in not facing up to the problem by an equivocation on the concept of 'voice'. He lumps together under 'voice' two phenomena which are quite different both in their attractions to individuals and in their effects on organizations. One form of voice—and the form relevant to Hirschman's argument that quality-conscious consumers who complain perform a service for all consumers—is protest or mobilization in order to secure a collective good in the form of a change of policy or an improvement in administration: the shareholders revolt, the parents press for better schools, the customers join a 'crusade' against lethal or polluting cars, non-returnable bottles, the failure of Distillers' to offer enough compensation to thalidomide children, or what have you. This is the case where the prospect of individual benefits is not likely to provide an adequate motive, but where, if for some reason voice *does* occur in sufficient volume, there will be an effect on overall quality.

The other phenomenon covered by Hirschman's use of the concept of 'voice' is that where the individual consumer pursues an individual benefit, that is to say a benefit private to himself rather than the public good of a change in the running of the organization as a whole. Thus, Hirschman includes as an example of voice the case in which 'dissatisfied consumers are able to turn in defective merchandise' (p. 35) and analyses in Appendix A a hypothetical situation in which 'half of the nonexiting customers complain and . . . the average complaint results in a cost that amounts to one-half of the article's sales price' (p. 131).

I think it is pushing the concept of 'voice' too far to include under it having a defect fixed while the item is under guarantee, but the terminological point is not the main issue. The crucial thing is that this kind of case can perfectly easily be accommodated within the calculus of individual costs and benefits but it is not of a kind that helps where the public good of a general improvement is at stake. It may encourage manufacturers to make their products more reliable (anyway while under guarantee) but does nothing for improvement in design to make the product safer, more convenient, less annoying to others besides the user, more aesthetically appealing, and so on.

Moreover, there may be many cases where only a minority of consumers are both quality-conscious and equipped with enough knowledge or self-confidence to make demands, and where the only effect on the system as a whole is to redistribute resources towards these articulate consumers at the expense of the rest, the net effect being virtually nil. Thus, I suspect that the demands for better individual service made by middle-class parents on the state school system or middle-class patients on the National Health Service have little effect on the average quality of the services but a great deal to do with the way in which the benefits provided are distributed between social classes.

The first part of my argument was that 'voice' in pursuit of a general increase in quality can rarely be expected to occur on Hirschman's premisses. The second part is that much exercise of 'voice' that does occur cannot be explained within Hirschman's theory. A good example is the 'consumer revolution' in the USA, which Hirschman claims to fit in by saying that 'recent experience even raises some doubts whether the structural constraints (availability of close substitutes, number of buyers, durability and standardization of the article, and so forth) deserve to be called "basic" when they can suddenly be overcome by a single individual such as Ralph Nader' (p. 43). But Nader himself can hardly be explained on the assumption that he is motivated by the increase in quality he might experience in the goods he himself buys. This would surely be burning down the house so as to have roast pig. And if Nader is explained quite differently, as a 'political entrepreneur' who draws (in Olson's terms) 'selective benefits' from running a crusade, there is still the problem that it would almost certainly not pay anybody else to contribute time or money to the crusade simply as a way of improving the quality of his own purchases. The answer, surely, is much more likely to be found by reflecting on the words—'revolution', 'crusade', or even the more neutral 'movement'—which are used to refer to the phenomenon. Such things are not, after all, usually characterized by a careful balancing of private costs and benefits.

The general point that has to be made here is that the purely instrumental attitude to voice—as a means to the improvement of one's own consumption—is itself not a constant but a variable. This variability of the instrumental orientation from one context to another is of course one of the great themes of sociology, from Tönnies' *Gemeinschaft* and *Gesellschaft* (community and association) to Talcott Parsons's pattern variables. In the rigorous, unified social science which is waiting to be born the relative strength of instrumental and non-instrumental orientations towards different kinds of groups will itself have to be explained and the appropriate forms of analysis for both developed. In the meantime, if Hirschman were really going to show economists what they have been missing, he would surely draw on the literature of non-instrumental voice, or in other words participation in a group for reasons other than the desire to modify its policy so as to secure a personal benefit. But his mode of analysis remains 'economic' throughout.

It is, of course, always possible to make an 'economic' analysis come out with the 'right answer' by manipulating the value of some cost or benefit so that the result of the postulated individual calculation corresponds to what has actually been observed to happen. But this merely shows that any phenomenon can be redescribed in 'economic' terminology: the 'economic' analysis has no bite unless at the least there is some way of saying before the fact when costs will be high and when they will be low, etc.[21]

Thus, we could always account for the exercise of voice in a given instance by adjusting the cost of voice *ex post* to make it pay, if necessary attributing a negative cost to the exercise of voice. This is, however, only a clumsy, and indeed misleading way of saying that

[21] These points are treated more fully in the context of Downs's and Olson's 'economic' explanations of political participation in my *Sociologists, Economists and Democracy*, ch. 2.

people sometimes *want* to exercise voice, irrespective of any calculation (explicit or implicit) that the expected value of the change in policy produced will outweigh the time and effort expended. I think it is reasonable to suggest that this is likely to happen in two very different kinds of social situation. The first is typified by the 'consumer crusade': it is a situation in which individuals are mobilized by some cause and may be prepared to incur considerable costs in pursuing it while the enthusiasm lasts. It is characteristic of mass societies and usually successive movements show a sharp rise and decline in support. It is probably best represented in 'economic' terms as a situation in which the benefits of the success of the cause are greatly inflated, though this is rather artificial and in any case leaves the phenomenon itself—the rise and fall of 'causes'—unexplained.

The second kind of situation is one in which voice in the form of participation in the affairs of some collectivity is simply a part of the form of life consisting of living as a member of that collectivity. An example might be provided by the traditional Swiss commune and many less formal collectivities. This kind of situation is not comparable with voice at the level of a mass society and is characteristically stable rather than fluctuating. Since it is not (as an ideal type) instrumental participation, it can continue even if the policy of the collectivity is considered completely satisfactory; and there is no reason to expect that participation will be increased by discontent with the 'quality of the product'. Indeed, the converse might be more correct, in as far as participation is an expression of membership. Thus, it will not do to say that the 'economic' calculus will still work provided we give the exercise of voice a negative cost. For we would then still be predicting variations above the baseline set by the fixed negative cost of voice, and there is no reason to expect these to occur in a situation where voice is not used simply with the object of securing an improvement in outcomes.

VI

If I have up till now kept the third member of the trio, loyalty, out of the way, it is because the attempt to treat it in economic terms seems to me much more fundamentally problematic than is the case with exit or voice. 'Loyalty' is regarded within the theory as a factor which operates so as to lower the benefit provided by the best competing alternative organization below that which it (as it were) intrinsically offers. As a way of explaining the absence of exit when it would be predicted by the calculus set out in the previous section, the manipulation of the benefit derived from the competing organization suffers from the same faults as does the manipulation of the cost of exercising voice in order to explain the presence of voice when its absence would be predicted by the calculus. Formally, the objection is that it is an *ad hoc* equation-filler. But this is important only because of the material objection that it does not capture a real social phenomenon.

The point here is that any equation can be made to 'work' if it has in it a constant which does not really function as a constant but rather as an error term. It is always possible to 'save the phenomena', as the pre-Copernican astronomers did by adding epicycles to the supposed circular motion of the sun and planets round the earth. Thus, to take a deliberately absurd example, suppose that someone were to put forward the hypothesis that the number of votes cast for candidates in parliamentary elections is proportional to the cube of the candidates' heights, plus or minus a factor of 'personal popularity/unpopularity' which could be different for each candidate. This hypothesis could be made always to fit the facts perfectly, provided its upholder were careful to wait until the election results were declared and then simply fill in whatever value for the personal popularity/unpopularity of each candidate could be calculated to make the answer come out right.

This is a grotesque example simply because the redundancy of the term relating electoral success to height would be apparent in advance from general experience and would also become clear by noticing the inverse correlation between the error term and the height term whenever some plausible factors were substituted for the 'personal popularity/unpopularity' term. The situation is less clear-cut in Hirschman's case, but the logic is exactly the same.

The probability of exit, in Hirschman's theory, is predicted by a two-term equation. The first is a cost-benefit calculation concerning the value of the best alternative and the probability of securing improvement in the existing product or organization at a given cost of voice. The second term is loyalty, conceived of as an imputed internalized tax on the competing product(s) or organization(s). Since loyalty is recognized only by its effects, the equation can always be made to fit the facts *ex post*, by imputing loyalty in sufficient quantity to a person who, on the basis of the first term (the cost-benefit calculation), should have switched but in fact has not done so.

There is, however, a difference between this case and my electoral example, since there is every reason to suppose that Hirschman's first term does correspond to a factor which really operates in at least a large proportion of all relevant situations. But since (as we have already suggested) the cost-benefit framework does not work at all in some kinds of organization, it will still be true that no consistent theory of the determinants of loyalty can be produced, where 'loyalty' is simply the name of the term which has to take up the slack left by the first term in order to get the 'right answer'. Instead of seeking to plug the gap left by cost-benefit calculations with an arbitrary imputed internalized tax, the only solution is to try to develop a more realistic understanding of the reasons why people leave organizations and why they stay in them.

Hirschman's interest in loyalty stems from his evaluative concerns. The starting-place of the whole book, as he tells us in the Preface (p. vii), was the observation that in some circumstances the possibility of exit actually makes things worse rather than better.

> In Nigeria, then, I had encountered a situation where the combination of exit and voice was particularly noxious for any recovery [in the performance of the railways]: exit did not have its usual attention-focusing effect because the loss of revenue was not a matter of the utmost gravity for management, while voice did not work as long as the most aroused and therefore the potentially most vocal customers were the first ones to abandon the railroads for the trucks (p. 45).

Since, therefore, exit hampers the operation of voice, it would seem to follow that a mechanism which would reduce the incidence of exit when it is institutionally available ought to increase the incidence of voice.

'Loyalty', as conceived by Hirschman, does tend to have this effect, but the effect is more conditional than Hirschman allows for. In saying that 'as a rule . . . loyalty holds exit at bay and activates voice' (p. 78), he falls into the trap of treating exit and voice as alternatives, whereas, as we have seen, each is one side of a dichotomy (the other side being doing nothing), so there is always the option of silent non-exit.[22] It will

[22] The exception which Hirschman goes on to allow to this 'rule' in the passage quoted is not in fact an exception at all, because it does not require loyalty, defined as a reduction in the benefit derived from the best competing organization. He says 'It is true that, in the face of discontent with the way things are going in an organization, an individual member can remain loyal without being influential himself, but hardly without the expectation that *someone* will act or *something* will happen to improve matters' (p. 78). This is quite consistent with the ordinary calculus set out in the previous section, since the person in question expects the present product to improve so that it is once again the best buy. All we need is some once-for-all cost of changing suppliers to prevent the person in question from exiting now and returning when things do get better again. (It is important to distinguish a cost of exit from a tax on the competing product, which is 'loyalty'.) Conversely, if loyalty *is* a tax on the competing product then it is perfectly

be recalled that the calculation facing the consumer is whether the expected value of the product after he has exercised voice is above or below the best available option not involving voice. If the best available option not involving voice is exit, then exit will be chosen; if it is the existing product (because it is still better than the rival or because it is expected to become better owing to the efforts of others) then the choice will be to stay and be silent, in other words to exercise neither 'exit' nor 'voice' options. The effect of loyalty on this calculation is simply to put a tax on the competing product. As Hirschman suggests (p. 136), we can conceptualize the position by subtracting the 'cost of disloyalty' from the value of the competing product. Thus, the value of the competing product may fall after the loyalty tax has been levied on it so that defecting to it is no longer superior to either staying and exercising voice or staying and doing nothing. It should be noticed that we cannot predict which of the remaining alternatives he will choose from the information that in a certain case loyalty has had the effect of inhibiting someone from choosing exit. All we can say is that whether he will stay and exercise voice or stay and suffer in silence will depend on which of these options would have been *second* on his list in the absence of any considerations of loyalty. But since one or other of these choices must be made if exit is abandoned, we can say a priori that the existence of loyalty must raise the probability of voice occurring.

The great problem, however, is not so much that loyalty, as conceptualized by Hirschman, has only limited efficacy in activating voice, but that it is not a significant phenomenon. And I retain enough confidence in the circumspect use of that ordinary-language philosopher's ultimate weapon, the Paradigm Case Argument, to suggest that there is more likely to be a real phenomenon corresponding to the ordinary meaning of 'loyalty' than to a construct which has little relation to this meaning.

To put it concretely, loyalty does not normally mean a mere reluctance to leave a collectivity, but rather a positive commitment to further its welfare by working for it, fighting for it and—where one thinks it has gone astray—seeking to change it. Thus, voice (as well as other forms of activity) is already built into the concept of loyalty. Reluctance to leave is not central, but is in many cases a logical implication of the requirements of loyalty since it is often only

consistent with the model that someone should stay indefinitely with a firm or organization he believes to be inferior, so long as the degree of inferiority is less than the 'tariff barrier' (an analogy Hirschman himself uses) represented by loyalty.

possible to further the welfare of a collectivity while belonging to it.[23] We can check this by noticing that typically disloyalty is predicated of someone who acts contrary to the interests of a collectivity (in the opinion of the speaker) while remaining a member of it. Someone who leaves is usually described as disloyal only if there is some special factor, for example that he has defected to another country, carrying military secrets with him.[24]

We can thus conclude that Hirschman puts things in the wrong logical relationship when he defines 'loyalty' so that it causes non-exit and it is then non-exit in turn which stimulates voice. Rather, loyalty is manifested, in certain circumstances, by voice, and may also require non-exit as a means to the exercise of voice or some other activity aimed at the welfare of the collectivity. It is interesting to notice that the only use of 'loyalty' which does fit Hirschman's definition is that occurring in the expression 'brand loyalty'. For brand loyalty, as I understand it, is precisely the unwillingness of a customer to switch from one brand to another even when the other brand is either objectively better or objectively identical but cheaper, more easily available, and so on. There is a certain irony in this since I suspect that Hirschman would agree that this is a debased form of 'loyalty' (indeed the application of a word like 'loyalty' to soap powder invites Marcusian invective), and in any case it is not loyalty to products on which he bases his hopes for the 'consumer voice'. The 'consumer crusade' à la Nader is a *general* onslaught on the suppliers of goods of a particular kind. It is not the reaction of an outraged 'brand loyalist' who would rather go to great trouble to improve his usual product than switch to a rival product he acknowledges to be perfectly satisfactory.

It would appear that Hirschman is uneasily aware that the move from loyalty to voice via non-exit has something fishy about it. But his efforts at remedying the defect lead him into literal nonsense. He suggests that the belief in one's influence (in the efficacy of one's voice) within an organization may itself result in loyalty. But the attempt to fit this idea into his framework comes to grief, as the following passage shows.

In terms of figure 3 of Appendix B, a person whose influence (that is, the

[23] In some cases, however, the welfare of a collectivity can be advanced only by leaving it. Thus, Irish or Pakistani emigrants are loyal to their family or village if they send back money from England or the USA.

[24] Consider the bumper-sticker of a few years ago: 'America—Love It or Leave It'. Presumably, those who professed this sentiment regarded active opposition to the Vietnam war from within the USA as more 'disloyal' than mere exit.

likelihood that he will be able to achieve full quality recuperation) is correctly expressed by a point as high as V_3 will be willing to trade off the certainty of the competing product against even a little hope of recuperation for the traditional product. Thus he will choose voice. He who has little influence and knows it, on the other hand, is not likely to take kindly to such a trade-off. If he is to opt for voice rather than exit [N.B. the false dichotomy] he will normally require the certain availability of the competing product to be matched by the near-certainty of recuperation for the traditional variety (p. 78n.).

The point V_3 in Figure 3 shows that the actor in question has about an almost fifty-fifty chance of securing a total recovery to the original quality if he chooses to exercise voice. As far as I can make out, Hirschman says that someone who has an almost fifty-fifty chance of securing 'full quality recuperation' 'will be willing to trade off the certainty of the competing product against even a little hope of recuperation for the traditional product'. This flat contradiction —which requires someone to believe simultaneously that he has a good chance and a very small chance of securing recovery—is merely the dramatic expression of the incompatibility of the whole notion with Hirschman's premisses.

What I think he wants to say here is that the experience of having had influence in a collectivity and the expectation of having influence in the future tend to increase a person's commitment to that collectivity, in other words his loyalty to it in the ordinary meaning of 'loyalty'. And since, as we have suggested, participation to try to put the collectivity back on the right track is a manifestation of loyalty, the more influential, tending to be more loyal, will also tend to be more active in exercising voice even if in a given case they do not expect it to be effective. But all this falls outside the framework set up by Hirschman.

VII

Before drawing this discussion to a close, I should like to look at the two chapters of Hirschman's book which are devoted specifically to applications of the basic ideas to political phenomena. One is a critique, using the model, of some central notions about party competition put forward in Downs's *An Economic Theory of Democracy*. The other uses the concepts to discuss the excessive 'loyalty' of President Johnson's 'official family', which led to a lack of 'exit' in the face of a deteriorating governmental product—the Vietnam war. Although I happen to be politically sympathetic to the conclusions reached, I regard these chapters as the weakest in the book. They do, however, raise some interesting analytical and evaluative points which will have to be met in any future attempt to use Hirschman's ideas in the development of political theory.

One important analytical point which has significant evaluative implications is that Hirschman introduces his two-party discussion by saying that, up to this point a deterioration in quality has been assumed to be something that all consumers would sooner not have (though some are more sensitive to it than others), but 'this assumption can and will now be dropped' (p. 62). This is to extend the analysis of changes in quality to an area where the whole conception of 'quality' is logically out of place. The concept of 'quality' presupposes a unidirectional standard of judgement, and this presupposition cannot blandly be withdrawn merely by saying one intends to do so. If we want to talk about left and right, or hawks and doves, we should cast our analysis in explicitly dimensional terms. Attempting to carry over into this context a form of analysis worked out in terms of distinctions between high and low quality is simply to invite trouble.

One form which this trouble takes is evaluative. Hirschman, as I mentioned earlier, makes or implies many judgements about the desirability of one thing or another, but never sets out his value premisses. Up to the point where the concept of quality is expanded so that a change in quality can be good or bad, it is fairly clear that the value premiss is that the quality of goods supplied in a market should be as high as possible, at any given price. This is certainly not uncontroversial, but it is the sort of value premiss economists have been using ever since Adam Smith: it assumes that consumption is the object of all economic activity. Thus, Hirschman does not ask whether the gain to consumers from the elimination of 'organizational slack' might be outweighed by the benefits to the managers of a quiet life, or (more seriously) whether it might not be more important for 'organizational slack' to be taken up by pressure within the firm for improvements in the conditions of the employees than in quality improvements to the product.[25]

The evaluative problem becomes much stickier, however, when we are talking not about quality at all but in fact about whether one lot of customers, members, etc. should get the outcome they want or

[25] One reader of an earlier draft has shrewdly observed that my opening remarks depend on the unstated assumption that the object of academic life is to maximize the advancement of the discipline and that most academics may prefer to use 'organizational slack' to grow roses, drink port, etc. I must plead guilty.

whether some other lot should do so, for an evaluation now involves a choice between incompatible preferences. This can be seen especially starkly in relation to Hirschman's criticism of the failure of the dissident members of the Johnson administration to resign and denounce the Vietnam war publicly. An obvious difficulty raised by this example is that one may accept Hirschman's arguments because one likes his conclusion. But it is of course possible to say that everyone who could have helped should have done all he could to stop the war, without accepting Hirschman's analysis, which applies to Presidents and their appointees generally. The best way to avoid this trap is to observe that if you buy Hirschman's argument you are committed to saying that, if there were Nixon appointees who were unhappy with the cease-fire terms in Vietnam, it is a pity that their loyalty prevented them from resigning with maximum publicity and trying to whip up feeling against the terms as a sell-out.

There are, actually, at least two separate points at which the analogy with consumers suffering from a decline in quality fails to hold for Presidential appointees suffering from qualms about government policy. First—the point already adumbrated—the talk of 'quality' conceals the fact that what we have in this case is simply a difference of opinion. 'Decline', in the analysis here, means 'decline from the point of view of the dissidents', and the fact that Hirschman (and probably most of his readers by now) agrees with them is neither here nor there since we may disagree with the dissidents equally strongly next time round. Second, the President's appointees are hardly to be assimilated to the consumers of a firm's product—these are surely the citizens at large—but are more similar to the board of directors. So what we would be saying if we bought Hirschman's recommendation is that the chairman should have less loyalty from the other directors. Even then, however, the analogy breaks down because the President is elected and the 'official family' is appointed by him. Democratic accountability rests entirely on the responsibility of the President for major policy decisions. To want, in general, more influence for the appointed at the expense of the elected is to undermine that principle.[26]

[26] One might, however, still in general (that is, without regard to the pros and cons of the particular President's policies) be in favour of more disloyalty, on condition that the main effect of disloyalty was not so much to make the President more responsive to his appointees as to make him more responsive to the Congress and the public at large. Watergate provides one example where loyalty to the President meant engaging in subversion of the democratic process itself. In the long run, however, the more important question (raised above all by the Pentagon Papers) is whether the Presidency has broken free of the checks envisaged by the constitution—whether, by a systematic policy of concealment and lies about its actions and its intentions, it can operate without any effective scrutiny, debate, or control by Congress and the public. To the

Analytically, too, Hirschman's discussion of what he calls 'the failure of "unhappy" top officials to resign over Vietnam' (p. vii) does not fit very happily into the framework of the book. It is introduced in partial fulfilment of his declared programme, that of encouraging 'neglected options': voice in economics and exit in politics. I have already suggested that voice is liable to be a weak reed in economic affairs.[27] And the case of the 'unhappy' officials hardly seems a good example of a situation in which exit might have been more efficacious than voice. Exit is supposed to operate on a firm by reducing its sales and profits, but what equivalent effect would more exit have had on President Johnson?

In fact, the question is not one of 'exit' as such at all. Hirschman, in a rather curious way, suddenly notices this in the last two pages of the chapter devoted to the subject. Here he points out that exit from a 'public good' is different from exit in the market. (And he might have added that exiting from the *production* of a 'public good' is different from exiting from the *consumption* of a 'private good'.) 'To exit now will mean to resign under protest and, in general, to denounce and fight the organization from without instead of working for change from within. In other words, the alternative is now not so much between voice and exit as between voice from within and voice from without (after exit)' (p. 105). Just so. But this effectively destroys the exit/voice symmetry between economics and politics. It looks, for all that Hirschman says to the contrary, as if there is no substitute for voice in politics, and that the only question is the choice of voice from inside or outside.[28] In fact, much more relevant to the idea of making

extent that this is so—and the process seems to me far advanced, to say no more—the maximum disloyalty is to be welcomed, especially in the form of leaks about what is really going on. Evaluatively this differs from the Hirschman case in that the desired result is accountability to the consumers (or their representatives in Congress) rather than accountability to the producers (the Presidential appointees). It also differs in that it does not require the disloyalty to be motivated by disapproval of the President's policies themselves. It could in principle be motivated simply by a dislike of concealment and lies or a belief that they are incompatible with free or democratic institutions.

[27] 'Organizational slack' in firms seems more likely to be deterred or corrected by (*a*) take-over bids by other firms; (*b*) state control, forced merger, or nationalization; or (*c*) more effective channels for employees to exert pressure on managers. None of these is considered by Hirschman.

[28] From this perspective it is clear that Hirschman's own description of the theme in the Preface—'the failure to resign'—is misleading. In the last few lines of the chapter he implicitly accepts that there were enough people who *resigned* over Vietnam and that the problem was rather their failure to *denounce* it, when he refers to 'the relief that *would* have been experienced if at least one of the public officials who "dropped out" of the Johnson administration over the Vietnam war had thereupon publicly fought official war policies' (p. 105). Compare the following from Louis Heren, reflecting on the same period: 'The responsibility [for the war] of course rested first with Kennedy and then with Johnson, but few of their advisers could see the

more use of exit in politics would have been a consideration of the possible scope for extending exit in relation to public goods, on Friedmanite lines, and also by giving different areas of a country the maximum chance of adopting radically different policies in relation to the use of cars, land use planning, etc.

VIII

Hirschman's chapter on party competition does not suffer to the same extent from confusions arising from the inappropriate retention of the terminology of 'quality', though it would read much more clearly if all occurrences of the word were struck out. There are still, however, both analytical and evaluative weaknesses.

The evaluative problem is very simple. Hirschman starts from the old Hotelling story about the two shops in the road inhabited along its length at uniform density by consumers who will take their custom to whichever shop is nearer. The 'social optimum'—the location which minimizes average travelling distance from the nearest shop—is for one shop to locate one-quarter of the way along the road and the other three-quarters of the way along, in other words for each to locate itself in the middle of half the customers. But if each shop seeks to maximize its number of customers they will converge towards the halfway point along the road and finish up next door to one another, one taking as customers all those to the left of the centre and the other all those to the right. When the story is carried over to parties (as by Hotelling in passing and by Downs at length) the implication is, of course, that in a two-party system where voters can be arrayed on a single dimension (e.g. left to right) and each voter votes for the party whose position is nearest his own, the parties will converge on the position of the median voter (the mid-point of the line if voters are uniformly distributed along its length).

Hirschman objects to this on a variety of grounds, but one is that Downsians are too complacent about such an outcome. Having set out the case of the location of shops he goes on: 'in a similar way it can be argued that it is probable, but socially undesirable, for parties in a two-party system to move ever closer together' (p. 67). He then confronts in a footnote the obvious objection that, whereas consumers only want a *shop* nearby, voters want not so much a *party* near

madness of it. Fewer were prepared to tell their master, preferring instead to slink back to Harvard and other academic and foundation boltholes.' Louis Heren, 'Pied Pipers at the White House', *The Times* (24 May 1973), 13.

themselves as as *government* near themselves. His reply is: 'it can be argued, however, that a two-party system implies a preference for a risky but meaningful over a meaningless choice' (p. 67n.). I do not, however, see why a two-party system implies any such preference, or indeed quite what is meant by saying that it implies anything. If the statement entails that the citizens of a country with a two-party system are on the average more supportive of the system when the parties are far apart than when they are close together, it is not, I think, in line with the historical record. And it does seem to be something like this that Hirschman intends since he glosses the sentence just quoted as follows: 'the average citizen may well prefer a situation in which a party with which he identifies closely has an even chance of beating one he sharply disagrees with, over a situation in which power is always held by a middle-of-the-road party which he neither likes nor dislikes strongly' (p. 67n.).[29]

Hirschman's objections to the Downsian model of two-party competition have some weight but are vitiated by a failure to relate them in the correct way to the model and also by incorrect analysis at a crucial point. The main objection is that Downs's theory predicts the convergence of parties on the middle of the spectrum and that 'hardly ever was a hypothesis so cruelly contradicted by the facts as were the predictions of the Hotelling–Downs theory by the Goldwater nomination' (p. 71). Presumably the McGovern candidature eight years later would have been adduced by Hirschman as an analogue on the Democratic side, had the book appeared in time to include it. What Hirschman makes much less of is that Goldwater was crushed in 1964—just as McGovern was in 1972. Yet this is crucial if we are to make a correct assessment of the Downsian analysis.

Downs's model is simply an axiomatic system, or more precisely a family of them, one being the one-dimensional two-party case discussed by Hirschman. It does not *predict*, as Hirschman seems to believe, except in the sense of predicting that when the axioms are satisfied the outcomes deduced from them will occur. The political system which Downs sets up in his axioms is unlike the USA in

[29] The preference for risk would have to be high if we accept an assumption put forward a little earlier in the chapter. Hirschman states this in words as: 'discontent rises more than proportionately with deviation of the actual from the preferred quality' (pp. 63–4n.). As the accompanying figure shows, what he intends by this is that discontent is not linear with distance but an increasing function of it. This entails that a person with a neutral attitude to risk, given a choice between an outcome a certain distance X from his most preferred outcome and a lottery of (say) a 0·5 chance of his preferred outcome and a 0·5 chance of one at a distance of $2X$, would always choose the first alternative.

a number of ways since it involves monolithic parties which by winning an election completely control the country's legislation and administration until the next election. As he himself observes, it comes closest to a tidied-up version of British politics. The separation of powers, party fragmentation, and the Federal Constitution of the USA depart so far from the conditions of the model that it ought to be regarded as a bonus if it works there at all.

Now, in addition to these structural axioms, Downs has an axiom to the effect that politicians seek to maximize votes, because they want to get into office for some reason or other. To the extent that parties are controlled by professional politicians this appears to me a remarkably powerful axiom. Thus, given the rest of Downs's analysis, it follows that in two-party systems the parties will converge in the middle—as the post-war experience of Britain, Australia, or New Zealand illustrates. The point about the USA is that the system of nominating conventions makes it possible for control to be wrested by zealots from the hands of the professional politicians. It still remains true that what the professionals want is a winner who will carry in as many lesser candidates as possible on his coat-tails and provide federal patronage. Where the professional politicians—the men in charge of the state machines, which are the only organizational reality American parties have—do control the nomination they have a pretty good record of going for the candidate they believe (rightly or wrongly) has the best chance of winning, whether they like him or not. (Thus, in 1960 they finally swallowed Kennedy on the basis of his record in primary elections and surveys commissioned and analysed by Kennedy staffers purporting to show him as having the best chance against Nixon.) The process by which right-wing enthusiasts took over state conventions in 1964 simply by turning up at normally routine meetings is described in detail by Theodore White, while in 1972 the new rules for selection of delegates opened the whole process up in the Democratic party.

Thus, what we can say is that American nominating conventions may be controlled by people who are not trying to maximize the number of votes garnered by the party standard-bearer. But the Downsian model still applies at the next stage in as far as voters satisfy the axiom stating that they vote for the ideologically closest candidate. And, as I have pointed out, this stage of the model stands up pretty well in that the two deviant candidates were defeated by spectacular margins.

It is here that Hirschman's argument seems to me to lack coherence.

Having suggested that the extremists will be mobilized by discontent with 'wishy-washy' policies to exercise voice and will thus be able to push their party away from the centre, he says that

there can be no guarantee that the voice mechanism will bring the party exactly back to the somewhat problematical 'social optimum' which, in analogy to Hotelling's treatment of the location problem, can be defined as the point at which the sum of the ideological distances between the party and its clients is minimized. The influence of those who have nowhere else to go may well make the party overshoot that point, with disastrous consequences for its vote-gathering objectives. This was essentially what happened to the Republican party in 1964 with the selection of Goldwater as its presidential nominee (p. 71).

One point which has to be clarified before we can discuss the main issue this raises is that the conditions of the 'social optimum' are incorrectly stated. Who 'the clients' of a party are in a two-party system is not predetermined but is a function simultaneously of its own position and the position of its opponent. A party would probably minimize the sum of ideological distances between itself and its clients by adopting a very extreme position. If the other party pursued a maximizing strategy by taking up a position close to it but nearer the median voter, this would of course mean that the extreme party had few clients. Having a small number of clients would in itself tend to produce a small sum of distances; and even if we ask (more sensibly) about the average distance, this would be low because the clients would be clustered at the end of the spectrum, while the other party would have all the rest of the voters as its clients. The 'social optimum' that Hirschman wants must be stated rather as a situation in which the average distance from the nearer of the two parties to the electorate as a whole is minimized. And this, where the electorate is spread uniformly along an ideological dimension, requires that the parties be one-quarter and three-quarters of the way along.

Now I have already argued that Hirschman does not provide adequate grounds for calling such a situation a 'social optimum'. My present concern, however, is with the analysis of party competition implied in the passage quoted. Hirschman assumes (a nice example of domination by a model, incidentally) that Goldwater's defeat must have been due to his 'overshooting' the socially optimum position. This would entail that less than a quarter of the voting population with an opinion found Goldwater too far left, in other words that Goldwater was further over to the right than the seventy-fifth percentile. Whether or not he was is an (in principle) empirical question which I shall not attempt to answer here. What I do wish to observe is that the assumption is not required in order to explain Goldwater's electoral defeat. Let us assume that Goldwater was exactly spot on the 'socially optimal' seventy-fifth percentile point and that Johnson occupied the 'middle ground' of the fiftieth percentile point (the position of the median voter). Following the Downsian assumption, which Hirschman does not challenge, that each elector votes for the candidate nearer his own position, this disposition of the candidates would predict victory for Johnson by a margin of 62·5 per cent of the vote to 37·5 per cent, which is not far off the actual result (Johnson, 61·0 per cent; Goldwater, 38·5 per cent).

The more general point underlying this is that a party following Hirschman's rule for a 'social optimum' will always be beaten by one closer to the median voter. Hirschman's reply would presumably be that, provided the extremist voice operates to the same degree in both parties, a stable equilibrium at the first and third quartiles can be maintained. But there are two problems with this. The first is that Hirschman's voice mechanism has no inherent tendency to finish up at the 'optimum' rather than at a more extreme or less extreme position, if we think of it as a process in which there is a tug-of-war between the professionals aiming at a candidate of the centre (so as to win) and the extremists aiming at a candidate of the extreme left or right (so as to have someone they identify with). More serious, however, is that even the most extreme zealot has an incentive to prefer moderate candidates provided he is really interested more in having the *Presidency* in the hands of someone relatively near his own position than merely in having a candidate doomed to defeat near his own position. For the Downsian analysis shows, as we have seen, that whichever candidate is nearer the centre will win. Let us imagine that the 'left' candidate is expected to be at (say) the thirtieth percentile from the left, and let us consider the calculus of an extreme right-wing zealot. (Put him, if you like, at even the hundredth point from the left.) A candidate near his own preferred position will be defeated, giving him a President seventy percentile points away. But a candidate more than thirty percentile points away from him (that is, less than seventy from the left) will be nearer the median than his opponent and will thus win. The choice is thus between a President seventy percentile points away and one only thirty-odd away.

We can, however, add to this that the left-wing zealots have exactly the same incentive towards moderation, if they too are concerned primarily to have a President relatively near themselves rather than a defeated candidate who is close. The equilibrium outcome, therefore, *even in a country where one party was run by extreme right-wingers and the other by extreme left-wingers*, would be exactly the same as Downs predicts on the assumption that politicians are concerned only to maximize votes, namely, that the parties would be next to one another round the position of the median voter.[30]

IX

I stated, at the end of section I, my belief that the existence of a growing core of concepts and associated theories had been on balance of advantage to the discipline of political science in the USA. How should we rate the concepts of exit, voice, and loyalty and the theory associated with them?

In order to answer this, we need to distinguish the leading ideas from the detailed analysis. The leading ideas are two: first, the idea of some sort of inverse relationship between exit and voice; and, second, the idea that under some circumstances exit may operate on those running a collectivity not as an incentive to improve but as a licence to deteriorate. I hope that I have shown these to be ideas of great fertility and synthesizing power.

The detailed analysis in which they are embedded is, as I have also tried to show, not satisfactory as it stands. In particular, although there is no question that a concept of loyalty is needed to account for the presence of voice and the absence of exit in some circumstances, the conceptualization offered by Hirschman is seriously defective. But this is not, of course, to say that he might just as well have stopped after setting out the basic ideas. By creating a theory with a clear logical structure he can be credited with having taken the major step towards a more adequate analysis.

It is a well-established academic custom to conclude an article by putting forward a programme of work for other people to do, so let me suggest that the first priority in developing an analysis is to look more systematically at the ways in which exit and voice can be related and to try to bring all the variables relevant to each kind of relationship into an explicit theoretical structure.

Thus, if we go back to the illustrations that were mentioned in section II, it seems to me that the only one fairly unambiguously exhibiting the kind of relation assumed by Hirschman was the case of

[30] For further discussion of this matter, see my *Sociologists, Economists and Democracy*, pp. 149–50.

educated Blacks leaving the southern USA, and thus failing to develop voice on behalf of the Black community. The other cases involved (or may well have involved) different or at least additional mechanisms. In particular we need to pay attention to the effects of exit other than those of removing potentially active carriers of voice.

In some kinds of situation, exit by some leaves those who remain behind better-off. Thus, up to some point (beyond which the community becomes unbalanced or unviable) emigration from an area in which land is in short supply makes the rest better-off by reducing subdivision of holdings or weakening the position of landlords. Voice may be decreased simply because the position improves.[31] In other situations, exit by some leaves those who remain worse off, quite apart from the fact that those who have left are not available as a source of voice. The most obvious example of this is the way in which the uncontrolled growth in the use of the private car makes public transport worse by taking away custom. The excellence of public transport in Venice is indeed due to everyone's being 'locked in', but the connection between the two probably owes at least as much to the fact that this provides plenty of customers for the *vaporetti* as to the fact that even influential Venetians have to use them.

[31] This presupposes that voice is inversely related to well-being. It seems plausible, however, that up to some threshold the struggle for existence is so grim as to leave no energy for voice. Thus, in the nineteenth century the Irish peasantry were politically inert during the terrible years of famine but became much more active when things improved—to a considerable extent as a result of massive emigration.

8

POWER

An Economic Analysis

I INTRODUCTION

Although controversy continues to rage about the proper definition and analysis of power, we find no great difficulty in understanding in a general way what is meant by ascriptions of power. The Norwegian government, for example, in a brochure for visitors entitled *Glimpses of Norway*, tells us: 'Today, Norway is a constitutional monarchy, with political power centered in the 150 member parliament (Storting).'[1] Obviously, political scientists might not be entirely happy with this. Stein Rokkan, in his contribution to *Political Oppositions in Western Democracies*[2] speaks of 'numerical democracy and corporate pluralism', suggesting that much of the power of the Storting has been delegated to corporate groups so that in practice the Storting often merely ratifies their deals. But even so the statement that political power is centred in the Storting serves to distinguish Norway from, for example, contemporary Chile, where it would not be true to say that the National Assembly has any political power at all, since it has been dissolved by the military junta. And we know roughly what is meant by saying that in Chile the President and the Assembly both *had* power until a group of generals *seized* power. One crude but practical criterion of power would be to ask: suppose you were an officer of the CIA or some multinational corporation with large funds available for buying favours in terms of public policy, what kind of person would it be rational to spend the money on? And it does seem reasonable to say that you could do worse than buy some members of the Storting (if any were for sale) but would be wasting your money in Chile on anything except a member of the government or perhaps the armed forces.

Robert Dahl's 'intuitive idea of power', in his essay on 'The Concept of Power', was that 'A has power over B to the extent that he

[1] *Glimpses of Norway* (Oslo: Royal Ministry of Foreign Affairs, n.d., *c.* 1971), 3.

[2] R. A. Dahl (ed.), *Political Oppositions in Western Democracies* (New Haven, Conn.: Yale University Press, 1966), 70–115.

can get B to do something that B would not otherwise do'.[3] Power is thus the ability to cause things to happen when the object is actions by other people. Bertrand Russell, in his book *Power*,[4] goes further and in effect identifies power with the ability to cause things to happen. He equates the use of power with the production of intended effects. The ability to cause actions of other people (social power) is then a subclass of power in general. The word 'power' is indeed employed in this general sense, as when we say that a man is 'powerfully built': we mean that he has strong muscles and is thus able to produce more intended effects by his own exertions than most people can. But there is no sense in looking for a general theory of power in this sense. We should simply be asking for a general theory of the ability to cause things to happen. Nor is it much more sensible to look for a general theory of social as against natural power. We should then be asking for a general theory of the ability to get people to do things.

What we have to do is divide up the phenomenon of getting other people to do things so that each method of getting people to do things can be analysed in the terms appropriate to it. And I think that as a first shot at this Talcott Parsons's division of the methods into four categories has much to commend it. He calls these methods 'activation of commitments', 'persuasion', 'inducement', and 'coercion'.[5] I propose to put inducement and coercion together but then add a further category, physical constraint, which has often been included—for example by Hobbes. I now want to explain these four categories and show that each calls for different techniques of analysis.

II FOUR VARIETIES OF POWER

Getting somebody to do something by 'activating a commitment' is a matter of cashing in on some norm that he already has to the effect that he *ought* to act in accord with a demand from a certain source. If *B* accepts a norm giving authority to *A*, then *A* has the ability to 'activate commitments' for *B*. To take a central political example, let us say that someone has a general belief that he ought to obey the law of the country in which he lives. A new law is passed by whatever procedure constitutes the 'rule of recognition' for a valid law in the country, and the person obeys it. Obviously, this process raises questions about the

[3] R. A. Dahl, 'The Concept of Power', *Behavioral Science*, 2 (1957), 201–15 repr. in Roderick Bell, David V. Edwards, and R. Harrison Wagner (eds.), *Political Power: A Reader in Theory and Research* (New York: Free Press, 1969), 79–93 at 80.

[4] B. Russell, *Power: A New Social Analysis* (London: George Allen and Unwin, 1938).

[5] Talcott Parsons, 'On the Concept of Political Power', in Bell, *et al.*, *Political Power*, pp. 251–84 at p. 258.

circumstances under which people acquire and retain such norms. The relevant studies are in the sociology of law and more generally of legitimate authority.

The second way of getting somebody to do something is to bring about a change of mind so that he does now want to do it. In principle we can distinguish between on the one hand supplying him with new information (whether true or false, sincerely or insincerely believed by the giver) which leads him to conclude that a different action will be a more effective means of reaching his goals, and on the other hand working on his goals by some method or another so that they become different. But in practice the distinction is often not clear because many goals are valued only (or partially) as means to something further. In any case, it is apparent that the kind of analytic tools necessary to discuss this phenomenon (Parsons's 'persuasion') are those relevant to the psychology and sociology of attitude change, the sociology of knowledge, propaganda analysis, and so on.

The third process involving power that I want to mention is one that Parsons does not. (It is, of course, characteristic that, compared with most discussions, he should include a normative conception that is not usually mentioned and leave out a conception involving the direct use of physical force.) Sir George Cornewall Lewis, in his *Remarks on the Use and Abuse of Some Political Terms*, said that the word 'power' 'appears to signify the possession of the means of influencing the will of another, either by persuasion or threats; or of constraining his person by means of physical force'.[6] This process is embodied in the usage of 'overpowering' someone and also (less explicitly) in that of 'having someone in one's power'. Notice that Lewis carefully sets off this kind of power from others in that it does not act on the will but directly reduces the range of actions open to the person over whom power is being exercised. By holding fast to this distinction we can see that power in this sense of incapacitation need not be embodied in anything as dramatic as chains or prison walls. If someone wants to do something that involves his travelling by car and I immobilize the only car available to him then I have prevented him from doing what he wanted more surely than if I had, say, threatened to burn down his house if he went.

An important case of physical constraint in this extended sense is that of reducing the capability of another to resist the imposition of sanctions, increasing his need to accept offered advantages, reducing

[6] Sir G. C. Lewis, *Remarks on the Use and Abuse of Some Political Terms* (Oxford: Clarendon Press, 1898), 92.

his capacity for doing similar things to oneself, or reducing his capacity to impose sanctions on oneself. Thus, in a war one side may improve its relative bargaining position by destroying the other side's anti-missile system so that its cities are more vulnerable, by destroying its stores of food so that the offer of food in return for compliance is more attractive, or (covering the last two categories) by destroying the other side's offensive capabilities. Thus, physical constraint may be used as an instrument for increasing power in the fourth sense, which I now discuss.

The fourth and final method by which one person (*A*) can get another (*B*) to do something is for *A* to change the incentives facing *B*. *A* can do this by attaching the promise of something *B* desires to gain to some action that he would not otherwise propose to do (Parsons's 'inducement'). Or *A* can do it by attaching the threat of something *B* desires to avoid to some action which he would otherwise propose to do (Parsons's 'coercion'). It is possible to combine a promise and a threat in respect of the same action.

This method of getting someone to do something he would not otherwise do is different from the 'activation of commitments' in that it appeals purely to self-interest. In effect, *A* says to *B*: 'I will make it worth your while to do *x*'. It differs from the second method—Parsons's 'persuasion'—because it does not alter the attractiveness of the action in question in the eyes of *B*. In itself, the action demanded by *A* remains unattractive. What happens is that, if *B*'s behaviour is successfully modified by *A*, this comes about because *B* has been convinced that *A* will provide rewards or sanctions, or refrain from providing them, according to the way *B* acts; and that the balance struck when he takes account of the direct effect of his own actions or inactions and the consequential actions or inactions of *A* is such as to make it more advantageous to do what *A* demands than not to do it. Finally, this fourth process of inducement and coercion differs from the third one in that, although force may be used, it is used in order to affect the will rather than to affect the capabilities. The distinction, which is central to Clausewitz's analysis, is between changing someone's choice among his options from what it would otherwise have been and actually removing some options from him.

For many purposes—ethical, legal, and (as we shall notice later) practical—threats have to be treated as different from promises. But for analytical purposes we can assimilate threats and promises into one theory. This is important because it means we can handle the case where *A* combines the two and says: 'If you don't comply with my demand I'll do something you don't like but if you do comply then I'll do something you do like.' Alexander George has remarked[7] that foreign policymakers tend to neglect the combined use of sticks and carrots. The Mafia, however, would appear to be well aware of the strategy, if they really go around saying 'I'll make him an offer he can't refuse'.

This fourth variety of power lends itself naturally to theoretical development from within an 'economic' or 'rational choice' framework. It falls within the province of ordinary economic theory, since an exchange in a market is in effect a case in which *A* promises *B* that he will do something that *B* likes (give him money or some commodity) on condition that *B* does something he would not otherwise do that *A* wants him to do (give him some commodity or some money). And obviously the whole subject is centrally related to bargaining theory and to the theory of games.

III POWER AND POLITICAL EXPLANATION

Since power is the *ability* to get people to do things, we can obviously construct a characterization of power corresponding to each of the four methods of getting people to do things that we have just outlined. Thus, power in the first sense is the ability to activate commitments: the capacity at one's own discretion to get people to do what they would not otherwise do by invoking some standing commitment to obey some source of instructions. Power in relation to the second process is the capacity at one's own discretion to change people's perceptions or goals by some means or other so that they want to do something they would not otherwise do. Power in relation to the third process is the capacity physically to restrain or constrain the actions of others. And, finally, power in the fourth sense is the possession by one actor (*A*) of the means of modifying the conduct of another actor (*B*) by means of an expectation in *B* that one or more of the alternative actions available to him will (with some probability) result in reward or punishment brought about by *A*. The exercise of power on a given occasion is the threat or promise by *A* of employing his means of modifying the conduct of *B* contingently upon *B*'s doing some action (or one of a set of actions) out of the alternatives open to him.

There are two points about this fourth variety of power which are worth clearing up at once. First, if *A* has the means of modifying the

[7] A. L. George, D. K. Hall, and W. E. Simons, *The Limits of Coercive Diplomacy: Laos, Cuba, Vietnam* (Boston, Mass: Little, Brown, 1971).

behaviour of *B* by making *B* better off or worse off contingently upon what *B* does, it must follow that *A* also has the ability to make *B* better off or worse off unconditionally. Thus, if *A* has power he has the means of making *B* better off or worse off than he would be if *A* did not exert himself. But if *A* in fact chooses to make *B* better off or worse off unconditionally this is not an exercise of power. The converse relationship usually but not invariably holds: if *A* can make *B* better off or worse off unconditionally he can normally also create an expectation in *B* that he will make him better or worse off depending on *B*'s actions. Thus, possession of the means of making someone better off or worse off normally constitutes power, that is to say possession of the means of modifying behaviour. But there are two prerequisites of there being a connection between the two. First, *A* must be able to communicate his threat or offer to *B*. And second, *A* must be able to find out whether *B* has in fact complied or not. Thus, as Schelling has suggested, if the families of kidnapped persons were locked up and kept incommunicado, this would make it impossible for kidnappers to get their demands through to their victims, thus making the kidnap pointless.[8] And the object of the secret ballot is to make people immune to threats and bribes.

Second, following on from this, it should be noted that the communication of threats and promises need not be explicit—all that is needed is that *A* should be able with some reliability to create an expectation in *B* that certain acts will have certain consequences brought about by *A*. This may be done explicitly or implicitly in speech, in writing, or even in gesture; or it may be done (where the situation is of an appropriate kind) purely by a sequence of reactions to moves by *B*. In other words, if every time *B* does something of a certain sort something nasty happens to him, or if every time he does something of another sort something nice happens, he is liable sooner or later to get the message, especially if *A* is visibly behind the nice or nasty things that happen each time.

Power, to repeat, is not an event but a possession. The event that is associated with this possession is the *exercise* of power. Someone *has* power over a period of time and during that time he has the means of modifying the behaviour of more or fewer people to a greater or lesser extent. He *exercises* power at a particular time within that period, in relation to a particular person or persons, and in respect of a particular modification of action. The exercise of power may of course be either

[8] T. C. Schelling, *The Strategy of Conflict* (Cambridge, Mass.: Harvard University Press, 1960), 39, n. 11.

successful in achieving its object or unsuccessful. Dahl remarks in 'The Concept of Power' that 'unfortunately, in the English language power is an awkward word, for unlike "influence" and "control" it has no convenient verb form. . . ."[9] But is this a mere grammatical deficiency in English (as, for example, the fact that there is no infinitive or past tense of 'must'), or does it (like most linguistic phenomena) reflect something about the nature of the concept itself? In the present case the answer is surely the latter. Since 'power', like 'wealth', refers to something possessed, there is no more sense in regretting the absence of a verb form than there is in regretting that there is no expression 'he wealths'. In both cases everything that can be said logically, given the meaning of the word, can be said with auxiliary verbs: he has power (or he has wealth); he exercised his power (or he spent his wealth).

If politics is, as Harold Lasswell said, the study of 'who gets what, when, how',[10] it is easy to see why we should feel that a knowledge of the distribution of power is so basic to the explanation of political events. But a knowledge of the distribution of power is not enough to enable us to predict with complete confidence who will get what. Someone may try to exercise his power but, through lack of skill, fail to alter behaviour in the way he wants. This possibility of slippage is not a defect but is in fact what saves the whole idea from triviality: it means that we have a framework for causal explanation. Weber and Dahl close the logical gap by equating power with the probability of one actor's being able to change the behaviour of someone in the direction desired. To say that *A* got *B* to do something that *B* would not otherwise have done because *A* had power over *B* becomes as vacuous as saying that someone became angry on a given occasion because he had an irascible temperament, or that opium makes people sleepy because it has the *virtus dormitiva*.

In any case, a complete explanation of 'who gets what' must take account of the fact that there are ways of getting things other than by the exercise of social power. First, you might get what you want by your own unaided efforts (the exercise of natural power). Second, there is the possibility of getting something without exercising power at all: people may simply give you what you want, either because they like you or feel a sense of duty to provide for your wants. And third, you may be able to benefit from the exercise of power by somebody

[9] Bell *et al.*, *Political Power*, p. 80.

[10] H. D. Lasswell, *Politics: Who Gets What, When, How* (with postscript) (New York: Meridian Books, 1958).

else without having to bestir yourself at all. The first of these does not have a great deal of importance in explaining difference in success between people in getting what they want. As Hobbes pointed out, the distribution of natural power is fairly equal—certainly such inequalities as there are in its distribution are dwarfed by the inequalities that exist in social power. Being lucky in your friends, guardians, or allies is of considerable significance in determining the degree to which different people get what they want. I shall not take it up in this chapter, but it will form a large part of the subject-matter of chapter 9.

IV THE MEASUREMENT OF COMPLIANCE

Power is the possession by *A* of the means of modifying the conduct of *B*. To begin with, then, we need some way of talking about how much the conduct of *B* is modified. In 'The Concept of Power', Dahl throws up his hands over this: there can be nothing except an unsorted list of things that *B* can be got to do. 'Suppose that I could induce my son to bathe every evening and to brush his teeth before going to bed and that my neighbour could induce his son to serve him breakfast in bed every morning. Are the two responses I can control to be counted as greater than the one response my neighbour can control?'[11] But there is not necessarily any difficulty about this. Surely, if both sons agree that providing breakfast is a bigger chore than bathing and brushing teeth, the neighbour is incontrovertibly obtaining more compliance than is Dahl.

This example is of course complicated by the fact that we are asked to compare responses of different people. Even here, as I have suggested, it can be done quite simply in some cases, but Dahl does not even suggest a technique for the easy case of comparing the responses of a single actor. Surely there is an obvious criterion: *A* can be said to secure more compliant behaviour from *B* the more *B* doesn't like complying with *A*'s demand. Thus, in any area where *A* and *B* have some conflict of goals (i.e. where the preference orderings of *A* and *B* for outcomes are not identical) we need to begin by constructing a compliance schedule for *B*. In its most modest form this can consist simply of a listing of all the possible demands that *A* might make, with at the top the item that *B* would least mind conceding, and then the other demands in order of increasing reluctance on *B*'s part to accede

[11] Bell *et al.*, *Political Power*, p. 84.

to them. When a negotiation is being undertaken by agents, the principal will normally brief them in precisely these terms.[12]

For the purpose of geometrical representation, let us put *B*'s degree of possible compliance on a horizontal axis, with zero compliance on the left and increasing compliance as we move right. In Figure 8.1, 0 represents zero compliance—the baseline against which the degree of compliance is to be measured. It is what *B* would choose to do if his behaviour were entirely unmodified by *A*. Moving right from 0, we get to *w*, which is the possible demand of *A* that *B* would least mind conceding. Compliance with successive demands as we move right would be increasingly objectionable to *B*. Let us call this horizontal axis *B*'s compliance line, since it is constructed from *B*'s compliance schedule. It is important to notice that compliance is measured entirely in terms of *B*'s reluctance and takes no account of *A*'s satisfaction. Zero compliance by *B* may in fact be quite satisfactory to *A* if what *B* most wants to do suits *A* well. And there is no suggestion that greater compliance by *B* is necessarily preferred by *A*.

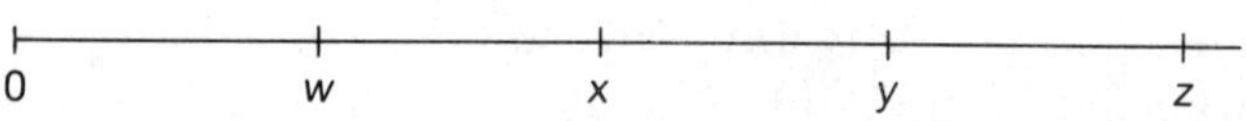

FIG. 8.1

For some purposes an ordinal scale is all that is needed. For other purposes, it is very useful to have a cardinal scale, and the obvious one is to have monetary units. Sometimes, money is actually the subject of *A*'s demand—as in blackmail, kidnapping, protection rackets, and all other forms of demanding money with menaces. In many others, money is not itself the subject of the demand, but it would make sense to ask *B* how much money he would have to be given to just compensate him for complying with each demand. Thus, we can now space out the four demands on a cardinal scale, as in Figure 8.2.

It is important to notice that 'getting someone to do what he does not want to do' must be understood to include 'inhibiting someone

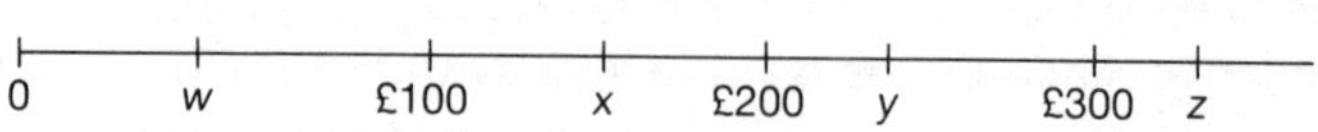

FIG. 8.2

[12] Fred C. Iklé, *How Nations Negotiate* (New York: Harper and Row, 1964).

from doing what he does want to do'. Both are equally an exercise of power. What this means in terms of the compliance line is that the zero point—no compliance by *A* with *B*'s demands—may be a point at which *B* is doing something that *A* does not like. The point at which *B* is *not* doing anything that has any interest for *A* may, by contrast, be a long way along the compliance line.

Figure 8.3 provides an illustration. Suppose that *B* owns the land at the bottom of *A*'s garden and has planning permission to erect four houses on it. *A* would most like the status quo, that is to say open space, but if there is to be any building he would prefer one house to two, two to three, and three to four. *B*'s preferences are the inverse, as shown in Figure 8.3: he would most like to build four houses and would like least the continuation of the status quo. Suppose now that *A* somehow has the means to make it worth *B*'s while to desist from building more than three houses. The outcome is that *B* builds three houses, but he is complying with *A*'s demand to the extent that he does not build the fourth house that he would otherwise have built.

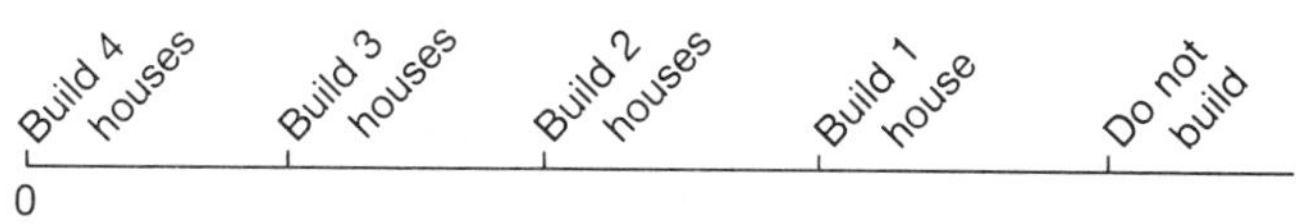

FIG. 8.3

That non-action can constitute compliance as well as can action has an obvious bearing on the 'community power' debate. Inaction where we might have expected action requires just as much explanation as action where we might have expected inaction. In both cases the answer may (though it may not) lie in discovering that the agent is complying with the wishes of someone else. Moreover, it is no refutation of the existence of a 'power élite' to show that some things happen contrary to the wishes of the putative power élite. There may nevertheless be many things that this power élite would intensely dislike that it is able to prevent from happening.

For example, a Labour government in Britain undoubtedly does things that the Confederation of British Industries dislikes. But are there other things that the CBI would dislike much more that the government would like to do and is inhibited from doing because of the sanctions that the members of the CBI could deploy? It seems as if the CBI believes so, since its spokesmen have developed over the years an elaborate Aesopian terminology for threatening Labour governments that unless 'business confidence' is created businessmen will not invest and may contract their operations.

The standard 'behaviouralist' objection to counting inaction as compliance is that we can see compliant action but we cannot see compliant inaction. This is an absurd piece of (to use a word of which the behaviouralists are fond) metaphysics. Action and inaction themselves are equally observable. On the other hand, *compliance* is never observable: to say that a piece of behaviour is compliant is always a theoretical statement entailing a counterfactual conditional. But this, again, is the same whether compliance is ascribed to action or to inaction. In one case we say that an actor is doing something that he would otherwise not do. In the other case we say that an actor is refraining from doing something he would otherwise do.

Obviously, this analysis of compliance fits most naturally into the analysis of our fourth variety of power, the ability to modify behaviour by the manipulation of rewards and costs. And it is on this that the rest of the chapter will concentrate. But consider also our first variety of power: your ability to get someone to do what he would not otherwise do by appealing to a norm that says he *ought* to obey you. Surely we wish to be able to say whether his accepting your authority and obeying your order changes his behaviour a lot or a little. And I do not see any alternative way of answering that question except by asking how much he has to give up by obeying—in other words what it costs him, taking as the baseline what he would have preferred to do in the absence of the order.

Our other two varieties of power require rather different treatment. Although both are instances of 'getting someone to do what he would not otherwise have done', neither is a case of 'securing compliance'. In the second case you persuade someone to change his preferences so that his 'zero compliance' position is nearer your own. You do not move him along his compliance line. And in the third case you reduce the number of alternatives open to him (in extreme cases to one), so that what he would originally have chosen to do (his original zero compliance position) is no longer available. In a different way, this is also therefore a matter of changing the compliance line rather than moving someone along it.

The analysis of the second and third varieties of power in terms of changing the compliance line is especially useful where one of these methods of changing behaviour is combined with one of the others. It enables us to think of the methods in relation to one another. Thus, for example, you might (starting from an initial position of sharply opposed goals) modify someone's behaviour in the desired direction partly by changing his mind so that his zero compliance position is no longer as distasteful to you as it was, and partly by operating on his new compliance schedule by offering rewards or threatening sanctions. Or, again, you might physically limit the alternatives open to someone (by putting a wall around him, for example) but then, within this restricted range of choices, attempt to elicit a choice he would not otherwise make by the exercise of authority or by offering a reward for certain behaviour.

V GAINS AND LOSSES FROM COMPLIANCE

It is tempting to pursue further the possibility of fitting into a broad framework the special analyses appropriate to each of our four varieties of power. But space limitations demand that if I am to reach some definite conclusions I must follow up only one line of analysis. In the rest of this chapter, therefore, I shall concentrate on the analysis of the fourth, 'economic', variety of power.

Obviously, such an analysis must rest on the relations of gains and losses for the actors. We therefore introduce these on the dimension lying at right angles to the compliance line. The vertical axis then measures various gains and losses for *A* and *B* associated with any given level of compliance on the part of *B*. The curve that can be drawn in most directly is the curve representing *B*'s loss from each level of compliance with *A*'s demands. Where the same units are used on both axes, the curve becomes quite trivial, since it is just a straight line running at 45° to the horizontal downwards to the right from the origin. But the units on the two axes do not, of course, have to be the same. Thus, if compliance is measured in money and loss in cardinal utility, we might suppose the curve to have the shape shown in Figure 8.4. The curve is marked '*B*'s gross loss from compliance' (the

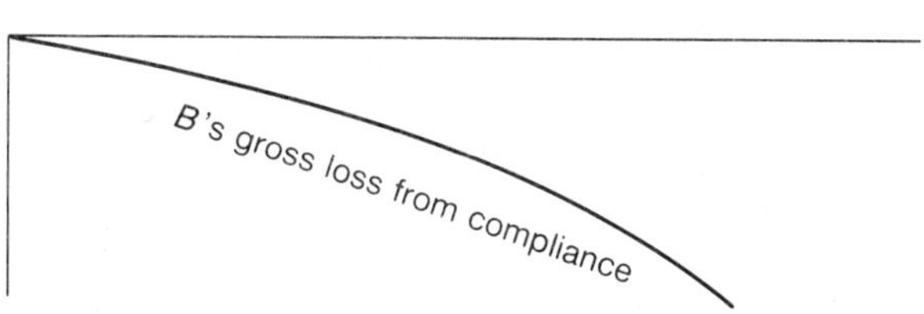

FIG. 8.4

significance of 'gross' will be explained below). The weakest interpretation of the vertical axis is that it measures ordinal utility, in other words that a greater distance from the origin measures a greater loss than a smaller distance (and the same for gains), but that any part of the vertical axis could be arbitrarily stretched or contracted without changing the information given. All we can say here, of course, is that the curve for *B*'s gross loss from compliance will slope down strictly monotonically from the origin. (In other words, it will go down all the way.) But any assertion about its shape would be meaningless. As I shall show, quite a lot can be got out of curves constructed on this very undemanding basis.

Let us now turn to *A*'s gross gain from *B*'s compliance. (The significance of 'gross' will, again, be explained below.) Everything that has been said about the units for measuring *B*'s loss applies here, but the question of the shape is much more interesting. We could say definitely that the curve for *B*'s gross loss from compliance must slope strictly monotonically down to the right, because this was guaranteed by the rules for constructing the horizontal axis: the further right, the more distasteful the thing in question. There is no such inevitability about the shape of *A*'s gross gain curve. It is quite possible for it to slope up to the right strictly monotonically, as in Figure 8.5. Here there is the maximum conflict of interest: the more *B* dislikes doing something, the more *A* would like him to do it. Situations which are straight transfers of money or of something else that is valued by both sides (e.g. territory for states) inevitably have this form. So are situations in which *B*'s suffering is itself the source of *A*'s satisfaction.

Many other situations, however, are not of this kind. These are situations with pockets of relative congruence of interest within a general context of conflict of interest. For example, T. R. Marmor and D. Thomas have pointed out that in negotiations between doctors and those responsible for running national health schemes, doctors are

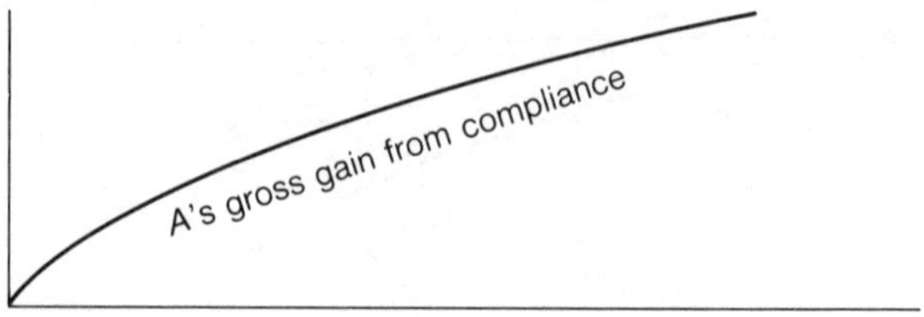

FIG. 8.5

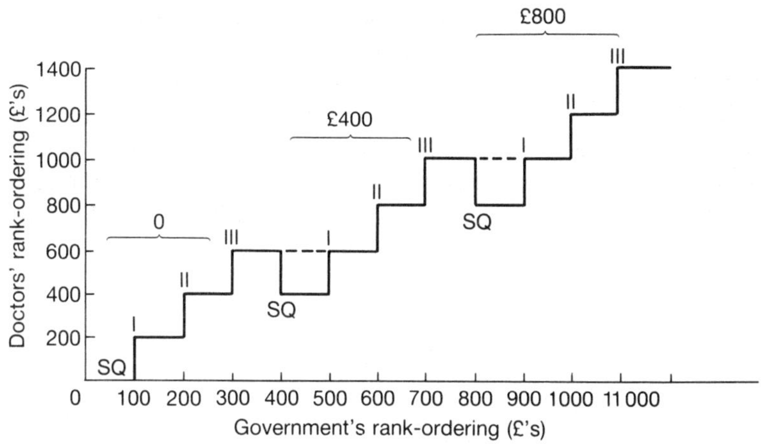

FIG. 8.6

deeply interested both in more money and in getting a method of payment that they like (in fact, normally what they have been used to). Governments, however, are interested almost entirely in keeping down the cost of the settlement, with the result that the deal always includes adoption of the doctors' preferred position on method of payment.[13]

Graphically, the doctor–government position might look something like Figure 8.6. The horizontal axis here represents compliance by the government with the doctors' demands and the curve represents the utility (which need be measured only ordinally) that the doctors get from each level of compliance. If each point on the compliance line represents some combination of total cost and method of payment, the far right end is obviously a very large total cost, plus the government's least relished payment method. Assuming that there is a conflict of goals over payment methods as well as total costs, but that the government cares less about payment methods relative to costs than do the doctors, we get the first trough (from the left) where the government, having begun by conceding on methods of payment, starts giving away more money; the second trough represents the same thing at a higher cost. On the figure it is imagined that there are three possible concessions on methods (I, II, III) and two on pay (£400, £800). If the concessions on methods are thought by the government

[13] T. R. Marmor and D. Thomas, 'Doctors, Politics and Pay Disputes: *Pressure Group Politics* Revisited', *British Journal of Political Science*, 2 (1972), 421–42.

to trade off against £100, £200, and £300 respectively, we get a compliance line as shown; and if the concessions on methods are worth £200, £400, and £600 respectively to the doctors, we get a curve for the doctors like that shown. This is of course a fairly mild coincidence of interest. If there is greater disparity in valuation between the parties, we get bigger dips in the curve. Thus, if the doctors value the three payment methods at £500, £1,000, and £1,500,

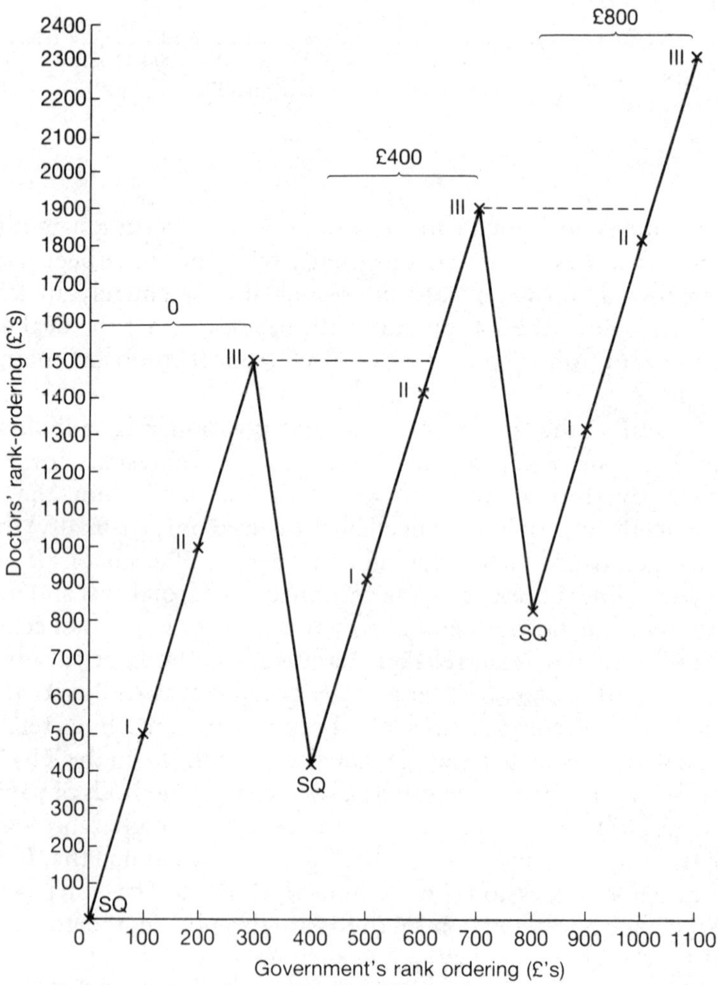

FIG. 8.7

we get Figure 8.7. In both these cases the thing most disliked by the government is still the thing most wanted by the doctors, but this is by no means inevitable. A blackmailer, for example, may be able to drive his victim to suicide but he would sooner stop short of exercising that degree of power at the point where his victim is paying as much as possible. We may thus often get a turning-point on the curve which does not again change direction or which at any rate has no higher peak to the right of it (see Figures 8.8 and 8.9).

The dotted horizontal lines in Figures 8.6–8.9 are there to assist the exposition of a simple theorem: that no point to the right of and below any other point on the gain-from-compliance curve can be an equilibrium position for a settlement. In other words, the sections of curve under a dotted line can be ignored as feasible outcomes. Thus, in Figure 8.8 there is no advantage to *A* in securing more compliance than O*x*, since he can gain no more than *px* and beyond *x* stands to gain less. And, in Figure 8.9, if the most compliance *A* can get is a little less than *u*, he cannot do better than get *t* compliance—as he moves to

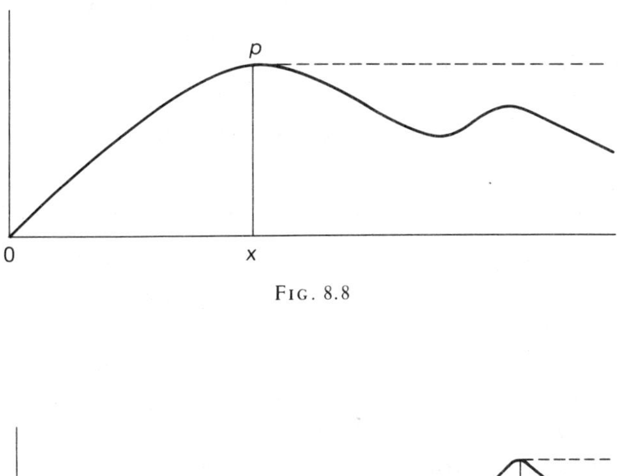

FIG. 8.8

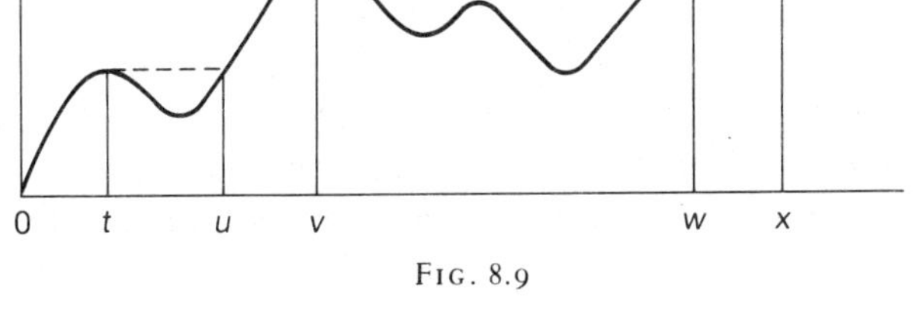

FIG. 8.9

the right from t he actually makes himself worse off. He is also, of course, making B worse off, but we can see from the shape of the curve that that in itself is not what he wants. (If A simply wants B to comply because it makes B suffer, A's curve must inevitably rise strictly monotonically; that is, it cannot have any dips or even flat sections in it.) In the same way, A can get no advantage from enforcing compliance between v and w or beyond x.

Naturally, other things being equal, the greater congruence of interest, the smaller the length of the compliance curve that forms a possible location for an equilibrium. Thus, in Figure 8.6, with only a relatively small congruence of interest between the doctors and the government, we can see that of the twelve possible outcomes (including that of no compliance with the doctors' demands by the government) only two are ruled out—£400 and £800 plus no change in payment methods. In Figure 8.7, however, where there is a bigger difference between the preference rankings of the two sides, six of the twelve possibilities are ruled out. In the combinations with £400 and £800 only payment method III stays in the set of equilibrium outcomes. (Incidentally, especially where the things at issue are finely divisible, there may be more than one outcome associated with a given degree of compliance by B. In such a case we need only take notice of A's highest-rated outcome at that point, since he would obviously not press for something equally hard to obtain but which he liked less.)

VI OBTAINING COMPLIANCE BY 'ECONOMIC' MEANS

Having now introduced the basic idea, I shall explain how the analysis of a given situation can be carried out, and then go on to discuss the implications for the study of power.

How does A actually get B to comply with his demands? The process we are analysing is one where A makes it worth B's while to comply. A must in other words make B believe that on balance he will be better off if he complies than if he does not. He must threaten B that, if B does not comply with the demand, A will see to it that he suffers a loss greater than the cost to B of complying. The incentives facing B are therefore rigged so he will be better off if he complies than if he does not comply. If A operates by means of promises, he must promise B that if he does comply he will receive a reward that will more than compensate for the loss represented by complying. Thus, taking the loss and the reward together, and comparing them with the no compliance/no reward alternative, B must find that he will be better off by complying than by not complying. Finally, if *A* employs a mixture of rewards and threats, he must ensure that between them they make the expectation of (compliance + reward + no sanction) preferable to the expectation of (non-compliance + no reward + sanction).

In all three cases, *B* must believe with some degree of confidence that *A* will carry out his promises and threats. He must also believe that *A* will not carry them out otherwise. *A*'s threat must be 'sanction if *and only if* non-compliance'. There is nothing to motivate *B* to comply in a belief that *A* will apply the same sanction even if he does comply. Conversely, the prospect of a reward following compliance will be effective only if *B* does not believe the reward would be forthcoming anyway.

We can see how all this works out diagrammatically by looking at Figure 8.10. Let us suppose that *A* wants to obtain an amount of compliance O*x* from *B*. (We shall ask what determines the level of *A*'s demand later.) This means that *A* is trying to get *B* to incur a loss of *rx*. This is *B*'s gross loss from compliance, and *r* is simply the point on *B*'s gross-loss-from-compliance curve perpendicular to the point *x* on the compliance line. Somehow, *A* has to overcome the degree of reluctance on the part of *B* expressed in the length of the line *rx*. How can he do it? As we have seen, he can use threats or promises, or he can use a combination of the two.

Let us suppose that *A* uses threats exclusively. He then has to make *B* believe that a sanction bigger than *rx* will be applied if he does not comply. If *B* believes this and consults his own short-term advantage,

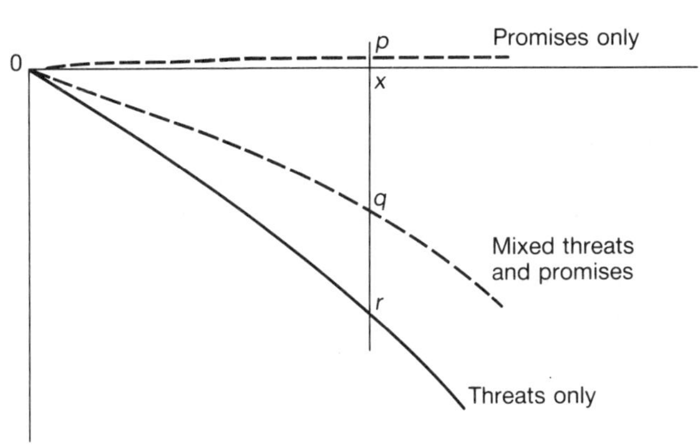

FIG. 8.10

we expect him to comply. The outcome therefore is that *B* complies (with a loss of *rx*) and *A* subsequently does nothing. If we define *B*'s *net* loss from compliance as the loss he suffers from compliance adjusted to take account of *A*'s actions in response, the net and gross losses are in this case the same, because there is no action by *A* in response to *B*'s compliance.

Now suppose that *A* operates entirely by means of promises. His task is then to convince *B* that the reward consequent upon compliance will more than outweigh the loss inherent in compliance, so that his gross loss is transformed into a net gain. Thus, in Figure 8.10, *A* is shown as offering a reward of *pr* to *B* in return for compliance. *B* therefore stands to make a net gain of *px*: his gross loss of *rx* is more than wiped out by his gain of *pr*.

Finally, suppose that *A* employs a combination of threats and promises. I have illustrated in Figure 8.10 one possible combination that should provide *B* with adequate motivation for compliance. *A* threatens *B* with a sanction of *qr* if he does comply. If he left it there, *B* would be better off not complying and suffering a loss of *qx* than complying and suffering a loss of *rx*. But *A* makes up the difference by also offering a reward of *pq* if *B* does comply. *B* therefore faces a net loss of $qr - px$ from compliance. This is less than his gross loss. He is thus better off than when being subjected to only threats but he is, of course, worse off than when *A* operates entirely by means of rewards.

For ease of exposition, I have carried out the analysis for just one point on the compliance line, namely, *x*. But the same analysis can be applied to every point along the compliance line. The result of joining up the points so obtained is the two curves for *B*'s net loss under conditions of promises only and mixed promises and threats. (The net and gross loss curves under conditions of threat only always coincide.)

Let us now turn to the other side of the relationship and focus on *A*, the actor making the demands on *B*. What, within our model, determines the demand that he makes—or indeed whether he makes any demand at all? To begin with, let us make the simplifying assumption that *A* has at his disposal means of rewarding and/or punishing *B* of infinite size, and that it costs *A* nothing to deploy these resources if he so chooses. We can in this case read off the demand that *A* will make from a knowledge of *A*'s gross gain curve. *A* will demand whatever degree of compliance maximizes his own gross gain. Thus, in Figure 8.11, we simply look for the point at which the gross gain curve reaches its greatest height *p*, and drop a perpendicular to the

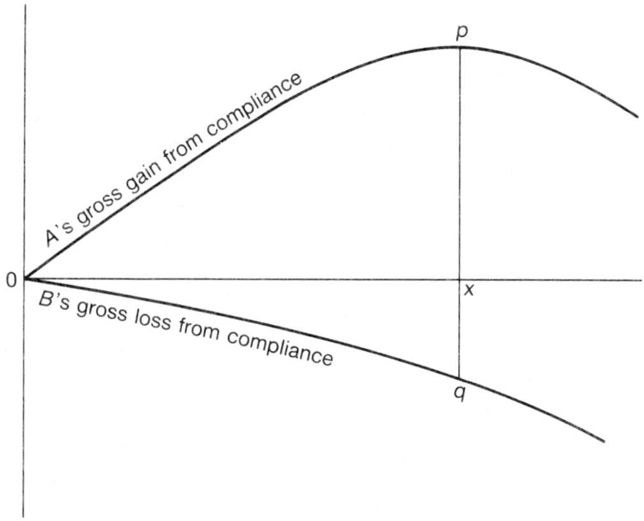

FIG. 8.11

compliance line. The point of intersection *x* gives the level of compliance *A* will demand.

Figure 8.11 also shows *B*'s gross loss curve. From our previous discussion we know that if *A*'s demand for the degree of compliance O*x* is to be successful, he must lead *B* to believe that he has a high probability of carrying out threats and/or promises, contingently on *B*'s behaviour, that make it preferable to comply (with the associated loss *qx*) than not to comply. In the present case, we are assuming that *A* disposes of infinite rewards and/or sanctions at zero cost. If *B* knows this then any threat or promise made by *A* will seem extremely plausible, since *B* knows that it will cost *A* nothing to carry it out. *A* simply has to make a threat and/or promise big enough to counterbalance the inherent loss *qx* involved in doing the thing demanded, and he wins. His gain from the operation is, of course, *px*.

However, the assumption that *A* has threats and promises of infinite size available for use at zero cost is not realistic. Normally, it costs something, in time, money, effort, personal risk, and so on, to carry out a promise or a threat. And, though there are no doubt exceptions, it is reasonable to suppose that in general the larger the threat or promise to be delivered on, the greater the cost of doing so. How should we work this fact into the model?

VII COSTS OF CARRYING OUT PROMISES

The situation is most straightforward in the case where *A* operates by making promises, so I shall take this one first. Let us assume that *A* does in fact intend to carry out the promise he makes to *B*, if only to maintain credibility with *B*—and whoever else knows about it—on future occasions. The anticipated cost to *A* of carrying out his promise may then be deducted from the anticipated gain from *B*'s compliance. The gross gain minus the cost of carrying out the promise gives us *A*'s anticipated profit from *B*'s compliance with any given demand.

Leaving aside for the moment the question of what now determines the level of demand made by *A*, let us take as given that *A* makes a particular demand upon *B*. What determines the cost to *A* of carrying out the promise appropriate to that demand? Pretty clearly, there are two factors involved. First, there is the size of the reward (measured in terms of *B*'s values) that *B* requires to compensate him for doing the thing demanded. The more distasteful the object of *A*'s demand the larger the reward *B* will require for compliance. The other factor is how much it costs *A* to generate any given level of reward for *B*. This is, if you like, the transformation function for *A*'s costs into *B*'s rewards.

Thus, the cost to *A* of producing the reward appropriate to elicit a given degree of compliance from *B* is given by the size of reward multiplied by the cost to *A* of producing a reward of that size. Given a certain transformation function, the cost to *A* of carrying out the appropriate promise will be lower the less onerous to *B* is the demand. Conversely, given the onerousness of the demand, the cost to *A* of carrying out the appropriate promise will be lower the less it costs *A* to provide any given amount of reward for *B*, measured in *B*'s terms.

It obviously follows from what has been said that we can in principle associate with each point along the compliance line a cost to *A* of carrying out the appropriate promise for securing that degree of compliance from *B*. If we draw *A*'s gross gain curve and at each point deduct from the gross gain the cost associated with obtaining it, we get a second curve under the first, giving *A*'s profit or net gain. The net gain curve will coincide with the gross gain curve at the origin, since zero compliance requires zero promises at zero cost. Thereafter, it will fall increasingly far below the gross gain curve if we accept that bigger promises cost more to carry out. Figure 8.12 illustrates the relation hypothesized between gross and net gain curves.

We are now in a position to return to the question of what

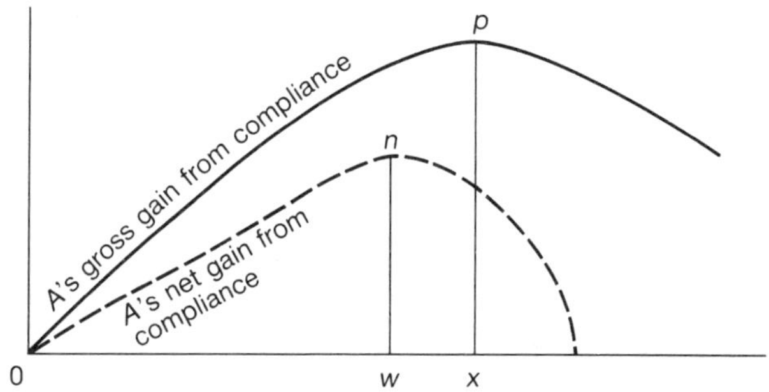

FIG. 8.12

determines *A*'s demands when it costs something to carry out promises. The answer is that the optimum demand for *A* is the one that maximizes his net gain. In Figure 8.12, *A*'s net gain curve reaches its highest point at *n*, which is perpendicular to *w* on the compliance line. *A* therefore demands O*w* degree of compliance from *B*. We can in fact now say looking back that our example with costless promises was a special case where the gross and net gain curves happen to coincide. It too therefore falls under the general rule that *A*'s optimal demand is the one that maximizes his net gain.

There are three implications for *A*'s optimal demand that are worth noticing. First, there will be many cases where *A*'s gross gain from *B*'s compliance would at every point be cancelled out by the cost of securing that compliance. Graphically, these are cases where, although the gross gain curve is (at least at some point along the compliance line) higher than the origin, the net gain curve is at no point higher than the origin. The maximum height of the net gain curve then occurs at the origin—in other words at the zero compliance point. The optimum demand by *A* would therefore be nothing (see Figure 8.13).

Situations of this kind are so ubiquitous that we do not usually even think about them. Almost any human being could find some way of benefiting from the compliance of almost any other human being. But the vast majority of these possibilities are never realized, or even contemplated, because the cost of securing any level of compliance would outweigh the gain. In a market economy there is no limit to the goods and services one can obtain from other people if one is willing and able to pay. But out of the vast gross gains obtainable from the shops we in fact pursue only that tiny fraction that we expect to yield a net gain. In political analysis, too, we do not bother to think about

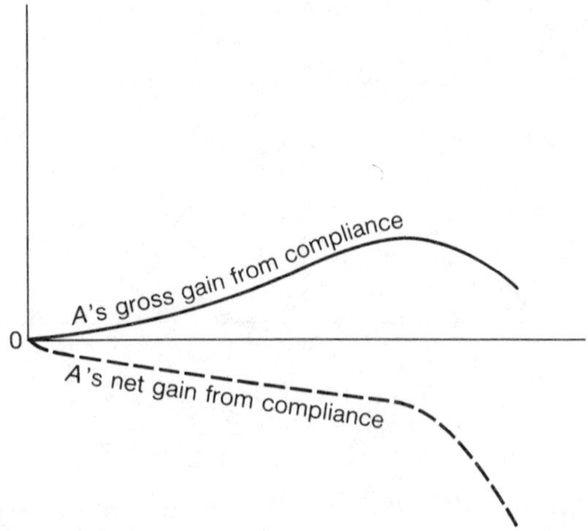

FIG. 8.13

gains, however large, that would obviously cost more than their value to obtain.

For the second point, we need to return to Figure 8.12. It may be seen there that, wherever the highest point on the gross gain curve occurs, the highest point on the net gain curve must fall to the left of it if there are costs of securing compliance and these costs increase strictly monotonically with the degree of compliance secured. What this means is that the existence of costs will always make the optimum demand less than it would be in the absence of costs. And we can add that, for any given gross gain curve, the higher the costs of securing compliance (and the greater the gap between gross and net gain curves) the smaller will be the optimum demand. Our first point, that the optimum demand may be zero, is simply a special case of this general implication of the existence of costs.

The third point is illustrated by Figure 8.14. This is like Figure 8.9 in that horizontal lines have been drawn from the top of each peak to indicate segments of the compliance line that it would not pay *A* to move *B* on to. But this time the same exercise has been carried out on both the gross gain curve and the net gain curve. It will be seen that the segments of the compliance line (*tu*, *vw*, and beyond *x*) that were unavailable even with zero cost of carrying out any promise are still unavailable when we allow for a gap between gross and net gain. But the segments that are unavailable when carrying out a promise has

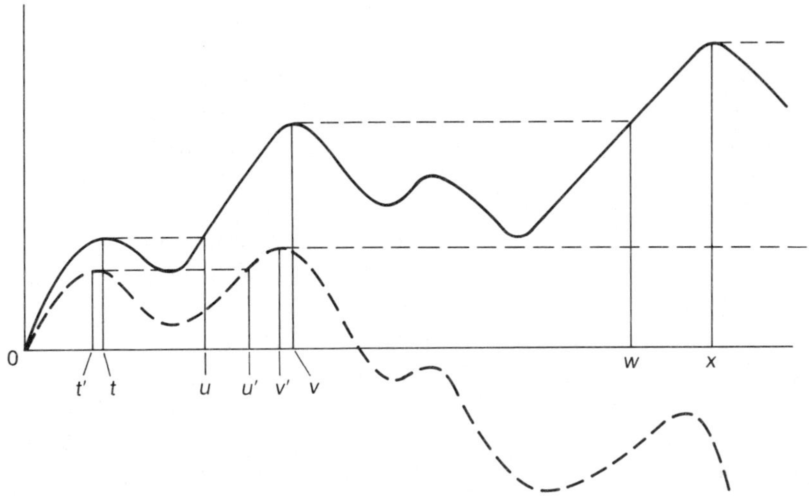

FIG. 8.14

costs may be seen to be greater: $t'u'$ and everything beyond v' are now ruled out. This is a necessary consequence of the assumption that the gap between gross and net gain increases the greater the degree of compliance demanded. We can say generally, then, that the unavailable segments where there are costs must include the segments that would be unavailable if there were no costs and will extend from these at both ends.

We might wish to relax the assumption that it always costs more to carry out a bigger promise. Rewards may be 'lumpy' rather than finely graded, so that the cheapest way for *A* to offer a reward over some size is to offer a reward that (in *B*'s eyes) is much bigger. All the intermediate degrees of compliance will then cost the same. In other words, costs of securing compliance will go up in steps instead of smoothly. If we have lumpy rewards like this, the truth of the first of our three implications of costs of promising remains intact. The other two, however, have to be withdrawn. It *may* still be that the optimal demand will be to the left of the maximum height of the gross gain curve, but all we can assert categorically is that it will never be to the right. And, similarly, although the available segments of the compliance line cannot exceed those available in a zero-cost situation, they will not necessarily be smaller.

VIII COSTS OF CARRYING OUT THREATS

It is my intention to analyse the use of threats using the same apparatus of gross and net gain as for promises. As before, it will be maintained that *A*'s optimum demand upon *B* for compliance is given by the point at which *A*'s net gain curve reaches its maximum height. But, because of the basic difference between the way in which promises operate and the way in which threats operate, the interpretation of *A*'s 'net gain' must inevitably be different for threats and, unfortunately, rather more complicated.

If *A* makes a promise to *B* and *B* does what is demanded, *A* has to provide the promised reward to maintain credibility. It is therefore reasonable to deduct the costs to *A* of providing the reward from the gain he would make from *B*'s compliance, and say that the result is *A*'s net gain from *B*'s compliance. For this simply reflects the nature of the process. But if *A* threatens *B* and *B* does what is demanded, *A* is committed to *not* doing anything. His total gain therefore is the whole of the gross gain that he derives from *B*'s compliance. It is only if *B* does not comply that *A* is committed to acting, and in that event *A*'s final position will be worse than it was before he made the threat, since he gains nothing from *B* but incurs the cost of carrying out the threat.

How, then, are we to interpret the notion of *A*'s net gain from *B*'s compliance? The answer is that we must understand it as the *expected value* of *A*'s gain from threatening *B*. 'Expected value' has its usual meaning here: the expected value of an action is the value of each of the possible outcomes discounted by the probability of its occurring. Just as we assumed that *A* will in fact carry out his promise if *B* complies, so let us simplify things here by assuming that *A* will in fact carry out his threat if *B* does not comply. We do not therefore allow for *A* to bluff in calculating *A*'s expected value of threatening. But we must allow for *A* to think that there is some probability that *B* will *believe* that *A* is bluffing. For suppose that *A* does not think that *B* will ever suspect him of bluffing—or, more precisely, suppose that *A* does not think that *B* will ever believe that *A* will fail to carry out his threat (whatever his intentions may have been at the time of making it) if *B* does not comply with *A*'s demand. On this supposition, it will always pay *B* to comply so long as *A*'s threatened penalty for non-compliance is greater than the costs to *B* of compliance. However great the cost to *A* of carrying out the threat would be, therefore, he will still expect with certainty that *B* will comply, even if (to borrow Schelling's example) *A*'s threat is that he will blow his brains out over *B*'s new suit unless *B* gives him the last slice of toast.[14] (We assume that *A* is sure that having to get the suit cleaned is worse for *B* than forgoing the toast.)

If we assume, then, that *A* will always in fact carry out his threat, but does not know whether or not *B* will comply, his expected value (or net gain) from threatening *B* is made up of two items. The first is the gross gain (G) from compliance discounted by the probability (p) of obtaining compliance. The second is the cost of carrying out the threat (C) discounted by the probability of having to carry it out. This probability is simply the probability that *B* will not comply, so that, if the probability of *B*'s complying is 0·9, the probability of having to carry out the threat is 0·1. The expected value (or net gain) is the expected gain minus the expected cost: symbolically, we can write it as follows: $pG-(1-p)C$.

Let us consider in more detail the precise mechanism by which threats work. We know already that, to have any hope of succeeding, the sanction threatened must be greater than the cost of compliance. Otherwise it would obviously always pay to accept the sanction —even if one were certain it would be applied—rather than comply. But this sets only the minimum level below which a threat will not be at all effective. If *B* has any doubt about *A*'s willingness (or ability) to apply the threatened sanction for non-compliance, he may not comply even if the sanction is a little greater than the cost of compliance. For any given expectation by *B* that *A* will carry out his threat (and let us suppose for now that this expectation is independent of the level of the threat), we can say that the probability of compliance is greater the more the sanction exceeds the cost of compliance.

Now turn the situation round and look at it from the point of view of *A*. For any given demand (represented by a point on the compliance line) he knows that there is a minimum threat below which *B* certainly will not comply. But beyond that minimum, the more he threatens the better becomes the chance of *B*'s complying. Thus, as the level of threat goes up pG increases. At the same time, however, $(1-p)C$ may or may not go up. C will definitely go up, if we assume that a greater sanction costs more to carry out. But $(1-p)$ will obviously go down, since p has gone up. In effect there is a trade-off between the advantage that *B* is more likely to comply and the disadvantage that if he nevertheless does not comply the cost of carrying out the threat will be greater.

[14] Schelling, *The Strategy of Conflict*, p. 127.

The optimum threat corresponding to any given demand will depend on the precise interaction between the cost of the sanction to *A* and the probability of compliance that a sanction of that size produces. For our present purpose we need only say that our 'net gain' curve will reflect the optimum choice corresponding to each point along the compliance line. We may note here that, if *A* can carry out costlessly a threat of infinite size, he will threaten an infinite sanction whatever the degree of compliance he demands. The earlier statement that the gross and net gain curves are identical for costless threats and promises can now be seen to require a slight qualification. The formula for net gain, as we know, is $pG-(1-p)C$. The second item $(1-p)C$ must be 0 because C is 0. But $pG = G$ only if $p = 1$. We should therefore say that gross and net gain are identical only if an infinitely large threat is certain to secure compliance. Provided that the cost of compliance is finite (as it was at the maximum point on the gross gain curve in Figure 8.11) this seems reasonable. But if the cost of compliance is also infinite the outcome is indeterminate: even the most appalling tortures do not always succeed in obtaining compliance.

Now that we have seen how *A*'s choice of threat is determined, we can raise the question of the relation between the gross and net gain curves. In Figure 8.15 we have taken two pairs of points, *q* and *r* and *u* and *v*, fairly close together on the compliance line. How does the gap between gross and net gains change as *A* moves from *q* to *r* and from *u* to *v*, making the optimal threat at each point? In terms of Figure 8.15, this means that we have to compare the lines *ah* with *bi* and *dk* with *el*.

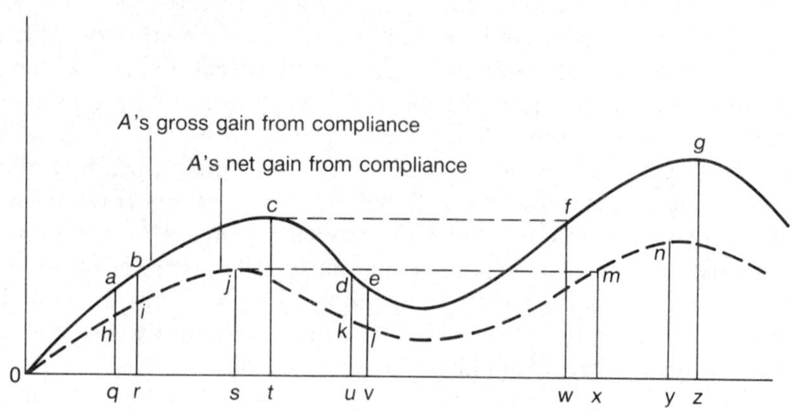

FIG. 8.15

It can be shown that, provided a bigger threat costs more to carry out, the gap necessarily widens as we move along the compliance curve under a gross gain curve that is rising to the right, and that no point at which it is falling is a possible point for a demand by *A*. Let us suppose that *A* has selected the optimum threat for the demand represented by *q* on the compliance line. He now wants to find the optimum threat for *r*. Let us consider two possibilities: that he maintains the same threat and that he maintains the same probability of compliance.

If *A* maintains the same threat, the probability that *B* will comply must go down because the cost of compliance relative to the sanction is higher. $(1-p)C$ will therefore increase, since the cost of carrying out the threat remains the same but the probability of having to carry it out increases. Whether pG goes up or down or stays the same depends on what happens to G as well as what happens to p. G is going up between q and r, and the gap between G and pG widens for two reasons. So long as $p<1$, the gap $(G-pG)$ will increase as G increases if p stays the same. But in addition p here declines as G increases, so the difference between G and pG is even greater.

We are looking for the way in which $G-[pG-(1-p)C]$ changes as we move along the compliance line. At points where G is increasing, both of the other expressions change in value to increase the gap: pG at best goes up more slowly than G and $(1-p)C$ increases. Where G is decreasing as we move to the right, $(1-p)C$ will still necessarily continue to increase, but the gap between G and pG need not increase, though pG will of course decline. This is because if p were to stay the same, the gap between G and pG would decrease as G declines. Whether or not the gap widens, however, the important fact is that net gain must decrease because pG is decreasing while $(1-p)C$ is increasing. It remains true therefore that points at which the gross gain curve is declining are not available as possible demands by *A*. Thus, in Figure 8.15 we have shown the gap narrowing between *u* and *v*. In other words, *dk* is greater than *el*. But the net gain curve is necessarily falling.

The same conclusions may be derived by supposing that, in moving from *q* to *r* or from *u* to *v*, *A* is concerned to keep the probability of *B*'s compliance constant. In this case pG must obviously stay the same as a proportion of G, while $(1-p)C$ will increase because the only way in which the same probability of compliance can be obtained for a demand further along the compliance line is to threaten a larger sanction, and we are assuming that a larger sanction costs more to carry out. Therefore, as before, the gap between the gross and net gain must increase while the gross gain curve rises, moving right along the compliance line, and when the gross gain curve falls the gap may widen or narrow but the net gain curve must move down.

In any particular case, the optimum move as the demand changes is hardly likely either to constitute keeping the threat exactly the same or to constitute keeping the probability of compliance exactly the same. But, since these two moves have the same general implications, so would the most likely actual optimum: a bigger threat but not sufficiently bigger to prevent the probability of compliance from falling.

What are the general implications? The answer is that all the general findings for promises carry over to threats. First, the net gain curve will always start turning down before the gross gain curve (provided the curve is smooth) because the gap between the two widens all the time the gross gain curve rises. The optimum demand by *A* will therefore always be less than it would be with costless threats or rewards (*y* as against *z*). And second, it remains true that all the segments of the compliance line that are ruled out because the gross gain curve is below a peak to its left (*tw*) are also ruled out because the net gain curve has a peak to its left. And, thirdly, more of the compliance line is ruled out on the basis of the net gain curve than the gross gain curve (*sx* as against *tw*).

IX CREDIBILITY AND COST OF THREAT

The analysis set out in the previous section may be strengthened by suggesting a further reason why the net gain curve will tend to fall relative to the gross gain curve as one moves along the compliance line. Until now we have assumed that the probability of *B*'s complying with *A*'s demand is a function of the difference between the cost to *B* of complying and the cost to *B* represented by the sanction threatened by *A*. But it is surely reasonable to postulate that *B* will also try to form an estimate of the likelihood that *A* will in fact be willing or able to enforce the sanction in the event that *B* does not comply with *A*'s demand. Other things being equal, the less likely *B* believes it to be that *A* will enforce the threat, the less likely *B* is to comply with *A*'s demand. And, other things being equal, the less likely *B* is to comply, the lower is pG and the higher is $(1-p)C$.

What determines *B*'s estimate of the likelihood of *A*'s enforcing his threat? No doubt there are many factors entering into the estimate, most of which cannot be accommodated within our simple model.

But I suggest that one factor is the cost to *A* of carrying out the threat. Other things being equal, the higher the cost to *A* of carrying out the threat, the less likely *B* is to believe that it will in fact be carried out if he fails to comply with *A*'s demand.

If this line of argument is acceptable, it means that an increase in C has a direct effect in depressing p, therefore lowering pG, and in increasing $(1-p)$, therefore raising $(1-p)C$ in two ways at once. Since we have been assuming all along that a bigger threat costs more to carry out, the addition of this new consideration means that it is more likely than we have suggested previously for any attempt by *A* to step up the level of threat to be self-defeating. So far we have envisaged the possibility that as *A* moves rightward along the compliance line he may increase the level of threat so as to keep the probability of compliance constant. The drawback so far emphasized has been that because $(1-p)C$ goes up as C goes up and p stays the same, it may not pay *A* to make a bigger threat, even if the gross gain from success in obtaining more compliance would be greater. Now, however, we have to add that increasing the threat will in itself have an adverse effect on p. The increase in threat that would otherwise have been necessary to maintain the level of p has to be augmented yet further to overcome the depressing effect on p of the cost of carrying out that greater threat. So the cost of maintaining the same probability of compliance goes up more than it would otherwise do.

Indeed, the cost may be infinite, as each increase in threat actually makes the goal of compliance recede further. This will be so if each successive dose of possible threat in relation to a given degree of compliance increases the cost to *A* of carrying it out so much that it more than counteracts in *B*'s mind the greater incentive to compliance contained in the greater excess of the sanction over the cost of compliance.

In other words, there may be no way of maintaining more than some particular probability of compliance at any given level of compliance, however great the cost that the party making the demand would in fact be prepared to bear in order to obtain compliance. This observation was reflected in the line of argument used by critics of the doctrine of 'massive retaliation' enunciated by President Eisenhower's Secretary of State, John Foster Dulles. According to this, any misbehaviour by the Soviet Union anywhere in the world would be met by a large-scale nuclear attack on the Soviet Union itself. The critics argued that there was simply no way in which Soviet leaders could ever be convinced that some minor move in an area not of vital importance to the USA would lead to the American President unleashing such devastation, with incalculable consequences for his own country.

It is true that the abandonment of 'massive retaliation' paved the way for the Vietnam War—a land war fought with conventional weapons in an area of very little strategic significance for US security. But this does not show that the critics were wrong. Rather, what happened was that the same mistake was repeated on a smaller scale. The leaders of North Vietnam and the Vietcong were simply not prepared to believe, however often American Presidents reiterated it, that the United States would indefinitely bear the costs of fighting in Vietnam when the real bearing of Vietnam on the security of the United States was so minimal—one might even say symbolic only. And in the long run they proved to be correct.

Incidentally, it should be borne in mind that among the costs of *A*'s carrying out threats is the repugnance that *A* may feel about it. This clearly played a part in the US withdrawal from Vietnam, and an even clearer example is provided by the way in which the death penalty for sheep stealing and theft of over £2 proved counterproductive in England in the eighteenth century because juries refused to convict even on clear evidence. At a more domestic level, a parent is more likely to obtain compliance by making a threat sufficiently moderate to make it plausible that he or she would be willing to carry it out than by uttering some blood-curdling threat like 'I'll skin you alive'.

So far we have been assuming that a bigger threat costs more to carry out. But, as with promises, this need not always be so. Threats, like promises, may be 'lumpy': if you want a sanction bigger than a certain size, there may be nothing efficient between it and a much bigger one. That is to say, intermediate-sized sanctions (if available at all) may be even more expensive to carry out than the much bigger one. The cost of making threats will thus go up in steps.

As with promises, once we allow for lumpiness we have to modify our arguments in some respects. It remains true that, if there are costs at all, the net gain curve will be below the gross gain curve at all points; and it will still be true that many cases in which a demand for compliance would be profitable with zero cost will show a net gain curve that is at no point positive once costs are taken into account. Moreover, the conclusions of section VIII remain valid. Whereas with promises lumpiness made it no longer true that the net gain curve would turn down before the gross gain curve, the effect of the size of the 'excess' sanction on the probability of compliance saves the relationship for threats. We are, *ex hypothesi*, dealing with a case where the size of the threatened sanction (and its cost, of course) stays the same along a stretch of the compliance line. This being so, p must decline and $(1-p)C$ increase as the demands become more unacceptable, so the gap between G and $pG-[(1-p)C]$ will increase while G increases and the net value itself $pG-[(1-p)C]$ will start to decline before G does.

All that is lost is the reinforcement for that conclusion provided by the present section, which does depend on the assumption that at each point there is a slightly bigger sanction available at a slightly higher cost.

X THE 'MYSTERY OF POWER'

I suggested at the beginning of section III that power in the 'economic' sense should be understood as the possession of the means of securing compliance by the manipulation of rewards or punishments; and I have now set out a model of the process by which rewards and punishments may be used to modify behaviour. It is now time to come back to the concept of power, and look at it in the light of this analysis. What are the problems with which we have to deal?

First, 'getting someone to do what he would not otherwise do' (Dahl's 'intuitive idea' of power) is not necessarily the same as 'getting someone to do what you want him to do'. *A* may be able to secure massive compliance from *B* without this enabling him to get *B* to do anything that he (*A*) wants him to do. For there may be nothing that *A* wants *B* to do. This might incline us to follow Alan Goldman and say that 'the extent of a person's power with respect to an issue is (*ceteris paribus*) inversely related to the degree of desire required for him to obtain a preferred outcome'.[15]

On the other hand, we might regard *A* as lucky rather than powerful if he can get something he wants a great deal by overcoming only small resistance on the part of *B*. To push it to an extreme: would we wish to say that *A* was exercising infinite power if he could get something he wanted very much from *B* merely by asking for it? If not, should we not concentrate on the amount of resistance *A* can overcome? We may then be inclined to adopt a definition of power like that of Karlsson,[16] according to which *A*'s power over *B* is a function of the difference between how *well off A* could make *B* if he tried and

[15] A. I. Goldman, 'Towards a Theory of Social Power', *Philosophical Studies*, 23 (1972), 221–68, at 253.

[16] Georg Karlsson, 'Some Aspects of Power in Small Groups', in Joan H. Criswell, Herbert Solomon, and Patrick Suppes (eds.), *Mathematical Methods in Small Group Processes* (Stanford, Calif.: Stanford University Press, 1962), 193–202.

how *badly off A* could make *B* if he tried. (See for further discussion chapter 11, below.)

These two approaches would lead us to say widely differing things about power in some situations, for the ability to get what you want and the ability to secure compliance need not be correlated. But both of these conceptions have one feature in common: they deal in terms of *A*'s *gross* gain and *B*'s *gross* loss. This itself seems implausible, however. If we concentrate on what *A* gains, should we not deduct the expected cost of getting it from the gross gain and say that *A* has more power the larger his *net* gain from securing compliance?

Alternatively, if we start from *B*'s end and identify power with compliance, do we really want to ignore the distinction between compliance secured by promises and compliance secured by threats? In other words, should we not look at *B*'s *net* loss (if any)? Perhaps we should not call a case where there is no net loss to *B* a case of 'power' at all: we might say that threats are associated with power and promises with exchange, as Blau does.[17]

Here then we have four quite different conceptions of *A*'s power over *B*: as *A*'s gross gain, *B*'s gross loss, *A*'s net gain and *B*'s net loss. More could be added. For example, we might identify *A*'s power with the smallness of the *difference* between his gross gain and his net gain. Nor is this the worst, for I have deliberately skated round the problematic relation between having power and exercising power. Obviously you can't exercise power that you don't have, but you can have power that you don't exercise. When we talk about power are we talking about what *A could* do or what *A does* do? Or should we perhaps be talking about what it would *pay A* to do?

It is not my intention exactly to *answer* these questions. In the tradition of philosophical analysis developed by Wittgenstein and Austin, I would say rather that my object is to attempt to dissolve the puzzlement that such questions reflect. My method, however, is not the orthodox 'linguistic' one of minute attention to nuances of meaning, but the construction of a model designed to give insight into the processes involved. When we see the way in which the various uses of 'power' reflect a concentration on different aspects of the process, we will be, I hope, relieved of the feeling that it matters to ask what is the meaning of power. What has been called ironically 'the mystery of power'[18] results from the fact that there are a number of

[17] P. M. Blau, *Exchange and Power in Social Life* (New York: Wiley, 1964).

[18] Herbert Kaufman and Victor Jones, 'The Mystery of Power', *Public Administration Review*, 14 (1954), 205–12.

aspects of power, and it is easy to move between them without noticing that they are different. De-mystification requires that we get them clear. Whether, after that, we want to go on using the word 'power' and, if so, how we use it, is of secondary importance.

XI A PARADIGM OF POWER

I think that the best way of approaching the analysis of power relationships in terms of the model is to construct a case such that nobody would have any doubts in saying that *A* did have power over *B*. I shall then offer an example. Finally, I shall take each element in turn and see what happens if we vary it.

I *A* has the opportunity of exercising power over *B*.

(1) *A* can communicate demands, threats [and offers*] to *B*.
(2) *A* can monitor *B*'s degree of compliance with his demands.
(3) *A* can, at low cost to himself, impose severe sanctions on *B* [and/or provide large rewards to *B**].

II *A* has the motive for exercising power over *B*.

(1) There is at least one demand on *B* that *A* could make, compliance with which by *B* would be (in gross terms) highly advantageous to *A* and highly disadvantageous to *B*.
(2) There is no alternative demand to that specified above that would be (again in gross terms) at least as advantageous to *A* while being less disadvantageous to *B*.

III *A* has an incentive to exercise power over *B*.

(1) There is at least one demand on *B* that *A* could make, compliance with which by *B* would be highly advantageous to *A* in net terms and highly disadvantageous to *B* in gross terms.
(2) There is no alternative demand to that specified above that would be at least as advantageous to *A* in net terms while being less disadvantageous to *B* in gross terms.

(N.B. If promises are to be included, the sections in brackets marked * should be included; if promises are to be excluded, the sections in brackets marked * should be excluded.)

Crudely, the logic of this is

I Could *A* probably obtain a lot of compliance cheaply if it paid him to?

II Would it pay *A* to attempt to obtain a lot of compliance if he could probably obtain it cheaply?

III Putting the two together: will it pay *A* to attempt to gain a lot of compliance, given the cheapness with which he can probably obtain it?

Thus, to give an example from industrial relations, the *opportunity* of a trade union to improve its members' pay by striking increases (i) the less the cost of a given length of strike (e.g. the more the state pays strikers or their families in lieu of wages), and (ii) the greater the cost to the employer of a given length of strike (e.g. the more capital-intensive the process and the more full the firm's order books). The *motive* of the trade union would be greater the more profitable the firm was, since this would mean that there was more in the kitty to share out.

An example that scores high on all the elements listed above may be drawn from Benjamin Barber's book about the history of the Swiss canton of Graubünden. After the Raetian Republic took possession of the fertile Tellina valley (now part of Italy) in 1512, 'the executive and judicial offices which comprised the colonial administration were officially put up for sale to the highest bidder' and 'corruption was limited only by the confines of the officeholders' imagination'. 'One judge . . . passed an arbitrary sentence of death on anyone who appeared before him, for whatever reason. It is a tribute to the catalyzing effect of fear on human generosity that this particular official amassed in fifteen months a fortune surpassing that of his most imaginative colleagues.'[19] Running through the list, it is clear that this provides for communication of threat, monitoring of compliance, and a low-cost means of applying a severe sanction. The Tellina valley was fertile and prosperous, so there were resources of high value to be transferred to the judge's pocket, and money has the characteristic that the more *A* gets the more *B* loses. These factors together meant that the judge was in fact in a position to extort large rewards at low cost.

XII ARE PROMISES AN EXERCISE OF POWER?

The first point we ought to take up is one that was left open in the paradigm for '*A* has power over *B*'. This is the question of whether compliance secured by offering a reward is an exercise of power. As I

[19] B. R. Barber, *The Death of Communal Liberty: A History of Freedom in a Swiss Mountain Canton* (Princeton, NJ: Princeton University Press, 1974), 152–3.

have already suggested, it matters less how we answer a question like this than that we should see what is at stake in giving different answers.

If we say that promises do constitute an exercise of power, we are saying that *A* can exercise power over *B* even if *B* actually gains in comparison with the *status quo ante*. Thus, we are in effect saying that *B* need suffer no net loss from compliance. What matters is simply that *A* should be able to secure *B*'s compliance at an acceptable cost to *A*.

Why might we wish to take this line? The argument would have to be that compliance is compliance whether it is induced or coerced. A rich man can have servants around him who will do his bidding. Is this not power? And when people (in either a capitalist or a socialist economy) work within some firm at the direction of others in return for pay, are they not subject to power?

The argument on the other side is that power should be contrasted with exchange. To be in someone's power is something we would prefer to avoid: people seek to escape from the power of others. But the possibility of exchange is never something that we would prefer to avoid, because it enlarges our freedom of choice without at the same time ruling out the opportunity of staying as we are if we do not like any of the additional alternatives. Here, too, plausible cases can be cited in support. If I buy a pound of parsnips in the greengrocer's shop, there is an exchange—money for parsnips—but am I exercising power over the shopkeeper by promising him money for complying with my demand for parsnips?

If we are unhappy about either saying that we look only at the degree of compliance (and therefore ignore the question of means) or saying that no case of gaining compliance by promises can ever be a case of exercising power, we must look for some other criterion that will sort out the cases in the way we feel happy with. I think this is the right move, but it is not at all easy to formulate the criterion precisely. There are two false trails that can I think be found in the literature.

One of these misguided suggestions is that we use 'power' only to refer to cases where someone can obtain a large amount of compliance with a high degree of probability, and it is simply a matter of fact that most cases of this sort are cases where the means are coercion rather than inducement. As a matter of usage, I think it is true that if we simply say that someone has power we imply that he has a lot of power. In the same way, though, if we say that someone has money we mean he has a lot of money. This does not entail that we cannot say someone has a little money, and similarly we can say someone has a little power.

The other misguided suggestion is that we use 'power' for relationships of which we disapprove, and that as a matter of fact we disapprove of coercive attempts to produce compliance rather than attempts employing the prospect of rewards. Again, usage is against this idea. It makes perfectly good sense to say that one approves of someone's power. Conversely, we may disapprove of attempts to modify behaviour by means of rewards. Bribery (of judges, for example) is almost by definition disapproved of, but it is not coercion.

I am myself inclined to think that the criterion for a power relation is an asymmetry between the parties. The tendency for power to be disapproved of could then be explained as a reflection of our disapproval of asymmetry in social relations, since there is a close connection, though not a perfect one, between asymmetry and unfairness. By 'asymmetry' I mean simply that one party stands to gain more out of the relationship than the other, because it is in a position to exploit the weakness or necessity or vulnerability of the other. (See for further discussion chapter 13 section II below.) By this criterion we get the result, which I think is in accordance with common usage, that threats are *always* an exercise of power, rewards only sometimes. If *A* is in a position to make a plausible threat against *B*, this must mean that he is able to exploit *B*'s vulnerability; and if he succeeds in obtaining compliance by issuing a plausible threat, then the transaction must be one-sided because it is inevitably one in which *A* gains and *B* loses. But an exchange may take place between parties with sufficiently equal positions to enable us to say that there is no asymmetry in the relationship. In terms of the model, we can indifferently describe an equal exchange as a case where *A* offers *B* a reward in return for compliance or a case where *B* offers *A* a reward in return for compliance. There is no reason in general why in an equal exchange both sides should not share the benefit arising from the transaction roughly equally. However, an exchange may be between unequally placed partners. If *A* is a single buyer or seller, facing an unorganized mass of sellers or buyers, he can set the price so as to get almost the whole surplus from the transaction. Similarly, as Marx correctly argued, the fact that a labourer in nineteenth-century Britain could survive only a short time without a job gave employers a great advantage in the labour market and enabled them to extract almost the whole surplus from the transaction of employment. Obviously, in terms of our model, to say that *A* is in a position to get nearly all the total gain out of the transaction is precisely to say that *A* can obtain a large amount of compliance of high value at low cost, while *B* has to accept, because of his weak position, compensation for the gross loss inherent in compliance that is only just enough to make compliance better on balance than non-compliance.

One final point. I noted before that if *A* makes *B* worse off unconditionally this is not an exercise of power, because it is not associated with any attempt to modify *B*'s behaviour. But suppose that after *A* has made *B* worse off he then comes along and, taking advantage of *B*'s distressed situation, is able to obtain compliance in return for an offer that *B* would have turned down before. Even more, suppose that *A*'s reduction of *B*'s well-being was deliberately designed to bring about a state of dependence. I think that in such a case we would be inclined to say that *A* was exercising power over *B* through offering rewards for compliance, even if we might not say the same if the relative positions of *A* and *B* had come about without the intervention of *A*. This has an obvious bearing on the question of whether the countries of the 'Third World' are subject to the power of the developed (and especially the ex-colonial) countries. Those who argue that they are not will point to the existing pattern of trade relations and say that these relations are mutually beneficial. But if what has just been said is true, the 'dependency' theorists are right to say that we have to ask how these patterns of trade came about in the first place.

XIII THREE CONCEPTS OF POWER

Having decided to admit the ability to make promises as a form of power under certain circumstances, we can now return to the other questions that were raised in section X. As I said there, I do not think that there is anything much to be gained from simply picking a definition and saying 'That's the one everybody ought to use'. But I do think that it is useful to see the implications of alternative definitions and to notice the way in which the choice of a definition is affected by what it is that we want to explain.

If we are interested in predicting how people will behave, then we want to know when it will *pay A* to try to get *B* to do something. It is no good *A*'s being able to derive enormous potential benefit from some compliant action by *B* if either *A* has no way of getting *B* to do it or if the cost to *A* of getting *B* to do it is so great as to cancel out the benefit. At the same time, it is also no good *A*'s being in a position to make sizeable threats or promises to *B* at low cost to himself if there is nothing that *B* has that *A* wants, or, more generally, if no compliant behaviour of *B* would produce a worthwhile gross gain for *A*.

In other words, if you are interested in predicting action—attempts by one actor to achieve compliance by another actor—you need both motive and opportunity. And that means that you have to insist on a certain amount of both **I** and **II** in the paradigm, such that between them they satisfy **III**. The resulting definition would be on the following lines: *A* has power over *B* if and only if *A* can profitably get *B* to do something *A* wants or, more formally, if and only if there is some level of compliance by *B* such that *A*'s net gain from it would be positive. The measure of power would be the maximum net gain obtainable by *A* at any level of compliance by *B*.

Notice that this definition concentrates on *A*'s net advantage from *B*'s compliance. Any given net advantage may arise either from x gross gain and y cost to *A* (e.g. a huge gross gain and high cost) or from $x-a$ gross gain and $y-a$ cost (e.g. a small gain and a minuscule cost). The present measure of power would produce the same result in both cases, and this is reasonable if what we are interested in is predicting action by *B*. For it is surely plausible, if we accept a general cost-benefit framework of analysis, to predict that the greater the profit to *A* that can be anticipated from action (in this case making an attempt to obtain compliance from *B*) the more likely *A* is to undertake that action.

But prediction of actions is not the only thing we may be interested in. I have already mentioned the Lasswellian conception of the *explananda* of politics as 'who gets what, when, how'. This implies a distributive focus to our inquiries: we are interested in the outcomes of social behaviour, in who gains and who loses. The obvious way of defining power from this point of view is in terms of inequality. *A*'s power over *B* will consist in *A*'s ability to gain at the expense of *B*.

In the simplest case this means that *A* has the ability to make a profit from gaining *B*'s compliance while *B* makes a net loss. In other words, *A*'s power consists in his ability profitably to coerce *B*. But, as I argued in section XII, there can also be an asymmetry in net gains. Suppose that both sides make a net gain from the transaction but that one of the parties (*A*) is able to appropriate almost all the profit by manœuvring the other (*B*) into a position where the choice is between the status quo and a small improvement on it. There is then an unequal distribution of the gains from trade between *A* and *B*.

The implication of this is that power should be defined in terms of the *difference* between what *A* gets and what *B* gets if *A* pursues the course most profitable to him. It would follow from this that there were two ways in which *A* might have no power over *B*. If it would not pay *A* to attempt to obtain compliance from *B*, the equilibrium position would obviously be one in which no attempt was made, and there would by definition be no gains and no losses to either party, so no power relation. But even if it would pay *A* to obtain compliance from *B* by offering a reward for compliance to *B*, there may still be no power relation because the outcome may be a fair exchange between *A* and *B* in which both make a roughly equal gain over their positions in the status quo ante. (Of course, *A* and *B* might both lose equally from an attempt by *A* to coerce *B* that fails. But it must be recalled that our analysis of net gains and losses is *ex ante* not *ex post*. If *ex ante* the net gain that *A* anticipates is negative, because the product of the probability of *B*'s non-compliance and the cost of carrying out the threat exceeds the product of *B*'s compliance and the gross gain from *B*'s compliance, then *A* has no incentive to attempt to obtain compliance. The case is therefore *ex ante* of the first type.)

Formally, then, the definition of power on this conception would be on the following lines: *A* has power over *B* if and only if the maximum net gain for *A* from compliance by *B* entails either a net loss by *B* or a smaller net gain by *B* than that enjoyed by *A*. And the measure of *A*'s power would be the size of the difference between *A*'s net gain and *B*'s net loss or between *A*'s net gain and *B*'s net gain, measuring these values at the equilibrium level of compliance demanded by *A*, that is to say the point that maximizes *A*'s net gain.

Unlike the first definition, this would enable us to predict changes in the pattern of distribution: if *A* has power over *B*, we predict that *A* will become better off and *B* worse off relative to the status quo. But it does not predict behaviour as well as the first definition does. First, all equal exchanges are simply ignored, so we eliminate a great deal of market behaviour. Second, if the probability of action by *A* is related to prospect of profit by *A*, the second definition, by contaminating *A*'s profit with *B*'s loss, entails that we can no longer move from power to motive so confidently. If what pays *A* most is to try to get *B* to do something he very much doesn't want to do, that must entail on this definition a great deal of power for *A*. Yet the net gain to *A* may be quite tiny, either because the gross gain is small (recall that *B*'s hating to do something does not entail that *A* loves having him do it) or because the cost of getting *B* to do it is so high that it almost outweighs a large gain. This observation of course illustrates the general point that different definitions serve different intellectual (or indeed practical) interests.

Both of the definitions canvassed so far have one thing in common: they both include within them a reference to the prospective gains of *A* from securing *B*'s compliance with a demand. And clearly to predict either behaviour or distributive outcomes we do need to take *A*'s prospective gains into account. But I think there is a further object we may have in attributing social power to people or groups and that in order to pursue that object we ought to leave *A*'s prospective gains out of the definition of power. I want to argue that, in some sense, we grasp social reality at a deeper level by looking at what *A* could get at low cost rather than what it actually pays *A* to get. In other words, I am suggesting that we might conceptualize power purely in terms of opportunity and not at all in terms of motive. *A*'s power would then consist simply of the ability to obtain low-cost compliance. Even if there were currently nothing *B* could do that *A* would wish him to do, *A* would still, on this conception, have the same amount of power as would be attributed to him if there were something *B* could do that *A* very much wanted him to do.

What interest would be served by such a definition? My answer is that an interest in *security* will lead us to such a definition, and that we ought to take an interest in security because of its importance for the dignity of individuals and societies and (related to this) their capacity to plan for the future with confidence. If *A* has power over *B* in the sense that *A* can at low cost to himself obtain compliance from *B*, then *A* has *B* in his power. *B* may not be subject to demands from *A* at the moment but he cannot count on that happy state of affairs continuing. *B*'s freedom depends on *A*'s not choosing to exercise his power. (In our cost-benefit framework this means that it depends on *A*'s net gain from securing compliance being negative, and if the cost of obtaining compliance is low this can come about only if *A*'s net gain is low.) If at any time *B* happens to get into a position where he does have something that *A* wants, to more than a negligible degree, he knows that *A* is in a position to demand it.

Let me give two examples of this kind of power in practice, the first from interpersonal relations, the second from international relations. The first is a little frivolous but illustrates an important point. It occurred to me, while reading an omnibus edition of the Jeeves short stories by P. G. Wodehouse, how often the plot turns around the dependence of one of Bertie Wooster's fellow Drones on an allowance from some aged relative, and on the need to meet (or appear to meet) the more or less cranky demands of this relative in order to keep the allowance. Even Bertie, in one of his more reflective moments, remarks that 'It's a curious thing how many of my pals seem to have aunts or uncles who are their main source of supply.'[20]

It may be noted that this constitutes a case where *A* (the aunt or uncle) operates on *B* (the Drone) by rewards rather than sanctions. The Drone would prefer a situation in which he has the option of complying with the whims of his aged relative and getting an allowance to a situation in which this option is withdrawn. (Of course, he would like even better to get the money without having to placate the aged relative, but this opportunity is not available, at any rate until the decease of the relative.) If we reflect on this, we can see that the relationship may not be one of power in the sense of an unequal exchange. It may be that the relative receives less benefit from the Drone's compliance than the Drone does from the allowance. But the point is that the Drone *is* dependent—his behaviour is open to control by the aunt or uncle—and the truth of this is not affected by the fact that he prefers dependence to independence on the only terms on which independence is available.

At the other extreme, many grave illustrations may be drawn from relations between states. If we define a weak state as one which at least one other state could, if it chose, occupy and control at fairly low cost, it must follow that the independence of a weak state at any time depends on its not having anything that makes it worth the while of a state that could occupy and control it to do so. Woe betide it if in an industrial era valuable raw materials are discovered on its territory or if economic and technical developments mean that its land and perhaps its inhabitants could be used profitably to grow some valuable cash crop like cotton, rubber, tea, or coffee. Woe betide it if, because of its location, it suddenly becomes strategically or commercially significant, as a coaling station or the site for a canal, for example. What has protected the independence of mountainous areas like Montenegro, Switzerland, or Ethiopia over the centuries? Partly the relative difficulty of conquering such mountainous territories but more, I suggest, the fact that their poverty has made them unattractive acquisitions. The possession of a mass of gold was the undoing of the Incas, and the Transvaal would no doubt have remained an independent state of poor farmers but for the discovery of diamonds in extraordinary quantity on the Rand. Again, Egypt lost its

[20] P. G. Wodehouse, *The World of Jeeves* (New York: Manor Books, 1973), 180.

independence to Britain and France largely to protect the Suez Canal, and the state of Panama was carved out by the United States to create a buffer for the Panama Canal.

The argument in favour of the conception of power as the ability to secure compliance at relatively low cost is that it focuses on the realities of dependence. Even if a state is independent, it is surely a relevant fact about it that its independence is contingent on the apathy of those states with power, and that its independence will be in jeopardy should it ever happen to become interesting to such a state.

XIV TECHNICAL LIMITATIONS OF THE ANALYSIS

I shall not expand any further on the limited scope of the 'economic' approach to the analysis of power. Instead I want to end this chapter by asking what are the limitations on the analysis that I have developed earlier *within* the general area where it applies. I shall consider three kinds of limitation: technical limitations, limitations on applicability (in the sense of operationalizability), and limitations on applicability in the sense of limitations on the usefulness of threats and promises themselves.

The model that has been presented here is extremely simple and primitive. Three technical limitations in it are, I think, especially serious. First, we were always considering cases where *A* is trying to get *B* to change his behaviour, but never cases where *B* is also trying to get *A* to change *his* behaviour. Of course, we can say that *B* is trying to change *A*'s behaviour if *B* refuses to comply until *A* offers a larger reward for compliance. And indeed the 'pure reward' case can often be equally well presented with either party as the active one trying to change the behaviour of the other. (For example, in an ordinary economic exchange we could make either party *A* or *B*.) But where each party has threats at its disposal and each is trying to move the other to a position worse than that of non-compliance, we do have to extend the model.

Second, we need to be able to allow for the fact that *B* may respond to a demand of *A* backed by a threat not merely by refusing to comply and then leaving *A* to decide whether it is worth the cost inherent in carrying out the threat: *B* may in addition attempt to reduce the probability of *A*'s carrying out the threat by making a conditional threat in turn to the effect that if *A* carries out his threat then *B* will do something to *A* that *A* will not like. (*A* may of course counter with a conditional threat against *B* to the effect that if *B* retaliates *A* will do something else.) The threat of retaliation differs from the case of mutual threats that I mentioned first in that *B*'s move here is defensive in nature: *B* is content to be left alone by *A* and simply to deter *A* from carrying out his threat, but *B* is not using his threat-capacity to attempt to get *A* to comply with a demand from *B* for a change in his behaviour.[21]

Third, there is a rather worrying tendency to slither between subjective and objective values in the model. Ideally, we want one set of curves to represent *A*'s actual benefits from any degree of compliance by *B* and the actual costs to *A* of carrying out any given threat or promise; and another set for *A*'s estimate of what a given degree of compliance would cost *B* and his estimate of what a given threat or promise would be worth to *B* if carried out. And the same *mutatis mutandis* for *B*.

I shall not discuss these three extensions any further here, since any attempt to incorporate them formally into the analysis would result in turning what is already a very long chapter into a treatise. I have, however, done enough work on the formalization of these extensions to have convinced myself that they can be accommodated within the general framework of 'economic' analysis put forward here. I have to warn, though, that the complexity of the analysis increases very rapidly as one adds refinements.

XV LIMITATIONS ON OPERATIONALIZABILITY

The next question that I want to raise concerns the possibility of getting actual measurements for the variables used in the analysis. Can this be done, and if not how serious a problem is this? I have three comments to make.

The first is that there is at the very least scope for experimental tests. Much work on threats and promises has already been done (as one can see by consulting *The Journal of Conflict Resolution*), but a good deal of this research has been carried out by social psychologists with a poor grasp of the relevant theory. The paucity of clear results is a reflection, I believe, of poor theory. It does not mean that experiments cannot yield clear results.

Second, I do not despair of the possibility of obtaining estimates even in real-life situations. It might be possible to get the actors in a

[21] I should perhaps mention, though, that in the US/Soviet example discussed in section IX I implicitly treated the Soviet response to an American nuclear attack as a cost to the USA of carrying out the policy of 'massive retaliation'.

real-life (but not life-and-death) negotiation to set down their own estimates of the quantities in advance, if necessary in a sealed envelope. One could then deduce from the theory the expected equilibrium outcome and compare it with the actual one. Of course, it is to be explicitly allowed that skill is an intervening factor between the model's predicted outcomes and actual outcomes. But over a number of cases it would become pretty clear whether skill was at all plausible as a gap-filler or whether there was something wrong with the theory's predictions in a more fundamental way.

Finally, my fall-back position is that a theory may throw light on real problems even if it cannot be operationalized. We may be better off with a formal model in our heads, even if we cannot make direct estimates of the variables. (It should be borne in mind that almost all of economics is like this. Nobody even tried to estimate a demand curve until the 1920s.) I may illustrate this by pointing out that what I have offered here could be looked at as a formalization of the purely verbal discussion of 'coercive diplomacy' and the alternatives in the book to which I referred at the beginning of this chapter, *The Limits of Coercive Diplomacy* (see note 7). As it happens, I did not read this book until I had gone through a number of drafts of this chapter, so the analysis contained in it is in no sense designed as a formalization of the implicit theory of the first chapter of *The Limits of Coercive Diplomacy*. It would, however, be an interesting exercise to have someone read that book and then this chapter and see if it helped in making clear the logic. I hope and believe that it would.

XVI LIMITATIONS ON THE USEFULNESS OF THREATS AND PROMISES

The question with which I shall conclude is the following: how useful are threats and promises, compared with other methods, in eliciting desired behaviour from other people? There is an obvious answer, namely, that what you can get is in any given case limited by the size of the threats and rewards you have at your disposal and your willingness to use them. This is primarily the sense in which 'coercive diplomacy' is deemed to have limits in the book to which I have just referred. Although there is not much theoretical interest here, it is of great practical importance. Thus, the protraction of the Vietnam war was caused, as the authors of that book argue, by the failure of American leaders to appreciate the size of the demand they were making on the leaders of North Vietnam in calling for them to give up the unification of the country. George Canning identified the phenomenon when he wrote a dispatch in rhyme to the British government to the effect that 'In matters of commerce / The fault of the Dutch / Is giving too little / And asking too much'.

Suppose, however, that someone were to say that the account just given of Pentagon policy, as based on a miscalculation, while perhaps true for the period up to the mid-60s, thereafter seems less and less applicable and that after that time collective psychopathology increasingly takes over as the right explanation. This would raise a new and more interesting issue about the usefulness of threats and promises. For we can see that, if threats and promises are to be of any use, both parties to the transaction must be minimally rational. The initiating party must be able to deliver what it threatens or promises, and also to withhold it. And there is no point in even trying to use threats or promises on someone who is too stupid to understand them or too lacking in self-control to act on them. We do not rely on deterrence with young children, for example: we put bars around the fire or across the windows. In other words we rely on what I called physical constraints.

The biggest questions along these lines about applicability arise when the actors are not individuals but collectivities (e.g. states). Obviously, all the difficulties that individuals experience in putting together coherent behaviour (in which information is processed, calculations made, and decisions reached and then implemented) are greatly magnified when a number of different people are involved in each stage. For this reason Graham Allison in his book *Essence of Decision*[22] cast doubt on the applicability of what he called a 'rational actor' model to international politics. I think that it is important to recognize limitations on the rationality of organizations, and in the case of relations among the superpowers this ought to entail very great caution in making use of strategies that rely on a quick and precisely calculated reaction by another.[23] But even so I think that Allison overstates the case for pensioning off the 'rational actor' model. For his other two models—that involving the examination of the standard operating procedure of an organization and that involving the analysis of in-fighting among top-level decisionmakers—can in my view be made sense of only in relation to the 'rational actor' model.

The bureaucratic machine, although it of course develops a life of its

[22] G. T. Allison, *Essence of Decision: Explaining the Cuban Missile Crisis* (Boston, Mass.: Little, Brown, 1971).

[23] J. P. Cornford, 'Review Article: The Illusion of Decision', *British Journal of Political Science*, 4 (1974), 231–43, at 233.

own, is after all set up with the object that it should serve the interests of the collectivity (say, the United States) rather than the individual interests of its members; and its 'standard operating procedures' are designed with the object of producing appropriate responses in the organization, 'appropriateness' again being conceived of in terms of serving some overall collective goal. Moreover, if a state (or any other organization) is to survive in a challenging environment, we can predict that constant efforts will have to be made to correct tendencies towards the pursuit of personal self-interest at the expense of organizational goals and tendencies for standard operating procedures to degenerate into rituals which play no useful role. We can only understand the notion of *correcting* tendencies in relation to some norm, and this norm is provided, I suggest, by the 'rational actor' model.

As far as political infighting is concerned, it is no doubt true that cabinet ministers fight for their departments. But this is built into the whole procedure for allocation, and may be regarded (analogously to 'multiple advocacy' in a trial) as contributing to rational decisionmaking. We should also not get too carried away by the idea that 'where you stand depends upon where you sit'. Allison's own analysis of the Cuban Missile Crisis does not, on the whole, suggest actors moved by a desire to aggrandize their own services or departments. The military were cautious, and Robert Kennedy, who played a key part, was hardly acting to build up the office of Attorney General.

A different though related question is that of the relative effectiveness of promises and threats as against alternative ways of getting people to do what you want. It may be possible to combine them so that their relative efficacy does not matter: for example in a smoothly running state the demands of the criminal law are backed both by normative acceptance—'mobilization of commitments'—and by sanctions. Here the existence of the sanctions does not detract from the authority of the law because the sanctions themselves are regarded as legitimate. But in other cases it seems likely that the introduction of promises and threats into a situation shifts people on to a self-interested way of looking at the matter, thus undermining the possibility of a normative appeal. This is the argument put forward by Richard Titmuss in his book *The Gift Relationship*,[24] where he suggests that the introduction of payment for blood has the effect of drying up the supply from voluntary unpaid donation of blood. The two kinds

[24] R. M. Titmuss, *The Gift Relationship: From Human Blood to Social Policy* (London: George Allen and Unwin, 1970).

of motive—in this case social responsibility and commercial self-interest—cannot, the argument goes, coexist in the same society in respect of the same category of transaction. Again, the attempt to mix punishment and rehabilitation in prisons may founder on the inflexibility of prison personnel, but it may also be affected by the problem of one method of eliciting desired behaviour cutting across another.

Finally, there is a point mentioned only in passing by George in *The Limits of Coercive Diplomacy* but which has big implications for the applicability of the 'economic' approach in both senses of 'applicability' that I have distinguished. George points out that an almost invariable effect of actually carrying out a threat—i.e. imposing sanctions—is to harden the attitude of the person subjected to the sanction to the original demand. In our terms, a given concession (expressed in descriptive terms) becomes greater in terms of the loss it would be felt to represent. To the extent that this is so we can say two things. The first is that recurrent demands backed by successively greater threats—even if the demand stays the same—may well actually fall further and further short of being sufficient to overcome resistance. The cost represented by the demand may, in other words, increase faster than the sanction for non-compliance. The other is that if we want to analyse a series of threats we may need to allow for a shift in curves between stages. We can of course carry out the analysis of each stage on the basis of a new set of curves giving us a comparative statics of bargaining with an equilibrium outcome corresponding to each set of curves. But how do we get from one set of curves to the next? That seems to take us outside the 'economic' approach. It requires some propositions in individual psychology (e.g. the frustration–aggression hypothesis) and, where groups are concerned, some notions about the way group solidarity intensifies as a result of common experience of deprivation.

9

IS IT BETTER TO BE POWERFUL OR LUCKY?

I

There are two ways of getting outcomes that you want. One is to bring them about yourself by exercising power. The other is to have them occur (often as the result of the exercise of power by others) without exercising any power yourself. Someone who is commonly in a position to obtain wanted outcomes by exercising power is powerful; someone who commonly obtains wanted outcomes without exercising any power is lucky. This chapter is devoted to an examination in depth of the relation between power and luck. That the relation is not straightforward should already have become apparent to anyone who has noticed that 'power' is defined as a capability whereas 'luck' is defined as a tendency or probability. I shall, in fact, argue that the concept parallel to luck is decisiveness. 'Power' can then be defined as the capacity for decisiveness.

My strategy in this chapter will be as follows. In section II I shall expound the two most well-known power indexes, that proposed by Lloyd Shapley and Martin Shubik and that proposed by John Banzhaf. Then in section III I shall offer a critique of both indexes. Section IV begins the constructive half of the chapter. Here I put forward a rigorous analysis of the relations between luck, decisiveness, and success, and on the basis of this analysis show how the so-called paradoxes of power generated by the standard power indexes can be dissolved. Section V applies the analysis to one historical example of great significance: the American Constitutional Convention of 1787 that created the present US constitution. This will, I hope, show the utility and plausibility of the analysis. Finally, in section VI, I offer a definition of power in terms of the conditions under which an actor can be decisive. I conclude by suggesting an answer to the question posed in the title of the chapter: power is more important to an actor, in relation to luck, the more uncertain that actor is of the likely alignment of forces within the relevant period of time.

Among the problems which I shall seek to illuminate by means of this analysis are the following. Is an increase in one's power always to be welcomed? Is it better to be powerful oneself or to have powerful friends? Must the power of a group be conceptualized as the sum of the power of each of the individual members of the group, or could a group be powerful while each of its members is individually powerless? I shall also seek to throw light on the so-called pluralist-élitist debate, arguing that each side's conclusions follow from its conception of the nature of power.

Let us begin by asking why anybody should ever want to have power. One answer would be that the possession and/or the exercise of power are intrinsically gratifying. It can hardly be doubted that the phenomenon exists. We can all think, for example, of academics who go around collecting committees in the way that Indian braves of an earlier day collected scalps. Some people, no doubt, get their kicks simply from taking part in decisionmaking, even if they are quite indifferent to the outcomes. But this enjoyment of power is parasitic upon the activities of those who do care about the outcomes and are prepared to work for the outcomes they want. A committee made up entirely of people who had no interest in pursuing some particular outcome but were fascinated by the process as such would be as frustrating as a brothel all of whose customers were voyeurs.

I think that the importance of the desire for power as an end in itself is often overestimated as a motive force in politics because of a tendency to conflate two phenomena that are analytically quite distinct. If a civil servant relishes power because this gives him a chance to further some policy to which he is attached—road pricing, free school meals, or whatever—this is a case where power is sought not for its own sake but in order to increase the chance that the favoured policy will be put into effect. The tendency to lump together the pursuit of power for some relatively disinterested public purpose and the pursuit of power as an end in itself comes about, I think, as a result of an implicit assumption that power must be sought either for some self-interested end or as an end in itself. If we take care to avoid this kind of cheap and fashionable cynicism we shall, I believe, conclude that in the great majority of cases people value power because of the chance it gives them to bring about states of affairs that they desire, and not primarily for any intrinsic gratification that they derive from power itself.

At any rate, for the purpose of this chapter I shall disregard the pleasures of power inasfar as they are detached from any notion of enabling one to bring about preferred outcomes. The view of the value of power to be adopted, then, is an instrumental one: power is desired because it gives its possessor the opportunity to change outcomes from what they would otherwise have been, in the direction that the possessor wishes. However, once we say that power is not going to be treated as an end in itself but only as a means to an end, we must define that end. Clearly, the end assumed in what I have just said is that of getting the outcomes you want. The question to which this chapter is addressed can then be put as follows: what is the relation between having power and getting the outcomes you want?

It should be apparent that there is no simple connection between the two. If an individual's power is defined as his ability to change outcomes from what they would otherwise have been in the direction he desires, the likelihood that outcomes will correspond to his desires does not depend solely on his power. It also depends on what the outcome would have been in the absence of his intervention. This is what I shall call luck. Someone with a little power (or no power) but a lot of luck may thus consistently obtain more of the outcomes he wants than someone who has a lot of power but only a little luck.

With enough power you can get everything you want without any luck. With enough luck you can get everything you want without any power. In between these two extremes, things get more complicated, and we need some more formal apparatus in order to keep clear heads. I shall provide that formalization in section IV. But before that let us see what can be learned from the most popular of the existing power indexes.

II

Although I have not so far made the limitation explicit, I am concerned in this chapter not with power in general but with political power. I shall take political power to be the ability of an individual or of a group to change the outcomes of some decisionmaking process from what they would otherwise have been in the direction desired by the person or group, where the decisions made are binding on some collectivity. For many purposes of analysis, it is convenient to consider a special case, namely the case of a body that reaches decisions binding on some collectivity by fixed rules that have the effect of aggregating the preferences expressed according to some specified means by the members of that body. Call such a body a committee and call the means for expressing preferences and the rules for aggregating them a voting procedure.

There are two standard 'power indexes' which purport to measure the relative power of the members of such a committee under alternative decisionmaking rules (weighted voting, chairman's casting vote, and so on). The older-established of the two is the Shapley–Shubik index, which was first put forward by Lloyd Shapley and Martin Shubik in 1954.[1] The other, the Banzhaf index, was introduced in 1965 by John F. Banzhaf III, and has been used by the New York State Court of Appeals.[2]

Briefly, they work as follows. To construct the Shapley–Shubik index for the power of each member of a committee under given voting rules, we consider every possible order in which all the members of the committee might vote in favour of the measure to be decided upon. Then, for each possible order, we identify the member of the committee whose vote pushes the measure over the line so that it wins. We call that voter 'pivotal' within that particular sequence. The power of any member of the committee is then simply the proportion of all the possible voting-orders in which that member is pivotal.

Thus, take the simple case of a committee operating under a majority-rule procedure with three members who have a vote each. The possible orderings are *A*(*B*)*C*, *A*(*C*)*B*, *B*(*A*)*C*, *B*(*C*)*A*, *C*(*A*)*B*, *C*(*B*)*A*. In each ordering, the bracketed member of the commitee is the pivotal one, since the second positive vote makes the measure pass or the second negative vote makes it fail. Out of the six possible permutations, each member of the committee is pivotal in two cases, so each has (unsurprisingly) a score of $\frac{1}{3}$ on the Shapley–Shubik index.

Whereas the Shapley–Shubik index is permutational, the Banzhaf index depends on counting coalitions. To establish the scores of committee members according to the Banzhaf index, we have to consider every possible minimum winning coalition, that is to say every set of committee members sufficient to carry a measure that would become insufficient if any member of the set were to withdraw. Thus, in the example given above, there are three minimum winning coalitions, that of *A* and *B*, *A* and *C*, and *B* and *C*. To get the score on the Banzhaf index we count the number of ways in which each actor

[1] L. S. Shapley and M. Shubik, 'A Method of Evaluating the Distribution of Power in a Committee System', *American Political Science Review*, 48 (1954), 787–92 (repr. in Roderick Bell, David V. Edwards, and R. Harrison Wagner (eds.), *Political Power* (New York: Free Press, 1969), 209–13). Page refs. are given to this reprint.

[2] J. F. Banzhaf III, 'Weighted Voting Doesn't Work: A Mathematical Analysis', *Rutgers Law Review*, 19 (1965), 317–43; and 'Multimember Electoral Districts: Do They Violate the "One Man, One Vote" Principle?', *Yale Law Journal*, 75 (1966), 1309–88.

could make a winning coalition into a non-winning one by withdrawing from it. (Each here could bring down two.) Then, in order to make the scores sum to unity, we simply divide each of them by the total. So, in the present case, the total is six, each committee member has a raw score of two, and the Banzhaf index, again not surprisingly, ascribes a final score of $\frac{1}{3}$ to each member.

Although the Shapley–Shubik and Banzhaf indexes are computed differently, and in any complex voting scheme usually produce different numerical results, it is generally the case that a change in voting rules that increases an actor's power on the Shapley–Shubik index also increases it on the Banzhaf index, and vice versa. In the example that was worked through above, the two indexes produced the same answers, but in such a simple case they could scarcely have failed to. If we constrain the answer so that the amount of power within the committee must sum to unity and must somehow be totally allocated among the individuals who make up the committee, we must expect that any completely symmetrical voting scheme will attribute equal power to each. This must be true simply because there is no basis on which to distinguish the members.

Note that the equality thus ascribed to the committee members in no way depends on the details of the actual scheme, so long as it treats all alike. Consider, for example, a rule requiring unanimous agreement. This would make the last voter pivotal in each of the six Shapley–Shubik permutations. We can see that each committee member is going to be last twice, giving each a score of $\frac{1}{3}$. On the Banzhaf measure there is only one minimum winning coalition (made up of *A*, *B* and *C*). Each committee member is thus in the single winning minimum coalition. The total score is therefore three, so we divide each individual's score by three, giving each $\frac{1}{3}$.

The point is, however, that we do not really need to carry out the calculations, because we can deduce directly from the symmetry of the voting rule that the power of the committee members is going to be equal. We may, of course, observe when we realize this that any measure of the distribution of power that is unable to distinguish between majority voting and a *liberum veto* is hardly telling us anything we would like to know. But that result is unavoidable right from the start once the commitment is made to treat power as something that must always be allocated to individuals in such a way that the individual scores sum to unity.

III

Both indexes are designed to try to capture the idea of an individual voter's chance of making a difference to the outcome. But both fail because they substitute something else. One counts the proportion of times an individual voter is pivotal out of all pivots, the other the proportion of defections from a minimal winning coalition an individual can engage in out of all such defections. But there is no reason for supposing that what we count is related in any direct way to what we want to know about.

The irrelevance of the measure advocated by Shapley and Shubik is patent. In their article they make the following claim: 'Our definition of the power of an individual member depends on [i.e. makes it depend on—B.B.] the chance he has of being critical to the success of a winning coalition.'[3] But their definition of a pivot does not in the least capture the notion of being critical to the success (or failure) of something. We can see this by thinking about the following case. Let us imagine that a million pounds has to be raised in a given time for some purpose—for example to prevent the export of a picture. And suppose that, as the deadline approaches, contributions to the appeal are coming in at the rate of a thousand pounds a day but that there is still a shortfall of a hundred thousand pounds. If some donor gives that amount, his contribution might well be said to have been critical to the success of the fundraising effort, because it is likely that in its absence the target would not have been reached. Now suppose instead that funds flow in at a rate of a thousand pounds per day and the target is reached with several days to spare. There was still some contribution that pushed the total over the line. But in this case it would be an abuse of language to call the donation critical, because if it had not been sent the target would still easily have been reached. Similarly, if a bridge has been weakened over the years by traffic, it would be unreasonable to say that its being crossed by the particular car that caused it to collapse was critical if there is every reason to suppose that the next car in line would have done the same thing. If, however, it was being crossed by a tank that made the bridge collapse, we might reasonably say that that was critical because with normal traffic the bridge would probably otherwise have lasted for many more years.

Thus, when we say that some event is critical for something's coming about, we are necessarily involved in a counterfactual

[3] Bell *et al.*, *Political Power*, p. 209.

assertion that, with everything else remaining the same, in the absence of the event in question the thing would not have happened. (There is an implicit qualification here: we mean that it would not have happened roughly at the same place or at the same time or in the same form. What constitutes sufficient closeness to count depends on the context.) In particular, an event is not critical if it could be foreseen with confidence that in its absence another event with the same effects would have occurred in its place.

Now recall how the Shapley–Shubik concept of a pivot is derived.

Let us consider the following scheme: There is a group of individuals all willing to vote for some bill. They vote in order. As soon as a majority has voted for it, it is declared passed, and the member who voted last is given credit for having passed it. Let us choose the voting order of the members randomly. Then we may compute the frequency with which an individual belongs to the group whose votes are used and, of more importance, we may compute how often he is *pivotal*. This latter number serves to give us our index. It measures the number of times that the action of the individual actually changes the state of affairs.[4]

I hope that it is not necessary to belabour the point that the pivot, so understood, does not in the relevant sense change the state of affairs. Since we have a group of individuals 'all willing to vote for some bill', it makes no difference who happens to provide the vote that gives the measure the winning margin, since, *ex hypothesi*, if any of the remaining members of the body had replaced that person in the sequence, he would have voted for the measure instead.

In other expositions, the pivot is said to be 'decisive', and this is the term that I propose to use later in developing a more satisfactory conception of power in a committee. But again it should be clear that the pivot in the Shapley–Shubik scheme is not decisive. Thus, Steven Brams writes:

For all the different ways in which the buildup of the grand coalition can occur through a sequence of additions of one player, there will be one player in each sequence who will be decisive to a coalition's becoming winning. We call this player, who makes the difference between a coalition's being winning or losing, the *pivot*. . . .[5]

But obviously, if what we have is 'the buildup of the grand coalition', the place of any member of the committee in the voting sequence is

[4] Ibid. 210, italics in original.

[5] Steven J. Brams, *Game Theory and Politics* (New York: Free Press, 1975), 162, italics in original.

neither here nor there. If a simple majority is all that is required and everybody is going to vote 'aye' anyway, then nobody is decisive because nobody individually makes a difference to the outcome.

To say, however, that no individual member of the committee has any power violates one of the postulates upon which the Shapley–Shubik index is constructed, namely that the power of the members of a committee must always sum to unity. The deeper point here is that the whole approach embodied in the Shapley–Shubik index is inappropriate. The index arises out of, and is indeed simply a special case of, Lloyd Shapley's work on the problem of the value of a game, and we need briefly to backtrack to look at that.

The question that Shapley set himself is a good one, and one of central importance to much political analysis. Indeed, one of my objects in this chapter is to provide a framework within which it can be answered (see sections V and VI below). The question is: how can we estimate a priori the value to someone of playing a certain game? It is evident that this is central to questions of accession and secession. The voters in the various American states had to estimate, for example, the value of the game constituted by the proposed Federal constitution. More recently, the British electorate had to estimate the value of the game constituted by the enlarged EEC. When the value of the game played within a state falls below some level we may expect that secession will begin to appeal. And so on.[6]

As Shapley wrote: 'In attempting to apply the theory [of games] to any field, one would normally expect to be permitted to include, in the class of "prospects", the prospect of having to play a game. The possibility of evaluating games is, therefore, of critical importance.'[7] Thus, we know that for zero-sum games there is a plausible case for assigning to each player his minimax value and calling that the value of the game to him: it is what, on the basis of sound theoretical arguments, he can expect to get. The problem is how to extend the assignment of the value of a game to other kinds of game. The Shapley value of a game to each player is derived by considering all subsets of

[6] See Ronald Rogowski, *Rational Legitimacy: A Theory of Political Support* (Princeton, N.J.: Princeton University Press, 1974) for an original analysis of legitimacy in terms of expectations about the course of decision making. Rogowski relates the acceptability of a regime to an actor to that actor's probability of 'uniquely determining' outcomes. This measure is a cousin of the Shapley–Shubik index: the total power of all actors sums to unity and each actor's score is supposed to reflect his individual responsibility for producing outcomes. Therefore the criticisms made here of the Shapley–Shubik index apply to Rogowski's treatment as well.

[7] L. S. Shapley, 'A Value for *n*-person Games', in H. W. Kuhn and A. W. Tucker (eds.), *Contributions to the Theory of Games II*, Annals of Mathematical Studies, 28 (Princeton, N.J.: Princeton University Press, 1953), 307–17, at 307.

one or more players that can be formed out of the set of players and treating each subset as equally probable. Some of these coalitions will have no value, others will (in the general case) have different values depending on their composition. The value of the game for each player is based on the increment that that player brings to each coalition. In other words, for each possible coalition (subset of players) we take its value and then subtract from that its value without the player for whom we are carrying out the calculation. (Obviously, if the player is not in a coalition, the difference must be zero.) That player is then credited with the whole of the increase in the value of the coalition that his presence brings to it.

The procedure can be stated in a way that brings out clearly the parentage of the Shapley–Shubik index: we can imagine

> the random formation of a coalition of all the players, starting with a single member and adding one player at a time. Each player is then assigned the advantage accruing to the coalition at the time of his admission. In this process of computing the expected value for an individual player all coalition formations are considered as equally likely.[8]

The Shapley–Shubik index may be seen as the Shapley value for the special case where coalitions do not have a variety of values but are either winning (value 1) or losing (value 0). Adding members to a coalition thus does not increase its value until the threshold of winning is reached; then, once the 'winning' point has been reached, adding more again does not increase the value further. The pivot—the member of the committee whose addition to a coalition changes it from losing to winning—thus gets credit for the whole value of a winning coalition.

The trouble is that the basic model is inappropriate to the typical phenomena of politics. It belongs to the branch of game theory that presupposes perfectly divisible and transferable utility—something like money only even better. When we spoke above about the 'value' of any given coalition we were talking about a substance—utility—that could be divided in any way among the members of the coalition in such a way that it remained the same size. This assumption violates the first principle of political analysis, which is that a public policy is a public good (or bad). If the death penalty is reintroduced, that pleases those who favour it and displeases those

[8] Kuhn and Tucker, *Contributions to the Theory of Games II*, p. 303. Cited in R. D. Luce and H. Raiffa, *Games and Decisions* (New York: Wiley, 1957), 250. See, generally, pp. 245–50 for a discussion of the Shapley value.

who do not. Similarly, a tax break is good or bad for people according to their situation. The gains are not confined to those who voted on the winning side nor are the losses confined to those who were on the losing side. The measure creates its own gainers and losers by its content: if you are advantaged or disadvantaged by it that will be so whether you voted in favour or against, or did not vote at all.

There are, of course, some cases in which people get paid off according to the way in which they vote. American presidential nominating conventions are the textbook example. Delegations are usually concerned with the symbolic/ideological characteristics of the candidates, and they also have a natural preference (at least *ceteris paribus*) for a candidate who has a good chance of winning the election. But, in addition, there is some advantage in having backed the candidate who actually gets the nomination—and to have backed him before it was clear that he was going to get it. The analysis of such a case in terms of transferable utility is at any rate partially appropriate in that we can think of a fixed amount of 'patronage' to be divided up among supporters. But it is, I suggest, a basic error to take a presidential nominating convention as a paradigm of political decisionmaking.

In saying this, I am not committed to a particularly high-minded view of politics. We can, if we wish, follow Lasswell's formulation and say that politics is 'who gets what, when, how'. The crucial question is precisely in virtue of what it is that they get whatever it is they get. What I am saying is that the standard way in which people get what they get is through the contents of public policies. Private pay-offs related to the way in which they vote are a by-product.

What about cases where a majority of legislators get together and cook up some scheme for providing geographically specific benefits for their own constituents? This presents no problem for the present analysis. That it is often thought of as a counter-example illustrates just how difficult it is to keep things clear. It is still true in such a case that the outcome is a public policy that distributes benefits and costs in a certain way. The benefits derive from the adoption of the policy, not from having voted for it. Naturally, we would expect the prospective beneficiaries (or their representatives) to be the ones to vote in favour and the prospective losers (or their representatives) to vote against. But the point is that there is no advantage in 'being a member of the winning coalition' if all we mean by this is voting for the measure. If one legislator whose constituents stand to benefit votes against, and one whose constituents stand to lose votes in favour, the measure is still passed and has exactly the same distributive effects. It is remarkable how much of the application of game theory to politics falls foul of this simple and elementary observation: the whole of William Riker's *The Theory of Political Coalitions*[9] is invalidated by it, and so is almost every analysis of power in decisionmaking bodies. They operate as if the pay-offs arising from a vote could be allocated according to the way people vote. They do not take account of the fact that a public policy is a public good.

On its own premisses, the Shapley–Shubik index is quite correct in identifying the value to an actor of taking part in a certain decision-making process with his power. If the utility arising from any play of the game (any vote of the committee) is divisible and transferable and it all goes to whoever makes the coalition win (the pivot), then indeed power and value are directly related to one another. But the whole point about a public good is that there is no way in which the person who provides it can appropriate all the value arising from it. There can thus be 'free riders', who gain the benefits without having done anything to bring the public good into existence. Hence the distinction on which I am insisting between power and luck as alternative ways of getting outcomes that you want. You may get them by exercising power and thus making them come about when they would not otherwise have done. But if you are lucky you will be able to take a 'free ride' on the efforts of others. Provided your policy preferences are like those of people who have power, you will finish up with no less than they get, even though you have done nothing to bring about the outcomes that are mutually desired. This shows plainly that if we are to talk sensibly about the anticipated value to an actor of a political process—a state, a federation, a common market or whatever, operating by known decisionmaking rules—we must break away from the approach embodied in the Shapley–Shubik index.

I have so far said nothing specifically in criticism of the Banzhaf index, but much less needs to be said. The Shapley–Shubik index is perfectly consistent, given its premisses (which happen to be inappli-

[9] William Riker, *The Theory of Political Coalitions* (New Haven: Yale University Press, 1962). Riker's notion that 'winning' is a universal value in politics depends on precisely the equivocation identified in the text, and his 'proof' of the minimum size principle depends upon the assumption of divisible, transferable utility. Riker's theory would work if politics were nothing but a matter of allocating spoils, in other words if it had no connection with policies that are public goods or bads. For a discussion of these two aspects of politics and of the problem of integrating them in a single analysis, see my 'Review Article: "Crisis, Choice, and Change", Part II, Games Theorists Play', *British Journal of Political Science*, 7 (1977), 217–53.

cable), and it has a certain theoretical elegance.[10] The Banzhaf index, by contrast, is a mere gimmick, with no coherent theoretical underpinnings. It has all the drawbacks of the Shapley–Shubik index in that it too assumes that the power in a committee sums to unity and can be exhaustively allocated among the members. But in addition it incorporates equiprobability in a very queer way by in effect assuming that each coalition should be weighted in the computation according to the number of different ways in which it can be brought down by the withdrawal of a member. Thus, in a committee with weighted voting it may be that a certain coalition is vulnerable to the defection of only one particular member, while another is vulnerable to defection by any of three members. (An example will be given a little later.) Then the Banzhaf index counts the first coalition towards one member's score, whereas the second coalition counts separately in the scores of three members. Yet, if one were going to depart from equiprobability, it would seem more plausible to go in exactly the opposite direction and assume that, the more different ways there are in which a coalition is open to being brought down by defection, the less likely it is to form.

Up to this point I have treated the Shapley–Shubik and Banzhaf indexes as a priori indexes, which in practice means that I have followed their authors in assuming that all orderings or defections from a minimum winning coalition are equally probable. But in real life we know very well that in any actual committee it would be very extraordinary for the votes of different members not to be related in some systematic way. Any adequate treatment of power in a committee must be able to deal with departures from equiprobability, and I shall show in the next section how that can be done within the framework of analysis I propose. The attempts that have been made to modify the application of the Shapley–Shubik and Banzhaf indexes, however, produce such absurdities that they underline the fundamental inadequacy of these indexes.

The method of analysis used is pretty crude. What is done is to postulate that some committee members always vote on the same side or always vote on different sides, and then see what this does to the power index for all the members of the committee. It is hardly surprising that the Shapley–Shubik index goes haywire when the attempt is made to move away from the equal probability of every ordering. The index is constructed, as we saw, by assuming that all the

[10] Luce and Raiffa, in *Games and Decisions*, pp. 245–50 and 253–5, provide a clear exposition of this point.

members of the committee vote in favour of a measure and by counting pivots. The introduction of the idea that some committee members vote one way and others vote the other way on the same measure therefore violates the assumption upon which the index is founded. What is done to fudge it is to assume that those who vote *before* the pivot must still all vote the same way, but that those who vote *after* the pivot can be allowed to vote either way. The Banzhaf index might appear less vulnerable, since we can always simply strike out some minimum winning coalitions on the basis of a stipulation that they will never form. But in practice both indexes give rise to exactly the same kinds of absurd conclusion.

The most dramatic illustration of this point is the so-called paradox of quarrelling members, described in the following terms by Steven Brams.

> We may suppose, for example, that two players are involved in a quarrel and refuse to join together to help form a winning coalition. Although one might suspect that they could only succeed in hurting each other, it is a curious fact that the quarrel between two players may actually redound to *their* benefit by increasing both their individual and combined voting power. We call this phenomenon the *paradox of quarreling members*.[11]

Consider an example in which there are three committee members, with weights of 3, 2, and 2 votes, and where 5 votes out of a total of 7 are needed for a committee decision. Call the player with 3 votes A and the other two B and C. Under normal circumstances the Shapley–Shubik values are $\frac{2}{3}$ for A and $\frac{1}{6}$ apiece for B and C, and the Banzhaf values are $\frac{3}{5}$ for A and $\frac{1}{5}$ apiece for B and C; but if for some reason B and C never agree the figures become $\frac{1}{2}$, $\frac{1}{4}$, $\frac{1}{4}$ on both indexes. Both indexes thus have the implication that B and C gain power by quarrelling.

On the Banzhaf criterion this is a result of the fact that when B and C quarrel only two minimum winning coalitions, that of A and B and that of A and C, are possible. Thus, A can bring down two coalitions (i.e. make them less than winning) while B and C can bring down one each. Thus, there are four possible ways of bringing down a coalition, two involving A and one each B and C. Hence the scores are: $A = \frac{1}{2}$, $B = \frac{1}{4}$, $C = \frac{1}{4}$. If the coalition of A, B, and C can form, however, we have an extra way in which a coalition can be brought down: by A's withdrawal from this 'grand coalition'. (Neither B nor C can bring it down by withdrawing from it since it would still have 5 votes. Thus, the coalition of A, B, and C is minimal with respect to A but not to B

[11] Brams, *Game Theory and Politics*, pp. 180–1, italics in original.

or *C*—an awkward notion but one integral to Banzhaf's way of doing the calculations.) Therefore, if all combinations are possible, there are 5 ways in which a coalition can be brought down, in 3 of which *A* figures, leaving one apiece for *B* and *C*. This produces the scores of $\frac{3}{5}$ for *A* and $\frac{1}{5}$ each for *B* and *C*.

On the Shapley–Shubik index it is a matter of the number of orderings in which each member is pivotal (i.e. makes up the required majority of 5 votes). *A*(*B*)*C*, *A*(*C*)*B*, *B*(*A*)*C*, and *C*(*A*)*B* are all the available permutations where *B* and *C* disagree, making *A* pivotal in 2 out of 4 and *B* and *C* pivotal in one each, producing scores of $\frac{1}{2}$, $\frac{1}{4}$, $\frac{1}{4}$. But if *B* and *C* do not necessarily disagree, there are also available *BC*(*A*) and *CB*(*A*), which add two more permutations where *A* is pivotal. (*A* is pivotal because *B* and *C* together do not make up the required 5 votes.) Thus, *A* would be pivotal in 4 cases out of 6 ($\frac{2}{3}$) and *B* and *C* in one each out of six ($\frac{1}{6}$). Yet the conclusion, that the power of *B* and *C* has increased, and that 'there is an incentive for them to quarrel and increase their share of the voting power'[12] is manifestly absurd. When *B* and *C* are always on opposite sides, this has the consequence that *A*, by casting his 3 votes, is always able to ensure 5 votes for the side he favours, since there will be 2 votes in favour of each side automatically.

Another so-called paradox, which either reduces to the paradox of quarrelling members or makes no sense, is one that says it is better (in the sense of producing more power) to split up than vote as a bloc. Thus, consider the same committee as before, with simple majority voting. The members might as well have one vote each, since no one and any two constitute a majority. The Shapley–Shubik and Banzhaf indexes therefore assign each member a score of $\frac{1}{3}$. 'Now assume that the 3-vote player breaks up into constituent 1-vote members.'[13] But *what* exactly are we to assume here? If the three members with one vote all vote the same way, nothing has changed. But if they vote differently (in accordance with the equiprobability assumptions of the two indexes), we have a change from (in effect) agreement between three voters to random association. The idea that a bloc whose members agree would split up and start voting against one another simply in order to increase their 'power' is bizarre, though not, it must be said, too bizarre to have inspired empirical research presented with a straight face.[14] In any case, if they do, the three members with a vote

[12] Ibid. 181.

[13] Ibid. 177.

[14] G. A. Schubert, 'The Study of Judicial Decision-Making as an Aspect of Political Behavior', *American Political Science Review*, 52 (1958), 1022–4; W. Riker, 'A Test of the

each increase their aggregate power from $\frac{1}{3}$ to $\frac{3}{7}$ on the Banzhaf index and $\frac{2}{5}$ on the Shapley–Shubik index.[15] But obviously it is better to have two allies on a committee than not, so this is an absurd conclusion. (For those who distrust their intuitions on this point, a demonstration is offered in the next section.)

Brams says of 'paradoxes' like these that 'this term is not meant to imply that they in any way invalidate the power indexes. Quite the contrary: They illustrate their usefulness in showing up aspects of voting power whose existence would have been difficult to demonstrate convincingly in the absence of precise quantitative concepts.'[16] I hope it is clear that these are not paradoxes in even the loosest sense of that much-abused term. Their only use is to drive home to anyone who is not persuaded by more abstract considerations the utter inadequacy of the indexes. Brams is like someone who owns a broken thermometer and says that the fact that it does not register a higher temperature when it is put in a flame shows us something new and interesting (albeit counter-intuitive) about the nature of heat.

IV

The approach that I shall take in developing an alternative to the measures of power considered and rejected is quite simple in principle. For the sake of ease of exposition, let us assume that any member of a committee has to choose only between acting and not acting in respect of any given proposal, and that each proposal admits only of a 'yes' or 'no' vote. It is an advantage of the analytic scheme to be put forward that it admits both of these restrictive assumptions to be relaxed, permitting us to consider different degrees of effort (for example, lobbying as well as voting) and also to consider cases where several alternatives are proposed. But let us for now follow the other indexes in taking the simplest kind of situation.

Suppose that the member of a committee does nothing in order to further the passage of a certain measure which he favours. (He may, for example, be ill and unable to attend the meeting at which it is voted on.) The outcome may nevertheless be the one he wants. We can estimate how often the outcome will correspond with the one he

Adequacy of the Power Index', *Behavioral Science*, 4 (1959), 276–90. I am not, of course, denying that those who are pivotal in a body whose members can be arrayed on one dimension get the outcomes they want. What I deny is that it makes sense for somebody to vote against what he is in favour of simply in order to be pivotal.

[15] Brams, *Game Theory and Politics*, pp. 177–8.

[16] Ibid. 181–2.

desires if he never does anything. Call the proportion of adventitious successes that this member of the committee has his *luck*. There is also some proportion of the time that the outcomes will correspond to his preferences if he does act. Call this his *success*: it represents how frequently he gets what he wants if he tries. Now take the difference between his success and his luck. This is his *decisiveness*: it represents the difference that acting makes to his success. The formula is then:

$$\text{success} = \text{luck} + \text{decisiveness}.$$

For any given individual each of these three measures will take a value between 0 and 1, but the scores of all the committee members do not have to sum to 1, and generally will not.

In order to apply this method of analysis to a committee we need to feed in some information about the degree of association between the votes of the different members of the committee. If we want to establish a priori values, we should assume that there is no association: that, from knowing how *A* voted, we are no better placed for guessing how *B* voted than if we knew nothing. Let us take the simple case of a three-member committee that decides by majority voting and where each member has one vote. Consider the situation from the point of view of *A*. We have to establish his luck and his success and we can then obtain his decisiveness by subtracting the first from the second.

To estimate his luck we need to know how often he will get the outcome he wants even if he does nothing. Suppose that he is in favour of a proposal. There is a fifty-fifty chance that *B* supports it and a fifty-fifty chance that *C* supports it. Since these probabilities are independent of one another, the probability that when *A* favours an outcome *B* and *C* will also do so is $\frac{1}{4}$. The probability that *B* and *C* will agree with each other but disagree with *A* is also $\frac{1}{4}$. The probability that *B* and *C* will be split is $\frac{1}{2}$. It may help to think of coin tosses. If you toss two coins, there is a one in four chance of getting two heads, a one in four chance of getting two tails and a one in two chance of getting a head and a tail.

Thus, if *A* does not act (i.e. abstains from voting), the measure that *A* favours will be carried one quarter of the time, will lose one quarter of the time, and will be tied half the time. If ties are resolved randomly, *A* may expect that half the ties will go in his favour and half against him. Thus, his expectation overall is that he will get what he wants half the time: this is his luck score.

Although I have worked it through here, this was not in fact necessary. For it must be the case that any actor whose preferences are randomly associated with a set of outcomes will on the average get the outcome he wants half the time. Think again of tossing coins. If you always pick your side on an issue by tossing a coin, you will inevitably like half the outcomes in the long run, *whatever* they are, just so long as the outcome in each case is independent of the result of your coin-toss. Even if all measures pass or all measures fail, you will still get half of the outcomes you want, provided that your preferences are randomly associated with these outcomes.

Now we have to ask what happens when *A* takes part in the proceedings. We know that a quarter of the time the measure he favours already has the votes of *B* and *C*, so it will pass without his help. And we also know that a quarter of the time *B* and *C* will agree in being against the measure, so it will still lose even with *A* voting in favour. In the remaining half of the cases, however, *B* and *C* are split and *A* is able to turn a tie into a win for the side he supports. All ties are now resolved in the direction he prefers, rather than only half of them. His success is therefore $\frac{3}{4}$. Since his luck is $\frac{1}{2}$, his decisiveness is $\frac{1}{4}$.

To extend the analysis, let us reconsider Brams's example of the 'paradox of quarrelling members'. This example will enable us to see how the method of analysis put forward deals with departures from equiprobability. It may be recalled that the example had another special feature, namely that a majority of five out of seven votes was needed for the passage of a measure. This requires us to treat 'yes' and 'no' votes separately, because the probabilities will be different. To take an extreme case, a committee every member of which had a veto would give each member the certainty of getting a 'no' outcome when he was against a measure, but only a low a priori probability of getting a 'yes' outcome when he favoured one. The question then arises of how to aggregate the probability of getting a desired 'yes' outcome and the probability of getting a desired 'no' outcome. I shall take the obvious step, in the absence of any reason for doing anything else, of averaging them. But for some purposes one may wish to consider them separately, and it is an advantage of the measure proposed that it enables us to do so.

The results can be presented in summary form as follows. We concentrate first on *A*'s scores. Table 9.1 is drawn up on the assumption that there is in each case a random association between *A*'s preferences and those of *B* and *C*, but that *B* and *C* may always disagree (I), have randomly associated preferences (II), or always agree (III). In all three conditions *B* and *C* cannot pass anything by themselves since they command only four votes between them and it

TABLE 9.1

Conditions	*A's success* (1)	*A's luck* (2)	*A's decisiveness* (3)=(1)−(2)
I. *B* and *C* always disagree	1	1/2	1/2
II. *B* and *C* have random association	7/8	1/2	3/8
III. *B* and *C* always agree	3/4	1/2	1/4

is stipulated that five votes are required. Therefore, if *A* does not take part, nothing is passed, which we assume suits *A* half the time on average. His luck is therefore $\frac{1}{2}$ in each of the three conditions defined by differing associations between the preferences of *B* and *C*.

If *A* votes, we get different results for each condition. We know that he can always have a 'no' outcome without taking part. But in condition I, *B* and *C* are always deadlocked 2–2, so whenever *A* is in favour of a measure he can make it win 5–2 by voting for it. *A* therefore has a success score of 1 (which must be correct since he always gets the outcome he wants) and a decisiveness score of $\frac{1}{2}$ (which we get by deducting his luck score of $\frac{1}{2}$, based on the assumption that he is against half of all measures).

In case II, where the preferences of *B* and *C* are associated at random with each other (and also with *A*'s preferences), *A* will get a 'yes' outcome by voting for a measure so long as *B* and *C* do not unite against it. Thus, *A* loses, in spite of using his vote when he is for something, when *B* is against it and when *C* is also against it. Since these are three independent probabilities of $\frac{1}{2}$, we multiply them together to get the probability of their joint occurrence and find that *A* loses $\frac{1}{8}$ of the time. The rest of the time when *A* favours something, either *B* is in favour and *C* against, or *B* is against and *C* in favour, or both are in favour. All three cases make *A* decisive, since they provide the margin of victory. Each has a probability of $\frac{1}{8}$, so *A* is decisive $\frac{3}{8}$ of the time, lucky $\frac{1}{2}$ of the time, and successful $\frac{7}{8}$ of the time.

Finally, in case III where *B* and *C* always agree, *A* loses in spite of voting whenever he is in favour of something and *B* and *C* are against it. Since, *ex hypothesi*, they always vote together in this case, we have only two independent probabilities to multiply together: the probability that *A* wants a 'yes' outcome and the probability that *B* and *C* want a 'no' outcome. Since these probabilities are independent, we multiply them together and get the answer that *A* loses $\frac{1}{4}$ of the time. He is decisive $\frac{1}{4}$ of the time (when he is in favour of something and *B*

TABLE 9.2

Conditions	*B's success* *(1)*	*B's luck* *(2)*	*B's decisiveness* *(3)=(1)−(2)*
I. *B* and *C* always disagree	1/2	1/4	1/4
II. *B* and *C* have random association	5/8	1/2	1/8
III. *B* and *C* always agree	3/4	3/4	0

and *C* are too) and lucky $\frac{1}{2}$ of the time (whenever he is against something), so he is successful $\frac{3}{4}$ of the time.

It may be recalled that the supposed paradox arose from the way in which the scores of *B* and *C* rose on the Shapley–Shubik and Banzhaf indexes when they quarrelled. It is therefore interesting to see how things appear from the point of view of *B* (who is of course isomorphic with *C*). The results are presented in Table 9.2. The underlying calculations can best be presented in tree form, as in Figures 9.1, 9.2, and 9.3. The trees show all the logically possible combinations of preferences that *A*, *B*, and *C* could have on some issue. The figures are probabilities. Thus, following down the leftmost line of Figure 9.1, the probability that *A* will be in favour (i.e. 'yes') on an issue is $\frac{1}{2}$; the probability that *B* will also be in favour is $\frac{1}{4}$, since there is no association between *A*'s and *B*'s preferences; but the probability that *C* will also be in favour is 0, since (in case I) *B* and *C* always disagree. The final row gives the result of each contingency from the point of view of *B*. Table 9.2 is derived by adding up the figures in this last row.

If we look at the two tables, Table 9.1 for *A* and Table 9.2 for *B*, we can see how this mode of analysis illuminates what is really going on in the example. Table 9.1 shows, as we should expect, that *A*'s success is least when *B* and *C* agree with each other, is intermediate when there is a random association between their preferences, and is at a maximum when they disagree. Since there is a random association between the preferences of *A* and those of *B* and *C*, his luck is constant and all the difference is made up by increased decisiveness. Thus, the analysis confirms the time-honoured view that it is better to face a divided opposition than a united one (*divide et impera*) and that the most advantageous position in a triad arises when the other members quarrel (*tertius gaudens*).[17]

[17] 'Literally, "the third who enjoys", that is, the third party which in some fashion or another draws advantage from the quarrel of two others.' Kurt H. Wolff (ed.), *The Sociology of Georg Simmel* (New York: The Free Press, 1950), 154n. The whole of Simmel's subtle discussion of the *Tertius Gaudens* and the principle of *Divide et impera* (pp. 154–62 and 162–9 respectively) is well worth reading.

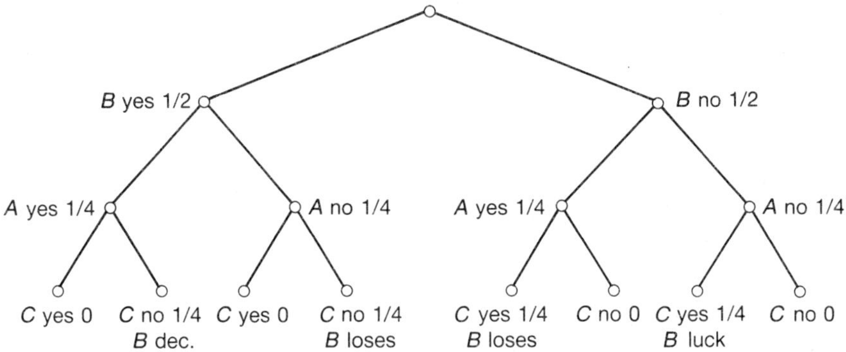

FIG. 9.1 Outcomes for *B* under condition I

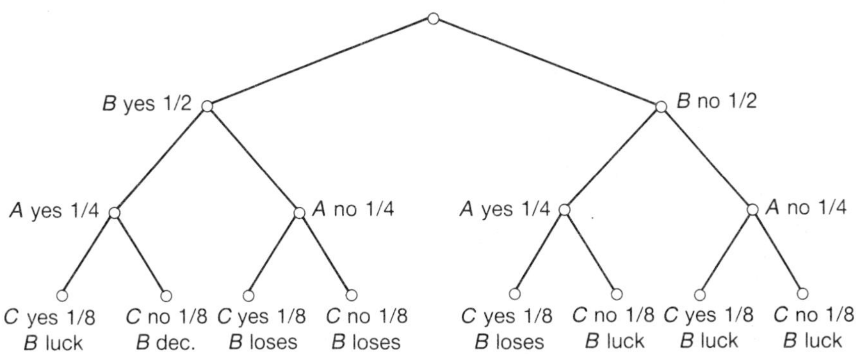

FIG. 9.2 Outcomes for *B* under condition II

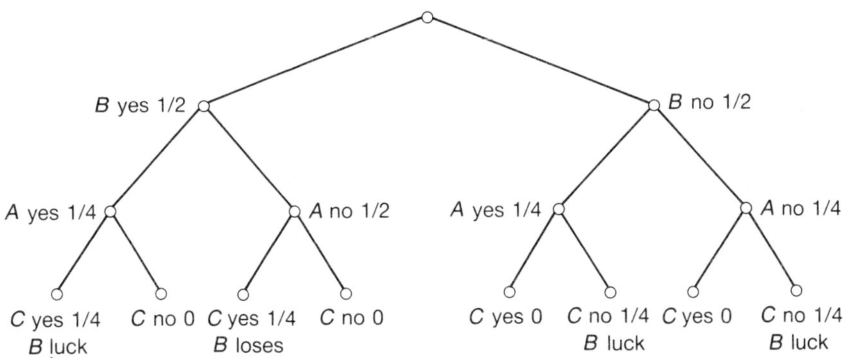

FIG. 9.3 Outcomes for *B* under condition III

Table 9.2 is more intriguing because it shows why, with a defective measure, the 'paradox' arose. We see here that *B* gets what he wants most often when he agrees with *C* all the time, loses most often when he disagrees with *C* all the time, and gets what he wants with an intermediate frequency when there is a random association between his and *C*'s preferences. This is all as we should expect, and shows that it is better to agree with others than to disagree with them.

However, when we look at the final column in Table 9.2, we see that decisiveness goes in the opposite direction to success, to the point where *B* has no decisiveness at all when he and *C* always agree. We can now see easily enough how the 'paradox' comes about: if we take decisiveness as something valued for its own sake, and compress the scores of the actors so that they sum to unity, we are bound to get the answer that *A*'s 'power' (i.e. decisiveness) goes down and that of *B* and *C* goes up when they quarrel. We can then derive the crazy conclusion that it pays them to quarrel. But by keeping decisiveness and success separate and not making the scores sum to unity we are able to see (1) that *A*'s decisiveness goes up when *B* and *C* quarrel; and (2) that, although the decisiveness of *B* and *C* goes up when they quarrel, their success rate goes down.

A moment's thought is sufficient to show why *B* is more successful but not at all decisive when *C* invariably agrees with him. If *B* is against something, *C* is (*ex hypothesi*) against it too. But, in the absence of any effort by *B*, a measure opposed by *C* will go down whatever *A*'s views about it. Therefore, whenever *B* is 'no' (half the time), he gets a 'no' outcome in virtue of *C*'s efforts. Half the time, then, he is lucky. When *B* is 'yes' (the other half of the time), *C* is also (*ex hypothesi*) 'yes'. If *A* is also 'yes' (which he will be in half of these cases), the measure will carry without needing *B*'s vote; but if *A* is 'no' (which will occur in the other half), the measure goes down anyway because no measure can pass unless *A* supports it. So, when *B* is 'yes', he has an equal chance of being lucky or losing. Overall, he is lucky three-quarters of the time and loses the remaining quarter of the time.

There is nothing strange about this result. What it says is simply that if *B* can count on *C* to vote in the direction that he favours he need not bother to exert himself. To make the point clearer, consider a committee that acts by majority vote (e.g. a parliament) and contains a bloc of committee members (e.g. a disciplined party) who always agree and constitute substantially more than a majority. No single member of this bloc has any decisiveness: so long as all the others vote, his absence will never make any difference to the outcome. Yet he always gets the outcomes he wants. Thus, his success is 1 while his decisiveness is 0.

This implies, of course, that there may be situations in which a group of people collectively bring about an outcome but none is individually decisive. There is nothing wrong in this conclusion: on the contrary, it is one of the defects of the Shapley–Shubik and Banzhaf indexes that they rule it out by insisting that 'power' must always sum to unity. But we must beware of deriving absurd conclusions by ignoring the relevance of levels of analysis. If six people shoot at somebody and any single shot would have been fatal, none of them was individually decisive (or critical) in causing the death. Yet they were certainly collectively responsible in that the victim would not have died if none of them had fired. We may therefore say—and must say—that a *party* was decisive even though no individual member of it was decisive. In other words, we must be prepared to carry on our analysis at the level of groups as well as individuals.

This has considerable relevance for the inconclusive pluralist–élitist debate about power. Both sides are probably right, given their level of analysis. This is why one has the impression of people talking past one another. The 'pluralists', who are really individualists, look at a situation and point out that no single actor—no single banker or industrialist, say—could have made much difference to what happened. They conclude from this observation—in most cases a perfectly reasonable one—that 'nobody has power'. The 'élitists' on the other hand insist that, if the whole group of bankers or industrialists wanted something different to happen they could make it happen, and tend to move from this to saying that individual members of the élite have power. Karl Marx showed a better grasp of the concept of power than either of these recent antagonists when he maintained both that the capitalist class has power and that individual capitalists are powerless.

As a coda to this section, I shall mention briefly that the second alleged paradox that I discussed in section III can be quite easily disposed of. It may be recalled that this involves a three-member committee with weighted voting as before (A with three votes, B and C with two votes each), but with a majority decision rule. For ease of exposition (and without affecting the analysis) let us think of A as a bloc of three members who always vote together, and B and C as blocs of two members who always vote together. The claim is, then, that if bloc A splits up and its members vote independently, they will in aggregate have more power than they did when they constituted bloc *A*. Before the split the situation is the same as it would be if each bloc had one vote, since no one and any two blocs constitutes a winning coalition. The figures in Table 9.1 therefore apply here. Now consider one of the members of bloc *A* after it has split up. (Call this member A_1.) His scores are given below those for *A* in Table 9.3. Thus, we get the reasonable answer that A_1 has the same luck as *A* (since their preferences are randomly associated with those of the others and this always provides a luck score of $\frac{1}{2}$), but *A* is more decisive than A_1 and therefore more successful by that margin. To ask whether the three successors of *A* (obviously A_2 and A_3 are isomorphic to A_1) are more decisive *together* is a senseless question, like asking if one bright person has more total intelligence than three dullards. Everything we need to know is contained in the table: a bloc with three votes is more successful than any of its constituents would be separately—and because public policies are public goods success is not a lump to be shared around. The idea that it would pay the members of the bloc to split up and start voting against each other can be seen to be absurd.

TABLE 9.3

	Success	*Luck*	*Decisiveness*
A (3 votes)	3/4	1/2	1/4
A_1 (1 vote)	5/8	1/2	1/8

V

One of the central problems of politics, I suggested earlier, is that of the expected utility of a regime. How can a country or a group, deciding whether or not to accede to a large political entity or secede from an existing one, form a sensible judgement without estimating the expected utility to be derived from the alternatives? But how is this to be done? The answer that flows from what has been said above is that the thing to concentrate on is the probability of getting desired outcomes, and not the probability of being decisive.

To illustrate this theme, I shall devote this section to a single case: the Constitution of the United States of America. The problem for the delegates to the constitutional convention was to come up with a proposed Constitution that could be ratified. The delegates of the smaller states maintained that they were afraid of their states' votes being swamped by those of the larger states in the new Congress. The delegates of the larger states tried to reassure them that they had nothing to fear, but in the end the smaller states prevailed and obtained the still existing system, according to which each state regardless of size, has two seats in the Senate.

James Madison, representing Virginia, the largest state, made a long speech (one of the very few that he records himself as making) in favour of the proposal to have both houses of the Congress elected on a basis that would tie representation to population. His speech was an extraordinarily acute attempt to argue that, if the small states paid attention to the probabilities of coinciding preferences, they need not fear that a coalition of the largest states would dominate the new federation.

TABLE 9.4

Va.	10	Va., Mass., Penn.	26
Mass., Penn.,	8		
NY., Md.	6	Others	39
Conn., NC, SC	5		
NJ	4		
NH, Ga.	3		
RI, Del.	1		
		Total	65

The numbers of seats allocated to the states in the House of Representatives had already been agreed on, and are as given in Table 9.4.[18] Thus, Virginia, Massachusetts, and Pennsylvania were between them only seven votes short of a majority. This was the context of Madison's speech, which, in part, ran as follows.

That it is not necessary to secure the small States agst the large ones he conceived to be equally obvious: Was a combination of the largest ones dreaded? this must arise either from some interest common to V^{a} Mas^{ts} & P^{a} distinguishing them from the other States or from the mere circumstance of similarity of size. Did any such common interest exist? In point of situation they could not have been more effectually separated from each other by the most jealous citizen of the most jealous State. In point of manners, Religion, and the other circumstances which sometimes beget affection between different communities, they were not more assimilated than the other

[18] James Madison, *Notes on Debates in the Federal Convention of 1787*, ed. with intro. by Adrienne Koch (Athens, Ohio: Ohio University Press, 1966), 617.

states—In point of the staple productions they were as dissimilar as any three other States in the Union. The Staple of Mas^{ts} was *fish*, of P^{a} *flower*, of V^{a} *Tob^{o}*. Was a combination to be apprehended from the mere circumstance of equality of size? Experience suggested no such danger. The journals of Cong^{s} did not present any peculiar association of these States in the votes recorded. It had never been seen that different Counties in the same State, conformable in extent, but disagreeing in other circumstances, betrayed a propensity to such combinations. Experience rather taught a contrary lesson. Among individuals of superior eminence & weight in Society, rivalships were much more frequent than coalitions. Among independent nations, pre-eminent over their neighbours, the same remark was verified. Carthage & Rome tore one another to pieces instead of uniting their forces to devour the weaker nations of the Earth. The Houses of Austria & France were hostile as long as they remained the greatest powers of Europe. England & France have succeeded to the pre-eminence & to the enmity. To this principle we owe perhaps our liberty. A coalition between those powers would have been fatal to us. Among the principal members of antient & Modern confederacies, we find the same effect from the same cause. The contentions, not the Coalitions of Sparta, Athens & Thebes, proved fatal to the smaller members of the Amphyctionic Confederacy. The contentions, not the combinations of Prussia & Austria, have distracted & oppressed the Germanic empire.[19]

It is interesting to apply the apparatus developed so far to the numbers in Table 9.4. First of all, we might ask: how reasonable were the fears of the small states that the 'big three' would dominate the Congress if both houses were filled on a basis proportional to population and the 'big three' voted together as a bloc? Obviously, before we can make any estimate of this we must postulate some probability of each other state's representatives voting the same way as the 'big three'. Let us make the 'neutral' assumption that when the 'big three' vote together any other state's representatives have a 0·5 probability of voting the same way. Further, let us assume that between the representatives of any two states outside the 'big three' there is a 0·5 probability of being on the same side of an issue where the 'big three' vote together. The last proviso is important. Suppose that each of the other states voted on the same side as the 'big three' half the time, but that they always voted the same way as one another. The 'other' states would then constitute a majority bloc which would always get what it wanted. The 'big three' would get what they wanted half the time, but only in virtue of wanting the same thing as the 'others' half the time. The 'big three' would never be decisive.

[19] Madison, *Notes on Debates*, pp. 205–6.

Take, then, the case where the 'big three' are united and the other states fragmented—as likely to agree with one another and with the 'big three' as not. What is the probability that the outcome will be 'yes' when the 'big three' vote 'yes', and that it will be 'no' when the 'big three' vote 'no'? The answer is 0·973. In other words, the 'big three' would be defeated only three times in a hundred votes. What about the expectations of the 'other states'? A state which had no vote or, because of the peculiarities of the distribution of votes, could never change the outcome from what it would be on the basis of the votes of the remaining states, would have a 0·5 chance of getting an outcome it would like. (This follows from the random association between the preferences of 'other states' and outcomes.) To the extent that a state has the possibility of altering an outcome by the direction of its vote, its probability of getting the outcomes it favours rises from 0·5. However, the range of increases is not very great. For New York or Maryland, the largest of the 'other states', the probability of getting a 'yes' outcome when the state's representatives vote 'yes' and a 'no' outcome when they vote 'no' is 0·525. For Rhode Island or Delaware, the smallest of the 'other states', the comparable figure is 0·506.

No doubt if we concentrate on the increase we can say that the difference is considerable. Rhode Island can raise its chance of getting an outcome it wants by 0·006 over the 0·5 it would have if it had no vote at all, whereas New York can raise it by 0·025—over four times as much. (It may be recalled that New York has six votes to Rhode Island's one.) But the point to emphasize is that even 0·025 is a tiny amount. It would be swamped by a relatively small downward adjustment in the estimate made of the probability of agreeing with the 'big three'. For example, it would obviously be preferable from the standpoint of 'rational legitimacy' to be Rhode Island, with its small addition to the basic probability of coinciding with the 'big three' but with a basic probability of 0·5 of agreeing with them, than to be New York with its larger addition to the basic probability of coinciding with the 'big three' if that basic probability were lowered to, say, 0·45. Rhode Island's probability of getting a desired outcome would be 0·506, while New York's would be 0·479.

This consideration should head off any recrudescence of the idea that decisiveness (in the sense of probability of changing the outcome) should be the basis of rational legitimacy. The significance of variations in decisiveness is liable to be smaller than even minor variations in probability of agreeing with other actors. Even worse, decisiveness may increase as the probability of getting an outcome one wants decreases. Thus, suppose that all the states except the 'big three' always voted together. Each member would then always get the outcome it wanted, however the 'big three' were to vote—even if the 'big three' were always on the other side. But since the majority over the 'big three' would be 39–26—a margin of thirteen votes—no single member of the 'other states' could make a difference to the outcome by casting its vote differently. Even if New York or Maryland were to change sides, the result would be a 33–32 vote in favour of the remaining 'others'. Thus, no single state would have any decisiveness, because the outcome would be the same however it voted. Yet it is surely plain that under the conditions stipulated the Union would be extremely attractive to the smaller states.

Madison's argument was that the relationships of interest or policy preference between states are more relevant to someone trying to decide if the new Constitution offers his state a good deal than are the relations of power between them. And the analysis I have offered supports that view. Luck is far more important than decisiveness within the range of votes allocated to the states, in that a quite large increase in votes is wiped out, in terms of any increased probability of success, by a quite small decline in luck. This seems no more than common sense. If no state has as much as a sixth of the votes, it is obvious that the most important determinant of success for a state is going to be how often other states agree with it. (Accession to the European Economic Community, which I mentioned above as another example, illustrates the same point.) But what do you do if you have no idea whether others will agree with you or not? Then you have to fall back on power. But what is power?

VI

I have so far defined luck, decisiveness, and success. But I have not defined power. It is tempting to identify power with decisiveness, and that is what the Shapley–Shubik and Banzhaf indexes would do if they worked. But the temptation must be resisted. Power is undoubtedly related to decisiveness but it is conceptually distinct. To put it in a slogan, decisiveness is a probability but power is a capability. An actor's power is his ability to overcome resistance—not his probability of overcoming resistance. For the probability of overcoming resistance depends on the probability of encountering resistance, and not just any resistance but resistance of the right amount. You can only overcome resistance if you meet some and if it is not too great for you to be able to overcome it.

The contrast between decisiveness and power can be seen more concretely if we consider the way in which the concepts of a dummy and a dictator should be defined within our scheme. Any satisfactory analysis should produce the result that a dummy—somebody who can never under any circumstances alter an outcome by his efforts from what it would otherwise be—has no power. At the other extreme, any satisfactory analysis should enable us to say that a dictator—that is, someone who can under all circumstances get the outcomes he wants—is all-powerful. Decisiveness will not give us the answers that we want. A dummy, it is true, is not at all decisive, but his being a dummy cannot be identified with his not being at all decisive. For a dictator may also not be at all decisive in some situations. If he is a very lucky dictator, all the outcomes he wants will occur even if he does nothing. Suppose, for example, that there is a National Council whose decisions the dictator can overrule whenever he wishes to. If it always does what he wants, the occasion never arises for him to overrule it. In this situation he is totally non-decisive: he never has occasion to change an outcome from what it would otherwise have been. But he is no less a dictator for that.

Clearly, what is missing is the counterfactual force of 'dummy' and 'dictator'—a counterfactual force which shows that they belong to the same logical family as 'power', which is also an inherently counterfactual notion. A dummy is someone who, however precisely matched the opposing sides might be, would still not be able to make the outcome shift in his preferred direction. A dictator is someone who, even if every other actor in the system had the opposite preferences to his own, could still bring about the outcome he wanted. Thus, if power is the ability to overcome resistance, a dummy has no power because he cannot affect outcomes even in the most favourable conditions, and a dictator is all-powerful because he can get the outcomes he wants even in the most unfavourable conditions.

It may be helpful to think of a physical analogy. Imagine a beam-balance from which weights of various sizes can be hung. If the aggregate weight on one side just matches the aggregate weight on the other, even a tiny weight will be sufficient to bring down the beam on the side to which it is added. Conversely, take the case where one weight can more than counterbalance all the other weights put together. Then we can say that, whenever that weight is placed on the balance, the beam will go down on its side regardless of the way in which the other weights are disposed. Power is the weight (metaphorically speaking) that an actor brings to the side he supports. To estimate an actor's power we need to find out how much of a disparity between the weight of the supporters and the weight of the opponents he can reverse by taking part in the decision on a measure. (It is worth noting that the metaphor of weight is in common use: Madison used it in the quotation given above.)

To put it non-metaphorically, we can describe an actor's power by cataloguing the kinds of situation in which he can change a prospective loss for the side he supports to a win for it. Consider, for example, a majority system in which there are three blocs, any two of which constitute a majority, and examine the situation from the point of view of one, bloc *A*. If the other two blocs disagree most of the time with each other and one of them agrees most of the time with bloc *A*, it both gets what it wants most of the time and gets it by being decisive most of the time. If the other two blocs agree with one another and disagree with *A* most of the time, *A* seldom gets what it wants and is seldom decisive. If the other two blocs agree with one another most of the time and also agree with *A*, then *A* gets what it wants most of the time but is seldom decisive. Thus, decisiveness and also success in getting desired outcomes vary according to the patterns of agreement and disagreement. Yet power—the ability to overcome resistance—is the same in all these cases. In each case, *A* can overcome the resistance of one bloc by forming an alliance with the other, but it cannot overcome the resistance of both the other blocs. There is no way of reducing that statement to any other.

Power is not an essentially contested concept but it is an essentially messy concept. There is no neat way of packaging together in a single index the ways in which actors can overcome some opposition with some allies to get a desired decision, block other unwanted decisions (perhaps with fewer allies or—in a *liberum veto* system—with no allies at all), and so on. But we can nevertheless say that some people have more power than others or that one person's power has increased over a period of time, so long as we recognize that this is a way of aggregating a lot of things without any precise rule for doing so. Not surprisingly, there is room for disagreement, but that does not mean that anything goes. (One might think in this context of the problems that arise in comparing the standard of living in different countries.)

One particular temptation that must be avoided is a return to the notion that the 'amount of power' in a system must add up to some fixed amount. Again, I think that we can illuminate the pluralist–élitist debate by seeing how the two sides arrive at their conclusions quite automatically, given their concepts.

Consider again the case of a dictator. If we say that a dictator has all the power, it might seem reasonable to conclude that nobody else has any power. But this is fallacious: it follows only if we are entitled to assume that the amount of power in the system adds up to 1, so that if a certain actor has 1 everybody else must have 0. Suppose *A* can overcome the opposition of *B* and *C* (the only other actors in the system). Then he has all the power in the sense that he can get whatever he wants against the opposition of the other two. But suppose that, whenever *A* does not care about the outcome on some issue and takes no part in the decision, *B* can always overcome the opposition of *C*. Then surely *B* has some power. There are some situations in which he can make a difference to an outcome. In terms of our physical analogy, if *A* outweighs *B* and *C* but *B* is heavier than *C*, *B* can tip the balance in its direction whenever *A* is not on the scales.[20]

This bears on the pluralist–élitist debate in the following way. The 'élitists' say that such-and-such people *could* get the outcomes they wanted if they tried and that they therefore have all the power. The 'pluralists' counter by saying that if you look at the day-to-day decisionmaking process you see that on most issues these people who are alleged to have all the power do not stir themselves and there are real struggles in which some actors win and some lose. They conclude from this observation that power is widely distributed. The answer that follows from my analysis is that both may be true at once, and it is a conceptual mistake to suppose that they are incompatible. The existence of a small group of people who could squelch any serious threat to their common interests does not entail that there is not real power exercised within the many policy areas where none of the proposed outcomes threatens those interests. But, conversely, the claim that there is an élite capable of overcoming the opposition of all other actors in the system is in no way disproved by showing that there are real stakes in the issues that are actually contended.

Let me try to draw all this together and then answer the question that I left dangling at the end of the previous section: how can you take rational decisions in the absence of estimates of the probability that

[20] It follows from this that a true case of a dummy on a committee with weighted voting is going to be very rare, since most so-called dummies could be decisive if some of the members of the committee did not vote. Indeed, in any committee with no minimum number of votes required for passage of a measure, no actor with a vote can be a dummy, since it is possible for all the others to abstain from voting.

others will agree or disagree with you on matters of public policy? To summarize: I assume that the thing to be valued in a political association is getting the outcomes you want. I call the probability of getting the outcomes you want success and I define success so that it is the sum of luck and decisiveness. Luck is the probability of getting what you want without trying and decisiveness is the increase in the probability of getting what you want that occurs if you try. Power cannot be defined directly in terms of any of these because it is a capability rather than a probability. An actor has more power the greater the range of unfavourable distributions of preferences within which he is decisive, in other words the more opposition he can overcome.

Given any specified amount of luck, it is better to be more powerful than less, because the more powerful you are the better your chance of being decisive; and, since success is the sum of luck and decisiveness, the more decisive you are the more successful you are, holding the amount of luck constant. Even if the particular constellation of preferences in which you find yourself is such that an increase in your power does not make you more decisive, it cannot make you less decisive, so at the worst your success rate remains the same—always assuming of course that your luck is unchanged.

On the other hand, if you could be equally successful with more or less power, it is by no means apparent that you should prefer to have more power. If you can get the same results either by engaging in political action or not, why not let others do the work? If power is not an end in itself, it would seem that it is better to have powerful friends than to be powerful yourself—provided, of course, that you have some way of being sure that they will remain your friends.

But that brings me to the question I left hanging: what happens if you cannot estimate future alignments? In that case you can only fall back on power. Thus, I would predict on the basis of this analysis that we will find a greater concern with the distribution of power the longer an association is to run (hence the concern for the distribution of power in constitutions), and a greater concern with the pattern of interests the shorter the period in which the decisionmaking body is to operate. For it is surely true that it becomes more and more difficult to predict the pattern of interests the further we look into the future.

It is important, however, to recognize how little surety about getting the outcomes one wants can be derived from any contemplation of the distribution of power if one insists on total agnosticism about the pattern of interests. (Random association of preferences is not, of course, agnosticism but a quite specific assumption.) It has often been remarked that those ordinary people who say in response to the surveys asked by political scientists that they personally could do something to change a national or even a local political decision of which they disapprove are not so much fine unalienated examples of the democratic citizen as—if they really mean it—sufferers from delusions of grandeur on a massive scale. I do not think that there is anything in this peculiar to liberal democratic regimes as they are in fact now organized. Even the most utopian set-up, if it gives equal power to everyone, is going to mean that (even in a society of a few thousands, let alone one of millions) the capacity of a single individual to overcome the resistance of others is going to be confined to those cases where the strength of his allies is very closely matched with the strength of his opponents. No individual can conceivably have the confidence that his power will be such as to change an outcome from one that he dislikes to one he likes where the balance of forces is significantly stronger (in the absence of his intervention) on the other side.[21]

The judgement about power must therefore be made about social groups, and any individual who is so agnostic about the future as to refuse to estimate with which groups his interests will lie must, I think, exclude himself from trying to make *any* rational estimate of his prospects within any polity. Even currently powerful individuals would presumably be unwise to count on remaining powerful in the future.

Looking at the future from the point of view of a social group rather than an individual, it would still be uncomfortable to have to rely on power as the sole basis on which to judge prospects of success. Unless one expects that the social group with which one's lot is bound up is always going to have all the power (in the sense in which I defined it), there must necessarily be some combinations of the other actors that can beat it. So in principle it could be on the losing side on every single

[21] This is a point that seems to be clearer to ordinary people than to social scientists. In the course of the research for her book *Beyond Adversary Democracy* (New York: Basic Books, 1980), Jane J. Mansbridge interviewed a number of the inhabitants of Selby, a small New England town. In her comments on an earlier draft of this chapter she recounted the following experience: 'When I was planning my Selby study, I originally included a set of questions from Almond and Verba's *The Civic Culture* [(Princeton, N.J.: Princeton University Press, 1963), p. 528]. Q. 22: "Suppose a regulation were being considered by the town of Selby that you considered very unjust or harmful. What do you think you could do? Anything else?" Q. 23: "If you made an effort to change this regulation, how likely is it that you would succeed?" In my pretest in a neighbouring town, several people answered the second question with some annoyance and surprise at my stupidity, "Why, it depends on how many people agreed with me, of course." I dropped the second question when I did my interviews in Selby.'

issue that comes up. It therefore seems that *some* estimate must be made of the likelihood that those combinations will in fact form. Otherwise, the whole notion of giving a value to a prospective association collapses.

10

THE OBSCURITIES OF POWER

The conceptual core of Steven Lukes's *Power: A Radical View*[1] is the contrast between three 'views' of power, which are called the one-dimensional, the two-dimensional, and the three-dimensional view. (The terms, it need hardly be said, are not neutral. Who would willingly accept a one-dimensional or two-dimensional view of something if a three-dimensional view were also available?) The author sets them out economically and I can do no better than to quote his description of each.

The 'first, one-dimensional view of power involves a focus on *behaviour* in the making of *decisions* on *issues* over which there is an observable *conflict* of (subjective) *interests*, seen as express policy preferences, revealed by political participation' (p. 15, italics in original). This is the 'pluralist' or 'decisionmaking' approach identified especially with Dahl, Polsby, and Wolfinger and articulated most fully in Polsby's *Community Power and Political Theory*.[2]

Lukes says that 'the two-dimensional view of power involves a *qualified critique* of the *behavioural focus* of the first view (I say qualified because it is still assumed that nondecision-making is a form of decision-making), and it allows for consideration of the ways in which *decisions* are prevented from being taken on *potential issues* over which there is an observable *conflict* of (subjective) *interests*, seen as embodied in express policy preferences and sub-political grievances' (p. 20, italics in original). This view (and the notion of two dimensions versus one) is drawn from Bachrach and Baratz, especially the version of 'Two Faces of Power' they published in *Power and Poverty*.[3]

The 'three-dimensional view of power involves a *throughgoing critique* of the *behavioural focus* of the first two views as too individualistic and allows for consideration of the many ways in which *potential issues* are kept out of politics, whether through the operation of social forces and institutional practices or through individuals' decisions.

[1] Steven Lukes, *Power: A Radical View* (London: Macmillan, 1974).

[2] Nelson W. Polsby, *Community Power and Political Theory* (New Haven: Yale University Press, 2nd edn., 1980).

[3] Peter Bachrach and Morton S. Baratz, *Power and Poverty* (New York: Oxford University Press, 1970), 3–16.

This, moreover, can occur in the absence of actual, observable conflict, which may have been successfully averted—though there remains here an implicit reference to potential conflict . . . [or] *latent conflict*, which consists in a contradiction between the interests of those exercising power and the *real interests* of those they exclude' (pp. 24–5, italics in original). This, as may be inferred, is Lukes's own preferred conception. It is obviously a descendant of the Marxist notion of 'false consciousness', especially as developed by Gramsci. It figured in a shadowy way in the original version of 'Two Faces of Power', before Bachrach and Baratz retreated in the face of hostile methodological criticism from the 'behavioural' camp, to produce an emasculated version in *Power and Poverty*. Lukes also finds an element of this 'three-dimensional' view in Matthew Crenson's book *The Un-politics of Air Pollution*,[4] in that Crenson takes it as axiomatic that human beings would prefer not to suffer the health and amenity costs of gross air pollution and therefore regards lack of any attempt to curb it as a phenomenon prima facie in need of explanation.

The point of the book is not simply to say that there are these three conceptions of power but to argue a thesis about them. This thesis seems to me both obscurantist and—even worse—obscure. The obscurity is partly a result of the fact that in a book of about twenty thousand words most of which is given over to exposition there is no space for the proper articulation of arguments. To give one example, the crucial thesis that every conception of power incorporates a distinctive concept of interest, and that 'the notion of "interest" is an irreducibly evaluative notion' (p. 34) is contained in a chapter of three hundred words! (Chapter 6). Lukes begins his argument for this: 'Extremely crudely, one might say. . . .' But should one say things 'extremely crudely', since there is presumably nothing (except possibly the prospect for Macmillans to make a quick killing—scarcely a cause which I would expect a self-styled radical like the author to look upon with favour) to prevent one from saying them in a way more in accordance with the normal canons of scholarly discourse?

But, even leaving aside the problems of horseback scholarship, there is still I suspect a deep obscurity at the heart of the author's own thought. For it appears that he wants to hold two positions simultaneously. The first is that the concept of power is 'essentially contested' (pp. 9, 26). Power is 'one of those concepts which is ineradicably value-dependent', so each of the three views of power

[4] Matthew Crenson, *The Un-Politics of Air Pollution: A Study of Non-Decisionmaking in the Cities* (Baltimore: Johns Hopkins University Press, 1971).

'arises out of and operates within a particular moral and political perspective' (p. 26). The second position is that the third ('three-dimensional') conception is *superior* to the others, where this apparently does not simply mean that it happens to fit in with Lukes's own values or moral and political perspective. He devotes a number of pages (especially chapter 7, 'The Three Views Compared') to trying to show that the other two views of power are inadequate, rather than simply distasteful to anyone who happens to share the author's own brand of radical politics.

He says, for example, that the one-dimensional view is 'blind to the ways in which [the] political agenda is controlled' (p. 57) and that the two-dimensional view 'remains superficial precisely because it confines itself to studying individual decisions made to avert potentially threatening demands from becoming politically dangerous' (pp. 37–8). By contrast, the three-dimensional view offers 'the prospect of a serious sociological and not merely personalised explanation of how political systems prevent demands from becoming political issues or even from being made' (p. 38). (So sociology really does equal socialism, just as those American Congressmen whom we laughed at believed all along!)

I do not see how, if the first proposition (irreducible value-conflict) is true, there can be any room for rational arguments of the second kind. Conversely, if it makes sense to assert, with the appearance of claiming the assent of anyone prepared to consider an argument, that one conception is 'blind' and another 'superficial' then I do not see how it can be true that our values and political outlooks automatically lock us into one or other conception of power. Presumably anybody who was convinced that his views were 'blind' or 'superficial' would be obliged, on pain of forfeiting his own self-respect and the regard of the scholarly community, to abandon them. But does that mean that he must become a convert to socialism?

Something has got to give. My own solution, for what it is worth, is that the superiority of the two-dimensional over the one-dimensional view is patent in that ability to control the agenda is obviously power. I would also say that one aspect of the three-dimensional view is also patently superior to either. It is simply obvious that a power relation may be exhibited (and in an extreme form) when the inferior does not raise an issue that he would like to, either because he knows it is hopeless and does not want to waste effort or because he fears that he will suffer a sanction even for raising it. Moreover, it need not be difficult to prove that somebody would like to raise an issue but does not do so for either of these reasons. We can simply ask him. (There is the risk that we may be putting the idea in his head for the first time but this can be got round by a suitably non-directive interviewing technique.) Up to this point it does not seem to me that there is any proper place for values or political outlooks. Anyone who denies what I have just said is either silly (and a lot of 'behavioural' fanatics were that) or is dishonestly trying to prevent awkward but clearly valid questions from being asked (and I am afraid some American political scientists in the late 1950s and early 1960s may have done that too).

On the other hand, when it comes to imputing 'real interests' to people and saying that they must be victims of power because they are not pursuing these 'real interests' (even if the reason is simply that they are not aware of these 'real interests'), we do have something that—at least on some interpretations—*is* a value dispute, in that it may turn on a non-empirical conception of human nature and its needs.

Suppose that two social scientists observed a society within which one group had a subordinate position, that this group was not being coerced into accepting its position, and that it was not subject to overt attempts at manipulation (e.g. by propaganda) by the superior group. And suppose that one social scientist concluded from these agreed facts that the subordinate group was not subject to power while the other concluded that it *must* be (even if there was nothing to observe) because it was contrary to human nature for a group authentically to accept a subordinate position. That would, I think, be a value dispute.

Notice, incidentally, that both these observers might agree in predicting that the subordinate group would be led to demand an end to their subordinate position if its members were subjected to a sufficiently intensive campaign from outside. But they would describe and explain it differently. One would say that their attitudes had been changed as a result of exposure to a propaganda campaign, and that this merely shows the plasticity (within certain limits) of attitudes. The other would say that they had been exposed to 'consciousness raising', that as a result their previous 'false consciousness' had been replaced by authentic consciousness, and that this shows how unnatural subordination is.

II

THE USES OF 'POWER'

Why are we interested in power? In an ambitious and admirable study, *Power: A Philosophical Analysis*,[1] Peter Morriss takes this question as his starting-point. There are, he suggests, three quite different contexts within which questions are asked about power. One is practical: we sometimes want to know who has power because we want to get something done or prevent something from happening. We therefore need to know who has to be mobilized or stopped. Sometimes a way of focusing this kind of inquiry is to ask: who is worth bribing?

The second context in which we want to know about power is 'the moral one of blaming, excusing and allocating responsibility' (p. 38). Here, Morriss rightly scotches the claim, made especially by William Connolly, that ascribing power is also ascribing responsibility. As Morriss points out, people are held responsible for what they do actually do (or fail to do), not for what they could do: 'we are blamed for our acts (and omissions), not for having power' (p. 39). The question of power arises here only because powerlessness in some matter necessarily negates responsibility for the outcome, while power to have prevented an outcome entails responsibility for it.

The third context Morriss calls 'evaluative'. Here what we are interested in is assessing the goodness or badness of a set of social arrangements. Morriss rejects the so-called 'radical' conception of power promoted by Steven Lukes and William Connolly, which entails that a set of social arrangements can be criticized only if we can lay responsibility on somebody for its existence. For, as he points out, we can perfectly well condemn a distribution of power without having to find culprits.

The work done by 'power' will differ in these three contexts, since the questions we shall be seeking to answer with its aid will be different. This has the implication 'that some arguments ostensibly about power (or about "power") are really arguments between competing perspectives. The CIA analyst [concerned with practice] and the democrat [concerned with evaluation] do not disagree about

[1] Peter Morriss, *Power: A Philosophical Analysis* (Manchester: Manchester University Press, 1988). Page references in the text are to this book.

the distribution of power: they have such different perspectives that they never reach the point of disagreement' (p. 205).

Despite the variety of contexts within which 'power' is deployed, it has, Morriss contends, a fixed core of meaning. All power, he says, is 'a sort of ability: the basic idea is that your powers are capacities to do things when you choose' (p. 49). This entails the rejection of the claim made by (among others) Dahl and Polsby to the effect that there is something epistemologically suspect in talking about anything except actual events. As Morriss says, we may in suitable circumstances have perfectly good evidence for the existence of a capacity, and this evidence need not consist of the actualization of that very capacity. 'When I go to a zoo, I can see that a lion is powerful enough to eat me up by observing its jaws, teeth and muscles, and combining these observations with my general knowledge of animals' masticatory performance. If I am still in doubt, I can observe what the lion does to a hunk of meat, and induce. Not even the most dogmatic positivist would declare that he couldn't know if the lion could eat him up until it had actually done so' (p. 16).

This is all well said, but what Morriss fails to make explicit is that, whereas all power is ability, not all ability is power. Notwithstanding Napoleon's palindromic lament 'Able was I ere I saw Elba', 'power' and 'ability' are not interchangeable. A case in point is Morriss's claim that, while both rich and poor have the physical ability to feed off caviar and champagne, in another sense of 'ability' the poor are unable to do so and must rest content with beer and pickles (p. 81). How does this translate into talk about power? We do unquestionably speak of natural strength as power. Hence we could quite accurately speak of the lion in the zoo as powerful. But we do not I believe regard the legally sanctioned ability of the rich to eat extravagantly as in itself a manifestation of power. They do indeed have means to the acquisition of power denied to the rest of us: they can, for example, hire people to do their bidding, or they can donate money to political causes and hence acquire political power in a very painless way. But they may not choose to employ their money in ways such as these. Then we may if we like say that they have the possibility of acquiring power in ways not open to the rest of us, but we cannot properly say that they actually have power. We must, then, insist that there is more to (social) power than being able to do what you choose to do. Your having power entails that you have the ability to overcome resistance or opposition and by this means achieve an outcome different from the one that would have occurred in the absence of your intervention.

In equating power with the capacity to do things, Morriss is reacting against what he sees as a misguided tendency in the academic literature to treat '*A* has power over *B*' as the paradigmatic use of the word 'power'. He argues (pp. 32–5) that this skews the whole analysis and that '*A* has power to do *x*' should instead be taken as the basic expression to be defined. For every use of 'power over' can be paraphased in terms of 'power to', whereas the reverse is not true.

In this context, Morriss notes that, although Robert Dahl's formal definition of power gives us a meaning for 'power over', 'in his empirical work he equates a person's power with their success on matters of key importance' (p. 35). It may perhaps help to make the point here more clear to consider the case of a voting bloc in a committee or legislature. Let us suppose that it achieves the outcome it wants by exercising its power. How might this come about? One way is that it might exercise power over other committee members or legislators, causing them to change their votes by blackmailing them (as it is said the Americans and Russians achieved power over Kurt Waldheim at the United Nations by threatening to expose his deception about his war record) or less colourfully by calling in some political debt for favours rendered in the past. But a bloc need not do any of this to exercise power, and in fact the standard way in which a bloc exercises power is simply to use the power inherent in its votes. By this means it may be able to swing the result of the vote from what it would have been if only the other blocs had participated to the outcome that it supports. This is 'power to' without 'power over'. But in taking 'power to' as the expression in terms of which others are to be defined, we should always bear in mind that power is not just a matter of getting what you want but of overcoming resistance or (net) opposition.

Having identified the common element in all uses of 'power', Morriss next draws an important distinction between power in a generic sense (what you *could* do under various conditions) and power in a particular sense (what you *can* do under the conditions that actually obtain). The first kind of power Morriss calls power as ability while for the second kind of power he revives the word 'ableness'. When we look at your power as ability we take your resources (the number of votes controlled by your bloc, or the sticks and carrots you can deploy) as given, but we allow the configuration of the other forces to vary. Thus, if your bloc has thirty votes in a hundred-seat legislature we ask what thirty seats are worth in enabling the bloc to bring about desired outcomes, abstracting from the possible ways in which the other seats might be divided among blocs and also from the extent to which those blocs might agree with one another or with your bloc. It would obviously be hopelessly cumbersome to list all the contingencies under which thirty votes would produce the desired outcome, so summary measures of power as ability (the typical a priori power indexes) are developed.

In interpersonal relations, power as ability is what you could achieve by overcoming resistance, if resistance were offered. But we must recognize that, as soon as we move away from the context of a decisionmaking body with precisely-defined criteria for winning, there is little hope of constructing a summary measure. A good deal of the difficulty in making empirical assessments of power lies precisely in the impossibility of stating in a concise form all the things that might be brought about by deploying a certain quantity of resources against varying degrees of resistance.

It would be highly convenient if 'power' could be made to work in the same way as 'income' does in economics, and much analysis has proceeded as if this were feasible. Economists would not have got very far if the only thing they could do was describe all the alternative baskets of goods that somebody could buy. The existence of a common set of prices enables them to avoid such catalogues and talk about income. But when we study power we do not have any similar way of rendering commensurable all the outcomes that people could get by overcoming resistance.

All we can say in general, then, is that power as ability is what you could achieve in various contingencies, where the contingencies are defined by the preferences of the other actors (including, in cases of committees or legislatures, their formation into voting blocs). If you could overcome a lot of resistance, or prevail over the combined force of all the committee members who do not belong to your bloc, then we can say that you have a lot of power as ability. If you could overcome only weak resistance, or prevail only over a divided opposition, then we can say that you have less power as ability. In contrast to power as ability, power as ableness is, Morriss suggests, 'measured by your set of compossible outcomes [i.e. outcomes that are obtainable together], and now the fewer obstacles in your path the better, if that allows you strength (or other resources) to achieve more. The less of your resources you have to expend, the more you have left over for doing other things, and therefore the more powerful you are' (p. 88). This should, let me point out, be read with the caveat already introduced, that not all ability is power. The ability to get something if there is nobody stopping you from getting it is not a form of (social) power. We are thus still concerned here with your ability to change outcomes from what they would otherwise have been. But we are now interested not in your ability to overcome *possible* resistance or opposition but in your ability to overcome *actual* resistance or opposition. This is your ableness, in Morriss's terminology.

We can illustrate ableness by going back over the two cases considered in the context of power as ability: power in interpersonal relations and power in a committee or legislature. I have power as ableness, then, in relation to you if I can overcome your actual resistance to what I want you to do. It is immaterial how slight this resistance is. What matters is that I should have the power (in the sense of ableness) to bring about the desired result by overcoming the resistance that exists. Thus, it could be that I have rather little power as ability in relation to you, in that I could not overcome very strong resistance on your part. But if you never resist very strongly anything I want, I have a full measure of power as ableness because I can always get the outcome I want over your resistance. Conversely, I may have quite a lot of power as ability, but if you are almost always violently against what I want, the result will be that I have little power as ableness.

How does power as ableness work when applied to a committee or legislature? Let us return to the case of a legislature in which your bloc, which we shall call bloc *C*, has 30 votes. Now let us add that there are two other blocs—bloc *A* with 40 votes, and bloc *B* which has 30 votes. The power of bloc *C* depends on the way in which the preferences of bloc *A* and bloc *B* are similar to one another and how similar the preferences of each of them are to those of bloc *C*.

Suppose, for example, that blocs *A* and *B* always voted together. Then bloc *C* would have no power as ableness because it would never be able to overcome the united forces of the other two blocs. But now imagine, conversely, that on every issue bloc *A* voted on the opposite side to bloc *B*. Then (so long as we assume that every issue has only two sides), bloc *C* would have total power as ableness, since it would always be in a position to obtain the outcome that it wanted by adding its votes to one or other bloc to make a majority.

There are two peculiarities about power as ableness. These make it a very tricky concept to work with and contribute a good deal to the confusion rampant in the literature on power. (Even Morriss is not entirely immune, as we shall see.) The first point about ableness is that it seems a bit strange to say that, while my power as ability remains unchanged, my power in some other sense waxes and wanes according to the preferences of others. Thus, suppose I have a certain amount of power as ability in relation to you: I can overcome a certain degree of resistance on your part. And suppose that I want you to do something that you do not want to do, but that my limited amount of power as ability is insufficient to overcome your reluctance to do it. Then my power as ableness is zero in this situation. But now let us imagine that for some reason your reluctance to do the thing in question decreases to an extent such that my power as ability becomes adequate to overcome your remaining resistance. Then I have suddenly acquired power as ableness while my power as ability has remained unchanged. Surely, however, the more natural way of describing the phenomenon is to say that my power, while remaining unchanged in amount, was insufficient to produce results initially but later became sufficient as a result of a change in the strength of your resistance. Obviously, the relevant sense of 'power' here is power as ability.

There is, nevertheless, an argument for keeping power as ableness in the vocabulary, while recognizing that it will sometimes lead us to say things that seem counter-intuitive. This is that in the context of committees and legislatures it does seem quite natural to talk of power in a way that is clearly power as ableness, even though such power has exactly the same disconcerting tendency to come and go as the environment changes. Thus, if we look at the US Supreme Court, it is manifest that, knowing only the voting rule for decisions of the Court, we must say that each Justice has an equal amount of power. This is power as ability: each Justice has an a priori equal chance of being able by his vote to bring about the outcome he favours. But now suppose that there are two blocs of four Justices which take opposite sides on every question that comes before the Court. We shall, I suspect, feel little reluctance in saying that the remaining Justice, who sometimes votes with one bloc and sometimes with the other, has more power than his brethren. We may, indeed, say that he has all the power since he is always in a position to ensure by his vote that the outcome will be the one that he favours. Clearly, this is power as ableness, since it depends on the distribution of preferences among the Justices.

Manifestly, the power of this Justice who occupies the pivotal position is fragile. All that is required is for one Justice to leave the bloc to which he belongs and join the other, or for one Justice to be replaced by an adherent of the opposite bloc's ideas, and the power of the erstwhile all-powerful Justice vanishes completely. In the new situation, there is a five-man bloc which can always get its way. We must now therefore say that the members of this bloc have all the power between them, and the previously pivotal Justice has none.

Although we recognize how evanescent is the power of the pivotal Justice, this does not inhibit us from being inclined to say that he truly is all-powerful so long as his good fortune lasts. This being so, we should perhaps reconcile ourselves to the idea that in interpersonal relations you have a lot of power if you are able to overcome the actual resistance you encounter, even if this power arises from your good fortune in not meeting much resistance.

The second peculiarity of power as ableness, which is again not crippling but requires careful handling, is that it is not always applicable. Consider an interpersonal case in which there is no resistance to overcome because the person whom you want to do something would do it anyway, or a legislative case in which the outcome your bloc wants would occur anyway because there is a majority for it without the votes of your bloc. We have no difficulty in ascribing power as ability to you in such a case because to say you have power in this sense is to say that you *could* overcome resistance if necessary, or that you *could* prevail over a certain balance of opposing votes if necessary. But we cannot intelligibly say that you have power as ableness in such a case. For it makes no sense to say that you can bring about over resistance or opposition an outcome that, given the actual preferences of the parties involved, will happen anyway. If power as ableness is the ability to overcome the actual resistance or opposition, it simply has no application when there is no resistance or opposition.

This is not an insuperable objection to power as ableness. Once we understand how the concept works, we should be prepared to recognize that it will not always have application to single-shot cases. Moreover, we can still apply the concept of power as ableness to a sequence of cases by simply leaving out of account the cases where it does not apply. Thus, we can say that I have complete power as ableness in relation to you so long as, whenever you do resist, I can overcome your resistance. Similarly, we can say that my bloc has complete power as ableness if it can change the outcome in the desired direction whenever it would otherwise be adverse.

An alternative way of formulating power as ableness over a sequence of cases would be to say that your power as ableness is the proportion of all cases in which (*a*) there is resistance or opposition, and (*b*) you can overcome it. This would entail that the power as ableness of bloc *C* in our example would be only one half if the outcome without its intervention (i.e. a win by bloc *A* with 40 votes over bloc *B* with 30 votes) were to be in line with its desires half the time and even less if its preferences were more congruent with those of bloc *A*. Such a measure would correspond to what I have called decisiveness: the proportion of all outcomes that are brought into line with your wishes by your intervention (see chapter 9 above). However, if we wish to use the language of power, I think that we shall reasonably wish to say that if you are in a pivotal position you have all the power, and we can achieve this by dropping from the denominator cases where you are successful without any need for intervention. The rationale is that, although the pivotal actor does not always win by using power, he always *can* win by using power. As far as I can see, Morriss wishes to operate with the concept of power as ableness in the way I have described (see p. 247 n. 5).

Power as ableness is the ability to bring about desired outcomes by deploying some resource to overcome resistance or opposition. But, as Morriss points out, for some purposes we may be interested in the ability (more precisely tendency or disposition) to finish up with desired outcomes, whether this occurs by the exercise of power as ableness or not. From some points of view, what matters most is the prospects of success, not the means by which success comes about. Thus, from ableness we can move to a different but related concept, which Morriss calls in the context of a committee or legislature the 'expected probability of winning' (EPW).[2]

This is all straightforward enough, but what makes it controversial is that Morriss wishes to describe success not arising from ableness as another kind of power, passive rather than active. Thus, he writes: 'when we investigate people's power to obtain some given end we sometimes find three sorts of people: those who have the power to obtain it; those who do not have the power to obtain it; and those who do not have the power to obtain it but obtain it anyway. . . . Sometimes we want to lump together people in the first and third groups; when we do, we can say that those in the third group have passive power' (p. 102). And again: 'we frequently don't want to

[2] Unfortunately, having made it clear that the EPW index includes success that falls outside the scope of ableness (pp. 171–2), Morriss goes on to call it an index of ableness (p. 179), and indeed entitles the chapter in which the EPW index is developed 'Measuring Ableness'. I shall assume, however, that the meaning of 'ableness' should be restricted to include what Morriss calls 'active power' (see below).

differentiate between people who do get something and people who *can* get it, but we want to distinguish these people from those who *cannot* get it. A concept of power that includes passive power does the job' (p. 100). No doubt it does—if we start with the assumption that all success should be attributed to some form or another of power. But why should we make that assumption?

Morriss distinguishes two kinds of passive power. One is getting things without intervening, where you could prevent the outcome you want by intervening against it. The other is getting things without intervening, where you could not prevent the outcome you want even if you intervened against it (see p. 102). Although Morriss makes much of the second case, and indeed some of the time seems to identify it with passive power (see pp. 99–100 and 172), I can see no reason for attaching any significance to the question of whether or not you could overturn a favourable outcome achievable without intervention if you were perverse enough to intervene in an attempt to stop it. A more important distinction, which may be at the back of Morriss's mind here, is the following. In some cases you can get what you want without exercising power as ableness because there is no resistance or opposition, but you have power as ability because you could overcome resistance or opposition if it existed. In other cases you can get what you want without exercising power as ableness, but you have no power as ability, so that if there were resistance or opposition you would lack the ableness to get the desired outcome.

Especially if we concentrate on the second kind of case, we must surely ask how it can contribute to clarification to make powerlessness a subclass of power. Morriss concedes that it is 'apparently bizarre' (p. 100), and I think that appearances here are veridical. We may agree that for some purposes it is convenient to group together all instances of being able to get what you want. But we still need an argument for calling them all instances of *power*, and this it seems to me Morriss does not supply.

There are, I believe, very good reasons for resisting the proposal that 'power' should be extended so as to include cases where desired outcomes occur with no intervention. For we surely want, in looking at people who do well under some set of arrangements, to distinguish between those who do well by exercising power and those who are the passive beneficiaries of the activities of others—the powerless members of a powerful class or clan, for example.

Thus, to move to the most significant issue that is implicated, when we find a pattern of privilege in a society we should surely wish to treat it as an empirical question how far this state of affairs arises as the result of the exercise of power by the beneficiaries. But if we equate power and success, the empirical gap is closed and it becomes a logical truth that the beneficiaries are powerful.

Here, I think, Nelson Polsby has the best of Morriss. Morriss quotes him as writing the following: 'Even if we can show that a given status quo benefits some people disproportionately (as I think we can for any real world status quo), such a demonstration falls short of showing that these beneficiaries created the status quo, act in any meaningful way to maintain it, or could, in the future, act effectively to deter changes in it' (p. 106).[3] Morriss's response runs as follows: 'Polsby is here quite right; but he is aiming at the wrong target. There is no need to claim that because someone benefits she must *cause* her good fortune, nor that she can control it. All one need do is note that a status quo that systematically benefits certain people (as Polsby agrees it does) is relevant in itself. One can deplore—or praise—such a situation without wishing to suggest that the beneficiaries cause it or (*pace* Lukes and Connolly) are somehow to blame for it' (p. 106, italics in original). Of course we can, and of course we may well be interested in inequality as such. But the context of the quotation from Polsby is his insistence that we should not move from the existence of inequality to the existence of power relations unless we *are* prepared to make assertions of the kind that he describes. Morriss, by extending the notion of power to include all cases of getting what you want, opens the way to just that move.

Ironically, Morriss is here engaging in a practice that he criticizes in others, namely, the use of tendentious definitions to score rhetorical victories. He thus criticizes William Connolly's idea that by redefining 'racism' so as to include 'institutional racism' (i.e. actual disadvantage, however caused) you have thereby shifted the terms of debate because people who do not want to think of themselves as racists in the old-fashioned sense now feel obliged to be against institutional racism as well. Obviously, any clear-headed anti-racist in the old-fashioned sense will be unmoved by the redefinition. It can therefore be effective only to the extent that it is a successful subterfuge.

As Morriss says, 'such tricks have absolutely nothing to do with philosophy and absolutely nothing to do with sorting out concepts. There is no doubt that institutional and old-fashioned racism are different concepts; that Connolly's "militant black activists" do not

[3] Nelson W. Polsby, *Community Power and Political Theory* (New Haven: Yale University Press, 2nd edn., 1980), 208.

like either; and that they can save themselves the trouble of showing exactly what is wrong with "institutional racism" if they can label it so that it looks like another sort of old-fashioned racism. This is a move that only a dishonest philosopher should applaud. If there *is* something wrong with institutional racism (and I agree with Connolly that there is), then it can be shown by reasoned argument, rather than by linguistic sleight-of-hand' (p. 204, italics in original).

Exactly the same analysis can be applied to Morriss's proposed extension of the concept of power, though I do not wish to accuse him of wilful obfuscation. We may suppose that many people would regard inequalities brought about by the exercise of power as more objectionable than the same inequalities *per se*. If so, then redefining 'power' so that all inequalities necessarily arise from the exercise of power saves the trouble of showing that they arise from the exercise of power in the ordinary sense. The move is exactly parallel to that from old-fashioned racism (active discrimination) to institutional racism (the bare existence of unequal outcomes between races). And the same objection can be made to both moves.

Leaving on one side the propriety of calling them all 'power', there can, however, be no doubt that we do need the concepts of power as ability and power as ableness, and also the broad concept of prospects of success, which includes in its scope what Morriss calls passive power. Let me conclude this review by giving examples of the ways in which we have to make use of these different concepts to deal with different problems.

I shall begin by considering the problems faced by a constitutional convention. Now, in drawing up a complex constitution, for example one that gives power to sub-units such as states and provinces in the national government, there are two possible approaches that may be followed. One is to rule out as irrelevant any speculation about the way in which these sub-units may be expected to form alliances on the basis of shared interests, ideologies, or membership of ethnic or racial groups. What we then want is to implement some distribution of a priori power, and this means that we shall be concerned with the power of sub-units in the sense of power as ability.

Alternatively, however, we may be concerned that what looks like a perfectly just a priori distribution of power will in fact result in a persistent pattern of alliances such that some groups in the society find themselves almost always on the winning side and others almost always on the losing side. To deal with this, we obviously need to think about power as ableness. Or perhaps we should think in terms of prospects of success, since it seems that we are more interested in the tendency of groups to win or lose than in their ableness, that is to say their ability to get the result they want by exercising power rather than being the passive beneficiaries of power exercised by others.

Another use of power as ability, which Morriss goes into at some length (pp. 183–97), is to deal with the problem of weighted voting. Where constituencies are of unequal size, representatives may be given unequal numbers of votes in a committee or assembly. But if their proportion of the votes is made equal to the proportion of the electors they represent, it can come about that some representatives have no power (they can never make a difference), while representatives of large constituencies will tend to have more than their 'fair share' of power. 'Power' here is invariably reckoned by taking the measure of the a priori probability of being decisive or forming part of a winning coalition. In these computations no account is taken of possible alliances between different representatives, so that a party's under-representation (in terms of a power index) in one constituency might be compensated for by its overrepresentation in another. The relevant notion is therefore one of power as ability.

In a pregnant sentence which is unfortunately not followed up, Morriss notes that 'the comparable problem with ableness is how to detect and eliminate gerrymandering' (p. 184). It is at any rate clear that power as ability is not relevant, since we can describe a partisan gerrymander only if we know the party preferences of voters in each area. A partisan gerrymander occurs where, in a system of single-member districts, boundaries are drawn so as to enable one party to maximize its number of seats. (Typically this is done by concentrating opposing voters in a few constituencies leaving the rest to be won by one's own side with modest majorities.)

Quite extreme gerrymandering is consistent with equal constituency sizes, and as far as power as ability is concerned equal constituencies give each voter the same a priori power. It is only by introducing the notion that if x per cent of the voters are Republicans they should get x per cent of the seats (or some more sophisticated variant) that we can talk about the unequal voting power of different voters depending on their party. (Typically this is expressed by objections that 'It takes x voters to elect a Democrat but y—some larger number—to elect a Republican'.)

Especially interesting in this context are the so-called benign gerrymanders designed to give racial or ethnic groups power by ensuring that they have a majority, or at any rate a strong presence, in a certain proportion of constituencies. The jurisprudence that has grown up around this in the USA is quite mind-boggling and could, I think, be used to illustrate the great difficulties that lie in the path of those who seek to deploy the concept of power as ableness. They would also, I think, lead us again to wonder if it is ableness or prospects of success that is relevant.

Although orientated to practice, these applications of the concepts of power (and the concept of prospects of success) should I take it be regarded as falling in Morriss's evaluative category. A more direct evaluative problem is the assessment of the distribution of power in a society. Suppose that there is a middle class facing a divided working class. It might be said that the middle class is not all-powerful because it could be defeated by a united working class (power as ability). It might also be said that, since the working class is in fact divided, the middle class is indeed all-powerful (power as ableness). And finally, it might be said that the middle class does in fact get the outcomes it wants—which is simply to report success. This is of course a very crude illustration, but it does, I think, illustrate that all three concepts have a use.

If we switch our attention to the practical use of 'power', we can immediately see that it is only worth bribing actors with power. But whether it is ability or ableness that is relevant depends on the context. Thus, if you did not know what the configuration of preferences was going to be but wanted to bribe someone to vote the way you directed, you would want an index of a priori power to tell you what each member of a complex decisionmaking body would be worth to have in your pocket. And Morriss argues ingeniously (pp. 162–5 and Appendix 4) that the Shapley–Shubik index can be made sense of as a measure of the worth of each actor to a potential briber. If, however, you knew what outcome you wanted and how everyone was disposed to vote, you would obviously be asking which combinations of people on the opposing side you would need to bribe in order to change the result from what it would otherwise be to the desired outcome. This would clearly involve some assessment of ableness: the ability of a member of a committee to change the outcome given the votes of the others.

A different action-orientated question is this: suppose that in a parliamentary system you, as monarch or president, are charged with the duty after a general election of inviting the leader of a political party to try to form a government. If one party has a majority of seats, the problem solves itself, but where no party has a majority the question arises of the criteria to be used in choosing a party leader to ask first. There are, as far as I know, only two criteria in use. One is that the leader of the largest party should get the first chance to form a government. This is obviously an application of power as ability since, a priori, the largest party has either more power than any other or at any rate no less than any other. The other criterion is that the job should be entrusted to the leader with the best prospects of attaining a parliamentary majority for a government containing his party. This is clearly not a question of power as ability, since it calls for attention to preferences: a small party of the centre would rate very low on any a priori power index but might be reckoned as an essential partner in any viable coalition, and hence the one whose leader should be asked first.

What is the relevant measure here? This question is discussed extensively by Morriss (pp. 169–81) and he quite rightly points out that ableness is not quite what is wanted since it is not relevant how far the party whose prospects we are assessing plays a role itself in producing a parliamentary majority. It is quite conceivable that in the case of a small party its own votes would much of the time be redundant, but this should certainly not be taken as a drawback to its prospects of having majority support. What we need is, as Morriss says, an index of the expected probability of winning or EPW (p. 172), which is a measure of prospects of success.

Morriss has the idea that a commission of experts could compile an EPW index for each party after an election had produced a hung parliament, and thus resolve the problem of choosing a Prime Minister designate. However, I think he misconstrues the job to be done. He imagines an attempt being made to estimate how often parties are likely to vote on the same side, and hence how often each is likely to find itself with a majorty on its side. This requires, though, that we conceive of a universe of policy issues that is somehow given, and votes cast purely on the basis of policy preferences. In practice, the policy issues that come up largely depend on the government's choice, and how parties vote depends on strategic considerations as well as policy preferences. Thus, the probability of a minority Labour government surviving with Liberal support in 1974 would not have been well estimated by looking at the degree of congruence between the parties' policy preferences across all issues. Rather, we would have to take into account that Labour would not introduce legislation known to be obnoxious to the Liberals and that the Liberals might vote for policies that were some way from their own most preferred outcomes because they feared the electoral consequences of precipitating an election.

It is a truism that, if the relevant criterion is the ability to form a government with majority support, the relevant index is one of expected probability of winning. But expected probability of winning cannot be analysed in terms simply of policy distances between parties and the outcomes of votes sincerely expressing their policy preferences. There could still, of course, be a commission of experts to give advice about the party leader to be called, even if we give up on the kind of calculations envisaged by Morriss. But we would then have to recognize that all they would be doing would be asking which party leader, all things considered, has the best chance of forming a government.

It may well appear from what has been said that power as ableness tends to get squeezed between power as ability and prospects of success. I think that this is indeed generally so. There is, however, a clear exception. Of the three uses of 'power' identified by Morriss, I have now discussed the evaluative use (judgement of the distribution of power in a system) and the practical use (estimation of who is in a position to do what). This leaves the moral use, which is concerned with the attribution of responsibility to actors by virtue of their relation to outcomes. Here I think it is clear that power as ableness comes into its own. If we ask whether somebody should be held responsible for failing to prevent some disaster, what we want to know is whether or not in the actual situation he could have done something to avert it. Power as ability does not enter in here: for the strictly limited purpose of assigning responsibility we are not interested in knowing what he could have done under other conditions. We are concerned with what he could have done in the actual conditions.

It is, I suggest, easy to see why 'power' gives so much trouble. The word is employed, as Morriss shows, in the context of three different kinds of inquiry. It is also apparent that 'power' is used both in the sense of power as ability and power as ableness. And although I do not believe that it is used self-consciously to include what Morriss calls passive power, it is very easy to slide from power as ableness to power as prospects of success, and there can be little doubt that this contributes to confusion. Although I have argued that Morriss's book is not without flaws, its publication without doubt marks a real step forward in our understanding of the uses of 'power'.

12

AND WHO IS MY NEIGHBOUR?[1]

> I remember, . . . about 1646 (or 1647) that Mr. John Maynard (now Sir John, and serjeant) came into Middle Temple hall, from Westminster-hall, weary with business, and hungry, when we had newly dined. He sate-downe by Mr. Bennet Hoskyns (the only son of Sergeant Hoskyns, the Poet) since Baronet, and some others; who having made an end of their Commons, fell unto various Discourse, and what was the meaning of the Text (Rom. v. 7.) 'For a just man one would dare to die; but for a good man one would willingly die.' They askt Mr. Maynard what was the difference between a just man and a good man. He was beginning to eate, and cryed:—Hoh, you have eaten your dinners, and now have leisure to discourse; I have not. He had eate but a Bitt or two when he reply'd:—I'le tell you the difference presently: serjeant Rolle is a just man, and Mathew Hale is a good man; and so fell to make an end of his dinner. And there could not be a better interpretation of this Text. For serjeant Rolle was just, but by nature penurious; and his wife made him worse: Mathew Hale was not only just, but wonderfully Charitable and open handed, and did not sound a trumpet neither, as the Hypocrites doe.
>
> J. Aubrey, *Brief Lives*

It is often said that the most important division in moral philosophy is between the view that what makes actions right or wrong is their consequences and the view that some kinds of actions are right or wrong intrinsically, and should be done or not done regardless of the consequences in any particular instance. The strongest objection to the first doctrine is that an adherent of it might be manipulated into doing something extremely evil by the threat on somebody else's part that he will otherwise do something with even more horrible consequences. The strongest objection to the second doctrine is that there seems to be something almost crazy in saying that, once an act has been

[1] This chapter departs from the original form of publication a good deal further than do any of the others in this volume. It is based on a revision of the original (1979) review essay which was carried out in 1983 with the objects of making the order of exposition more natural and also making the discussion relatively independent of the terms set by a rather crass book. At that time the discussion of the relevant literature was carried up to 1983.

determined to fall under a certain description, no consideration of consequences can be relevant in assessing the moral quality of that act.

I believe that both objections are well taken and that any satisfactory view of the matter must accommodate both of them. In this chapter I shall argue for a position that does this. It denies that any act can be immune to moral censure simply in virtue of its falling under some description. But at the same time it allows what an unqualified consequentialist doctrine cannot allow, namely that it makes a difference in the moral quality of an act whether its foreseeably bad consequences follow directly from it or whether they arise from the act's occasioning the predictably wrong act of another.

The doctrine that some kinds of acts are intrinsically right or wrong, irrespective of their consequences, must of course be filled out by specifying what it is about actions that makes them right or wrong. One view that has achieved some considerable currency is this: what makes an act wrong is that it injures somebody and what makes an act right (which in this context means 'permissible' rather than 'required') is that the actor had a right to do it, or, in different words, that the act fell within his sphere of absolute discretion. I shall criticize both halves of this theory.

An even more fundamental question in moral philosophy is whether morality rests on convention or whether some things would be wrong in a society whatever its institutions and whatever the beliefs of its members. I shall not be so bold as to tackle this great question head on but I shall nevertheless try to throw some light on it. I shall, as before, suggest that the strongest arguments on both sides are correct. It is true that much adverse judgement of other cultures is mere prejudice. The stock example of missionaries objecting to the scanty clothing of their 'natives' is entirely to the point here. But it is also true that genocide is wrong whatever the social context in which it occurs. I shall seek to put forward a view that gives full weight to the moral relevance of convention without collapsing into total relativism.

The essay will be cast in the form of a critique of a book published in 1978, Charles Fried's *Right and Wrong*.[2] I shall at times wander pretty far from Fried's text, but the book still provides the framework for my discussion. Although it must be conceded that Fried is hardly the subtlest of thinkers, there are some advantages in having the view to be discussed presented in a fairly stark form. If Fried is willing to draw conclusions from which others who share his outlook might shrink,

[2] Page references in the text of this chapter are to Charles Fried, *Right and Wrong* (Cambridge, Mass.: Harvard University Press, 1978).

that is surely to his credit. Truth, as Bacon said, arises more readily from error than from confusion.

I shall set out my criticisms under two heads: that Fried is mistaken in reducing morality to a matter of rights and wrongs (sections I and II); and that the notion of saving one's soul does not survive translation into secular terms (section III). I shall take up the question of convention in the course of the discussion in section II. I shall conclude (section IV) by returning to the question with which I opened this chapter and ask where the intervening discussion leaves the doctrine of consequentialism.

I WRONGS

The title of Fried's book is *Right and Wrong*; and, not being a man inhibited by excessive modesty, he claims to be able to tell us what is right and what is wrong. However, the two major parts into which the book is divided are called 'Wrongs' and 'Rights'.[3] The shift from right and wrong to rights and wrongs is momentous. Wrongs are things we do to particular people: we wrong them when we do certain things to them. To assume, as Fried does, that we can talk about wrong by talking about wrongs is to commit ourselves to a substantive moral doctrine of a peculiar kind. Other things being equal (at least), it is wrong to wrong people. But cannot there be wrong without anyone being wronged?

Consider these examples. First, let us suppose that a woman could conceive a child now, while she is taking a drug that will cause her child to be gravely deformed at birth; or she could postpone conception for a few months and have a normal child. If the woman goes ahead and conceives the defective child, we can say that the child she bears is much worse off than the child she might have borne later. But we cannot say that the woman has harmed the child that is born, because that child would not have otherwise existed. The child therefore has not been wronged, unless we say that bringing it into existence at all was wronging it (a case of wrongful birth). Let us stipulate, however, that the child is not so miserable as to regret having been born. It still seems reasonable to say that the woman did wrong by conceiving the defective child, and to say this without

[3] There is also a third part of the book (pp. 165–94) which consists of only one chapter. This is entitled 'Roles' and discusses the implications of the theory for professional ethics. Although I regard the chapter as highly obnoxious I shall not take it up here since the rest of the book is self-contained without it.

taking into consideration the effects of the birth on other people who would have existed anyway. We can maintain that the woman did wrong, however, only if we accept that it is possible to do wrong without wronging anybody.[4]

What is in effect a generalization of the same example is the following. Suppose those currently alive deplete resources and create pollution with the result that subsequent generations suffer great hardship. Provided this course of action results in different people being born, compared with what would have happened if a more responsible course had been followed, nobody is wronged. For the would-be complainants would not otherwise have come into existence.[5] Yet it seems absurd to suggest that the members of the current generation are not open to moral criticism for their conduct.

If the only points at which the equation of wrong with wronging came unstuck were those involving alternative populations, we might feel secure in saying that under normal circumstances doing wrong and wronging can be identified. For problems involving possible people are very hard to make sense of anyway. (For a review of the difficulties, see chapter 18 below.) But I believe that the same slippage between wrongdoing and wronging also occurs in cases where the population affected is given. It is still possible to do wrong in relation to people without wronging anybody.

Imagine, then, that a hospital has a limited supply of a scarce drug. The doctor in charge could either use the drug in one massive shot to save the life of one person (less will be of no use to him) or divide it into five equal doses which will save the lives of five people. Would he do wrong to give all of the drug to the one person rather than to divide it among the five?[6] Or, imagine that several people are stranded on one rock, and that one person is stranded on another rock. Assuming that there is not enough time to rescue the people on both rocks before the tide rises and drowns them, does someone with a boat do wrong by rescuing only the lone person? The reason for saying that the doctor or the man with the boat does not do wrong would be that nobody is wronged. Nobody has any cause for complaint, the argument goes, so long as the drug or the boat was used and not wasted.

[4] This example was introduced by Derek Parfit. The best exposition of his views is to be found in his *Reasons and Persons* (Oxford: Clarendon Press, 1984), 351–79.

[5] This is seriously maintained by Thomas Schwartz 'Obligations to Posterity', in R. I. Sikora and Brian Barry (eds.), *Obligations to Future Generations* (Philadelphia: Temple University Press, 1978), thus illustrating the point that one person's proof is another's *reductio ad absurdum*.

[6] The example was introduced by Philippa Foot, 'Abortion and Double Effect', *Oxford Review*, 5 (1967), 5–15, at 9.

As Miss Anscombe put it: 'Why, just because he was one of the five who could have been saved [by the drug], is he wronged in not being saved, if someone is supplied with it who needed it? What is *his* claim, except the claim that what was needed go to him rather than be wasted? But it was not wasted. So he was not wronged. So who was wronged? And if no one was wronged, what injury did I do?' Similarly, the man with the boat 'doesn't act badly if he uses his resources to save X, or X, Y and Z, *for no bad reason*, and is not affected by the consideration that he could save a larger number of people. For, once more, who can say he is wronged? And if no one is wronged, how does the rescuer commit any wrong?'[7]

We can be grateful to Miss Anscombe for making it so clear that the argument rests on the assumption that if no one is wronged nobody can have done wrong. But why should we accept that assumption? Why should we not say that it would be wrong to save fewer lives rather than more? It seems to me spurious to argue that the drug or the boat were not wasted: they were wasted in the sense that they were not used to the best advantage. Suppose the doctor treated one of the five patients with an adequate dose and poured the remaining four-fifths of it down the sink. If giving all the drug to one patient would have been all right, is there anything wrong with that? If so, why? In both cases one person is saved where five might have been. Or suppose that the man with the boat goes to the rock with lots of people and takes off just one person picked at random. He is surely wasting life-saving space in the boat as much as if he went to the rock on which just one person is stranded and rescued that person. The question 'Who is wronged?' is irrelevant. We need not show that anyone is wronged before we can say that it would have been better to use the life-saving resource to save more lives.

Someone who agrees that saving fewer is wrong might try to salvage the equation of wrongdoing and wronging by suggesting that the greater number who might have been saved but were not can legitimately be said to have been wronged. I am inclined to think that this claim would appeal only to someone who was for some reason already committed to the principle that wrongdoing requires a wronged party. It is, of course, true that the greater number suffer grievously as a result of the wrong choice made by the possessor of the medicine or the boat. But all that can be claimed of each of the losers is that it would have been efficient (in life-saving terms) to have saved the group of which he or she was a member. The same person, by

[7] G. E. M. Anscombe, 'Who is Wronged?', *Oxford Review*, 5 (1967), 16–17, at 17.

happening to go to the rock with the smaller number of people, would have lost the claim to be saved. But it seems to me that it is one thing to say that a calculus of life-saving shows that so-and-so was a member of the group that should have been saved and another to say that so-and-so was wronged by the failure to follow the results of applying that calculus. To anticipate the discussion in the next section for a moment, let us pose the question in terms of rights: did each member of the larger group have a right to be saved? If we want to say that wrongdoing is the violation of somebody's rights, we may be driven by the wish to conclude that it is wrong not to save the larger number into saying that each of them has a right to be saved. I cannot see any knockdown argument to show that this is a mistake but I would again ask if one would ever feel drawn to say that the larger number had a right to be saved while the smaller number did not except in order to arrive at the conclusion that it was wrong not to rescue the larger number.

What, after all, is going on here? There is no way of saying who has the right to be saved until the calculation has been carried out to determine which course of action will be most efficacious in saving lives. The only thing that distinguishes those with the right to be saved from those with no right to be saved is that the former emerge from the calculation as those whom it is more efficient to save. This state of affairs does not seem to me to be very perspicuously rendered by talking about some people having a right to be saved and others not. Such talk makes it sound as if the members of the larger group have a right to be saved and therefore ought to be saved, whereas it is actually the other way round: they ought to be saved and, once we have determined that, we could if we choose say (but without adding any new point) that they have a right to be saved.

In the course of his discussion, Fried refers to an article later than Miss Anscombe's which, he says (p. 219), develops the argument with 'great power and subtlety'. Although I should myself be inclined to substitute 'perversity' for 'subtlety', I do think that the central point that the article makes is important and must be faced in any analysis of the notion of a duty to rescue. The author, John Taurek, puts forward the following case.[8] Suppose that we have once again the situation in which the available amount of some drug could save one person in a single dose or some larger number of people divided into smaller doses. And now suppose further that the person who would require

[8] John Taurek, 'Should the Numbers Count?', *Philosophy & Public Affairs*, 6 (1977), 293–316.

the whole amount to be saved owned it. Would we say that he was morally condemnable if he used it on himself? If we would not, then, Taurek argues, this must show that there is no duty to maximize the number of lives saved. So we can generalize the case and say that if some third party owned the drug, we could not consistently say that he was wrong to give it to the one rather than the five.

This argument clearly depends, if it is to be valid, on our acceptance of the proposition that, if *A* cannot be blamed for doing something to save his own life at the expense of several other people's lives, then nobody else can be criticized for choosing to save *A*'s life at the expense of those other people. But this move seems to me to be without foundation. It is true that in 'common sense morality' we make allowances for people in extreme situations. We do not condemn people for failing to be heroes, and to hand over the drug that would save your life so that the lives of five others could be saved would surely be heroic. But that certainly does not mean it would not be better if the five lives were saved instead of the one.[9] Since it would not be heroic for a third party who owned the drug to give it to the five rather than the one, he *can* be criticized for not doing so.

How, then, should we deal with the case of the man with the boat, to take account of what is valid in Taurek's argument without drawing his invalid conclusions? The answer I wish to give is that, instead of asking simply 'Was what he did right or wrong?' we shall ask more fine-grained questions, and according to the answers respond in a variety of ways. Thus, in some circumstances we would treat him as a moral leper if he failed to rescue the people—he happened to be passing the rock anyway, the sea was calm, and he could have taken them off at almost no inconvenience or risk to himself. In others, we might award him a medal for heroism—the sea was stormy and he was putting his own life at risk by going out to rescue the people. In between is a continuous gradation: the further the rock, the severer the storm, the less seaworthy the boat, the less robust the man's health, for example, the better his deed in rescuing the people.

If the man would be risking his life, many other questions become relevant. How did these people come to be stranded? Did they go on to the rocks knowing and accepting the risk? If they did not know, should they have known? Or did they know of the risk but thought they had covered it by arranging to be taken off by a boat which has

[9] Cf. Derek Parfit, 'Innumerate Ethics', *Philosophy & Public Affairs*, 7 (1978), 285–301, and Gregory S. Kavka, 'The Numbers Should Count', *Philosophical Studies*, 36 (1979), 285–94.

failed to appear? And what about the man? What dependants has he? Given their particular circumstances and the prevailing social system, how will they fare if he dies in the rescue attempt? And so on. That these questions are relevant shows that we cannot simply postulate a duty to do as much good as possible, counting in one's own welfare as one unit among many. But they also show the inadequacy of the idea that it would be wrong to save nobody but beyond moral criticism to save one rather than many.

After saying everything that can be said about the situation, we may ask whether, taking everything into account, rescuing should be regarded as praiseworthy and not rescuing as acceptable conduct in the circumstances, or whether not rescuing should be regarded as blameworthy and rescuing as no more than could be reasonably expected of any decent person in the circumstances. But people will probably not all draw the line in exactly the same place: some people set higher standards (for themselves and for others) than do the rest of us. And it does not have to be a *line* at all. After the morally relevant facts have all been established, we may feel disinclined either to say that, in that situation, rescuing was praiseworthy or not rescuing blameworthy. (This is not, of course, to deny that rescuing would always be better than not rescuing.)

What about 'wrong'? We can certainly say that what the man with the boat did was wrong, if it falls so far below the minimum standards of conduct required by the social norms of our community as to lead to universal disapprobation; or we can say more loosely that what he did was wrong if we believe that the social norms should be such as would lead to his severe condemnation. The only thing we cannot do is pretend that we are trying to duplicate the actions of a sort of secular equivalent of the Recording Angel.[10]

II RIGHTS

The strong drive underlying Fried's *Right and Wrong* is the wish to come up with a fixed and finite list of things that people can be morally required to do such that if they do not infringe these rules they can count as 'morally good'. The opening sentence runs: 'This book is about how a moral man lives his life' (p. 1), and the connection between sticking to the rules and being 'morally good' comes out later in, for example, this passage from near the end of the book:

[10] Cf. Joel Feinberg, 'On Being "Morally Speaking a Murderer"', in *Doing and Deserving: Essays on the Theory of Responsibility* (Princeton, NJ: Princeton University Press, 1970), 38–54.

We must recognize a discontinuity: Between the merely just man and the chiseler comes the dividing line of right and wrong, while the whole distance between the saint and the merely just man occurs within the range of the morally good, and thus the categories of condemnation and compulsion are wholly inappropriate within that range. At most, what are in order are judgments of regret, but even those are questionable. The scale of judgement is marked, if at all, in degrees of praise only (pp. 175–6).

This Pharasaical conception of moral goodness as the satisfaction of certain rule-based minimal requirements can be questioned on two grounds. First, we can point out that it has had a long run for its money and if it has fallen into disrepute this was for good reasons, based on extensive experience with it. Victorian novels and biographies are thickly populated with self-righteous prigs who never did anything wrong in Fried's sense but still managed to make life hell for everyone around them. (One might recall the description of Dr Temple, the mid-Victorian headmaster of Rugby School, as 'a beast: but a just beast'.)

The second point that can be made goes to the root of the whole conception. Is a legal or theological model appropriate to what purports to be a secular account of the content of morality? In law and in any rule-based religious system, there is no room for better or worse, only for right and wrong, or, more precisely, permitted, required, and prohibited. Any act is either legal or illegal. There are no degrees of legality. Similarly, an act can be more or less sinful only in the sense that it constitutes a more or less grave sin. The borderline of any given category of sin is an area of increasing doubt about its application, not a continuum of decreasing sinfulness.[11]

The question that must be raised is whether it makes sense to construe morality on the legal model, as Fried does, in the absence of a divine lawgiver. Miss Anscombe observes that 'it is not possible to have [a *law* conception of ethics] unless you believe in God as a law-giver: like Jews, Stoics and Christians'.[12] I think she is right. Since Fried does not call on supernatural authority to underwrite his theory, we must say that his 'wrong' is, to adapt Hobbes, the ghost of sin sitting upon the grave thereof.

We can see both the inadequacy and the arbitrariness of this law conception of morality by examining Fried's doctrine of rights. The

[11] See G. E. M. Anscombe, 'Modern Moral Philosophy', *Philosophy*, 33 (1958), 1–19; reprinted in Judith J. Thomson and Gerald Dworkin (eds.), *Ethics* (New York: Harper & Row, 1968), 186–210, at 201. (All page references in this chapter are to the reprint.)

[12] Ibid. 192.

drive to establish minimal standards the meeting of which absolves anyone from criticism emerges very clearly in the definition of a right that is offered by Fried:

> I want to do something. It is not wrong, but it has (bad) unfortunate concomitants. Do I have to weight these, and forbear if the balance is unfavorable? Usually yes, *unless I have a right to do whatever it is I am doing*. If I have a right to marry whom I want (who wants to marry me), then this just means I do not have to consider how our happiness compares to the unhappiness our marriage will cause my rivals or hers, our parents, the neighbors (pp. 83–4, italics in original).

Fried claims to give us 'an account of moral choice and substantive moral values that is rich, complex and true to the facts' (p. 2). This claim is palpably false. Whatever plausibility Fried's claim may have is gained entirely from the false dilemma he constantly poses that, if one rejects his theory, there is no alternative to accepting universalistic consequentialism—that is to say, the theory that we have a duty to maximize total human wellbeing.

In fact, however, any account fully sensitive to the complexities would regard almost all the substance of morality as falling outside either the sphere of rights or wrongs (understood as Fried proposes to understand them) or the sphere of universal consequences. Counting everyone's interests equally is something legislators and administrators often should do. For a private individual to adopt it, counting himself as one, is (depending on the context) heroic, selfish, meddlesome, or crazy. But, equally, there are very few kinds of case where consequences can be totally discounted in arriving at a moral judgement. Rape and physical injury would be among the few examples to the contrary: nobody would be criticized for refusing to submit in such instances however a utilitarian balance of advantage might come out. Marriage, Fried's own example, surely is not such a case.

If a right is what Fried says it is, there is no right to marry whom you please. (Of course there is, and ought to be, a legal right. But there are many reasons why people should have legal rights, and none of them depends on the existence of moral rights in Fried's sense.) If I have a right to marry whom I please, let us recall, 'I do not have to consider how our happiness compares' to that of others affected. It would be one thing to say that, having considered everything, I would rarely be blameable for preferring my interest to that of third parties. But that is a far cry from saying it is totally irrelevant to any judgement of the moral quality of my act how others would be affected. In this context, it is interesting that P. H. Nowell-Smith, in his book *Ethics*, gives just two illustrations of 'moral obligation', of which the second is: 'I am not free to marry the girl of my choice, because I know that it would break my mother's heart and I am obliged by filial duty.'[13] If the case of marriage fails to convince, take divorce. There is and ought to be a legal right to divorce, but surely the decision to seek a divorce is open to evaluation on the basis of its impact on the interests of all those affected?

If a right were what Fried says it is, there would be no rights to act. For there is no class of actions (such as decisions about whom to marry) with the property that any choice made is beyond moral criticism. The only rights would be rights not to be wronged. We could speak of a right not to be assaulted or raped. This would be a way of saying that assault and rape are always subject to condemnation, whatever the circumstances. But there are no actions of a kind that are never liable to criticism.

We should observe that none of this entails that there are not rights to act in a sense other than a legal one. But it does mean that such rights cannot be construed on the lines proposed by Fried. Thus, we recognize moral rights as well as legal rights. These arise out of the positive morality of a society in a way parallel to that in which legal rights arise from the positive law of a society. We are here concerned with the sphere within which morality (*mores*) can properly be assimilated to the legal model. Thus, just as contracts give rise to legal rights, so promises give rise to moral rights. If you have promised me something, then, whether or not the promise is legally binding, I have a right to demand fulfilment, even if it would be burdensome to you to carry out your promise and of trivial advantage to me to have you do so.

But there is a disanalogy between moral and legal rights, and I suspect it is failure to take account of it that leads Fried into error. If I have a legal right to do something, I never do wrong legally by exercising it, however inopportunely. Substituting 'moral' for 'legal' in both places turns a correct statement into an incorrect one. It is not true that if I have a moral right to do something I never do wrong by exercising it, however inopportunely. The analogy between moral and legal rights, is, rather, that the exercise of either a moral or legal right is always open to moral appraisal and, potentially, to moral condemnation. As Justice Frankfurter put it, 'much that is legally

[13] P. H. Nowell-Smith, *Ethics* (Harmondsworth: Pelican, 1954), 210.

permitted is repugnant to the civilized mind'.[14] The same may be said of moral rights.

Thus, suppose that I have a moral right (based, say, on an earlier agreement that is not legally binding) to play the piano for an hour every evening in the apartment above yours. That means you cannot require me to refrain; but if I do not enjoy it much and you hate it, I would certainly be a better person if I chose not to exercise my moral right to play. Thus, we often say both that somebody is 'within his rights' in doing something and wrong to do it.[15] That is a kind of complexity that Fried cannot accommodate in his theory of rights.

Just as we found Fried's ideas about wrongs more sharply presented by other writers, Anscombe and Taurek, so here we can fruitfully shift our discussion to Judith Jarvis Thomson's well-known argument against rights of recipience, in her article 'A Defense of Abortion'.[16] This is particularly handy for the continuation of the discussion begun in section I in that it bears on the duty to rescue.

Thomson supposes that you have been kidnapped by a society of music-lovers and that a famous violinist has been plugged into your kidneys for nine months of recuperation. If you unplug him he will die. The question she asks about your accepting this and not unplugging the violinist is posed as follows: 'Is it morally incumbent on you to accede to this situation? No doubt it would be very nice if you did, a great kindness. But do you *have* to accede to it?'[17] Before we know where we are, this is turned into the question whether the violinist has a 'right to life' that trumps your right to determine the use your own kidneys are put to. The answer is 'no', and that is equally true, according to Mrs Thomson, if he only needs to be plugged into your circulation for an hour.[18]

In a second example, we are to suppose that your life would be saved by the cool touch of Henry Fonda's hand upon your fevered brow.[19] Does he have to supply it? If we look closely at what she says about the case, it again becomes clear that she sees the question as one about what you have a right to receive from Henry Fonda. If we feel any temptation to say you have a right to have him cross the room to soothe your fevered brow, how far exactly does he have to come

[14] Gerald Grant, 'The Character of Education and the Education of Character', *Daedelus*, 110 (1981), 135–49 at 141.

[15] See Jeremy Waldron, 'A Right to Do Wrong', *Ethics*, 92 (1981), 21–39.

[16] J. J. Thomson, 'A Defense of Abortion', *Philosophy & Public Affairs*, 1 (1971), 47–66; reprinted in R. M. Dworkin (ed.), *The Philosophy of Law* (Oxford: Oxford University Press, 1977), 112–28. (Page references to reprint.)

[17] Ibid. 113. [18] Ibid. 123. [19] Ibid. 118.

before the right ceases to exist? Across the street, across town, halfway round the world? Any particular cut-off point seems absurd. 'So I have a right to it when it's easy for him to provide it, though no right when it's hard? It's a rather shocking idea that anyone's rights should fade away and disappear as it gets harder and harder to accord them to him.'[20] We are thus driven to conclude that you either have an unconditional right to a touch of his cool hand on your fevered brow or you do not, and in that case it seems evident that you have no such right. But why cannot we simply say (as I suggested we should in the case of the man with the boat) that the further he has to come the less badly we think of him if he does not? And cannot we condemn him for not crossing the room, *just because* it would be so easy? This would be like the man with the boat passing right by the rock and refusing to rescue the people from drowning even though he could do so in perfect safety and at very little personal inconvenience. Why need we seek to say more?

I am perfectly well aware that lurking in the background of all this talk about 'rights' by Mrs Thomson is a policy question about positive law: should the law enforce a 'right to life'? But why should we suppose that in order to answer a question about what the law should be we must first find out about the existence or non-existence of some other, spooky, kind of right? In the end, it turns out, even Mrs Thomson concedes that what she calls 'Minimally Decent Samaritan laws' could be defended.[21] But does that not mean that saving a life by crossing a room (a less fanciful analogy would be going a few yards out of your way to pull a drowning child out of a puddle) could be made (or, indeed, morally just *is*) something you 'have to' do? If so, it must be that the person you 'have to' save does not have a 'right' to be saved (in the 'natural right' sense) because we should then get back into the position of having to say that the right comes and goes according to whether or not there happens to be somebody around who could save him while being no more than Minimally Decent. But if we can argue about the pros and cons of enforcing (either by legal sanctions or social pressure) Minimally Decent Samaritanism, without ever mentioning natural rights, why cannot we do the same for Good Samaritanism? I shall argue below that we can.

Fried, like Mrs Thomson, poses the question: what right do others have to demand services from us, over and above not deliberately being harmed? And he comes up with the answer: precious little. The

[20] Ibid. 123. [21] Ibid. 125.

'negative right' not to contribute to the good of others if we choose not to has the effect of ruling out just about any enforced beneficence. Most of Fried's discussion of enforced beneficence is carried out as if the kind of 'enforcement' in question was solely legal enforcement. Thus, in his discussion of blood and kidney donors, he writes as if there were only two alternatives: *either* people have a right (of bodily integrity) to do what they like with their blood and tissues (including giving them, selling them, or keeping them) *or* it would be permissible for a squad of medical policemen to drag you off, clamp you to a table, and extract your blood or organs without your consent (p. 140).

Fried then applies his conclusion (that forced donation is out) to the question of whether people must develop and employ their talents to benefit the community. Fried construes talents on the model of blood and kidneys: you can use your talents to benefit yourself or to benefit others. (In the latter case you can either sell them or give them away.) You can choose not to develop your talents, or, if you have developed your talents, you can let them deteriorate or simply not use them. Thus, a tax on people's earning potential would be bad because it would penalize those who choose to be lazy; an income tax is bad (though less bad) because it penalizes those who choose to be hard-working (pp. 143–7).

Towards the end of the book, Fried suddenly extends all this earlier discussion of legal enforcement to exclude moral criticism of refusal to help other individuals or serve the community.

> It would violate the rights of individuals, to *enforce* notions of fairness or efficiency in respect to the deployment of what I have called a man's discretionary resources. But should we not at least recognize a *moral* duty to use these resources for the good of all mankind—fairly and efficiently? Yet if a man may not be compelled but may be blamed (and should blame himself) if he does not use his liberty to maximize the good of all mankind, then we have accomplished very little by affirming that negative rights establish the core of moral personality. For if total claims upon us, while not enforceable, are nevertheless morally valid, then moral personality is established on a foundation which makes it morally immune only from coercion but not from condemnation. But surely we would want moral personality to have a more secure foundation. It is not enough that a man cannot be forced to act like a utilitarian maximizer; it should also be the case that he cannot be morally condemned if he does not act that way (p. 172, italics in original).

I hope that by this point it is not necessary to emphasize that the choice posed here between being free from any possibility of moral criticism for not doing something for others and being morally required to act as a 'utilitarian maximizer' is a wholly bogus one. What I do want to argue is that Fried's case against 'positive rights' is given a quite unwarranted plausibility by his first presenting it as if it were a question of legal enforcement and then calling on the conclusion of that discussion later to rule out moral criticism. A society may well establish a legal right of its members not to have their blood taken without their consent or not to contribute their talents to the common good if they choose not to. But there are many reasons why something should not be made subject to legal enforcement. The case against may be quite strong without in the least implying that there is a 'right' in Fried's sense not to do it, that is to say that the decision not to contribute must be beyond moral criticism. We can therefore agree that it should not be legally required to give blood or contribute to the common good, without agreeing that people should not feel bad (or be made to feel bad) about failing to do so. Why it should be an assault on somebody's integrity to feel that the decent thing to do would be to give blood is completely beyond me.

I cannot create a full-blown alternative here but let me sketch what one might look like. I suggest, then, that the value of fairness calls for doing good to others in so far as there exist widely practised social norms that one should do that kind of good. People can quite properly be criticized for failing to live up to such norms. The basic idea is that a whole variety of alternative norms would be consistent with the requirements of justice. Which norms exist in a society is a matter of culture and tradition. One can criticize these norms even if the existing norms fall within the range of justice. A utilitarian may say they should be more stringent; a libertarian that they are too stringent, for example. As a theory about the basis for appraising such norms, 'actual rule utilitarianism'—that norms should be judged by the consequences of observing them—was inadequate but not a bad first shot. What sank it was the idea that, in order to be consistently utilitarian, one must try to show that each instance of obeying the rule would help maximize total utility. On the view I am proposing, however, the moral basis for obeying the existing rule is that it is unfair to be a 'free rider', taking advantage of the contributions of others and not contributing yourself.[22]

This general idea is familiar enough where the source of the norm is a legal enactment. Thus, within broad limits the level of taxation is

[22] H. L. A. Hart, 'Are There Any Natural Rights?', *Philosophical Review*, 64 (1955), 175–91. Reprinted in F. A. Olafson (ed.), *Society, Law and Morality* (Englewood Cliffs, NJ: Prentice-Hall, 1961), 173–86.

neither just nor unjust, but if others with your income are paying their assessed share it is unfair of you not to. It is neither just nor unjust to ban open fires in the middle of a city to cut down air pollution, but if others comply it is unfair of you not to. Note that it is the behaviour creating the benefits that creates the obligation of fairness, not the law itself. Thus, if nobody else takes any notice of the city ordinance requiring owners of dogs to clean up after them, it is not unfair if you do not either.

The positive morality of a community can be the source of benefit-creating behaviour just as can its positive law, and the same analysis can be applied. Let us call the degree to which people expect and are expected to help one another individually and contribute to the common good the *level of public morality* of a society. This level will be different in different societies. It is, for example, relatively high in small, ethnically and socially homogeneous countries such as New Zealand, lower in Britain, and lower still in the USA.

The argument I am making is that the different levels of public morality in different societies are conventional (in at any rate one sense of the term) but that they provide the basis for judgements of fair and unfair behaviour, and for criticizing those who fall too far short of the standard. What would be an unfair refusal to help others in New Zealand would be perfectly fair among the Ik of Uganda, of whom Colin Turnbull wrote in the Acknowledgements of his book about them: 'It is difficult to know how to thank the Ik; perhaps it should be for having treated me as one of themselves, which is about as badly as anyone can be treated.'[23] (Note, again, that one can treat people *badly*, even among the Ik; one simply cannot treat them *unfairly*.)

Fried's theory entails that it would be wrong, because it is an attack on inalienable negative rights, for a society to have a high level of public morality. I suggest, on the contrary, that to erect to the status of natural law the alienation of contemporary American society is provincialism, and to put forward as binding on all mankind the latest intellectual fashion in Cambridge, Mass., is parochialism.

It is also, I believe, limited imagination rather than superior insight into the 'nature of things' that leads Fried to regard the idea that being a kidney-donor might be a matter of morality as so utterly absurd that it can be used as the cornerstone of a whole theory of negative rights. There are, I think, three features of being a kidney-donor that make it relatively unsuitable to be the subject of a social norm, as against, for

[23] Colin M. Turnbull, *The Mountain People* (New York: Simon and Schuster, 1972), 13.

example, being a blood-donor.[24] First, giving up a kidney involves a serious operation and some increased risk of eventual renal failure (though the prospect of this would be much less grim if one could be sure of a ready supply of donors in case one's remaining kidney were to fail). Second, rather a small proportion of the population would be donors, even if all who could benefit from a transplant got one, raising the question 'Why me?' (Similarly, conscription runs into increasing trouble the *smaller* the proportion of those eligible who are drafted.)[25] And, third, the question 'Why me?' is less persuasively answered by saying 'Because our tissue-typing shows that you are the person in the whole country who is most compatible with somebody who needs a transplant' than is the answer 'Because you're there' when you are the only person on the beach and somebody is drowning just offshore.

For all these reasons, it may well be that kidney-donation by live donors never becomes a social norm anywhere. Even in conscript armies, the Western tradition has been that dangerous missions requiring small numbers should be filled by volunteers, and giving a kidney seems most aptly assimilated to that kind of exceptionally meritorious offering of oneself for the good of others. (A closer equivalent to blood-donation would be giving permission for one's organs to be used for transplants after death, and it seems to me quite possible that this will some day be the norm in countries with a high level of public morality.)

The upshot is that the donation of kidneys, so far from being a case from which we can confidently move to others, is in a number of ways quite distinctive. Anybody who has clear intuitions that even the mildest form of social pressure towards being a kidney-donor would be unjust should beware of being stampeded into the kind of reckless generalization from that case engaged in by Fried and Nozick.

And what if it *did* become a norm, to (say) the weak extent that being a blood-donor in Britain (particularly in the case of those with a rare blood group) might be thought of as a norm? Would that really be such a terrible assault on individual integrity? Or would it be one of the highest expressions of human fellowship?

[24] See Richard M. Titmuss, *The Gift Relationship: From Human Blood to Social Policy* (London: George Allen and Unwin, 1970), 215, 225, 242–3.

[25] See for a discussion of conscription chapter 14 of this book.

III FROM SOUL-SAVING TO FACE-SAVING

In the introduction to *Right and Wrong*, Fried writes as follows:

> Individualism is often seen as a selfish doctrine allowing individuals to ignore the interests of others. Right and wrong, however, emphasize not the individual's selfish concerns but his moral integrity, and in this we come closer to the historic heart of individualism. If deontology, the theory of right and wrong, is solicitous of the individual, it is primarily solicitous of his claim to preserve his moral integrity, to refrain from being the agent of wrong, even if such fastidiousness means forgoing the opportunity to promote great good or to prevent great harm. In this respect the primacy of right and wrong is a doctrine that shows its traditional religious origins in contrast to the secular, melioristic foundations of those theories which hold that it is consequences alone which count. . . . Religious views . . . expect the secular future to share the imperfections and suffering of the present and the past. With such expectations it follows that the focus must be on personal moral perfection. Thus Christianity rejects consequentialism on the (consequentialist) ground that man is unlikely to gain the whole world (or its betterment) even if he were prepared to lose his soul. And of course one need believe neither in original sin nor in any theology at all to share this sense of our situation (p. 2).

I believe that the 'of course' in the last sentence here is too easy. If we substitute 'moral perfection' for 'a state of grace' and replace 'saving your soul' with 'protecting your moral integrity', it is in my view a serious question whether we are left with a credible (or creditable) doctrine.

To illustrate, let me turn to Fried's chapter on the absolute wrongness of lying, whatever the human consequences of telling the truth. In the course of his discussion, Fried cites Augustine's *De mendacio*.

> Having argued that God destroys all who tell lies, he [Augustine] asks: If this truth be granted, who of those who assent will be shaken by such argument as are given by those who say: 'What if a man should flee to you, who by your lie can be saved from death?' . . . In very truth, some are indignant and angry if someone is unwilling to lose his soul by telling a lie so that another may grow a little older in the flesh (p. 70).

Granted the premisses, this seems fair enough. If life on earth is the blink of an eyelid compared to eternity, which is going to be spent in bliss or torment depending on how you conduct yourself here, and if telling a lie will shift you from being saved to being damned (or even has any finite probability of doing so), you would surely be quixotic to lie in order to add a few years to somebody else's life on earth (which is also the blink of an eyelid). If that is really how things are, Augustine is quite right. But suppose that none of it is true: there is no God, this is the only life we have, and violent death is one of the greatest evils we know. Is anything left of the argument? Fried says that he can offer 'secular versions' of Augustine's arguments, and the one corresponding to that quoted above is as follows:

> The frequent references to lying as defilement might fairly be given the following interpretation: if lying is (absolutely) wrong, then to treat lying as something which is simply bad, undesirable, but to be traded off to procure other goods, to avoid worse harms, is to pursue good ends by impermissible means. To use a Kantian formulation, the violation of the categorical imperative is inestimably worse than any harm one may fend off by such a violation, since the categorical imperative and our obligation under it are what found our moral nature. Any violation for a mere contingent good trades what gives us moral status at all for something which has moral status only insofar as it is attributable to a moral being. This, then, is the Kantian version of the notion of gaining the whole world but losing one's soul (pp. 70–1).

I have to say that I find the secular translation a step from the sublime to the ridiculous. We are, after all, talking about a case where, by telling a lie, you can save a man's life. If I were the man who was fleeing death, I should not think much of the moral nature or moral status of somebody who was agonizing about whether to pollute his precious 'integrity' to save my life. 'Moral status' is a very poor substitute for 'soul'. It seems to me that the moral theory being put forward by Fried needs the original article. 'Moral status' simply will not carry the weight. If we take God and the soul out of the picture, the emphasis on 'integrity' becomes a form of narcissism. The question Fried would have us keep in the forefront of our minds is always 'How do I come out of this looking?' There certainly are people like this, but the idea that we should be expected to admire them seems to me bizarre.

The reasoning which this moral dandy is supposed to offer to the refugee runs as follows:

> We are responsible for the wrongs we do ourselves and not for those which by our wrong we fail to prevent others from committing. This argument is necessary . . . to maintain the distinction between the wrong and the bad. The category of the wrong speaks in the first or second person, but not in the third person: it tells me what I must not do, and I violate it just by doing the forbidden thing. But though the norm is universal in its application, a violation by another person is not a wrong except in relation to that other

person. In relation to me it is bad, so that my lying to prevent a wrong by another is a case of my doing wrong in order to prevent something which *from my point of view* is a bad. To be sure, what the other will do *is* wrong, but it is *his* wrong (p. 71, italics in original).

Thus, the fact that by revealing your whereabouts, I give the pursuer the opportunity to work his nefarious will is neither here nor there. That he will kill you is the foreseeable but unintended consequence of my act; and anyway, it is his wrong, not mine. If this is Kant, I prefer to spell it with a *c*.

To keep the record straight, I should add that Fried finally extricates himself from the conclusion that it is wrong to lie in this case by adducing a complicated argument extending over seven pages to the effect that the pursuer has no right to the truth so he is not wronged by being lied to. (See pp. 72–8.) However, the point is not whether or not it is possible with enough of a struggle to get out the obviously right answer. The point is that, as Fried admits, 'a struggle is necessary in the context of my argument' (p. 72). Bernard Williams has correctly argued that the object of setting up hard cases for utilitarians is not to see if the right answer can be arrived at by utilitarian calculation with enough effort, but to point out that the effort is needed.[26] The same argument can, I suggest, be deployed against Fried here. Any theory that requires seven pages of fancy footwork to establish that it is all right to lie to a would-be murderer in order to save his prospective victim's life has something seriously wrong with it.

The last long quotation raises two questions, one about double effect, the other about responsibility. In my view, the first is fairly straightforward, the second far more complicated than Fried, with his sweeping metaphysical assumptions, admits. Fried raises the issues in the following example: a man seeking to free a prisoner (1) blows up the prison wall with the predictable consequence that a guard will be killed by falling masonry or (2) shoots the guard so as to obtain the keys. (See p. 23.) Fried apparently wants to say that there is a difference in the moral quality of the two acts: in the first case the death of the guard is a foreseen but unwanted by-product of blowing up the wall, whereas in the second case the guard's death is deliberately brought about as a means to the escape. But in my view, not only is the man who brings about the guard's death equally responsible in both cases, but he is equally culpable. That the death of the guard is in the first case a by-product and in the second case a means is irrelevant, and

[26] Bernard Williams, 'A Critique of Utilitarianism', in J. J. C. Smart and Bernard Williams, *Utilitarianism: For and Against* (Cambridge: Cambridge University Press, 1973), 99, 117.

if the doctrine of double effect implies the contrary (as Fried apparently holds) that is sufficient basis for dismissing it.

As another example, take the much discussed case of bombing in wartime. Suppose that it is known that (given the inaccuracy and dispersion inherent in aerial bombing) the only way to have a reasonable chance of hitting an important military installation is to drop a number of bombs that can be foreseen to kill thousands of civilians. Can the man who plans the raid say: 'I am not responsible for the civilian deaths—they are the foreseen but unintended by-product of the raid on the military target'?

I think not. Fried cites with approval 'the international law of war' as condemning 'intentional infliction of civilian casualties, while permitting the causing of such casualties as a side-effect, even a certain one, of military action against military targets' (p. 21). But surely the *responsibility* for the outcome is just the same whatever the intention of the actor. It is monstrous if (as seems to follow from Fried's views) a man can disclaim responsibility for almost anything that happens as a result of what he does just so long as he picks his intentions carefully enough.

Holding the military planner responsible for all the consequences—both the destroyed military installation and the dead civilians—does not preclude our condemning him if he aims at the civilians while acquitting him of a war crime if he aims at the military installation and hits the civilians as a by-product. But he must *answer* for all the consequences. He must, to be excused, show that the military target was really important, that there was no way of hitting it at reasonable cost to his own side that would have killed fewer civilians, and so on. Relieving him of responsibility for the foreseen but unintended consequences of ordering the bombing raid would mean that he did not have to justify it in terms of the balance between (military) gains and (civilian) losses.

Consider any situation in which it is claimed (1) that we properly hold somebody fully responsible for an act of his under some description (e.g. aiming at a military target, organizing a peaceful civil rights march) but (2) that we should acquit him (wholly or partly) of responsibility for (some of) the consequences of the act (e.g. killing innocent people, creating the occasion for a race riot). I suggest that, whenever the claim is plausible, we will find it to be a case where we hold somebody else (partly or wholly) responsible for those consequences. The simplest way in which somebody other than the actor is held responsible is where there is a *novus actus interveniens* between the actor and the foreseeable consequence of his act. The more subtle way is where, although the act produces its natural consequences without any other act coming between, we hold someone responsible for the circumstances in which that act has those consequences.

Thus, Alan Donagan has argued that, in a war that is legitimately being fought, 'the deaths of noncombatants who are killed in direct attacks on military installations are to be deemed accidental, on the ground that it is the enemy's fault that noncombatants are there'.[27] This seems to me implausible, if such things as munitions factories, railway marshalling yards, and so on, are military targets, given the radius within which bombs aimed at them are bound to fall. But the point that the responsibility may shift to those who create the circumstance seems reasonable. If the enemy puts civilian hostages on military trains[28] or straps innocent persons to the front of its tanks 'so that the tanks cannot be hit without hitting them'[29] it is responsible for their deaths. But notice that responsibility here is assigned by saying something like, 'You can't expect people fighting a war to call it off because the other side fixes things so as to make it impossible to fight without killing innocent people.' Some judgement about what it is reasonable to expect cannot be escaped here.

Suppose, to modify the example of the tanks, that I am tired of people driving too close behind me so I grab a child who is playing in the street and lash it to the back of my car before setting off. If you drive behind me at a distance that does not leave you with ample room to avoid running into my car (even if it would be considered enough normally), then I would say that, in the event of a collision, you are partly responsible for the resulting injuries to the child. Why? Because in this case 'business as usual' is *not* reasonable.

In the case of the *novus actus interveniens*, Fried regards the solution as simple: an act always breaks the chain of responsibility. So the last actor before the consequence is always responsible for the consequence—subject, of course, to the proviso about responsibility for the circumstances being what they are in the first place. Thus, 'we must not do wrong even in order to prevent more, greater wrongs by others. If those others do wrong it is their wrong, for which they are responsible' (p. 2). Once again, I find Fried's theory too simplistic.

Fried is haunted by the nightmare of our being saddled with

[27] Alan Donagan, *The Theory of Morality* (Chicago: University of Chicago Press, 1977), 87.

[28] See Michael Walzer, *Just and Unjust Wars: A Moral Argument with Historical Illustrations* (New York: Basic Books, 1977), 174, for an example from the Franco-Prussian War of 1870.

[29] Robert Nozick, *Anarchy, State, and Utopia* (New York: Basic Books, 1974), 35.

excessive personal responsibility for the state of the world. Thus, in his opening paragraph he writes:

> My central concern is to discern structure and limits in the demands morality makes upon us. . . . We are constrained but not smothered by morality once we acknowledge that there are limits to our responsibility for the world's good and ill, that we are responsible for some things but not everything (p. 1).

Within limits, the concern to restrict our liability for consequences is quite appropriate. It would, indeed, be intolerable if people could always get us to do things by suffering if we didn't do them.[30] It would be even worse if we could always be manipulated by people threatening bad consequences unless we did what they demanded. But Fried's desperate struggles to escape suffocation take him much too far. In slashing away at the clammy tentacles of consequentialism he also cuts off a large chunk of live morality.

The legal model again misleads here. In the law, people are in general held solely responsible for their own actions. But moral judgements can be far more finely nuanced. We can allow for all kinds of relations between the actions of different people that would, and should, never get into a court of law. As Hart and Honoré put the point:

> The use of the legal sanctions of imprisonment, or forced monetary compensation against individuals, has such formidable repercussions on the general life of society that the fact that individuals have a type of connexion with harm which is adequate for moral censure or claims for compensation is only *one* of the factors which the law must consider, in defining the kinds of connexion between actions and harm for which it will hold individuals legally responsible.[31]

A good example of the point at issue here is provided by advice-giving. Except in special cases such as professional advisers or counsellors of crime people are not legally responsible for the advice they give others, even if following it has disastrous consequences. The responsibility falls squarely on the person who decides whether or not to take the advice. Morally, however, if someone does something bad on our advice, especially if the advice pertained to a matter of

[30] One might recall Scobie, in *The Heart of the Matter*: 'He had always been prepared to accept the responsibility for his actions, and he had always been aware too, from the time he made his terrible vow that [Louise] should be happy, how far *this* action might carry him.' Philip Stratford (ed.), *The Portable Graham Greene* (New York: Viking Press, 1973), 92–367, at 154.

[31] H. L. A. Hart and A. M. Honoré, *Causation and the Law* (Oxford: Clarendon Press, 1959), 62.

fundamental choice rather than the means to an end the person definitely was going to pursue anyway, we share the responsibility.[32] Other examples are provocation and temptation. From a moral point of view we tend to hold people rather widely responsible for provoking and tempting others—far more widely than in law.

More generally, it seems to me that we cannot absolve ourselves totally from responsibility for the foreseeable actions that others do as a result of our actions. Suppose that I have a contractual right to keep my employee late at work once a week. I know, however, that he tends to beat his wife when I keep him at work late, and that he rarely does so at other times. No doubt the beating is the employee's wrong, not mine. But if I know what the facts are and still keep the employee late, do I not have some moral responsibility too? Should I be able to excuse myself on the ground that the result, although foreseen, was not intended?

Again, suppose that Martin Luther King announces a civil rights march in some Southern town, and the local worthies prophesy violence. Or suppose that somebody proposes to deliver a speech on some controversial topic and zealots on the other side threaten to break it up. It seems to me important here to keep two things in focus, and not let either force out the other. One is that the racists and bigots are fully responsible for whatever bloodshed occurs. The other is that the organizers of the march or rally are also responsible for the bloodshed: not necessarily blameable but answerable.[33] Their answer may be a satisfactory one that relieves them of blame (and it need not be couched in terms of strictly utilitarian considerations). But they must be prepared to answer. Otherwise, if we simply say of the racists and bigots 'It's their wrong,' we cannot say that the organizers were wrong not to take every precaution to minimize violence, consistent with carrying out their object. Yet this is surely morally relevant. That the organizers did not intend that their actions should lead to violence but merely foresaw violence as a consequence is undeniably relevant but not the end of the story. What the law should be is another matter and there may be good reasons founded in the value of free speech and

[32] 'If people ever took advice', Virginia Woolf noted defensively in her diary, 'I should feel a little responsible for making up Ralph's mind [to marry Carrington]. I mean I am not sure that this marriage is not more risky than most.' Her biographer comments: 'Her doubts were well-founded. . . .' Although there is no question that Ralph Partridge did the marrying—it was his act—Virginia Woolf was surely right to feel qualms about her role. See Quentin Bell, *Virginia Woolf: A Biography* (New York: Harcourt Brace Jovanovich, 1974), 80, 81.

[33] For the suggestion that the root meaning of 'responsible' is 'answerable', see H. L. A. Hart, *Punishment and Responsibility: Essays in the Philosophy of Law* (London: Oxford University Press, 1968), 264–5.

assembly for saying that the responsibility for violence should be laid solely at the door of those who commit it and that those who provide the occasion for it should not be held legally responsible for failing to minimize the risk, provided their contribution does not amount to what the law will take cognizance of as provocation.[34]

Fried is concerned that too strong a sense of responsibility for the world's sufferings will be bad for our moral health. (See pp. 34–5.) As the old Chinese song put it:

> Don't escort the big chariot;
> You will only make yourself dusty.
> Don't think about the sorrows of the world;
> You will only make yourself wretched.[35]

I am inclined to believe that there is relatively little risk, in the countries where Fried's book is most likely to be read, of that danger. In arguing so strenuously for limited liability, Fried is simply telling us what we would like to hear. Think of the kind of context in which people characteristically say things like: 'My conscience is clear.' This is generally a defensive statement made to deny responsiblity for the consequences of one's acts: the ruin of a business competitor, the suicide of a subordinate, and so on. Fried would say that, provided it was not your intention to procure the competitor's ruin or deliberately drive the subordinate to suicide, your conscience is quite properly clear. I suggest that it is a lot less simple than that. We do not have to choose between holding someone responsible for all the consequences of his acts and limiting liability for consequences as stringently as Fried does.

Obviously, if this is so, the right answer is going to be very complicated. In developing it I predict that we shall get more help from the novelists than from the lawyers. One particular way in which the law is a poor model is that, where responsibility for an outcome is divided, the total normally adds up to 100 per cent: if one driver was 70 per cent responsible for the collision at an intersection then the other one contributed 30 per cent to it. Fried, following this logic, assumes that, if we are to hold one person 100 per cent responsible for his actions we must absolve everybody else of responsibility for them. But attributing moral responsibility is not a fixed-sum game. Just as there can be overdetermination of events there can be, so to speak, overresponsibility for outcomes.

[34] See Hart and Honoré, *Causation and the Law*, pp. 333–4 for a somewhat inconclusive account of English law on this point.

[35] Arthur Waley, *The Book of Songs* (London: George Allen, 1937), No. 286.

Underlying all of Fried's book is, as he often repeats, a Kantian notion of human freedom according to which we do not merely have the freedom to choose what to do but also the freedom to choose what to choose: we are literally responsible for making ourselves.

> I choose my life plan freely. . . . Though the system of wants I have constructed for myself is supremely important to me, it is after all I who have constructed it. . . . The . . . conception I offer holds a man responsible for his wants. . . . The respect we are entitled to as regards our wants . . . depends on the fact that as free beings we have freely chosen this conception of the good (pp. 124–6).

If Fried's theory is correct, society is due for a great leap backward. Marx and Freud—and everything they stand for—will go out of the window. There can be no room for the subversive notion that people are the products of their social environment or that their actions may have deep-rooted psychological causes. You can do anything if you try, and it is metaphysically guaranteed that you can always try. So out go any suggestions that there are causes of suicide, recidivism, alcoholism, baby-battering, inability to hold a job, failure to use contraception, and so on. Pleas of insanity or diminished responsibility will disappear from the legal system. Social workers and psychiatrists will be out of a job. Society will inscribe on its banner not, as Marx thought, 'From each according to his ability, to each according to his need' but:

> It matters not how strait the gate,
> How charged with punishment the scroll,
> I am the master of my fate:
> I am the captain of my soul.[36]

Fried might reply that this is to take him too literally. But if we once allow Fried's metaphysical absolute to be turned into an empirical claim about actual people, I do not see how we can avoid concluding that nobody fully has the ability and opportunity to shape his own life. And can we avoid concluding that the extent to which people are in fact able to shape their own lives varies greatly from country to country and within countries from class to class?

Fried at no point offers any defence of his conception of freedom. At one point he says that 'in moral philosophy we may often be forced to swallow some quite unchewed metaphysical morsels' (p. 20). But

[36] W. E. Henley in F. T. Palgrave (ed.), *The Golden Treasury* (London: Oxford University Press, 1929), No. 397, p. 476.

does that also apply to forcing these unchewed morsels on everybody? In a liberal society everyone has the privilege of believing what he likes—even that the earth is flat or that men are noumenal beings. But when it comes to questions of public policy, it matters a lot to everyone whether the premisses on which proposals are made are in fact true.

Let us grant that the freedom to shape our own lives and achieve our own ends is of central importance. As Fried puts it: 'Happiness is . . . the aim and outcome of individual *choice*, the success of the self in realizing its own values through its own choices and efficacy' (p. 34, italics in original). I maintain that it is nothing better than a cruel hoax to say that everyone has such freedom by virtue of being a noumenal self. Only a privileged minority of the human race have ever had the opportunity either to choose their own ends (to the extent that anyone can ever do so) or to be efficacious in pursuing self-chosen goals. To develop a core of identity, to be able to integrate short-term and long-term aims into a coherent 'life plan', and to acquire the skills necessary for having a reasonable opportunity to carry out that plan: none of these abilities just accrues to people as a concomitant of their metaphysical status. What chance has an unemployed high-school dropout in the ghetto or a Mississippi plantation worker to 'realize his own values' through his own 'choices and efficacy'?

It makes a big difference politically whether or not we swallow the unchewed metaphysical morsels that Fried offers us. If we say that freedom is something human beings are guaranteed metaphysically, we almost inevitably finish up with Fried's complacent kind of liberal conservatism. If, by contrast, we take freedom as empirically problematic, as something that has to be created, we find ourselves committed to a social and economic revolution to create the conditions in which alone freedom can thrive.

IV THE REVOLT AGAINST CONSEQUENTIALISM

Although not much is left by this stage of Fried's *Right and Wrong*, it is still significant as a straw in the wind—the wind of anti-consequentialism that has been blowing with increasing force since the 1960s. In this concluding section, I shall put Fried's book in its context and ask how we should assess consequentialism.

Let us begin with the term 'consequentialism' itself. It was, I believe, introduced into Anglo-American philosophical discourse by Elizabeth Anscombe in 1958 to mean the doctrine that one should judge the morality of an action by its consequences.[37] The contrast is with an act's being judged by its nature. The judgement of an action would then turn on its being an action of a certain sort, where 'being of a certain sort' could not include 'having such-and-such consequences'. Candidates for the role of a 'sort of action' might be specific descriptions ('killing an innocent person' or 'betraying a friend') or more general characterizations such as the Kantian one of 'treating a person as a means only and not as an end in himself'.

In principle, a consequentialist could have any criterion for judging consequences as better or worse, however bizarre: he could say that good actions are those that have the effect of raising the level of the sea, increasing the amount of radiation at certain frequencies, and so on. But, in practice, the consequences are usually defined in terms of human interests. Thus, an egoistic consequentialist judges actions by the way they affect himself, a patriotic consequentialist by the way they affect his country, and a universal consequentialist by the way they affect all human beings. (A 'non-speciesist' universalist might judge actions by their consequences for all sentient beings. I shall not consider this extension of universalism in the present discussion.)

The most familiar version of consequentialism is utilitarianism, the doctrine that one act (or policy, institution, etc.) is better than another if it yields more aggregate happiness to human beings. We should note, however, to avoid confusion, that the term 'utilitarianism' is often extended to include the whole of what I am calling consequentialism. Thus, for example, G. E. Moore proposed an 'ideal utilitarianism' according to which value inheres in such things as the existence of beautiful objects and the creation of certain kinds of personal relationships, and acts are to be assessed in terms of their value-producing effects.[38] I have not followed this usage. I take utilitarianism (as I have defined it) as the prime example of consequentialism, because of its historical importance and its relatively definite specification.

What we have seen in recent years is, I believe, a shift from consequentialism, the doctrine that actions are right or wrong according to their consequences, to absolutism, the doctrine that actions are right or wrong according to their nature. In Anglo-American philosophy, the prevailing way of looking at morality used to be consequentialist, with some qualms about lying, breaking promises or killing innocent people in a good cause. It has now shifted towards

[37] See Anscombe, 'Modern Moral Philosophy', p. 8. Cf. Donagan, *Theory of Morality*, p. 190; Williams in Smart and Williams (ed.), *Utilitarianism: For and Against*, p. 84.

[38] G. E. Moore, *Principia Ethica* (Cambridge: Cambridge University Press, 1903).

absolutism, with residual doubts about catastrophic consequences. The conclusions may not have altered drastically but there has been a sea-change in the premisses. It may be asked whether it matters much what the premisses are if there is so much play in their application. The answer is, I think, that it does in the long run make a difference where you start. For this will determine what you take to be the easy problems. Thus, you can start from consequentialism and then build in some side-constraints on particularly repellent actions or you can start from absolutism and add some escape clause for situations where the consequences of following such a rule would be too horrendous. In principle, it is indeed possible to imagine that you could get to the same concrete judgements starting from either end. But in practice it tends to make a big difference which cases are taken as clear and central and which as difficult and exceptional. For what is at stake is no less than one's fundamental conception of what morality is all about, and it would be surprising if that did not have some implications for conduct. I do think that in fact the shift to absolutism has a quite clear tendency to reduce the scope of the diffuse obligations to others that are generated by universal consequentialism.

This kind of shift is nothing new: we can find a number of analogues. The most striking was perhaps the rapid repudiation of logical positivism after the Second World War which led A. J. Ayer to complain that he went from being a Young Turk to being old hat without an intervening period of solid respectability.[39] Putting it very schematically, we might think of a shift in starting-point as having four stages. In the first stage, a dominant paradigm (to use the inevitable Kuhnian terminology[40]) rides high. Scholars devote their research to developing the dominant paradigm, exploring its implications, and trying to clear up anomalies. There are some objectors, either left over from a previous paradigm or reacting on their own initiative against the dominant paradigm, but they are voices crying in the wilderness. In the next stage, the criticisms of the dominant paradigm build up but it still remains true that the paradigm holds the field. It is still, as it were, the thing to beat. The decisive stage is the third one in which a new paradigm is established and becomes the focus of attention. Taking the offensive is not always the way to conduct a war (as Marshall Foch demonstrated) but in the war

[39] A. J. Ayer, *A Part of My Life: The Memoirs of a Philosopher* (London: Oxford University Press, 1978), 294–5.

[40] Thomas S. Kuhn, *The Structure of Scientific Revolutions* (Chicago: Chicago University Press, 2nd edn., 1970).

between paradigms it is critical. As Imre Lakatos in particular emphasized, a paradigm becomes dominant when it generates a research programme that looks interesting and holds out hopes of being feasible.[41] As the new paradigm begins to take hold, those who continue to support the previously dominant one are relegated to the wilderness. The final stage is that in which the new paradigm is triumphantly established. History is now rewritten—history is, of course, always written by the victors—so that those who in some way anticipated the current paradigm (and especially the prophets who were previously crying in the wilderness) are presented as the major figures while the heroes of the earlier paradigm fall into obscurity.

I may, of course, be hopelessly wrong in my reading of the entrails. But it seems to me that the evidence for some fundamental shift is persuasive. Ten or twenty years ago, such work as was being published on substantive questions of morality was almost all located within the utilitarian paradigm. As I have emphasized, to say that work is located within a paradigm is to say only that the paradigm provides the focus of attention; the attention may be either positive or negative. In this respect, we can, I suggest, trace a change between the 1950s and the 1960s. Although the period of the mid-1950s hardly corresponds fully to my ideal typical first stage, it would not, I hope, be over-intepretation to sum up the prevailing mood as follows: utilitarianism, in some shape or form, has just *got* to be the right general answer, and the research programme is to apply enough technical ingenuity to crack the problems of application (thresholds, co-ordination, etc.) in order to get out the right specific answers. This was the period of mixed strategies, varieties of rule utilitarianism, and so on.[42] If we now turn to the books and articles of the mid-1960s we find very few people investing in attempts of this kind to make utilitarianism work. At any rate with hindsight, we can see that period as a classical pre-revolutionary one. The old regime still survives, but it is the subject of widespread yet diffuse disaffection and finds few

[41] Imre Lakatos, 'Falsification and the Methodology of Scientific Research Programmes' in Imre Lakatos and Alan Musgrave (eds.), *Criticism and the Growth of Knowledge* (Cambridge: Cambridge University Press, 1970), 91–197.

[42] The basic approach was well expressed by Samuel Gorovitz as follows: 'As a normative principle, the principle of utilitarianism has an enormous intuitive appeal. It calls on an agent to perform that action which will do more good for more people than any other, and it is hard to imagine how such an action could fail to be the right thing to do. Even though many objections to utilitarianism as a moral theory have been raised, this basic appeal remains for many people, who are more inclined to try to meet the objections than to abandon what is initially such a plausible moral theory.' Introduction to Samuel Gorovitz (ed.), *Utilitarianism, John Stuart Mill, with Critical Essays* (Indianapolis: Bobbs-Merrill, 1971), p. xiii. This is a useful selection of the kind of work I am referring to; it is noticeable that the bulk of the pieces are from the mid-1950s.

thoroughly convinced defenders. By 1973, we find Bernard Williams pronouncing sentence of death: 'The important issues that utilitarianism raises should be discussed in contexts more rewarding than that of utilitarianism itself. The day cannot be too far off in which we hear no more of it.'[43]

It is instructive to review the career of John Rawls in this context. His early 'Two Concepts of Rules' is presented as a variant of utilitarianism, closely related to Urmson's interpretation of Mill.[44] By the time of *A Theory of Justice*,[45] the theory is presented as an alternative to utilitarianism, but it is clear from the form of the argument that the object is taken to be weaning the reader away from his putatively utilitarian loyalties. At the same time, the line of analysis developed, especially in the second half of the book, makes the theory really incommensurable with utilitarianism. The question is not (as it might first appear) between average and maximin utility but between basically incompatible visions of man and society. Subsequent developments in Rawls's thinking carry this process further. Meanwhile, the rewriting of history is taking place with respect to *A Theory of Justice*: I would hazard the guess that most people now read it in a more Kantian light than when it first appeared, both because of Rawls's own subsequent glosses on it and the concomitant changes in the mental climate that I am trying to depict here. Thus, although *A Theory of Justice* did not shift the paradigm when it appeared, it can be mobilized to form an important part of the intellectual ammunition of the neo-Kantians.

In order for the critics of the old paradigm to go from the defensive to the offensive, it is necessary to have a critical mass of work that exemplifies the new approach and provides handholds for those less adept to scramble up after the virtuosi. Or, to put it more mundanely, you cannot have articles until you have books. You can, of course, have a lot of articles peppering the old paradigm; but to obtain the reassuring sense of cumulative development characteristic of 'normal science' there must be a solid body of literature forming a common reference point.

Right and Wrong may be seen as a contribution to the building up of that critical mass. To appreciate it in this context, one must also

[43] Williams in Smart and Williams (eds.), *Utilitarianism: For and Against*, p. 150.

[44] John Rawls, 'Two Concepts of Rules', *The Philosophical Review*, 64 (1955), 3–32; J. O. Urmson, 'The Interpretation of the Moral Philosophy of J. S. Mill', *The Philosophical Quarterly*, 3 (1953), 33–9. Both reprinted in Gorovitz (ed.), *Utilitarianism* on pp. 175–94 and 168–74 respectively.

[45] John Rawls, *A Theory of Justice* (Cambridge, Mass.: Harvard University Press, 1971).

consider two books that were published at about the same time: Alan Donagan's *The Theory of Morality* and Michael Walzer's *Just and Unjust Wars*. The three books are different but complementary. Donagan's is the most ambitious work. In a relatively brief compass, *The Theory of Morality* undertakes to expound the substance of what Donagan calls the Hebrew-Christian moral tradition and also to ground it in a Kantian meta-theory of morality. The book is sharp, spare, and clear. Walzer's book, in contrast, is diffuse and theoretically unrigorous. (It may even be ultimately incoherent.) But its bulk provides one essential ingredient: it gets onto the table a mass of problems in one large and important area of morality that can be referred to and worked over by others. Fried's book is different again. The talent that is most on display in *Right and Wrong* is a talent for synthesizing the work of other recent writers with his own earlier work.[46] But if it is potential influence that we are concerned with, we should never underestimate the importance of a work of synthesis.

The books by Fried, Walzer, and Donagan are not primarily critiques of consequentialism. They are devoted to the working out of a non-consequentialist ethic, and their criticisms of consequentialism are incidental to that purpose. More important, if we are looking for a body of work that will form a common reference point, is that all three ground their non-consequentialist systems in traditional Hebrew and Christian religious morality. Its major interpreters such as Aquinas and Maimonides are referred to as authorities. If the essence of a paradigm shift is a shift in focus, these books certainly provide it. All three, for example, devote careful and detailed attention to the doctrine of double effect, and I quoted from all three in my discussion of the doctrine in section III. As it happens, they come out in different places: Fried embraces it with uncritical enthusiasm, Walzer accepts it with substantial qualifications, while Donagan in the end rejects it. But, to repeat, the important thing is what is regarded as an important question, not what is said about it. So the point here is that we find three highly respected academics taking seriously a doctrine that most people had thought of as a quaint survival from the Middle Ages, like the custom of venerating the relics of saints. At the same time, fine discriminations between different varieties of utilitarian theory that would until recently have been treated as raising serious issues tend to be dismissed summarily. The function of the term 'consequentialism' is indeed to make this change of focus seem natural.

[46] There is a valuable reference section at the end of the book (pp. 197–219), which is not keyed to specific points in the text but provides a kind of running bibliographic commentary on the sources (many of them also at Harvard) drawn upon.

As with all the best historical stages, each of the ones I have outlined develops within the womb of the preceding one, and we can already begin to discern roughly how the anti-consequentialist history of morality is going to look. First there was Hebrew and Christian traditional morality and its scholarly expositors. Then there came the dark age of utilitarianism during which the traditional doctrines took refuge in Roman Catholic moral theology. Miss Anscombe's 'Modern Moral Philosophy' may well be the only piece of academic moral philosophy to be rescued out of the period 1870–1970. The 1970s, beginning with *A Theory of Justice*, will then presumably count as the beginning of a new era.[47]

Fried's role in all this is primarily as a sort of intellectual broker. He brings together two anti-consequentialist lines of thought: the Hebrew-Christian tradition of 'Thou shalt not' and the 'libertarian' doctrine of natural rights which has recently enjoyed such a curious revival in American academic philosophy. He then adds some 'integrity' from Bernard Williams: in conjunction with the first, integrity means keeping your hands clean, while, in the second, it means doing your own thing. The result is a potent brew with something for (almost) all tastes. It is quite a feat to accommodate within a single theory the God of the Pentateuch, Robert Nozick, Pontius Pilate, and Henry David Thoreau. (A quotation from Thoreau's 'On Civil Disobedience' leads off the book.) Of the mainstream moralists recognized in Britain and North America only Jesus and John Stuart Mill are left out in the cold.[48]

I must now confess that I have been using the term 'consequentialism' with less precision than I might have done. However, I can immediately add that I have in this been reflecting a similar lack of precision that runs through the literature. I began this section by ascribing the word 'consequentialism' to Elizabeth Anscombe, and defined it as the doctrine that all actions are to be judged by their consequences. However, Miss Anscombe did not actually define the term in the article I referred to, and the form of words I used is capable of being interpreted in (at least) two ways. According to one interpret-

[47] The reference notes in Fried's book may be read as a first sketch of this revisionist history.

[48] As Miss Anscombe says, 'Christianity derived its ethical notions from the Torah.' 'Modern Moral Philosophy', p. 191. That traditional Christianity has more in common with the Torah than with the Gospels was a commonplace of classical utilitarianism: we find it in both Bentham and John Stuart Mill. The same incompatibility was noted by Maimonides, who wrote that 'Jesus the Nazarene, may his bones be ground to dust . . ., interpreted the Torah and its precepts in such a fashion as to lead to their total annulment, to the abolition of all its commandments and to the violation of its prohibitions.' 'Epistle to Yemen', in Isadore Twersky (ed.), *A Maimonides Reader* (New York: Behrman House, 1972), 441.

ation, consequentialism may be defined as a negative doctrine: it denies that it is possible to specify a list of act-descriptions in terms of their 'nature' such that it would never under any circumstances —whatever the consequences—be right to do an act of a kind that was on the list. This appears to be what Miss Anscombe had in mind by 'consequentialism'. Her point was to contrast it with what she called the 'Hebrew-Christian ethic', according to which 'you are not to be tempted by fear or hope of consequences'. As she says: 'the prohibition of certain things simply in virtue of their description as such-and-such identifiable kinds of action, regardless of further consequences is . . . a noteworthy feature of [this ethic].' But 'it is pretty well taken for obvious among [modern academic philosophers] that a prohibition such as that on murder does not operate in face of some consequences.'[49]

Ironically, Fried, for all his expressed admiration for Miss Anscombe, is himself a consequentialist in her terms. For he says that 'we can imagine extreme cases where killing an innocent person may save a whole nation. In such cases it seems fanatical to maintain the absoluteness of the judgement, to do right even if the heavens will in fact fall' (p. 10). Interestingly enough, Miss Anscombe mentioned exactly this case in her dismissal of any claim that the 'Oxford Objectivists' (of whom the best known is Sir David Ross) could be exempted from the charge of consequentialism. 'Oxford Objectivists of course distinguish between "consequences" and "intrinsic values" and so produce a misleading appearance of not being "consequentialists". But they do not hold—and Ross explicitly denies—the gravity of, e.g., procuring the condemnation of the innocent, is such that it cannot be outweighed by, e.g., national interest.'[50]

Fried is himself a consequentialist, then, in what I shall call the weak sense of the term. In this sense, to recapitulate, consequentialism is the doctrine that it is possible for any prohibition based on the 'nature' of an act to be overridden if the consequences of adhering to the prohibition are sufficiently horrendous. What, then, we are bound to ask, is the object of Fried's crusade? In what sense of 'consequentialism' can he be counted as an anti-consequentialist?

The alternative conception of consequentialism, which I shall call the strong conception, is the doctrine that each person has a duty to act

[49] All quotations from Anscombe, 'Modern Moral Philosophy', 198. Alan Donagan, who follows Miss Anscombe by claiming to expound 'the Hebrew-Christian ethic', also understands consequentialism in this way, as the denial of absolute prohibitions.

[50] Anscombe, 'Modern Moral Philosophy', p. 196 n. 4.

at all times so as to maximize the total amount of good. Fried's identification of the enemy with 'utilitarian maximizing' clearly shows that the consequentialism with which he contrasts his own theory is to be understood in this way.[51]

It is curious to note that this strong consequentialist doctrine has exactly the same formal characteristics as Fried's own theory, for it too divides all acts into the required, the prohibited, and the permissible, with no room for the better or worse. Consequentialism is a particularly implausible way of assigning content to the trichotomy because it narrows the range of moral indifference to cases where two or more acts would have equally good consequences. One way of looking at Fried's theory is to say that he takes over the framework and simply expands the area of the morally permitted with his doctrine of negative rights.

There is no question that strong consequentialism is defective. By demanding that everyone's interests count equally in the computation (including the agent's) and then making it a duty that the agent act to maximize net benefit, it makes acts that would be heroic into routine duties. It also, in its hedonist form, entails that 'a man who, *ceteris paribus*, chooses the inferior of two musical comedies for an evening's entertainment has done a moral wrong, and this is preposterous'.[52] Notice, however, that there is nothing at all preposterous in saying that, if the alternative theatres were equally conveniently located and equally comfortable (etc.) and if nobody else was affected one way or the other by the choice, it would certainly have been *better* if this man had gone to the more enjoyable show. In fact, it is hard to see how anyone could deny it.

The decline in popularity of utilitarianism as a moral theory in recent years can, I think, be to some extent explained by the way in which utilitarianism has come to be understood as a variety of strong consequentialism. We may observe that strong consequentialism goes back to William Godwin, who, in *Political Justice*, quite explicitly maintained the duty of each person to maximize the aggregate happiness.[53] It then seems to have become dormant until G. E. Moore maintained in *Principia Ethica* that 'the assertion "I am morally bound to perform this action" is identical with the assertion "this action will

[51] Similarly, Bernard Williams's attack on 'utilitarianism' makes sense only as an attack on consequentialism in this strict sense.

[52] Urmson, 'The Interpretation of the Moral Philosophy of J. S. Mill', p. 170 in Gorovitz (ed.), *Utilitarianism*.

[53] William Godwin, *An Inquiry Into Political Justice*, abridged and edited by K. Codell Carter (Oxford: Clarendon Press, 1971).

produce the greatest possible amount of good in the Universe"'.[54] To find out what one must do it was necessary to determine what constituted 'the good', and one answer could be that given by utilitarianism.

The resulting conception of utilitarianism, as a strong consequentialist doctrine, would not fit Bentham or J. S. Mill, neither of whom asserted a duty to maximize aggregate happiness. Bentham seems to have thought of the problem of practical morality as one of setting up institutions that would result in people who are pursuing their own interest acting at the same time in ways that conduce to the general interest. The market, as understood by Adam Smith and Bentham, is, of course, the paradigm institution here, but all of Bentham's pieces of social invention—for choosing governments, for getting officials to behave honestly, and so on—can be seen as attempts to pull off the same trick of creating conditions in which a 'hidden hand' will guide individuals motivated by self-interest in the direction indicated by the greatest happiness principle. This does not mean that he did not believe in non-self-interested behaviour. He acknowledged its existence but, like Hobbes and Hume, he thought benevolence was too weak a force to rely on for achieving anything important in society. As he wrote: 'All that the most public-spirited, which is as much as to say the most virtuous of men can do, is to do what depends upon himself towards bringing the public interest, that is, his own personal share in the public interest, to a state as nearly approaching to coincidence, and on as few occasions amounting to a state of repugnance, as possible with his private interest.'[55]

Mill was (perhaps deliberately) ambiguous and trying to decide what he 'really meant' in *Utilitarianism* is probably unfruitful. But chapter V does explicitly say that 'duty' can be understood only within the context of a system of social norms. The criterion of a good state of the world and the ultimate test of the system of rules constituting a society's positive morality is general happiness. It is clear, however, that this is not equivalent to defining the duty of each individual as being the maximization of happiness.[56]

A version of utilitarianism that would avoid the disadvantages of strict consequentialism and would, I believe, articulate the common ideas of Bentham and Mill might run something like this:

[54] *Principia Ethica*, Ch. V, sec. 89. See also G. E. Moore, *Ethics* (London: Oxford University Press, 1912), 140.

[55] Quoted in David Baumgardt, *Bentham and the Ethics of Today with Bentham Manuscripts Hitherto Unpublished* (Princeton: Princeton University Press, 1952), 423.

[56] J. S. Mill, *Utilitarianism* in Gorovitz (ed.), *Utilitarianism*, pp. 13–57.

Utilitarianism is a theory about what constitutes good states of the world. It is no part of utilitarianism so understood to try to answer the question how far individuals can be 'required' to sacrifice themselves for the greater good of others, if this is taken to be a question asked in abstraction from any legal system or set of social norms, for we acknowledge no supernatural source of 'requirements'. All we can say is that a society is likely to be a better society the more its members have a self-sacrificing disposition. For, given the tendencies to self-interest in human beings, it is hardly likely that people will be so self-sacrificing as to reduce the amount of good in the world by acting in accord with an excessively self-sacrificing disposition. We can add the advice that moral rules and institutions are better the better the state of the world they give rise to, given whatever general level of self-sacrifice can be predicted to occur in the society; and, to the extent that the moral rules and institutions themselves affect the general level of self-sacrifice, institutions that elicit more self-sacrifice are better than those that elicit less, other things being equal.

I believe that a general framework like this can, indeed, be put to good use even if we drop the classical utilitarian postulate that the criterion for testing institutions is their contribution to aggregate happiness. I should like to claim as much for the sketch of an alternative to Fried's theory that was put forward in section II. The criteria for judging moral norms that were there employed included fairness as well as utility, but the overall approach was, I think, the one just outlined.

Let me conclude by comparing the strong and the weak forms of consequentialism. Weak consequentialism holds that there is no class of cases, definable in advance, such that the consequences are never relevant to the question of what is the right thing to do. Strong consequentialism holds that there is at all times a duty to act so as to maximize the amount of good—to maximize aggregate happiness if one is a utilitarian, to maximize something else if not. Strong consequentialism entails weak consequentialism and the denial of weak consequentialism entails the denial of strong consequentialism. But it is logically possible to accept weak consequentialism and reject strong consequentialism. In fact, Fried does this and so do I.

If we agree about both types of consequentialism, how can we disagree about so much else? The answer is, of course, that our being able to do so illustrates how weak is weak consequentialism and how strong is strong consequentialism. To accept weak consequentialism requires only that, for any proposed absolute prohibition, one can think of *some* hypothetical set of circumstances in which it should be departed from. To deny strong consequentialism requires only that one should be able to find one hypothetical case in which an act admitted to have the best consequences is not considered to be a duty. It should be plain that a vast range of positions on real issues are compatible with the acceptance of weak consequentialism and the denial of strong consequentialism.

I can illustrate this by referring to Bernard Williams's much-discussed example of Jim, who, while on a botanical expedition, 'finds himself in the central square of a small South American town' where a 'captain' is about to shoot twenty Indians, following 'recent acts of protest against the government'. The captain, Pedro, offers Jim the privilege of shooting one Indian, upon which he will let the others go. If Jim refuses, the twenty Indians will be killed as planned.[57] What should Jim do? A number of commentators have protested at the artificiality of the dilemma as presented: how, for example, does Jim know that Pedro will shoot all the Indians if he does not shoot one; or release the rest of them if he does? However, I think that the case will do with no more than probabilities attached to the alternatives. For the point of the example is that both strong consequentialists and deniers of weak consequentialism have no need to find the problem difficult. If Jim is a strict consequentialist, the fact that it is he who is to shoot an Indian has no moral significance (though if he has squeamish feelings about killing that should go into the calculation as a psychological datum). His only qualms should be over the probabilities. But if the evidence for Pedro's intentions is clear (for example, he has already shot one batch of twenty when Jim arrives) and Jim sees after he has shot one that the rest are released, he can feel that he has done a good job in saving nineteen Indians, and that is all there is to be said. Equally, if Jim does not accept weak consequentialism, he need feel no responsibility for the deaths of the Indians, since he can say of Pedro (in Fried's words) 'It's *his* wrong'. If we find both of these reactions too simple, we must, it seems to me, accept weak consequentialism and reject strong consequentialism.

My complaint against Fried is that he treats the rejection of strict consequentialism as if it licensed him to move to a position in which consequences play a role only in very occasional and extreme cases. His only example of something that would compensate for doing wrong is 'saving a whole nation'. Fried's argument, such as it is, proceeds much of the time as if it were only necessary to mention the implications of 'utilitarian maximization' to derive his own conclusions. I have suggested here that there are many reasons for rejecting his conclusions while agreeing with the rejection of strong consequentialism.

[57] Williams in Smart and Williams (ed.), *Utilitarianism: For and Against*, p. 98.

13

LADY CHATTERLEY'S LOVER AND DOCTOR FISCHER'S BOMB PARTY

Liberalism, Pareto Optimality, and the Problem of Objectionable Preferences

In the ten years since Amartya Sen announced 'the impossibility of a Paretian liberal', the alleged 'liberal paradox' has come in for a good deal of critical discussion.[1] I shall argue in the first section, 'Lady Chatterley's Lover', that, on a sensible understanding of 'liberalism' and of the significance of something's being 'socially preferred' (in the sense of being picked out by a social welfare function), there is no incompatibility between liberalism and Pareto optimality. In the second section, which is called 'Doctor Fischer's Bomb Party', I ask on what grounds we might nevertheless disapprove of deals that the parties have a right to make. This is, in my view, the serious question of substantive morality that is left after we have cleared away the problems that are internal to social choice theory. In the third section, 'What's Wrong with Social Choice?', I broaden the discussion to argue that the so-called liberal paradox illustrates the general weakness of social choice theory as a mode of political philosophizing. The basic conception of a 'social welfare function' constructed out of 'preferences' is, I suggest, fundamentally misguided. The fourth and final section, 'Paradox Lost', attempts to make clear exactly what my dissolution of the liberal paradox amounts to. (This part of the chapter has not previously been published.)

I LADY CHATTERLEY'S LOVER

The basic idea of the impossibility result is simple enough. Suppose that we take three conditions that we should like a social welfare function to satisfy: unrestricted domain (*U*), Pareto optimality (*P*),

[1] A. K. Sen, 'The Impossibility of a Paretian Liberal', *Journal of Political Economy*, 78 (1970), 152–7; and *Collective Choice and Social Welfare* (San Francisco, Calif.: Holden-Day, 1970), 78–88. An extensive review is provided by A. K. Sen, 'Liberty, Unanimity and Rights', *Economica*, 43 (1976), 217–45. The two articles are reprinted in Amartya Sen, *Choice, Welfare and Measurement* (Cambridge, Mass.: MIT Press, 1962), 285–90 and 291–326.

and liberalism (L). Then the theorem is that these three requirements, U, P, and L, are incompatible. 'Unrestricted domain' means that we do not place any restrictions on the range of individual preferences entering into the social welfare function. Pareto optimality is the requirement that if everybody prefers one state of affairs to a second then the first state of affairs is 'socially preferred'—that is to say, ranked higher on the social welfare function. (The question of what exactly is the significance of a social welfare function is one that I shall duck here, not because I want to slight its importance but because I want to take it up at length later.) What the liberal condition means here is that each individual should be 'socially decisive' over some pairs of alternative social outcomes. Candidates for the role of such pairs would be the two states of the world that are identical in every respect except that in one I sleep on my belly and in the other I sleep on my back, or that in one my kitchen walls are painted pink while in the other they are painted crimson. In other words, if I prefer to lie on my belly rather than on my back, the social welfare function should produce the conclusion that, of two states of the world differing only in respect of which way up I lie, the state of the world in which I lie on my belly is socially preferred.

We had better at this point, for the sake of brevity, resort to *p*s and *q*s. L specifies that for each i there is a pair of alternatives p and q such that if i prefers p to q, the social welfare function ranks p above q (and conversely if i prefers q to p); and P specifies that, if everyone prefers p to q, the social welfare function ranks p above q. The thesis of the 'impossibility of a Paretian liberal' states that conditions L and P are inconsistent, given U. The proof is very simple and, as far as it goes, incontestable. It runs as follows. Let i be decisive over the pair $\langle p, q \rangle$ and j be decisive over the pair $\langle r, s \rangle$. If i prefers p to q and j prefers r to s, then, by condition L, p is socially preferred to q and r is socially preferred to s. But if i and j both also prefer q to r and s to p, then, by condition P, q is socially preferred to r and s is socially preferred to p. So p is preferred to q, q to r, r to s, and s to p. This is, obviously, a violation of 'acyclicity', which is normally taken as an absolutely minimal demand to make of a social welfare function.

The entire literature tends to revolve around an example which Sen introduced in 1970 involving the reading of D. H. Lawrence's novel *Lady Chatterley's Lover*. (This of course dates the original treatment fairly precisely, for today stronger meat might be required to make the case plausible.) The example runs as follows. Mr A (the prude) has the following preference order with regard to this supposedly lubricious book: $\bar{a}\bar{b}$ (nobody read it); $a\bar{b}$ (he read it rather than contemplate the lewd Mr *B* wallowing in that filth); $\bar{a}b$ (Mr *B* read it); then ab (both read it). Mr *B* has the following preference order: ab (it would do Mr *A* good to read it and he would enjoy reading it himself); $a\bar{b}$ (if only one is to read it, let Mr *A* widen his literary horizons); $\bar{a}b$ (read it himself); $\bar{a}\bar{b}$ (waste of a good book).

It may help to set this out in tabular form. The preferences, then, are in the following order:

A (the prude)	*B (the lewd)*
$\bar{a}\bar{b}$	ab
$a\bar{b}$	$a\bar{b}$
$\bar{a}b$	$\bar{a}b$
ab	$\bar{a}\bar{b}$

As may immediately be seen, $a\bar{b}$ is Pareto-superior to $\bar{a}b$. That is to say, both *A* and *B* prefer it. Yet the liberal principle, according to Sen, demands that the lewd Mr *B* should read the book and the prudish Mr *A* should not, since each should decide on his own reading matter. Since I want to maintain that there is no such liberal (or libertarian) principle entailing this conclusion, it would be as well to quote Sen's words:

On libertarian grounds, it is better that the lewd reads the book rather than nobody, since what the lewd reads is his own business and the lewd does want to read the book; hence [$\bar{a}b$] is socially better than [$\bar{a}\bar{b}$]. On libertarian grounds again, it is better that nobody reads the book rather than the prude, since whether the prude should read a book or not is his own business, and he does not wish to read the book; hence [$\bar{a}\bar{b}$] is better than [$a\bar{b}$].[2]

Thus, we get the 'preference cycle' that constitutes the 'liberal paradox'.

What drives this result is, of course, the fact that both *A* and *B* have what Sen calls 'nosy' preferences: *A*, the prude, is more concerned to prevent *B*, the lewd, from reading what he regards as a pornographic book than he is to avoid reading it himself (either to save *B*'s soul or because he can't bear to think of him enjoying it); and *B* is more interested (whether maliciously or in a missionary spirit) in inflicting *Lady Chatterley* on *A* than he is in reading it himself.[3] But is it true that

[2] A. K. Sen, 'Personal Utilities and Public Judgments: or What's Wrong with Welfare Economics', *Economic Journal*, 89 (1979), 537–58, at 550. Cf. Sen, 'Liberty, Unanimity and Rights', p. 218.

[3] Note that it is not merely that *A* and *B* have 'nosy preferences', in the sense of caring about each other's reading habits, but that they have *strong* nosy preferences. That is, the 'paradox'

such nosy preferences subvert liberalism? It seems to me that this is not so. Sen claims, as we have seen, that the liberal principle says that it is 'socially better' that the lewd read *Lady Chatterley* and the prude not, but I simply deny there is any such liberal principle. Hence Sen's claim that he has shown 'the incompatibility of the Pareto principle . . . with some relatively mild requirements of personal liberty, for consistent social decisions, given unrestricted domain'[4] simply falls to the ground. For liberal principles do not say in a context like the *Lady Chatterley* case who should read what; rather, liberalism is a doctrine about who should have a right to decide who reads what. Sen, citing Mill and Hayek, suggests that 'considerations of liberty require specification of . . . e.g. whether a particular choice is self-regarding or not . . . , or as falling within a person's "protected sphere"'.[5] Quite so, but let us take note of the purpose for which this information is required. It is brought in at the stage at which we argue about the allocation of rights: we say that when it comes to (say) what they read, people should have power to take their own decisions because this is 'self-regarding' or should be within the 'protected sphere'. But we do not then judge the *use made* of these rights in terms of any principle of liberty: the notion that any principle of liberty that would be endorsed by Mill or Hayek is violated by the prude choosing to read *Lady Chatterley* and the lewd not doing so (provided, of course, that they are freely exercising their rights, as in the case stated) is pure fantasy.

Liberalism cannot be connected up to Sen's statement of an alleged liberal principle because it is not a doctrine about what constitutes a 'socially better' state of affairs, where a state is defined by things like '*A* reads *Lady Chatterley* and *B* doesn't'. Rather it is a doctrine about who has what rights to control what. When the liberal principle says that there should be a protected sphere,[6] what that means is that there are some things (e.g. which way up to lie in bed, what colour to paint one's kitchen, or how to spend one's money) about which an individual should be able to decide what to do, without any coercive

would not arise if each had a preference concerning the other's behaviour but, when it came to the crunch, cared more about his own. This would yield the following orderings:

A	B
$\bar{a}\bar{b}$	ab
$\bar{a}b$	$\bar{a}b$
$a\bar{b}$	$a\bar{b}$
ab	$\bar{a}\bar{b}$

Since both prefer $\bar{a}b$ to $a\bar{b}$, conditions L and P both endorse the same outcome here.

[4] Sen, 'Personal Utilities and Public Judgments', p. 549.

[5] Ibid.

[6] Sen, 'Liberty, Unanimity and Rights', p. 218.

interference by or on behalf of society. Indeed, further than that, the force of society will be put behind the claim of each individual to do what he likes in such a protected sphere without being subject to coercion by anybody else.

We can express this idea perspicuously by making use of the conceptual apparatus developed by James Coleman.[7] In this schema, actors can control certain events, either individually or jointly. They also have interests in events—not necessarily the same ones as those over which they have control. In the case of a binary choice, an actor's interest in getting the alternative that he prefers may be understood as the difference between the utility that he expects to derive from the favoured alternative and the utility that he expects to derive from the less favoured one. Clearly, as Coleman says, a utility-maximizing actor will seek to 'do two things: first, gain control over those events that interest him, and secondly, exercise that control in such a direction that the outcome he favors occurs'.[8]

And, once we have a structure of rights to control events and of interests in those events:

> the principal activities of actors in attempting to realize their interests consist of actions through which they gain effective control of events they are interested in, through giving up effective control over events they are not [or less—B.B.] interested in. In economic activities, this consists of an explicit exchange of control; in other areas of life, including political activities, it consists of less explicit exchange of control often based on informal agreements.[9]

Let us apply these notions to the *Lady Chatterley* case. The initial distribution of control over events provided by a liberal scheme for assigning rights is as follows:

A (the prude)	controls	{ *A* read *Lady Chatterley* *A* not read *Lady Chatterley*
B (the lewd)	controls	{ *B* read *Lady Chatterley* *B* not read *Lady Chatterley*

If each makes his choice independently, *A* will choose not to read *Lady Chatterley* and *B* will choose to do so. However, if we look at the structure of interests, we see that, because both actors have nosy preferences, the structure of rights is out of alignment with the

[7] J. S. Coleman, *The Mathematics of Collective Action* (London: Heinemann Educational, 1973), Ch. 3. [8] Ibid. 73. [9] Ibid. 75.

structure of control. Each is more interested in what the other does than in what he does himself.

Ranking of interests by A	*Ranking of interests by B*
1. *B* not read *Lady Chatterley*	1. *A* read *Lady Chatterley*
2. *A* not read *Lady Chatterley*	2. *B* read *Lady Chatterley*

It is this structure that makes it mutually advantageous to the two parties to exchange control over the event in which they are less interested for control over the event in which they are more interested. *A* surrenders his right not to read *Lady Chatterley* in return for the more valued control over the reading matter of *B*, and *B* in return surrenders his right to read *Lady Chatterley* in return for the ability, which is more important to him, to have *A* read it.

It is essential to notice that the initial assignment of rights plays a crucial role in bringing about this post-trade outcome in which the prude finishes up reading *Lady Chatterley* and the lewd finishes up not reading it.[10] Suppose, for example, that the rights were not distributed so as to give each actor control over his own reading-matter, but instead that the prude could determine both what he himself read and also what the lewd read (a lewd minor, perhaps). Then, the outcome that would be brought about by an own-utility-maximizing prude (one, for example, not constrained by considerations of fairness in deciding how to exercise his rights) would be one in which neither reads *Lady Chatterley*.

It should be borne in mind that Pareto optimality is in itself indifferent to distributive considerations. Thus, for example, the outcome in which neither reads *Lady Chatterley's Lover* would be Pareto-optimal, since there is no alternative to it that both parties would prefer. This is the outcome we might expect if the initial assignment of rights allowed the prude to decide on both what he himself reads and what the lewd reads. For clearly, since the lewd has no rights over his reading-matter, he has no bargaining counter to offer in order to gain control over events controlled by the prude and move the outcome in a direction he favours. To put it another way, since the prude has all the power, the Pareto-optimal outcome is simply the one that puts *him* as high up his preference rankings as he

[10] Of course, if symmetry were maintained but the initial assignment of rights gave each control over the other's reading-matter, there would be no transfer of control (given the nosy preferences that we are postulating) because the structure of control and the structure of interest would then be congruent. However, if each were more interested in what he read than in what the other read, they would transfer control so that the prude did not read *Lady Chatterley* and the lewd did.

can get, and to hell with the preferences of the lewd. An exception would arise if the lewd were lucky enough to have his preferences enter into the prude's utility function—but presumably the prude, being a meddlesome prude, does not give weight to others' lewd preferences in arriving at his own preference ordering of outcomes.

The essential point about Pareto optimality, then, is that it simply calls for all mutually advantageous deals to be made, but to pick one Pareto-optimal outcome out of the infinite number of Pareto-optimal outcomes we have to have an initial assignment of rights. The liberal principle is a criterion for the assignment of these rights which tells us who should start with the power to control what events. If we knew the assignment of rights and what Coleman calls the structure of interests, we could, given his own theory, in principle work out the unique Pareto-optimal outcome corresponding to that assignment of rights. In the absence of such a strong theory as Coleman's, the assumption that mutually advantageous exchanges of control over events would be made until no opportunities remained would not generate a unique outcome. There might, in other words, be alternative Pareto-optimal outcomes compatible with a given initial assignment of rights. (We might recall that in the theory of economic bargaining—over an exchange of apples for oranges, say—it requires a very strong theory to pick out a unique point on the contract curve.)

It is important to be clear that there is all the difference in the world between having a right to decide something, where the contents of the decision may be made contingent on the offers other people make in order to influence that decision, and not having a right at all. Only by eliding that distinction can Sen achieve the effect of making us think that there is nothing between totally isolated decisionmaking in personal matters and a situation in which all preferences, including nosy ones, are thrown into a common pot and some sort of utilitarian calculus applied to them to arrive at politically enforced decisions about what people must or must not do (in effect, a set-up in which there are no rights at all).

Thus, in considering how one might come to drop the condition of liberalism, Sen offers this possible argument for doing so: 'The idea that certain things are a person's "personal" affair is insupportable. If the color of Mr. *A*'s walls disturbs Mr. *B*, then it is Mr. *B*'s business as well. If it makes Mr. *A* unhappy that Mr. *B* should lie on his belly while asleep, or that he should read *Lady Chatterly's* [*sic*] *Lover* while awake, then Mr. *A* is a relevant party to the choice.' He then goes on to say: 'This is, undoubtedly, a possible point of view, and the popularity of rules such as a ban on smoking marijuana, or suppression of homosexual practices or pornography, reflect, at least partly, such a point of view. Public policy is often aimed at imposing on individuals the will of others even in matters that may directly concern only those individuals.'[11] But, he says, to deny the weak liberal condition (which after all requires only that there be *some* alternative over which each person is decisive) is to 'deny even the most limited expressions of individual freedom. And also to deny privacy, since the choice between x and y may be that between being forced to confess on one's personal affairs (x) and not being so forced (y).'[12]

I hope it will be clear by now that this confuses two quite different ideas: that people should never fail to act on their personal preferences in what 'directly concerns' them, and that people should not be *required* to violate their personal preferences in what 'directly concerns' them. The second is, indeed, an authentically liberal idea. But the first is not, as Sen suggests, an essential part of every reasonable conception of liberalism. It might even be said to be antithetical to a conception of liberalism that emphasizes the freedom of individuals to make their own choices with as few constraints as possible. For surely we are more free to choose if we can trade a decision over something we have a right to control in return for control over a decision that we value more, which some other person has a right to take, than we are if some agent of the social welfare function restrains us from doing so. The simple answer, then, is that there is no inconsistency in principle between liberalism and Pareto optimality. Liberalism is, indeed, a principle that picks out a protected sphere, but one that is protected against unwanted interference, not against use in trading with others.

To sum up, if a social welfare function tells us what constitutes a better state of the world, there can be no conflict between any social welfare function, whatever its content, and the principle that there should be a protected sphere within which people shall be legally free to do what they choose. For the two have different subject-matters: one is about what is 'socially better', the other about what people shall be able to do without legal coercion.

The only way in which we can create a conflict between a social welfare function and a genuinely liberal principle of this kind is by supposing that what is socially better should be enforced. But then no elaborate argument is needed to establish incompatibility, since that idea is *itself* in conflict with the liberal principle. Thus, again, nothing

[11] Sen, *Collective Choice and Social Welfare*, p. 82. [12] Ibid. 83.

turns on the particular content of the social welfare function. If the choice between x and y is within A's protected sphere, this entails that A should neither be forced to do x nor be forced to do y.

To ask (on this interpretation of what it implies to say something is socially better) how we should determine, in accordance with liberalism, whether x or y is socially better is a question obviously doomed to produce an absurd answer, so it is hardly surprising that it is possible to show that any particular answer is absurd. To say 'A's own preference shall determine whether x or y is socially better' is not a 'liberal' answer, because it still presupposes (on this interpretation of what it means to say that something is socially better) that either x or y should be enforced—yet this is exactly what the notion of a protected sphere is designed to deny.

II DOCTOR FISCHER'S BOMB PARTY

So far in this chapter I have sounded, most of the time, like a born-again disciple of Milton Friedman, with the slogan 'Free to Choose' inscribed on my banner. It is now time to dispel that impression. As I said at the outset, I do not find Sen's *Lady Chatterley* example very compelling. But I do share the intuition that seems to lie behind Sen's anti-Paretianism: that some Paretian deals raise problems. However, Sen has misdiagnosed the issue by talking about a 'liberal paradox'. And he has, subsequent to 1970, compounded the error by saying that he prefers 'libertarian' to 'liberal'.[13] For, in the contemporary jargon, a libertarian is precisely somebody who believes that no limits should be set on the drive towards Pareto optimality. The state should not, for example, step in between a willing seller of labour (willing, that is, compared to the alternatives) and a willing buyer by prescribing minimum wage rates. Nor should it prevent people from entering into onerous contracts (e.g. at usurious rates of interest) if they regard that as advantageous to themselves. Thus, it is clear that libertarianism, so conceived, is in no sense incompatible with Pareto optimality. Rather, Pareto optimality is a natural part of the kind of social philosophy (in effect an ideology constructed out of outdated introductory economics textbooks) known as libertarianism.

This ideology assumes, in effect, that if people are to have a right in general to do what they choose in some area (e.g. buy or sell labour, lend or borrow money), it is better for there to be no legal restrictions

[13] Sen, 'Liberty, Unanimity and Rights', p. 218.

on the exercise of the right. But there are in some cases good reasons for setting limits to the range of transactions that should be permitted. Minimum wage laws and usury laws can operate so as to strengthen the position of the weak, providing by legal enactment the equivalent of an agreement that the weaker parties would have found it advantageous to conclude among themselves, if the problem of collective action did not arise. On somewhat similar lines, legal systems characteristically do not allow the consent of the victim to count as a defence to a charge of inflicting bodily harm or death. The rationale is, plausibly, that the position of potential victims would be weakened if they could validly consent. The prohibition of contracts of servitude and of debt peonage can be justified in the same way. These limitations do, of course, prevent the achievement of Pareto optimality, if we take a regime of unrestricted rights as our baseline and look at potential transactions one by one. But it is also inconsistent with libertarianism, as I have defined it.

It is, then, quite reasonable to assign rights in society so as to take account of the strategic relations of the parties. In the cases I gave, one side actually has an interest in being prevented from entering into certain kinds of legally effective agreements, thus illustrating, *contra* Friedman, that it is not always advantageous to be 'free to choose'. Although in general people can do better for themselves (i.e. achieve more preferred outcomes) by being legally free to deploy their rights in any way they wish, there are some cases where they can achieve a more preferred outcome if their rights are restricted so that they are prevented from giving up their rights or from exchanging them on particular terms.

At this point, however, we may begin to wonder whether the notion of Pareto optimality is well defined in such contexts. I said that limits on the exercise of a right prevent the achievement of Pareto optimality if we take as a baseline the absence of restrictions and if we consider the potential transactions one by one, independently of one another. But why should we? What we have here is a situation in which someone may be better off doing a certain deal than not doing it if he is permitted to do it, but would be better off still if he were not permitted to do it. Since *ex hypothesi* his position in the second rights regime is preferable to any open to him (either by dealing or not dealing) in the first rights regime, we cannot say that either of the regimes is Pareto-superior to the other. We have, rather, two regimes with different distributions among the actors, neither of which dominates the other. On this line of reasoning, we can say that both regimes have the possibility within them of attaining (different) Pareto-optimal outcomes.

Fortunately, conundrums of this kind do not have to be straightened out before I can present the problem to which this section of the chapter is devoted. Let us suppose that we have some system of rights established, and that it is of a conventional liberal nature. That is to say, although it restricts the exercise of rights along some of the lines just mentioned, it leaves open a wide range of discretionary behaviour. In addition to the resources for exchange offered by the market, then, we will suppose that people have many other opportunities to trade rights over things they control for things that other people control.

The question I want to raise is the following. When people operate within this established framework of rights, are there Pareto-optimal deals which they can properly be condemned for making? We are thus looking at cases where someone uses a right he unquestionably has (e.g. to read or not read *Lady Chatterley*) in order to try to influence, by making a contingent offer to act one way rather than another, the use another person makes of a right that *he* unquestionably has (e.g. to read or not read *Lady Chatterley*). Interestingly enough, Sen himself, in an article written three years after the survey article from which I was quoting before, broke away far enough from the social choice terminology to present the question in these terms, though without repudiating the implicit claim that what he said could be translated into the language of social welfare functions. He said there that a trade between the lewd and the prude:

> raises a deeper question, viz., whether *having a right* based on the 'personal' nature of some decisions (in this case the right to read what one likes and shun what one does not wish to read) must invariably imply being free *to trade that right* for some other gain, irrespective of the nature of the gain (in this case the lewd's gain consists in getting pleasure from the prude's discomfiture, and the prude's gain in avoiding the discomfort of knowing that the lewd is reading a book that he—the prude—disapproves of). If the answer to this question is yes, then clearly the criticism of the Pareto principle would not apply to this case. I believe it is possible to question such an affirmative answer, but I resist the temptation to go further into this complex issue.[14]

It is precisely that complex issue that I wish to address here.

To begin with, let us get it quite clear that there is nothing wrong in general with attempts to manipulate one's use of rights to advance

[14] Sen, 'Personal Utilities and Public Judgments', p. 552, italics in original.

nosy preferences. Suppose that I have a purely disinterested nosy preference for your giving up smoking (it is not that the smoke bothers me, etc.) and you have likewise a preference for my losing weight based on a disinterested concern for my health rather than a desire to look at someone trimmer. It seems hard to see how any moralist could object to our making a deal in order to further our nosy ends. There is, surely, a version of the *Lady Chatterley* case that comes close to this, where the contingent offers are well intentioned in a somewhat parallel way. It is only by attributing nasty motives to the lewd (making the prude squirm) and reducing the prude's concern for the lewd to a self-centred one (avoiding his own discomfort at knowing the lewd is reading the book) that Sen is able to make us feel any qualms at all about the propriety of a trade. Even then, the case is one that I find hard to take seriously. There is no question that the lewd and the prude of Sen's depiction would be better people if they had different preferences but, given the preferences they have, I still feel reluctant to say that they should not act to further them. In fact, it seems to me that they deserve one another.

Let me take up instead the second novel that I have included in my title, Graham Greene's *Doctor Fischer of Geneva or the Bomb Party*.[15] The eponymous Dr Fischer is a very rich Swiss who, for reasons that we need not enter into here, wishes to have his contempt for the human race reinforced and justified. To this end he assembles a group of wealthy toadies (or Toads, as his daughter calls them) who endure all kinds of insults and humiliations at the hands of Dr Fischer in return for lavish gifts. Although they could, as Dr Fischer frequently emphasizes, quite well afford to buy the same things for themselves, they are too mean to spend their own money and greedy enough to put up with a lot of indignities in order to get them free. The climactic 'bomb party'[16] is unsuitable for our purposes because I suspect that, even under Swiss law, consent is no defence to a charge of bodily harm, and Dr Fischer, by offering his guests Christmas crackers which have either a large cheque or a small bomb in them, and inviting them to pull one each and take the consequences, is on shaky legal ground. And even if he is not legally guilty, we may still wish to hold the right to bodily integrity to be morally inalienable. Let us therefore take the earlier dinner party which the narrator (who is married to Dr Fischer's daughter) attends, since this raises no problems of violating

[15] Graham Greene, *Doctor Fischer of Geneva or the Bomb Party* (New York: Simon and Schuster, 1980).

[16] Ibid. 65–6.

the rights of the guests. At this party, Dr Fischer dines on caviare, while his guests are offered nothing but cold porridge. As Dr Fischer points out, they are perfectly free not to eat it if they choose not to. As the narrator recounts it to his wife afterwards:

'Mrs. Montgomery [one of the Toads] said I should have been sent from the table as soon as I refused to eat the porridge. "Any of you could have done the same," your father said. "Then what would you have done with all the presents?" she asked. "Perhaps I would have doubled the stakes next time," he said.'

'Stakes? What did he mean?'

'I suppose he meant his bet on their greed against their humiliation.'[17]

I shall take it as uncontroversial that Dr Fischer would have been a better man if he had not had the desires that led him to give such dinner parties. But can we say that Dr Fischer ought, morally, not to have acted as he did? Can we say that it was not merely bad-producing conduct (like painting one's kitchen in clashing colours) but wrong?

I do myself feel strongly inclined to say this. If I try to determine what special features of the case make me want to say that it was wrong for Dr Fischer to act on his objectionable preferences, I seem to find two. The first is that this is a case of playing on a weakness of character—in this case greed—for one's own satisfaction. The other, somewhat related point is that Dr Fischer is deliberately corrupting the Toads, that is to say, making their characters worse in respect of the flaw of excessive greed. When Dr Fischer's invitation to the narrator to come to the dinner party arrives, his wife says: 'He wants you to join the Toads.' The following dialogue ensues: 'But I've nothing against the Toads. Are they really as bad as you say? . . .' 'They weren't always Toads, I suppose. He's corrupted all of them.'[18]

Dr Fischer played on human weakness. Another type of case is that where what is taken advantage of is economic weakness. Thus, where there are great disparities in economic circumstances between the parties, and in particular where one is in desperate need, the other (better-off) party may take advantage of the economically weaker one. Note that the resultant deal is certainly Pareto optimal in that the weaker party prefers the deal to the status quo ante. Our criticism is of the stronger party for offering those terms. The underlying idea is again that there are ways in which people should not treat others.

Examples of this second kind of case would be as follows:

(*a*) Offers that express contempt, by emphasizing the worthlessness

[17] Ibid. 73–4. [18] Ibid. 40–1.

of the person. An example would be paying people to dig holes and fill them up again. We might contrast this with the superficially similar case of a landlord paying men (as sometimes happened in earlier centuries) to carry out ornamental work on his estate purely in order to provide employment for them. In such a case, one may well object to the distribution of initial resources that puts the parties in the position where that is a Pareto-optimal deal but not, it seems to me, to the transaction itself.

(*b*) Offers that are intrinsically degrading—to do such things as eating excrement, blaspheming against one's religion, prostitution. (This is, of course, on the analysis that prostitution is taking advantage of poor alternative employment for women. Note, however, that this analysis can be used either to criticize prostitution or to criticize the economic position of women. In other words, if you cannot convince people that working in a match factory or a sewing room for the available pay is bad, you may still be able to convince them by pointing out that many girls prefer prostitution. This was, of course, Shaw's strategy in *Mrs Warren's Profession.*)

A third case of offers that ought not to be made is, I would suggest, those that are really coercive offers even though they are not caught within the usual (or legally enforceable) conception. In effect, these involve not appealing to psychological or economic weakness but to the recipient's better nature in an inappropriate way. Examples would be: 'If you don't marry me, I'll kill myself'; 'If you don't give me the job, it will blight my life'; 'Only by doing what I want can you save me from committing a mortal sin.' The point of these cases is that the person is not making a threat ruled out by the usual bans on coercion. Yet at the same time there is no doubt that the other person's decision is taken under duress. 'If you don't do it, I'll kill myself' may well be much more really coercive than 'If you don't do it, I'll punch you on the nose.'

To sum up, the question has been one of actions taken to encourage someone to do what you want him to, taken against a background where he is free to choose to accept or reject whatever offer you make. I have suggested that everything turns on that phrase 'free to choose': being free to choose is not simply equivalent to not being coerced, in the sense of threatened with the deprivation of a right. It has got to include the idea that not going along with the deal that is offered is an acceptable state of affairs. The second and third types of exception I gave are both ways in which this condition fails: in the third you are going to be made to feel bad if you do not accept (so it may be treated as an implicit sanction) and in the second you are not really free to reject it because the status quo is so unbearable that you have to take anything that promises to alleviate it. (A subset that gets closer to implicit coercion is where in the absence of a deal things get worse and worse, not because of the other's action but simply in the nature of the case—the obvious examples being where you are running out of money without a job, running out of water in the desert, etc.) The Dr Fischer case fits in more awkwardly, but we might say that weakness of will in the face of temptation is a lack of freedom to choose. In the absence of such conditions—so that the person to whom the offer is made is genuinely free to refuse it—is there any reason why, *given* the preferences, it is wrong to try to change the incentives facing somebody?

I do not think so. When it comes down to it, the only really objectionable cases do seem to be the three kinds of case I have picked out already. And the only plausible way of getting the *Lady Chatterley* case in is by imagining that the prude is presented with the offer as a challenge to his integrity. Suppose that the lewd says 'You always say that it matters a lot to you that people don't degrade themselves by reading filth. Here's a chance to stop me doing so, and the only cost to you is reading it yourself—and you're so incorruptible it won't matter to you.'

Examples of objectionable attempts to get compliance with nosy preferences generally rely on a background of inequality. For example, the efforts of the Victorian middle class to regulate the lives of their servants over and above what was defined in doing the job for which they were employed is no doubt revolting to any reasonable person. But is this not because their market position was such that they could impose these conditions as the norm? Suppose that a couple now wanted to employ a live-in nanny for their children and insisted on no visits from boyfriends. In the present market this would presumably require quite a hefty premium over the standard pay for the job. But then if somebody thinks it is worth the premium and takes the job on those conditions do we have any reason to think that that is a bad arrangement? Given a correct distribution of rights, then, my conclusion is that we can afford to be pretty tolerant of efforts to further nosy preferences, even unworthy ones.

III WHAT'S WRONG WITH SOCIAL CHOICE?

This chapter has raised two questions. The first is whether there is some inherent conflict between the Pareto principle and some liberal principle of a kind that would be endorsed by J. S. Mill or F. A. von Hayek. The second is whether we have grounds for the moral condemnation of the use people sometimes make of the area of discretion granted them by a system of rights in offering to act in a certain way in return for some change in behaviour by another. This may be paraphrased as a question of whether Pareto-optimal moves can be undesirable. The answer to the first question is a clearcut 'no': there is no such contradiction. The answer to the second is a more hesitant 'yes': under some circumstances mutually preferred actions may be open to censure.

The key to the first question is that the Pareto principle and the liberal principle have different subject-matters, so they cannot conflict directly. The Pareto principle is a criterion for judging the goodness or badness of states of affairs, whereas the liberal principle à la Mill or Hayek is a criterion for assigning rights to individuals (and perhaps collectivities).

To spell this out a little more fully, here is a statement by Leontief of the Pareto principle, as quoted by Sen: 'The social welfare is increased whenever at least one of the individual utilities on which it depends is raised while none is reduced.'[19] And, in Sen's translation into his own lingo: 'For all pairs of states x, y, . . . if everyone has at least as much utility in x as in y, and someone has more utility in x than in y, then x is socially better than y.'[20] Note that this is a statement about what makes social welfare greater or makes one state of affairs socially better than another. It says nothing about what rights individuals should have or indeed what use they can, with propriety, make of those rights.

Now recall Mill's famous 'simple principle', which is, I suppose, a paradigmatic statement of the kind of liberal principle that is supposed to conflict with the Pareto principle:

> The object of this Essay is to assert one very simple principle, as entitled to govern absolutely the dealings of society with the individual in the way of compulsion and control, whether the means used be physical force in the form of legal penalties, or the moral coercion of public opinion. That principle is, that the sole end for which mankind is warranted, individually or collectively, in interfering with the liberty of action of any of their number, is self-protection. That the only purpose for which power can be rightfully

[19] Sen, 'Personal Utilities and Public Judgments', p. 537. [20] Ibid. 538.

exercised over any member of a civilized community, against his will, is to prevent harm to others. His own good, either physical or moral, is not a sufficient warrant. He cannot rightfully be compelled to do or forbear because it will be better for him to do so, because it will make him happier, because, in the opinions of others, to do so would be wise, or even right. These are good reasons for remonstrating with him, or reasoning with him, or persuading him, or entreating him, but not for compelling him, or visiting him with any evil in case he do otherwise.[21]

Not only does this not conflict with principles for the evaluation of states of affairs but it presupposes them. For Mill's whole point is that an individual's own good might be increased by his doing something where nobody else is adversely affected, and that this is nevertheless no ground for 'interfering' by means of legal or social sanctions. (Note, however, that 'remonstrance' is not a sanction.) It is thus historically bizarre to suppose that Mill would be fazed by any 'dilemma of a Paretian liberal', since he quite explicitly dissociated his 'simple principle' from any judgement of consequences. He accepts that an individual may, in exercising his rights, pass up a chance to make himself better off and nobody else worse off; but he denies that that is any reason for the rest of us to make him do it if he chooses not to.

There is no need for present purposes to take up the hoary question of whether, if the run is sufficiently long (e.g. measured in centuries), and the definition of utility sufficiently elastic (e.g. 'the permanent interests of man as a progressive being'), Mill's 'simple principle' is compatible with a very indirect sort of utilitarianism. The point that matters here is that a conflict between a liberal system of rights and the Pareto principle can arise only if (*a*) every single act is to be assessed according to the Pareto principle; and if (*b*) enforcement is considered to be an appropriate response to infractions of it. And it is made quite clear by Mill that this is exactly what he wants to deny; in fact the 'simple principle' might be said to consist of the denial.

It is, then, undeniable that if we propose a criterion for a good state of affairs like Pareto optimality, or, more full-bloodedly, maximizing aggregate utility, and if we also say that legislators and government officials should seek on a case-by-case basis to enforce the pursuit of this end, then farewell legal rights. And if we also assign a duty to everybody to co-ordinate social sanctions in order to maintain pressure towards the pursuit of the collective end, we have Mill's night-

[21] J. S. Mill, 'On Liberty', in J. M. Robson (ed.), *Essays on Politics and Society* (Toronto: University of Toronto Press, 1977), vol. i, pp. 213–310, at 223–4.

mare (how quaint it seems now!) of an excessive weight of public opinion on individual freedom. But what must be emphasized is that there is absolutely no inconsistency between holding that it would be a better state of the world if someone refrained from doing *x* (because doing it will be 'physically' or 'morally'—Mill's terms—deleterious to him, with no offsetting gains to others), and at the same time holding that he should not be legally or socially coerced into refraining from doing *x*.

It should be observed that I have been talking about the absence of enforcement (legal and, in Mill's extension, social) in certain areas as the essence of liberalism, and this seems to me historically correct. There is no inconsistency between liberalism and the view that, as a matter of individual morality, each person has a duty to maximize the amount of good in the universe. Thus, Godwin, in *Political Justice*, is archetypically liberal (even anticipating Mill's extension of the doctrine from law to public opinion) in looking forward to the end of all legal and social sanctions, while at the same time putting forward a fanatically rigorous doctrine of individual morality according to which every shilling in my pocket has its destined recipient, namely the person in all the world who will derive the most happiness from spending it.[22] This kind of strict consequentialist doctrine has few adherents as a theory and probably none in practice, but there is nothing anti-liberal about it. It can be combined, as it was in Godwin's case, with a strong endorsement of individual rights against coercion. Indeed, there is much to be said for Godwin's view that the relaxation of legal and social controls can be tolerated only when it occurs in a society within which stringent standards of individual morality are widespread. These standards need not be strictly consequentialist but they must acknowledge, in Justice Frankfurter's words, that 'much that is legally permitted is repugnant to the civilized mind'.[23]

To sum up, we can say that there are (at least) three things to be distinguished: what constitutes a good state of the world (this is what a social welfare function [SWF] should tell us); what rights individuals should be granted, that is to say in what areas of conduct they should be free from legal and (if we follow Mill) social coercion; and what, morally speaking, individuals have a duty to do. ('Duty' is of course just one out of the family of terms used in moral judgement, which are

[22] W. Godwin, *Enquiry Concerning Political Justice with Selections from Godwin's Other Writings*, abr. & ed. K. C. Carter (Oxford: Clarendon Press, 1971).

[23] Quoted by Gerald Grant, 'The Character of Education and the Education of Character', *Daedalus*, 110 (1981), 135–49, at 141.

not interchangeable. For the present strictly limited purpose, however, it can stand in for the rest.) How these three are related is a question, or set of questions, in moral and political philosophy. It is a substantive issue and is not to be settled by consulting the meanings of words. (Moore, for example, was simply wrong in regarding the proposition that one has a duty to maximize the amount of good in the universe as an analytic truth.) This is not the place to discuss the substantive issue. The point that has to be made here is that the *only* way in which a conflict arises between liberalism and Pareto optimality is if we adopt the meta-principle that not only do individuals have a moral duty to pursue the good (i.e. implement the SWF), but that 'mankind, individually or collectively' is warranted in *enforcing* the SWF, using legal or social sanctions. But, to repeat, there is nothing in the notion of an SWF that entails that what is 'socially better' must be (or may be) brought about by coercion.

Suppose that my 'personal' preference (i.e. consulting nobody but myself) is to have a crimson kitchen or to read *Lady Chatterley's Lover*. And now suppose that somebody with nosy preferences makes me an offer to change my mind, e.g. offers me $1,000 to switch to pink (thus appealing to my preference for more rather than less disposable income), or offers to read *Lady Chatterley* if I do not (thus appealing to *my* nosy preference in regard to his reading-matter). And suppose that the offer is, given my overall preference scheme, attractive: I was almost indifferent between crimson and pink anyway, and would actually have been happy to change for $10; I was only mildly keen on reading *Lady Chatterley* but attach great importance to the other's reading it. Then clearly Pareto optimality (which does here seem to be no more than an expression of elementary rationality) says that it is a better state of the world if I accept the offer: both parties gain and nobody else is affected either way. But nothing immediately follows from this about social intervention. Unless we adopt the additional principle that the SWF is to be enforced, I still have the right to paint my kitchen any colour I like or read whatever books I like. If I choose to act like a damn fool and turn down a deal that would move me up my preference ordering, the fact that I am also failing to move the outcome up a notch on the SWF does not mean that anybody can call a policeman and make me consummate the deal.

It is essential to distinguish between, on the one hand, an actual system—a constitution and a set of laws—that specifies who can control what events and, on the other hand, a criterion on the basis of which one might judge that a certain state of society is morally preferable to some alternative state of society. An SWF is a proposal for a criterion that will tell us what is a better state of society. Sen, by talking about 'social decision functions' and 'collective choice rules' as well as 'social welfare functions', makes it sound, to the unwary reader, as if the topic under discussion were actual constitutional rules. But it is not. It is still simply ideas people might have about what are better or worse states of affairs.

Now it is, of course, true that an interesting theoretical question arises if I support some decisionmaking rule, that is to say some actual system for the allocation of power, and disapprove of what comes out of it. For example, I may think that the majority has (via some representative system) a right to decide what is done about something and regard the majority decision as unjust. Or I may think that you quite properly have the right to the last word about the colour of your kitchen walls but also think that your decision is deplorable. Undeniably, I may say, you should have the right to decide on their colour. But why should that choice be beyond criticism on the basis of some reasonable criteria for good outcomes? Pareto optimality is by no means the only criterion for criticizing the choice of colour scheme. It might be said that, although you are quite within your rights in having any colours you choose in your kitchen, it would have been better if you had taken account of the sensibilities of others, or shown a less vulgar taste, or spent the money on something other than redecoration, or any of a thousand things. Liberalism says that nobody can make you paint your kitchen any colour you don't want it painted. It does not say that everybody else has to like it, or agree that your choice is the 'socially best' one.

The point is in fact a quite general one that applies either to (real) social decision procedures or to individual rights. In the first case it spawns the so-called 'paradox in the theory of democracy' (not to be confused with the 'paradox of voting') that Richard Wollheim claimed to have discovered.[24] In the second case it gives us the puzzle of how there can be a 'right to do wrong'—for a right only to do right would be no right at all.[25] However, we do not in practice find any great difficulty in voting one way and still accepting that, if we were in the minority, the actual decision should go with the majority. Similarly, we do not in practice (most of us, anyway) feel that there is really any contradiction in saying that somebody should have a right to do either

[24] R. Wollheim, 'A Paradox in the Theory of Democracy', in P. Laslett and W. G. Runciman (eds.), *Philosophy, Politics and Society*, 2nd ser. (Oxford: Basil Blackwell, 1962), 71–87.

[25] See J. Waldron, 'A Right to do Wrong', *Ethics*, 92 (1981), 21–39.

x or y but that what he or she really ought to do is x—even if y is the choice made by the right-holder. And in my view we are quite correct in this.[26]

It must be acknowledged that if one believes that each individual has a duty to maximize the good, and if the good (or SWF) includes Pareto optimality among its criteria, there will be a moral duty to pursue Pareto optimality wherever it leads. This would clearly entail that, if nobody else was affected, you would have a duty to get as high up your own preference rankings as possible. And it would mean that, since your all-things-considered highest preference on almost anything could always be changed by a big enough contingent offer, you could be manipulated into finding that almost anything might be your duty.

Of course, problems arise here about the meaning of 'preference'. If we say that the desire not to be manipulated is itself a wish that can enter into an all-things-considered preference, you may be able to say that you *prefer* not to accept a fantastic offer. But then preferences and actions become analytically indistinguishable. If we retain a more normal concept of preference (of the kind that Sen himself requires) so that we can say that something is preferable, on my scale of preferences, but I nevertheless choose not to do it, we will have to conclude that a duty to pursue Pareto optimality will be a moral constraint on what might reasonably be thought of as an area of individual discretion. The solution if we do not like this is to reject the premiss that gives the trouble: the idea that each person has at every moment a duty to pursue the good (including his or her own good where that of others does not enter into competition with it).

One possible way of accounting for Sen's invention of condition L—but I must insist that this is speculative—is that it is an attempt to incorporate a sphere of moral indifference into a strictly consequentialist moral system. There is some evidence for this interpretation in that he began a relatively recent article by saying that in it, 'without disputing the acceptability of consequentialism', he intended, among other things, to argue that Paretianism 'deserves rejection in its general form'.[27] And one way of interpreting the driving force behind condition L is that there ought to be not merely a protected sphere in the Mill/Hayek sense of one immune to legal or social coercion, but one in which what I do is *morally* my own business, in other words

[26] I have tried to make this clear in 'Wollheim's Paradox: Comment', *Political Theory*, 1 (1973), 317–22.

[27] A. K. Sen, 'Utilitarianism and Welfarism', *Journal of Philosophy*, 76 (1979), 463–89, at 463–4.

where I have no duty to do one thing *or* the other. If this is the intention lying behind condition *L* then it seems to me misguided. For there is a much more direct way of getting rid of the problem of a vanishingly small sphere of moral indifference if that is the worry, namely abandoning strict consequentialism. And Sen's attempt to incorporate a condition guaranteeing a sphere of moral indifference into a consequentialist morality has the unfortunate effect of undermining the judgements of outcomes that we should actually be prepared to make.

We can see how this happens by following Sen's development of condition *L*. His informal statement of the principle of 'personal liberty' runs as follows: 'There are certain personal matters in which a person should be free to decide what should happen, and in choices over these things whatever he or she thinks is better must be taken to be better for the society as a whole, no matter what others think.'[28] Now the first half of this is fair enough. And it is precisely what is guaranteed by a set of liberal rights. The second half could scarcely be said (as Sen claims) to be one of the 'more widely used principles in evaluating social states',[29] since it is not even intelligible as it stands. The assertion has to be interpreted within the framework of social choice theory.

'Socially better' means 'picked out by the social welfare function', and condition *L* means that over certain pairs of choices (at least one pair) each person should be decisive in determining what is picked out by the SWF. Clearly, the question to be raised here is: why should it be supposed that a liberal (or indeed anyone else) would wish to endorse Sen's condition *L*? Why should I wish to insist not only that I should be able actually to decide what happens, e.g. whether my kitchen walls are pink or crimson, but also whether or not it will be 'socially better' that my walls be pink rather than crimson? On the face of it, the latter has less to do with individual autonomy than with megalomania. Surely it ought to be enough that I can decide what colour my kitchen walls are. To ask to be 'socially decisive' in the recondite sense given to that term by social choice theory seems ridiculously presumptuous.

Why would we want to make such a claim? The only explanation I can think of is that, given consequentialism, this is a way of squeezing in an area of moral indifference. But the trouble with this is that, while we may not want to insist that people have a *duty* to (say) act in accordance with the Pareto principle, we may often want to say that it would be a better state of the world if they did, and this possibility is denied by condition *L*.

[28] Sen, 'Liberty, Unanimity and Rights', p. 217. [29] Ibid.

Thus, Sen has written that it could be that

> while I would prefer you to read what I consider to be good literature as opposed to what appears to me to be muck, I do not want my preferences to count in the social evaluation as to whether it is better that you read good literature or bury yourself in muck. I might accept taste differences as legitimate and accept the greater relevance of your taste in matters that I agree are essentially your 'concern'.[30]

But the notion that what you read is your business does not entail *de gustibus non est disputandum.* Your taste should, if you insist on following it, have not merely greater but exclusive relevance to the question of what you actually do. But surely I must, if I believe that I have any judgements of taste about literature or colour schemes (as against merely 'knowing what I like'), apply *my* standards to your reading matter or your kitchen walls. If I believe that *Lady Chatterley* is muck, or that crimson walls are inappropriate to a kitchen, then that is what I think. I cannot be expected to change my mind merely because you happen to think otherwise.

Perhaps the underlying problem here is that the word 'preference' is being grossly overworked. Part of the logical positivist baggage that orthodox welfare economics carries around with it is the idea that judgements of better and worse have no cognitive content but are simply expressions of attitudes. Hence, they can be assimilated quite properly to other forms of preference. When we combine this with the other dogma derived (incorrectly) from crude verificationism to the effect that 'interpersonal comparisons of utility' are 'meaningless' (or themselves express a 'value judgement' construed as something without cognitive content), we get the characteristic form of post-Arrow welfare economics in which 'social welfare' is derived from some process of aggregating preferences.

Sen wants to challenge this kind of 'welfarism', but he is insufficiently iconoclastic. The conclusion he wishes to draw from the Paretian liberal dilemma is that we need more than utility information (i.e. in this case preference information) in order to assess social welfare. We need, for example, to know the source of the preference: why does the lewd prefer that the prude read *Lady Chatterley's Lover*? But what he does not challenge is the idea that moral or aesthetic judgements should be treated as preferences and put into an SWF. The only question he raises is whether all preferences should 'count in determining social choice'.[31] So, he implies, nosy (or at any rate

[30] Ibid. 236. [31] Ibid.

nastily nosy) preferences should count less than 'personal' ones, or perhaps they should not count at all.

This, however, is an attempt to stop the mischief at too late a point. The move that should be blocked is the one that treats moral or aesthetic judgements as preferences to be cranked into an SWF along with other preferences. If I believe that *Lady Chatterley's Lover* is muck, or that crimson walls are unsuitable for a kitchen, then I presumably think it would be a better state of the world if you did not read *Lady Chatterley* or paint your kitchen walls crimson. But the fact that I believe that is not *itself* what makes it better—nor does it contribute even a tiny bit to making it better. If we add strict consequentialism, so that you have a duty to go for the best state of affairs possible, it will follow from my beliefs that you have a moral duty not to read *Lady Chatterley* or paint your kitchen walls crimson. But the ground for the duty is that (I believe) doing those things would bring about an inferior state of affairs to some other that it is open to you to bring about. The ground is *not* that I would 'prefer' you to refrain—or that I and many other judges of literature or colour schemes share the same 'preference'. I may not, indeed, have any preference in the matter at all, in any ordinary sense of the term. I may simply have formed a quite disinterested aesthetic judgement on the question of *Lady Chatterley* or crimson decor. I may not care a bit what you do, but that obviously doesn't give me any reason for withdrawing my judgement.

We might do better, if we are going to assimilate moral and aesthetic judgements to any other kind of thing, to assimilate them to beliefs about matters of fact. If I believe that the Sears Tower in Chicago is taller than the Eiffel Tower, we are presumably under no temptation to turn that into a statement of a preference. And if I have the (fairly incontrovertible) view that it is better that people believe what is true than what is false, it will follow that I think it would be better for people to believe that the Sears Tower is taller than the Eiffel Tower. But surely it should be plain here that they should (in my view) believe it because it is (in my belief) true—not to please me by falling in with my 'preference in the matter'.

Thus, the belief that it would be a better state of the world if you didn't read *Lady Chatterley's Lover* is itself a social welfare judgement, which I arrive at after taking account of the fact that you would like to read the book (and giving that whatever weight I think appropriate), the effects I think the book would have on you, and anything else that seems to me relevant. My belief is just that, and there is no reason on earth why anybody else (or I myself) should treat it as a preference and put it in with other preferences to determine what would advance 'social welfare'. I have already, *ex hypothesi*, taken account of everything I consider relevant in arriving at my judgement about where the social welfare lies. If somebody else were trying to form a judgement on this point, he too would have to form an opinion of what the book would do to you, find out if you wanted to read it, and so on. But he would be rather eccentric to take account of *my* judgement as an ingredient in *his* judgement about social welfare. (He might of course regard me as a literary, or moral, authority, but then he would follow my judgement in reaching his own, not incorporate it as a 'preference'.)

If Sen's concern is with the construction of SWFs out of ill-assorted materials, it is entirely well placed. Indeed, I hope it will not be too self-indulgent to point out that I said this myself, five years before Sen published his Paretian liberal paradox, in my *Political Argument*. In discussing majoritarianism—the idea that things should be done if a majority wants them done—I suggested that we should, if we apply the principle at all, count only privately orientated wants:

> The justification for counting only privately-oriented wants is that it avoids at one stroke the most objectionable feature of the majoritarian principle, namely the way in which it commits one to handing over questions of right and wrong, justice and injustice, to the majority of a group in which one's own voice counts only as one. Yet at the same time the amendment leaves one free to take account of desires which are put forward simply by people as wants in matters affecting themselves. This may seem high-handed at first sight, but further reflection suggests that what I have called 'publicly-oriented wants' are not actually put forward as wants at all. To treat them as wants is to degrade them and to fall into absurdity.
>
> Suppose that I am making up my mind whether it is fair for the *A*'s to get more of something than the *B*'s; and the *A*'s and the *B*'s are the only people directly affected by the division, in the sense of 'affected' which I have defined. Should I, in making up my mind, take account of the opinions of the *C*'s in the matter? I may, of course, let them weigh with me as having a certain authority, but surely it would be ridiculous to mix in the wants of the *C*'s for, say, the *A*'s to win, consequential on their belief that the *A*'s have the best case, on an equal footing with the privately-oriented wants of the *A*'s and *B*'s.[32]

The relevance of this for social choice theory is fairly radical, because it entails that we should reject the whole idea of aggregating preferences —including individuals' judgements about social welfare—into some

[32] B. M. Barry, *Political Argument* (London: Routledge and Kegan Paul, 1965), 63–4.

sort of *social* SWF. The error of supposing that this is a sensible thing to try to do goes back to Kenneth Arrow's book *Social Choice and Individual Values*[33] (though, as far as I can tell, no further). And a devastating criticism of it was made as early as the next year by Ian Little, who wrote:

[Arrow] calls his function both a social welfare function and a decision-making process. He believes that 'one of the great advantages of abstract postulational methods is the fact that the same system may be given different interpretations permitting a considerable saving of time.' Yes, but we must be careful not to give such a system a nonsensical interpretation, and it will be my contention that to interpret it as a social welfare function *is* to give a nonsensical interpretation.

Imagine the system as a machine which produces a card on which it is written 'x is better than y,' or vice versa, when all individual answers to the question 'Is x better than y?' have been fed into it. What significance are we to attach to the sentence on the card, i.e. to the resulting 'master'-order? First, it is clear that the sentence, although it is a sentence employing ethical terms, is not a value *judgment*. Every value judgment must be *someone*'s judgment of values. If there are n people filling in cards to be fed into the machine, then we have n value judgments, not $n+1$. The sentence which the machine produces expresses a ruling, or decision, which is different in kind from what is expressed by the sentences fed into it. The latter express value judgments; the former expresses a ruling between these judgments. Thus we can legitimately call the machine, or function, a decision-making process.

But what would it mean to call the machine a social welfare function? One would be asserting, in effect, that if the machine decided in favour of x rather than in favour of y, then x would produce more social welfare than y or simply be more desirable than y. This is clearly a value judgment, but it is, of course, a value judgment made by the person who calls the machine a social welfare function.[34]

There is only one point on which I would like to modify what Little said. I do not think that it makes any more sense to say that individual judgements are aggregated into a ruling or decision than it does to say that they are aggregated into a social welfare judgement. What goes into a social decision (that is to say, a real decision with real effects) is votes, not expressions of views about social welfare. What comes out (say of referendums) are decisions but on what is to be done, not a ruling between competing judgements about what social welfare

[33] Kenneth J. Arrow, *Social Choice and Individual Values* (New York: John Wiley and Sons, 1951).

[34] I. M. D. Little, 'Social Choice and Individual Values', *Journal of Political Economy*, 60 (1952), 422–32, repr. in Brian Barry and Russell Hardin (eds.), *Rational Man and Irrational Society? An Introduction and Sourcebook* (Beverly Hills, Calif.: Sage, 1982), 269–82, at 275–6.

requires. To tie this together with the earlier discussion of (legal) rights, we may say that rights and votes go together in one box (the box marked 'control over actions') while judgements of social welfare go into another box. And this second box does not in addition contain anything corresponding to a vote tally. There simply is no such thing as a social welfare judgement compounded out of social welfare judgements. The thing is a logical monstrosity. As Little said, if you feel you should take account of other people's judgements of social welfare, not merely as suggesting where the truth lies but as preferences to be incorporated into your own 'social welfare function', that is logically possible—though, I would immediately wish to add, morally obtuse. But then the result of that process is *your* judgement about where the social welfare lies. It is not some sort of superordinate judgement that is nobody's judgement and everybody's judgement at the same time.

It may then be asked 'But what happens if the people in a society reach different conclusions about the social welfare?' The answer is, of course: what happens now. Different people do, indeed, disagree about what would make the world better. They argue about it, but there is no guarantee that they will finish up by agreeing. What we neither have nor could have is some algorithm for taking these divergent judgements and producing some 'social' judgement.

What we do need, in order to have a stable society, is a constitution that specifies how collectively binding *decisions* are to be taken. And if the society is to be liberal as well as stable, either the constitution or the legislation enacted under it should set out individual rights. But this is, again, in the sphere of control, not the sphere of judgement.

These rights, since they specify what actions people will be allowed to take without being exposed to legal or (in Mill's extension) social sanctions, have no direct connection with anybody's judgements about what makes a better or worse state of affairs. What Sen offers as his liberal principle—condition *L*—has no connection with rights, and thus no connection with liberalism à la Mill or Hayek. It is concerned with the relation between individual preferences and the SWF. There is, undeniably, a conflict between condition *L* and the Pareto principle, because they both deal in outcomes and set up contradictory criteria for a 'socially better' state of affairs. But this merely reinforces the point that condition *L* is not a liberal principle.

I fear that all this may appear like a minor skirmish on the borders of social choice theory, the details of which can be of no possible interest to anyone except Sen and myself. I want to emphasize that this is not so. If I am correct, the implication is that we cannot expect to get any help from social choice theory in analysing rights because the whole concept of social choice or social preference is too simple to accommodate the concept of a right. Sen's proffered translation of Mill and Hayek into the language of SWFs comes up with altogether the wrong kind of thing.

Since the world is full of social choice theorists and many of them are very clever, I had better be more specific. I do not see how one could deny in advance that it may be possible to carry out some complicated translation of what we actually want to say into some extension of the language of social choice. What I do feel fairly safe in denying is that the result will illuminate any significant problem in moral or political philosophy. Rather, it will continue to generate its own internal puzzles out of its own inadequacies.

The reason for this is that social choice theory is a theory producing orderings of outcomes (states of the world). But the theories we require must include concepts such as the right of an actor (which might be an individual or a collectivity like a governmental sub-unit or a country) to make certain choices, and the notion that an actor ought or ought not to do certain things within the range of things it has a right to do. These simply cannot be connected directly to a system for generating rankings of outcomes, which is what social choice theory is.

Thus, Sen's idea that the solution lies in changing the utility information (so that the lewd and the prude might choose not to have their nosy preferences counted in the SWF) is fundamentally misguided. For the question of the socially preferred outcome (according to the SWF) is different in nature from the question of the rights people should have. There is no need to mess about with the SWF. It may really be that the world would be a better place if the prude widened his horizons and the lewd did not skim novels for the dirty bits and that they are quite right in agreeing this is better than the reverse. But it does not follow that it is morally permissible for them to bring it about if that can be done only by interfering with one another's freedom. The whole idea of anti-paternalism is, after all, that some consequences admitted to be superior should not be brought about if the means are a reduction of freedom of choice. I believe myself that anti-paternalism has got completely out of hand when it issues in objections to the mandatory use of seatbelts or crash helmets. But hardly anybody would wish to say that a reduction in freedom of choice is *always* permissible (still less required) whenever it brings about better outcomes, and that is all we require for the present case.

The second claim mentioned at the beginning of this section is more substantively interesting, and is one that Sen himself has not explicitly defended, though, as I have noted, he has said that he thinks it can be defended. This is the claim that, when rights have been assigned in an ethically acceptable way, it may be wrong for one person to offer to use his rights in a certain way with the object of inducing another to use his rights in a way he would not otherwise choose. I have suggested that such cases can arise, but they all seem to be subsumable under the objection that the freedom to choose is more apparent than real.

It should be emphasized that a positive response to the second claim in no sense rehabilitates the 'liberal paradox'. Suppose we conclude for some reason that I ought not to offer you $10 never to wear that tie again even though I am clear that it would be worth it to me and even though you would be happy to close with the offer. We should not rush to the conclusion that Pareto optimality fails *because* it conflicts with the liberal principle establishing (among other things) your right to wear whatever tie you like. All that can be deduced is that not every Pareto-optimal outcome available under the system of designated rights should be brought about. But the rejection of the view that all Pareto-optimal moves are desirable is a position with respect to the use people ought to make of their rights. It is logically quite independent of the case for establishing rights. We could equally well support exactly the same system of rights and at the same time maintain that the more Pareto-optimal deals that are consummated the better.

If we support a set of rights but believe that not all Pareto-optimal moves are desirable, we will be committed to saying that sometimes people do things they have a right to do but that they should not do. If we support a set of rights and believe that Pareto optimality is one criterion of a desirable outcome, we will find ourselves saying that sometimes it would be better if people were to make some Pareto-optimal deal but that they have a right not to if they choose not to. Both positions are consistent.

Even if there is no logical connection there, it may be asked how my rather indulgent views of trades conforming to the Pareto principle can be reconciled with my earlier-expressed view that judgements about better or worse states of affairs (e.g. that it would be better if you did not read *Lady Chatterley*) should not be treated as preferences and cranked into an SWF. My answer is that there is no inconsistency here because the second question is not whether the fact that the prude thinks it is socially better for the lewd not to read *Lady Chatterley* provides a reason for somebody else (the lewd or anybody else forming a social welfare judgement) to conclude that it would be better for the lewd not to read it. (The prude must of course think it better, but not that it's better *because* he thinks it's better; rather that he thinks it's better because it *is* better.) The second question that I took up is, instead: given that (on the basis of the contingent offers) the prude wants to read *Lady Chatterley* and the lewd does not, is there any reason for us (or them) to conclude that they ought not to do so? In other words, this is a case where, *ex hypothesi*, each does have a preference for what the other does, and these preferences are so strong that each cares more about what the other reads than he does about what he reads himself. Given this highly unusual situation, the question is whether there is anything wrong in their doing what they both prefer, so that the prude reads and the lewd does not. My answer that this is probably all right, given the preferences, does not conflict with my view that the assignment of rights should be done on quite separate criteria from those on which we judge the use people make of them, and my view that in general judgements of social welfare should be distinguished from preferences. The lewd and the prude *do* have strong preferences as regards one another's behaviour; but that is no reason for concluding that beliefs about what is better or worse are usually no more than weaker preferences (or, as Hume might have said, calmer passions) than the kind of preference we may have for vanilla over strawberry ice-cream.

IV PARADOX LOST

Those who have thought at all about the liberal paradox fall into two groups. There are those who are firmly convinced that it constitutes a serious problem for liberalism, at any rate if one accepts the principle of Pareto optimality, and find it hard to imagine how anyone can think otherwise; and there are those who do not see any incompatibility between liberalism and the Pareto principle, and find it hard to see how anyone could think that there is. As a result of hearing the arguments contained in this chapter, a number of people whose acumen I respect have moved from the first group to the second, but the point of interest here is that the process of conversion has in all cases been swift and painless, without any intermediate stage of doubt.

The explanation for this phenomenon is, I suggest, that everything depends on where you start from. If you begin by rejecting the premiss that individual decisiveness over the social welfare function is an inherent element in liberalism, you can accept the validity of Sen's proof without suffering a pang. From this point of view, the impossibility of reconciling condition *L* (or any variant on it) with Pareto optimality is of no concern, because condition *L* has no ethical significance in the first place.

If, however, you start from the premiss that liberalism requires individual decisiveness over the social welfare function, you are trapped in the labyrinth. The only means of escape appears to be to modify condition *L* in some way so as to render it compatible with Pareto optimality. Sen reviewed a number of these attempts at solving the problem in its own terms in 'Liberty, Unanimity and Rights'. Hardly surprisingly, he found them wanting. Every failed attempt at escape, however, reinforces the conviction that one has uncovered some deep contradiction in social choice theory.[35] Thus, in the commentary which Sen wrote on the original version of this chapter,[36] he incorporated chunks of boilerplate from earlier reviews of the literature which consisted of long series of references to articles related to the liberal paradox. Their function was, I think, intended to be to suggest that the liberal paradox must be a real problem to have collected such a large bibliography around it.

Another occupational risk from immersion in the literature is a tendency to assimilate a new criticism that challenges the framework to an old one that presupposes the framework. Sen's commentary also provides an example of this, and I think the point is worth pursuing, since it will enable me to set out as clearly as possible the distinctive nature of my line on the liberal paradox.

According to Sen, what I have done is to offer a solution to the problem that is similar in essence to that proposed by Robert Nozick.

[35] A parallel, and much more important, case is that of Arrow's General Possibility Theorem. Enormous efforts have gone into trying to modify Arrow's conditions so as to make them consistent with one another, and the negative results have reinforced the sense that Arrow's theorem is a major stumbling-block for the concept of social welfare. Yet, as I pointed out in section III of chapter 2 above, even if all of Arrow's conditions were fulfilled simultaneously, this would do nothing to guarantee that the outcome would increase social welfare on any interpretation of the words that was evaluatively significant. Thus, from Arrow's point of view, we have a determinate outcome whenever there are only two options to choose among and also whenever there are more than two but the preferences happen to be single-peaked. But the outcome preferred by a majority to the other(s) might be to exterminate all the members of the minority—scarcely a contribution to social welfare in any interesting sense of the expression!

[36] Amartya Sen, 'Foundations of Social Choice Theory: An Epilogue', in Jon Elster and Aanund Hylland (eds.), *Foundations of Social Choice Theory* (Cambridge: Cambridge University Press, 1986), 213–48, esp. 223–32.

Nozick's position is that, once a set of rights has been assigned to individuals, there is no room for a social welfare function. People must be allowed to do whatever they choose to do with their rights, and any authoritative social decision to the effect that one outcome is better than another must involve an interference with that free exercise of rights.[37]

Now it should be evident, even from this brief exposition, that Nozick implicitly accepts the premisses from which the liberal paradox is generated, in that he assumes an incompatibility between rights and a social welfare function. His 'solution' simply consists in saying 'So much the worse for the social welfare function'. In total contrast to this, what I am maintaining is that there is no way in which a social welfare function can be a threat to individual rights because the two things have different subject-matters. Rights are about what people should be allowed to do, whereas a social welfare function is about what constitutes a good state of affairs. Even if we endorse individual rights for consequentialist reasons only (because we mistrust the intelligence or goodwill of the state, or are concerned about costs of enforcement), we shall still often be led to conclude that people have used their rights on particular occasions in ways that make for a worse outcome than could have been achieved if they had done something else that was legally open to them. There is absolutely no incoherence in saying both that people should have rights that leave them with several options and also that the results of their using their rights will sometimes be less than optimal. It will sometimes be manifestly clear that a choice other than the one actually made would have brought about a better state of affairs. On occasion, the actor himself or herself may admit this.

To sum up, what I offer is not yet another 'solution' to the problem of the impossibility of a Paretian liberal. Instead, my argument is that there is no such problem. What the liberal paradox calls for is not solution but dissolution.

[37] Robert Nozick, *Anarchy, State, and Utopia* (New York: Basic Books, 1974), 165–6.

14

TRAGIC CHOICES

Tragic Choices, by Guido Calabresi and Philip Bobbitt, is an unusually serious effort at relating the principles discussed by political philosophers to real issues in public policy.[1] It continues, with good reason, to be widely cited. I want here to raise two questions that are central to the interpretation and evaluation of the book. First, I shall analyse the notion of a tragic choice. I shall argue that the definition proposed by the authors is methodologically inconvenient and depends on implicit and highly controversial philosophical premisses. Second, I shall take up some points in the substantive chapters and argue in particular that the authors give unnecessary hostages to economic orthodoxy by failing to recognize where it has valid arguments and by making errors in economic analysis themselves which, although they are not crucial to their general case, will tend to discredit it with economists. Since I sympathize with the overall thrust of their challenge to the apostles of the market, my aim here is the constructive one of trying to strengthen it by detaching it from various assertions and denials that seem to me unfounded.

I THE CONCEPT OF A TRAGIC CHOICE

What makes a choice a 'tragic' one? One way in which we can approach this question is by way of ostensive definition. What are the actual examples of tragic choices cited in the book? I have tried to collect together all the references to cases in the book, and, although I cannot claim that the list is exhaustive, I do not think that any example discussed for a full paragraph or more has escaped me.

Because it is given the fullest treatment, is referred to the most often, and is described by Calabresi and Bobbitt as 'paradigmatic' (p. 177), pride of place should go to the provision of haemodialysis machines (artificial kidneys). More generally, scarce medical resources are also referred to a number of times, and occasionally other examples such as iron lungs and cardiac shunt operations are

[1] Guido Calabresi and Philip Bobbitt, *Tragic Choices* (New York: W. W. Norton and Co., 1978). Page references in the text are to this book.

mentioned. Following haemodialysis and its attendant medical cases, we can rank roughly level two others: the military draft (including such questions as the right to buy substitutes) and the right to have children. These three cases, or sets of cases, account for almost all the space given to examples. Of the rest, only one gets any extended analysis, namely, immigration policy in the United States, and it is not altogether clear whether this is regarded as lying within the sphere of tragic choices or as illustrating the more general point that in many areas collective choices cannot but display a differential value placed on the characteristics of different people. The others to get at least a little discussion are: the provision of grade crossings as a road safety measure; the death penalty; distributing food in a famine or water in a drought; choosing occupants of a lifeboat if there is not enough space for all; and choosing subjects for medical experimentation. Others are only mentioned in passing: adoption; child custody; quarantine; what to do about hostages; and abortion. Again, however, it may be that not all of these are to be thought of as examples of tragic choices but rather as illustrations of more general features that tragic choices share: not enough is said to make this clear.

Based on this list, and the order of priority given to the examples within it, we might plausibly construct a definition along the following lines:

> A 'tragic choice' is one involving life and death (at least probabilistically) or—less centrally—other vital personal goods such as childbearing, where alternative technically feasible policies will have the effect (whether or not they have the intention) of distributing these goods and bads (or the probability of incurring them) in different amounts and/or in different ways among individual recipients.

The various features of this definition are drawn up with an eye on the list so as to get the right inclusions and exclusions. I think that the definition I have put forward would specify a field of enquiry which, while not self-contained (since whatever might be said of things falling within it would also be true of some others outside), has enough interesting special features to be worth picking out for special study.[2] We might denote it by the oversimplified but adequately mnemonic tag 'life and death cases'.

Although I believe that Calabresi and Bobbitt would have done well

[2] An illustration of the fact that there is, as it were, a rational core to this way of grouping subjects for analysis is perhaps suggested by the fact that the authors' list has much in common with the list of cases discussed by Jonathan Glover in his *Causing Death and Saving Lives* (Harmondsworth: Penguin Books, 1977).

to adopt some such definition of the sphere of tragic choices as I have just put forward, the course they in fact follow is quite otherwise. According to them there is no such thing, strictly speaking, as a tragic *situation*. Tragedy, rather, is coextensive with the existence of irreconcilable values in some matter. (In spite of this they do in fact quite often talk about 'tragic situations', but I take it that they would say that such talk is to be understood as shorthand, where the unpacked form would be something like 'a situation in which, according to some given set of values, unresolvable value conflicts come into play'.) Since the book is about social policy, rather than individual decisionmaking (e.g. a certain individual's decision as to whether or not to stop smoking or to wear a seat belt), the locus of these conflicts must be 'society'. But such a manner of speaking involves a crucial ambiguity. We might say that a society is subject to irreconcilable conflict when different groups within it have different views and these are held in an absolute way that does not permit compromise (e.g. the 'right to life' vs. the 'right to choose' in contemporary American sloganeering about abortion). But the same phrase might mean instead that the individuals within the society hold irreconcilable values. And, of course, there could be a combination of both phenomena at the same time in the same society, with some irreconcilable conflicts between different people and others within some individuals.

Unfortunately, Calabresi and Bobbitt do not address this issue frontally, and I think that their analysis gains a certain unwarranted plausibility from their implicitly playing fast and loose with the distinction between distributive and collective sense of the word 'we'. They tend to imply that 'we' are subject to such and such a conflict, where the reality would perhaps more plausibly be put by saying not that each and every one of us is subject to it but that society as a whole is subject to conflict between its members.[3]

[3] The most relevant statement comes right at the beginning of the book, where it is said that 'the use of examples may lead the reader to conclude that what we mean by tragic is subjective to each individual, that tragic choices are those that each of us finds appalling. Instead, we intend to discuss the tragedies of cultures; it is the values accepted by a society as fundamental that mark some choices as tragic. The critic of social values may object strongly to decisions his society finds quite acceptable, and readily approve of other choices that his society must make and yet cannot stomach; moreover, he may be right. But it is not with him or with our own imperatives that we are concerned; it is rather with those choices which the society finds intolerable' (pp. 17–18). A contrast is drawn here between what a 'society' or 'culture' finds 'acceptable' or 'intolerable' and what individuals—presumably members of that society or culture—believe about the same matters. This might make it sound as if the societal or cultural conflict is between rather than within individuals. But I think that the more plausible reading is that there are widespread though not universal beliefs held by the members of the society or culture that give

I shall return to this point in a little while. Before doing so, however, I should ask how the author's explicit definition of a tragic choice in terms of value conflicts (pp. 17–19, 22–3, 149–50, 195–6) relates to the definition in terms of 'life and death cases' that, I have already said, fits the authors' actual list of examples. If I am right in thinking that at least some of their illustrations of irreconcilable conflict of values are not intended to be 'tragic' ones, the implication must be that a 'tragic choice' is defined neither simply as a life-and-death case, nor simply as a value conflict case, but as a case of unresolvable value conflict *in the context of* a life-and-death case. If this is so, it of course raises the question of why the intersection of these two sets should be taken as the subject of special study and given the special name 'tragic choices'. The answer could be that life-and-death cases provide a particularly convenient context in which to study unresolvable value conflicts because of the extra urgency of such conflicts in these cases and hence the extra effort that is likely to go into trying to cope with them. Such an answer, if given, would seem to me quite reasonable.

Having said that, however, I must return to the question of whether it would not be better to focus on the way in which societies deal with life-and-death problems, leaving it open as to whether (or how frequently) there are irreconcilable conflicts, and studying the process just as seriously whether there are or not. There are two reasons for preferring such a course to the one actually followed in this book. The first is that it seems to me inconvenient to have one's subject matter so liable to come and go depending on what people think. If some particular question (e.g. provision of expensive medical care) is seen in some societies at times as involving a 'tragic choice' but in others as not (because 'everybody' agrees that it should go to those who can afford it, or to a privileged racial minority only), is that a sound methodological basis for studying the allocation in the first set of cases but not the second? I do not see that it is.

My second point about the idea of tragic choices, as formulated by Calabresi and Bobbitt, is that it seems to me to rest on a suspect ethical assumption. Of course, values conflict, in the sense that there are always, say, problems of equitable distribution versus perverse incentives, or between process values (e.g. fair trial, individual liberties) and outcome values (e.g. reducing crime, cutting the accident toll). But why should this everyday fact be taken to give rise to the

rise to conflicts within those individuals, and that these occasion the 'tragic choices' to be discussed in the book.

conclusion that all we can do is 'limit the spreading stain' (pp. 149–50) or that 'we cannot be barred from using flawed methods since they are all we shall have in the tragic situation' (pp. 61–2)? Why cannot we simply determine in some case what is the best thing to do, taking account of the relevant values? The results may indeed excite emotion, but must we accept that, when the decision is to provide some with dialysis but not all, the authors' quotation from an article on Greek tragedy is appropriate? 'We have a prospect of insuperable moral difficulty, a nightmare of injustice in which the assertion of any right involves further wrong, in which fate is set against fate in an intolerable necessary sequence of violence' (p. 18). It is important to recognize that this is not just a matter of rhetorical excess. Unless the 'tragic choices' analysed by Calabresi and Bobbitt really have this property, much of what they say in the book ceases to be convincing.

There is a large problem lurking here. As is well known, some philosophers hold that in any situation, however sticky, there is always a (relatively) best thing to do. There cannot be a situation in which all alternatives are wrong. Even if every alternative conflicts with a 'prima facie duty', there has to be one that is less bad than the others. That is the alternative which one ought 'all things considered' to choose. The competing view is that in some situations whatever is chosen will be wrong. But this claim is quite plausibly qualified by saying that such a situation can arise only because of the wrongdoing of somebody (who may or may not be the agent), so there is no inconsistency in the moral system considered as one of 'strict compliance'. For example, if you promise to do something intrinsically wrong you must either break a promise or do something wrong. If you make two incompatible promises you must break one. But you are at fault for getting into the situation in the first place. If you are forced to choose between complying with a hijacker's demand or allowing innocent people to be killed, it might be held that either choice is wrong; but you would not be faced with the choice except for the unjust acts of the hijacker. And so on.

It appears to me that the strongest reason for adopting the second view is an unwillingness to concede that one can lightheartedly do something terrible if it is the best thing in the situation. But there is no need to be lighthearted about it. Someone who says that there is always a best thing to do can perfectly well still feel remorse if the choice is between bads but the situation could have been avoided by different action earlier, or regret if the choice is forced by the wrong action of another. But suppose we have a 'trolley case'[4] where none of this applies (the runaway trolley is not due to poor maintenance or a malicious attempt at homicide), then should one feel guilty about switching the trolley from a track that kills six to a track that kills one? It seems not. Remorse or even regret seem out of place—only the feeling that the situation is unfortunate though nobody's fault.

Calabresi and Bobbitt create the impression that life-and-death situations are liable to involve tragic choices in their sense by making a move that seems to me illegitimate. This is the claim, frequently repeated in this book, that there is a widespread social or cultural value to the effect that human life is priceless and should be saved at any cost, however high. 'Our values and institutions depend on the notion that life is beyond price' (p. 39). But we surely ought to ask whether there is any such commitment to the infinite value of life, that no sacrifice is too great to save life, and so on. We do not act as if we thought so, and, although this is more difficult to prove, I do not believe that we think it either. I am inclined to think that the idea is a piece of sentimentality that simply will not stand up to scrutiny.

Since Calabresi and Bobbitt offer no evidence in favour of the claim that there is such an absolute value in 'our' society and culture, I shall not try to assemble any evidence to the contrary. But I do want to point out how central it is to their argument. Thus, to return again to the statement (pp. 61–2) that 'we cannot be barred from using flawed methods since they are all we shall have in the tragic situation', we may ask: Why so? In my view this has not been established by any argument of a specific nature. For anything specific said to the contrary, one is free to believe that the right method can be used in the right kind of case. No: the assertion is really a dogma derived from the idea that no outcome can be justified if it causes some to live and some to die, because life has 'infinite value'. If we drop this assumption, there will still indeed be tough choices to be made, but it does not follow that any procedure for carrying them out must be flawed.

This point can be pursued further in the context of the authors' summary (on pp. 49–50) of what is wrong with each of the 'pure' allocational procedures. In each case, the notion of the 'infinite value of life' is pressed into service—and since no procedure can possibly

[4] 'Trolley cases' involve the dilemma of someone standing by the switching gear when a runaway trolley comes down the track. The case envisaged in the text is one where, if the points are left as set, six people at the end of the track will be killed; if the trolley is switched to the other track one person at the end of that track will be killed. Those unfamiliar with contemporary moral philosophy may perhaps be surprised to learn that there is an entire literature devoted to 'trolley problems'.

satisfy that without sacrificing every other possible value, this makes it easy to show that each procedure is, when measured against 'our' or 'society's' values, defective. In each case, Calabresi and Bobbitt mention other problems with each method of allocation, but if we subtract the 'infinite value of life' point from each, we have what seems to me a much more tractable problem in which values will have to be traded off against one another.

I wish to suggest that this notion of tragic choices infects the whole analysis with a kind of fundamental irrationalism. For if life and death cases are indeed (at least potentially) tragic in the sense defined—'a nightmare of injustice in which the assertion of any right involves a further wrong'—all we can do in order to escape intolerable psychological pressure is try to pretend that they don't exist. And, much of the time, the book gives the impression that that is what it is about: not how societies cope with tragic choices but how they attempt to deny their existence. It is not very easy to show this by selective quotation, but I think that anyone who has read the book is likely to have come away from it with the feeling that the book is about fudging rather than facing policy choices in life-and-death cases.

There is, however, an apparent difficulty in treating value conflicts as a source of psychic strain or discomfort. If what really drives social policy is cognitive dissonance reduction, why should societies go to such lengths to accommodate the conflicting values or to arrange institutions so that the conflict is not too overt? Surely it would have been much easier (not to mention cheaper) to change one's values so as to avoid the discomfort in the first place.

If this move is resisted (and I agree that it should be) this is presumably because people not only want to avoid discomfort but really do hold the values. But then we can ask whether they *ought* to hold those values. It may be possible to convince them not to hold a value such as that of the infinite value of life, but to accept that trade-offs are unavoidable and should be faced rationally. Institutional changes may still be required to get to a good trade-off, but this is different from trying to make the problem disappear by sleight of hand. The way in which Calabresi and Bobbitt set it up, the principles tend to be rather crude. A lot of room is then left for juggling to accommodate them, and this is presented as a fairly irrational business. For example: *either* we give all lives a single (maybe implicit) monetary value and trade off between intensive care units, ambulance services, biomedical research, elimination of grade crossings, median barriers on highways, safety of nuclear power plants, aeroplane safety (etc.) *or* we simply follow different strategies in different areas and avoid noticing that this is 'irrational'. The alternative which I would prefer is to try to make sense of the relevant distinctions between different kinds of situations, then see if there are still inconsistencies in the ways in which we deal with them. For example, we might conclude that there is a relevant difference between an improbable large catastrophe and the certainty of a small number of deaths, even if the 'expected' loss of life (i.e. number discounted by probability) is equal. Or we might decide that it makes a difference whether people have a choice of assuming a risk in return for a benefit to them or not. Having done this, we might still conclude that in a relatively narrow area (e.g. medical) or even narrower (e.g. the distribution of services in hospitals) there are inconsistencies that cannot be accounted for by invoking any plausibly relevant differences. But we shall have got away from the simplistic idea (common among economists) that a society must be 'irrational' if the value it implicitly assigns to saving a life is different in different areas.

I believe that the appropriate approach is one combining 'interpretative charity' with independent standards of judgement. That is, I think that it is important to try to see what can be made of the discriminations between cases that people (including ourselves in off-duty moments) feel inclined to make, rather than simply imposing some schematic formula and dismissing any distinctions that cannot be fitted in. But at the same time I see no reason for accepting our unreflective judgements as the last word. Surely it ought to be possible by thinking systematically about things to refine our ideas. That is at any rate the minimally rationalistic premiss from which I would start.

II MARKETS AND MORALS

The Pareto principle (see chapter 13) has two interpretations, one broad and trivial, the other narrower and inherently contentious. In the broad sense it says that if everybody in a society prefers x to y, then it is better for x to be the state of affairs than y. Barring external intervention, it is hard to see how this could be controversial, since *ex hypothesi* there would be nobody within the society to disagree. In this sense, however, 'prefer' has to be given a sense that will allow us to say that one prefers x to y for any reason, including thinking as a matter of abstract justice that x is right or wishing to live in the kind of society that has x instead of y. It should be clear that the policy prescriptions characteristic of economists cannot be derived from this interpretation of the Pareto principle. Wherever some programme provides goods in kind (food, clothing, or housing, for example) an economist will normally observe that it would be Pareto superior to give the recipients the cash value of the goods instead. (This of course presupposes that the good in question can be bought on the market.) Similarly, for any scheme that sets quantitative standards to limit, say, air or water pollution by factories, an economist will typically maintain that there exists in principle some Pareto-superior alternative using pricing (effluent taxes). But on the first interpretation of the Pareto principle, it requires only one person to dissent for any reason to stop any such policy in its tracks.

These characteristic prescriptions follow only if the principle is understood as telling people what preferences they *ought* to include in their judgements. Thus, for example, in a sprightly defence of the standard economist's line, Thomas Schelling says of a hypothetical situation in which money originally allocated for airport safety is given as cash and used for something else: 'And I don't care. I'd rather have the money, the lower taxes [than your having it], but if you are entitled to the money and would rather have the money than [airport] lights, I'll get no satisfaction out of making you buy the lights.'[5] This could be treated as a purely autobiographical assertion, throwing a (not altogether flattering) light on the range of things Schelling cares about. But of course in the context what it means is 'I don't care and you shouldn't either.' It is legitimate for me to have a concern for your utility (preference-satisfaction), but not for your safety, except to the exact extent that it forms part of your utility (as *you* judge it). '*You* may have put too low a value on your life, but I don't know why I should feel guilty about that.'[6] Why is guilt the only appropriate response; how about action to ensure that you do spend the right amount?

In the debate between the economists and just about everybody else, Calabresi and Bobbitt are on the side of the angels but are less help to the angelic hosts than they might be, for two main reasons. First, because of the resolutely 'non-judgemental' (to use a hateful expression) character of the book, they make it too easy for an economist to say: 'Yes, unfortunately people are funny like that, but that simply shows they should either be ignored or straightened out.' (Schelling claims that it takes two hours to convert the average public policy student.)

[5] Thomas Schelling, 'Economic Reasoning and the Ethics of Policy', *Public Interest*, 63 (1981), 37–61, at 49.

[6] Ibid. 47.

Second, I believe that at a pre-analytic level Calabresi and Bobbitt concede far too much to the economists' general approach. At a number of points in the text, the authors come close to accepting the underlying idea that the object of social policy is to produce an equitable and/or efficient distribution of utility. They differ from economic orthodoxy by wanting to talk about the intensity of utility. But to allow that intensity of *desire* is the factor that should ideally enter into policy is already to concede the fundamental idea: that it is utility that matters, rather than the nature of specific actions, relationships, or conditions.

Thus, for example, in their discussion of political allocation, the authors in effect accept that the standard against which you judge any actual procedure is an ideal market (one with equitable or equal incomes). But there is simply no reason for accepting this. That a political allocation will not take account of the intensity of different people's relative desires to live (p. 36) or serve in the armed forces (p. 42) is an advantage rather than a disadvantage. Why should one suppose that intensity of desire should be the relevant feature, rather than something more objective such as relative need, against a background of equal priority for all, or equal priority for those of the same age? For many allocations, the appropriate criterion will refer to the resources directly and not to the utilities that we might conjecture are produced by them. Thus, the 'intensity' issue raised on pages 111–14 seems to me a red herring.

The same point is at issue in another discussion, in which Calabresi and Bobbitt consider a proposal that the length of national service in different branches of the armed services might be adjusted on a 'market-clearing' basis. That is to say, the less popular forms of military service would require a shorter period of conscription. They reject it by saying (pp. 92–3) that people value their time unequally. This objection seems to me either irrelevant or confused. What is the numeraire in terms of which this unequal value is supposed to be expressed? If money, all this shows is that rich people value everything more—expressed in terms of money—than do poor ones. But it is surely no valid objection to a scheme for distributing the burden of national service that it does not equate the money value of different people's time. That the rich value their time more highly in monetary terms than do the poor should be irrelevant here.

If money is not the numeraire, then what possibly could be? Since time is something that everybody has the same amount of, saying that some people value their lives more than others has no obvious meaning. It could be a way of suggesting that some people's lives are intrinsically more valuable than those of others (for example, that the lives of Whites are worth more than those of Blacks). Or it might be a way of suggesting that some people get more pleasure, happiness or whatever out of their lives than do other people. Neither consideration, however, seems to me one that social policy should take cognizance of in any society committed to the proposition that all citizens should be treated equally. The obnoxiousness of the first is patent. But the second also systematically advantages some over others by giving those who experience things more intensely than others an extra claim on resources. Yet as far as I can see, it is precisely this objectionable kind of comparison that Calabresi and Bobbitt have in mind when they speak (p. 92) of 'relative intensity' as something that allocations should reflect. It is, of course, perfectly valid to take into account the relative intensity of desire for different things *within* one person's life. But the kind of global judgement of relative intensity across people that Calabresi and Bobbitt apparently envisage should have no place.

Precisely because time is a resource that everyone has an equal amount of, the proposal for having different lengths of national service established to 'clear the market' seems to me a good one. It is, incidentally, an application of Bernard Shaw's proposal that everybody should be paid the same but that hours of work should be adjusted on a market-clearing basis so that those in jobs nobody wanted to do would work fewer hours. This is open to the objection that some people might prefer to work longer hours for more money or fewer hours for less, and it is hard to see why they should be prevented from doing so. But no similar objection can be made to the proposal for adjusting lengths of military service to clear the market, because the norm from which the bidding starts is clearly one of an equal length of service for all.

Calabresi and Bobbitt also object to queuing as a method of allocation on the same grounds, namely, that people value their time unequally. This is again a misguided objection. In so far as queuing simply measures the amount of time that people are prepared to give up in order to obtain something, it is an excellent way of allocating something scarce where ability to pay is considered an inappropriate criterion. The popularity of queuing as a method of allocation arises, indeed, precisely from its approximating a measure of the amount of time people are willing to give up in order to, for example, see a certain exhibition.

The objections to queuing are quite otherwise. The first is that it is only a rough and ready measure of willingness to give up time. It discriminates against the aged and infirm, and also favours those with flexible schedules over those with inflexible ones. But the most serious drawback is that the queuing itself constitutes a massive deadweight loss arising from the procedure. If willingness to queue could be established without actually making people queue there would be far more to be said for it.

In putting forward their case against allocating certain things such as medical care through the ordinary market mechanism, the authors take on board so much of the baggage of orthodox welfare economics that their argument fails to get off the ground. By accepting value-individualism (or ethereal anti-paternalism) they open themselves to destructive criticism in its own terms from the partisans of Pareto. And their proposal of 'wealth-neutral' markets is I think hard to defend against the kind of criticism Schelling would bring against it without bringing in staunchly paternalistic or 'merit want' considerations that the authors eschew in their discussion.

This requires some clarification, since the authors do make use of the notion of merit wants, but unfortunately they get it wrong, and this makes their discussion rather difficult to follow. According to them, the phenomenon of merit wants arises only from the maldistribution of income. (See p. 89 and n. 3 on p. 202.) Merit wants occur, they say, when the poor buy less of something than they would if they had more money *and* where this generates what the authors unfortunately fall in with the economists in calling 'external costs', which can include simply the fact that some people in the society do not feel that the resultant distribution of the thing is ethically right. However, if we go back to the original introduction of the term by Richard Musgrave, we can see that merit wants should be thought of as arising whenever the amount of something purchased by somebody on the market is thought (by someone) to be too small.[7] Questions of maldistribution of income thus need not come into it at all. The governments of Western Europe that put big subsidies into opera houses do not do so because operagoers enjoy below average incomes, nor is relative income of users the reason for subsidizing public libraries or national parks. These are thought to be things that a civilized society should provide. The case for providing them free or below costs is derived from 'quality of life' considerations, not distributive ones.

[7] R. A. Musgrave, *Theory of Public Finance* (New York: McGraw-Hill, 1959), 13.

Now we can obviously bring such things as health care and housing under Musgrave's notion of merit goods, by saying that they are good things that people should have. From this point of view it is immaterial whether they would buy more at cost price if they had more income or whether they would prefer the cash equivalent of the subsidy to spend on something else. But notice that this does entail an ineluctably paternalistic view. The alternative 'external costs' approach taken up by Calabresi and Bobbitt under the confusing title of 'merit wants' is, by contrast, indefensible. Either (unlike Schelling) I do care about your having medical care (as against having the equivalent in cash to spend as you like) or I do not. If I do, then it should be whatever *reason* I have for caring that should itself be the reason for your getting the care but not the cash. That is to say, I must be prepared to offer some reason for medical care being important and for its being right to provide it for you even if you would sooner take the cost of it in the form of cash instead and use it on drink with which to drown your sorrows. If my only reason for saying medical care but not money should be provided is that I happen to feel bad about your lack of medical care but not about your lack of money, and I think that social policy should be designed to make me feel good, I am justly open to the scorn of a Schelling. Couldn't I—*shouldn't* I—try to train myself to care about your utility rather than your medical care? If it is simply a matter of how I happen to feel about it, then I surely should.

This point can be made concrete by examining briefly the authors' idea of 'wealth-neutral' markets for, say, the right to have children or for medical insurance. The basic notion here is that the prices or subsidies should be set for each income stratum in the population (e.g. each quintile) so that on average people in each stratum will buy the same amount (have the same number of children, take the same value of insurance, etc.).[8] There is an obvious problem here that is glanced at by the authors but not taken seriously enough, namely, that people in different income bands may have different tastes, so that, for example,

[8] There is, incidentally, an error in reasoning on pp. 101–2 about the implications of a mixed price and subsidy scheme for children. The authors suggest that, if some have to pay to have children and others are paid not to, there must be some income group that achieves the putative ideal of 2.1 children without incentives. This is not so. What *is* true is that, if some mix of payments from people to have children and payments to people not to have children is used, there may be some group such that at some point the *pay-out* is zero. For example, if $2,000 a year is paid to couples in some income group not to have any children, $1,000 a year for having only one, and zero for having two, while $1,000 a year is to be paid by them for having a third child, $2,000 a year for having a fourth, and so on, there will be no payment for two children, in either direction. But of course such a couple still faces an effective cost of $1,000 for each child from the first to the *n*th.

the very rich might have to pay less for the right to have a child than the less rich. On the other hand, if there is likely to be uniformity across *individuals*, there is no point in creating anything so elaborate as a wealth-neutral market rather than simply providing everyone with the same amount—and indeed that is in my view the case for publicly provided health services rather than the authors' wealth-neutral market for insurance.

However, the obvious objection, to which Calabresi and Bobbitt do not pay any attention, is that a wealth-neutral market might well be colossally inefficient in the usual Pareto sense. Suppose that, to get the poorest group to buy on average as much health insurance as the richest group, one had to add nine dollars to every one dollar the poorest are prepared to pay themselves. Clearly, in line with standard consumer theory, one would not expect that a poor person who is given an extra nine dollars to spend will spend it all on medical insurance (or indeed on any one thing). Therefore, an economist will always point out, the poor person would get more utility (that is, prefer the resulting consumption bundle) if he were given the nine dollars in cash and left to spend it how he pleased, rather than being permitted to take it only in the form of extra medical insurance. Giving money allows for the attainment of Pareto optimality; giving it in kind generally precludes it.

Now it is true that one could not in practice guarantee that every poor person would gain from a switch to cash. For as a matter of practical implementation we could not actually offer the cash equivalent. It would obviously be open to gross strategic manipulation simply to ask each poor person how much he would have been willing to spend on medical insurance if a scheme to add nine dollars to every one dollar he spent himself had been in operation, and then give him in cash the amount of subsidization he would have received by spending that amount. We cannot therefore say that it would be a Pareto-superior move to take the money we expected to spend on the first scheme (assuming that we could estimate this by sample surveys) and divide it equally among the poor. (A Pareto-optimal situation is not of course Pareto-superior to every non-Pareto-optimal situation.) On the other hand, we can certainly say with confidence that *most* poor people will prefer getting the average amount that the scheme would have cost. Suppose that it would have cost $900 per head of the poorest section of the population. That implies that each would have spent, on average, $100 of his own money on insurance to get a total benefit of $1,000 in insurance. Now it is clear (on the basis of the standard reasoning) that someone who would have spent the average amount ($100) on insurance and got the average subsidy ($900) is no *worse* off by getting the $900 in cash instead, since he can put the cash into insurance if he chooses. He is almost certainly better off, since he almost certainly will not put more than a proportion of it into insurance. *A fortiori*, anyone who would have spent less than the average and got less than the average subsidy is definitely better off with the cash. This leaves those who would have spent more than $100 and would thus have got more than $900 in subsidy, and here the answer is indefinite. But we certainly cannot, of course, say that such people are necessarily worse off (measured in terms of their own preferences) with the $900 in cash. Suppose somebody would have spent $200 of his own money to get $1,800 in free supplementary medical insurance. The question is whether he values $900 in cash more than $1,800 in insurance: had he been offered a choice between those two options, which would he have taken? Some, we can assume, would prefer the insurance to a smaller amount in cash, and they are the losers from the alternative scheme. But their losses will, we can know for certain, be smaller in aggregate than the gains of those who gain. Thus, the alternative satisfies the two criteria of potential Pareto optimality *and* no adverse distributive effects between poor and rich. The redistribution is among the poor from those who have a greatly above-average taste for medical insurance to those with an average or below-average taste for it.

But this way of putting the point raises a deeper question, namely, whether it is possible to construct a coherent ethical rationale for wealth-neutral markets. I am not at all confident that it is. I have already argued against the 'external costs' approach. If we try to find a more secure foundation, it seems to me that it must be paternalistic; but I believe that this is liable to lead us to something other than wealth-neutral markets. Let me explain.

On the one hand, we have something which we shall call X (it may be the right to bear children or to obtain medical insurance, for example) which, *ex hypothesi*, has been judged appropriate for allocation through a market. This means (*a*) that people are to be faced with a choice between having more of X and spending more on other consumption items such as cigarettes or cinema tickets; and (*b*) that we will not do anything to stop somebody spending little or nothing on X if he chooses. On the other hand, we are concerned that, with an ordinary market, the poor will finish up with less (on the average) of X than the rich, and we want to prevent that from happening. We therefore arrange things so that, although they do (on the average) *spend* less, they *get* the same amount (on the average) of *X*.

The problem of ethical coherence, as I see it, is this. If we take the line that this thing, *X*, is 'too important to be left to the market', that is, that the amount of *X* someone gets should not depend on his income, do we not have to say that *X* has some intrinsic importance over and above its contribution to people's utility? For if it is important only in so far as it conduces to utility, there seems to be an obvious case for taking the money put into creating a wealth-neutral market for *X* and giving it to people as cash. Then, if they agree that *X* is as important as you think it is for their utility, they will in any case spend it on *X*. If they do not agree with you, they will spend it on something else, and (trivially, given the definition) get more utility. But if we say that *X* has some special virtue over and above its conduciveness to utility, why should the amount of it that people get be related (even via a modified market) to their willingness to give up other marketed things for it? If we once say that *X* has an importance not measured by utility, does this perhaps commit us to saying that people ought to get it whether they are willing to pay for it or not? If so, it looks as if we can justify a move away from a straight market only if we adopt a paternalistic position and attribute a virtue to *X* that is not reducible to its conduciveness to utility (i.e. its tendency to be chosen). But once we adopt that position we seem to be committed to going beyond a wealth-neutral market and saying that the allocation should not be related to tastes at all. The authors' halfway house between an ordinary market and a paternalistically based overriding of individual preferences thus seems to me to be insecurely founded.

This discussion bears on a related policy question that arises at the level of collectivities rather than individuals. Periodically the idea surfaces that the level of educational expenditures (and perhaps other 'essential services') should be related to 'tax effort'. That is to say, within some wider area (e.g. the State of California) each taxing authority (e.g. school district) should be provided with supplemental funds so that the product of a mil (a tenth of a cent) in property tax (or it could be a given rate of income tax or sales tax) is an equal per capita amount of revenue. So, somewhat parallel to the medical insurance case, a district which raises ten times less than the most prosperous one per mil will get nine dollars added to every one it raises. Then an equal 'tax effort' will give rise to an equal per capita expenditure.

But surely the problem just set out for the wealth-neutral market arises here. If education is simply another public good, producing utility for its consumers, why doesn't Schelling's analysis of the municipal airport lighting apply? That is to say, why not estimate the cost of the scheme and give the money as a block grant to school districts or municipalities so that the poorest ones get the most and so on, leaving them to spend it on anything they like? On the other hand, if education is a 'basic right', why should a child's educational opportunities (inasfar as these are affected by money spent on schools) depend on the willingness to pay of the voters in its school district, any more than it should depend on their *capacity* to pay? Once again, it seems hard to rationalize the intermediate stage between (*a*) adjusting incomes (not necessarily to the 'right' level but to the extent implied by a Calabresian wealth-neutral scheme) and then letting things rip, or (*b*) providing a uniform level of service regardless of either capacity *or* willingness to pay.

It may be that the wealth-neutral pricing idea can be revived not to carry the main burden of allocation of some merit good but to trim demand for it at the margin so as to reduce congestion. Suppose that we have made art galleries free or have provided a national health service without any user charges. We now find that there are too many people in front of the pictures and too many people in the doctors' waiting rooms. We might then be tempted to introduce some modest price arrangement to reduce the burden on other mechanisms (mainly queuing and administrative selection) that will be needed to control numbers. Clearly, the ideal would be to set before each person an equal-sized hurdle (a difficult idea to make precise let alone operational, but I take it as intuitively intelligible) so that two people with a sore throat of equal severity or an equal yen to see the treasures of King Tut will be deterred to just the same degree by the price levied. This could obviously be done only by making the price sensitive to income, and this is the basic notion of the wealth-neutral market. In practice, of course, nothing very refined is ever done along these lines. Art galleries with charges for admission have a regular rate and then lower rates for members of groups with low average incomes—the young, the old, and the unemployed. Prescription charges under the National Health Service are waived for those already certified as poor and receiving cash benefits. There are also 'season tickets' for the chronically sick and usually for art museum enthusiasts, in order to work in 'special needs'. Since this structure of pricing is obviously far too crude to present anything like equal deterrence (especially among those who pay the standard price) it cannot be relied on to do much: in practice other restrictions have to be used, and we in fact find queues for popular exhibitions and congested doctors' waiting rooms.

This analysis suggests that the most plausible case for wealth-neutral pricing is to deter. The obverse of deterrence is inducement. And I think that my argument about the relative suitability of wealth-neutral markets for deterrence can be strengthened by noting that the use of such markets seems especially unattractive for inducement. Consider the idea tossed out in passing by the authors (p. 140) for a 'wealth-neutral market for subjects in medical experimentation'. This might involve paying people in the top tranche (those with an income of over, say, $100,000 per annum) several thousands of dollars to get enough of them to undergo some experiment that an equal proportion of people in, say, the poorest 10 per cent of the population could be induced to undergo for less than $100. Since a wealth-neutral market is by definition one in which each income group has to be induced to produce an equal proportion of 'volunteers', the richest segment of the population can in effect hold out for being paid a great deal just because they do not need the money and thus have to be bribed heavily to accept some given degree of inconvenience, discomfort, or health risk. Conversely, the very poor, just because they desperately need the money, lose out. The willingness of many of them to become experimental subjects in return for a relatively small amount of compensation means that they will in fact get paid only a little.

Again, consider the all-volunteer army. A lot of people in the USA are worried about the fact that this (inevitably) attracts disproportionate numbers of Blacks, since they are the people to whom the jobs, given their actual alternatives, look most attractive. This concern is partly political—especially for those who hope to see American troops fighting Communism in Africa in the next few decades—but there is also a rather fuzzy moral sentiment about Blacks carrying an 'unfair share' of the risks involved in defending the country. The obvious 'Calabresian' response would be to have low pay rates for Blacks and high pay rates for Whites, adjusted until Whites and Blacks are proportionately represented in the army. (Not too appetizing as a piece of public policy!) Similarly, an objection to paid blood donation on the line that the poor (and racial minorities) will finish up by giving most of the blood could be met by paying more to middle-class Whites.

My own view is that the fundamental issue in these cases is whether to recruit by appealing to pure self-interest ('Do it if, consulting your own private preferences, the price makes it worth it') or whether to make it a matter of social obligation, either giving rise to appeals to altruism (British blood donorship or volunteering for the British Expeditionary Force in 1914–16)[9] or to authoritative political decision (the draft or perhaps a lottery for experimental subjects). If you opt for the market approach to recruitment, then it seems to me you must accept that the effect will be to attract disproportionately those to whom a given amount of money in return for a given obligation looks most attractive, that is to say, those with fewer alternative opportunities. If you are queasy about that outcome, you should prefer an alternative method of recruitment.

[9] There is a subtle but all-important difference, which could not be captured in any standard economic analysis, between paying people *who* volunteer and paying people *to* volunteer. Volunteers are always paid by the army: the question is whether the pay is (and is supposed to be) the sole motivation. Thus, the evidence from the time makes it clear that the overwhelming majority of those who joined the British Expeditionary Force in the first year of the First World War did so because they saw it as a patriotic duty, not because the career prospects looked attractive in relation to civilian alternatives. I doubt if any major country has come as close this century to regarding its regular army as a collection of mercenaries who just happen to be citizens as has the contemporary USA. One might speculate that this can occur only in a country that never expects to use its army to repel an invasion: the French had the Foreign Legion for fighting overseas but assumed that direct threats to *la patrie* would be met by the draft.

15

CAN STATES BE MORAL?

International Morality and the Compliance Problem

> It is quite a mistake to suppose that real dishonesty is at all common. The number of rogues is about equal to the number of men who act honestly; and it is very small. The great majority would sooner behave honestly than not. The reason why they do not give way to this natural preference for humanity is that they are afraid that others will not; and the others do not because they are afraid that *they* will not. Thus it comes about that, while behaviour which looks dishonest is fairly common, sincere dishonesty is about as rare as the courage to evoke good faith in your neighbours by showing that you trust them.
>
> F. M. Cornford, *Microcosmographia Academica*

I

In the last few years I have presented a number of papers to various audiences on issues of international morality and have also conducted several courses for college students and professionals. From experience, I can safely make the generalization that in any such context sooner or later (and usually sooner) the objection will come up that this is merely flailing the air. For, it is said, the conduct of states is not an appropriate subject for moral evaluation or censure. Of course, some people will suggest that there is no point in moral discourse in any sphere of life. This kind of universal moral scepticism raises deep philosophical issues which would be well worth discussing on some other occasion. But for the present purpose I wish to direct my attention to those who do not deny the appropriateness of moral appraisal in ordinary life but who do nevertheless hold that it is inappropriate in the international arena.

Why might someone make a distinction along these lines? Two reasons seem to be most commonly put forward for scepticism specifically about international morality. The first is that governments almost invariably pursue the national interest whenever it conflicts with the interests of other countries, and in any case they have a duty to their citizens to do so. The second reason has been expressed as follows by Terry Nardin (although this is not his own view):

> The international system is not to any appreciable extent a society united by common rules, but simply an aggregate of separate societies each pursuing its own purposes, and linked with one another in ways that are essentially ad hoc, unstable, and transitory. The conduct of each state may in fact be rule-governed, in the sense that each observes rules of its own choosing. But because the decisions of each are governed by different rules, the separate states cannot be said to be members of a single society of states united by common rules of conduct—rules whose authority is acknowledged by all states.[1]

The reasoning that connects the two is, roughly speaking, that if each state pursues its own national interest, a given state will comply with common rules only to the extent that it can be made to be in that state's interest to comply. But, in the absence of 'a common Power to keep them all in awe', as Hobbes put it,[2] there is no way of ensuring that most states will comply most of the time with any set of rules. So there are not, in any real sense, any rules governing international conduct.

Before going any further, it is worth observing that both of these points have analogues in common-sense morality as it operates within societies. This would cut no ice if we were dealing with a universal moral sceptic. But since we are not this is a potentially significant finding. Thus, in common-sense morality it is generally held to be acceptable (and indeed under some conditions praiseworthy) for different people to have different 'moral aims'.[3] That is, we do not believe there is a single good that all have an equal moral obligation to pursue. Instead we believe, for example, that it is right for a given individual to pay more attention (or give more weight) to the interests of persons to whom he or she is related by ties of family or other association and commitment than to the interests of others. (This includes giving more weight to one's own interests than to those of randomly selected others.)

In common-sense morality it is also generally thought that there is a class of social norms to which adherence is morally obligatory only if

[1] Terry Nardin, *Law, Morality, and the Relations of States* (Princeton, NJ: Princeton University Press, 1983), 36.

[2] Thomas Hobbes, *Leviathan*, C. B. Macpherson (ed.) (Harmondsworth: Penguin Books, 1981), ch. 13, p. 185.

[3] Derek Parfit, *Reasons and Persons* (Oxford: Clarendon Press, 1984). For an earlier, simpler, and clearer exposition, see 'Prudence, Morality, and the Prisoner's Dilemma', *Proceedings of the British Academy*, 65 (1979), 539–64, esp. p. 559.

enough other people adhere to them. With a practice that is collectively beneficial provided that it is generally observed (the standard philosophical example is refraining from wearing a path by taking a short cut across a lawn), the presumption is that fairness requires each person to observe it on the condition that enough others do so to achieve the object served by the norm. On the other hand, if the norm is not efficacious in providing people with a reason that they accept (and act on) for eschewing their private, antisocial interests, then the moral obligation on each one to observe the norm tends to evaporate.

I am being deliberately vague about the form of the relation between compliance by others and the obligation to conform to a rule oneself because I believe that relation will vary according to the details of the case. In some instances, just one bit of non-compliance releases everyone else from an obligation to refrain from doing what the norm prohibits. If one neighbour shatters the peace of the neighbourhood by using a power mower early on a Sunday morning, it does not make much difference if others do so too. But in other instances much of the collective benefit may be achieved even with a substantial amount of non-compliance.[4] If only three-quarters of householders in a city centre comply with a rule against burning garden refuse, the air may be much less dirty than if there were no restraint, and this might plausibly be thought to generate an obligation of fairness to comply, albeit a weaker one than if compliance were closer to being universal.

I should emphasize that the structure of common-sense morality is not utilitarian, since this may not be apparent from these examples. The question is not simply which act—compliance or non-compliance—would have the most net beneficial consequences, given what all the others are doing. It is true that in some cases the dictates of common sense will coincide with those of utilitarianism. If, for example, so many people have already walked across the grass that a path of completely bare earth has been created, utilitarianism and common sense would agree that there is no moral obligation on anyone to refrain from taking the short cut. This can be called the 'threshold effect'. Here utilitarianism and common sense unite in dissenting from the view held by some philosophers that, even when some threshold has been passed, the right thing to do is unaffected by the absence of beneficial consequences.

Such a view is characteristically arrived at by taking a framework for moral decisionmaking that is not unreasonable in itself, but then

[4] Brian Barry and Russell Hardin (eds.), *Rational Man and Irrational Society? An Introduction and Sourcebook* (Beverly Hills, Calif.: Sage, 1982), 108.

applying it too immediately and simplistically, without recognizing the need for institutional mediation between the ultimate criterion and the demands of morality in concrete situations. One way in which this happens is that Kant's formulation of the categorical imperative—that one must be able to will the maxim of one's action as a universal law—is misapplied. (One can with perfect consistency will universal adoption of the maxim that one walks across the grass whenever, because of the actions of others, there is no point in not doing so.) Another route which can lead to the same conclusion is to take ideal rule utilitarianism—the doctrine that the best set of rules is that which would have the best consequences if it enjoyed general adherence—and then to say that the right thing to do in any actual situation is to act on the rules of ideal morality so understood, whether or not others either recognize or act on these rules.

According to common sense it is mere quixotry to feel obliged to do something that is in fact pointless simply because it would have a point in some counterfactual state of the world. And I think the common-sense position will withstand any amount of philosophical scrutiny. There are some who claim to find an argument against utilitarianism (that is, act utilitarianism, not the curious form of ideal rule utilitarianism mentioned above) in that it gets what they regard as the 'wrong answer' in threshold cases. They are, in my view, kicking the ball through their own goal: what they regard as an argument is actually a *reductio ad absurdum*.

Common-sense morality is thus not unconcerned with beneficial overall consequences in evaluating actions. But it differs from utilitarianism in that it is not concerned solely with the production of beneficial overall consequences. The prescriptions of the two will normally coincide in threshold cases, but even then the way in which they reach their shared conclusions is not quite the same. For utilitarianism the decisive point—and the only one that could possibly matter—is simply that, given that others have already worn a path in the grass, there is no collective benefit gained from walking around the edge that can be set against the benefit the agent himself gains from cutting across. There is obviously then a net overall benefit from cutting across. The line taken by common-sense morality includes all of the above considerations, but it does not stop there. It goes on to say that there is no collective benefit that others can help provide: if other people go to the trouble of walking around, they are merely taking gratuitous exercise. Since there is no collective benefit from which one gains as a result of the forbearances of others, there can be no unfairness in not contributing to it oneself, and this is the real reason why it is morally permissible to walk across the grass. To introduce a new metaphor, one cannot properly be accused of being a free rider if the train never leaves the station.

In a threshold case, this extra loop is trivial because there is no way in which one can help provide any collective benefit by one's own action, even if one wishes to. This is precisely the reason for the conclusion of common-sense morality coinciding with that of utilitarianism. Fairness does not enter in because the issue of fairness is pre-empted by the recognition that the 'co-operative' move does not in fact do anybody any good. We might say that the utilitarian conclusion is determined by its own single criterion, whereas the more complex common-sense conclusion is overdetermined.

To see that there really is a difference between the practical implications of common sense and those of utilitarianism, we need only look at a non-threshold case. It does not have to be one in which the net benefit from an agent's contributing to a public good is invariant with respect to the number of others who contribute. That is the simplest case. But the general form of the relation we require is simply that, even when few other people are contributing, there is still a net benefit to be gained from any given agent's contribution (after subtracting the cost to the agent of producing the increment of collective benefit enjoyed by all). Such cases are quite common in real life, though it will often be hard to establish the amount of collective gain from a single contribution in order to compare it to the cost of that contribution to the actor. But Derek Parfit is correct in calling it a 'mistake in moral mathematics' to suppose that a small effect diffused over a large number of people is not a real effect; it may be significant in determining the moral quality of the act that brings it about.[5]

Returning to the example of air pollution, we may observe that there may be no upper threshold in many cases. Even if everyone living in the city centre except me is burning soft coal, it is quite possible that there is still a net benefit from my refraining from doing so: the overall reduction in air pollution outweighs the cost to me of using some alternative means of heating. On the utilitarian criterion, this is enough to generate the conclusion that I have a moral obligation to refrain from adding my smoke to the pall already created by the others. But, according to the dictates of common-sense morality, I have no such obligation. The failure of the others to contribute to the

[5] Parfit, *Reasons and Persons*, pp. 78–82.

collective good—clean air—releases me from the moral obligation to do so myself. I cannot reasonably be accused of behaving unfairly if I fail to act on a norm that so many others who are similarly situated are failing to act on.

We can again make the point by using the 'free rider' metaphor. In the previous case there was nothing I could do by myself to make the train go. Here the point is simply that, even if I do not pay my fare, I am not riding at the expense of others. In this case, my fare would suffice to move the train a minute fraction of an inch, but then the others would be free riding at my expense. I have no obligation to give them a free—even if extremely short—ride.

Common-sense morality is capable of discriminating between different kinds of moral judgement. Thus, although in the situation described it would not be morally obligatory to refrain from burning soft coal, it would certainly be admirable. Anyone who did so would be exhibiting the virtue of beneficence. Common-sense morality differs from utilitarianism in that it denies that what does the most good is in general obligatory and that it recognizes other virtues besides beneficence, such as that of behaving justly towards others.

For utilitarianism, then, the relevance of what other people are doing is purely contingent: we need to know what they are doing simply because it may make a difference to the net benefit that a single act of contribution would bring. But once the presence of a net benefit has been established, there is an obligation to contribute, regardless of how few others are contributing. Indeed, we can imagine a case, such as traffic congestion, in which the fewer who contribute by refraining from driving, the larger the net benefit from a single act of contribution. Then, by the utilitarian criterion, the obligation to contribute becomes more stringent the smaller the proportion of others who contribute. According to common-sense morality, however, the obligation of fair play would always diminish as the number of contributors diminished. None the less, if a single contribution would do a lot of good, and particularly if it would alleviate suffering or destitution, then it might be required by common-sense morality as an obligation of humanity. Normally, however, benefits that fit this description are not collective in character.

II

So far I have suggested that the two grounds most often advanced for denying that international affairs can be subjected to moral appraisal have clear analogues in what common-sense morality holds about morality within societies. Corresponding to the claim that political leaders have a right, perhaps even a duty, to pursue the national interest is the notion that people have their own legitimately differing 'moral ends', which will permit or possibly even require them to give more weight to their own interests and to those of people connected to them than they give to the interests of others. And, corresponding to the claim that the lack of assurance that other states will comply with international norms releases states from any obligation to observe them, there is in common-sense morality a complex connection between the degree of compliance by others and the obligation to conform to a norm oneself.

My purpose in pointing out these connections is simply to examine the following question: if these two features of common-sense morality are not usually thought to cause it to self-destruct as a source of moral obligations and other moral phenomena (and I believe that in fact they do not), why should it be supposed that their international analogues must have such devastating implications for the possibility of moral appraisal in international affairs?

Let us take up in turn the two alleged grounds for the amorality of the international order. The relevant implication for states of the notion of different 'moral ends' is that governments have some duties—possibly quite extensive—towards their own citizens that they do not owe to citizens of other countries. (Those who prefer to formulate issues of political obligation in lateral rather than hierarchical terms could express this by saying that citizens of a single country owe one another things that they do not owe citizens of other countries.) But this does not mean that anything goes. Generally speaking, my special obligation to my family does not legitimate lying, stealing, cheating, or killing on their behalf. The special obligation is set in a context of constraints on the morally acceptable means of advancing my moral ends.

It would seem that countries are in a position exactly analogous to this. We can easily allow that a government has duties to its own citizens that it does not owe to people in other countries. But again, this does not mean that the government has a moral licence to do anything to advance the national interest without regard to possible violation of the legitimate interests of others. (Is there anything magical, after all, about one particular grouping—a nation-state—that can dissolve all wider moral considerations? Why should this one level of association be exempted from moral constraints that apply to all others?)

To the extent that we can talk about a common international morality, it takes the form of a belief that there are morally binding constraints on how governments can pursue their national interest. This raises the second alleged ground for the amorality of the international order: how can there be morally binding constraints without a centralized agency of enforcement? In the Hobbesian 'condition of mere Nature' which characterizes the relations of states with one another, would not anyone adhering to moral constraints 'but betray himself to his enemy'? 'For he that would be modest, and tractable, and perform all he promises, in such time, and place, where no man else should do so, should but make himself a prey to others, and secure his own certain ruine.'[6]

The simple answer, which is not complete but is still worth giving, is that the moral norms that govern everyday life in a society are generally not backed by legal sanctions either but are none the less quite broadly effective in restraining conduct. The response will inevitably come that this evades the issue because the security provided by legal enforcement provides the essential underpinnings of a whole system of mutual restraint within a society. This argument undeniably has an element of truth. International relations, in contrast, are fundamentally conditioned by the absence of an agency capable of enforcing compliance. A state normally commands a monopoly on the use of violence within its territory, whereas international law and morality permit the waging of war under certain conditions. However, the notion that in the absence of a core of centrally enforced norms there can be no others that are effective is simply erroneous. Huge numbers of international transactions take place every day on the basis of norms that the parties rely on and, in fact, adhere to—some codified into international law and others developed through custom.

It is true that much of the compliance with these norms can be accounted for by the rational pursuit of interest. It is to a state's advantage to not be excluded from the system of diplomatic relations, to have a reputation as a reliable trading partner, and so on. Hobbes, who is often regarded as an authority by the realists, deduced from the postulate of survival that one should 'seek peace' in the state of nature. He drew up a long list of prescriptions—'laws of nature'—that should be acted upon as long as doing so is compatible with safety. 'He that having sufficient Security, that others shall observe the same Lawes

[6] Hobbes, *Leviathan*, ch. 14, p. 196; ch. 15, p. 215.

towards him, observes them not himself, seeketh not Peace, but War; & consequently the destruction of his Nature by Violence.'[7]

In practice, states can often follow the (admittedly quite undemanding) prescriptions of positive international morality without putting their security at risk in the slightest. It is equally true that much of the time there are self-interested motives for sticking to the prescriptions of common-sense morality in everyday life. And ordinary experience shows that, to the extent that others observe the norms, we feel an obligation to do so too. Perhaps the truth is that most of the time we do not inquire too minutely into the reasons for doing what is required. We recognize the general advantageousness of the system and accept its authority in guiding our actions. States are, I would suggest, not very different in this respect. Their standard operating procedures are to adhere to the appropriate international norms; it would actually be unworkable to have to determine on every occasion where the exact balance of long-term and overall interest lies before taking action.

I have conceded, however, that because common international morality does not ask a lot, the question of reasons for adhering to it is not a very pressing one. Nardin has summed it up as follows:

> The moral element in international law is to be found in those general principles of international association that constitute customary international law, and above all in the most fundamental of those principles, such as the ones specifying the rights of independence, legal equality, and self-defense, and the duties to observe treaties, to respect the immunity of ambassadors, to refrain from aggression, to conduct hostilities in war in accordance with the laws of war, to respect human rights, and to cooperate in the peaceful settlement of disputes.[8]

When we look at economic affairs, what is striking is the absence of any international system comparable to that within nations to tax those who can afford it to provide assistance to those who would otherwise be destitute. This does not mean that there is no mechanism for international redistribution: the World Bank does after all make loans on favourable terms to poor countries. But these are discretionary and in any case do not represent a sizeable transfer. The domestic analogue would be closer to a system of soft loans from the government to small businesses than to a welfare system. Here, no doubt, the absence of coercion makes itself strongly felt. If contributions to government coffers were raised by voluntary subscription, even tax

[7] Ibid., ch. 15, p. 215.

[8] Nardin, *Law, Morality, and the Relations of States*, p. 23.

rates of 10 per cent would be regarded as visionary and utopian, as they are in the international context. We would hear that it asks far too much of human nature for the wealthy to tithe themselves to benefit the poor. The affluent countries are committed in principle to give 0.7 per cent of gross national product as official aid, but even that rate greatly exceeds the amount that almost any country actually provides.

III

Is this an inevitable consequence of the lack of an international sovereign? The best way to approach this question is indirectly. Let us first ask what the ideal would be if we were to ignore the problem of compliance, and then see what adaptations would be required. We must know our aim before we can tell how far short of the target we are bound to fall.

What exactly do we mean by 'ideal morality'? Derek Parfit, who makes heavy use of the notion, defines an 'ideal act theory' as one that 'says what we should all try to do, simply on the assumptions that we all try, and all succeed'.[9] This is not quite right, because ideal morality should not include prescriptions to attempt things that we have good reason to believe people, or collectivities such as states, could not succeed in doing if they tried. We are interested here in utopian thinking—not science fiction. In constructing a 'full compliance' theory of morality,[10] we should look for one that abstracts from what I have called the 'compliance problem'. This is the problem that people may not act on the prescriptions embodied in a normative system that covers them, even though they could do so perfectly well if they chose. We normally focus on the prospect that people will fail to comply because prescriptions of morality ask them to act in some way that runs contrary to (what they perceive as) their self-interest. But we must also allow for the prospect that people may simply not accept as valid the particular set of prescriptions with which we are concerned.

Since many people are familiar with the concept of 'ideal theory' as introduced by John Rawls in *A Theory of Justice*, it may avoid confusion if I discuss the ways in which my notion of ideal theory agrees with or departs from his. The point of similarity is that Rawls equates ideal theory with what he calls 'strict compliance theory',[11] by which he means a theory of justice constructed on the assumption that

[9] Parfit, *Reasons and Persons*, p. 99.
[10] Ibid.
[11] John Rawls, *A Theory of Justice* (Cambridge, Mass.: Harvard University Press, 1971), 8, 9.

'the parties can depend on one another to conform to them'.[12] But my conception of ideal theory diverges sharply from that of Rawls in an important way.

In constructing an ideal theory we must, Rawls says, address what he calls 'the strains of commitment'. By this he means that people may find it difficult or impossible to adhere to some sets of principles.[13] This might be interpreted as being equivalent to my demand for utopia rather than science fiction: we do not want principles that require people to do what is impossible or even difficult if this implies that people are liable to fail if they try. But this is not what Rawls has in mind.

Rawls says that, even when designing an ideal theory, we should throw out 'principles which may have consequences so extreme that [people] could not accept them in practice'. And his example of an 'extreme' principle is the utilitarian principle that people should act to maximize overall well-being. For this requires some people 'to accept lower prospects of life for the sake of others'. (By lower prospects Rawls presumably means lower than the prospects under some alternative principle.) Thus, the utilitarian principle as a basis for a social ethic 'is threatened with instability unless sympathy and benevolence can be widely and intensively cultivated'. Without a word of discussion, Rawls assumes that this cannot be done, and immediately concludes that we should 'reject the principle of utility'.[14]

This cavalier disposition of an important and difficult psychological question illustrates precisely what is wrong with Rawls's conception of ideal theory. By incorporating the problem of compliance (as I have defined it) under the description of 'the strains of commitment', Rawls moves too fast in the direction of practicality, while at the same time stopping short of it. His 'ideal theory' is an unsatisfactory hybrid of ideal and practical considerations—and is neither really ideal nor really practical.

The theory makes large concessions (perhaps too large) to the fact that people may not be willing to do things that are perfectly within their power but which would require them to make sacrifices. At the same time, the theory assumes that, provided some threshold of 'non-demandingness' is passed—Rawls supposes that his own theory passes this threshold—we can assume absolute and invariable compliance with the dictates of the theory. It is hard to know what to do with such a theory. It seems better to start from an ideal uncontaminated by the

[12] Ibid. 145. [13] Ibid.
[14] All quotes in this para. are from ibid., p. 178.

compliance problem and then, moving away from that point, to introduce *all* the problems of compliance in their awful variety and complexity.

In thinking about the dimensions of the compliance problem, we should notice that there are two ways in which an ideal theory may run into difficulties with compliance. These two ways do not invariably go together and there is some reason to believe that they tend to be inversely related. First, an ideal theory of morality may run into practical difficulties because it is excessively *liable* to non-compliance. Second, it may run into difficulties if it is excessively *vulnerable* to non-compliance.

Other things being equal, a rule will be less liable to non-compliance the less that conformity with it entails a conflict with some strong desire, the more readily that non-compliance can be monitored by others, and the more incentive that others have to react to non-compliance in a way that reduces or eliminates the advantage gained. Other things being equal, a rule will be less vulnerable to non-compliance the less any level of non-compliance affects the value of the rule. In particular, it is important that the point of the rule—the ends that justify it—should not be frustrated by a small number of cases of non-compliance.

IV

I shall return to non-compliance later. For now let me relax the constraint imposed by problems of compliance and ask what an ideal set of international norms would look like, focusing particularly on the question of international economic distribution.

There is an influential view (put forward by among others John Rawls in *A Theory of Justice*) that distributive justice can be predicated only on relations within a society, where a society is understood as a scheme for mutual advantage through joint participation in co-operative undertakings. The idea is that distributive justice concerns the distribution of gains from social co-operation. This seems mistaken if it is seen as setting the limits of distributive justice.

If one country builds tall smokestacks and pumps sulphur into the atmosphere, which descends on another country downwind in the form of acid rain, then it has injured the other and, as a matter of justice, should either clean up its industry or compensate the other country. There need be no reciprocal advantage or even any other form of relationship between the two. Not all economic value is created by the co-operative effort that goes into it; production requires a production site, capital, and usually raw materials. The notion that claims of justice can arise only among those engaging in a co-operative enterprise puts things backwards. Before co-operation can occur, distributive questions must have already been answered about rights over land, resources, and other advantages that would-be co-operators did not themselves create. As a matter of ideal morality, the answer currently accepted in the international community—that each state has an absolute right to everything within, under, over, and extending two hundred miles beyond its national boundary—is a rotten one. But my present point is simply that an answer must be given to these distributive questions, and that that answer will establish a global distribution of some kind among countries that need have no co-operative relations at all.

The insistence on co-operation as a condition of morality stems from a conception of morality as a scheme of mutual advantage from mutual restraint. This, however, introduces the compliance issue too soon and too strongly. It provides a self-interested motive for compliance with moral norms by making the content of moral norms entirely coincident with what a sophisticated calculation of self-interest would require.

There is an alternative conception of morality that can be found in Rawls, sitting uneasily alongside the one discussed above—one which has been put forward most clearly by Thomas Scanlon,[15] although it was anticipated by, for example, David Hume and Adam Smith. According to this tradition of thought, there is a strong connection between morality and impartiality. A moral position is one that can be accepted from any viewpoint. It is not enough for me to say, 'This arrangement suits me.' The arrangement must be capable of being defended to all those affected; if any other person affected could not reasonably be expected to accept it in the absence of coercion, then the arrangement cannot be morally justified. I have already pointed out that much of the time there are good reasons of self-interest for doing what the moral norms of one's society require. According to this alternative conception of morality, the primary motive for behaving morally for its own sake is simply 'the desire to be able to justify one's actions to others on grounds they could not reasonably reject', where

[15] Thomas M. Scanlon, 'Contractualism and Utilitarianism', in Amartya Sen and Bernard Williams (eds.), *Utilitarianism and Beyond* (Cambridge: Cambridge University Press, 1982), 103–28.

the basis for others' reasonable rejection of one's actions is given by *their* 'desire to find principles which others similarly motivated could not reasonably reject'.[16]

This may appear to be a circular definition of morality and the moral motive because the notion of 'reasonableness' already presupposes that people have some moral ideas. I am not sure how Scanlon would reply to this charge, but I believe it ought to be admitted. There are two ways in which we can avoid giving reasonableness a moral tinge, but both of them mask the central idea of the theory in the process of tidying it up.

One possibility is to impute to the parties purely self-interested motivations, so that each will agree only to whatever will best serve his or her interests. Reasonableness is thus construed as if it corresponded to the 'rationality' of game theorists and decision theorists, and indeed, this interpretation of reasonableness would make moral theory a subject for one or the other of those disciplines.

If we set things up so that the parties have conflicting ends (as they usually do in real life) we get a problem for game theory. It seems plausible that there must be some arrangement that is better for everybody than a free-for-all. The problem is to identify the pay-offs offered by a free-for-all and then to devise some rule for distributing the gains that can be achieved by moving away from a free-for-all towards this other arrangement. We thus arrive at a theory like that of David Gauthier,[17] behind whom stands the sardonic figure of Hobbes.

If, on the other hand, we eliminate conflicting interests by introducing constraints on the information available to the parties about their respective positions—a 'veil of ignorance', as Rawls calls it—we get a decision-theoretic problem. Since the veil of ignorance, whatever the precise details of its construction, gives each party identical information to work with—information laundered of any clues that would enable them to differentiate among themselves—they are all faced with the same set of calculations. Hence, we can represent the problem as one presented to a single decisionmaker. This produces theories such as Harsanyi's derivation of utilitarianism from the maximizing of expected utility,[18] or one strand of Rawls's theory of justice, where a conservative, risk-aversive (maximin) rule for making choices under uncertainty is seen as leading to the difference principle, which

[16] Ibid. 116; 116 n. 12.

[17] David Gauthier, *Morals by Agreement* (New York: Oxford University Press, 1986).

[18] John C. Harsanyi, 'Cardinal Welfare, Individualistic Ethics, and Interpersonal Comparisons of Utility', *Journal of Political Economy*, 63 (1955), 309–21.

prescribes that the position of those who are worst off should be raised to as high a level as possible.[19]

The other method we could use to purge the notion of reasonableness of any moral content would be to take Scanlon's formula literally and suppose that the parties are *solely* motivated by the desire to reach agreement. Under this version we would not impute to them any substantive views at all about the acceptability of one outcome over any other. This line of thought would bring the problem of the terms of agreement under yet a third branch of formal theory. We would look to the work on pure co-ordination problems pioneered by Thomas Schelling in *The Strategy of Conflict*[20]—the sort of problem that arises when two people want to meet in a town without having made prior arrangements, and therefore each tries to decide where he will have the best chance of meeting the other, given the knowledge that the other is trying to make the same decision.[21] The moral theory that arises from this is conventionalism: the content of morality is arbitrary, but it is still binding because it matters that we all act on the same rules, whatever they may be. Morality, in this view, becomes the search for 'prominent solutions' (or 'Schelling points', as they have come to be known) in situations where some rule is needed.[22]

The youthful David Hume, ever on the look-out for paradoxes with which to jolt the world of polite learning into paying him some attention, came close in the *Treatise* to maintaining that rules governing property are conventional in this way. The operations of the 'fancy'—the disposition of the human mind to make associations between different ideas where there is no connection in reality—were invoked to explain why the details of the rules about property took the form they did.[23] But by the time he wrote the *Enquiry*,[24] Hume had modified his position and maintained only that fanciful analogies or associations of ideas might come into play in order to settle the issue between two or more alternative rules that were equally beneficial.

[19] See Brian Barry, *The Liberal Theory of Justice* (Oxford: Clarendon Press, 1973), ch. 9, pp. 87–107; and Rolf E. Sartorius, *Individual Conduct and Social Norms* (Encino, Calif.: Dickenson, 1975), 122–9.

[20] Thomas C. Schelling, *The Strategy of Conflict* (Cambridge, Mass.: Harvard University Press, 1960), ch. 4, pp. 83–118.

[21] See also David Lewis, *Convention* (Cambridge, Mass.: Harvard University Press, 1969).

[22] See Karol Sołtan, *The Causal Theory of Justice* (Berkeley and Los Angeles: University of California Press, 1987).

[23] David Hume, *A Treatise of Human Nature*, L. A. Selby-Bigge (ed.), 2nd edn. by P. H. Niddich (Oxford: Clarendon Press, 1978), vol. iii. sec. 3, pp. 501–13.

[24] David Hume, *An Enquiry Concerning the Principles of Morals*, in *Enquiries*, L. A. Selby-Bigge (ed.), 3rd edn. by P. H. Niddich (Oxford: Clarendon Press, 1975).

This is surely much more plausible. The rule, for example, which assigns the lambs to the owner of the ewe stems not merely from a tendency for the 'fancy' to run from the one to the other but also from the rule's convenience and its avoiding the creation of perverse incentives.[25] The rule of the road—to drive on the right or to drive on the left—is scarcely the paradigm of a moral rule. Usually it does make a difference what the content of the rule is.

I have spoken of two ways to construe the notion of reasonableness so as to purge it of distinctly moral content. If we assimilate reasonableness to the rational pursuit of self-interest, we get a problem in game theory or in decision theory, depending upon what we do about information conditions. If we press to the limit the idea of seeking an agreement with others who are also seeking one, we get a problem of co-ordinating expectations. I have mentioned in passing the great implausibility of the second approach. Regarding the first, I shall only say that seeking to transform what was intended as a guide for thinking about morality into a calculus capable of deriving moral conclusions from premisses devoid of any moral content seems to me to miss the original point.

The notion of reasonableness is admittedly indefinite, but it is not devoid of content. What we need to do to build up the theory is to specify it further, not substitute some simpler and more tractable notion. Thus, if we say that somebody has made a reasonable offer, we generally mean that it is an offer that the other party would be reasonable in accepting. A reasonable person is one who has a tendency to make—and accept—reasonable offers. We will have to tighten this definition if we want to characterize further the range of reasonable offers in some specific situation (and it is likely to be a range rather than a unique position). But even without going further, we can be quite sure that a reasonable offer will not be identified with a rationally maximizing offer, either with full information or behind some kind of veil of ignorance.

I do not now have the fully developed theory in hand, though I hope to in a few years' time.[26] For now I must press on with the problem of this chapter. So far I have only pointed at the way in which morality might be understood as that which it would be reasonable for all to accept. Let me suggest, without filling in all the steps, how evidence

[25] Ibid. 195–6.

[26] The first instalment of what is promised here is *Theories of Justice* (Berkeley and Los Angeles: University of California Press, 1989). This is the first volume in a 3-volume *Treatise on Social Justice* which will, taken together, constitute my attempt to give substance to the approach laid out in this chapter.

from the real world can be brought to bear in order to establish what this conception of morality dictates for international distribution.

As the theory stands, it sets up an ideal decisionmaking context of uncoerced agreement that is found only rarely and, it seems safe to say, never in large groups such as states.[27] Nevertheless, societies approach the ideal to varying degrees, and it is not mere sentimentalism or unreflective submission to the local ideology to suggest that the modern, Western liberal-democratic states are, by comparative and historical standards, relatively high on the criterion of unforced agreement. With obvious exceptions such as Northern Ireland, the gaols do not contain many political prisoners, and no sizeable section of the population is thoroughly alienated from the society's major institutions. Suppose, then, that we look for invariant features of these societies. If we find them, can we not at least say that we have a presumption in favour of assuming that these features are ones that arise in conditions of uncoerced agreement? There are two features that are common to all liberal-democratic societies. They may not be equally well-developed in all of these societies, but there is a positive correlation between the degree to which these features are present and the extent of universal, uncoerced consent.

The first feature is this: these countries are all to some extent market societies, and wherever the operations of the market cause people's incomes to vary widely from year to year, owing to factors outside their control, the state will suppress or heavily intervene in the market to mitigate or eliminate these effects. An obvious and striking example is responses to the income levels of the agricultural sector. The United States—that bastion of the free market—no less than the countries of the European Economic Community (EEC) has an elaborate system of quotas, subsidies, and price supports to cushion farmers from the rigours of the market.

The second invariant feature of these countries is that they have some kind of system for the relief of indigence caused by illness or injury, unemployment, age, or youth. The well-being of those who, for some reason beyond their control, are unable to maintain themselves

[27] It is commonplace in the literature that Rawls's 'original position' has some similarities to Habermas's 'ideal speech situation'. More interesting are their dissimilarities. The spirit of the present enterprise is I believe closer to Habermas, who writes: 'it is a question of finding arrangements which can ground the presumption that the basic institutions of the society and the basic political decisions would meet with the unforced agreement of all those involved, if they could participate, as free and equal, in discursive will-formation'. See Jürgen Habermas, 'Legitimation Problems in the Modern State', in *Communication and the Evolution of Society*, Thomas McCarthy (tr.) (Boston, Mass.: Beacon Press, 1979), 186; see also Joshua Cohen and Joel Rogers, *On Democracy* (Harmondsworth: Penguin Books, 1983), ch. 6, pp. 146–83.

at a certain minimum standard is regarded as the responsibility of society, with the state collecting the taxes necessary to make the required payments. That a mechanism of this kind is crucial for the uncoerced acceptance of basic social institutions is evidenced by the way in which such schemes have typically expanded as suffrage has been extended to new groups further down the social hierarchy. It is particularly significant that in some cases welfare legislation was introduced by a conservative government as a concomitant of the extension of the franchise precisely in order to forestall destabilizing demands on the system (Bismarck's Germany being the famous example).

When we turn from this domestic intervention and redistribution to the world economy, we are immediately struck by the absence of anything remotely comparable to either feature. Countries with one-crop or one-mineral economies are at the mercy of the ups and downs of the international market with only very spotty exceptions (e.g. the STABEX scheme for certain primary commodities operated by the EEC countries and their former colonial dependencies). There is no scheme for the systematic transfer of funds from affluent countries to poor ones, although there have been proposals: the demands of Third World countries for a New International Economic Order centre around the attempt to bring commodity markets under some kind of international control, and proposals for the continuous creation under the International Monetary Fund of Special Drawing Rights for poor countries might be seen as an imperfect way of easing the constraints on their economies.

Both lines of initiative have foundered on the unwillingness of rich countries, led by the US, with Japan, Germany, and, lately, Britain in support, to countenance any steps towards a new deal for the poor countries. It seems clear that this refusal sticks only because the rich countries have the power to make it stick. The poor countries do not accept the reasonableness of the status quo, and neither would we if we were in their position. I have argued that it is a basic presupposition of the domestic politics of all countries in which the basic institutions achieve a fair level of popular consent that people should not face ruin and destitution as a result of circumstances beyond their control. This presupposition should also apply in international situations, where people's life chances are set primarily by their having been born into a particular social position in a certain country, and where no plausible amount of personal exertion can raise the majority of people in a desperately poor country above poverty.

It is not necessary to argue here the precise implications of these ideas for the amount and nature of international redistribution that is called for as a matter of ideal morality. I shall assume, however, that it is very much larger than the current level of transfers, including the maximum of 1 per cent of GNP currently given by any of the relatively wealthy countries. There must be practical limits on what the poorer countries can absorb, and these might well limit transfers. But the point is that there is no need to settle these questions in order to see the direction in which things ought to go.

V

Let us now return to the problem of compliance. The immediate question is: wherein does the compliance problem actually reside? It would be easy to assume that we need to come up with a scheme that all actors—in this case states—find to be in their interest to comply with. But this was not how we approached it in discussing compliance in everyday life. There it was argued that the system of obligations should not be too prone to subversion by non-compliance. The analysis had two components. First, I suggested that liability to non-compliance is a function of the sacrifice demanded and the degree to which non-compliance could be monitored and sanctioned by others. Second, I treated vulnerability to non-compliance as a matter of how serious a threat was posed to the achievement of one's 'moral ends' by the non-compliance of others.

If we relate this approach to international affairs, we can conclude, perhaps surprisingly, that the problem of compliance is not a serious impediment to moving towards a much greater degree of international co-operation on economic matters and a greater international redistribution of income. Looking first at vulnerability, it seems clear that no government's moral ends would be gravely jeopardized if it co-operated in an international scheme (say, that proposed in the Law of the Sea Convention) with which there was some non-compliance. The state can cease to comply or pull out if enough others do so, and in the meantime the relative disadvantage from complying where others do not is unlikely to be of disastrous proportions. Similarly, for countries that pay their share in some redistributive arrangement (say, a percentage of GNP into some international fund), it is irritating but not a major setback to their interests if some countries pay less than their share. We might say that the self-sufficiency of states, in comparison with individuals, has the implication that norms for states are generally less vulnerable to non-compliance than norms for individuals.

Of course, it might be thought that international norms would for the same reason be particularly liable to non-compliance. Because states are less dependent on the co-operation of others to achieve their moral ends, they have less of a self-interested motive for observing any set of international norms. I have already noted the obvious point that legal sanctions of the centralized kind available within countries do not exist internationally. But that should not blind us to the ways in which states already feel constrained, not by fear of military force directed against them, but simply by the anticipated consequences of violating international norms. The standard case is the reluctance of governments to repudiate loans, even when the regime has changed and the previous regime's loans were misappropriated (as in Nicaragua). A more complex example is that of the EEC, which has a system of taxation and a body of economic regulations but has no sanctions except the disadvantages to a member state of withdrawing or being expelled. In other words, to the extent that interdependence exists, it tends to make compliance with the norms defining that interdependence more reliable.

The number of states in the world is small enough for there to be some real chance of monitoring compliance with a set of norms which have been defined as states' obligations, and of making continuation of the arrangement dependent on the achievement of a certain level of compliance. There is nothing in the problem of compliance to prevent governments from looking for ways of implementing the requirements of ideal justice by setting up international schemes. What makes such moves so difficult is not compliance but motivation, and one of my major aims in this chapter has been to try to avoid confounding the two. The problem of compliance, as I have presented it, presupposes some willingness to act morally simply for the sake of acting morally, but allows for a legitimate concern about the performance of others. The structure is, in terms of game theory, an assurance game rather than a prisoner's dilemma: so long as others co-operate, co-operation is preferred to non-co-operation.

F. M. Cornford, in his classic analysis of academic politics, *Microcosmographia Academica*, remarked that there is only one argument for doing something—that it is the right thing to do—and all the rest are arguments for doing nothing.[28] It sounds much more portentous to

[28] F. M. Cornford, *Microcosmographia Academica* (London: Bowes and Bowes, 6th edn. 1964), 22.

say that a desirable change is unfeasible because it depends on too many other people doing the right thing than to confess simply that you choose not to make the change because, although it is the right thing to do, by doing it you would incur some cost.

The current celebration of selfishness at home and chauvinism abroad that is apparently electorally popular in both Britain and the US may mean that hypocrisy—the tribute paid by vice to virtue—is no longer in fashion. The pure assertion of naked national self-interest may not raise a blush. Unfortunately, in the account of morality I have relied on here there is no way of making logically coercive arguments to get people to behave morally. I cannot, for example, maintain that those who violate the requirements of morality are engaged in some kind of self-contradiction. In the view I have advanced, people must want to behave in a way that can be defended impartially—in a way that has a chance of being accepted by others without coercion—for moral motivation to take hold. This is a psychological phenomenon rather than a logical one. Once people have moral motivation, rational argument has a place in helping to determine what the concrete requirements of morality are. But people cannot be persuaded into having moral motivation if they lack it. Psychopaths are not necessarily lacking in ratiocinative capacity.

If this is correct, it is natural to ask what conditions predispose people to acquire moral motivation, or, in other words, what conditions arouse the moral motive. I speculate that part of the answer is that the experience of dependence on others is an important predisposing factor. Those who are in a position to control the lives of others commonly become tyrannical. They behave in ways that they would not voluntarily accept if they were on the receiving end. It is in situations where one must gain the co-operation of others in order to achieve one's own ends that one cultivates the habit of looking at things from the other person's point of view and considering what type of conduct the other person might reasonably find acceptable.

As a proposition of speculative moral psychology, the suggestion is that equality of power—or at least not too extreme an inequality of power—is conducive to the formation and elicitation of moral motivation. But I do not mean to reinstate the Hobbes/Gauthier conception of morality through a back door; I am not saying that the *reason* for acting morally is that, under conditions of approximately equal power, it is necessary for the pursuit of one's own advantage to co-operate with others on terms that can be mutually accepted as reasonable. The motive for acting morally remains what I have said:

the desire to be able to justify our conduct. And that desire is more likely to come to the fore in conditions of approximately equal power than in conditions of serious inequality.

If there is anything to all of this, the application at the international level is fairly apparent. The world is a place in which states are unequal in power. The question is whether to follow Robert Tucker in rejoicing in this fact, as he did as an adviser to President Reagan in the 1980 election campaign and in his book *The Inequality of Nations*,[29] or whether to regard it as regrettable. Clearly, for anyone who would like to see more moral motivation in the conduct of international relations, the current degree of inequality must be seen as a great misfortune. The problem is not only one of global inequalities of power, but one of extreme regional imbalances of power as well. The Soviet invasion of Afghanistan and the US invasion of Grenada are paralleled by the Israeli invasion of Lebanon and the South African invasion of Angola—all were carried out in the face of virtually unanimous disapproval from the rest of the world. There could be no better illustration of Lord Acton's dictum that all power tends to corrupt than the arrogant reactions of all four of those governments to international criticism, as typified by Reagan's reaction to the UN vote (108 to 9) condemning the invasion of Grenada: 'It didn't upset my breakfast at all.'[30]

The best prospect for the future is the hope that the present extreme inequalities of power among nations will be reduced. And there is some hope for the long run. The period since the Second World War has seen massive decolonization and the creation of new states that, though individually weak, are certainly better placed to defend their interests than they were before independence. The American post-war hegemony has also ended: the economic preponderance of the USA in the world economy was inevitable in the aftermath of the Second World War but was bound to disappear once recovery set in. There seems to be a long-term trend towards a more interdependent world.

Unfortunately, however, it looks as if this evolution will be opposed by the superpowers with all the forces at their command: covert destabilization operations, military aid to regional surrogates, and, if all else fails, direct intervention. It seems doubtful that this will prevent the equalization of power in the long run. But in a world

[29] See Jeff McMahan, *Reagan and the World* (London: Pluto Press, 1984), 11; Robert Tucker, *The Inequality of Nations* (New York: Basic Books, 1977).

[30] McMahan, *Reagan and the World*, p. 166.

brimming with nuclear weapons there is the danger that, adapting Keynes's aphorism, in the medium run we shall all be dead. Ultimately, if we are to be saved, it will be by political action rather than by political philosophy.

16

HUMANITY AND JUSTICE IN GLOBAL PERSPECTIVE

This chapter has three sections. The first argues that considerations of humanity require that rich countries give aid to poor ones. The second argues that considerations of justice require transfers of economic resources from rich countries to poor ones. The third picks up the distinction between aid and transfer and argues that, when we get into detail, the obligations imposed by humanity and justice are different, although not incompatible.

I HUMANITY

What is it to act in a way called for by humanity? A humane act is a beneficent act, but not every beneficent act is a humane one. To do something that helps to make someone who is already very happy even happier is certainly beneficent, but it would not naturally be described as an act called for by considerations of humanity.

The Oxford English Dictionary defines humanity as 'Disposition to treat human beings and animals with consideration and compassion, and to relieve their distresses; kindness, benevolence.'[1] In this chapter I shall understand by 'humanity' the relief of distress. As a matter of usage, it seems to me that the *OED* is right to put this before the more extended sense of kindness or benevolence in general. In any case, it is this notion that I want to discuss, and the word 'humanity' is the closest representation of it in common use.

There are three questions to be dealt with. First, is it morally obligatory to behave humanely, or is it simply laudable but not morally delinquent to fail so to act? Second, if it is morally obligatory, what implications does it have, if any, for the obligations of rich countries to aid poor ones? Third, if (as I shall suggest) rich countries have a humanitarian obligation to aid poor ones, by what criterion can

[1] *The Oxford English Dictionary*, sub. Humanity, 3b. In the light of the central example to be discussed below, it is interesting to note that the title of a society founded in England for the rescuing of drowning persons in 1774 was the Humane Society (*OED*, sub. Humane, 1c).

we determine how much sacrifice the rich countries should be prepared to make?

I shall begin my discussion by taking up and considering the argument put forward by Peter Singer in his article 'Famine, Affluence and Morality'.[2] Singer puts forward a simple, clear, and forceful case for a humanitarian obligation for those in rich countries to give economic aid to those in poor countries. The premisses of his argument are as follows. The first is 'that suffering and death from lack of food, shelter, and medical care are bad'. The second is given in two alternative forms. One is that 'if it is in our power to prevent something bad from happening, without thereby sacrificing anything of comparable moral importance, we ought, morally, to do it'. The other, and weaker, form is that 'if it is in our power to prevent something very bad from happening, without sacrificing anything morally significant, we ought, morally, to do it'. He goes on to say that 'an application of this principle [i.e. the second version] would be as follows: if I am walking past a shallow pond and see a child drowning in it, I ought to wade in and pull the child out. This will mean getting my clothes muddy, but this is insignificant, while the death of the child would presumably be a very bad thing.' All that has to be added is that the application of the second premiss is unaffected by proximity or distance and 'makes no distinction between cases in which I am the only person who could possibly do anything and cases in which I am just one among millions in the same position'.[3] If we accept these premisses we are committed, Singer claims, to the conclusion that people in the rich countries have a moral obligation to help those in the poor countries.

For the purpose of this chapter, I am going to take it as common ground that one would indeed be doing wrong to walk past Peter Singer's drowning child and do nothing to save it. This of course entails that, at least in the most favourable cases, duties of humanity must exist. In the space available, it hardly makes sense to try to argue for a complete theory of morality from which this can be deduced, and in any case I myself am more sure of the conclusion than of any of the alternative premisses from which it would follow. Anyone who disagrees with the claim that there is an obligation to rescue the child in the case as stated will not find what follows persuasive, since I

[2] Peter Singer, 'Famine, Affluence and Morality', *Philosophy & Public Affairs*, 1 (1972), 229–43. See, for a briefer and more recent statement of the same basic case, Peter Singer, *Practical Ethics* (Cambridge: Cambridge University Press, 1979), ch. 8, pp. 158–81.

[3] All quotations in this paragraph from Singer, 'Famine, Affluence and Morality', p. 231.

certainly do not think that the case for international aid on humanitarian grounds is *stronger* than the case for rescuing the drowning child.

The extension of the drowning child case may be challenged along several lines. Here I can only state them and say briefly why I do not think that they undercut the claim that the case for an obligation to save the drowning child applies also to giving international aid. (The appearance of dogmatism here is purely a result of compression.)

The first argument is that the child may be supposed not to be responsible for his plight (or at any rate it may be on that supposition that the example gets to us) but that countries are responsible for their economic problems. My comments here are two. First, even if it were true that the death by disease and/or starvation of somebody in a poor country were to some degree the result of past acts or omissions by the entire population, that scarcely makes it morally decent to hold the individual responsible for his plight; nor, similarly, if his predicament could have been avoided had the policies of his government been different.

Let us move on to consider another way in which a challenge may be mounted to Singer's extension of the argument for a duty to aid from the case of the drowning child to that of famine relief. It may be recalled that Singer explicitly made the shift from one case to the other via the statement that neither proximity nor the one-to-one relation between the victim and the potential rescuer makes any moral difference. Clearly, if this claim is denied, we can again agree on the duty to rescue the drowning child but deny that this is an appropriate analogue to the putative duty of people in rich countries to aid those in poor ones. A number of philosophers have tried to drive a wedge between the cases in this way, but I have to say that I am not very impressed by their efforts. The argument for proximity as a relevant factor is that, if we posit a duty to rescue those near at hand, we keep the duty within narrow bounds and thus do not let it interfere with people's life plans; but, if we allow the duty to range over the whole of mankind, it becomes too demanding. Although some people see merit in this, it appears to me that it is invoked simply because it provides a way of arbitrarily truncating the application of the principle so as to arrive at a convenient answer. I shall go on later to agree that there are limits to what people can be required to sacrifice. But I see no ethically defensible reason for saying that, if we cannot (or cannot be required to) do anything we might, we should simply contract the geographical scope of the principle that we are obliged to relieve suffering. Perhaps we should channel our limited humanitarian efforts to where they are most needed, which, if we live in a relatively rich country, is likely to be outside its boundaries.

Singer also made it explicit that, if the case of the drowning child were to be extended to international aid, one would have to rule out the one-to-one relation between the rescuer and the potential rescuee as a morally relevant factor. Attempts have been made to do so, but they likewise seem to me to lack merit. If there are several people who could save the drowning child, it is sometimes said that none of them is particularly responsible for saving it. But if the child drowns because none of them saves it, they are all morally responsible for its death. Conversely, suppose that several people are drowning at some distance from one another, that there is only one person around to save them, and that he can save any one of them but no more than one. It has been argued that this person cannot do his duty, defined as saving all those whom he might save, since he could save any of them. It is then concluded that, since there can be no duty to do the impossible, no duty to rescue exists in such a case. The conclusion is, however, fallacious. For the terms of the duty have been misstated. There is indeed no duty to save all of the drowning people. But there is in the case as stated a duty to save one of them. That the duty does not have a determinate object is no objection to its standing. It does not pick out a particular person to save but it still insists that somebody should be saved.

Finally, it might be accepted that the case of the drowning child would extend to international aid if the aid would do any good, but then denied that it will. The main lines of this argument are two. The first is the one from waste and inefficiency: aid does not get to the right people; development projects are a disaster; and so on. But I would claim that even if waste is endemic in aid to poor (and probably ill-organized) countries, the difference it makes to health and nutrition is sufficient to make it worth giving even if only part of it gets to the people it is supposed to get to. And if, as is all too true, aid in the past has often been inappropriate, the answer is not to withhold aid but to make it more appropriate: no more massive dams, electricity-generating stations, or steel mills, but cheaper, less complex, and more decentralized technology.

The second line of argument is the neo-Malthusian: that the only effect of aid in the long run is to lead to population increase and thus to even more suffering. I agree that if this is the only effect of aid the humanitarian case for it falls to the ground. But it is clear that economic development combined with appropriate social policies and the widespread availability of contraception can acually reduce the rate of population growth. The implication is thus that aid should be given in large amounts where the social and political conditions are right, so as to get countries through the demographic transition from high birth-rate and high death-rate to low birth-rate and low death-rate as rapidly as possible.

Where ideological or religious dogmas result in pro-natalist government policies or rejection of contraception by the population, one might conclude that aid would be better withheld, since the only foreseeable effect of economic improvement will be to increase numbers. But can we really be so sure that attitudes will not change? The election of a relatively young and doctrinally reactionary Pope does not encourage hopes of any early change in official doctrine. But even without any change at that level, it is striking how, in the developed countries, the practices of Roman Catholics have altered dramatically in just a couple of decades. For example, in the Province of Quebec, which had for more than two centuries a birth-rate close to the physical maximum, with families of more than ten children being quite common, the birth-rate fell over the course of just a few years to one that is among the lowest in North America.

If we accept the conclusion that the rich have some obligation on humanitarian grounds to provide economic aid to the poor, the next question is, how much sacrifice is required? In my view, no simple and determinate criterion is available. This is a problem of the obligation of humanity in general, not a peculiarity of the international context. In the standard case of rescuing someone in danger of drowning, the usual guidance one gets from moral philosophers is that the obligation does not extend to risking one's life, though it does require that one suffer a fair amount of inconvenience. However, the decision in cases such as that of Singer's drowning child characteristically has clear and finite limits to its implications. But, given the failure of most people or governments in rich countries to give much aid, it would clearly be possible for individuals to give up a high proportion of their incomes without risking their lives and still leave millions of saveable lives in poor countries unsaved. Thus, the question of limits is pressing.

There is an answer that is, in principle, straightforward. It is the one embodied in Singer's claim that one is obliged to help up to the point at which one is sacrificing something of 'comparable moral importance'. This is, of course, a maximizing form of consequentialism. If you say that pains and pleasures are what is of moral importance, you get Benthamite utilitarianism (in the traditional interpretation, anyway);

if you say it is the enjoyment of beauty and personal relationships, you get G. E. Moore's ideal consequentialism; and so on. The trouble with this is, needless to say, that most of us do not see any reason for accepting an obligation to maximize the total amount of good in the universe. (See above, chapter XII.)

Singer's weaker principle is that we should give aid up to the point at which we are sacrificing anything of moral importance. But this seems to me useless: for a Benthamite utilitarian, for example, even getting one's trousers muddy would be in itself an evil—not one comparable to the death of a child, but an evil none the less. Even Singer's chosen case would therefore be eliminated on this criterion, let alone any more strenuous sacrifices.

I conclude, provisionally and in the absence of any plausible alternative, that there is no firm criterion for the amount of sacrifice required to relieve distress. This does not mean that nothing can be said. It is fairly clear that there is a greater obligation the more severe the distress, the better off the potential helper would still be after helping, and the higher the ratio of benefit to cost. What is indefinite is where the line is to be drawn. In the words of C. D. Broad, in what may be the best single article in philosophical ethics ever written, 'it is no objection to say that it is totally impossible to determine exactly where this point comes in any particular case. This is quite true, but it is too common a difficulty in ethics to worry us, and we know that we are lucky in ethical questions if we can state upper and lower limits that are not too ridiculously far apart.'[4]

What, in any case, are we talking about here as the range? We could perhaps wonder whether the level of aid from a country like the United States should be 3 per cent of GNP (the level of Marshall aid), or 10, or 25 per cent. But, unless we reject the idea of an obligation to aid those in distress altogether, we can hardly doubt that one quarter of one per cent is grotesquely too little.

II JUSTICE

'Are we not trying to pack too much into the concept of justice and the correlative concept of rights? The question of whether it is *wrong* to act in certain ways is not the same question as whether it is *unjust* so to act.'[5] I think the answer to John Passmore's rhetorical question is in the

[4] C. D. Broad, 'On the Function of False Hypotheses in Ethics', *International Journal of Ethics*, 26 (1916), 377–97, at 389–90.

[5] John Passmore, 'Civil Justice and Its Rivals', in Eugene Kamenka and Alice Erh-Soon Tay (eds.), *Justice* (London: Edward Arnold, 1979), 25–49, at 47 (italics in original).

affirmative. We should not expect to get out of 'justice' a blueprint for the good society—nor should we wish to, since that degree of specificity would inevitably limit potential applicability. Surely it ought to be possible for a just society to be rich or poor, cultivated or philistine, religious or secular, and (within some limits that are inherent in justice itself) to have more or less of liberty, equality, and fraternity.

Up to this point I have studiously avoided any reference to justice. I have been talking about the obligation to relieve suffering as a matter of humanity. The fact that the obligation is not derived from justice does not make it a matter of generosity, nor does it entail that it should be left to voluntary action to adhere to it. It is an obligation that it would be wrong not to carry out and that could quite properly be enforced upon rich countries if the world political system made this feasible. And the core of the discussion has been the claim that the obligation to help (and *a fortiori* the obligation not to harm) is not limited in its application to those who form a single political community.

It is of course open to anyone who wishes to do so to argue that, if the rich have a properly enforceable obligation to give, this is all we need in order to be able to say that the rich must give to the poor as a matter of justice. I have no way of proving that it is a mistake to use the term 'just' to mark out the line between, on the one hand, what is morally required and, on the other, what is praiseworthy to do but not wrong to omit doing. All I can say is that such a way of talking seems to me to result in the blunting of our moral vocabulary and therefore a loss of precision in our moral thinking. Justice, I wish to maintain, is not merely one end of a monochromatic scale that has at the other end sacrifice of self-interest for the good of others to a heroic or saintly degree. Rather, it points to a particular set of reasons why people (or societies) may have duties to one another and picks out particular features of institutions that make them morally condemnable.[6]

I shall return to the distinction between humanity and justice in section III, where I shall be able to refer to the results of my discussions of each of them. My plan is to analyse justice under two heads. The first is justice as reciprocity; the second, justice as equal rights. These are both familiar ideas, though I shall give the second a slightly unfamiliar twist. Justice as reciprocity I will discuss in three aspects: justice as fidelity, justice as requital, and justice as fair play. (The

[6] For a sustained argument along these lines, see T. D. Campbell, 'Humanity before Justice', *British Journal of Political Science*, 4 (1974), 1–16.

analysis of justice as reciprocity is carried out in a much extended form in chapter 17 below.)

The notion of justice as fidelity is that of keeping faith. In addition to covering contracts and promises, it extends, in a rather indefinite way, to meeting legitimate expectations not derived from explicit voluntary agreement. Clearly it is an essentially conservative principle and tends if anything to operate contrary to the interests of poor countries, in so far as they often find themselves in the position of seeking to renegotiate disadvantageous deals with transnational corporations within their territories.

Justice as requital is also a basically conservative principle but can, on occasion, have revisionist implications *vis-à-vis* justice as fidelity. No simple rule governs what happens when they conflict. Henry Sidgwick, with characteristic caution, said that we have two standards of justice, as the customary distribution and as the ideal distribution, and added that 'it is the reconciliation between these two views which is the problem of political justice'.[7] I shall not take up that large challenge here. I shall confine myself to an exploration of the possible implications of justice as requital for international distribution.

The idea of justice as requital is that of a fair return: a fair exchange, a fair share of benefits from common endeavour, and so on. The most obvious application in the relations between rich and poor countries is in prompting us to ask whether poor countries are getting fair prices for their exports and paying fair prices for their imports. This raises the obvious question of what the criterion of a 'fair price' is. Suppose, however, that we say, minimally, that it is the prevailing world price. Then it seems clear that, even on this criterion, many poor countries have legitimate complaints about the transfer pricing of transnational corporations. For example, when in the late 1960s the Andean Pact countries (Bolivia, Colombia, Ecuador, and Peru) started taking a serious interest in the pricing policies of transnational corporations operating within their territories, they found overpricing of imports to be the norm, sometimes by factors of hundreds of per cent, and, less spectacularly but still significantly, underpricing of the value of exports.[8] This enabled the companies to attain rates of return on capital of often more than 100 per cent while at the same time evading government limits on repatriation of profits. Since the Andean Pact countries have been politically independent for a century and a half

[7] Henry Sidgwick, *The Methods of Ethics* (London: Macmillan, 7th edn. 1907), 273.

[8] Constantine V. Vaitsos, *Intercountry Income Distribution and Transnational Enterprises* (Oxford: Clarendon Press, 1974), esp. ch. 4.

and have relatively sophisticated bureaucracies compared with those of most countries in the Third World, it is inconceivable that similar practices do not obtain in other, more vulnerable countries.

When we turn to the structure of world prices itself, the criterion of justice as requital becomes less helpful. The countries of the Third World, as part of their demands for a 'New International Economic Order', have demanded an 'Integrated Program' of commodity management that would be designed to push up the prices of raw materials in relation to manufactured products.

The success of the Organization of Petroleum Exporting Countries (OPEC) was unquestionably significant here in providing a dazzling example of the effectiveness of a producer cartel. Oil, however, seems to be unique in that it is so cheap to extract and worth so much to consumers. This means that it has always, since the days of the Pennsylvania oilfields, yielded enormous economic rents. The only question has been who captured them. And clearly, until 1973, the Middle Eastern oil producers were getting only a small proportion of the economic rent.

Other commodities are not like oil. It may indeed be possible to push up the prices by restricting supply, but substitution or recycling is likely to set in. From the long-run point of view of the world, this pressure towards conservation would be desirable, no doubt, but the point is that it does not spell a bonanza for the raw material producers.

Clearly, this is only scratching the surface, but I think that it is at any rate important to keep in mind that, even if commodity prices could be raised substantially across the board, this would not make most poor countries *appreciably* better off; and it would make some, including almost all of the world's most desperately poor countries, worse off. Whatever conclusion one wishes to draw, therefore, about the applicability to world prices of justice as requital, the implications are not going to be such as to solve the problem of poor countries that are also resource poor.

We still have to see if any redistributive implications flow from the third branch of justice as reciprocity: justice as fair play. The idea here is that, if one benefits (or stands to benefit) from some co-operative practice, one should not be a 'free rider' by taking the benefits (or being ready to take them if the occasion arises) while failing to do one's part in sustaining the practice when it is one's turn to do so. Thus, if others burn smokeless fuel in their fireplaces, take their litter home from the countryside, or clean up after their dogs, it is unfair for you to refuse to do the same.

The principle of fair play has a potentiality for underwriting a certain amount of redistribution from rich to poor in so far as one practice that might be regarded as prospectively beneficial to all concerned would be the practice of helping those in need. If such a practice existed, it would operate analogously to insurance, which is a contractual way of transferring money from those who have not suffered from certain specified calamities to those who have. The principle of fair play would then hold that it would be unfair to be a free rider on a scheme of helping those in need by refusing to do your part when called upon.

The invocation of this notion of what the sociobiologists call 'reciprocal altruism' may appear to provide a new way of distinguishing the drowning child case from that of international aid. Perhaps what motivates us in agreeing that there is an obligation to rescue the child is an unarticulated contextual assumption that the child belongs to our community (however widely we may conceive that 'community') and that there are norms within that community calling for low-cost rescue—norms from which we stand to gain if ever we find ourselves in need of rescue. Such feelings of obligation as we have in this case can therefore be adequately explained by supposing that they arise from the application of the principle of fair play. It was, thus, an error to have taken it for granted that an acknowledgement of an obligation to help in the drowning child case must show that we accepted a general principle of an obligation to aid those in distress.

I believe that the objection is formally valid. That is to say, it is possible by invoking the principle of fair play to underwrite the obligation to rescue the drowning child without committing oneself to a universal obligation to rescue. One could respond to this by arguing that the conclusions in section I of this chapter can be reinstated by deriving universal obligations from the existence of a world community. I shall consider this argument below. But before doing so, I should like to follow an alternative and more aggressive line.

The point to observe is that, although we may indeed be motivated to agree that we ought to rescue the drowning child by considerations of justice as reciprocity, it does not follow that we are motivated solely by those considerations. Suppose that you are briefly visiting a foreign country, with an entirely alien culture, and have no idea about the local norms of rescue. Would you, if you came across Singer's drowning child, have an obligation to wade in and rescue it? I think that most people would say yes in answer to that question. And, clearly, those who do so are acknowledging obligations of humanity as distinct from obligations of justice.

None of this, of course, is intended to suggest that the difficulties in moving from a general obligation of humanity to an obligation on the part of rich countries to give economic aid to poor ones is any less problematic than it appeared earlier. But it does fend off a possible challenge to the move from the drowning child case to the universal obligation to aid. The view I want to maintain is that the answer in the drowning child case is over-determined where the duty of fair play also underwrites rescue. The strength of the obligation depends upon the circumstances, but it never disappears. Both psychologically and morally, the obligation to aid would be strongest if there were an explicit and generally observed agreement among a group of parents to keep an eye on one another's children: humanity, fidelity, and fair play would then coincide and reinforce each other. The obligation would be perhaps a little less strong but still very strong in a small, stable, and close-knit community with a well-developed tradition of 'neighbourliness', since the obligation of fair play would here have maximum force. It would be less strong if the norm of rescue were more widely diffused over a whole society, and would of course vary according to the society. (New Zealand would rate much higher than the United States on the strength of the norm of helping strangers within the society, for example.) And, finally, in the absence of any established practice of aiding strangers that would give rise to obligations of fair play, there is still, I am suggesting, an obligation of humanity that does not in any way depend upon considerations of reciprocity. (See above, chapter 12 section II for an amplification of these ideas.)

I have been taking for granted that the existence of a practice of rescue does give rise to an obligation to play one's part. This can be questioned. Somebody might say: 'Why should I co-operate with the scheme if I'm willing to renounce any benefits that might be due to me under it?'[9] But the cogency of the objection depends upon the existence of stringent conditions of publicity: it must be possible to make this declaration known to all those in the scheme and everyone

[9] Adam Smith expressed this view: 'As a man doth, so it shall be done to him, and retaliation seems to be the great law which is dictated to us by nature. Beneficence and generosity we think due to the generous and beneficent. Those whose hearts never open to the feelings of humanity should, we think, be shut out in the same manner, from the affections of all their fellow-creatures, and be allowed to live in the midst of society, as in a great desert, where there is nobody to care for them, or to enquire after them.' Adam Smith, *The Theory of Moral Sentiments* (Indianapolis, Ind.: Liberty Classics, n.d.), 160.

must thereafter remember its having been made. (This is essential, since many transfers to those in need are going to be predominantly from the young and middle-aged to the old, so it would undermine the integrity of any such co-operative scheme if people could change their minds about its value as they got older.) Neither condition is generally met. Consider a practice of rescuing the victims of accidents—drowning swimmers are the case that is usually cited. If this practice exists in a whole society, it is not feasible for those who wish to opt out to notify everybody else in advance. And how many could be counted on to be strong-minded enough to wave away a would-be rescuer when they were in need of help themselves? Even if they could, in many cases the rescuer has to incur the trouble and risk in order to get there (as with rescuing a swimmer), or the victim may be unconscious and thus incapable of spurning help.

It is crucially important to notice, however, that the principle of fair play is conditional: that is to say, it stipulates that it is unfair to be a free rider on a co-operative practice that actually exists, and that it *would* be unfair to free ride on other mutually beneficial practices if they did exist. But it does not say that it is unfair for a practice not to exist that would be mutually beneficial if it existed.

As anyone familiar with Rawls's theory of justice will have been aware for some time, we are here on the edge of deep waters. For one strand of Rawls's theory is precisely the notion of justice as reciprocity that is embodied in the principle of fair play. According to Rawls, a society is a scheme of social co-operation, and from this fact we can generate, via the notion of fair play, principles of justice. But, clearly, any actual society simply generates whatever is generated by its actual co-operative practices. If it provides retirement pensions out of social security taxes, it is unfair to be a free rider on the scheme by dodging your share of the cost. And so on. But if I am right about the applicability of the principle of fair play, the most Rawls can say about a society that does not have such a scheme is that it suffers from collective irrationality in that it is passing up a chance to do itself some good. He cannot employ the principle as a step in an argument that such a society is unjust.

I make this point because Charles Beitz, in the last part of his admirable book, *Political Philosophy and International Relations*,[10] has argued, within a Rawlsian framework, for a global difference

[10] Charles Beitz, *Political Philosophy and International Relations* (Princeton, NJ: Princeton University Press, 1979). The part of the book in question was first published in substantially the same form as 'Justice and International Relations', *Philosophy & Public Affairs*, 4 (1975), 360–89.

principle. That is to say, income should be redistributed internationally so that the worst-off representative individual in the world is as well off as possible. Beitz acknowledges that he is taking for granted the general validity of Rawls's theory and is simply arguing from within its basic premisses for the dropping of Rawls's restriction on the application of the two principles of justice to societies. I have been suggesting that, even within a society, one cannot use the fact that it is a co-operative scheme to argue that it is unfair not to have more extensive co-operation, though not to do so may be collectively irrational. But the international scene presents two further difficulties. First, I think that Rawls is broadly right in (implicitly) denying that the whole world constitutes a single co-operative partnership in the required sense. Second, I do not think that international redistribution can plausibly be said to be advantageous to rich as well as poor countries. Rawls is therefore probably correct in deducing from his system only non-aggression, diplomatic immunity, and the like as mutually advantageous to countries and thus, on the principle of fair play, just. If I am right, however, they are simply collectively rational and give rise to duties of fair play only to the extent that they are instantiated in actual practice.

Beitz's argument for extending the Rawlsian difference principle is in essence that the network of international trade is sufficiently extensive to draw all countries together in a single co-operative scheme. But it seems to me that trade, however multilateral, does not constitute a co-operative scheme of the relevant kind. Trade, if freely undertaken, is (presumably) beneficial to the exchanging parties, but it is not the kind of relationship that gives rise to duties of fair play. To the extent that justice is involved it is justice as requital, that is, giving a fair return. Justice as fair play arises not from simple exchange but either from the provision of public goods that are collectively enjoyed (parks, defence, a litter-free or unpolluted environment, and so on) or from quasi-insurance schemes for mutual aid of the kind just discussed. Trade in pottery, ornamentation, and weapons can be traced back to prehistoric times, but we would hardly feel inclined to think of, say, the Beaker Folk as forming a single co-operative enterprise with their trading partners on the Mediterranean. No more did the spice trade unite East and West.

To the extent that we are inclined to think of the world as more of a co-operative enterprise now, this is not because trade is more extensive or multilateral, but because there really are rudimentary organs of international co-operation in the form of United Nations agencies and such entities as the International Monetary Fund and the World Bank. But the resulting relationships clearly fall short of those of mutual dependence found within societies. And my second point comes in here to draw attention to the fact that the extent of increased co-operation that would really be mutually beneficial is probably quite limited. In particular, redistribution on the insurance principle seems to have little appeal to rich countries. In the foreseeable future, aid to the needy is going to flow from, say, the United States to Bangladesh rather than vice versa. The conditions for reciprocity—that all the parties stand prospectively to benefit from the scheme—simply do not exist. One could again retreat behind the 'veil of ignorance' and argue that, if people did not know to which society they belonged, they would surely choose something like a global difference principle—or at any rate a floor below which nobody should be allowed to fall. And this seems plausible enough. (I have argued it myself in an earlier work.[11]) But this move clearly points up even more sharply than in the case of a single society the degree to which inserting the 'veil of ignorance' takes us away from the sphere of the principle of fair play.

In his well-known article, 'Are There Any Natural Rights?',[12] H. L. A. Hart argued that special rights must presuppose general rights. Before people can act in ways that modify their rights and those of others (paradigmatically by promising) they must, as a matter of elementary logic, have rights that do not stem from such modifications. Putting this in terms of the present discussion, we can say that justice as reciprocity needs a prior assignment of rights before it can get off the ground.

Now we might try to solve the problem by sanctifying the status quo. We could, in other words, simply declare that we are going to push the principle of justice as the fulfilment of reasonable expectations to the limit, and say that whatever rights somebody now has are to be taken as the baseline in relation to which all future developments must satisfy the requirements of fidelity, requital, and fair play. If we note that the conservation of value is akin to the Pareto principle, we may observe that this would give us the Virginia school of political economy especially associated with James Buchanan.

I have criticized his approach elsewhere,[13] and I shall not repeat my criticisms here. But it is surely enough for the present purpose to point out that, on the principle of the unquestioned justice of the status quo,

[11] Brian Barry, *The Liberal Theory of Justice* (Oxford: Clarendon Press, 1973), ch. 12.

[12] H. L. A. Hart, 'Are There Any Natural Rights?', *Philosophical Review*, 64 (1955), 175–91.

[13] See my extended review of Buchanan's ideas in *Theory and Decision*, 12 (1980), 95–106.

the most grotesque features of the existing allocation of rights would be frozen in place forever unless those who suffered from them could find some quid pro quo that would make it worth the while of, say, a Shah of Iran or a General Somoza to accept change. But that would be, if it could be found, an improvement in efficiency arising from the reallocation of the existing rights. It would not face the real problem, which was of course the injustice of the initial allocation of rights.

Hart's answer to his own question is that the general right that is presupposed by any special rights is an equal right to liberty. He does not give any explicit argument, as far as I can see, for its being equal. But I take the point to be that, since a general right is something that is necessarily anterior to any act giving rise to a special right, there is simply no basis for discriminating among people in respect of general rights. In order to discriminate, one would either have to do so on the basis of some quality that is obviously irrelevant to the assignment of rights (e.g. skin colour), or on the basis of something the person has done (e.g. made a promise) that provides a reason for attributing different rights to him. But then we get back to the original point, namely that such a differentiation in rights entails that we have an idea of the proper distribution of rights without the special factor adduced. And that must, it seems, be an equal distribution.

In this chapter I want to take this idea and apply it to the case of natural resources. I shall suggest that they fit all the requirements for being the subjects of a general right and that therefore everyone has an equal right to enjoy their benefits.

As Hillel Steiner has remarked, 'Nozick rightly insists that our commonsense view of what is just—of what is owed to individuals by right—is inextricably bound up with what they *have done* . . . [but] unlike other objects, the objects of appropriative rights . . . are *not* the results of individuals' past actions. . . . Appropriative claims, and the rules governing them, can have nothing to do with desert.'[14] Consider, for example, Bruce Ackerman's fable of the spaceship and the manna. One of the claimants, 'Rusher', says: 'I say that the first person who grabs a piece of manna should be recognized as its true owner' and, when asked for a reason, says, 'Because people who grab first are better than people who grab second.'[15] That, I think, illustrates my

[14] Hillel Steiner, 'The Natural Right to the Means of Production', *The Philosophical Quarterly*, 27 (1977), 41–9 at 44–5 (italics in original). The reference to Robert Nozick is to *Anarchy, State, and Utopia* (New York: Basic Books, 1974), 154.

[15] Bruce A. Ackerman, *Social Justice in the Liberal State* (New Haven: Yale University Press, 1980), 38.

point. What exactly is supposed to be the virtue of getting there first, or in merely having some ancestor who got there first?

The position with regard to countries is parallel to that of individuals. Today the basis of state sovereignty over natural resources is convention reinforced by international declarations such as votes of the United Nations General Assembly in 1970, 1972, and 1974 to the effect that each country has 'permanent sovereignty over natural resources' within its territory.[16] It is easy enough to see the basis of the convention. It has a transcendent simplicity and definiteness that must recommend it in international relations. For, in the absence of a 'common power', stability depends heavily on conventions that leave the minimum amount of room for interpretation. Within a municipal legal system, by contrast, it is possible to introduce and enforce complex rules limiting the rights of individual appropriation (e.g. restricting the amount of water that can be drawn off from a river) and transferring a portion of the economic rent from the property owner to the state. Moreover, in the absence of a 'common power', it is a convention that is relatively easy to enforce—at any rate easier than any alternative. For a state may be presumed, other things being equal, to be in a better position to control the appropriation of the natural resources of its own territory than to control those of some other country.

In practice things are not always equal, and many Third World countries have found that controlling foreign companies that own their natural resources is no easy matter: an unholy alliance of multinational corporations and their patron governments (for most, this is the United States) stands ready to organize international boycotts, to manipulate institutions such as the World Bank and the IMF against them, and, if all else fails, go in for 'destabilization' on the Chilean model. The problem is exacerbated when a country seeks to gain control of the exploitation of its own natural resources by expropriating the foreign-based companies that have been there, often long before the country became independent. For the issue of compensation then arises, and this is likely to be contentious, not only because of the possibility of dispute about the current value of the investment, but also because the country may claim compensation for inadequate (or no) royalties paid on extraction in the past—a claim that (as we noted above) falls validly under the heading of justice as requital.

[16] Oscar Schachter, *Sharing the World's Resources* (New York: Columbia University Press, 1977), 124, references in n. 52, p. 159.

However, no substantial body of opinion in either the North or the South (or, perhaps more remarkably, in the East or the West) is adverse to the principle that each country is entitled to benefit exclusively from its own natural resources and to take decisions about their exploitation. In recent years, practice has increasingly come into line with the principle. The outstanding illustration is OPEC, but the same pattern of improved royalties and more control over how much and what is extracted obtains also in other countries and for other commodities.

It would hardly be surprising if, when the principle of national sovereignty over natural resources has been so recently and precariously established, Third World countries should be highly suspicious of any suggestion that natural resources should in future be treated as collective international property. They may well wonder whether this is anything more than a cover for the reintroduction of colonialism. I do not see how such doubts can be allayed by mere assertion. Clearly, everything would depend on the principle's being applied across the board rather than in a one-sided way that lets the industrialized countries act on the maxim 'What's yours is mine and what's mine is my own.' So far, that is precisely how it has been used, as in the proposals of American chauvinists such as Robert Tucker that the United States should be prepared to occupy the Saudi Arabian oilfields by military force in order to maintain the flow of oil at a 'reasonable' price, so that Americans can continue to use up a grossly disproportionate share of the world's oil. Since the United States, if it used only domestically produced oil, would still have one of the world's highest per capita levels of consumption, the effrontery of this proposal for the international control of other countries' oil would be hard to beat.

If the Third World countries were too weak to do anything more than hang on to the present position of national sovereignty over natural resources, we would have to regard that as the best outcome that could be obtained. It is clearly preferable to the earlier set-up, in which countries with the power to do so controlled the natural resources of others. For, although the distribution of natural resources is entirely arbitrary from a moral point of view, it has at any rate the kind of fairness displayed by a lottery. That is presumably better than a situation in which the weak are despoiled of their prizes by force and fraud.

In spite of these forebodings about the potential misuse of the principle that natural resources are the joint possession of the human race as a whole, I think it is worth pursuing. For it is scarcely possible to be satisfied with the present situation from any angle except that of extreme pessimism about the chances of changing it for the better rather than for the worse. The overwhelming fact about the existing system is that it makes the economic prospects of a country depend, to a significant degree, on something for which its inhabitants (present or past) can take absolutely no credit and to whose benefits they can lay no just claim, namely its natural resources—including in this soil, water, minerals, sunlight, and so on. The claims of collectivities to appropriate natural resources rest, as do those of individuals, on convention or on law (in this case, such quasi-law as the United Nations resolutions cited above). No doubt the point has been impressed on people in the West by examples such as Kuwait, the United Arab Emirates, or Saudi Arabia, and it may be that such small numbers of people have never before become so rich without any effort on their own part, simply as a result of sitting on top of rich deposits. But I see no coherent way of saying why there is anything grotesque about, say, the case of Kuwait, without acknowledging that the fault lies in the whole principle of national sovereignty over natural resources. If it were simply a matter of a few million people hitting the jackpot things would not be bad, but of course the obverse of that is the existence of countries that have poor land, or little land per head, and few mineral resources or other sources of energy such as hydroelectric power.

Obviously, some countries are richer than others for many reasons, and some, like Japan, are among the more affluent in spite of having to import almost all their oil and the greatest part of many other natural resources. What, then, about the other advantages that the people in the rich countries inherit—productive capital, good systems of communications, orderly administration, well-developed systems of education and training, and so on? If the point about special rights is that someone must have done something to acquire a special right, what have the fortunate inheritors of all these advantages done to give them an exclusive claim to the benefits flowing from them?

The answer that the defenders of property rights normally give at this point is that, although the inheritors have done nothing to establish any special rights, those who left it to them did do something (namely, help to create the advantages) and had a right to dispose of it to some rather than to others. The special rights of those in the present generation thus derive from the use made by those in the previous generation of *their* special rights.

I cannot, in this already long chapter, undertake here to ask how far this answer takes us. We would have to get into questions that seem to me very difficult, such as the extent to which the fact that people who are no longer alive wanted something to happen, and perhaps even made sacrifices in order to insure that it could happen, provides any basis in justice for determining what those now alive should do. (See chapter 6 *ad fin.* for a discussion of this question.) I shall simply say here that I regard any claims that those now alive can make to special advantages derived from the efforts of their ancestors as quite limited. First, the inheritance must itself have been justly acquired in the first place, and that cannot be said of any country that violated the equal claims of all on natural resources—which means almost all industrial countries. Second, the claims to inheritance seem to me to attenuate with time, so that, although the present generation might legitimately derive some special advantages from the efforts of the preceding one, and perhaps the one before that, the part of what they passed on that was in turn inherited from their predecessors should be regarded as by now forming part of the common heritage of mankind.

Obviously, making this case out would require elaboration beyond the space available. But I do want to emphasize that what follows constitutes, in my view, a minimalist strategy. That is to say, whatever obligations of justice follow from it represent the absolutely rock-bottom requirements of justice in international affairs. To the extent that other advantages can be brought within the net of the principle of equal rights, the obligations of rich countries go beyond what is argued for here.

It would be ridiculous to spend time here on a blueprint for a scheme to put into effect the principle that I have been advancing. Its implementation on a world-wide scale, if it happens at all, is going to occur over a period measured in decades and, indeed, centuries. It will depend both on fundamental changes in outlook and on the development of international organs capable of taking decisions and carrying them out with reasonable efficiency and honesty.

The history of domestic redistribution is very much to the point here in suggesting that there is a virtuous circle in which the existence of redistributive institutions and beliefs in the legitimacy of redistribution are mutually reinforcing and have a strong tendency to become more extensive together over time. When Hume discussed redistribution in the *Enquiry*, the only form of it that he considered was 'perfect equality of possessions'.[17] The notion of continuous redistribution of

[17] David Hume, *An Enquiry Concerning the Principles of Morals*, in *Enquiries*, L. A. Selby-Bigge (ed.), 3rd edn. by P. H. Niddich (Oxford: Clarendon Press, 1975), 193–4.

income through a system of progressive taxation does not seem to have occurred to him. The Poor Law did, of course, provide a minimum of relief to the indigent, but it was organized by parishes and it is doubtful that the amateurish and nepotistic central administration of the eighteenth century could have handled a national scheme. The introduction of unemployment and sickness benefits and old age pensions in one Western European country after another from the late nineteenth century onward was made possible by the development of competent national administrations.

At the same time, these programmes constituted a political response to the extension of the suffrage, or one might more precisely say a response to conditions that, among other things, made the extension of the suffrage necessary for the continued legitimacy of the state. A certain measure of redistribution was the price the privileged were prepared to pay for mass acceptance of their remaining advantages. Once in place, however, such programmes have shown a universal tendency to take on a life of their own and to grow incrementally as gaps in the original coverage are filled in and the whole level of benefits is gradually raised. Indeed, it has been found in cross-national studies that the best predictor of the relative size of a given programme (say, aid to the blind) within the whole welfare system is the amount of time the programme has been running compared with others. In the long run the programme seems to generate supporting sentiments, so that even Margaret Thatcher and Ronald Reagan propose only reductions of a few percentage points in programmes that only thirty years ago would have seemed quite ambitious.

I do not want to drive the comparison with the international arena into the ground, but I think that, if nothing else, reflecting on domestic experience ought to lead us to look at international transfers from an appropriate time perspective. The United Nations Organization obviously has a lot wrong with it, for example, but its administration is probably less corrupt, self-serving, and inefficient than that which served Sir Robert Walpole. If one takes a time span of thirty years, it is, I suggest, more remarkable that the network of international co-operation has developed as far as it has than that it has not gone further. And in the realm of ideas the notion that poor countries have claims of one sort or another to aid from rich ones has moved from being quite exotic to one that is widely accepted in principle. At any rate in public, the representatives of the rich countries on international bodies no longer deny such a responsibility. They merely seek to evade any binding commitment based on it. But in the long run what is professed in public makes a difference to what gets done because it sets the terms of the discussion.

It is not at all difficult to come up with proposals for a system by which revenues would be raised on a regular basis from the rich countries and transferred to the poor ones. If any such scheme ever gained enough momentum to be a serious international issue, economists and accountants would no doubt have a field day arguing about the details and there is no point in anticipating such arguments here. However, the small amount of space I shall devote to redistributive mechanisms does not mean that I do not regard them as being of crucial importance.

Now, broadly speaking, two alternative approaches are possible. One would be to take up each of the aspects of international justice that have been discussed—and whatever others might be raised—and to base a system of taxes and receipts upon each. This would be messy and endlessly contentious. The alternative, which is, I predict, the only way in which any systematic redistribution will ever take place, if it ever does, is to have one or two comprehensive taxes and to distribute the proceeds according to some relatively simple formula among the poor countries.

The most obvious, and in my view the best, would be a tax on the governments of rich countries, assessed as a proportion of gross national product that increases with per capita income, the proceeds to be distributed to poor countries on a parallel basis of negative income tax. Gross national product reflects, roughly, the use of irreplaceable natural resources, the burden on the ecosphere, and advantages derived from the efforts of past generations and past exploitation of other countries. Ideally, this tax would be supplemented by a severance tax on the extraction of mineral resources and a shadow tax on the value of land and similar resources. (States could be left to collect the money by any means they chose. But their aggregate liability would be assessed by valuing the taxable base and applying the set rate.) This would certainly be required to take care of some glaring inequities that would still otherwise remain. But the simple system of transfer based on gross national product would be such an advance over the status quo that it would be a mistake to miss any chance to implement it by pursuing further refinements.

I believe that any other kinds of general tax, that is to say, taxes not related specifically to some aspect of justice, should be rejected. For example, a tax on foreign trade or on foreign trade in fossil fuels has been proposed.[18] This is so obviously arbitrary that it is hard to see how anyone can have considered it worth mooting. It has the manifest effect of penalizing small countries and countries that export coal and oil—and those that import it as well, if one believes that the incidence of the tax would be shifted to the consumer. Conversely, it has an absurdly favourable effect on very large countries that import and export little in relation to the size of their GNP and are relatively self-sufficient in energy derived from fossil fuels. No doubt the US State Department loves it, but why anyone else should be imposed on is a mystery to me.

I have assumed without discussion that resources transferred to satisfy the requirements of justice should go straight to poor countries rather than being channelled through international agencies and dispensed in the form of aid for specific projects. I shall spell out the rationale for this in the next section. But I will simply remark here that nothing I have said about justice rules out additional humanitarian transfers. And these would appropriately be administered by international organizations. The basis for raising such revenues for humanitarian aid would very reasonably be a progressive international shadow income tax, since this would perfectly reflect ability to pay. We might thus envisage a dual system of international taxation—one part, corresponding to the requirements of justice, going directly to poor countries to be spent at their own discretion; the other going to the World Bank or some successor organization less dominated by the donor countries.

III THE RELATIONS BETWEEN HUMANITY AND JUSTICE

I have been arguing that both humanity and justice require a substantial expansion in the scale of economic transfers from rich countries to poor ones. I should now like to show that, as the two rationales are very different, so are their practical implications. This point is worth emphasizing because those who pride themselves on the possession of sturdy Anglo-Saxon 'common sense' tend to conclude that, if we agree on the humanitarian obligation, we are wasting our breath in arguing about claims of injustice—claims for the rectification of alleged unrequited transfers from poor to rich countries in the past that are hard to assess and impossible to quantify, or involve more or less abstruse doctrines about the nature of justice in the contemporary

[18] Eleanor B. Steinberg and Joseph Y. Yager (eds.), *New Means of Financing International Needs* (Washington, DC: The Brookings Institution, 1978), ch. 3.

world. If we recognize the case for action on simple and straightforward humanitarian grounds, the idea goes, should we not concentrate on putting into place the appropriate aid policies, rather than allow ourselves to get sidetracked into fruitless wrangles about justice? In this context it is often said that the demands made by the countries of the South are 'symbolic' or 'ideological' and have the effect only of making more difficult the real, practical task of negotiating actual concessions by the countries of the North. The question that seems to me of more import is the following: if an obligation of humanity is accepted, under whatever name, how much difference does it make whether or not the kinds of claims I have been discussing under the heading of 'justice' are also conceded?

The answer is I believe that it makes a great deal of difference. Putting it in the most abstract terms, the obligations of humanity are goal-based, whereas those of justice are rights-based.[19] I would once have expressed the distinction between humanity and justice as one between an aggregative principle and a distributive principle.[20] I now, however, regard that distinction as less fundamental than the one I wish to mark by talking of goal-based and rights-based obligations. The point is that humanity and justice are not simply alternative prescriptions with respect to the same thing. Rather, they have different subject-matters.

Humanity, understood as a principle that directs us not to cause suffering and to relieve it where it occurs, is a leading member of a family of principles concerned with what happens to people (and other sentient creatures)—with what I shall call their well-being, intending to include in this such notions as welfare, happiness, self-fulfilment, freedom from malnutrition and disease, and satisfaction of basic needs. Justice, by contrast, is not directly concerned with such matters at all. As well as principles that tell us what are good and bad states of affairs and what responsibilities we have to foster the one and to avert the other, we also have principles that tell us how control over resources should be allocated. If we understand 'resources' in a very wide sense, so that it includes all kinds of rights to act without interference from others, to constrain the actions of others, and to bring about changes in the non-human environment, then we can say that the subject-matter of justice (at any rate in modern usage) is the

[19] For a distinction stated in these terms see Ronald Dworkin, 'The Original Position', *Chicago Law Review*, 4 (1973), 500–33, repr. in Norman Daniels (ed.), *Reading Rawls* (Oxford: Basil Blackwell, 1975), 16–53. The relevant discussion is on pp. 38–40 of this reprint.

[20] Brian Barry, *Political Argument* (London: Routledge and Kegan Paul, 1965), 43–4.

distribution of control over material resources. At this high level of generality, it is complemented by the principle of equal liberty, which is concerned with the control over non-material resources. To put it in a slogan, which has the advantages as well as the disadvantages of any slogan: humanity is a question of doing good whereas justice is a question of power.

When the contrast is stated in those terms, it might seem that bothering about justice is indeed a waste of time and that the bluff Anglo-Saxon advocates of common-sensical utilitarianism have the best of it after all. Why, it may naturally be asked, should we care about the distribution of *stuff* as against the distribution of *welfare*? Is this not simply commodity fetishism in a new guise?

The easy but inadequate answer is that the concept of justice is concerned not only with any old stuff but with the kind of stuff that has the capacity to provide those who use it with the material means of well-being: food, housing, clothing, medical care, and so on. This is correct as far as it goes and shows that being concerned with justice is not irrational. But it is inadequate because it leaves the supporter of justice open to an obvious flanking movement. His opponent may reply: 'You say that the only reason for concern about the distribution of the things whose proper allocation constitutes the subject-matter of justice is that they are the means to well-being. Very well. But are you not then in effect conceding that your "deep theory" is goal-based? For what you are saying is that we really are ultimately concerned with the distribution of well-being. We simply take an interest in the distribution of the means of well-being because they are what we can actually allocate. But this means that justice is a derivative principle.'

There are two lines of response open at this point. One is to concede that criteria for the distribution of resources are ultimately to be referred to the goal of well-being, but at the same time to deny that it follows from that concession that we can cut out the middleman and set out our principles for the allocation of resources with an eye directly on the well-being they are likely to produce. Or, more precisely, we may say that among the constituents of well-being is autonomy, and autonomy includes the power to choose frivolously or imprudently. Thus, on one (admittedly controversial) interpretation, John Stuart Mill's talk of justice in Book v of *Utilitarianism* and his presentation of the 'simple principle' of *On Liberty* in terms of rights is all consistent with an underlying utilitarian commitment if we allow for the importance to people of being able to plan their own lives and make their own decisions.

I think that this is by no means an unreasonable view and has more to be said for it than is, perhaps, fashionable to admit. Anyone who wishes at all costs to hold up a monistic ethical position is, I suspect, almost bound to finish up by trying to make some such argument as this. But I think that it is, nevertheless, in the last analysis a heroic attempt to fudge the issue by using the concept of autonomy to smuggle a basically foreign idea into the goal-based notion of advancing well-being.

The alternative is to deny that, in conceding that control over resources is important only because of the connection between resources and well-being, one is thereby committed to the view that principles for the distribution of resources are derivative. According to this view, there simply are two separate kinds of question. One concerns the deployment of resources to promote happiness and reduce misery. The other concerns the ethically defensible basis for allocating control over resources. Neither is reducible, even circuitously, to the other. When they conflict, we get hard questions, such as those involved in the whole issue of paternalism. But there is no overarching criterion within which such conflicts can be solved as is offered (at least in principle) by the idea that autonomy is an important, but not the only, ingredient in well-being.

As may be gathered, this is the position that I hold. In what follows, I want to show what difference it makes to employ an independent principle of justice in considering issues of international distribution. To make the discussion as clear as possible, I shall draw my contrast with a principle of humanity understood in the kind of pretty straightforward way exemplified in section I of this chapter. The contrast would be softened the more weight we were to give to autonomy as a component in well-being. Note, however, that even those who might wish to emphasize the importance of individual autonomy are likely to doubt the value to individual well-being of autonomy for states; yet it is precisely the question of autonomy for states that is going to turn out to be the main dividing line between humanity and justice at the international level.

The point is one of control. The rich countries already mostly concede, at least in verbal declarations, that they have a humanitarian obligation to assist the poor countries economically. The importance to the future of the world of their beginning to live up to those declarations can scarcely be overestimated. I trust that nothing in this chapter will be taken as disparaging humanitarian aid. To the extent that it does in fact relieve problems of poverty, disease, malnutrition, and population growth it is, obviously, of enormous value.

But to see its limitations, let us be really utopian about humanitarian aid. Let us imagine that it is collected on a regular and automatic basis from rich countries according to some formula that more or less reflects ability to pay; for example, a shadow tax on GNP graduated by the level of GNP per capita. And suppose that the proceeds were pooled and dispersed through agencies of the United Nations, according to general criteria for entitlement to assistance.

Now, undoubtedly, such a world would be an immense improvement on the present one, just as the modern welfare state has transformed, say, Henry Mayhew's London. But it would still leave us with a division between the donor countries, free to spend 'their' incomes as they pleased, and the recipient countries, which would have to spend their incomes 'responsibly'. No doubt, this would be less objectionable if the criteria for 'responsible' expenditures were drawn up in partnership between donor and recipient countries rather than, as now, being laid down by bodies such as the IMF and the World Bank in whose governing councils the rich countries have a preponderant voice. But funds earmarked and conditional upon approved use would still be basically different from income of the usual kind.

In contrast, transfers that were consequential upon considerations of justice would simply reduce the resources of one set of countries and augment those of another set. The distribution of control of resources would actually be shifted. It is therefore easy to see that the question of justice in the relations between rich and poor countries is by no means a purely 'symbolic' one. Real issues are at stake, and it is no self-delusion that leads the poor countries to press for a recognition of the claims of justice and the rich countries to resist these claims.

The conclusion we have reached, then, is that the crucial characteristic of justice is that the obligation to make the transfers required by it does not depend upon the use made of them by the recipient. At this point, I find that the following kinds of objection are usually made. What if the recipient country wastes the resources transferred to it? What if it is going to spend the money on armaments? What if it has a very unequal distribution of income and the additional income will be divided in the same unequal way? Such objections illustrate how difficult it is to get across the idea that, if some share of resources is justly owed to a country, then the money is (even before it has actually been transferred) as much that country's as the rest of its income.

The answer that I give is that there are extreme circumstances in which the international community or some particular donor country would be justified in withholding resources owed as a matter of justice to some country. But these are exactly the same extreme conditions under which it would also be justifiable to refuse to pay debts to it, to freeze its assets overseas, to subject it to economic sanctions, or perhaps to intervene with force to change its government.

One could envisage a world in which there were indeed an international authority that allowed countries to keep only that portion of the national income that was justly distributed internally and used in approved, non-wasteful ways. Such a world would not be at all like ours, since it would accept no principle of national autonomy. It would be one in which a global society (not now in existence) had inscribed on its banner: 'From each according to his ability, to each according to his needs.'

The alternative to that world, so different from ours, is one in which the general presumption is of national autonomy, with countries being treated as units capable of determining the use of those resources to which they were justly entitled. This is the world that we now have, and the only modification in the status quo I am arguing for is a redefinition of what justly belongs to a country. Inevitably, as the price of autonomy, it permits countries to use resources that are justly theirs in wasteful ways, and it does not insist that a country that allows some to live in luxury while others have basic needs unfulfilled should lose income to which it is entitled as a matter of justice.

My point here is that both of the models I have sketched are internally consistent. We could have a system in which there are no entitlements based on justice and in which, assuming that states are still the administrative intermediaries, funds are allocated for worthy purposes and cut off if they are misspent, just as in the United States the Federal government cuts off funds to state and local governments that do not comply with various guidelines. Or we could have a world in which, once the demands of just distribution between countries are satisfied, we say that we have justice at the world level, and the question of domestic distribution and national priorities then becomes one for each country to decide for itself.

What is not consistent is to have a world in which those countries that are required by international justice to be donors live under the easygoing second system while those that are recipients live under the stern dispensation of the first. If the idea is going to be that countries should have their entitlements reduced if they are wasteful and fail in internal equity, then the obvious place to start is not with some poor country in sub-Saharan Africa or South Asia but with, say, a country that burns one ninth of the world's daily oil consumption on its roads alone and that, in spite of having a quarter of the world's GNP, is unable to provide decent medical care for much of its population, while a substantial proportion live in material conditions of abject squalor that (except for being more dirty and dangerous) recall the cities of Germany and Britain in the aftermath of the Second World War.

None of this, let me emphasize, denies the independent significance of humanity as a criterion in international morality. But we cannot sensibly talk about humanity unless we have a baseline set by justice. To talk about what I ought, as a matter of humanity, to do with what is mine makes no sense until we have established what is mine in the first place. If I have stolen what is rightfully somebody else's property, or if I have borrowed from him and refuse to repay the debt when it is due and as a result he is destitute, it would be unbecoming on my part to dole out some part of the money that should belong to him, with various strings attached as to the way in which he should spend it, and then go around posing as a great humanitarian. That is an exact description of the position in which the rich countries have currently placed themselves.

The need for humanitarian aid would be reduced in a world that had a basically just international distribution. It would still be required to meet special problems caused by crop failure owing to drought, destruction owing to floods and earthquakes, and similar losses resulting from other natural disasters. It would also, unhappily, continue to be required to cope with the massive refugee problems that periodically arise from political upheavals.

Beyond that, humanitarian aid in the form of food, technical assistance, or plain money is no doubt always a good thing. How much the rich countries would have to give on the basis of an obligation of humanity depends first on the extent of redistribution we hold to be required by justice and, second, on the stringency that we assign to the obligation of humanity—how much sacrifice can be demanded to deal with what level of need.

As will be clear, this chapter is concerned only with a preliminary investigation of the principles relevant to an ethical appraisal of international distribution and redistribution. I must therefore leave any more precise statement of implications for future discussions —and not necessarily by me. Ultimately, if anything is to be done, it will require a widespread shift in ideas. Greater precision can be expected to develop *pari passu* with such a shift. I very much doubt the value of single-handed attempts to produce a blueprint in advance of that.

17

JUSTICE AS RECIPROCITY

I INTRODUCTION

What, if anything, do rich nations owe to poor ones? What, if anything, does the present generation owe to those who are to come after it? In the last few years we have seen an enormous increase in the salience of these questions. The poor countries have a comfortable majority in the General Assembly of the United Nations and have established in UNCTAD a permanent international organization dedicated to furthering their interests. The spectacular success of OPEC has forcibly drawn attention to the extent to which the prices of raw materials are subject to economic power and thus brought commodity prices more explicitly into the political arena. The East-West theme of cold war confrontation that ran through the third quarter of the century is being replaced in the final quarter by the North-South theme of confrontation between rich and poor nations.[1] At the same time, a new understanding of the complex interrelations that make life possible on earth has made us more aware of the way in which quite minor alterations of the ecological balance may have catastrophic long-run consequences. The interests of our remote descendants have started to figure explicitly in debates on the disposal of nuclear waste and the proposal to ban fluorocarbon aerosol propellants. Moreover, the literature of 'limits to growth', 'spaceship earth', and so on has served to emphasize the fact that, however sanguine one might be about new discoveries of raw materials and substitutes, resources are finite and we cannot therefore avoid facing the fact that the more we use the less there will be left for our descendants.

Most of us have only the haziest ideas about what justice requires in these cases. Even worse, we feel that the framework within which we normally think about justice—the framework that serves us well enough for thinking about relations among contemporaries in the same society—fails to give us a grip on these problems of international and intergenerational justice. In this chapter I shall explore them by

[1] See, for an analysis of the changing character of international politics, Robert O. Keohane and Joseph S. Nye, *Power and Interdependence: World Politics In Transition* (Boston, Mass.: Little Brown, 1977).

setting out this framework of everyday thought, seeing exactly how international and intergenerational justice relate to it and then arguing that there is another conception of justice, also deeply rooted in our common ideas, that provides a key to the problems of justice between countries and between generations.

The framework within which we ordinarily discuss questions of justice among contemporaries who are members of the same society is, I suggest, that of justice as reciprocity. Every society of which I have read has some notion as to the rightness of meeting reasonable expectations that a favour will be returned, of pulling one's weight in co-operative enterprises, of keeping agreements that provide for mutual benefits, and so on.[2] Thus, Marcel Mauss, in his classic *The Gift*, 'stresses that there is a universally recognized obligation to reciprocate gifts which have been accepted', while A. R. Radcliffe-Brown 'assumed a principle of reciprocity which he called "the principle of equivalent return". This he held was expressed in the *lex talionis*, in the principle of indemnification for injury, and in the principle that those who give benefits should receive equivalent benefits.'[3]

Again, the most significant recent work of political philosophy, *A Theory of Justice* by John Rawls,[4] is built around the notion of justice as reciprocity. It has been said correctly that 'it is the contractualist conception of equality as reciprocity that is at the root of Rawls's interpretation of justice'.[5] The essence of justice as reciprocity for Rawls is what in his article 'Justice as Fairness' he called the duty of fair play: 'the obligation which participants who have knowingly accepted the benefits of their common practice owe to each other to act in accordance with it when their performance falls due'.[6] 'Fair play' in this sense is an important part of justice as reciprocity but we have many other usages involving the concepts of fairness which we employ to assess the extent to which reciprocity is being satisfied or violated. Thus, we speak of a fair exchange when the values of the

[2] See Alvin W. Gouldner, 'The Norm of Reciprocity', *American Sociological Review*, 25 (1960), 161–78 and 'Reciprocity and Autonomy in Functional Theory', in N. J. Demerath III and Richard A. Peterson (eds.), *System, Change, and Conflict* (New York: Free Press, 1967), 141–69.

[3] Quotations from Gouldner, 'Reciprocity and Autonomy', p. 150 nn. 17 and 18. The first refers to Marcel Mauss, *The Gift* (Glencoe, Ill.: Free Press, 1954), the second to a Chicago University seminar of 1937, 'The Nature of a Theoretical Science of Society'.

[4] John Rawls, *A Theory of Justice* (Cambridge, Mass.: Harvard University Press, 1971).

[5] John W. Chapman, *Nomos*, 6, Carl J. Friedrich and John W. Chapman (eds.) (New York: Atherton Press, 1963), 147–69, at 149.

[6] John Rawls, 'Justice as Fairness', repr. in P. Laslett and W. G. Runciman (eds.), *Philosophy, Politics and Society*, 2nd ser. (Oxford: Basil Blackwell, 1962), 132–57, at 146.

things exchanged are equivalent, and of a fair offer as a proposal for a fair exchange. We speak of fair compensation when the value of the compensation matches the loss sustained. And we speak of fairness not only in relation to the way in which the burdens of a common enterprise are distributed but also in relation to the way in which the benefits are distributed. Other things being equal, if one person puts more into an activity yielding a common benefit, it is considered fair that he should get more out.[7]

The first half of this chapter will be devoted to the further analysis of justice as reciprocity. I shall look at justice as reciprocity under three heads. The first is justice as requital, that is to say, making a fair return for benefits received (section II). The second is justice as fidelity, that is to say, carrying out one's side of a bargain voluntarily entered into (section III). The third is justice as mutual aid, that is to say, playing one's part in a practice of helping those in need (section IV).

The second half of the chapter will be concerned with the limitations of justice as reciprocity, even when its bounds are drawn quite widely as in my discussion. After pointing out these limitations in relation to justice between countries (section V) and justice between generations (section VI), I shall put forward another conception of justice—justice as equal opportunity (section VII). In conclusion (section VIII) I shall sketch in the implications of this conception for justice between nations and justice between generations.

II JUSTICE AS REQUITAL

I intend under this heading to include a mixed bag, united only by the general idea of *quid pro quo*. Thus, I include fair dealing in explicit trading situations and the more diffuse notion of making an adequate return contained in the notion that 'one good turn deserves another'. The converse of this, for bad turns, is that anyone who harms another should provide compensation or suffer punishment. I include Rawls's duty of fair play, which calls on those who have enjoyed, or stand to enjoy, a public good to be willing to contribute to the cost of

[7] See George Caspar Homans, *Social Behavior: Its Elementary Forms* (London: Routledge and Kegan Paul, 1961), ch. 12, for an exposition of the view that 'men are alike in holding the notion of proportionality between investment and profit that lies at the heart of distributive justice' (p. 246). Homans explicitly equates distributive justice and fair exchange: 'Fair exchange, or distributive justice in the relations among men, is realized when the profit, or reward less cost, of each man is directly proportional to his investments' (p. 264). See Elaine Walster and G. William Walster, 'Equity and Social Justice', *Journal of Social Issues*, 31 (1975), 21–43 for a review of the small-group literature subsequent to *Social Behavior*.

providing it. (In 'Justice as Fairness' Rawls gave the examples of taxes for the provision of government services and of trade union dues.[8]) The converse of the 'anti-free rider' principle is that anyone who contributes especially effectively to the provision of a collective benefit is in fairness entitled to be rewarded more highly by the (other) recipients of the benefit. Clearly, justice as requital could be analysed in much more detail and the types of justice as requital roughly distinguished here could be further developed. But for my present purpose it is enough if I have pointed in an unambiguous way to a conception of justice that is at least in some forms non-controversial and universal.[9]

III JUSTICE AS FIDELITY

This is the aspect of justice that was for Hobbes the whole of it: 'that men perform their covenants made'. The connection between fidelity and reciprocity is obvious, so much so that it is not surprising to find the part taken for the whole and all of justice as reciprocity reduced to contractual relations. Thus, Hobbes takes up two aspects of what I have been calling justice as requital: commutative justice as 'equality of value of the things contracted for' and distributive justice as 'the distribution of equal benefit, to men of equal merit'. And he disposes of them as criteria of justice by arguing, against the first, that 'the just value, is that which [the contractors] be contented to give', and, against the second, that 'Merit . . . is not due by Justice; but is rewarded of Grace only'.[10] This, however, simply presupposes the definition of 'justice' that Hobbes has already given, in terms of keeping covenant.

Charles Fried has expressed the Hobbesian position on the first as follows:

The plausibility of [mutual promising] as showing the kind of practice which must be considered just depends on this—that the sacrifices which are made

[8] Rawls, 'Justice as Fairness', p. 146. The inadequacy of voluntary contributions as a way of supporting the cost of public goods is argued in Mancur Olson, Jr., *The Logic of Collective Action* (Cambridge, Mass.: Harvard University Press, 1965). For a sophisticated formal analysis which explores the question of under what circumstances co-operative behaviour can be maintained without coercion, see Michael Taylor, *Anarchy and Cooperation* (Chichester: Wiley, 1967) revised as *The Possibility of Cooperation* (Cambridge: University of Cambridge Press, 1987).

[9] For a discussion of some of the ramifications of justice as requital and the difficulties that arise in applying it, see Robert E. Goodin, *The Politics of Rational Man* (Chichester: Wiley, 1976), chs. 6 and 7.

[10] Thomas Hobbes, *Leviathan*, C. B. Macpherson (ed.) (Harmondsworth: Penguin, 1968), ch. 15, p. 208.

by each individual are by hypothesis less than the gain to that individual. Furthermore, we need not determine whether any individual has in fact received full value, and more, for his sacrifice, since as the practice is defined, it is the individual himself who approves the exchange.[11]

Consider a case such as one reads of now and then, of somebody who digs out a picture or a stamp collection that has been gathering dust in the attic and sells it to a dealer at a fraction of its market value. The dealer has not used force or fraud and was under no legal obligation to supply information as to the true value of the object purchased. And the object was clearly less valuable to the seller at the time of the sale than the money he was offered for it, otherwise he would not have chosen to sell. Yet there is surely a perfectly clear sense in which this deal is unfair: the profit from the transaction is too unequally divided between the parties. Notice that we may say that a morally scrupulous dealer would not have taken unfair advantage of the seller's inexperience in this way without committing ourselves to the view that the law should void the contract or even to the view that the dealer had violated a duty. Yet the basis of our judgement that the dealer would have been more admirable if he had behaved differently is surely not that he would have shown himself generous or benevolent but that he would have shown sensitivity to the requirements of fairness.

Thus we can, and do, say intelligibly that a contract is unfair between the parties because the value of the things exchanged is unequal, although it is still a contract. And we do, quite rightly, say that it is unfair if 'men of equal merit' are treated differently, even if the giving of a reward is a matter of grace. The parable of the labourer in the vineyard (Matthew 20: 1–16) illustrates the point. That the lord of the vineyard gave more than the customary rate to those who had worked less than a full stint was a matter of 'grace' in Hobbes's terminology, and the lord's reply to one who had 'borne the burden and heat of the day'—'Friend, I do thee no wrong; didst not thou agree with me for a penny?'—is undeniably to the point. But there is surely also a genuine issue of fairness embodied in the complaint, 'these last have wrought but one hour, and thou hast made them equal to us'. Indeed, unless it is assumed that there is a natural sentiment of fairness—equal pay for equal work—that is being flouted, the parable loses its force which is, I take it, to emphasize the difference between the grace of God and human justice.

Hobbes had an ulterior political motive in denying that there were

[11] Charles Fried, 'Justice and Liberty', *Nomos*, 6, pp. 126–46, at 133.

alternative criteria of justice: he did not want to provide any excuses for non-performance of covenants since that might weaken the absolute claims of the sovereign. But it is quite consistent to say that a contract you entered into is unfair in that it does not exchange equal values or give a greater return for a greater contribution but that it would be unfair not to carry out your side of a bargain freely agreed to.

A quite different ulterior political motive has led Robert Nozick, in *Anarchy, State, and Utopia*, to deprecate the Rawlsian duty of 'fair play'. Nozick's fear is that it will license any group of people to create a duty to contribute to some common enterprise simply by providing unasked-for benefits. 'One cannot, whatever one's purposes, just act so as to give people benefits and then demand (or seize) payment. Nor can a group of people do this.'[12] He therefore wants to insist that there must be actual consent before it is legitimate to coerce people to contribute to a common good. Once again, the implication is that justice as reciprocity is reduced to contractual relations.

Characteristically, Nozick does not bother to offer any arguments, and rests the burden of his case on an eccentric example involving a public address system and 'some of the people in your neighbourhood' who put down everybody's name on a list to broadcast over it for a day.[13] It is indeed doubtful whether the case as stated gives rise to a duty to broadcast, still less that it gives the others a right to coerce you to do so (though I do think that as a matter of decency you should give advance notice of your intention not to perform). However, it is far from clear that the case as stated falls under Rawls's principle of fair play. For Rawls defined the duty of fair play by saying that 'a person is required to do his part as defined by the rules of an institution when two conditions are met: first the institution is just (or fair) . . . and second, one has voluntarily accepted the benefits of the arrangement or taken advantage of the opportunities it offers to further one's interests'.[14] Nozick's case may be defective as a counter-example on all three possible counts: it does not constitute an example of an 'institution' for the purpose of the principle; it is not just for 'some people' in the neighbourhood to arrogate to themselves the right to direct the use others make of their time; and listening to the public address system is scarcely voluntary.

If we turn to the real-life analogue of Nozick's example, it seems

[12] Robert Nozick, *Anarchy, State, and Utopia* (New York: Basic Books, 1974), 95.

[13] Ibid. 93–5.

[14] Rawls, *A Theory of Justice*, pp. 111–12. I am indebted to the comments on Nozick's example in Thomas Scanlon, 'Nozick on Rights, Liberty, and Property', *Philosophy & Public Affairs*, 6 (1976), 3–25, at 15–17.

clear to me that the American public television stations have a good case for appealing (as they do) to the sense of fairness of those 'free riders' who choose to watch but do not contribute to the expenses of running the service. And I would add that considerations of fairness legitimate (if they do not require) that public television should be supported by a compulsory levy on the owners of television sets, as it is in many countries. It may be argued, of course, that this is unfair because some will be forced to contribute who do not watch public television or (in a country where there is no commercial television) would prefer having commercial television to paying for a licence. But to anyone except a fanatic the issue presents itself as a choice between the unfairness of permitting 'free riders' and the unfairness of collecting from non-beneficiaries, and there is no reason why the judgement should always go the same way. Let us leave aside the question of enforcement, however. The crucial point for present purposes is the simple one that the public television stations do have a legitimate claim in terms of fairness against those who benefit from the programmes but fail to contribute—a claim that Nozick's thesis would render unintelligible.[15]

The Rawlsian duty of fair play, as I noted above, requires that the benefits should have been accepted voluntarily. However, the general anti-free-rider principle is not limited in this way. It is unfair to enjoy the benefits of a practice without doing your part, even if you could not avoid enjoying these benefits. For example, if you live in an area where only smokeless fuel is permitted to be burned, you cannot help breathing cleaner air, having to wash curtains less often, and so on, but that does not in any way diminish your obligation to play your part and burn only smokeless fuel. Similarly, if other visitors to some remote beauty spot obey the rule that they should take their litter away with them, you cannot help enjoying the absence of litter, but again that would not make it any less unfair for you to leave yours behind.

Nozick's nightmare of people arbitrarily being able to impose obligations of fairness on you by doing you favours fails to take account of the fact that it takes more to create a practice (or in Rawls's terms an institution) than a few people getting together and starting to provide benefits for others. One of the main purposes of law is to define practices and thus create well-defined duties of fairness. The

[15] For an analysis of the implications for the provision of public goods of a morality favouring each person who benefits giving his 'fair share' of the costs, see Russell Hardin, *Collective Action* (Baltimore: The Johns Hopkins University Press for Resources for the Future, 1982), ch. 6. Hardin notes the importance of setting a standard 'membership fee' to create a 'uniquely prominent, relatively fair solution for cost-sharing'.

threat of criminal penalties is not very important as a motive for compliance with rules against domestic air pollution or littering. The law is, however, significant as a co-ordinating device, defining a standard of conduct that it would be fair for all to adhere to provided that others do so too. Nozick's idea, that if a random collection of self-appointed do-gooders cannot create obligations of fairness then neither can a public authority, entirely misses the point.

'The law', Paul Freund has said, 'is addicted to the device of finding "implied" contracts as a way out of novel problems, and of assimilating relations—such as public utility and customer—to a contractual mold'.[16] No doubt there are good technical reasons for this device, but in general the argument against trying to cram all cases of reciprocity into contract is an extension of that deployed by David Hume against the use of a fictitious 'original contract' to underwrite political obligation. If the real point is that of reciprocal advantage, nothing is gained by going through an extra loop and saying that the obligation derives from the fact that it would have been worth contracting had the occasion arisen.[17]

I have criticized the reduction of requital to fidelity. Rawls, in *A Theory of Justice*, goes in the other direction. He says that 'the principle of fidelity is but a special case of the principle of fairness applied to the social practice of promising' and that 'the obligation to keep a promise is a consequence of the principle of fairness'.[18] If he meant simply that the principle of fidelity and the principle of fair play both derive from justice as reciprocity this would be unexceptionable. But to assimilate them, as Rawls does, results in slighting the significance of voluntary agreement.

In the case of practices where participation is not optional, Rawls says (reasonably enough) that the duty of fair play comes into operation to require performance only when the practice is itself just in the way in which it distributes benefits and burdens. He tries to extend this to promising by saying that the principle of fairness makes the carrying out of promises obligatory only where the practice of

[16] Paul A. Freund, 'Social Justice and the Law', in *On Law and Justice* (Cambridge, Mass.: Harvard University Press, 1968), 82–107, at 84.

[17] Freund's remarks on the history of Roman and English contract law seem to me to suggest that the notion of justice as fidelity was a development out of that of justice as requital. According to Freund, the generalized notion of a contract arose in Roman law from 'either a delivery of a thing in expectation of a performance . . . or . . . the performance of an act in expectation of counterperformance' (p. 84), while in English law 'the elements of both *quid pro quo* and reliance entered into its inheritance' (p. 85). It is worth noting that these are precisely the bases of an enforceable duty of fair play ridiculed by Nozick.

[18] Rawls, *A Theory of Justice*, pp. 344, 346.

promising is itself just. An example of an unjust practice of promising would be one in which people were 'bound by words uttered while asleep, or extorted by force'.[19] This is of course right but it does not establish what Rawls wants. For the analogy of a particular non-voluntary practice is not the general practice of promising but 'a particular pattern of transactions' established by a set of mutual promises.[20] And the point is that justice as fidelity requires performance even if the 'small-scale scheme of cooperation' established by this set of mutual promises violates justice as requital in the way in which it distributes benefits and burdens among the participants. This is simply to reiterate that justice as requital and justice as fidelity are independent derivations from the generic notion of justice as reciprocity, and may on occasion conflict.

IV JUSTICE AS MUTUAL AID

Consider, to begin with, an ordinary case of voluntary insurance—against fire, theft, or accident, for example. If we look at the operation of the scheme within a certain slice of time, and overlook the contractual basis of the arrangements, we see a large number of fortunate citizens who have not had fires (and so on) in the period each paying in money which is dispensed to the small number who have been unfortunate. Simply observing the pattern of transfers we could not distinguish the insurance company from a charitable institution appealing to the generosity of the fortunate to give succour to the unfortunate. What makes the difference is reciprocity. Even the most coldly calculating egoist will, if he is rational and risk-averse, willingly pay insurance premiums because only by doing so can he establish a claim to compensation for unlikely but potentially devastating contingencies.

Private insurance is, as I have said, based on contractual relationships. Inasfar as it exhibits reciprocity, it is the kind dealt with in my remarks on justice as fidelity. The exchange is simply of a regular premium for a right to be paid in some contingency. The reason for beginning my discussion of justice as mutual aid with it is that it illustrates how, even in a society made up of devotees of Ayn Rand, there would be continuous redistribution from the fortunate to the unfortunate—on a purely voluntary basis. In what follows I shall argue that the insurance model can be extended to (*a*) a non-

[19] Ibid. 345. [20] Ibid. 346.

contractual practice of mutual aid; and (*b*) a non-voluntary system of redistribution.

Imagine a small community a hundred miles from the nearest town. Each family possesses a car, but cars are, of course, liable to break down. To meet this contingency a two-part practice has developed: anyone who is going into town anyway should be prepared to give a ride to a person whose car is not in use, even at some minor inconvenience of scheduling, picking up, setting down, and so on; and in case of genuine emergency anyone for whom it is not unduly inconvenient should be prepared to make a special trip into town. This practice would, I suggest, generate a duty of mutual aid derived from the general notion of justice as reciprocity.

It is interesting to speculate how the practice of mutual aid might extend to those without a car at all. Suppose that, because of either loss of earnings or increasing infirmity, some of the old people in the community are no longer able to run a car. It might seem that, since they can no longer pay the 'premium'—the liability to give lifts to others—the insurance model should entail that they be excluded from the benefits. Any help they receive would then have to be put down to charity rather than reciprocity. But those who have cause to fear that they may some day themselves be reduced to the same circumstances will favour extending the benefits of the practice as an insurance measure.

This is still reciprocity but in a more complex form. Those who contribute benefits in a given period do not necessarily have any expectation of being able to claim them in future from the present beneficiaries. But they expect to be able to make claims themselves in the future on others, as defined by the practice. At any given time, the young could get a short-run gain by reneging on the extension of mutual aid to the old. But a social practice defined by informal norms and underwritten by informal sanctions (the exclusion from benefits of those who violate 'fair play' by failing to perform when required to) cannot simply be stopped and then started up again later. The age cohort that is thinking of reneging on its obligations to the old cannot, therefore, reasonably expect to be able to impose the same obligation later on its juniors.

The young have reason, derived from the insurance motive, for maintaining the extended practice in order to be in a position to benefit from it later themselves if they need to. This, it should be conceded, presupposes that those who make the sacrifices now will actually be around when they will stand to benefit from the operation of the same practice. We should therefore anticipate that reciprocity of this intertemporal kind will be weakened by mobility, and this does indeed seem to accord with experience. If the community were known to be due to be dissolved in a few years' time (suppose, for example, that its economy is entirely based on the exploitation of a non-renewable natural resource and that when that comes to an end its members will scatter), then we have to say that giving lifts to those without cars would switch from reciprocity to charity.

It should be observed that waiving the 'premium' for some does not entail waiving it for all. Anyone who, relying on the practice to get him out of trouble, chose to save the expense of having a car or ran one that was notoriously unreliable would be condemned as a free (or cheap) rider. If he has no less reason for paying the premium than anyone else, it is unfair of him not to. He would therefore be excluded or—given that there is a humanitarian duty in life-and-death emergencies to help, which is not dependent on reciprocity—subject to condemnation. (We could extend the story to more generalized reciprocity, so that someone who relied on others for transport provided some other service to members of the community, but there is no need to get into such further extensions here.)

I now have to say a little about the way in which justice as mutual aid underwrites compulsory redistribution. This theme has in recent years been taken up by economists under the label 'Pareto-optimal redistribution'.[21] Saying that a redistribution is Pareto optimal is to say that everybody prefers the distribution after redistribution has been carried out to the one before. The apparent paradox involved in saying that all might gain from redistribution is resolved by recalling that those who did not have a fire in a certain year have had their premiums redistributed to those that did; yet at the start of the year they thought they were better off with the insurance than without it, otherwise they presumably would not have chosen to buy it. I shall not discuss other things that economists include under 'Pareto-optimal redistribution', such as redistribution required by altruism (feeling better if others are happy) or malice (feeling better if others are unhappy), since these do not have any relevance to justice. Some economists even include relief from individual or collective violence

[21] See Geoffrey Brennan, 'Pareto-Desirable Redistribution: the Non-Altruistic Dimension', *Public Choice*, 14 (1973), 43–67; and three essays in Harold H. Hochman and George E. Peterson (eds.), *Redistribution through Public Choice* (New York: Columbia University Press, 1974): James D. Rodgers, 'Explaining Income Redistribution' (pp. 165–205); Richard Zeckhauser, 'Risk Spreading and Distribution' (pp. 206–28); and A. Mitchell Polinsky, 'Imperfect Capital Markets, Intertemporal Redistribution and Progressive Taxation' (pp. 229–58).

from the poor as a motive for 'Pareto-optimal redistribution', but this makes sense only if we count handing over one's wallet to a mugger as a Pareto-optimal redistribution. I shall divide the case for redistribution deriving from reciprocity into three elements: first, insurance for categorical contingencies; second, insurance for non-categorical contingencies; and, third, redistribution through time.

First, then, by 'categorical contingencies' I mean specifiable misfortunes: being sick, going blind, being thrown out of work by a general recession or a sudden fall in the market for one's skills (for example the redundancies of engineers and draughtsmen attendant upon the cut-back of the US aerospace industry). The state can accept risks (like that of compensation for long-term unemployment) that a private insurance company cannot. Suppose, for example, that a company were to offer a medical insurance policy to all in good health at age 21, with a guarantee that it would never cancel it and that premiums would not reflect subsequent individual experience or health prospects. Rational risk-averse people would welcome such a policy; but, if they are free to opt out at any time, then those whose health is still good twenty or thirty years later would have an incentive to join a scheme that offered lower rates than those it accepted after a medical examination. The original scheme would thus be undermined, since only those in poor health would be left in it and would in effect form a pool of bad risks. This is a sort of prisoner's dilemma situation: at age 21 everyone would prefer the scheme with everyone staying in, but those who remain healthy have an incentive to defect. The solution is for the state to collect the premiums from everyone through ordinary taxes or a special social security levy.

Over and above this, it would be rational to insure against 'bad luck', and this is what I mean by the second head of insurance against non-categorical contingencies. Looking at his prospects at the age of 21, say, a person with normal tastes would be willing to buy insurance, if it could be purchased, that would take some of his income if he is lucky enough to make a lot and give him some if he is unsuccessful. The state can achieve this by positive and negative taxation and, again, unless the state is going to enforce insurance agreements that do not allow for withdrawal on either side any time during the life of the insured person, only the state can bring about this kind of redistribution.

There are two obvious constraints on the amount of redistribution that would be generated by the state providing 'luck insurance' in the amount that would be purchased voluntarily. First, the redistribution package offered to each person would have to be related to his expected income: redistribution from those with good prospects at age 21 to those with poor prospects at age 21 falls outside the present rationale.[22] And second, since the 'bad luck' to be insured against is simply imputed from an income that falls below the average for one with such prospects at age 21, the problem of 'moral hazard'—the bane of all insurers—rears its ugly head. The perfect insurance (considered aside from moral hazard) makes the client indifferent between escaping the contingency insured against and suffering the contingency plus getting the compensation. But that means there is no incentive to avoid the contingency—to lock doors, check wiring, avoid health risks, and so on. Where the probability of the contingency's occurring can be affected by choices, therefore, insurance must be less than perfect to avoid skyrocketing premiums or the bankruptcy of the insurance scheme. If each person were offered a guaranteed income equal to the average for those with his prospects (that is, 100 per cent tax on income above and 100 per cent supplementation of income below), bad luck would be seriously contaminated by lack of exertion and the scheme would be in danger of going broke because of actual average incomes falling below those projected.

Finally, we should consider redistribution through time. If the normal human career is to have no earned income in the early years of one's life and again after retirement, then a lot of what looks like interpersonal redistribution when viewed at a single point in time, may be thought of alternatively as intertemporal redistribution within each person's lifetime income. Economists have been particularly concerned with the state's role in distributing income backward. Babies and children cannot (legally) borrow to get themselves a good education, medical and dental care, a nutritious diet, and so on; yet someone might see clearly, on reaching the age of majority, that it would have been worth paying money out in the future to have had those things earlier on. Even when the legal bar to borrowing falls at the age of majority, it is difficult to borrow much on future earnings. The problems set by making loans to be repaid out of future income over a long period are illustrated by the high rate of default in the USA on loans to college students. The state can overcome these problems by providing benefits, in the form of education, free milk, subsidized

[22] If we assume that the best the insurer could do in setting rates was to use educational level, achievement test scores, socio-economic background, race, and so on as evidence, the risk to be insured against would be 'luck' as defined by Christopher Jencks in *Inequality: A Reassessment of the Effect of Family and Schooling in America* (London: Allen Lane, 1973)—that variation in lifetime earnings not explained by such factors.

school meals, medical services, child allowances, and so on, and then collecting the cost later in taxes.

Redistribution forward is easier to the extent that saving is easier than borrowing. But in an uncertain world, where in many countries no form of investment yields a positive (inflation-discounted) return, it is highly rational to want to have any private superannuation scheme or savings programme underpinned by a scheme of state pensions that is, when it comes down to it (whatever its insurance trimmings may be), a scheme for transferring from those who are earning to those who are retired. It may be noted that such a (non-actuarial) scheme corresponds to the extended practice of mutual aid in my example of the isolated community.

V RECIPROCITY AND RELATIONS BETWEEN COUNTRIES

From the viewpoint of justice as reciprocity, we must say that even the meagre redistribution that takes place now (in the form of aid, soft loans, and commodity contracts at above world prices) has to be counted as charity rather than justice. Justice as fidelity does not help: poor countries tend to break contracts (whether excusably or not need not be asked here) more often than rich countries. Justice as requital is a complicated matter. Obviously, in the imperialist period raw materials were extracted and labour employed without adequate return, and there is now a case for reparations. It may be said that the descendants of the exploiters have no obligation to atone for the injustice of their ancestors; but surely they do if they are themselves richer as a result of that injustice and the descendants of the exploited are poorer.[23]

It is a good deal harder to show that current transactions fail to meet the standard of justice as requital. To my knowledge, the most elaborate and sustained attempt to argue that international trade between rich and poor countries is a process by which the rich exploit the poor is Arghiri Emmanuel's book *Unequal Exchange*.[24] According to Emmanuel, 'as far as the underdeveloped countries are concerned . . . international aid has ceased to be regarded as a one-sided and gratuitous act on the part of the rich countries and is seen as an obligation that corresponds to a certain right of compensation'.

[23] For an analysis of some of the problems arising from group reparations for misdeeds of earlier generations, see Boris I. Bittker, *The Case for Black Reparations* (New York: Random House, 1973).

[24] Arghiri Emmanuel, *Unequal Exchange: A Study of the Imperialism of Trade* (New York: Monthly Review Press, 1972).

He goes on: 'Compensation for what? That is indeed the question, and this is what I have tried to answer'.[25] As I understand it, the essence of his answer is that the large difference in wages paid in different countries for the same number of hours of qualitatively similar work (measured in terms of skill, physical exertion, and so on) shows that the system of international exchange is unequal. Thus, he says:

While one may be able to find reasons, whether good or bad, to explain the difference between the wages of an American metal worker who controls a power press worth a million dollars and those of a worker on a Brazilian coffee plantation who uses only a simple machete, it is much harder to explain why a building worker who puts up a bungalow in the suburbs of New York has to be paid thirty times as much as his counterpart in the Lebanon, though both of them use the same tools and perform exactly the same movements as their Assyrian fellow worker of four thousand years ago.[26]

Surely it would be harder to explain how it would be possible to find building workers in New York at Lebanese (or Assyrian) rates of pay. Assuming the existence of some kind of labour market, any work in rich countries will be better paid across the board than the same kind of work in poor countries—hence the rule of thumb that the quickest way of judging the standard of living of a country is to see what a haircut costs, because a haircut is a standardized service almost all of whose price is made up of labour costs.

On Emmanuel's theory, the scale of unequal exchange in international trade today is truly enormous: it can be measured by asking what the terms of trade would be if wage rates were the same in all countries, and comparing that hypothetical state of affairs with the status quo.

If we assume that wages account for fifty per cent of the cost of [Third World] exports, and that the relevant rate of wages is one-twentieth of that prevailing in the advanced countries, a simple calculation will show us that the difference between the present value and the equivalence value is . . . a difference . . . in hundreds of thousands of millions. If fifty sacks of coffee are at present exchanged for one automobile, whereas, in order to pay coffee plantation workers at the same rate as workers in the automobile industry, fifty sacks would have to be exchanged for ten automobiles, the loss suffered by the coffee producers and the gain made by the other party in this transaction are not *less than* the value of fifty sacks, but *nine times as much*.[27]

[25] Ibid. 264.

[26] Ibid. 263–4.

[27] Ibid. 368 (italics in original). Notice that this passage shows a shift in ground from the earlier one quoted, in that the standard is now taken to be one in which the pay of the machete-wielding coffee worker and the power press operative in the car plant is equalized.

Now I think it is a perfectly intelligible view of the requirements of international justice that being born into one country rather than another should not determine one's fate to the extent that it does now, so that a person born into a poor society is condemned to almost certain disease, malnutrition, and poverty, while another, who has the good fortune to be born into a rich society, has an excellent chance of living a healthy and comfortable life. Later in the chapter (see below, section VI), I shall examine the conception of justice—justice as equal opportunity—from which such a view might be derived. But it seems to me simply perverse to try to derive any such notion from justice as requital, that is from the criterion of fair exchange.

To say, for example, that the poor countries actually lose from trading with the rich ones immediately raises the question of why they should choose to trade at all in that case. Unless trade benefits both parties (compared with the absence of trade), the general presumption is that it does not take place. Doubtless, Brazilians would prefer obtaining ten automobiles in exchange for fifty sacks of coffee to obtaining one automobile; but, if we are asking whether or not Brazilians actually *lose* from exchange, the relevant question is whether or not they would be better off keeping the coffee themselves. Emmanuel nowhere suggests that they would be, and I see no reason to believe they would.

In this context, we must, however, be careful not to abstract from the possibility of conflicts of interest within the poorer countries. 'Brazilians' do not, for example, collectively decide how much coffee to exchange for so many automobiles. One strand in the critique of the contemporary international economic order is that in many countries there is an alliance between foreign corporations and a small stratum of indigenous beneficiaries (importers, franchise-holders, and so on) at the expense of the rest of the population. A poor country may therefore engage in uncoerced exchanges that are actually worse for the bulk of the population than no exchange at all. But we should not regard any one pattern as universal. What is in fact striking is the very wide range of ways in which poor countries handle their trading relations with the developed world.[28] I am inclined to doubt that a great deal of trade is literally worse for the Third World country concerned than no trade at all. In any case, it seems clear that the elimination of all such trade would do very little to narrow the gap that now exists between rich and poor countries.

[28] See Michael Moran, 'Review Article: The Politics of International Business', *British Journal of Political Science*, 8 (1978), 217–36.

Justice as requital in exchanges is not, indeed, to be identified with a condition in which all that can be said is that both parties gain something from trade. As I suggested earlier (in section III), the criterion is that both sides gain equally from an exchange. Some economists would say that this is a hopelessly metaphysical notion. At any rate in simple cases, however, its application seems fairly straightforward. Suppose someone is selling a house and there is one interested buyer. The seller would rather keep the house than accept less than £100,000, while the buyer would rather keep his money than pay more than £120,000 for the house. If the price is close to £100,000 the buyer realizes almost all the gain from the exchange; and if the price is close to £120,000 the seller realizes almost all the gain. Surely the gain is shared equally if the price is roughly half way between the two figures. Where variable amounts may be traded between the parties, the analysis is more complicated than where the only question is what price something like a house sells at. But the idea of an equal gain from the whole transaction (with the amount traded being whatever the parties agree on at the price set) still seems to me to make sense, at least in that gross departures may be detected.

We may now introduce another strand in the critique of contemporary international economics, which is popular in UNCTAD. This is that there is an asymmetry between the way in which goods typically exported by rich countries are priced and the way in which those typically exported by poor countries are priced. A car manufacturer sets his price and sells however many cars he can sell at that price, whereas the raw materials and agricultural products that form the bulk of exports of most poor countries are much more likely to be sold on a competitive world market in which sellers will unload their goods at any price that leaves them better off selling than not selling. There is thus, it is argued, a built-in advantage for the industrial nations in international trade, because they can control production so as to obtain the profit margins they aim for.

As it stands, this claim is clearly overstated, since it is apparent that there is a good deal of competition in world markets between, say, the car manufacturers of different countries. A firm which arbitrarily decrees a certain profit margin and refuses to sell at any price that does not yield that margin is liable to find itself out of business. Suppose, however, that it were accepted that the industrial nations do gain differentially from the present set-up. How different would the distribution of income over the world look if the poor countries were to succeed in controlling the prices of their exports through some system of collective action? The answer is, as far as I can tell, that it would not look greatly different from the way it is now.

This may appear perverse when one considers the dramatic improvement in the economic circumstances of the oil-producing states that was brought about by OPEC. But oil has two remarkable characteristics. First, the cost of extracting the oil from the largest deposits (in Saudi Arabia and the Persian Gulf) is a matter of a few cents per barrel: in Kuwait it does not even need to be pumped out, and all that has to be done is fill the tankers.[29] Second, for some uses there is no feasible substitute for oil, and these include the important ones of fuelling the internal combustion engine and providing raw materials for the petrochemical industry; and for the rest (especially heating and electricity generation) the substitutes available in most places are much more expensive, like coal or atomic power. Oil thus generates a lot of economic rent, and the appropriation of a much larger share of this economic rent by the countries with the oil naturally makes a noticeable difference.

At the opposite end of the spectrum from oil are commodities such as sisal and jute whose maximum price is set by the point at which it is cheaper for users to switch to other fibres (including synthetics). Even ironclad controls over price could do little in these cases to redistribute income towards the producers. Justice as requital is satisfied even at a low price because, although the seller is not gaining much (compared with the next best use of the land or doing nothing at all with it), the buyer is also not gaining much (compared with the next most expensive alternative purchase). Equal exchange, it must be emphasized, has no inherent tendency to equalize the overall position of the parties. It is concerned purely with the distribution of the gains from the transaction between them.

Obviously, the crucial question is whether most of the commodities exported by Third World countries are more like oil or more like sisal and jute, and the answer is apparently that, although they form a spectrum, they lie mostly towards the sisal and jute end. It may be possible, for many products, to raise the price without too serious a drop in sales in the short run, but in the long run it will pay users to adapt to the higher prices by substituting other materials, using less, recycling, and so on. It may be recalled, incidentally, that Emmanuel, in calculating the 'loss' from exchange to the poorer countries, took the amount they would get if they were able to sell the *present* amount

[29] Anthony Sampson, *The Seven Sisters: The Great Oil Companies and The World they Shaped* (New York: The Viking Press, 1975), 94.

of exports at a price *ten times higher*. But this figure has no significance because the sales at ten times the price would be far smaller. Perhaps in the long run tea will go the same way as handmade lace—too labour-intensive to be affordable. Perhaps it should. But it does not seem to me very sensible to say that tea is 'really' worth ten times what it costs now, and that tea pickers are being exploited by tea drinkers, if the effect of increasing the price of tea ten times would be simply to throw the tea pickers out of work.

Even leaving aside the tendency over a period of a few years for users to find substitutes, the introduction of an international cartel in commodities other than oil (the 'Integrated Programme') has only limited prospects. David McNicol has calculated, using short-run elasticities of demand, that a doubling of the prices of fourteen commodities would increase the incomes of the LDCs ('less developed countries') by $20.5 billion per year.[30] This is an amount less than twice the present sum of international economic assistance and is to be compared with the $80 billion by which the OPEC countries increased their oil revenues in *each* of 1974, 1975, and 1976.[31]

Even more serious than the relatively limited overall impact of these increases is their distribution among countries.

> The principal *gainers* would be the major producers of cocoa, coffee, cotton, copper and sugar. . . . The *losers* would be nations who export relatively low-value commodities and who import substantial quantities of other commodities—especially cotton, copper, sugar and wool. . . . India, the nations just below the Sahara, and many of the nations in northern Africa and southeast Asia export relatively low-value crops; and there is some indication that they tend to be importers of agricultural products. These nations, which are a majority of the poorest of the LDCs, would probably be net losers under a system of restrictive commodity agreements.[32]

Thus, the final result would actually be a widening of the existing gap between rich and poor countries.

I have been assuming that the Integrated Programme would operate on the basis of price-fixing and production quotas, with the redistribution from rich countries to poor countries proceeding from the higher revenues generated by the increased prices. It would, of course, be

[30] David L. McNicol, *Commodity Agreements and the New Economic Order* (California Institute of Technology Social Science Working Paper, 1976). The fourteen commodities are cocoa, coffee, tea, wool, cotton, sugar, bananas, jute, sisal, beef, copper, tin, and iron. Wheat and rice are imported heavily by Third World countries and McNicol assumes that they would be excluded from price-raising efforts.

[31] Ibid. 133.

[32] Ibid. 132–3.

possible in principle (though hardly politically realistic in the foreseeable future) for the rich countries to go further and offer to pay for more of the controlled commodities than could be cleared on the market. In the short run, the surplus could be stored. But eventually only two solutions would be open. One would be to subsidize sales so as to increase demand either on a regular basis (British agricultural policy until the 1970s) or in order to dump a particular 'mountain' that has accumulated (as the EEC has done). The other would be to restrict supply by paying for non-production on the lines of the US 'acreage retirement' schemes. Subsidization would reduce the objectionable distributive effects of the straight production-quota scheme, whereas paying for non-production would do nothing about them. But both would be enormously expensive, and would constitute an irrational, inefficient, and inequitable way of transferring income from rich countries to poor ones. The lessons of British and American policies towards farming would be equally applicable to global analogues: 'In the United States, as in Britain, farm subsidies have been both economically inefficient and socially indefensible, distributing benefits preponderantly to the wealthiest minority of farmers.'[33]

We still have to ask whether any case for international redistribution from rich countries to poor ones could be established under the third heading of justice as reciprocity—justice as mutual aid. The answer is negative. And it is negative precisely because the minimal similarity of circumstances required to underwrite obligations of mutual aid is lacking here. Justice as reciprocity, we must again emphasize, has no comfort to offer to those who are chronically bad risks. Just as banks prefer to lend to the rich rather than the poor, mutual aid extends only to those who are sufficiently well off to have a reasonable prospect of being able to reciprocate any aid they may receive when the occasion to do so arises.

> Such endeavours as the organized efforts in international development aid, or the objectives of the European Development Fund, and the proposed Southeast Asian Development Fund cannot be adequately understood in terms of reciprocity. . . . [The law governing diplomatic immunity] is strictly conditioned upon reciprocal interest and reciprocal enforcement. . . . In any meaningful sense, however, there is no reciprocity between the interest of the United States or Britain or France in assisting, bilaterally and through multilateral institutions, the development of Tanzania or India or Colombia and the interest of these countries in receiving such assistance.[34]

[33] Graham K. Wilson, *Special Interests and Policymaking: Agricultural Policies and Politics in Britain and the United States of America, 1956–70* (London: John Wiley and Sons, 1977), 73.

[34] Wolfgang Friedmann, 'The Relevance of International Law to the Processes of Economic

To illustrate the point, even if the USA were hit in one year by a major earthquake, a serious drought and several disastrous hurricanes, it could still pull through economically by borrowing or realizing foreign assets. The probability, in the lifetime of anyone now alive, that the USA will be asking Bangladesh for aid is so low as to mean that aid from the USA simply cannot be construed as mutual aid.

VI RECIPROCITY AND RELATIONS BETWEEN GENERATIONS

On the face of it, there is no room for justice as reciprocity to operate between people who are not alive at the same time. The man who asked what posterity has ever done for us got to the heart of the problem.[35] Since, in the nature of the case, posterity cannot do anything for us, there can be no obligation arising from justice as reciprocity to do anything for posterity. However, there are two possible escape routes, and they are worth some examination.

The first line of escape has a powerful intuitive appeal to many people, for I have found that whenever I press the conclusion that justice as reciprocity does not have application to future generations somebody proposes it. I have not found it worked out in print, though Edmund Burke's *Reflections on the Revolution in France* contains some ideas in the general area. There is his famous vision of society as 'a partnership between those who are living, those who are dead, and those who are to be born'.[36] And there is the panegyric on the 'idea of inheritance': 'People will not look forward to their posterity, who never look backward to their ancestors. . . . The institutions of policy, the goods of fortune, the gifts of providence, are handed down to us, and from us, in the same course and order'.[37]

The line of argument is, I take it, as follows: since we have received benefits from our predecessors, some notion of equity requires us to provide benefits for our successors. The notion of equity involved is, it would appear, somehow related to reciprocity. In my discussion of justice as mutual aid (above, section IV), I considered a case in which the young provide transport for the old in the expectation that when

and Social Development', in Richard A. Falk and Cyril E. Black (eds.), *The Future of the International Legal Order* ii: *Wealth and Resources* (Princeton, NJ: Princeton University Press, 1970), 3–35, at 12 and 13.

35 '"We are always doing", says he, "something for Posterity, but I would fain see Posterity do something for us."' Joseph Addison, *The Spectator*, No. 583.

36 Edmund Burke, *Reflections on the Revolution in France*, in A. J. Grieve (ed.), *Reflections on the French Revolution and Other Essays* (London: J. M. Dent, 1910), 93.

37 Ibid. 31.

they themselves are old the young will do the same for them. I emphasized there the advantage to all (taking a long time span) of maintaining the practice. We can add that, even if the young could somehow get away with neglecting the old now and reintroducing the practice in time to benefit when they are old themselves, it would be unfair—a violation of justice as reciprocity—for them to do so. The extended reciprocity here runs in the opposite direction: having received benefits, we have an obligation of justice to pass on comparable benefits. The analogy lies in the fact that in both instances there is an ongoing practice from which we stand to benefit and which therefore creates a duty of 'fair play' to do our part in it.

I do not think that it is possible to sustain a completely general principle to the effect that the receipt of a benefit creates a prima facie obligation to pass on a similar benefit to others. R. M. Hare put forward such a principle in a context somewhat analogous to the present one in that it involves the question of bringing people into existence as against providing for them. Hare argued that, if we are glad we were born, this entails that we ought (in the absence of countervailing reasons) to maximize the number of people born. And he derives this from what he calls a 'logical extension' of the Golden Rule, which he takes to mean that 'we should do to others as we wish them to do to us'. The extension is 'to say that we should do to others what *we are glad was* done to us'.[38]

There are two arguments against this extended Golden Rule. First, the result it reaches for issues of population is ridiculous. This, however, may be circumvented if it can be shown that the extended Golden Rule does not have these implications.[39] The more serious argument is simply that the extended Golden Rule is silly in quite straightforward cases not involving the difficulties imported by worrying about the claims of potential people. If someone offers me a toffee apple, out of the blue, and I accept it, does my enjoyment of the toffee apple create even the tiniest obligation to distribute toffee apples to others? I do not see that it does. If it would spread happiness to give away toffee apples, *that* is no doubt a reason for doing so (though hardly one amounting to an obligation). But the reason thus generated does not seem to be in any way affected by whether or not I happen to have myself been the lucky recipient of a toffee apple. As a matter of moral psychology, it may be that receiving a toffee apple is what it

[38] R. M. Hare, 'Abortion and the Golden Rule', *Philosophy & Public Affairs*, 6 (1977), 185–90, at 208 (italics in original).

[39] For an argument, which seems to me plausible, to that effect, see George Sher, 'Hare, Abortion, and the Golden Rule', *Philosophy & Public Affairs*, 6 (1977), 185–90.

takes to get my sluggish benevolent tendencies going, in bringing to my attention how much others might enjoy one. But that is another matter.

In my view, the so-called extended Golden Rule is plausible only in the context of a practice, when it becomes synonymous with justice as reciprocity (see above, section III). If there is a practice of handing round toffee apples and I have taken and enjoyed those given out by others it is unfair not to hand round some myself, just as someone who ducks out when it gets to his turn to buy a round of drinks is behaving unfairly.

If we could establish the existence of a practice of looking after the interests of later generations, there would seem to be some sort of case, based on justice as reciprocity, for saying we should play our part in the practice and take account of the interests of our successors. The obligation would not fit very well into the threefold classification I developed earlier, but I suppose it would best be regarded as a sort of extension of justice as requital.

The question then is, does such a practice exist, of which we are the beneficiaries? I am not sure exactly what kind of evidence is relevant to this question, but I would take it that the kind of thing we should look for is (*a*) evidence that our ancestors had a norm to the effect that the interests of future generations should be given serious weight in decisionmaking; and (*b*) evidence that such a norm, if it was generally professed, was acted on. I cannot hope here to enter in any systematic way into such an enquiry. But it does not appear to me that the interests of later generations have ever played a very important role in public deliberations, still less in actual decisions. Let us take up the central issue—the degrading of the environment and the exhaustion of non-replaceable natural resources. My impression is that the only reason why our ancestors did not do more damage is that they lacked the technology to do so. I can see little evidence that they held back from anything that was technologically feasible and immediately profitable from any consideration about the costs they were imposing on their descendants. I do not therefore think that we would be under much of an obligation to our own descendants if we were constrained by nothing more stringent than the ecological morality of our ancestors. I am inclined, therefore, to suggest that the only implication of justice as reciprocity in this extended form is to give us an extra reason for adopting a more responsible attitude towards our successors. If we have some reason to do so anyway (which still remains to be shown), there is a bonus from justice as reciprocity in that we may be in on the foundation of a practice that will make it more likely that our successors will do likewise.

I now come to the second argument against the conclusion that we have no obligation to our successors derived from justice as reciprocity. This also appeals to the duty of fair play, but this time it is fair play among contemporaries rather than fair play over the generations. The argument is that, although we do not have obligations *to* future generations, we may have obligations *with respect to* future generations. The idea here is that, to the extent that the welfare of future generations is something nearly all of us as a matter of fact care about, it can be treated as a public good; and justice as requital (it will be recalled) requires us to play a fair part in contributing to a public good from which we benefit. That the 'benefit' is, as it were, a sentimental one directed at the future, rather than a personal one here and now, does not affect the logic.[40]

The obvious limitation to this argument is that the obligation with respect to future generations is entirely parasitic upon our actual sentiments about them. If we care about their welfare (or more specifically if enough of us care about their welfare to make it qualify as a public good), we can generate a derivative obligation among ourselves. But there is nothing in the argument that says we should care for their welfare. Since in practice it does not appear that many people have a time-horizon for public policy extending much beyond thirty years, this does not get us very far.

Discussions by experts of threatened crises in raw materials, energy, pollution, food shortages, and so on generally appear to be founded on the belief that they have shown fears to be alarmist if they can produce evidence that we can probably get through the next thirty years without catastrophe. The notion that we should be thinking how to arrange things so that the human race has even a fighting chance of getting through the next ten thousand or hundred thousand years would, I am sure, be regarded by these experts as bizarre. The question of justice between generations is precisely the question of whether we *should* care about the welfare of our successors, and what sacrifices we ought to be prepared to make now in their interests. I am not impressed by the bland assurance that all we have to do is feed in our own prejudices and they will come out as obligations of justice.[41]

[40] See D. Clayton Hubin, 'Justice and Future Generations', *Philosophy & Public Affairs*, 6 (1976), 70–83, and Thomas Schwartz, 'Obligations to Posterity', in R. I. Sikora and Brian Barry (eds.), *Obligations to Future Generations* (Philadelphia: Temple University Press, 1978).

[41] For a more extended discussion of this point see my paper 'The Circumstances of Justice and Future Generations', in Sikora and Barry (eds.), *Obligations to Future Generations*.

VII ANOTHER PRINCIPLE OF JUSTICE

My primary aim in this chapter has been to analyse the principle of justice as reciprocity and to show how limited it is in its application to problems of justice between nations and justice between generations. I have also tried to show that the attempt to derive more acceptable conclusions from justice as reciprocity than those that appear at first sight to follow (and I share the views of those who find those conclusions unacceptable) are pursuing an unprofitable enterprise. Their efforts are a tribute to the power and appeal of the paradigm of justice as reciprocity. But I am convinced that the way forward is not to devote further efforts to trying to square the circle, that is to say, trying to get non-outrageous conclusions from justice as reciprocity. The solution is rather, I suggest, to see if there is not some principle of justice complementary to justice as reciprocity that comes into its own when we move outside the special case of justice among contemporaries who are members of the same society.

I emphasize that it must be complementary because I believe that justice as reciprocity is here to stay. It is (as I suggested earlier in section I) a cultural universal, and anyway it makes a lot of sense. Any theory of justice that tried to eliminate justice as reciprocity would be doomed from the start. We must therefore seek to show how justice as reciprocity needs to be supplemented, not displaced.

I believe that this can be done without great difficulty. The glaring limitation of justice as reciprocity is that it can say nothing about the initial control over natural resources. Once ownership rights are assigned, justice as reciprocity can tell us about fair trading. But it is silent on the crucial first stage. Theorists who wish to place fair exchange at the centre of their conceptions of justice, from John Locke to James Buchanan and Robert Nozick, have always recognized that some other kind of theory has to be brought in to get things started or that one must simply be agnostic about the initial distribution of resources.

We could, of course, take the heroic path of saying that justice as reciprocity is the only sort of justice and that, however we may characterize the initial distribution of resources, 'just' and 'unjust' are not appropriate words. But that seems rather preposterous, since we surely want to have some distributive concept to evaluate distributions. If we can't have 'just' (or 'fair') we will have to invent some other; but we will surely want some distributive criterion.

Consider a 'state of nature' story. A number of people occupy a certain territory and live by hunting. It has been found by experience that bands of six are the most efficient for hunting, and on the principle of requital it is just for members of each band to be rewarded in accordance with their contribution to its success. Justice as mutual aid requires that a band experiencing a run of bad luck in hunting should be saved from starvation by others. But this does not entail systematic transfer from a more skilful band to a less skilful one.

So far so good. But now consider a development in this story. Suppose that in one half of the territory the terrain is more favourable so that game is more easy to catch. Specifically, let us assume that for any band (whatever its level of skill) exactly half as much effort is required in the more favoured half of the territory to catch any given amount of game. Now suppose that one half of the people in the area declare that access to the more favoured half of the territory is henceforth to be controlled by them. And suppose also that they somehow succeed in enforcing this against the others. (Call them the 'dominant group' and the others the 'subordinate group'.) The dominant group now has a choice. The members can hunt for themselves, catching an adequate supply of game with half the effort that the subordinate group has to exert to make the same catch. Or they can permit the members of the subordinate group to hunt in the favoured territory on condition that they hand over a share of whatever they catch.

According to a common view, it makes a big difference to the analysis of the situation which of these paths is taken. If the dominant group offer a deal to the subordinate group and it is accepted, the members of the dominant group are living off the labour of the others; whereas if they simply exclude the others and hunt for themselves they are not. But this seems to me a misguided way of looking at the position. The advantage lies in controlling access to the favoured part of the territory, and the question of what use that advantage is put to is secondary. *Given* that the advantage is going to be maintained, the subordinate group would rationally prefer to have the option of hunting in the more favoured territory in return for giving up a share of the catch. So it would seem strange if the dominant group were to be judged more severely for providing the option to the subordinate group than otherwise.

What has justice as reciprocity to say about all this? If the dominant group excludes the subordinate group, it has nothing to say. If the dominant group permits the subordinate group to hunt in return for a share of the proceeds, justice as requital says that there should be a fair exchange. But since an hour spent hunting in the more favoured terrain is twice as productive as an hour spent outside it, it is obviously a fair exchange that the privilege should cost a share of the catch. On the question of whether it is just for the dominant group to control access, justice as reciprocity is silent. If we want to make a judgement about the justice of that, it looks as if we must go to some sense of justice not derivable from justice as reciprocity. Tentatively, let me suggest that the principle is one of justice as equal access to natural resources.

To reinforce but at the same time refine this idea, let us turn to a society that is, by almost universal agreement, exceedingly unjust —South Africa. I believe that, although some countries may be more violent and others more repressive, South Africa is *the* most unjust society in the world, but nothing I have to say turns on the acceptance of that view, which would require for its support much more about the distinction between injustice and other evils.

Let us now ask what it is that makes South Africa *economically* unjust. I suggest that there are at least these three features:

1. Non-Whites are not allowed to unionize, and are paid less than the value they contribute to the economy.
2. Non-Whites are provided with poor opportunities for acquiring education, and are prevented by the job reservation system from filling the better-paid jobs, even if they are qualified.
3. Under apartheid, non-Whites are prohibited from owning land in any of the more productive areas of the country. The so-called 'tribal homelands' are carefully chosen to be barren and devoid of mineral resources.[42]

The first of these points falls squarely within the scope of justice as reciprocity: non-Whites are not allowed a fair bargaining position and are not receiving fair exchange for the value of their work. But the other two points cannot be related to justice as reciprocity. Suppose that non-Whites *were* paid the full value of their product: the other two points would still be valid. Justice demands not only that people should be paid the value they contribute but that they should have a fair opportunity to increase the value they contribute. Justice as reciprocity has nothing to say about this.

It might perhaps be suggested that justice as requital can be employed to argue that non-Whites are not getting their fair share of

[42] See Pierre van den Berghe, *South Africa: A Study in Conflict* (Berkeley and Los Angeles: University of California Press, 1967), 196–8.

school expenditures, in that per capita educational costs of White children are many times those of non-White children. But it must be recalled that justice as requital demands only that benefits received should be matched to taxes paid. Apologists of the South African regime can say quite truthfully that since Whites pay most of the taxes it is just, in this sense, for Whites to receive most of the benefits. This illustrates the way in which, given a fundamental pattern of injustice, justice as reciprocity operates merely so as to maintain it in equilibrium.

I think that this discussion of South Africa, sketchy as it is, can form the basis for a second shot at the principle we are looking for. It is, I suggest, none other than equality of opportunity, understood in a very broad sense that goes way beyond equal chances to get ahead in a meritocratic rat-race. The minimal claim of equal opportunity is an equal claim on the earth's natural resources. The maximum claim is that the same abilities and efforts should reap the same rewards. This, it may be noticed, is the driving force behind Emmanuel's criticism of the present international economic order. His error was, I believe, not in saying that there is something unjust about one person getting a huge multiple of the other's pay for performing the identical task, but rather in attempting to fit this idea in to the framework of justice as reciprocity.

VIII SOME IMPLICATIONS OF THE PRINCIPLE

I realize that there are many difficulties in clarifying the conception of equal opportunity and also in thinking through its implications. In this closing section, I shall therefore tackle a more modest (but still formidable) task. I shall take up the narrow conception and ask what implications it has for international and intergenerational justice. This discussion is offered as a sketch of what might be said; I hope elsewhere to expand and refine it. (See below, chapter 19.)

The main implication is that the claim of each country to control access to the natural resources of its territory cannot be accepted as absolute, nor can the claim of any given generation to use the earth's resources as it sees fit. It is wrong (to quote Burke again) for 'the temporary possessors and life-renters in [the commonwealth . . . to] act as if they were the entire masters . . . [to] cut off the entail, or commit waste on the inheritance'.[43] The planet is the common

[43] Burke, *Reflections on the Revolution in France*, p. 137.

heritage of all men at all times and any appropriation of its resources must be subject to appraisal from the point of view of justice.

It has to be said that recent moves in international forums do not suggest an easy road for the principle that the world's resources are a common possession of all human beings. The United Nations General Assembly has declared the 'permanent sovereignty over natural resources' of the country in which the natural resources occur.[44] The International Law of the Sea convention is apparently going to move away from the ocean as a 'common' by extending national territorial claims over the sea-bed and marine life rather than by internationalizing the sea's resources. And the emphasis that the Third World countries are putting (through UNCTAD) on the raising of commodity prices as the favoured means of international redistribution is also inauspicious. As we have seen (section V), it has the same effect as the other two moves: it is good for those countries with resources but is if anything on balance disadvantageous for countries whose problem is that they are resource-poor. However, if it is assumed (not implausibly) that the only realistic alternative at present to national sovereignty is letting the rich countries have a free hand in using up the world's natural resources and that the citizens of rich countries will accept higher prices but not higher taxes, these moves can be understood as defining a politically feasible second-best.[45]

It is important to see that, if it is a matter of justice to give countries more equal access to the world's resources, the duty to make transfers to a resource-poor country does not depend on the use made of the additional income by that country.[46] This is how justice differs from charity. If a man approaches me and asks for money to feed his wife and children, I can quite properly ask myself if there is reason to believe that he will spend anything I give him on buying alcohol. But an employer may not legitimately refuse to pay his employee what he owes him on the ground that he disapproves of the way it is going to get spent. This is not to say that there should not be some requirement that the employee support his wife and children; but there are two separate issues which should be kept distinct.

[44] Charles R. Beitz, 'Justice and International Relations', *Philosophy & Public Affairs*, 4 (1975), 360–89, at 371 n. 9.

[45] For a useful introduction to these questions see Oscar Schachter, *Sharing the World's Resources* (New York: Columbia University Press, 1977).

[46] Conservatives (or, if they are a distinguishable category, those who are reluctant to give up what they have got) naturally fasten on to the argument that the obligation to redistribute is voided by the nature of the regime. See, for a string of similar arguments against redistribution, Robert W. Tucker, *The Inequality of Nations* (New York: Basic Books, 1977).

The application of this example in international affairs is as follows:

1. Where aid is given as charity to relieve suffering, it is legitimate for the donor country to insist that the aid be disbursed to the needy within the recipient country.
2. In as far as redistribution is required by the demands of justice, the criterion of justice is that countries, as collectivities, should have their fair share of the world's resources.
3. Failure of a country to have a just internal distribution does not relieve donor countries of the obligations of international justice.
4. International pressure, economic sanctions, or even military intervention may sometimes be legitimate as a way of improving the internal justice of a society.
5. The right of other countries to apply such pressure is not increased if the country in question is a beneficiary of international transfers based on justice. Nor is the right decreased if the country in question is a net contributor. (Of course, it is politically *easier* to bring pressure on poor countries, but that is a separate question.)

One final point. We might agree that the employer could, without committing injustice, withhold the pay he owes the employee if he knows that the employee is going to use it to buy an armoury and terrorize the neighbourhood or to destroy his family. But in an extreme case like that the employer (or anybody else) would also be justified in taking away money the employee already has. The international analogy is that a transfer to a country whose government plans to buy weapons for external aggression or internal repression may legitimately be cancelled; but in any situation where that would be legitimate it would also be legitimate to withhold any other payments that were due. (The UK government's freezing of all financial obligations to Rhodesia after the latter's Unilateral Declaration of Independence would be a case in point.)

What about intergenerational relations? I believe that the notion of fair access to resources can be deployed to deal with them. In my 'state of nature' example it would surely be unfair (in a sense which has nothing to do with reciprocity) for one generation of hunters to hunt the game to extinction and leave their successors to starve. Access to the earth's resources can be unfairly distributed over time as well as over space.

What justice requires is that the range of opportunities open to successor generations should not be narrowed. If some openings are closed off by depletion or other irreversible damage to the environment, others should be created (if necessary at the cost of some sacrifice) to make up. (See chapter 19 below.)

This conception of intergenerational justice has several attractive features. First, it is a global extension of a principle that families with possessions to pass on have traditionally espoused: 'Keep the capital intact!' Second, it underwrites the asymmetry that many people (including myself) feel between making successors better off, which is a nice thing to do but not required by justice, and not making them worse off, which *is* required by justice. And third, it does not make the demands of justice to our successors depend on our knowing their tastes—still less on our approving of them.[47] (The notion that our obligations depend on our empathy with future generations is discussed further in chapter 18 below.)

[47] See M. P. Golding, 'Obligations to Future Generations', *Monist*, 56 (1972), 85–99.

18

JUSTICE BETWEEN GENERATIONS

> Suppose that, as a result of using up all the world's resources, human life did come to an end. So what? What is so desirable about an indefinite continuation of the human species, religious convictions apart?
>
> Wilfred Beckerman, 'The Myth of "Finite" Resources'

My object in this chapter is to ask what if anything those alive at any given time owe their descendants, whether in the form of positive efforts (e.g. investment in capital goods) or in the form of forbearance from possible actions (e.g. those causing irreversible damage to the natural environment). We scan the 'classics' in vain for guidance on this question, and for understandable reasons. Among human beings, unlike (say) mayflies, generations do not succeed one another in the sense that one is off the scene before the next comes into existence. 'Generations' are an abstraction from a continuous process of population replacement. Prudent provision for the welfare of all those currently alive therefore entails some considerable regard for the future. The way we get into problems that cannot be handled in this way is that there may be 'sleepers' (actions taken at one time that have much more significant effects in the long run than in the short run) or actions that are on balance beneficial in the short run and harmful in the long run (or vice versa).

More precisely, the problem arises (as a problem requiring decision) not when actions actually have long-run effects that are different in scale or direction from their short-run effects but when they are *believed* to do so. The increased salience of the problem for us comes about not just because we are more likely to have the opportunity, thanks to technology, of doing things with long-run consequences not mediated by similar short-run consequences but also because there is more chance of our knowing about it. A useful new technology that we have no reason to believe has adverse long-term effects does not present any problem of decisionmaking for us, even if, unknown to us, it actually has the most deleterious long-run consequences. Conversely, new knowledge may suggest that things we have been doing for some time have harmful long-term effects. Even if people have been doing something with adverse long-term effects for hundreds or thousands of years, so that we are currently experiencing the ill effects in the form of, say, higher disease rates or lower crop yields than we should otherwise be enjoying, it may still require some breakthrough in scientific understanding to show that the current situation has been brought about by certain human practices.

In recent years we have all been made aware by the 'ecological' movement how delicately balanced are the processes that support life on the earth's surface and how easily some disequilibrium may ramify through a variety of processes with cumulative effects. The stage is set for some potentially very awkward decisions by this increased awareness that apparently insignificant impacts on the environment may, by the time they have fully worked themselves through, have serious consequences for human life. We may, any day, be confronted with convincing evidence for believing that something on which we rely heavily—the internal-combustion engine, say—is doing irreversible damage to the ecosystem, even if the effects of our current actions will not build up to a catastrophic deterioration for many years (perhaps centuries) to come.

If we ask what makes our relations with our successors in hundreds of years' time so different from our relations with our contemporaries as to challenge the ordinary moral notions that we use in everyday affairs, there are two candidates that come to mind, one concerned with power and one with knowledge. I shall consider these in turn.

A truistic but fundamental difference between our relations with our successors and our relations with our contemporaries, then, is the absolute difference in power. The present inhabitants of Britain may believe that, although they have some discretion in the amount of aid they give to the people of Bangladesh, they have little to hope or fear from the present inhabitants of Bangladesh in return. But they cannot be sure that later geopolitical events may not change this in their own lifetime. We can be quite certain, however, that people alive in several centuries' time will not be able to do anything that will make us better off or worse off now, although we can to some degree make them better off or worse off.

Admittedly, our successors have absolute control of something in the future that we may care about now: our reputations. It is up to them to decide what they think of us—or indeed whether they think about us at all. And presumably what, or whether, they think of us is going to be in some way affected by the way that we act towards them. I must confess, however, to doubting that this does much to level up the asymmetry of power between us and our successors, for two reasons. First, although they control a resource which may matter to us, we have no way of negotiating an agreement with them to the effect that they will treat our reputations in a certain way if we behave now in a certain way. We therefore have to guess how they will react to the way we behave, and in the nature of the case such guesses are bound to be inexact. Second, and more important, although individuals are undoubtedly moved by thoughts of posthumous fame for their artistic achievements or political records, it does not seem plausible to suppose that the same motivation would operate collectively so as to lead a mass electorate to support, say, measures of energy conservation. Altogether, therefore, I do not think that the fact of later generations determining our reputations deserves to be given much weight as an offset to the otherwise completely unilateral power that we have over our successors.

How important is this asymmetry of power between us and our successors—the fact that we can help or hurt them but they cannot help or hurt us? It is tempting to say at once that this cannot possibly in itself make any moral difference. Yet it is perhaps surprising to realize that a variety of commonly held views about the basis of morality seem to entail that the absence of reciprocal power relations eliminates the possibility of our having moral obligations (or at any rate obligations of justice) to our successors.

There is a tradition of thought running from Hobbes and Hume to Hart and Warnock according to which the point of morality is that it offers (in Hobbes's terms) 'convenient articles of peace': human beings are sufficiently equal in their capacity to hurt one another, and in their dependence on one another's co-operation to live well, that it is mutually advantageous to all of them to support an institution designed to give people artificial motives for respecting the interests of others.

It seems plain that such a view cannot generate the conclusion that we have moral obligations to those who will not be alive until long after we are dead. Thus, G. J. Warnock, in *The Object of Morality*, offers two reasons for saying that moral principles should have universal application rather than being confined to particular groups. 'First, everyone presumably will be a non-member of some group, and cannot in general have any absolute guarantee that he will encounter no members of groups that are not his own; thus if principles are group-bound, he remains, so to speak, at risk. . . .

Second . . . if conduct is to be seen as regulated only *within* groups, we still have the possibility of unrestricted hostility and conflict *between* groups. . . . '[1] Obviously, neither of these reasons carries weight in relation to our successors, since we do precisely have an absolute guarantee that we shall never encounter them and cannot conceivably suffer from their hostility to us. It should be added in fairness to Warnock that he himself suggests that morality requires us to take account of the interests of future generations and also of animals. But my point is that I do not see how this squares with his premisses.

It is, indeed, possible to get some distance by invoking the fact with which I began this chapter, that the notion of 'successive generations' is an artificial one since there is a continuous process of replacement in human populations. Once we have universalized our moral principles to apply to everyone alive now, there are because of this continuity severe practical problems in drawing a neat cut-off point in the future. In the absence of a definite cut-off point, it may seem natural to say that our moral principles hold without temporal limit. But could what is in effect no stronger force than inertia be sufficient to lead us to make big sacrifices for remote generations if these seemed to be called for by atemporal morality? Surely, if morality is at base no more than mutual self-defence, we would (whether or not we made it explicit) agree to ignore the interests of those coming hundreds of years after us.

There is an alternative line of argument about the basis of moral obligations, also involving reciprocity, from which the denial of obligations to future generations follows directly. This view is seldom put forward systematically though it crops up often enough in conversation. This is the idea that by living in a society one gets caught up in a network of interdependencies and from these somehow arise obligations. A recent statement of this view may be found in Burton Zwiebach, who says that 'the basis of our obligation is the common life'.[2] The same idea—that obligations to others arise from actual relations with them—underlies Michael Walzer's *Obligations*.[3] Obviously, this more parochial view, which makes obligations depend on actual rather than potential reciprocal relationships, rules out any obligations to subsequent generations, since there is no reciprocity with them.

As T. D. Weldon recognized when he put forward a similar view in

[1] G. J. Warnock, *The Object of Morality* (London: Methuen, 1967), 150.

[2] Burton Zwiebach, *Civility and Disobedience* (London: Cambridge University Press, 1975), 75.

[3] Michael Walzer, *Obligations* (Cambridge, Mass.: Harvard University Press, 1970).

the last chapter of *States and Morals*,[4] it is very close to basing obligations on sentiments. This further move is made in one of the very few papers addressed explicitly to the present topic[5] and permits some consideration to be given to future generations—but in a way that I personally find more morally offensive than a blunt disregard of all future interests. According to Martin Golding, obligations rest on a sense of 'moral community'. Whether or not we have any obligations to future generations depends on whether we expect them to live in ways that would lead us to regard them as part of our 'moral community'. If we think they will develop in ways we disapprove of, we have no obligations to them. This view is obviously a diachronic version of the common American attitude that famine need only be relieved in countries with the right attitude to capitalism.

A third view which appears to leave little room for obligations to future generations is the kind of Lockean philosophy recently revived by Robert Nozick in *Anarchy, State, and Utopia*.[6] Indeed, it is scarcely accidental that the uniquely short-sighted destruction of trees, animals, and soil in the United States should have been perpetrated by believers in a natural right to property. According to Nozick, any attempt to use the state to redistribute resources among contemporaries in order to bring about some 'end state' is illegitimate, so presumably by the same token any deliberate collective action aimed at distributing resources over time would fall under the same ban. Provided an individual has come by a good justly, he may justly dispose of it in any way he likes—by giving it away or bequeathing it, trading it for something else, consuming it, or destroying it. No question of justice arises in all this so long as he does not injure the rights to property and security from physical harm of anyone else. Since we have a right to dispose of our property as we wish, subsequent generations could not charge us with injustice if we were to consume whatever we could in our own lifetimes and direct that what was left should be destroyed at our deaths. (Having one's property destroyed at death has been popular at various times and places and could presumably become so again.) It would clearly be, on Nozick's view, unjust for the survivors to fail to carry out such directions.

Once again we can see that the problem is the lack of bargaining power in the hands of later generations. Those without bargaining

[4] T. D. Weldon, *States and Morals* (London: John Murray, 1946).
[5] M. P. Golding, 'Obligations to Future Generations', *Monist*, 56 (1972), 85–99.
[6] Robert Nozick, *Anarchy, State, and Utopia* (New York: Basic Books, 1974).

power may appeal to the generous sentiments of others but they cannot make legitimate moral demands, as Nozick's examples of the men on their desert islands vividly illustrates. He asks us to imagine a number of men washed up on desert islands, with the possibility of sending goods to each other and transmitting messages by radio transmitter, but with no means of travelling themselves. Sternly resisting the temptation to comment further on the outlook of a man for whom the paradigm of human relations is a number of adult males on desert islands, let us ask what moral obligations they have to each other. Nozick's answer is simple: none. Even if one has the good fortune to have landed on an island flowing with milk and honey while his neighbour is gradually starving on a barren waste, there is no obligation on one to supply the other's needs. Where could such an obligation possibly come from? To get a parallel with the relations between generations all we have to do is imagine that the islands are situated along an ocean current. Goods can be dispatched in one direction only, down the current. Even if those further down the line could call for help (as later generations in fact cannot) they could make no moral claims on those higher up.

I have so far concentrated on one potentially relevant fact about our relations with our successors: the asymmetry of power. The second one, which is invariably mentioned in this context, is the fact that we have less and less knowledge about the future the more remote the time ahead we are thinking about. Whether or not this is (like the asymmetry of power relations) an absolutely necessary truth derivable from the very concept of the future is a question any attempt to answer which would involve opening the can of worms labelled 'Determinism'. I shall therefore simply accept the basic assertion as true—since it is surely true for us now, anyway—and ask what its implications are.

The answer seems to be fairly clear. As far as I can see, no theory that survives the first consideration and still holds that we have some sort of obligation to take account of the interests of remote future generations would have its conclusions upset by our unavoidable ignorance about the future. It may, of course, be held that we have *no* knowledge of the way in which our present actions will affect the interests of those who come after us in more than *k* years' time—either because we don't know what effects our actions will have on the state of the universe then or because we can have no idea what their interests will be. In that case, it obviously follows that our accepting an obligation to concern ourselves with their interests does not entail our behaving any differently from the way we would behave if we did not accept such an obligation. We can decide what to do without having to bother about any effects it may have beyond *k* years' time. But the obligation still remains latent in the sense that, if at some future date we do come to believe that we have relevant information about the effects of our actions on people living in more than *k* years' time, we should take account of it in determining our actions. The obligation would have been activated.

Ignorance of the future may be invoked to deny that obligations to remote descendants have any practical implications so that we can ignore them with a good conscience in deciding what to do. Thus, John Passmore, in his book *Man's Responsibility for Nature*,[7] canvasses among other possibilities the rigorous atemporal utilitarianism put forward by Sidgwick, according to which 'the time at which a man exists cannot affect the value of his happiness from a universal point of view'.[8] But he says that, because of the existence of uncertainty, even Sidgwick's approach would lead us to the conclusion that 'our obligations are to *immediate* posterity, we ought to try to improve the world so that we shall be able to hand it over to our immediate successors in a better condition, and that is all'.[9]

I think this all too convenient conclusion ought to be treated with great mistrust. It is true that we do not know what the precise tastes of our remote descendants will be, but they are unlikely to include a desire for skin cancer, soil erosion, or the inundation of all low-lying areas as a result of the melting of the ice-caps. And, other things being equal, the interests of future generations cannot be harmed by our leaving them more choices rather than fewer.

Even more dubious, it seems to me, is the habit (especially common among economists for some reason) of drawing blank cheques on the future to cover our own deficiencies. The shortages, pollution, over-population, etc. that we leave behind will be no problem for our successors because, it is said, they will invent ways of dealing with them. This Micawberish attitude of expecting something to turn up would be rightly considered imprudent in an individual and I do not see how it is any less so when extended to our successors.

My own view is that, especially in the context of universalistic utilitarianism, the appeal to ignorance normally functions as a smoke-screen, to conceal the fact that we are simply not willing to act in the kind of saintly way that a serious application of the doctrine must

[7] John Passmore, *Man's Responsibility for Nature* (London: Duckworth, 1974).
[8] Henry Sidgwick, *The Methods of Ethics* (London: Macmillan, 7th edn., 1907), 414.
[9] Passmore, *Man's Responsibility for Nature*, p. 91 (itals. in original).

entail. Passmore writes (claiming to paraphrase Rawls) that 'the utilitarian principle of impartiality, taken literally, demands too much of us; we cannot reasonably be expected to share our resources with the whole of posterity'.[10] He is more to the point here than when introducing ignorance as a 'fudge factor' to make the answer come out where in any case he feels it should be.

I entirely share the reluctance I have attributed to others to accept the full rigours of universal utilitarianism. Admittedly reluctance to accept a theory about our obligations is hardly enough to disqualify it. After all, the whole idea of talking about obligations is presumably to put to us a motive for doing things that we would (at least sometimes) not be inclined to do otherwise. But the demands of universal utilitarianism—that I should always act in such a way as to maximize the sum of happiness over the future course of human (or maybe sentient) history—are so extreme that I cannot bring myself to believe that there is any such obligation.

At the same time, I find it impossible to believe that it can be right to disregard totally the interests of even remotely future generations, to the extent that we have some idea of the way in which our current actions will affect those interests. If I am correct in saying that it is an implication of the three theories of morality considered earlier that there are no obligations to distant future generations, they too have to be rejected.

But if we dump mutual self-protection, entitlement, and community (with which we may roughly identify the holy trinity of political theory, first identified by T. H. Green and still faithfully worshipped by the Oxford Modern Greats degree—Hobbes, Locke, and Rousseau) what are we left with? Unless we are prepared to fall back on an appeal to intuitions (and it may come to that), the only general approach remaining is as far as I can see some sort of ideal contractarian construction: what is required by justice is that we should be prepared to do what we would demand of others if we didn't know the details of our situation or theirs.

The name of Rawls naturally, and rightly, springs to mind here. But it should be recognized that the ideal contractarian formula is open-ended and does not have to be identified with Rawls's use of it. Nevertheless, Rawls's *A Theory of Justice*[11] is the obvious place to start and I shall therefore now set out and criticize Rawls's contribution to the problem of justice between generations. The first point to notice is

[10] Ibid. 86.

[11] John Rawls, *A Theory of Justice* (Cambridge, Mass.: Harvard University Press, 1971).

that Rawls discusses the problem only in the context of the 'just savings rate' and this imposes two limitations on the generality of his conclusions. The obvious one is that if we concentrate on the question of how much we are obliged to make our successors better off, we miss the whole question of whether there may not be an obligation to avoid harm to people that is stronger than any obligation to make them better off. This is after all a common view about relations among contemporaries.

The second, and ultimately perhaps more serious, limitation is that investment has a characteristic that enables discussion of it to dodge the most awkward difficulties. The only way in which we can leave people in n years (where n is a large number) more productive capital than they would otherwise have had is to create the additional capital now and hope that the intervening generations will pass it on; or, more precisely, to create it now and hope our immediate descendants and their successors will each pass on a larger total to *their* successors than they would have done had we left them less ourselves. If they do, then thanks to our efforts members of remote future generations will indeed be better off than they would otherwise have been. But there is no way in which we can be confident that our efforts will have any net effect, because everything depends on the behaviour of the intervening generations, whom we have no way of binding.

Although it does not strictly follow from all this, it is easy to reach the conclusion if we concentrate on the 'just savings rate' that the problem of relations between generations can be reduced to the question of the relations between one generation and its immediate successors. There is no way of making remoter generations better off by making savings now that does not involve making nearer generations better off; conversely, if we make our immediate successors better off by making savings now we at any rate make it possible for them to make *their* successors better off than they would otherwise have been.

Obviously, it might still be held that if we take account of remoter generations this should lay on us a greater obligation to build up capital now than would arise if we knew that our immediate successors would be the last generation ever. But since we have no way of ensuring that our immediate successors will not go on a binge and run down the capital we leave them this must surely weaken the case for our having to make extra efforts to save merely so as to make it *possible* for our immediate successors to pass on more than they would otherwise have done.

When, by contrast, we look at the bads rather than the goods that we have the opportunity of passing on to our successors, we can see that the same convenient assumption is not generally applicable. True, resource depletion has something of the same characteristic. The only way in which we can leave more to our remote successors is to leave more to our immediate successors; and if we make extra efforts to conserve resources so as to give our immediate successors more scope to pass on resources in their turn, we take the risk that they will simply blue the lot anyway. (See further on this chapter 19 below.)

But this is not necessarily the case with other bads that we might pass on. There could in principle be some ecological sleeper-effect that we set off now with no ill effects for some hundreds of years and then catastrophic effects. And there are in any case real examples (such as the use of fluorocarbon sprays) of things that we do now that may well have continuous and irreversible ill effects during the rest of the period during which there is life on the planet and that can either not be counteracted at all or only counteracted at great cost or inconvenience.

Our successors may indeed make things even worse for remotely future generations, adding further ecological damage to that done by us. And if we refrain from causing some kind of ecological damage, there can be no guarantee that our successors will not cause it themselves. But this does not suffice to destroy the distinction between investment, which has the property that our successors can choose whether or not to pass on the benefits we leave them, and ecological damage, which has its own adverse effects on remote future generations whether or not our successors add to it. I suspect that it is because of the reduction of the problem that follows from taking investment as the paradigm of relations between generations that Rawls is satisfied with a solution that would otherwise be manifestly inadequate.

He postulates throughout *A Theory of Justice* (without ever adequately explaining why) that the people in the 'original position' (whose choices from behind the 'veil of ignorance' are to constitute principles of justice) know that they are all contemporaries, although they do not know to which generation they belong. The obvious problem that this raises is a sort of n-generation prisoner's dilemma. Generation k, who happen to be behind the veil of ignorance, may be willing to save on condition that their predecessors have saved. But there is no way in which they can take a conditional decision of this kind because there is no way of reaching a binding agreement (or indeed any agreement) with their predecessors. All *they* can do is to decide themselves whether to save or not. As Rawls says, setting out the problem: 'Either previous generations have saved or they have not; there is nothing the parties [in the original position] can do to affect it.'[12] How can we escape this difficulty?

It might appear that the obvious way out of the difficulty is to drop the postulate that the people in the 'original position' are contemporaries, and this is I believe the path that Rawls should have taken to be true to his own theory. But he does not take it. Instead, the tack that he takes is, he says, to 'make a motivational assumption'. The 'goodwill' of the parties in the original position 'stretches over at least two generations'. We may, though we need not, 'think of the parties as heads of families, and therefore as having a desire to further the welfare of their nearest descendants'. He concludes as follows:

> What is essential is that each person in the original position should care about the well-being of some of those in the next generation, it being presumed that their concern is for different individuals in each case. Moreover for anyone in the next generation, there is someone who cares for him in the present generation. Thus the interests of all are looked after and, given the 'veil of ignorance', the whole strand is tied together.[13]

One slightly technical objection that must be made to this is that the conditions stated by Rawls as necessary for the interests of all to be looked after are unnecessarily strong. Given the veil of ignorance, it is not necessary for each party to be certain that there is someone in the next generation he cares about. He will have a motive to support principles giving weight to the welfare of the next generation provided he knows that he will probably care about somebody in the next generation. Similarly, there is no need for everybody in the next generation to have someone who cares for him in this one so long as the uncared-for cannot be identified as a category and thus made the object of discriminatory principle-choosing from behind the veil of ignorance. And as far as I can see they are pretty safe from that risk.

This, however, is just a skirmish. There are two powerful objections to the use Rawls makes of his 'motivational assumption'. The first, which I have already foreshadowed, is that even if it does everything Rawls wants it to do, that is still not enough. The really nasty problems (to some extent actual but even more potential) involve obligations to remote descendants rather than immediate descendants and on these Rawls has nothing to say. It has been suggested that we might boost the extension of concern into the future

[12] Ibid. 292. [13] Ibid., all quotes in this paragraph from pp. 128–9.

derivable from sentiment (which is what Rawls's derivation amounts to) by pointing to the fact that if we care about our grandchildren and they care about their grandchildren we should care about our grandchildren's grandchildren, and so on *ad infinitum*. But those who base themselves on sentiment must follow where it leads, and if primary concern is as short-winded as Rawls suggests, it is scarcely plausible that secondary concern will alter the picture much. Certainly, by a few centuries' time it would be asymptotically approaching zero.

The second objection, which seems to me decisive, is that the derivation of obligations to future generations from the 'motivational assumption' is a pretty thin performance. The only justification offered for the 'motivational assumption' is that it enables Rawls to derive obligations to future generations. But surely this is a little too easy, like a conjurer putting a rabbit in a hat, taking it out again and expecting a round of applause. What it comes to is that we impute to the people in the original position a desire for the welfare of their descendants; on the basis of this we 'deduce' that they will choose principles requiring some action in pursuit of that welfare; and on the basis of the general theory that what would be chosen in the original position constitutes principles of justice we say that the principle governing savings that they would choose is the 'just savings principle'. But if it is acceptable to introduce desires for the welfare of immediate descendants into the original position simply in order to get them out again as obligations, what grounds can there be for refusing to put into the original position a desire for the welfare of at least some contemporaries?

For the whole idea—and the intellectual fascination—of 'justice as fairness' is that it takes self-interested agents, and, by the alchemy of the 'original position', forces them to choose principles of universal scope. In relation to subsequent generations, the postulate of self-interest is relaxed to allow concern for successors, but this naturally limited sympathy is not forced by the logic of the 'original position' to be extended any further than it extends naturally. Our limited sympathies towards our successors are fed into the sausage-machine of 'justice as fairness' and returned to us duly certified as obligations. We come seeking moral guidance and simply get our existing prejudices underwritten—hardly what one would expect from a rationalist philosopher.

The alternative route out of Rawls's difficulties is to pursue the logic of his own analysis more rigorously. This entails scrapping the part of the construction specifying that all the people in the 'original position' are contemporaries and know that they are. We should now have to imagine that there is a meeting to decide on intergenerational relationships at which all generations are represented. Clearly, the 'veil of ignorance' would be required to conceal from them which generation each of them belonged to. Otherwise, an earlier generation would always have the whip-hand over a later one in the negotiations.

There are, obviously, formidable difficulties involved in the very notion of a meeting of all generations. But those difficulties are equally inherent in the bare notion of an individual choosing criteria for relations between generations either without knowing to which he belongs (Rawlsian individual choice) or on the basis that whatever criteria he chooses will apply to all generations (Kantian individual choice). It might therefore be offered as a point in favour of the 'general meeting' construction that it brings out the difficulties graphically.

If the whole notion of collecting representatives from all generations is difficult in itself, there is a special problem introduced by the fact that actions taken at one time may affect the number of subsequent generations by making the tenure of human life on the planet longer or shorter than it would otherwise have been. (In the extreme case, the actions of one generation may be such as to make it the last.) If every generation that *might* exist is represented at the meeting, everybody knows that the criteria chosen may turn out to make his or her generation non-existent.

This is an awkward problem and it is understandable that David Richards, who differs from Rawls in saying that 'the class of members of the original position includes, in a hypothetical sense, *all* persons, who have lived, live now, or will live'[14], suggests that the rational contractors would adopt a principle limiting population so as to make those who do live as well off as possible (I omit the details). He adds that 'the egoistic desire to exist of the contractors does not influence their consideration of this problem, for *ex hypothesi* the contractors know they exist in some point of time, and are thus only concerned to ensure that their existence be as satisfying as possible'.[15]

There are two objections to this way of disposing of the problem. First, although we may in the end want to say that people who do not get born do not count, this should surely be the conclusion rather than the premiss built in by virtue of the construction. Second, we must ask if there is not something incoherent in putting together (*a*) the idea that

[14] David A. J. Richards, *A Theory of Reasons for Action* (Oxford: Clarendon Press, 1971), 81 and 134 (itals. in original).

[15] Ibid. 134.

people in the original position are choosing among policies that will produce different total numbers of people and (*b*) the idea that they know at the outset that they are all the people who ever have existed or ever will exist. It is surely a curious sort of choice if the results of it are already instantiated in the composition of the group of people doing the choosing!

We cannot therefore avoid having to ask whether the interests of potential people in being born should be taken into account or whether each possible decision-rule should be evaluated simply by estimating how those who would actually be born under it would fare, and ignoring those who might have been born under some other decision-rule.

I confess that this is an area in which the light is, for me, fitful. One point, however, seems to me clear, though it is admittedly only a negative one. This is that we should not call one situation better than another simply because it contains some extra people whose lives are worth living. The attraction of such a view derives from two things, I suspect. One is an illegitimate extension of the Pareto principle. This says that one situation is better than another if everything else is the same but at least one person prefers the first to the second. The principle is hard to deny in general (see chapter 13 above) but its plausibility extends only to cases where there are the same people in the two situations.[16] To say that a hypothetical person is made better off by being actualized is an abuse of language.

The second cause of misplaced sentiment about the unborn is a tendency to think of them inhabiting 'never never land' while waiting anxiously for the chance to be born. The unborn have no regrets about not being born because they do not exist. It is essential, as Doctor Johnson said, to 'clear the mind of cant', and in particular of Victorian whimsy. In this context I may remark that it is a serious drawback to the idea of a convention of all possible generations (or all possible people) that it makes it almost impossible to escape from such a way of thinking. Not to be born after you have already attended a meeting of representatives takes on too much of the aspect of dying extremely prematurely. Admittedly, David Hume remarked on his death-bed that there is no more to being dead than to not having been born, but there is the crucial difference between them that one can have a conscious prospect of being dead but not one of not being born.

[16] As Ian Little pointed out in *A Critique of Welfare Economics* (Oxford: Clarendon Press, 1950, 2nd edn., 1957), if someone dies we cannot compare his welfare before and after (p. 49), and the same is true if someone is not born in one situation and is born in another.

However, if we can somehow exclude this artefact of the construction, I do not see how coming into existence can itself be regarded as a good from the point of view of the potential person, since potential people do not have points of view. And yet I must admit to feeling uneasy with the alternative conclusion that we should take into account only the conscious states of those who get born.

I find no difficulty in accepting this with regard to the numbers of people alive at any one time. In asking whether the world will be better off in the year 2000 with seven billion inhabitants than it is with four billion now, I do not feel any temptation to say that the extra numbers are themselves, other things being equal, an improvement —even if most of the enlarged population do not regret having been born. But in asking whether it would matter for human beings (or life on earth in general) to come to an end in five hundred years' time rather than 500,000, I do not find irrelevant the fact that in the first case many generations that might have come into existence will not have the opportunity of doing so.

It may, of course, be argued that good reasons can be given in terms of the interests of actual human beings for not choosing to do something that brings about a substantial risk of ending human life in five hundred years' time. The people in the original position would not care to risk the distress at the prospect or the suffering entailed in the process. But human life will presumably come to an end eventually anyway and in a congress at which all potential generations are represented, the risk of being the last generation that actually exists is the same whether that occurs early or late, and the risk of being non-existent (we are saying) is not to count. In any case, I feel fairly sure that my conviction that it would be monstrous to take risks with the existence of future generations in order to secure advantages or avoid hardships for those who will live during the shortened time span left does not rest on such calculations.

The Hobbesian, Lockean, and Rousseauan theories give only the most tenuous and contingent security to the interests of future generations. It now appears that no theory confining its attention to the states of actual human beings will do. If we say that those who do not get born do not count in the choice of an 'ideal contract', the relatively early end of the human race may be preferred to a longer history at a somewhat lower level. The solution chosen would not be exactly equivalent to average utilitarianism (maximizing the average happiness of those who actually live) if we accept Rawls's arguments that people choosing in the 'original position' would be more concerned to avoid very bad outcomes than to obtain very good ones. But we can certainly say that 'average utilitarianism' where only those who get born count in the denominator runs into the same problem as an 'ideal contract' where only those who get born have a vote. The highest average for those who live may entail not merely a relatively small population at any given time (which seems to me a quite unexceptionable conclusion) but a relatively short time span for the human race, as those who are alive splurge all the earth's resources with an attitude of *après nous le déluge*.

The 'total utility' view (that the sum total of happiness should be maximized) in effect enfranchises potential people.[17] However, the unpalatibility of this form of utilitarianism, which I have already remarked upon, seems to me greatly increased when we realize that it would call upon us to make sacrifices merely so that there could be more people, so long as each extra person adds any positive amount to the notional sum total of happiness. It may also be noted that, although the total utility doctrine is biased towards actualizing a lot of potential people, it is not biased towards spreading them over a long time span. It is consistent with total utilitarianism that we should have a massive population for another two centuries and then nothing. Perhaps it is unlikely that this is the way to maximize total happiness, but the point is that at any rate as far as I am concerned the continuation of human life into the future is something to be sought (or at least not sabotaged) even if it does not make for the maximum total happiness.

Certainly, if I try to analyse the source of my own strong conviction that we would be wrong to take risks with the continuation of human life, I find that it does not lie in any sense of injury to the interests of people who will not get born but rather in a sense of its cosmic impertinence—that we should be grossly abusing our position by taking it upon ourselves to put a term on human life and its possibilities. I must confess to feeling great intellectual discomfort in moving outside a framework in which ethical principles are related to human interests, but if I am right then these are the terms in which we have to start thinking. In contrast to Passmore, I conclude that those who say we need a 'new ethic' are in fact right. It need not entail the kind of

[17] It does not, however, follow that an 'ideal contract' chosen by all potential people—if we can make sense of that notion—would be for maximizing total happiness. If they were, in Rawlsian fashion, much more concerned to avoid very bad outcomes than to obtain very good ones, it would seem prudent to vote for not bringing the human race into existence. All this would require would be that there should be *some* people of whom Sophocles' 'highest of all is not to be born' would apply.

half-baked ideas that Passmore criticizes, but should surely as a minimum include the notion that those alive at any time are custodians rather than owners of the planet, and ought to pass it on in at least no worse shape than they found it in.

19

THE ETHICS OF RESOURCE DEPLETION

Why does the exploitation of non-renewable natural resources raise a special problem in intergenerational equity? The reason is, simply, that any resources we use will not be available in the future. It is true that most minerals can be recycled, and scrap metal is, indeed, an important constituent in goods manufactured today. But we are still digging out ore at a great rate. And it should be borne in mind that non-renewable energy resources—fossil fuels—cannot be recycled. Once they have been burned, they have gone forever, as far as any use to human beings is concerned.

It is true that there are estimated to be enormous quantities of minerals in the top mile of the earth's crust. However, much of the supply is inconveniently located in relation to demand and presents great difficulties in extracting it. (A great deal of it is under the deep seabed and Antarctica.) Future generations therefore face progressively greater costs in getting access to non-renewable resources.

It might appear at first blush that the only equitable solution is to ensure that future generations face the same stock of resources as we do. This, however, would obviously imply that no non-renewable resources should ever be used. The logic would be on a par with that of the (possibly apocryphal) town council which passed an ordinance to the effect that there should always be at least one taxi waiting at the station to ensure that taxis would be available for arriving passengers. We must come up with a criterion that allows for some exploitation of non-renewable resources even when that is going to mean that, other things being equal, future generations will inherit a diminished stock.

The solution that I propose is intended as a practical application of the intuition that underlay the solution that I have just rejected. That intuition was that we should not make the position of future generations worse than ours by our depletion of non-renewable resources. We can, I suggest, capture the spirit of this by stipulating that future generations are owed compensation in other ways for our reducing their access to easily extracted and conveniently located natural resources. In practice, this entails that the combination of improved technology and increased capital investment should be such as to offset the effects of depletion.

What, precisely, constitutes 'offsetting'? There are two possible interpretations. The one that would naturally occur to economists —and not only to economists—would be to define offsetting in terms of utility: we should do whatever is necessary to provide future generations with the same level of utility as they would have had if we had not depleted the natural resources. There are all kinds of difficulties in drawing practical implications from this idea, but the objection that I shall put is pitched at a level of principle and would still be relevant even if all the practical problems could be swept away.

The alternative that I wish to defend is that what constitutes offsetting the depletion of natural resources is the replacement of the productive opportunities we have destroyed by the creation of alternative ones. In other words, when we say that resource depletion makes future generations worse off than we are, this should be taken to mean that they will be worse off in terms of productive potential; and it is that loss of productive potential for which justice requires us to compensate. (The notion of productive potential will be explained below.) Questions immediately arise. What is an acceptable alternative, and what happens if future people have different tastes from ours (as seems a priori very likely)? I shall discuss these and other problems in due course.

First, I want to offer a general argument for defining the criterion in terms of opportunities rather than utilities. My answer is that this is true of justice in all contexts, so that intergenerational justice is simply an application of the general idea. We therefore need a discussion of the broad thesis rather than one confined to future generations, for the conclusion will surely be stronger for the rather strange case of future generations if it can be shown to be plausible in more familiar cases. To this end, let me return to the alternative interpretation of the criterion of compensation for resource depletion, that it should be defined in terms of utility. This idea stems from a general conception of what should be the subject-matter of moral assessment: that, although we perforce distribute rights, opportunities, or material goods rather than utility, the ultimate standard of judgement should be the utility to people that arises from those resources.

Utilitarianism, understood as the theory that the aggregate amount of utility should be maximized, is the best-known example of a theory that takes utility as the only thing that matters, in the last analysis.

Thus, as Sidgwick put it, utilitarianism is concerned with 'the distribution of *Happiness*, not the means of happiness'.[1] Ted Honderich advanced a 'Principle of Equality' defined not in terms of equal treatment but in terms of 'the qualities of the experience of individuals'. The principle was then 'that things should be so arranged that we approach as close as we can, which may not be all that close, to equality in satisfaction and distress'.[2] Again, Amartya Sen began an article by saying: 'Usual measures of economic inequality concentrate on income, but frequently one's interest may lie in the inequality of welfare rather than of income as such.' And he went on to say that this raises problems not only of 'interpersonal comparisons of welfare, but also those arising from differences in non-income circumstances, e.g. age, the state of one's health, the pattern of love, friendship, concern and hatred surrounding a person'.[3]

It is generally agreed that there are, in practice, severe limits to the extent to which distribution can be individuated so as to take account of the way in which different people either get different amounts of happiness from some baseline amount of the means of happiness, or gain unequal amounts of happiness from the same increments in the means of happiness. Thus, the relevant information is difficult to come by—some would say that the problem is not even well defined. Collecting the information would in any case intrude on personal privacy. The policy would place a premium on dissimulation, as people would try to give the appearance of having a utility function of a kind that would provide them with a large allocation of income or other means of happiness. And the implementation of a programme of adapting distribution to individual psychological characteristics would obviously place vast powers in the hands of those doing the allocating—powers to make decisions on a largely discretionary basis, because of the lack of precisely defined objective criteria for establishing the susceptibility of different people to external advantages or disadvantages.

For all these reasons it might be admitted that in practice idiosyncratic differences in the way people convert the means of happiness into happiness itself should be disregarded for purposes of public policy. And it might plausibly be added that the case for disregarding idiosyncrasies becomes overwhelming when we know nothing

[1] Henry Sidgwick, *The Methods of Ethics* (London: Macmillan and Co., 7th edn., 1907), 47 n. 1.

[2] Ted Honderich, *Three Essays on Political Violence* (Oxford: Basil Blackwell, 1976), 41.

[3] Amartya Sen, 'Welfare Inequalities and Rawlsian Axiomatics', *Theory and Decision*, 7 (1976), 243–62, at 243.

definite about the people concerned—as must be the case with people as yet unborn. We *could* therefore, by invoking ignorance, get from the premiss that the ultimate object of distribution is utility to the conclusion that justice between generations should be defined in terms of resources: in the absence of the appropriate information we must fall back on distributing resources without looking beyond resources to utilities. Instead, however, I want to suggest that the whole idea of treating utility as the object of distribution is wrong.

To strip away the practical complications, imagine that by some incredible advance in psychometric technology it became possible to fit people with tiny, tamper-proof 'black boxes' implanted under the skin, and that these 'black boxes' measured (and somehow could be shown to measure to the satisfaction of anyone with enough training in neurophysiology and electronics) the amount of utility received by the recipient within, say, a period of a year. I do not think that the availability of this kind of publicly verifiable information would eliminate the case against allocating the means of happiness so as to achieve a certain distribution of happiness. For my view is that such information is in principle irrelevant when it comes to determining a just distribution.

Suppose we believe that two people should be paid the same amount: they do the same work equally well, have equal seniority in the same firm, and so on. What this means is that they have an equal claim on the resources of society to do what they like with that chunk of resources. (Taking account of market distortions, we can say that prices do roughly correspond to the real claim on resources at the margin represented by alternative purchases.) Justice consists in their getting an equal crack at society's resources, without any mention of comparative utility. If we discover that one of them gets more fun out of spending his income than does the other, this is no reason for transferring income from the one who derives more utility to the one who derives less. Similarly, if the price of something one of them enjoys goes up (e.g. because of an increased demand for it), this is no reason for increasing his income in compensation. For he had no special claim on the amount of utility he was getting before. All he had a claim on was a fair share of resources.

The argument as applied to future generations is, then, that we should not hold ourselves responsible for the satisfaction they derive from their opportunities. What is important from the point of view of justice is the range of choice open to them, rather than what they get out of it. But choice of what? The range of choice I have so far discussed has been the range of consumption choices. Broadly speaking, I have been making the case for defining justice in terms of income rather than utility.

But this is not the whole story. For we obviously cannot literally provide people not yet born with income, any more than we can provide them with utility. The question is, in either case, whether we need to predict how much they will actually get if we do one thing rather than another. Even if this were feasible (which it is not), it would still be beside the point.

The important thing is that we should compensate for the reduction in opportunities to produce that are brought about by our depleting the supply of natural resources, and that compensation should be defined in terms of productive potential. If we could somehow predict that there would be a general decline in working hours or in the amount of effort people put into work, this would be no reason for saying that we must hand over additional productive resources to future generations. This notion of productive potential will be analysed below. For the present, all we need to grasp is that productive potential is equal in two situations if the same effort would produce the same output.

Two questions follow from this. First, why should future generations be left not worse off (in opportunity terms) than they would have been in the absence of our having depleted the resources? And second, if we say that our depletion of resources should not leave future generations with a smaller range of opportunities than they would otherwise have had, this requires us to have some standard on the basis of which we can establish what opportunities they would otherwise have had. What is the appropriate standard?

Let me begin with the first point. The basic argument for an equal claim on natural resources is that none of the usual justifications for an unequal claim—special relationships arising in virtue of past services, promises, etc.—applies here. From an atemporal perspective, no one generation has a better or worse claim than any other to enjoy the earth's resources. In the absence of any powerful argument to the contrary, there would seem to be a strong presumption in favour of arranging things so that, as far as possible, each generation faces the same range of opportunities with respect to natural resources. I must confess that I can see no further positive argument to be made at this point. All I can do is counter what may be arguments on the other side. Is there any way in which the present generation can claim that it is entitled to a larger share of the goods supplied by nature than its successors? If not, then equal shares is the only solution compatible with justice.

The only theory of distributive justice that might appear to have implications inconsistent with the equality of generations is the Lockean one of a 'natural right' to appropriate by 'mixing one's labour' with natural resources. This might be taken to imply that there is no criterion by which the collective exploitation of natural resources by a generation can be judged, as long as the individualistic requirements of the Lockean theory are met. However, even taking that theory seriously for a moment, we should bear in mind that Locke said that legitimate appropriation was limited by the proviso that 'enough and as good' should be left for others. If we interpret 'others' to include later generations as well as contemporaries, we get the notion of equality between generations. And Locke's attempt to fudge the application of the proviso once people have 'consented to the use of money', which is a fraud anyway, cannot even get a foothold in the intergenerational case, since future generations are obviously in no position to consent to our exploitation of natural resources in a way that fails to leave 'as good' for them.

Clearly, if each generation has an equal right to enjoy the productive opportunities provided by natural resources, it does not necessarily follow that compensation for violating that right is acceptable. We will all agree that doing harm is in general not cancelled out by doing good, and conversely that doing some good does not license one to do harm provided it does not exceed the amount of good. For example, if you paid for the realignment of a dangerous highway intersection and saved an average of two lives a year, that would not mean that you could shoot one motorist per year and simply reckon on coming out ahead.

That example, however, involves gratuitous infliction of harm. In the case of resources and future generations, the crucial feature is that we cannot possibly avoid harming them by using up some non-renewable resources, given the existing population level and the technology that has developed to sustain that level. So the choice is not between reducing the resource base for future generations and keeping it intact, but between depletion with compensation and depletion without compensation. The analogy is therefore with the traveller caught in a blizzard who, in order to survive, breaks into somebody's empty weekend cottage, builds a fire, and helps himself to food. Even the most obtuse defender of property rights would scarcely deny that this is a legitimate use of another's property without his permission. It will be generally agreed, also, that while the unauthorized taking of another's property was entirely justifiable in the circumstances, the traveller is not absolved from making restitution for whatever he damaged or consumed.

The second problem arises in this way. Suppose we say that justice requires us to compensate future generations for depleted resources, so that they have as much productive potential as they would have inherited had the resources not been depleted. To give this criterion any operational significance, we must obviously give some definite content to the notion of the amount of productive potential that future generations would have enjoyed in the absence of resource depletion. Otherwise we have no means of deciding what is required by justice in the way of compensation.

We cannot say that 'the productive potential that future generations would otherwise have enjoyed' is to be settled by *predicting*. Perhaps, in the absence of resource depletion, we would in fact be inclined to leave future generations with far less productive potential than, as a matter of justice, we ought to leave them with. If we were to leave them an inadequate amount plus an amount calculated to compensate for resource depletion, we would then be behaving unjustly. Conversely, in the absence of resource depletion, maybe we would leave future generations with far more productive potential than is required by justice—whatever that is. In that case, even when resource depletion is taken into account, the same amount would still more than satisfy the requirements of justice.

It is apparent, therefore, that 'the productive potential that future generations would otherwise have enjoyed' must be defined in terms of justice. We must understand it to mean the following: what future generations would justly have enjoyed in the absence of resource depletion. But how much is that? The answer is critical in determining the whole outcome of our enquiry. To make the most extreme case, suppose we said that the only things we owe to future generations are whatever natural resources we inherited plus due compensation (measured in terms of productive capacity) for what we depleted. If we left anything more than a few picks and shovels they would be ahead, since they would then be in a better position to exploit natural resources than if they had to use their bare hands. Anything more than that would go beyond the demands of justice. But human generations do not succeed one another with one generation marching off the stage as another marches on, so self-interest on the part of the living will in any case ensure that far more than that is handed on. However selfishly those alive at any given time behave, they can scarcely avoid passing on to their successors a pretty large capital stock that embodies thousands of years of technological development. Hence, the principle of compensation for the depletion of natural resources could be accepted without the slightest implication that more should be done to protect the interests of future generations than would inevitably be done as a by-product of the pursuit of self-interest by the current generation.

I imagine that few would really want to say that we would be beyond criticism on grounds of justice if we ran down capital and used up natural resources in whatever way best suited us, as long as we left our successors somewhat better equipped than people were in the Stone Age. But it is hard to come up with a clear-cut principle to say exactly how far the bounds of justice extend. I believe, however, that there are some leading ideas which can guide us.

Most of our technology and the capital stock embodying it are not by any stretch of the imagination the sole creation of the present generation; we cannot therefore claim exclusive credit for it. The whole process of capital formation presupposes an inheritance of capital and technology. To a considerable extent, then, we can say that, from the standpoint of the current generation, natural resources are not really as sharply distinguished from capital and technology as might at first appear. Both are originally inherited, and thus fall outside any special claims based on the present generation's having done something to deserve them. We can therefore make no special claim on *our* side. But can others (those who did create them) claim that they can endow us with exclusive control over what we inherit? This raises complicated issues.

It seems to me that inherited capital can be looked at from two standpoints, that of the creators and that of the receivers, and that the trick is to give weight to both perspectives. From the side of the recipients, inherited capital is exactly like inherited natural resources —the present generation can claim credit for neither. From the side of the earlier generations, on the other hand, accumulated capital and natural resources that are handed on have different statuses, in that capital is created and natural resources are not. Yet no generation creates from scratch all the capital it hands on. It seems reasonable to suggest that it should get credit at the most only for the capital it adds.

This gives us a rough basis for proceeding. Let us say that, as a reasonable reconciliation of the two perspectives, each generation's sacrifices (if any) to increase the capital stock it passes on give it a claim to some consideration by the following generation of its objectives in making these sacrifices. Beyond one generation, its specific wishes for the disposition of the increment become progressively less significant as constituting claims on the decisions of the living.

We can now venture a statement of what is required by justice towards future generations. As far as natural resources are concerned, depletion should be compensated for in the sense that later generations should be left no worse off (in terms of productive capacity) than they would have been without the depletion. And how well off they would have been is to be determined by applying the principles that have been worked out above. As a starting-point, we may say that the capital stock inherited should be passed on without diminution, but this can be modified somewhat to accommodate the claims of past generations. If we suppose, for example, that the previous generation made sacrifices to permit the present generation a higher standard of living without any expectation that this generation would pass it on, it would seem legitimate for the present generation to pass on slightly less. On the other hand, if one believes that successive past generations made sacrifices in the (no doubt vague) expectation that each generation would pass on more than it inherited, this would constitute a prima facie case for saying that the present generation has a certain obligation to continue with this process. The whole notion of obligations to continue the undertakings of past generations, however, raises difficulties that need further work. (See above, chapter 6.) I do not think we should go far wrong here if we set it aside and simply say that compensation should be reckoned as what is required to maintain productive potential.

Three practical problems arise in any attempt to apply the conclusions of this abstract discussion. The first is whether the compensation criterion can be given a workable significance. The second is where issues of intragenerational distribution fit in. And the third is how to deal with the difficulty that alternative policies have results in the future that are associated with varying degrees of uncertainty.

On the feasibility of the compensation criterion, the apparent problem is this: oil is oil is oil. How do we decide what is adequate compensation for running down the world's reserves of oil? In the most favourable case, it may be possible to compensate in a quite direct way. If we run down the oil by 10 per cent but develop technology that makes it possible to extract 10 per cent more oil from any given deposit, we have in effect left future generations with as much (exploitable) oil as we found. Or if we develop internal combustion engines that produce more power per gallon of petrol used, we have made the remaining stock of oil go further, measured in output terms—which is what counts—than it would otherwise have done. And so on.

I do not want to suggest that this will solve all the problems of implementation; where it is not applicable, we have to fall back on the more general idea of maintaining productive capacity. Within limits, which over a long time period may be very wide, it is always possible to substitute capital for raw materials by recycling, cutting down waste, and making things get results by being complicated and well engineered rather than big and heavy. Energy may appear unamenable to this treatment. But it can still be economized by a greater expenditure of capital, and the performance of Western economies in the period since 1973 has illustrated the way in which, with the right incentives, capital expenditure will be substituted for energy.

The second practical problem is this: what happens when the principles for justice between generations are combined with moral principles governing distribution among people who are contemporaries, whether they live now or in the future? One reason for confronting the question of intragenerational distribution is that there are some who profess impatience with a concern for the interests of unborn generations when there are so many existing people now starving or suffering from preventable malnutrition and disease. I must admit to some sympathy with this impatience. I have a possibly prejudiced idea that one could run in Marin County[4] more successfully on a platform of doing good things for future generations than of transferring money to poor people now, either domestically or internationally. Being in favour of future generations is somehow more antiseptically apolitical than being in favour of one's contemporaries, and also, in an odd way, gives an impression of being more high-minded.

If it were really necessary to make a choice between intragenerational and intergenerational justice, it would be a tough one. But in my view there is no such dilemma, because I do not believe that there will turn out to be any inconsistency between the requirements of each. In the absence of a full theory of both, I cannot show this. But I

[4] See Cyra McFadden, *The Serial: A Year in the Life of Marin County* (New York: Alfred A. Knopf, 1977). Of a typical couple in this affluent area north of San Francisco it is remarked that they 'belonged to the ACLU and the Sierra Club and went to the Mozart Festival at Stolte Grove every year with the picnic of the month from *Sunset* in a Cost Plus hamper. . . .' (p. 8).

predict that whatever redistribution among contemporaries is required by justice will also be able to observe the constraints that the interests of future generations be protected.

Of course, if citizens and governments in the rich countries are willing to make only token sacrifices to meet the demands of either intragenerational or intergenerational justice, a choice will have to be made. But we ought then to be clear that the necessity for choice arises not from any real incompatibility, but simply from the not unusual phenomenon that people are not prepared to behave justly when it is contrary to their immediate interests, unless they are somehow coerced into doing so. And while poor countries have a certain amount of ability to cause trouble to rich ones, future generations obviously have no way of enforcing a fair deal on the present generation. (See above, chapter 18.)

It will be apparent that the principles already enunciated for justice among generations may be applied equally well to relations among contemporaries. (See above, chapter 16.) Thus, the argument that there is no act by which the value of natural resources may be regarded as earned or deserved by whoever happens to find them suggests an equal claim of all contemporaries on that value. Similarly, the idea that inherited capital and technology gradually merge into the 'common heritage of mankind' clearly implies a just claim by poor countries on rich ones.

Intragenerational justice would best be met by a combination of a self-balancing, shadow (positive and negative) income tax on countries and a severance tax on the exploitation of natural resources, the proceeds being transferred to resource-poor countries such as India, Bangladesh, or some Central African countries. This would, in an admittedly rough and ready way (but no other is to be expected), make tax liability depend on both the special advantages arising from possession of rich natural resources and the more general advantages that make for high per capita income. Intergenerational justice requires, as we have seen, maintenance of capital (with certain modest exceptions) plus the creation of additional technology and capital to compensate for resource depletion. Yet this has an intragenerational aspect too. To say that 'the present generation' should pass on certain productive capabilities to 'future generations' leaves open the question of how the burdens and the benefits should be distributed among contemporaries, now and in the future. What can be said about this?

It is legitimate for those who form the current generation in a country to make special efforts to provide extra benefits for their own descendants if they choose to do so, since this is more than is called for by justice anyway. This is in effect an intergenerational gift of resources whose disposition the people in that country have a just claim to control. But the mere passing along of the amount of capital inherited draws no credit. And, as I have suggested, the wishes of those who originally made the sacrifices to accumulate it should be regarded as fading out over the course of a few generations. This implies that some of the capital stock should be diffused as claims to special benefits run out, in the same way as patents and copyrights expire with time.

The problem of resource depletion by those living in some country can be divided into two parts: who should provide the compensation, and who should receive it? I suggest that those countries which consume the largest quantities of non-renewable natural resources should be responsible for the bulk of the effort to provide the technology and capital formation to substitute for them.

On the other hand, I wish to argue that it would be extremely inequitable if the compensatory technology and capital were passed on for the exclusive benefit of the successors of those in the countries who depleted the natural resources. Since running down any natural resources deprives all future inhabitants of the world of the production from any given combination of capital and labour, the compensation is owed not to descendants of the current heavy users only, but to all in the future who are disadvantaged by that use—in fact, everybody.

The redistributive case is even stronger than this. For industrial countries have achieved their present prosperity by first using their own natural resources and then, when these began to get scarce, by using those of the rest of the world at relatively low cost to themselves—in the case of oil, for example, for a few cents per gallon through the 1950s and 1960s. In effect, this bonanza has been turned into accumulated capital that is regarded by these countries as their private property to do with as they choose. But it is obviously harder for countries that missed out on this era of cheap resources to undertake a similar course of economic development in the future. (The effect of oil price increases on Indian economic planning is a dramatic illustration, and many others could be offered.) The poor countries, therefore, have been especially disadvantaged because, unlike the rich countries, they have nothing to show for the past depletion of world resources except perhaps in free access to some unpatented technology that was part and parcel of Western development.

The upshot of this discussion is that, generally speaking, the countries with the highest per capita production and the highest use of non-renewable natural resources (the two are highly correlated) should be making transfers to the poor countries to meet the requirements of intergenerational justice. This clearly overlaps with the requirements of purely intragenerational justice that were outlined earlier. An across-the-board international income tax (levied on countries, to be raised through their own domestic tax systems), whether or not supplemented by a severance tax on the extraction of mineral resources, would meet all the requirements, as long as part of the proceeds of the tax were devoted to the building up of technology and capital in the recipient countries, and as long as those in the rich countries did not treat payment of the tax as an alternative to accumulating capital domestically to enable their own descendants to offset the effects of resource depletion.

The final problem is that of uncertainty. It cannot be avoided because, in deciding what technologies we ought to develop to compensate future generations for the depletion of resources, we must somehow deal with the fact that the risks and benefits are, to some degree, speculative. Suppose most competent authorities agree that there is a possibility (i.e. it cannot be excluded on the basis of existing scientific knowledge) that some action taken now (e.g. burying nuclear wastes deep underground, releasing fluorocarbons into the atmosphere, or carrying out experiments on recombinant DNA) will have serious and irreversible (or only doubtfully/expensively/gradually reversible) adverse consequences in the long term; and suppose further that either there is disagreement on the likelihood of these adverse consequences coming to pass or agreement on the impossibility, in the present state of knowledge, of quantifying the risk (or some mixture of the two). The question, then, is how we should react to this state of affairs. Should we say that the profound uncertainty makes it unreasonable (or 'premature', if one is optimistic about the prospects for finding out more in the future) to decide against taking the action? Or should we say that, in the absence of better information, the possibility of disastrous consequences is a decisive reason for not acting? *Ex hypothesi*, methods of decisionmaking that discount alternative outcomes by their probabilities of occurrence are not available here.

The simplest argument for giving the second answer rather than the first is a two-part one: (*a*) in the case of an individual making a choice that affects only himself, we should regard anyone who acted on the basis of the first alternative as crazy; and (*b*) when we change the case to one that involves millions of people and extends over many centuries, the same reasoning applies with increased force.

The best way to establish (*a*) is by means of an example. Imagine that your dentist were to say: 'The only way of saving this tooth is by means of a new procedure. There is every reason to believe that the procedure will succeed in saving the tooth, but it's conceivable that it will kill you. It may be that, however many times it were done, nobody would ever be killed by it. But it can't be ruled out on the basis of anything we currently know about physiology that it's highly lethal. It's not impossible that it has one chance in a hundred of killing you. Since we have no idea of the magnitude of the risks involved, I draw two conclusions: more research is needed, and in the meantime you should undergo the procedure.' I predict that not only would you decline his suggestion, but you would also think he should have his licence withdrawn for professional incompetence.

As far as (*b*) is concerned, I need only say that there is no prima facie reason for supposing that changing the case so that the numbers involved are larger and extend over a longer time is going to make the choice associated with an uncertain potential for catastrophe more palatable rather than less. If anything, the argument is even strengthened. Let me conclude by offering three considerations.

First, we might ask whether genocide is universally abhorred for no other reason than that it entails killing a large number of individual human beings. Or is it worse to wipe out an entire people than to kill an equal number of individuals scattered throughout the world? One answer might be that genocide is worse because it is the expression of an evil theory—that of racial superiority and inferiority. But genocidal attempts antedated the Nazis (e.g. the 'Armenian massacres' and the hunting to extinction of the native populations of Tasmania and California in the nineteenth century), yet those cases were no less terrible.

We can approach what I consider the critical point by discussing what has been called 'cultural genocide'—the practice of systematically exterminating the intelligentsia—the professionals, writers, journalists, students, and anyone with an above-average level of education. Those with greater knowledge of history than I can no doubt cite examples going back thousands of years, but well-attested examples from recent decades are Pakistan (the early stages of the civil war that led to the creation of Bangladesh) and Burundi. These examples of 'cultural genocide' seem to me less terrible than the destruction of the entire Bengali or Hutu populations would have been—numbers obviously do make a difference. At the same time they are, in my view, worse than random killing of the same numbers of the same populations.

My point is that the destruction of cultures is a bad over and above the physical destruction of its bearers. This, then, gives us a reason for holding that destroying a large population is more serious than killing the same number of random individuals. And this in turn is another reason why remote possibilities of catastrophic accidents (e.g. in nuclear reactors) should be treated as especially grave threats, and not simply balanced against the number of deaths from bronchitis or lung cancer that can be associated with the use of fossil fuel as an alternative. One chance in a million per annum of wiping out New York simply is not the same as having ten more people die each year.

Risk may be acceptable if it is accepted voluntarily in the pursuit of something that seems valuable to the person who chooses it. If somebody wishes to risk his or her life gratuitously by rock climbing or white-water canoeing, one might say that there is no case for preventing or discouraging these freely chosen activities. But the risks of, say, nuclear power generation are not at all plausibly construed on that model. The risk cannot be confined to the beneficiaries. We have a public good and a public bad; people who use the electricity get the good, and those who live near the plant get the bad, irrespective of whether they would prefer to do without both. If we were to respond that in the nature of the case consent cannot be obtained from everyone affected before any piece of collective action is undertaken, I would of course agree. But then the question of distributive equity arises. The canoeist gets the risk *and* the benefit. But with larger-scale projects, it is unlikely that the risks and the benefits will be distributed to each person in the same proportions. If nuclear plants are located in the country and mainly supply the cities, the rural people get a disproportionate share of the risks, while the city people benefit.

These problems are exacerbated across generations. First, cultural impoverishment is irreversible and continues to impoverish all successive generations. Second, if we do things now that impose risks on future people, there is clearly no way of getting their consent. And, finally, with some examples such as nuclear power plants, the benefits and risks are asymmetrically distributed across time: the benefits disproportionately occur while the plant is producing electricity, and the risks continue in some form for thousands of years, until the radioactivity of the waste decays to a safe level.

20

THE CONTINUING RELEVANCE OF SOCIALISM

I

A century ago Sir William Harcourt proclaimed 'We're all socialists now.' Today we have a Prime Minister whose declared purpose is to wipe socialism off the political map, and a Leader of the Labour Party who rarely uses the word except among gatherings of the faithful. I am therefore swimming against the current in arguing, as I propose to do here, that socialism is a doctrine that speaks to contemporary conditions in societies such as ours. But I believe that the case can be made. I make my claim only, of course, for socialism as I shall define it. But I wish to maintain that my definition captures the common core of socialism that united such disparate figures as Marx and the Fabians, and thus has good historical support.

Sir William Harcourt was, no doubt, exaggerating. But the element of truth in what he said is that, from the 1880s onwards, a broad agreement developed about the responsibilities of the state. Among the propositions that would have found general support, I shall pick out two: one is that taxes on wealth and income should be seen not only as a way of raising revenue but also as a way of bringing about a fairer distribution of wealth and income; the other is that the state should define a level of material well-being below which none of its citizens should fall, and then provide the resources necessary to ensure that nobody does fall below that level. The significance of Mrs Thatcher's term of office as Prime Minister is that we can no longer take it for granted that the government is committed to propositions such as the two I have just listed. Although she and her ministers may not have explicitly repudiated them, their actions have been such as to lead us to the conclusion that they have in fact abandoned them as guides to policy.

The easing of death duties, the abolition of the long-standing tax relief for earned income, and the reduction of the highest rate of income tax to 40 per cent all suggest a shift away from the notion that taxes should contribute to overall equity. And it is surely relevant in this context that the last of these measures was defended primarily as a 'simplification' of the tax system. On the face of it, there is something bizarre about treating a change that makes a well-off minority far better off as if its distributive implications were merely a by-product of administrative convenience. But it makes sense if we assume that the overall distribution of income is simply not seen as raising any moral issue.

The evidence for the government's repudiation of the second proposition is more direct. Under the reform of the welfare system inaugurated in April 1988, the arrangements under which payments were made to cover special expenses such as clothing or household necessities have been abolished, and replaced by a so-called Social Fund. The particular feature of this that is relevant here is that it has pre-set cash limits, which means that each local office has only a certain amount of money to give out, however many people may qualify for payments. (A further turn of the screw is that if someone is unlucky enough to apply for money when the local office has run out of the month's quota, that person cannot apply again until six months have elapsed, whatever the merits of the claim.[1]) Thus, for the first time in over fifty years—and perhaps for the first time since the Elizabethan Poor Law was enacted in 1601—the government has formally abandoned the undertaking to meet all the claims that are valid according to its own criteria, introducing instead a scheme under which it is predictable that many eligible claimants will be refused benefits simply on the grounds that the funds provided are inadequate.

As a political philosopher, if not as a citizen, I can only welcome the advent of Mrs Thatcher. By opening up to debate issues that had for a long time been regarded as closed she has extended our scope. Although she does not appear to be a very reflective person, I think that she should be given credit for having a coherent social vision, and one that is profoundly antithetical to socialism. In what follows I shall try to identify its roots in a certain kind of individualism, and argue that individualism so understood is a fatally flawed doctrine. I define socialism as the denial of the claims of individualism. If I succeed, therefore, in showing the limitations of individualism, I shall also have made out my case for the continuing relevance of socialism.

[1] Christian Wolmer, 'The New Poor Law', *Observer* (10 Apr. 1988), 15.

II

What is socialism? In proposing a definition, I want to steer between two common notions. One is that 'socialism' is simply a word to be applied nowadays to relatively egalitarian liberals. The other is that socialism is a kind of religion, which hopes for a transformation of human nature and rests on a series of predictions about historical events. Such a view is supported, for example, by *Pears' Cyclopaedia* (1967) where, in the 'Ideas and Beliefs' section, 'Socialism' is followed by Southcottism—the belief in the predictions of Joanna Southcott—and Spiritualism. The conception of socialism that I intend to put forward does not depend in any way on beliefs about the course of history and does not require a transformation of human nature. I can best approach it by asking what socialism is contrasted with. The two pairings that immediately come to mind are 'socialism versus capitalism' and 'socialism versus individualism'.

What can we learn from the opposition of socialism to capitalism and individualism? I think that both contrasts fit together with the following definition of socialism: A socialist society is one in which the citizens of that society are able, by acting together, to control the major features of the society and, in particular, to overcome the undesirable consequences of individual actions. Thus conceived, socialism is above all a theory of citizenship: it is concerned with empowering citizens to act collectively in pursuit of the interests and ideals that they share with one another and that can be realized only by collective action. Gaetano Mosca was, on this analysis, quite right to see Rousseau as the progenitor of the socialist idea.

Let me briefly follow through the relations between socialism as I have just defined it and the two contrasting terms, capitalism and individualism. The most prominent contemporary defenders of capitalism, Milton Friedman and F. A. Hayek, constantly claim that its primary virtue is its automatism. Thus, Friedman, in his well-known essay, 'Capitalism and Freedom', argued that in a capitalist society nobody exercises any power—even the managers of massive corporations—because all actors are so tightly constrained by the discipline of the market that on any given occasion only one course is open to them. Those who do anything different disappear from the system as a result of bankruptcy.[2] And, in his book *The Mirage of Social Justice*, Hayek argues that, precisely because the distribution of income

[2] Milton Friedman, *Capitalism and Freedom* (Chicago: Chicago University Press, 1963).

does not arise from any central decisionmaking process but from millions of independent decisions, the concept of social justice is inapplicable to market outcomes.[3]

Whether we look for our historical antecedents to Marxism or to Fabianism, I believe we are safe in saying that the core of socialism has always been the rejection of claims such as those of Friedman and Hayek. Where Friedman sees the market as a realm of freedom because nobody has any power, the socialist sees it as a realm of necessity, for precisely the same reason. The transformation from a society ruled by the tyranny of the market to one of freedom requires collective control over the economy. Similarly, the socialist turns Hayek's argument on its head. It is precisely because the market is incompatible with the introduction of considerations of distributive justice that it cannot be accepted as the arbiter of income distribution.

As I am presenting it, the core of socialism in its economic aspect is the constraint and modification of the market to accommodate the interests of people as workers, consumers, and citizens. The citizens of any society are quite naturally and rightly concerned with large accumulations of power in private hands, and it is a consequence of such a concern that socialism is opposed to private ownership of the means of production. It must, however, be emphasized that no reorganization of ownership (including ownership by the workers in a firm) can overcome the inadequacies of the market that I shall sketch in a moment. If so-called 'market socialism' denies this, then it is in my view a contradiction in terms.

I have been talking up to now about socialism versus capitalism. What about socialism versus individualism? Individualism is best seen, both historically and analytically, as the generalization of the case for capitalism to non-economic matters. It is no accident, I suggest, that the notion of the hidden hand originated in the heyday of deism. According to the deistic picture of the universe, God, having arranged things to operate according to universal laws, did not intervene any further in his creation. What appeared to be imperfections were merely the unavoidable by-products of the best possible set of general laws. The parallel with the standard rationale of the market could scarcely be clearer. Hayek particularly, who has often said that he finds himself most at home intellectually in the late eighteenth century, is identified strongly with the ideologically loaded concept of the 'rule of law'. According to this, states must operate by general

[3] Friedrich A. Hayek, *Law, Legislation, and Liberty*, vol. ii, *The Mirage of Social Justice* (Chicago: Chicago University Press, 1976).

laws only, and not intervene in the workings of the economy in order to bring about specific outcomes. And, like Leibniz, Hayek assures us that, even if the results in individual cases sometimes appear unfortunate, all is for the best in the best of all possible worlds so long as we have the best set of general laws.

Individualism, I suggest, is simply what you get if you take the optimistic analysis of the market and extend it beyond economics to the whole of social life. The market paradigm says that, given the right framework of general rules (enforcement of property rights and contracts, maintenance of competition, etc.), pursuit of individual self-interest is transmuted into social good. Individualism—epitomized, for example, in Mill's *On Liberty*—takes this structure of thought and makes it the basis for a whole theory of society.[4] So-called libertarianism, represented by, for example, Ayn Rand, Murray Rothbard, and their disciple Robert Nozick, is simply individualism that has run amok. Indeed, libertarianism has been well defined as the form taken by liberalism as common sense asymptotically approaches zero.

What marks liberal individualists of all kinds is a distaste, amounting in some cases to detestation, for politics. The wheeling and dealing, the messy compromises that are inseparable from politics, are anathema to them. To such people, the worst thing you can say about some area—education, say, or public transport—is that it has become 'politicized'. It might be naïvely supposed that, in what is supposed to be a democracy, subjecting important areas of public policy to political scrutiny and control would be thought of as a good thing. But no: according to the tenets of individualism, once the general rules have been laid down, people are free to act individually, but not collectively.

Some observers claim to have found something paradoxical in the fact that the Thatcher regime combines liberal individualist rhetoric with authoritarian action. But there is no paradox at all. The two are in fact simply opposite sides of the same coin. Even under the most repressive conditions—in Soweto or the Gaza Strip and the West Bank, say—people seek to act collectively in order to improve things for themselves, and it requires an enormous exercise of brutal coercion in order to fragment these efforts at organization and force people to pursue their interests individually. Things are no different here: left to themselves, people will inevitably tend to pursue their interests

[4] John Stuart Mill, *On Liberty*, in *Essays on Politics and Society*, ed. J. M. Robson (Toronto: Toronto University Press, 1977), i. pp. 213–310.

through collective action—in trade unions, tenants' associations, community organizations, and local government, for example. Only the pretty ruthless exercise of central power can defeat these tendencies: hence the common association between individualism and authoritarianism, well exemplified in the fact that the countries held up as models by the free-marketeers are, without exception, authoritarian regimes.

It was at one time fashionable to suggest that socialism should be defined as the pursuit of equality. There is, however, nothing distinctively socialist about equality: there can be (and are) egalitarian anarchists and egalitarian liberals as well as egalitarian socialists. Socialism thus has no monopoly on egalitarianism; but more than that, there is nothing in socialism itself that commits one to equality. The central demand of socialism is that outcomes—and this obviously includes the distribution of income—should fall under collective control. But this leaves open what the distribution of income ought to be. Some socialists believe that those who contribute more to the society through their work should get more; others believe that the ability to contribute more arises from good fortune and does not constitute a valid claim to finish up with more. I am inclined to think that the ultimate resolution of this issue depends on a satisfactory solution to the problem of free will, and I do not think this can be expected soon. (It is significant that the fallen angels in *Paradise Lost* pitched on this as a topic good for a few million years of debate.) Anyway, pending the cracking of the problem of free will, socialists can, I suggest, legitimately disagree about equality.

III

The idea has been put about that socialism is bound to be unattractive to most people because it demands too much in the way of sacrifice. In fact the paradigm of socialism is the prisoner's dilemma, where what is most in the interest of each prisoner individually—to confess—is contrary to the interests of both of them together.[5] Examples abound in real life: if we all try to drive our cars at once, the roads become so congested that none of us can get anywhere; if we all have garden bonfires whenever we wish, none of us can hang out the washing or sit outside in comfort; and so on. The remarkable ideological success of

[5] For an exposition and a discussion of the significance of the prisoner's dilemma see Brian Barry and Russell Hardin (eds.), *Rational Man and Irrational Society? An Introduction and Sourcebook* (Beverly Hills, Calif.: Sage, 1982), Pt. I.

Thatcherism is to identify the selfish, antisocial choice with self-interest. Obviously, if socialism is to succeed, this ideological obfuscation has to be removed; but it is important to recognize that the task is one of education rather than one of mass conversion to altruism. What is called for is not self-sacrifice but simply playing one's part in a collectively beneficial practice.

To any socialist, the operations of the market provide an unending source of illustrations for the thesis that the aggregate results of the pursuit of private interest may well be collectively damaging. The pollution created by firms in the course of profit-maximization is a hackneyed but none the less central example. I can see no incompatibility between the politics of red and green; on the contrary, socialism seems to me to provide the essential intellectual framework for environmental concerns. It should be conceded that one of the most arrogant, obstructive, and unconscionable polluters in Britain is the Central Electricity Generating Board. But all that shows is the inappropriateness of this kind of public corporation as a socialist instrument.

Pollution by producers is a form of market failure in that there is no way in which the market can incorporate into its calculations the economic costs, aesthetic damage, and threats to health and life itself created by pollution. The citizens must, acting through the instrumentality of the state, step in to curb the pursuit of profit—and let me emphasize that this is equally true whether the producers are privately owned firms, public corporations charged with acting commercially, or workers' co-operatives.

The evil is generated by the logic of the market mechanism itself. To the degree that it works in the way postulated by the elementary textbooks, that is to say to the degree that it is genuinely competitive, it forces firms on pain of bankruptcy to do whatever is legal (or more precisely whatever is cost-effective, taking into account the probability and cost of conviction) in the pursuit of profit—however injurious this may be to the labour-force, to those living in the neighbourhood, or indeed to the purchasers of their products.

There are more subtle forms of market failure, which again illustrate the way in which uncoordinated individual decisions may add up to outcomes that are not desired. There is no way in which a market can register the willingness to pay for having a service available. Many of us attach a good deal of importance to having public telephones disseminated over the country in case we are stranded and need them, yet it may well be that a large number of these public telephones do not get enough use to 'pay for themselves'. Acting according to a commercial criterion here would be failing to provide people with what they want and are willing to pay for. A fanatical marketeer could, presumably, suggest that everyone should adopt a telephone kiosk in some remote village and drive out periodically to it with a sackful of coins to make long telephone calls to Australia. I need not insult your intelligence by pointing out what is wrong with this proposal.

There are also, of course, distributive arguments in favour of retaining a dense network of public telephones, and the same mix of collective benefit and distributive considerations can be invoked in many other areas, of which public transport is probably the most important: here again, the value of public transport is not adequately measured by the fares that are collected because its very existence has a value. Even someone who always drives derives a benefit from public transport in the form of insurance against a breakdown.

In these examples, the market can be shown to fail in its own terms: it does not manage to come up with the goods that we want in our capacity as consumers. But the market can also fail in ways that take us beyond the limited perspective of consumerism. If we want to see some beautiful stretch of coastline protected for ever against development, or the ancient quarter of some city saved from demolition, the reason may indeed be that we want to preserve the option of going and looking at it ourselves some day. Here, the state has to step in to provide us with a certain form of 'consumption' that can be enjoyed only if private preferences for buying and selling are overridden by the preference for a public good. But we may instead step outside our role as consumers altogether, and support preservation simply because we think that it is good and right for the country to be one in which natural beauty and artefacts of historical interest or aesthetic value are preserved.

Another very significant illustration of the potential clash between market forces and the wishes we have as citizens is this. In very many countries, and sometimes localities within countries, people feel an intense sense of discomfort if more than a certain proportion of the real estate and productive capacity fall into the hands of non-nationals. As individuals they may be quite willing to sell to the highest bidder but as citizens they may at the same time vote to set a limit to the proportion of total assets that can be held in foreign hands. The socialist principle is that what people want as citizens should prevail over what they want as private buyers or sellers.

The distribution of income and wealth in a society can be analysed with the same apparatus. According to the by now notorious argument of Robert Nozick,[6] if a large number of people voluntarily pay, say, 50 pence to watch some star performer, they can obviously have no valid objection to whatever distribution of income arises from it, even if the result of this set of transactions and innumerable other sets of transactions like it is to create a grossly unequal distribution. The argument, if such it can be called, is obviously a variant on Locke's suggestion that by 'consenting to the use of money' people consent to whatever distribution of income and wealth comes about. You might as well say that every time we turn on a light we consent to nuclear reactors and acid rain, or that by not—between us—putting some arbitrary amount of money per year into a public call box somewhere on the Yorkshire moors, we consent to its being carted away.

All that can be deduced here is that a lot of people, taking independent decisions, preferred paying 50 pence to missing the star's performance. We cannot say that they approved of the resulting distribution of income, because that was not a choice on offer. The distribution of income is an aggregate outcome, and can be chosen only by a collective decision. We have already seen how we may choose collectively to modify the outcomes we would bring about individually—preventing development that our decisions as consumers would make profitable or barring sales to foreigners that would pay us as individual sellers. And so here too we may for a whole variety of reasons—distribution of power, concern for the quality of social relationships, as well as considerations of equality—wish to change by collective action the outcome of a mass of individual decisions.

IV

I said in my opening remarks that the present government has opened up conflicts of principle where before there was consensus, and this is nowhere better illustrated than in relation to schooling. I am not concerned here with the details of the government's policies but with the underlying principle, which is very plainly the individualistic one of turning decisions over to the operation of a market or quasi-market. What I want to do quite briefly is to show how the socialist critique of individualism applies here.

[6] Robert Nozick, *Anarchy, State, and Utopia* (New York: Basic Books, 1974), 160–4. This is usually referred to as the Wilt Chamberlain example, since it is built around the case of a well-known American basketball player.

Let us simplify the analysis by contrasting two ideal types of educational system. In one, children are allocated to schools so that each school will be representative of the social class and ethnic mix of the district—say the area of the local authority. In the other, parents either have educational vouchers which can be used at any school or have the right to apply for their children's admission to any school in the appropriate age-range run by the local authority. The schools in turn can select children from among the applicants.

We may now look at the operation of the second system. The result of all the decisions by parents and schools will be some pattern of allocation which nobody chose and perhaps nobody wants. Typically, it will be one in which there is a pecking order of schools. Even if all the schools in an area have equally good facilities and equally good teachers, all that is needed to create a hierarchy is a preference by parents for schools with more rather than fewer children of high academic attainment and selection by schools among applicants on the basis of academic attainment.

From a consumer point of view, this may be a quite unattractive outcome. If there are five schools and everyone wants to get into one of them, four-fifths of the parents are going to be disappointed. Freedom of choice is really no more than freedom to apply: the only school that can be chosen unconditionally is the one at the bottom of the heap—precisely because few choose it. There is no way in which it can be shown a priori that parents or children will be more satisfied on average with such a system of so-called parental choice than with one in which each child is allocated to a school whose composition is similar to that of the others in the area.

Suppose, however, that parents were happy enough to have their children educated in schools that were relatively homogeneous with respect to social class and ethnicity. The system of parental choice could then count as a success from the consumer point of view. But we should still have to ask how this system should be regarded from the point of view of the citizens—those with children currently in the school system and those without. I think the answer is that it should be looked on with misgivings. We live in a society where racial and ethnic tensions have already given rise to large-scale riots. We live in a society where the frustration and resentment of losers leads to vandalism and violence. Does it make sense to perpetuate the divisions of class and ethnic group in the schools? If we leave the composition of the schools to parental choice that is what we shall be doing even though the choice will not be made explicitly.

The relevance of socialism is here, as in my other examples, to insist that an outcome is not saved from critical assessment by its origin in individual choices. The overall result of a lot of choices made by parents and schools has to be compared with what can be achieved by allocating children to schools with the object of creating a microcosm of the area in each school, and then trying, by precept and practice, to encourage equal respect and understanding among children of different backgrounds.

Miracles are not to be expected from schools: they cannot themselves compensate for everything else that is wrong in a society. But what must be emphasized is that, whether by default or by explicit action, every society chooses either to perpetuate and intensify its divisions in its schools or to make some effort to overcome them.

V

The core of socialism, as I have presented it, is that people should act collectively through central and local government to attain ends that cannot be achieved by individual effort. Needless to say, collective action for shared ends can also be undertaken by people outside the framework of government. Trade unions are an excellent example: though not in themselves socialist, because they pursue a partial interest, they provide a model of socialism in action. Hence their importance in the history of socialism.

The trade union model of collective self-help is also of great significance for social welfare policy because trade unions all over Europe in the course of the nineteenth century developed schemes of insurance as a natural extension of their other activities in pursuit of the collective benefit of their members. Now in most continental European countries (the Scandinavian ones taking the lead) these mutual benefit societies were first subsidized and rationalized by the state and then finally more or less completely absorbed in schemes of universal social insurance. The usual way in which these schemes operate is that both contributions and benefits are roughly proportional to income, subject to some minimum level of benefit. There is, therefore, not a great deal of transfer between income strata, and this has the implication that those with higher incomes have no self-interested reason to resist a generous level of provision. The question people in each stratum are invited to ask themselves is: what level of benefits do I want to pay for? And the answer has turned out to be: a lot. It is a commonplace that, in the last forty years, the scale of transfer payments in Western Europe outside this country has grown phenomenally, so that costs now run at between a fifth and a quarter of the national income in most countries.

Meanwhile, the British experience has been strikingly different from that of the rest of Western Europe. Starting in the immediate post-war period with one of the best-funded systems, Britain has by now slipped below most of the others in the proportion of its gross national product that goes on income maintenance. Why is this? One possible explanation is that in the same period Britain has slipped from having the highest income per head in Western Europe to having one of the lowest, and therefore cannot 'afford' as much as the others. But why should relative poverty produce a lower *proportional* expenditure? One might think that if anything insurance would be relatively more important the less well off people are.

We should I think look for an answer in the mind-set that thinks in terms of 'what the country can afford' instead of 'what coverage people want to pay for'. Abstracting from their variations, let us say that the continental systems exhibit the 'insurance model'. How then shall we describe the underlying ethos of the British system, as it has developed over the course of this century? I suggest that it should be called the 'needs model'. By this I understand the following guiding idea: that payments should be made only to those who are in need, and should be set at a level sufficient to get them above some defined poverty level.

I shall not stop to belabour all the differences between a pure insurance model and a pure need model, but it is I hope evident that they are opposed at every turn. The most striking contrast between them is that the needs model entails means-testing for all benefits, whereas the insurance model in its pure form has no room for means-testing at all. Thus, under the insurance model people who are sick or unemployed will automatically receive, say, three-quarters of their previous income, while under a needs model they may receive nothing if they have too much money in the bank or a continuing source of family income. From the insurance point of view, this is as bad as an insurance company's refusing to compensate for a burglary on the grounds that the policyholder can perfectly well afford to replace the stolen items out of his or her own pocket. Conversely, from the needs point of view, paying out a lot of money to someone who is already well off is a 'waste' of resources that could be better 'targeted' on the 'needy'.

Life never makes things completely easy for the makers of models.

Although the bulk of the money disbursed within the continental systems falls under the insurance model, each country also has some kind of means-tested assistance for people who fall between the cracks. Conversely, the British system is some way from exemplifying the needs model exclusively. Formally, the system is one of social insurance with flat-rate benefits. There are, however, two observations to be made. The first is that flat-rate benefits, the legacy of the wartime Beveridge Report, violate the insurance concept, which is one of income replacement. A flat-rate scheme is like a system of fire insurance in which every houseowner gets just enough to rebuild a minimal house whatever the size of the one that has burnt down. It is clear that, in spite of its insurance trappings, a flat-rate system is best seen as a way of meeting needs—something that Beveridge himself acknowledged.

The second point to make is that, in any case, Beveridge's flat-rate benefits have never been set at a level above the official poverty line. The result has been that at no time since the war have there been fewer than millions of people on means-tested supplementary benefits. If the insurance-related benefits have to be topped up in this way, it seems fair to say that the system as a whole conforms primarily to the needs model.

As a further support for this view of the matter, I can adduce the fact that the surviving elements of the insurance model are seen as anomalies. Why, it is asked recurrently by some wiseacre, should 'we' be paying good money to people who do not need it? The solution, which is constantly being independently discovered, is a negative income tax which would put all benefits on a means-tested basis. (The change in name to negative taxation is thought for some reason to solve all the existing problems of means-tested benefits.)

On the face of it, the needs model is rather attractive: those who can afford it give, and those who need it receive. It is noteworthy that with almost no exceptions Anglophone philosophers who have written about the foundations of the 'Welfare State' have seen the task as one of defending the claims of need. The needs model is Good Samaritanism writ large, and indeed arguments in favour of it often start by appealing to cases where one person can save another from some situation of dire need. The basis of Good Samaritanism is that the aid is given without any expectation of return. The Samaritan may, of course, hope that somebody will do the same for him if the occasion ever arises, but there is no link between his present altruistic act and what may or may not happen to him in some like contingency in the future.

I expect that what I have just said will already have reminded a number of you of Richard Titmuss's argument in *The Gift Relationship*.[7] In that book voluntary blood donation, an act of unconditional altruism, was advanced as a paradigm for social policy generally. Now blood donation is significantly different from other areas of collective provision precisely in that it is voluntary: no supporter of a general scheme of transfer payments is going to suggest that the wherewithal should come from voluntary contributions. The relevance of blood donation is, however, taken to be this. Blood donation may be regarded as an expression of social solidarity, which we may understand as the generalization of Good Samaritanism. And social policy might then be seen as an expression of social solidarity too, here understood as universal and compulsory Good Samaritanism. Concretely, this would entail those who can afford it voting out of a sense of empathy to pay taxes to support those in need.

Titmuss believed that the moral basis of the post-war Welfare State was laid in the experience of the Second World War and in particular the sense of common vulnerability and interdependence generated by the blitz. There is much plausibility in this.[8] That disasters, natural or man-made, stimulate social solidarity is one of the best-documented findings in social science. But what is equally well established is that after things return to normal solidarity gradually diminishes, and Britain in the post-war period also illustrates this.

What happens when a system founded on an assumption of a high level of social solidarity has to exist in a society where that assumption has failed to be true? The answer is, I suggest: what has actually happened in this country over the past forty years. The system becomes meaner and meaner as time goes on. Where does this leave us? Fortunately, it leaves us still in a good position. The insurance model is, I wish to say, the implementation of the socialist principle with regard to social security. Insurance by its very nature requires a lot of people to get together, and the best insurance occurs when everyone is in it, with the power of the fisc as the ultimate underwriter. The reasons for state insurance are as strong now as they were when the mutual benefit societies were absorbed on the continent of Europe. Unemployment, for example, has never been satisfactorily

[7] R. M. Titmuss, *The Gift Relationship: From Human Blood to Social Policy* (London: George Allen and Unwin, 1970).

[8] See for support of this view Robert E. Goodin and John Dryzek, 'Risk sharing and Social Justice: The Motivational Foundations of the Post-War Welfare State', in Robert E. Goodin and Julian Le Grand, *Not Only the Poor: The Middle Classes and the Welfare State* (London: Allen and Unwin, 1977), 37–73.

insured against in the private market. And it is inevitable that private sickness pay insurance—like medical insurance—will charge higher premiums to those who are poorer health risks, or even refuse to insure them altogether. (We can see this phenomenon at work in the distasteful but entirely logical efforts of insurance companies to exclude from life insurance coverage those whom they regard as being at risk from AIDS.)

What I have just said should bring out an important point about social insurance. It is not the object of social insurance simply to ape the workings of private insurance, but to provide coverage for everybody without discriminating against bad risks. This is one of the ways in which social insurance is better than private insurance. The point of insurance is to provide protection against misfortunes, but no private scheme will provide protection against the misfortune of being a bad risk in the first place. Social insurance can and does.

Now it is of course true that, as a result of this, some very fortunate people would be better off in a hypothetical private market than under a social insurance scheme—though we should not forget the very high overheads of private insurance, overheads that are inherent in the attempt to keep out poor prospects. It is often suggested that, because of this, social insurance is not really insurance at all. The suggestion is obtuse in presupposing that private insurance is the only kind of insurance. Social insurance is a different and better kind of insurance because it is, as the cliché has it, 'from the cradle to the grave' (or 'from womb to tomb') and membership in it is not voluntary.

Because membership is compulsory, there is no necessity to treat bad risks less well than good ones. Moreover, those who are severely disabled from birth, so that they have no prospects of ever earning enough to pay insurance contributions, can be included by a simple and obvious extension of the insurance idea: that, of all the things we would wish to insure against if we could, being severely disabled at birth must surely head the list.

It is apparent that social insurance calls upon a certain degree of solidarity in that, for example, people of voting age know whether or not they are severely disabled, and the great majority are not. It is, however, in the nature of all public goods that some people get more out of them than others, and the disproportion between contribution and expected benefit is probably less for a system of social insurance than for almost any other public good. And I think that, if once people see the logic of social insurance, they should be able to see that it would be an anomaly to discriminate against or exclude the bad or hopeless risks.

VI

It is time to draw these remarks to a close. The fundamental argument for socialism, as I hope I have illustrated in my various examples, is simply that it is the only way of satisfying a lot of important desires. Undeniably, the antithesis of socialism—capitalism or individualism—gives us some of what we want. But it forces all aspirations into the one narrow channel of making and spending money. There is nothing about socialism that is incompatible with making and spending money, but, as I have tried to show, the object of socialism is to provide us with options in our capacity as citizens as well as in our capacity as individual consumers.

Acting through the market, we can do nothing to change a grotesquely unjust distribution of income, to create an adequate system of income-maintenance, to prevent industries from polluting and farmers from destroying the countryside, or to provide ourselves with properly funded public services of all kinds. Only in our capacity as citizens can we, acting collectively through local and national governments, bring about the outcomes that we want.

But do we really want them? I think it must be conceded that it is possible to create a society in which the response to market failure is not a swing to socialism, but an exacerbation of individual efforts to stay ahead by making and spending yet more money. Does the public health service have long waiting lists and inadequate facilities? Buy private insurance. Has public transport broken down? Buy a car for each member of the family above driving age. Has the countryside been built over or the footpaths eradicated? Buy some elaborate exercise machinery and work out at home. Is air pollution intolerable? Buy an air-filtering unit and stay indoors. Is what comes out of the tap foul to the taste and chock-full of carcinogens? Buy bottled water. And so on. We know it can all happen because it has: I have been doing little more than describing Southern California.

Now it is worth noticing two things about the private substitutes that I have described. The first is that in the aggregate they are probably much more expensive than would be the implementation of the appropriate public policy. The second is that they are extremely poor replacements for the missing outcomes of good public policy.

Nevertheless, it is plain that the members of a society can become so alienated from one another, so mistrustful of any form of collective action, that they prefer to go it alone.

We need not feel too sorry for the inhabitants of Southern California. Most of them have enough money to carry out the project of extreme privatization in style—and anyway there is all that sunshine. What is much less of a joke is the prospect of the same thing in a country with a third of the income and even less than a third of the sunshine.

Can it happen here? The object of the present government is undoubtedly to create the conditions for its happening. By systematically reducing the quality of public services of all kinds, it hopes to turn people away from them and encourage them to seek solutions individually. There is, it seems to me, no guarantee that this strategy will fail. As I said before, I do not regard socialism as coming with built-in prophecies. Perhaps, however perverse it may be, most people will get locked into pursuing private solutions to public deficiencies. But I hope not, because this would result in all of us living more limited and impoverished lives.

INDEX